Social Welfare

SOCIAL WELFARE

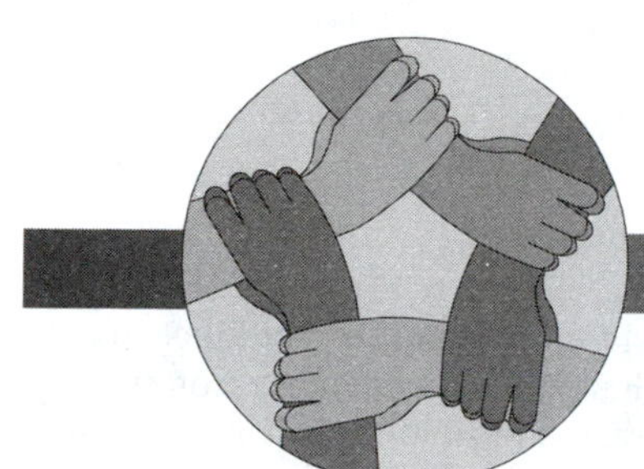

Politics and Public Policy

Fifth Edition

STUDY EDITION

Diana M. DiNitto
The University of Texas at Austin

Boston New York San Francisco
Mexico City Montreal Toronto London Madrid Munich Paris
Hong Kong Singapore Tokyo Cape Town Sydney

Series Editor: Judy Fifer
Editor-in-Chief; Social Sciences: Karen Hanson
Editorial Assistant: Julianna M. Cancio
Marketing Manager: Jackie Aaron
Editorial-Production Service: Melanie Field/Strawberry Field Publishing
Text Designer: Menagerie Design and Composition
Cover Administrator: Linda Knowles
Cover Designer: Studio Nine
Composition Buyer: Linda Cox
Manufacturing Buyer: Julie McNeil

A previous edition was published under *Social Welfare: Politics and Public Policy,* Fifth Edition, copyright © 2000, 1995, 1991, and 1983 by Allyn and Bacon.

ISBN 0-205-37824-2

Printed in the United States of America

10 9 8 7 6 5 4 3 2 RRD/VA 08 07 06 05 04 03

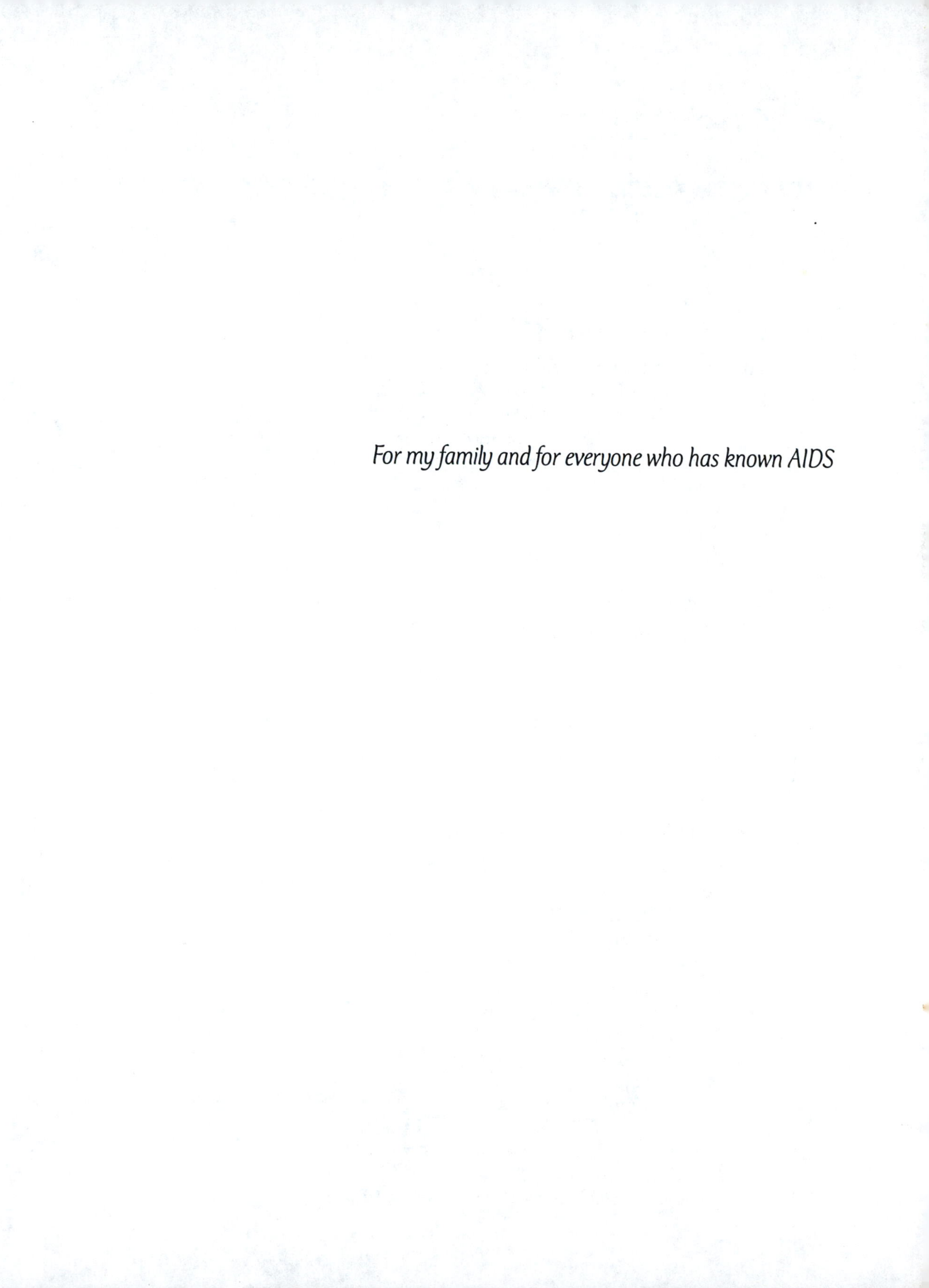

For my family and for everyone who has known AIDS

Contents

Preface

Social Welfare: Politics and Public Policy, Fifth Edition, is intended to introduce students to the major social welfare policies and programs in the United States and to stimulate them to think about major conflicts in social welfare today. The focus of the book is on *issues,* and it emphasizes that social welfare in the United States involves a series of *political* questions about what should be done for groups such as the poor, the near poor, and the nonpoor—or whether anything should be done at all.

Social Welfare: Politics and Public Policy describes the major social welfare programs—their histories, trends, and current problems and prospects. But more importantly, it tackles the difficult conflicts and controversies that surround these programs. Social welfare policy is *not* presented as a series of solutions to social problems. Instead, social policy is portrayed as public conflict over the nature and causes of social welfare problems; over what, if anything, should be done about them; over who should do it; and over who should decide about it.

Some of the major policies and programs covered in this book are

- Social Security
- Unemployment compensation
- Workers' compensation
- Supplemental Security Income
- Vocational rehabilitation
- The Americans with Disabilities Act
- Child support enforcement
- Temporary Assistance for Needy Families (formerly Aid to Families with Dependent Children)
- General Assistance
- Food Stamp Program
- School lunch and breakfast programs
- Special Supplemental Nutrition Program for Women, Infants, and Children
- Community action programs
- Job Training Partnership Act and other job programs
- Mental health services
- The Older Americans Act
- Child welfare services
- Medicare
- Medicaid
- Civil rights legislation
- Immigration legislation

Although it is impossible to capture all the complexities of social welfare in the United States in a single volume, these policies and programs are described and analyzed, and alternative proposals and "reforms" are considered. Public policies that address gender inequities and the inequities faced by members of various ethnic groups are also addressed.

This book is designed for undergraduate and beginning graduate courses in social welfare policy. It does not require prior knowledge of social welfare, and it may serve as a springboard to further interest in social welfare policies and programs.

Many texts on social policy treat social insurance, public assistance, and social service programs *descriptively*; by so doing, they tend to obscure important conflicts and issues. Other books treat these programs *prescriptively*; by so doing, they imply that there is a "right" way to resolve social problems. *Social Welfare: Politics and Public Policy* views social policy as a *continuing political struggle* over the issues posed by poverty and other social welfare problems in society—different goals and objectives, competing definitions of problems, alternative approaches and strategies, multiple programs and policies, competing proposals for "reform," and different ideas about how decisions should be made in social welfare policy.

An accompanying website and other technology-assisted supplements are available to accompany the text; the website address is www.abacon.com/dinitto.

I owe a special debt to Professor Thomas R. Dye. Although he no longer appears as a coauthor of the book, without him there would never have been a book at all. I wish to thank the reviewers who commented on previous editions, including reviewers of the Third Edition: Professor Doris Burton, Indiana University; Professor Matthew Kinkley, Lima Technical College; and Professor Lon Johnston, University of Mary Hardin-Baylor, and reviewers of the Fourth Edition: Stephen C. Anderson, University of Oklahoma; Daniel R. Meyer, University of Wisconsin–Madison; Edward W. Ihle, Syracuse University; and Carole C. Upshur, University of Massachusetts, Boston. I wish to especially thank Professor Robert B. Hudson of Boston University who has provided extensive commentary on previous editions and on the draft of the Fifth Edition. Thanks also to Amy Dolejs, Mary Margaret Just, Kelly Larson, Melanie Sinclair, and Jaclyn Smith for their assistance in helping me complete this edition. Several users of the book, both faculty and students, have communicated with me about previous editions. I appreciate their interest and look forward to further contacts with readers.

D.M.D.

CHAPTER

Politics, Rationalism, and Social Welfare

POLITICS AND SOCIAL WELFARE POLICY

No one is happy with the nation's public assistance system—not the working taxpayers who must support it, not the social welfare professionals who must administer it, and certainly not the poor who must live under it. Even the nation's social insurance system has become a source of controversy. Since the Social Security Act of 1935, the federal government has tried to develop a rational social welfare system for the entire nation. Today a wide variety of federal programs serve people who are aged, poor, disabled, sick, or have other social needs. **Income maintenance** (social insurance and public assistance) is now the largest single item in the federal budget, easily surpassing national defense. The Social Security Administration has the largest budget of any federal agency. The budget of the U.S. Department of Health and Human Services is not far behind, and many additional social welfare programs are administered by other departments. Yet even after sixty-five years of large-scale, direct federal involvement, social welfare policy remains a central issue in U.S. politics.

Social welfare policy involves a series of *political* issues about what should be done for the poor, the near-poor, and the nonpoor—or whether anything should be done at all. The real problems in social welfare are not problems of organization, administration, or service delivery. Rather, they involve political conflicts over the nature and causes of poverty and inequality, the role of government in society, the burdens to be carried by taxpayers, the appropriate strategies for coping with social problems, the issues posed by specific social insurance and public assistance programs, the relative reliance to be placed on providing cash rather than services to the poor, the need for reform, and the nature of the decision-making process itself. In short, social welfare policy is a continuing political struggle over the issues posed by poverty and inequality and by other social problems in society.

Policymaking is frequently portrayed as a *rational* process in which policymakers identify social problems, explore all the solutions to a problem, forecast all the benefits and costs of each solution, compare benefits to costs for each solution, and select the best ratio of benefits to costs. In examining social welfare policy, this book considers both the strengths and weaknesses of this rational model.

More importantly, it portrays social welfare policy as a political process—as conflict over the nature and causes of poverty and other social problems and over what, if anything, should be done about them. Social welfare policy is political because of disagreements about the nature of the problems confronting society, about what should be considered "benefits" and "costs," about how to estimate and compare benefits and costs, about the likely consequences of alternative policies, about the importance of one's own needs and aspirations in relation to those of others, and about the ability of government to do anything "rationally." As you will see, the political barriers to rational policymaking are indeed very great.

Scope of Social Welfare Policy

Social welfare policy is anything a government chooses to do, or not to do, that affects the quality of life of its people. Broadly conceived, social welfare policy includes nearly everything government does—from taxation, national defense, and energy conservation, to health care, housing, and public assistance. More elaborate definitions of social welfare policy are available;[1] most refer to actions of government that have an "impact on the welfare of citizens by providing them with services or income."[2]

Some scholars have insisted that government activities must have "a goal, objective, or purpose," in order to be labeled a "policy."[3] This definition implies a difference between governmental actions in general and an overall plan of action toward a specific goal. The problem, however, in insisting that government actions must have goals in order to be labeled as "policy" is that we can never be sure what the goal of a particular government action is. We generally assume that if a government chooses to do something there must be a goal, objective, or purpose, but often we find that bureaucrats who helped write the law, lobbyists who pushed for its enactment, and members of Congress who voted for it all had different goals, objectives, and purposes in mind! Multiple goals are not necessarily a bad thing, especially when they mean that more people stand to benefit from a policy, but any of the intentions of a law (stated or not) may also be quite different from what government agencies actually do. All we can really observe is what governments choose to do or not do.

Political scientists Heinz Eulau and Kenneth Prewitt supply still another definition of public policy: "Policy is defined as a 'standing decision' characterized by behavioral consistency and repetitiveness on the part of those who make it and those who abide by it."[4] It might be a wonderful thing if government activities were characterized by "consistency and repetitiveness"—that they seem to have "rhyme and reason"—but it is doubtful that we would ever find a public policy in government if we insisted on these criteria. As you shall see, much of what government does is neither consistent nor repetitive.

Note that this book focuses not only on government action but also on government *in*action—that is, on what governments choose *not* to do. Government inaction can have just as important an impact on society as government action.

For practical purposes, much of the discussion presented here is limited to the policies of government that directly affect the income, services, and opportunities available to people who are aged, poor, disabled, ill, or otherwise vulnerable. I discourage lengthy discussions of the definition of social welfare policy. These discussions are often futile, even exasperating, since few people can agree on a single definition of social welfare policy. Moreover, these discussions divert attention away from the study of specific social welfare policies.

The boundaries of social welfare policy are indeed fuzzy, but clarifying subjects of concern and interest can be viewed as a challenge, not an obstacle. Specifically, this book addresses major government programs in

Income maintenance
- Social Security
- Unemployment compensation
- Workers' compensation
- Supplemental Security Income (SSI)
- Temporary Assistance for Needy Families (TANF, formerly Aid to Families with Dependent Children)
- General Assistance

Nutrition
- Food stamps
- School lunches and breakfasts
- Special Supplemental Nutrition Program for Women, Infants, and Children (WIC)
- Congregate meals
- Meals-on-wheels

Health
- Medicaid
- Medicare
- Public health

Social services
- Child protective services
- Family preservation services
- Community mental health services
- Day care and preschool education for children
- Employment services
- Job training
- Independent living and long-term care services for people who are elderly or disabled
- Vocational rehabilitation

Some of these social welfare programs are called **public assistance** because people must be poor (according to legal standards) in order to receive benefits; benefits are paid out of general-revenue funds. Public assistance programs (what most people simply call "welfare") include TANF, food stamps, Medicaid, SSI, school lunches and breakfasts, and General Assistance. Other social welfare programs are called **social insurance** because they are designed to prevent poverty. Workers, as well as their employers, pay into these programs; then, upon retirement or disability, these former workers are entitled to benefits, regardless of their wealth. Social insurance programs include Social Security, Medicare, unemployment compensation, and workers' compensation. Still other social welfare programs are labeled **social services** because they provide care, counseling, education, or other forms of assistance to children, elderly individuals, those with disabilities, and others with particular needs. Child protective services, day care, early education, homemaker services, job training, mental health care, and vocational rehabilitation are all examples of social services. Also considered are a number of issues that affect the provision of social welfare services, such as civil rights legislation, the status of women and certain ethnic or racial groups in society, and the influx of immigrants to the United States.

This book seeks, first of all, to describe the country's major social welfare programs. But it is also concerned with the causes of social welfare policy—why policy is what it is. In order to understand contemporary social welfare policy, it is necessary to learn about some of the social, economic, and political forces that have shaped social welfare policy in America. This book is concerned with how social welfare policies have developed and changed over time. It is also concerned with the consequences of social welfare policies—their effects on target groups and on society in general. Furthermore, the chapters that follow consider some alternative policies—possible changes, "reforms," improvements, or phaseouts. Finally, this book is concerned with political conflict over the nature and causes of poverty and other social problems—and conflict over what, if anything, should be done about them.

Social Welfare Policy: A Rational Approach

Ideally, social welfare policy ought to be rational. A policy is rational if the ratio between the values it achieves and the values it sacrifices is positive and higher than any other policy alternative. Although this might be viewed as a strictly economic (cost–benefit) approach, we should not measure benefits and costs only in a narrow dollar-and-cents framework while ignoring basic social values. The idea of rationalism involves the calculation of *all* social, political, and economic values sacrificed or achieved by a public policy, not just those that can be measured in dollars.

Rationalism has been proposed as an "ideal" approach to both studying and making public policy.[5] Indeed, it has been argued that rationalism provides a single "model of choice" that can be applied to all kinds of problems, large and small, public and private.[6] Most government policies are far from being entirely rational. Even so, the model remains important because it helps identify barriers to rationality. It helps us pose the question "Why is policymaking not a more rational process?"

Let us examine the conditions for rational policymaking more closely:

1. Society must be able to identify and define social problems and agree there is a need to resolve these problems.
2. All the values of society must be known and weighed.
3. All possible alternative policies must be identified and considered.
4. The consequences of each alternative must be fully understood in terms of both costs and benefits, for the present and for the future, and for target groups and the rest of society.
5. Policymakers must calculate the ratio of benefits to costs for each alternative.
6. Policymakers must choose the policy that maximizes *net* values—the alternative that achieves the greatest benefit at the lowest cost.

Because this notion of rationality assumes that the values of society as a whole can be known and weighed, it is not enough to know the values of some groups and not others. There must be a common understanding of societal values. Rational policymaking also requires information about alternative policies and the predictive capacity to foresee accurately the consequences of each alternative. Rationality requires the intelligence to calculate correctly the ratio of costs to benefits for each policy alternative. This means calculating all present and future benefits and costs to both the target groups and nontarget groups in society. Finally, rationalism requires a policymaking system that facilitates rationality in policy formation.

Identifying **target groups** means defining the segment of the population for whom the policy is intended—those who are aged, poor, ill, disabled, or abused, or who have other needs. Then the desired effect of the program on the target groups must be determined. Is it to change their physical or economic condition—for example, to increase the cash income of poor people, to improve the housing conditions of inner-city residents, to improve the treatment of children, or to improve the health of the elderly? Or is the program designed to change their knowledge, attitudes, or behavior—for example, to provide job skills, to improve literacy, or to increase awareness of legal rights? If several different effects are desired, what are the priorities among them? And what are the possible unintended or unanticipated consequences on target groups—for example, does public housing provide shelter for poor people at the cost of increasing housing segregation between African Americans and whites? Or do emergency shelters for homeless people risk forgoing the establishment of permanent housing units? What is the impact of a policy on the target group in proportion to that group's total need? A program that promises to meet a recognized national need—for example, to eradicate poverty—but actually meets only a small percentage of that need, may generate great praise at first but bitterness and frustration later when it becomes known how insufficient the impact really is.

Policies are likely to have different effects on various segments of the population. Identifying the effects of policy on important **nontarget groups** is crucial, but it can be difficult. For example, what is the impact of welfare reform proposals—such as a guaranteed annual income—on groups other than the poor (working families and government bureaucrats)? Rational policymaking also requires consideration of these **externalities** or **spillover effects.** These nontarget effects may be benefits as well as costs—for example, the benefits to the housing industry from public housing projects or the benefits to farmers, food manufacturers, and retailers from the Food Stamp Program.

When will the benefits or costs be felt? Is the policy designed for short-term emergency situations, or is it a long-term developmental effort? If it is short term, what will prevent bureaucrats from turning it into a long-term program, even after immediate needs are met? Many studies have shown that new or innovative programs have positive effects initially—for example, model preschool programs and job training programs. However, the positive effects sometimes disappear as the novelty and enthusiasm of new programs wear off. Other programs experience difficulties at first. For example, physicians and other health care providers were strongly opposed to the Medicare and Medicaid programs. But these programs turned out to have "sleeper" effects. Today Medicare and Medicaid have achieved widespread acceptance and provide vast sums of money to the health care industry.

Rational policymakers must measure benefits and costs in terms of general social well-being. Government agencies have developed various forms of cost–benefits analysis to identify the direct costs and benefits (usually, but not always, in dollars) of providing aid and assistance to the *average* family, worker, or job trainee. It is more difficult to identify and measure general units of social well-being. We need to know, for example, how better to measure health, job skills, and employment opportunities. We are still struggling with ways to measure these social values.

Comprehensive rationality in public policy not only fails to occur in the political environment, it may actually not be rational. This apparent contradiction was noted many years ago by Herbert A. Simon, a Nobel Prize winner for his studies of the decision-making process in large organizations. It is so costly and time consuming to learn about *all* the policy alternatives available to decision makers, to investigate *all* the possible consequences of each alternative, and to calculate the cost–benefit ratio of *every* alternative, that the improvement in the policy selected is not worth the extra effort required to make a comprehensive rational selection. Simon developed a theory of **bounded rationality,** which recognizes the practical limits to complete rationality. He wrote, "It is impossible for the behavior of a single, isolated individual to reach any high degree of rationality. The number of alternatives . . . [to be] explore[d] is so great, the information . . . to evaluate them so vast that even an approximation to objective rationality is hard to conceive."[7]

In contrast to completely rational decision making, Simon's notion of bounded rationality means that policymakers consider a limited number of alternatives, estimate these consequences using the best available means, and select the alternative that appears to achieve the most important values without incurring unacceptable costs. Instead of maximizing the ratio of benefits to costs, policymakers search for a "satisfying" choice—an alternative that is good enough to produce the desired benefits at a reasonable cost. This means that policymakers do not try to create the best of all possible worlds but rather seek to get by, to come out all right, to avoid trouble, to compromise.

Rationalism, then, presents an ideal model of policymaking—in social welfare and in other policy fields. But policymaking in "the real world" is not usually a rational process. Policymaking occurs in a political context that places severe limits on rationality.

Social Welfare Policy: A Political Approach

Social welfare policy is political. By political I mean that social welfare policy arises out of conflict over the nature of the problems confronting society and what, if anything, should be done about them.

Politics has been described by political scientist Harold Lasswell as "who gets what, when, and how";[8] it is an activity through which people try to get more of whatever there is to get—money, jobs, prestige, prosperity, respect, and power itself. Politics, then, is conflict over the allocation of values in society, and this conflict is central to politics and policymaking. "Politics arises out of conflicts, and it consists of the activities—for example, reasonable discussion, impassioned oratory, balloting, and street fighting—by which conflict is carried on."[9]

Why do we expect conflict in society over who gets what? Why can't we agree on "a theory of justice" according to which everyone would agree on what is fair for all members of society, particularly those who are most vulnerable to social problems?[10] Why can't we have a harmonious, loving, caring, sharing society of equals? Philosophers have pondered these questions for centuries. James Madison, perhaps the first American to write seriously about politics, believed that the causes of "faction" (conflict) are found in human diversity—"a zeal for different opinions concerning religion, concerning government, and many other points . . . [and] an attachment of different leaders ambitiously contending for pre-eminence and power." More importantly, according to Madison, "the most common and durable source of factions has been the various and unequal distribution of property. Those who hold and those who are without property have ever formed distinct interests in society."[11] In short, class differences among people, particularly in the sources and amount of their wealth, are the root cause of social conflict.

It is the task of government to regulate conflict. It does so by (1) establishing and enforcing general rules by which conflict is carried on, (2) arranging compromises and balancing interests in public policy, and (3) imposing settlements that the parties to a dispute must accept. Governments arrange settlements in the form of public policies that allocate values in such a way that they will be accepted by both "winners" and "losers," at least temporarily. Finally, governments must impose these settlements by enforcing public policy and by promising rewards or threatening punishments.

From a political perspective, public policy is the outcome of conflicts in government over who gets what, and when and how they get it. A policy may be considered *politically rational* when it succeeds in winning enough support to be enacted into law, implemented by executive agencies, and enforced by the courts. Or it may be considered *politically rational* if it is supported by influential groups and believed to be popular among the voters. But this certainly differs from the type of rationality described earlier in the rational model.

Indeed, the political approach raises serious questions about rationality in policymaking. It suggests that

1. **Few social values are generally agreed on; more often there are only the values of specific groups and individuals, many of which are conflicting.** For example, even if we did agree that poor people need help in securing an adequate diet, whether they should receive food, food stamps or electronically distributed benefits, or cash is an ongoing political debate. On many issues, there is no fundamental agreement on the goal to be achieved. For example, there is little likelihood that antiabortion and prochoice forces will ever agree on the issue of access to abortion.

2. **Problems cannot be defined, because people do not agree on what the problems are. And what is a problem to one group may be a benefit to another group.** Consider discussion of what causes poverty. Explanations range from the willful behavior of those who prefer not to work, to discrimination and structural barriers to participation in gainful, economic activity. Remedies include low public assistance payments that provide a very meager standard of living for the poor, but save taxpayers' money, at least in the short run. Meager welfare payments may also force unemployed people to accept low-wage jobs benefitting industries that rely on this cheap labor pool. Or consider that saving the spotted owl would be viewed as a great benefit to some environmentalists but would represent a serious cost to those who rely on the logging industry for a living.

3. **Many conflicting costs and values cannot be compared or weighed.** For example, how can we compare the value of individual dignity with the cost of a general tax increase? Policymakers at all levels—local, state, and federal—face these challenges every day. A city or county government may choose to fund a residential program for people with developmental disabilities, rather than a drug detoxification program. Perhaps they view people with developmental disabilities as a more deserving clientele; perhaps they believe that program will be better administered. But they do not really know if their choice will achieve greater social values. In fact, many local governments appoint citizen advisory groups to recommend allocations of human service funding, because it takes the political pressure off elected officials in trying to distinguish one seemingly good cause from another.

4. **Policymakers, even with most advanced computerized analytic techniques, cannot accurately forecast or predict the consequences of various policy alternatives or calculate their cost–benefit ratios when many diverse social, economic, and political values are involved.** Perhaps the best example of this concerns difficulties in economic forecasting. We may try to predict the effects of a general tax cut on consumer buying power, but other economic forces that cannot be foreseen well in advance—downturns in particular industrial sectors of the economy such as occurred in the auto and steel industries—may offset any beneficial effects on the country's overall economic well-being. Many other events happen over which we have no control, such as earthquakes in California and floods in the Midwest. Even though we try to respond rationally to these natural disasters, they may divert funds and at-

tention from other activities already in place. Finally, there is fallout from events that perhaps could be predicted, but that we choose to ignore, such as events leading to city riots during the civil rights unrest of the 1960s, or the Los Angeles riots that erupted after the trial in the Rodney King police brutality case in 1992.

5. **The environment of policymakers, particularly the political system of power and influence, makes it virtually impossible to discern all social values, particularly those that do not have active or powerful proponents in or near government.** Those who are poor or ill may have little access to governmental representation, even though their needs are great. Children in the United States face high rates of poverty, abuse, and neglect, yet they have no direct voice in the political arena.

6. **Policymakers are not necessarily motivated to make decisions on the basis of social values. Instead they often seek to maximize their own rewards—power, status, re-election, money, and so on.** Policymakers have their own needs, ambitions, and inadequacies, all of which can prevent them from performing in a highly rational manner. For instance, there is general agreement that the federal debt is a severe strain on the country, yet members of Congress have often done little about it, because any tax increase or budget cut may mean lost votes for some senator or representative anxious for re-election. Congressmembers also do their best to support pet projects in their districts to gain favor with constituents, whether or not these projects are good for the nation as a whole.

7. **Large, segmented government bureaucracies create barriers to coordinated policymaking.** It is difficult to bring all the interested individuals, groups, and experts together at the point of decision. Governmental decision making is so disjointed that it is a wonder how any legislation gets passed and any programs get implemented. Anyone who remembers the diagrams of "How a Bill Becomes a Law" from junior high civics classes knows that the maze of readings and calendars works to prevent most proposals from ever being seriously considered. Even when proposed legislation is considered, lawmakers use many tactics to pass or to defeat it, from filibusters to riders attached to other, sometimes unrelated, bills. Only a tiny fraction of legislation that is introduced to Congress and state legislatures ever makes it through the gauntlet (see Illustration 1-1, "Special Tips for the Legislative Process"). As described in Chapter 12, the process of implementing policy is no less cumbersome.

How can we bridge the differences between an ideal model of rational policymaking and the realization that policymaking is a political activity? Political scientist Charles E. Lindblom first presented an **incremental model** of policymaking as a critique of the rational model.[12] Lindblom observed that government policymakers do *not* annually review the entire range of existing and proposed policies, or identify all of society's goals, or research the benefits and costs of all alternative policies to achieve these goals. They, therefore, do not make their selections on the basis of *all* relevant information. Limits of time, knowledge, and costs pose innumerable obstacles in identifying the full range of policy alternatives and predicting their consequences. Political

ILLUSTRATION 1-1

Special Tips for the Legislative Process

Very few of the bills introduced in any body become law. In the U.S. Congress as well as most states, only about 10–15% of the bills introduced become law. A classic study by Ron Dear and Rino Patti of the bills introduced over several years in the Washington state legislature yielded seven tactics that were likely to improve a bill's chances of success. The bills that made it out of committee and onto the floor tended to share the following characteristics.

FACTORS THAT FOSTER SUCCESS

Early Introduction. If your state allows bills to be prefiled before the session formally begins, that's a good time to get your bill introduced. It means there will be more time to consider it, hold hearings on it, build support for it, raise and answer questions about it.

Multiple Sponsors. A bill that has several sponsors from the outset tends to look more like a winner. Bills with only one sponsor, by contrast, are sometimes assumed to be introduced just to please a constituent or do somebody a favor but not as a serious legislative proposal. Multiple sponsors increase credibility and also the number of advocates working for its success.

Bipartisan Sponsorship. It is always essential to have sponsors from the party in the majority, but unless the legislature is overwhelmingly dominated by one party, it helps a bill's credibility and chances if its sponsors come from both parties. (On the national level, and anywhere that margins are close or party discipline is unreliable, bipartisan sponsorship is essential.)

Support of Governor and Relevant Executive Agency. Since the executive branch will have to administer the resulting program (and in any case tends to have data, information, and expertise), legislators often are influenced by their support or opposition. If support is out of the question, the next best option is executive branch neutrality. The worst posture is outright opposition.

Influential Sponsors. The job of getting a bill through hearings and out to the floor will be much easier if the chair or highest-ranking minority members of the subcommittees and committees are sponsors of the bill. If they, or highly respected senior members of the body, become sponsors and use their influence on its behalf, that's half the battle.

Open Hearings. Hearings are a good opportunity to make a public record, bring an issue before the public, get questions and points of opposition out in the open and dealt with, and to give the advocacy groups a rallying point.

Amendments. Some advocates think their proposal has to be enacted exactly as they conceived it. That rarely happens. In fact, bills that are not amended tend to die. That's because everyone who amends a proposal has to be familiar with it and develops a bit of "ownership," a stake in its future if you will. Encourage amendments; they'll increase your bill's chances of success.

Ultimately, even these seven tactics are no guarantee of success. Bills are more likely to pass if they involve low costs, noncontroversial beneficiaries and purposes, and little

continued

ILLUSTRATION 1-1 *(continued)*

significant change. Bills to create "National Tuna Week," or name a building, have an easier time than bills to provide comprehensive health or human services to low-income families. Knowing the process won't ensure victory, but not knowing it makes it hard to even be a player.

Just keep reminding yourself: laws will be passed with you or without you. The choice is yours.

Source: Nancy Amidei, *So You Want to Make a Difference: A Key to Advocacy* (Washington, DC: OMB Watch, June 1991), pp. 19–20. Based on Ronald B. Dear and Rino J. Patti, "Legislative Advocacy: Seven Effective Tactics," *Social Work*, Vol. 26, No. 4, 1981, pp. 289–296. Copyright 1981, National Association of Social Workers, Inc., SOCIAL WORK.

limitations prevent the establishment of clear-cut societal goals and the accurate calculation of cost–benefit ratios. The incremental model recognizes the impracticality of comprehensive rational policymaking and describes a more conservative process of public decision making.

Incremental policymaking considers existing policies, programs, and expenditures as a base. It concentrates attention on newly proposed policies and programs and on increases, decreases, or other modifications in existing programs. Incrementalism is conservative in that policymakers generally accept the legitimacy of established policies and programs. The focus of attention is on proposed changes in these policies and programs. This narrows the attention of policymakers to a limited number of new initiatives and increases or decreases in the budget.

There are important political advantages to incrementalism in policymaking. Conflict is reduced if the items in dispute are only increases or decreases in existing budgets or modifications of existing programs. Conflict would be greater if policymaking focused on major policy shifts involving great gains or losses for various groups in society or "all or nothing," "yes or no" policy decisions. To reconsider existing policies every year would generate a great deal of conflict; it is easier politically to continue previously accepted policies.

Policymakers may also continue existing policies because of uncertainty about the consequences of completely new or different policies. It is safer to stick with known programs when the consequences of new programs cannot be accurately predicted. Under conditions of uncertainty, policymakers continue past policies or programs whether they have proven effective or not. Only in a "crisis" do political decision makers begin to consider new and untried policies over existing ones. Thus, groups and individuals who seek more than incremental change in public policy usually try to generate a "crisis" atmosphere. A case in point is the view of some Americans that the country is facing a "health care crisis" necessitating a new program of national health insurance. A substantial number of people contend that either there is no crisis (most Americans have public or private health insurance, and there is a system of remedial care for others) or that the so-called crisis has been blown way out of proportion.

Those who see a crisis advocate a major shift in health care delivery in the United States, while the remainder may prefer a more conservative course of action—trying some pilot or demonstration programs or using strategies that address only people who currently have no health care coverage.

Policymakers also realize that individuals and organizations—executive agencies, congressional committees, interest groups—accumulate commitments to existing policies and programs. For example, it is accepted wisdom in Washington that bureaucracies persist over time regardless of their utility, that they develop routines that are difficult to alter, and that individuals develop a personal stake in the continuation of organizations and programs. These commitments are serious obstacles to major change. It is politically easier for policymakers to seek alternatives that involve only a minimum of budgetary, organizational, or administrative change.

Finally, in the absence of generally agreed-on social goals or values, it is politically expedient for governments to pursue a variety of different programs and policies simultaneously, even if some of them are overlapping or even conflicting. In this way, a wider variety of individuals and groups in society are "satisfied." Comprehensive policy planning for specific social goals may maximize some people's values, but it may also generate extreme opposition from others. A government that pursues multiple policies may be politically more suitable to a pluralistic society comprised of people with varying values.

THE POLICYMAKING PROCESS

Policymaking involves a combination of processes. These processes are not always clear-cut and distinguishable, but we can identify them for purposes of analysis. They include the following:

- *Identifying policy problems.* Publicized demands for government action can lead to identification of policy problems.
- *Formulating policy proposals.* Policy proposals can be formulated through political channels by policy-planning organizations, interest groups, government bureaucracies, state legislatures, and the president and Congress.
- *Legitimizing public policy.* Policy is legitimized as a result of the public statements or actions of government officials, both elected and appointed—the president, Congress, state legislators, agency officials, and the courts. This includes executive orders, budgets, laws and appropriations, rules and regulations, and decisions and interpretations that have the effect of setting policy directions.
- *Implementing public policy.* Policy is implemented through the activities of public bureaucracies and the expenditure of public funds.
- *Evaluating public policy.* Policies are formally and informally evaluated by government agencies, by outside consultants, by interest groups, by the mass media, and by the public.

This is a formal breakdown of the policymaking process used by many students of public policy.[13] What it says is that some groups succeed, usually through the help of the mass media, in capturing public attention for their own definition of a problem. Various government bureaucracies, private organizations, and influential individuals, then, propose solutions in terms of new laws or programs, new government agencies, or new public expenditures. These proposals twist their way through the labyrinths of government and eventually emerge (generally after many alterations and amendments) as laws and appropriations. Government bureaucracies are created to carry out these laws and spend these funds. Eventually, either through informal feedback or formal evaluation studies, the successes and failures of these laws, bureaucracies, and expenditures are examined.

All this activity involves both attempts at rational problem solving *and* political conflict. This is true whether we are describing Social Security or the Food Stamp Program, employment training or access to an abortion. Both rational and political considerations enter into each stage of the policymaking process.

Agenda Setting

Deciding what is to be decided is the most important stage of the policymaking process. We might refer to this stage as "agenda setting." Societal conditions not defined as problems never become policy issues. These conditions never get on the "agenda" of policymakers. Government does nothing, and conditions improve, remain the same, or worsen. But if conditions in society are defined as problems, then they become policy issues, and government is forced to decide what to do.

Think of all the conditions that existed for many years but were nonissues until they were broadly publicized. The "separate but equal" doctrine remained in place for decades until the civil rights movement swept the country, complete with marches, sit-ins, and even riots. Poverty has always been with us, but it first became a political issue in the 1960s with the help of television documentaries. Policy issues do not just happen. Creating an issue, dramatizing it, calling attention to it, and pressuring government to do something about it are important political tactics. These tactics are employed by influential individuals, organized interest groups, policy-planning organizations, political candidates and officeholders, and perhaps most importantly, the mass media. These are the tactics of agenda setting.

Nondecisions

Preventing certain conditions in society from becoming policy issues is also an important political tactic. "Nondecision making" occurs when influential individuals or groups act to prevent the emergence of challenges to their own interests in society. According to political scientists Peter Bachrach and Morton Baratz,

> *Non-decision making is a means by which demands for change in the existing allocation of benefits and privileges in the community can be suffocated before they are even*

voiced; or kept covert; or killed before they gain access to the relevant decision-making arena; or failing all these things, maimed or destroyed in the decision-implementing stage of the policy process.[14]

Nondecision making occurs when powerful individuals, groups, or organizations act to suppress an issue because they fear that if public attention is focused on it, something not in their best interest may be done. Nondecision making also occurs when political candidates, officeholders, or administrative officials anticipate that powerful individuals or groups will not favor a particular idea. They therefore do not pursue the idea because they do not want to rock the boat. Such was the case with publicly supported health insurance. Until the 1960s, powerful medical lobbies were successful in blocking serious consideration of these health care initiatives.

The Mass Media

The power of the mass media is their ability to set the agenda for decision making—to decide what problems will be given attention and what problems will be ignored.[15] Deciding what is "news" and who is "newsworthy" is a powerful political weapon. Television executives and producers and newspaper and magazine editors decide what people, organizations, and events will be given public attention. Without media coverage, the general public would not know about many of the conditions or government programs affecting poor people or other groups or about alternative policies or programs. Without media coverage, these topics would not likely become objects of political discussion, nor would they likely be considered important by government officials, even if they knew about them. Media attention creates issues and personalities. Media inattention can doom issues and personalities to obscurity.

The media, especially the major television networks, are often accused of having a liberal bias.[16] Even if this is true, today, countervailing opinions get their share of coverage from conservative television and radio commentators, talk show hosts, and newspaper columnists, and special television channels devoted to their opinions.

Perhaps the real danger today is that we are overwhelmed with the number of issues that have caught the media's attention. The media themselves are competing for attention to issues. Government inaction and public indifference may result when people feel that there are too many problems to consider or that problems continue to grow even when we try to intervene. The media work most effectively to bring light to a cause when there is some consensus about the problems to be addressed. But often, such consensus is elusive.

The Budget

The budget is the single most important policy statement of any government. The expenditure side of the budget tells us who gets what in public money, and the revenue side of the budget tells us who pays the cost. There are few government activities or programs that do not require an expenditure of funds, and no public funds may be spent without legislative authority. The budgetary process provides a mechanism for reviewing government programs, assessing their costs, relating them to financial resources, and making choices among expenditures. Budgets determine what programs and policies are to be increased, decreased, allowed to lapse, initiated, or renewed. The budget lies at the heart of all public policies.

In the federal government, the Office of Management and Budget (OMB), located in the Executive Office of the President, has the key responsibility for budget preparation. OMB begins preparing a budget more than a year before the beginning of the fiscal year for which it is intended (for example, work began in January 1998 on the budget for the fiscal year beginning October 1, 1999, and ending September 30, 2000). Budget materials and general instructions go out from OMB to departments and agencies, which are required to submit their budget requests for increases or decreases in existing programs and for new programs to OMB. With requests for spending from departments and agencies in hand, OMB begins its own budget review. Hearings are held for each agency. Top agency officials support their requests as convincingly as possible. On rare occasions, a dissatisfied department head may ask the OMB director to present the department's case directly to the president. As the following January approaches, the president and the OMB director devote a great deal of time to the budget document, which is nearing its final stages of assembly. Then, in January, the president sends his proposal—*The Budget of the United States Government*—to the Congress. After the budget is in Congress's hands, the president may recommend further amendments as needs dictate.

Congress has established separate House and Senate Budget Committees and a joint Congressional Budget Office to review the president's budget after its submission to Congress. These committees initially draft a concurrent resolution setting target totals to guide congressional actions on appropriations and revenue bills considered throughout the year. Thus, congressional committees considering specific budget appropriations have the president's recommendations to guide them and the guidelines of the budget committees. If an appropriations bill exceeds the target set by the earlier resolution, it is sent back to the budget committees for reconciliation.

Consideration of specific appropriations is a function of the Appropriations Committee in each house. Both of these important committees have about ten fairly independent subcommittees to review the budget requests of particular agencies or groups of related functions. These subcommittees hold hearings in which department and agency officials, interest groups, and other witnesses testify about new and existing programs and proposed increases or decreases in spending. The appropriations subcommittees are very important, because neither the full committees nor the Congress has the time or expertise to conduct indepth reviews of programs and funding. Although the work of the subcommittees is reviewed by the full committee, and the appropriations acts must be passed by the full Congress, in practice most subcommittee decisions are routinely accepted.

Even after all its work, Congress usually makes no more than small changes in the total budget figure recommended by the president. This is not to say that major struggles do not ensue over particular programs. On some social welfare spending issues (big ones like Medicare and smaller ones like the voluntary service program called AmeriCorps), budget battles have been especially acrimonious. Political partisanship is contributing to a more contentious budget process, but there are so many appropriations that most are still determined by executive agencies interacting with the OMB, and Congress usually makes only minor adjustments in them.

This description of the federal government's budget process may make it sound as if it were the most rational aspect of policymaking, but it is no less political than other aspects. This is because government spending is very big business. The president's proposed budget for fiscal year 2000 is \$1.8 trillion.[17] Methods such as "planning, programming, and budgeting systems" and "zero-based budgeting" have been introduced over the years to make budgeting more rational, but in the long run,

> *if politics is regarded in part as conflict over whose preferences shall prevail in the determination of national policy, then the budget records the outcomes of this struggle. . . . The size and shape of the budget is a matter of serious contention in our political life. Presidents, political parties, administrators, congressmen, interest groups, and interested citizens vie with one another to have their preferences recorded in the budget. The victories and defeats, the compromises and the bargains, the realms of agreement and the spheres of conflict in regard to the role of the national government in our society all appear in the budget. In the most integral sense, budgeting—that is, attempts to allocate scarce financial resources through political processes in order to realize disparate visions of the good life—lies at the heart of the political process.*[18]

Implementation

Policy implementation includes all the activities that result from the official adoption of a policy. Policy implementation is what happens after a law is passed. We should never assume that the passage of a law is the end of the policymaking process. Sometimes laws are passed and nothing happens! Sometimes laws are passed and executive agencies, presuming to act under these laws, do a great deal more than Congress ever intended. Political scientist Robert Lineberry writes,

> *The implementation process is not the end of policy-making, but a* continuation of policy-making by other means. *When policy is pronounced, the implementation process begins. What happens in it may, over the long run, have more impact on the ultimate distribution of policy than the intentions of the policy's framers.*[19]

Specifically, policy implementation involves

1. The creation, organization, and staffing of new agencies to carry out the new policy, or the assignment of new responsibilities to existing agencies and staff.
2. The development of specific directives, rules, regulations, or guidelines to translate new policies into courses of action.
3. The direction and coordination of personnel and expenditures toward the achievement of policy objectives.

The best-laid plans of policymakers often do not work. Before a policy can have any impact, it must be implemented. And what governments say they are going to do is not always what they end up doing.

Traditionally, the implementation of public policy was the subject matter of public administration. And traditionally, administration was supposed to be free of politics. Indeed, the separation of "politics" from "administration" was once thought to be the cornerstone of a scientific approach to administration. But today it is clear that politics and administration cannot be separated. Opponents of policies do not end their opposition after a law is passed. They continue their opposition in the implementation phase of the policy process by opposing attempts to organize, fund, staff, regulate, direct, and coordinate the program. If opponents are unsuccessful in delaying or halting programs in implementation, they may seek to delay or halt them in endless court battles. In short, conflict is a continuing activity in policy implementation.

The federal bureaucracy makes major decisions about the implementation of public policy. There are about two million civilian employees of the federal government (not counting the 750,000 civilian employees of the Department of Defense).[20] This huge bureaucracy has become a major base of power in America—independent of the Congress, the president, the courts, or the people. The bureaucracy does more than fill in the details of congressional policies, although this is one power of bureaucratic authority. Bureaucracies also make important policies on their own by (1) proposing legislation for Congress to pass; (2) writing rules, regulations, and guidelines to implement laws passed by Congress; and (3) deciding specific cases in the application of laws or rules.

In the course of implementing public policy, federal bureaucracies have decided such important questions as the extent to which women and members of particular ethnic groups will benefit from affirmative action programs in education and employment, whether opposition political parties or candidates will be allowed on television to challenge a presidential speech or press conference, and whether welfare agencies will search Social Security Administration files to locate nonsupporting parents. The decisions of bureaucracies can be overturned by Congress or the courts if sufficient opposition develops. But most of these bureaucratic decisions go unchallenged, and there are analogous layers of bureaucracy at the state and local levels.

THE AMERICAN PUBLIC AND SOCIAL WELFARE

Even in a democracy, public opinion may not determine public policy, but politicians are mindful of what their constituents—particularly their powerful constituents—think. Of course, the public, like politicians, frequently do not agree on public policy issues, and its own views are often inconsistent. For example, an analysis of public opinion surveys showed that although Americans tend to express resentment for "welfare" programs, they also say that they want to help people in need.[21] Historically, Americans, young and old, have voiced strong support for the nation's Social Security program.[22]

There is less consensus on spending for public assistance. In the late 1980s, Americans voiced greater support for increased health, education, and nutrition spending than for defense spending,[23] but they were generally not disposed to pay much more in taxes to support programs for the poor.[24] By 1996, 53 percent were against cuts in social spending and 54 percent were against cutting defense spending.[25]

The Gallup Poll keeps its finger on the pulse of the country with continuous telephone surveys of scientifically selected samples of adult Americans. Since 1935 it has asked Americans what they think is the country's most important problem. From 1935 until the late 1980s, Americans were either most concerned about economic issues—unemployment, inflation, high living costs—or wars and related international matters, although racial problems and civil rights did appear at the top of the list a few times in the 1950s and 1960s.[26] Then in 1989, drugs topped the list for the first time and remained there through 1991 when the economy and unemployment again took precedence.[27] In 1994 these issues gave way to what the country now sees as its most important problem—crime.

There is actually considerable variation in what Americans see as the country's most important problem. For example, in April of 1998, 20 percent thought that crime and violence was the most important problem, while 16 percent thought it was a decline in ethics, morals, and the family, 13 percent named education, 12 percent named drugs, and 10 percent said it was poverty and homelessness, followed by a range of other issues.[28]

In 1996 Gallup polled Americans by asking them, "Suppose that on election day this year you could vote on key issues as well as candidates. Please tell me whether you would vote for or against each one of the following propositions."[29] Interviewers then named 27 items in random order. There was at least 80 percent agreement that the federal government should balance the budget, raise the minimum wage, make English the country's official language, impose life sentences for drug dealers, and not give racial preferences on the job and at school. Congress and the president have made progress in balancing the budget (see Chapter 2), raising the minimum wage (see Chapter 9), and in toughening sentences for drug dealers (see Chapter 10). Some states and courts have moved to limit racial preferences (see Chapter 11), and nearly half the states have made English their official language (though it is already the nation's first language). The poll also indicated that Americans are much more divided on issues such as whether social and defense spending should be reduced or whether a flat tax system should be adopted.

Also of interest is how much agreement there is on these issues among particular segments of the population. Take, for example, the issues of a balanced budget, cuts in social spending, restricted abortions, and school busing. As seen in Table 1-1, there is considerable support among all segments of the population for a balanced budget amendment—83 percent were for and 14 percent were against. Men and women were almost equally supportive of the need to balance the budget. Within age groups, a majority of those 50 to 64 years old also favored a balanced budget, but they were less likely to do so than those of other ages. Geographic region of the country made little difference in how people felt on this issue, but those in urban communities were

TABLE 1-1

A Closer Look at How Americans Would Vote on Some of the Issues[a,b]

	Balanced budget amendment		Cuts in social spending		Restricted abortions		School busing for racial balance	
	For	*Against*	*For*	*Against*	*For*	*Against*	*For*	*Against*
National	83%	14%	44%	53%	42%	56%	34%	62%
Sex								
Male	82	16	42	54	41	56	34	64
Female	84	12	46	51	43	55	34	61
Age								
18–29 years	88	11	44	56	45	54	50	48
30–49 years	85	12	41	56	41	57	33	64
50–64 years	74	20	36	58	36	61	28	70
65 & older	82	15	59	36	45	50	24	68
Region								
East	85	13	37	60	35	62	31	65
Midwest	82	13	48	50	44	51	37	60
South	82	15	46	50	46	53	35	60
West	84	13	47	50	41	58	35	64
Community								
Urban	78	19	45	54	40	59	39	58
Suburban	86	12	40	55	39	57	31	65
Rural	86	9	50	47	51	47	33	63
Race								
White	84	12	44	52	43	54	30	66
Non-white	77	22	47	53	36	62	56	39
Education								
College postgraduate	71	28	32	64	27	70	32	61
Bachelor's only	87	10	40	57	40	59	25	73
Some college	87	10	41	56	40	56	32	66
High school or less	83	12	51	45	47	51	39	57
Politics								
Republicans	93	6	49	48	51	47	24	73
Democrats	76	20	37	61	39	58	42	53
Independents	82	13	47	49	37	60	35	62
Ideology								
Liberal	71	24	39	60	30	67	50	47
Moderate	83	14	40	58	40	59	34	62
Conservative	89	8	53	42	52	46	25	71
Income								
$75,000 & over	80	19	38	60	27	70	25	73
$50,000 & over	84	13	40	58	34	63	25	72
$30,000–49,999	87	10	40	56	44	55	34	63
$20,000–29,999	83	14	46	51	47	52	37	60
Under $20,000	79	17	50	46	46	50	42	53

Source: Lydia Saad, "Issues Referendum Reveals Populist Leanings," *The Gallup Poll Monthly,* May 1996, p. 6.

[a]Responses are based on 922 interviews.

[b]Responses of "No opinion" are omitted from the table.

somewhat less likely than suburban and rural residents to support a balanced budget. Whites were somewhat more likely than those of other racial groups to favor balancing the budget. Those with postgraduate education were least likely to see the need for a balanced budget. Republicans were most supportive of a balanced budget, and Democrats were the least supportive, with Independents falling in between. Similarly, conservatives were most supportive while liberals were least supportive and moderates fell in between. Finally, middle income earners were most supportive of a balanced budget while those in the highest and lowest income groups were less supportive.

There is much more disagreement about cuts in social spending, with 44 percent of Americans polled for and 53 percent against cuts. Interestingly, women were slightly more inclined to support cuts, a finding that differs from many previous polls. Older Americans were more likely than other groups to say they favored cuts, also interesting in light of the fact that the elderly receive more of the country's social welfare dollars than younger Americans. People living in the eastern United States were less likely than those living in other areas to support social spending cuts, while those in rural areas were more likely to support cuts than those living in other types of communities. Also interesting is that there was little difference in how white Americans and Americans of other racial groups felt about social spending cuts. Americans with less formal education were more likely to support cuts than those with more education, and those who earned less tended to favor spending cuts more than those in other income groups, even though those with less education and less income often rely more on social welfare programs than those with more education and income. As might be expected, Republicans and conservatives were more likely to favor social spending cuts than those of other parties and other political ideologies.

A majority of Americans oppose restrictions on abortion, but those most likely to oppose restrictions have postgraduate education and earn the most money. With regard to school busing, about two-thirds of Americans are opposed to this method of achieving racial balance. These percentages are reflected across most segments of the population except that those 18 to 29 years old are about equally divided on the issue, and more whites, Republicans, and conservatives oppose busing than other groups. As income increases, support for school busing also declines.

In addition to the problems that Americans believe should be addressed most urgently, another important question is who should address them. A synthesis of public opinion polls indicates that confidence in government, especially the federal government, fell substantially from the 1970s to the 1990s, and that citizens decidedly felt that the federal government gave them the least for their money compared to state and local governments.[30] Citizens also felt that the states should assume more responsibilities now held by the federal government. A majority thought that the states should take the lead in improving education (72 percent), reducing crime (68 percent), and providing job training (55 percent). There was not a clear majority on reforming welfare or improving health care, but citizens felt that the federal government should take the lead in protecting civil rights (67 percent) and in strengthening the economy (64 percent).

America's Capacity for Giving

In addition to government expenditures for social welfare, we must consider private philanthropy and volunteerism as important sources of aid. Volunteers in the United States spend countless hours helping those less fortunate than themselves—they visit elderly people in nursing homes, tutor children from disadvantaged environments, dish out meals in soup kitchens, assist people with AIDS, and perform many other services, all without much government help.

Independent Sector, an association of private, foundation, and voluntary organizations, reports that approximately half of all adults volunteer, and they spend a little over 4 hours a week doing so.[31] Those 45 to 54 years old are most likely to volunteer (55 percent), and those 18 to 24 and 75 years and older are least likely to volunteer (38 percent and 34 percent, respectively). Volunteers also tend to be white, women, college graduates, and those in higher income brackets. Volunteers are most likely to invest their efforts in religious or church-related activities (26 percent), followed by a variety of informal activities (20 percent), educational activities (18 percent), youth development (15 percent), health (13 percent), human services (13 percent), and many other activities from international efforts to the arts.

A number of Americans also dig into their pockets to help. According to the American Association of Fund-Raising Counsel (AAFRC) Trust for Philanthropy, in 1997 Americans gave nearly $143 billion, an increase of $10 billion from 1996, fueled largely by a strong economy.[32] Individual Americans are the biggest contributors, having given $109 billion. In 1995 contributing households gave an average of $1,017, or a little more than 2 percent of their income.[33] Although this is considerably less than the 10 percent that many churches encourage their members to tithe, it represents a substantial amount of the funds donated to charities. Foundations and corporations provided far less than individuals; in 1997 their contributions were $13 billion and $8 billion, respectively.[34] Religious organizations received the greatest share of all the funds donated ($75 billion) while education received $22 billion, health received $14 billion, human services received $13 billion, and the arts received $11 billion. For 1997, *The Chronicle of Philanthropy* reports that the Salvation Army was the biggest recipient of charitable donations, taking in $1.2 billion, twice as much as the next largest recipient, the YMCA.[35] Volunteerism and philanthropy allow Americans to channel their efforts and funds where they feel the needs are greatest.

Americans' tradition of service is also exemplified in federal organizations like the Peace Corps and the Corporation for National Service. The Peace Corps supplies volunteers to other countries to assist with community development efforts. The Corporation for National Service operates AmeriCorps, the Volunteers in Service to America (VISTA) program, the Retired and Senior Volunteer Program, and several other domestic volunteer programs.

Saying that the government could not possibly meet all the country's social service needs, former President George Bush tried to encourage even more volunteer efforts during his term in office. Bush referred to the country's many volunteers as "1,000 points of light," and he supported the idea of a national service program for young people run by a foundation with substantial federal funding. Similar plans, many urging voluntary participation by youth in return for educational benefits to attend college or vocational schools, had been proposed for many years. Some people believe that such service should be required of all young people, similar to a military draft. President Clinton also sees the power of volunteer efforts. Early in his administration he pushed for a national service program that would allow Americans of any age to serve their country in exchange for help in obtaining a college education. The president was successful in getting his AmeriCorps program enacted, although he had hoped for a larger program (see Chapter 9). During Clinton's second term, he convened the President's Summit for America's Future with the support of all the surviving former presidents. The summit was a kick-off to a two-year campaign chaired by retired General Colin Powell to promote volunteerism with an emphasis on helping children in disadvantaged situations through tutoring and other services.

Everyone appreciates the efforts of those who are willing to give their time or money to help others. It is difficult for Americans to imagine a society where such assistance is not available. Citizen involvement is important to public, private, and church-affiliated social service agencies. Volunteers do much to aid their communities by helping these agencies provide more and better services. Like President Bush, President Clinton has said that "Much of the work of America cannot be done by government."[36] Conversely, much of the work of America cannot be done by volunteers alone. Illustration 1-2 puts these roles into perspective. As Bishop John Ricard of the U.S. Catholic Conference commented on voluntary efforts to feed the hungry:

> *Our efforts cannot and should not substitute for just public policies and effective programs to meet the needs of the hungry. . . . [These efforts] should not be misread as a sign of success for volunteerism, but rather a desperate attempt to feed hungry people when others have abandoned their responsibility.*[37]

And specifically in regard to the Clinton administration's efforts to recruit corporations' help, Liz Krueger of the Community Food Resource Center in New York City said, "What I fear is the perception that these companies, or the public as a whole, can take the place of radically reduced government assistance."[38] Many people—those in need of job training or mental health care—need professional assistance. Volunteers alone cannot make up for gaps in social services when professional help is needed. One challenge of our social welfare system is to determine the best mix of public and private, professional and voluntary efforts to help those in need.

Political Ideology and Social Welfare

If Americans were pure in their political ideology, there would be clear differences in the conservative, liberal, and moderate agendas for the country. Just who fits each of these categories? According to the *New Political Dictionary,* a **conservative** is "a defender of the status quo"; "the more rigid conservative generally opposes virtually all government regulation of the economy, . . . favors local and state action over federal

ILLUSTRATION 1-2

We Can Take Care of Our Own . . . Or Can We?

by Julian Wolpert

Arguing that giving more responsibility for social programs to the states and less to Congress and the president will not shred the safety net, [former] Sen. Robert Packwood of Oregon [once] said . . . "For us to presume that they're Scrooges and we're Midases is wrong."

Unfortunately, the data shows clearly that Scrooge's descendants are alive and well, and in control of some parts of our nation. And in other places, deep recession or long-term poverty requires help from outsiders that cannot be provided by local government or charities.

A glance at the tables in the current *Statistical Abstract* is enough to show that three-person households on welfare in Texas and Alabama receive monthly payments equal to only one-seventh of those states' per capita income. At the other extreme, welfare recipients in Minnesota get benefits three-and-a-half times greater than in Texas or Alabama—but still less than half the per capita income in *their* state. In contrast, Texans, Alabamans, and Minnesotans receiving Social Security are all eligible for the same benefits because, as a federal program, Social Security doesn't penalize anyone for where they happen to live. None of this should come as a surprise: when Washington folks speak disparagingly of people on welfare why would there be any reason to think that local folks would think or act differently? At least programs originating in Washington treat everyone the same.

What about the ability of charities to make up the difference? In saying that he favors greater dependency on local charities for safety net support, [former] House Speaker Newt Gingrich expresse[d] a noble sentiment, but one that is not backed up by performance. The findings from *Patterns of Generosity in America,* a . . . Twentieth Century Fund study, shows how far-fetched it is to expect that charities can fill the gaps left by the less generous state and local governments. Indeed, we found that where state and local governments are most generous to their neediest residents, charitable donations are highest; where government is relatively stingy, so are private donors.

Overall, donations to charities are a meager 2 percent of personal income, despite the fact that contributions are tax deductible. And contributions have remained at that level for two decades, whether the economy was in boom or recession. If the level of giving could be raised to 5 percent—an implausibly high figure—that would still fall far short of matching even the amount of money currently being proposed for cuts in federal social service programs.

Furthermore, charity organizations are overwhelmingly locally based in the strictest sense of the word: most of the money they raise is spent on services and projects within the community itself. With our communities increasingly becoming segregated by income level and most charities doing their work closest to home, little of what is raised crosses over community or ethnic lines except in cases of temporary disasters.

It also is true that contribution levels do not correlate with the affluence of a

continued

ILLUSTRATION 1-2 *(continued)*

community or the depth of distress there. Some communities are, for whatever reasons, generous. They raise much more for the United Way, Jewish Federation, and Catholic Charities for local services than do others. Cities in Ohio, for example, are twice as generous as cities in Texas in their contributions per employee to the United Way.

The typical beneficiaries of most are community churches and synagogues, YMCAs and related organizations, museums, public radio and television, universities, and parochial schools. In short, donors tend to give to charities for services the donors themselves use, and not to sustain safety nets. Those charitable agencies that do provide assistance to the economically needy and the handicapped rely overwhelmingly, not on individual largesse, but on money from federal, state, and local government.

Unquestionably, charities add to the variety and quality of the life we enjoy in our communities. For this, they deserve our continued support. But we shouldn't expect too much. Even the most generous communities lack the organization and resources needed for the much larger job of addressing serious inequality in income, education, health care, nutrition, and other areas for which we rely today on the federal government for assistance.

If devolution is a ruse for simply doing less, its supporters should come clean and let the nation have a debate on the merits of the proposition. But if [former] Senator Packwood, [former] Speaker Gingrich, and the others really believe more can be done with less if it is done by state and local governments and private charities, the responsible thing to do would be to ask the Office of Management and Budget or the General Accounting Office, or some legitimate think tank to conduct a rigorous study of the implications of devolution to states, localities, and charities.

Or, they might start with demonstration projects in different parts of our nation before rushing into a change of this magnitude. Congress and the public need an honest appraisal of what "taking care of our own" really implies.

Julian Wolpert is a professor at Princeton University's Woodrow Wilson School and the author of the Twentieth Century Fund report, *Patterns of Generosity in America.* The Twentieth Century Fund is now the Century Foundation.

Source: Julian Wolpert, "We Can Take Care of Our Own . . . Or Can We?" *The Washington Post,* June 29, 1995, http://epn.org/tcf/xxwhos01.html.

action, and emphasizes fiscal responsibility, most notably in the form of balanced budgets." But not all conservatives are this rigid. On the other hand, a **liberal** is "one who believes in more government action to meet individual need."[39] Many Americans fall somewhere in between these extremes.

The Republican party platform as of late has been highly conservative, especially on social issues such as abortion and gay rights. Many Republican members of Congress have also resisted broad-scale health care reform, preferring a more incremental and narrowly targeted approach. Some Republicans think that their party has moved too far to the right.[40] Although they may favor the Republican ideology on spending and taxing matters, they are unhappy with the party's stance on abortion and gay rights. Meanwhile, many people who espouse the liberal agenda, which remains consistent in its prochoice and pro gay rights stances, have become more cautious in their approach to government spending. Although the term *liberal* (sometimes referred to as the "L" word) is most often associated with the Democratic party, not all Democrats are happy with the liberal agenda for the country. Democrats of more moderate or conservative persuasions may align themselves with the need for strengthening some social programs, but there are Democrats whose religious and moral convictions persuade them that access to abortion and gay rights are not issues they can support. Except for the most strident of ideologies, the lines between liberal and conservative, Democrat and Republican can be difficult to draw.

To the liberal and conservative rhetoric of the country, we must now add the rhetoric of family and social values. The country has long debated the effects that out-of-wedlock births, divorce, and desertion have on its moral fiber. The media seized the opportunity to exploit the issue when former Vice President Dan Quayle tried to make the Republican pitch for family values by criticizing TV character Murphy Brown for having a baby outside of marriage. When Gallup pollsters said to Americans, "Some people think the government should promote traditional values in our society. Others think that the government should not favor any particular set of values. Which comes closer to your own view?," 53 percent favored promoting traditional values while 42 percent believed that the government should not favor any particular set of values.[41] "Traditional values," however, may mean different things to different people.

The Republican platform on traditional family matters sits quite well with the "religious right" of this country. No longer content to focus on matters of religion alone, this movement, the so-called *moral majority,* has taken a high profile on certain political issues, especially abortion. As one source described it, the religious right believes that "Government should enforce scriptural law," while "most mainstream religious people support the separation of church and state to ensure freedom of religion and speech for all."[42] Though the religious right would like to see less government involvement in issues like education and public assistance, it would like more government intervention to outlaw abortion and restrict the behavior of gay men and lesbians. The ranks of the religious right feel that they hold the ideal for family values in the United States, even if public opinion polls show that most Americans favor access to abortion on some level. Of course, virtually all Americans believe in family values, even if they don't agree with the moral majority on what constitutes a family and how best to preserve these values. Interest in the role of religion in politics and public life seems to be growing.[43] Certainly, many individuals' stances on public policy issues are influenced by their religious orientation, and these orientations vary as much as do individuals' political leanings.

The presidency of William Jefferson Clinton provides its own study in political ideology. The president, a Southern Baptist, is well informed about scripture. During his first run for the presidency in 1992, Clinton called for a "new covenant" for social welfare. He wanted more job training and child care in return for greater responsibility on the part of AFDC recipients through stiffer work requirements, caps on the amounts given to those who have more children while receiving public assistance, and limits on the amount of time families can receive benefits—not what Americans think of as typical liberal rhetoric from a Democratic president. Those who espouse this combination of views may be called "New Democrats" or "centrists."

On entering office in 1993, President Clinton demonstrated his concern for American families by signing the Family and Medical Leave Act. The act provides 12 weeks of unpaid leave to workers when a new baby arrives or there is a family illness. President Bush never signed this bill, because he claimed it would stymie business. But the moral majority has been clearly upset by President Clinton's strong support of abortion rights and by his support of gay rights. The country's discussion of family values in the context of political life has taken on broader meaning as the president's extramarital behavior (and that of some Republican Congressmembers) has dominated the media. Although the religious right has been rocked from time to time by the scandals of some of its own high profile televangelists, the president's admitted marital infidelity has given the movement more grist for its mill. Americans have spent a good deal of time contemplating the relationship between personal values and public life.

PACs and Social Welfare

The political model of policymaking provides a clear indication of the importance of influence in the political arena, but the poor and disadvantaged, who need help the most, are not represented in Washington in the same fashion as other groups in society.[44] They rarely write letters to members of Congress, and they do not make significant campaign contributions. They are rarely found on a representative's home state lecture circuit—service club lunches, civic meetings, and dedications. The poor cannot afford to come to Washington to visit their representatives' offices. Indeed, they do not turn out at the polls to vote as often as the nonpoor.

To the extent that the poor and disadvantaged are represented at all in Washington, they are represented by "proxies"—groups that are not poor or disadvantaged themselves but that claim to represent these groups. Many of these proxy groups have organized and reorganized themselves under various names over the years—the National Welfare Rights Organization (dissolved in the mid-1970s), the Children's Defense Fund, the Low Income Housing Coalition, the Food Research and Action Center.

Lobbyists for the poor can be divided roughly into three categories: (1) churches, civil rights groups, and liberal organizations; (2) organized labor; and (3) welfare program administrators and lawyers. The churches (the National Conference of Catholic Bishops, the National Council of Churches, B'nai Brith, and others) often support programs for the poor out of a sense of moral obligation. Likewise, liberal activist groups (Common Cause, Americans for Democratic Action, and others) often support social programs out of an ideological commitment. Civil rights organizations—the National Urban League, the National Association for the Advancement of Colored People (NAACP), the Mexican American Legal Defense and Education Fund (MALDEF), and others—support programs for the poor and disadvantaged as a part of their general concern for the conditions affecting particular ethnic groups.

The success of lobbying efforts on behalf of the poor can also depend on the addition of organized labor's political power to the coalition of churches, civil rights groups, and liberal activists. Even though the clout of organized labor has waned in recent years with declining union membership, the AFL-CIO rallied during the 1996 election in an effort to reverse the poor treatment that members felt labor issues had received at the hands of Republicans. Labor groups like the AFL-CIO do all the things that poor and disadvantaged members of society find difficult to do in politics: political organizing, campaign financing, letter writing, and personal lobbying. Historically, organized labor has tended to support programs for the poor, even though union pay scales have moved a great distance from the poverty line. Among those who comprise organized labor, labor leaders may be more likely to support social programs than the rank-and-file membership. Of course, the first concern of organized labor is labor legislation—labor relations, minimum wages, fair labor standards, and so on—but when labor leaders join other members of the welfare lobby in support of social programs, the result is a stronger political coalition.[45]

Welfare program administrators and lawyers have a direct financial interest in supporting social welfare spending, and they may take the lead in organizing the others into coalitions that support particular programs. Their opponents—those who favor reduced spending for social programs—complain, "Virtually all of the lobbying has come from people who are involved directly or indirectly in administering these programs."[46] The welfare bureaucracy is said to create a *poverty lobby,* which consists of "people doing well by the government's doing good."

Prominent among the organizations representing social program administrators and lawyers is the American Federation of State, County, and Municipal Employees (AFSCME). Affiliated with the AFL-CIO, AFSCME is a labor union that includes many public workers whose jobs are directly affected by cutbacks in social programs. Another organization concerned about social welfare services is the Legal Service Corporation (LSC), whose attorneys provide legal assistance to poor and disadvantaged individuals. The LSC is chartered as an independent corporation, but much of its funding comes from the federal government. The LSC has come under a great deal of criticism for what conservative congressmembers see as lobbying on its own behalf. Of course, there are very few government bureaucracies—from the Defense Department, to the National Aeronautics and Space Administration, to the Department of Agriculture—that do not, directly or indirectly, lobby Congress for their own programs.

While the welfare lobby continues to go about its work, an anti-welfare lobby has grown increasingly vocal in this country. This sentiment has been fueled by the positions of authors such as Charles Murray who believe that public assistance programs are the cause, not the cure, of welfare dependency,[47] and conservative radio personality Rush Limbaugh who railed against the Clinton health care reform proposal and just about anything else the president tries to do. The religious right has also had success in promoting its social welfare agenda by getting anti-gay rights measures on the ballots in several states, by influencing school board elections, and with its untiring efforts to erode reproductive freedoms.[48]

Lobbying for or against social welfare issues is a form of political activity that goes on every day with members of Congress and state legislatures. An even more important form of political activity is support of individual candidates. Those interested in seeing specific types of legislation passed or defeated naturally support candidates who share their views. Support may come verbally through endorsements, and financially through campaign contributions at election time. Today, many candidates and special interests are supported through the use of **political action committees** (PACs). PACs are used by all types of interest groups. The American Medical Association operates a very wealthy and influential PAC. Virtually all forms of business and industry—real estate, agriculture, automobile, insurance, hospital—have PACs. The National Association of Social Workers, AFSCME, and other groups of social welfare service providers also operate some form of PAC. Although it does not identify itself as a PAC, the most prominent politically active group of the religious right is the Christian Coalition, founded by preacher Pat Robertson. There were 608 PACs in 1974 and 3,798 in 1999.[49] From 1995 through 1996, PACs raised $438 million.[50]

Many PACs have a vested interest in social welfare spending. The American Medical Association, long opposed to government intervention in the health care arena, now has a very large stake in the Medicare and Medicaid programs. The AMA closely monitors attempts to change the nature of health care delivery in the United States. So does the Health Insurance Association of America which spent millions to influence the shape of health care when the Clinton administration tried to substantially alter the role of insurers in health delivery (see Chapter 8). Other groups that provide social welfare services also want to make sure that they are not adversely affected by new legislation, budget cuts, and government regulations, and they raise money to see that just the opposite happens.

A few politicians refuse to accept PAC money. Although this number may be growing, support of candidates through PACs remains a crucial feature of election campaigns. The PAC that contributed the most ($2.6 million) to candidates in 1995 and 1996 was the Democratic Republican Independent Voter Education Committee.[51] Other PACs that contributed at least $2 million represented a mix of professionals and trade organizations: AFSCME, United Auto Workers, Association of Trial Lawyers, National Automobile Dealers Association, National Education Association, American Medical Association, Realtors Political Action Committee, International Brotherhood of Electrical Workers, and United Food & Commercial Workers International. Candidates generally prominently display the endorsements they receive from such organizations. The fear, of course, is that elected officials who are beholden to these special interests have a difficult time resolving public policy issues. For this reason, many individuals concerned about political ethics and campaign reform have proposed legislation to limit the use of PAC funds to support individual candidates.

Professional and trade group PACs are not the only big political contributors. So called "soft money" contributions also allow corporations and individuals associated with corporations, as well as other individuals, labor groups, and PACs, to give substantial sums of money—more than can be given to candidates directly—to party committees. The committees can then distribute this largesse to candidates running for state and local offices. The Federal Election Commission continues to state that "soft" money "cannot be used in connection with federal elections."[52] Newspaper accounts give another impression, indicating that "soft money" is being used to provide at least some forms of assistance to federal office seekers, especially following a June 1996 Supreme Court ruling based on First Amendment protections of free speech.[53] The nonpartisan Center for Responsive Politics reports that the largest soft money contributors in the 1995–1996 election cycle were Philip Morris, Joseph E. Seagrams & Sons, RJR Nabisco, Walt Disney Co., and Atlantic Richfield.[54] When most types of contributions are added together, tobacco giant Philip Morris was the largest overall contributor in the 1995–1996 election cycle, giving over $4 million.[55]

Campaign finance reform is an important topic on the political agenda. The influence that particular individuals and groups may yield through their contributions is one concern that may warrant change; so are the campaign finance scandals we so often hear about. It is no wonder that the "little person" feels it is hard to be heard.

SUMMARY

Although there are elements of rationalism in policymaking, the policy process is largely political. Our abilities to develop policies rationally are limited because we cannot agree on what constitute social problems and on what, if anything, should be done to alleviate these problems. We also hesitate to take bold, new directions in our current social welfare system, because we fear making large, costly errors that may be difficult to reverse.

Many energetic lobbies and political action committees in the United States work to influence elected officials every day. The work of politicians is difficult because the values espoused by these competing interest groups can differ widely. When it comes to social welfare policy, Americans represent the political spectrum from conservatives to middle-of-the-road centrists to liberals. This diversity of opinion causes the country to pursue a pluralist approach to social welfare policymaking. Policymakers follow several lines of thinking and arrive at policies and programs that are often contradictory and overlapping because they try to see that there is something there for everyone.

Social welfare policy development and implementation are much more a political "art and craft"[56] than a rational science. It is not enough for human service professionals to know the needs of people and to want to pass policies and provide services to help them. Given the backlash against some forms of social welfare policy, especially public assistance, policy advocates for the disenfranchised must both understand the political process and be adept at working within it if they are to have a voice in shaping social policy.

NOTES

1. See, for example, David G. Gil, "A Systematic Approach to Social Policy Analysis," *Social Service Review,* Vol. 44, December 1970, pp. 411–426.

2. T. H. Marshall, *Social Policy* (London: Hutchison University Library, 1955), p. 7. Also see the discussion in Neil Gilbert and Paul Terrell, *Dimensions of Social Welfare Policy,* 4th ed. (Boston: Allyn and Bacon, 1998), Chapter 1. The distinction between *social policy* and *social welfare policy* is discussed in George Rohrlich, "Social Policy and Income Distribution," in Robert Morris, ed., *Encyclopedia of Social Work,* 16th ed. (New York: National Association of Social Workers, 1971), pp. 1385–1386.

3. See Carl T. Friedrich, *Man and His Government* (New York: McGraw-Hill, 1963), p. 70; Harold Lasswell and Abraham Kaplan, *Power and Society* (New Haven, CT: Yale University Press, 1970), p. 71.

4. Heinz Eulau and Kenneth Prewitt, *Labyrinths of Democracy* (Indianapolis: Bobbs-Merrill, 1973), p. 465.

5. Other major theoretical approaches to the study of public policy include institutionalism, elite theory, group theory, systems theory, and incrementalism. For an introduction to these approaches, see Thomas R. Dye, *Understanding Public Policy,* 9th ed. (Englewood Cliffs, NJ: Prentice Hall, 1998), especially chapter 2.

6. Edith Stokey and Richard Zeckhauser, *A Primer of Policy Analysis* (New York: Norton, 1978).

7. Herbert A. Simon, *Administrative Behavior* (New York: Macmillan, 1945), p. 79. See also his *Models of Man* (New York: Wiley, 1957) and *The Sciences of the Artificial* (New York: Wiley, 1970). Simon was trained as a political scientist; he won the Nobel Prize in economics in 1978.

8. Harold Lasswell, *Politics: Who Gets What, When, How* (New York: Free Press, 1936).

9. Edward C. Banfield and James Q. Wilson, *City Politics* (Cambridge, MA: Harvard University Press, 1963), p. 7.

10. John Rawls, *A Theory of Justice* (Cambridge, MA: Harvard University Press, 1972).

11. James Madison, *The Federalist, No. X,* November 23, 1787, reprinted in *The Federalist; or, The New Constitution* (London: Dent, 1911), pp. 41–48.

12. Charles E. Lindblom, "The Science of 'Muddling Through,'" *Public Administration Review,* Vol. 19, Spring 1959, pp. 79–88.

13. See Charles O. Jones, *An Introduction to the Study of Public Policy,* 2nd ed. (North Scituate, MA: Duxbury Press, 1978); Dye, *Understanding Public Policy,* 9th ed.

14. Peter Bachrach and Morton S. Baratz, *Power and Poverty* (New York: Oxford University Press, 1979), p. 7.

15. Thomas R. Dye and Harmon Zeigler, *American Politics in the Media Age,* 3rd ed. (Monterey, CA: Brooks/Cole, 1989), especially chapter 5.

16. See Christopher Hewitt, "Estimating the Number of Homeless: Media Misrepresentation of an Urban Problem," *Journal of Urban Affairs,* Vol. 18, No. 3, 1996, pp. 431–447, especially p. 440.

17. Executive Office of the President, Office of Management and Budget, *Budget of the United States Government, Fiscal Year 2000* (Washington, DC: U.S. Government Printing Office, 1999).

18. Aaron Wildavsky, *The New Politics of the Budgetary Process* (Glenview, IL: Scott Foresman, 1988), p. 8.

19. Robert L. Lineberry, *American Public Policy* (New York: Harper & Row, 1977), p. 71.

20. U.S. Bureau of the Census, *Statistical Abstract of the United States, 1998* (Washington, DC: U.S. Government Printing Office, 1998), Table No. 559, p. 353.

21. R. Kent Weaver, Robert Y. Shapiro, and Lawrence R. Jacobs, "Welfare (The Polls-Trends)," *Public Opinion Quarterly,* Vol. 59, No. 4, 1995, pp. 606–627.

22. Fay Lomax Cook, "Congress and the Public: Convergent and Divergent Opinions on Social Security," in Henry J. Aaron, ed., *Social Security and the Budget: Proceedings of the First Conference of the National Academy of Social Insurance* (New York: University Press of America, 1990), pp. 79–107.

23. *The Gallup Report,* Report No. 274, July 1988, pp. 4–9.

24. Jon Noble and Keith Melville, "The Public's Social Welfare Mandate," *Public Opinion,* January/February 1989, pp. 45–49, 59.

25. Lydia Saad, "Issues Referendum Reveals Populist Leanings," *The Gallup Poll Monthly,* May 1996, pp. 2–6.

26. Karen Branch, "An Eye on Drugs," *Austin American-Statesman,* August 29, 1989, http://archives.statesman.com.

27. "Most Important Problem," Public releases from Gallup Poll results, December 1997, http://www.gallup.com/poll/data/problem.html.

28. "Most Important Problem," *The Gallup Poll Organization,* http://www.gallup.com/Gallup_Poll_Data/mood/problem.htm, accessed December 29, 1998.

29. Saad, "Issues Referendum Reveals Populist Leanings."

30. This paragraph relies on Timothy J. Conlan and James D. Riggle, "New Opportunities/Nagging Questions: The Politics of State Policymaking in the Nineties," November 27, 1995; "Changing Public Attitudes on Government and Taxes," U.S. Advisory Commission on Intergovernmental Relations, 1994; Yankelovich/Time/

CNN, Roper Center for Public Opinion Research, January 25–26, 1995, all reported in Kenneth Jost, "The States and Federalism," *Congressional Quarterly Researcher,* September 13, 1996, pp. 795–815; also see Charles Murray, "Americans Remain Wary of Washington," *Wall Street Journal,* December 23, 1997, p. A14.

31. This paragraph relies on Virginia Hodgkinson, Murray Weitzman, and the Gallup Organization, Inc., *Giving and Volunteering in the United States: 1996 Edition* (Washington, DC: Independent Sector, 1996) cited in *U.S. Bureau of the Census, Statistical Abstract of the United States: 1998* (Washington, DC: U.S. Government Printing Office, 1998), Table No. 638, p. 396.

32. AAFRC Trust for Philanthropy, "*Giving U.S.A. 1998.* Announces Charitable Giving Increased 7.5% in 1997," May 27, 1998, http://www.aafrc.org/NEWS.HTM.

33. Hodgkinson et al., *Giving and Volunteering in the United States: 1996 Edition,* cited in *U.S. Bureau of the Census, Statistical Abstract of the United States: 1998,* Table No. 639, p. 396.

34. Figures in this sentence and the next rely on AAFRC Trust for Philanthropy, "*Giving U.S.A. 1998* Announces Charitable Giving Increased 7.5% in 1997."

35. Debra E. Blum, Paul Demko, Marilyn Dickey, Holly Hall, and Domenica Marchetti, "A Banner Year for Big Charities," *The Chronicle of Philanthropy,* November 5, 1998, http://philanthropy.com/premium/search.htm.

36. Quoted in Scott Shepard, "Summit to Tap Volunteer Spirit," *Austin American Statesman,* April 27, 1997, pp. A1, 21.

37. Bishop John Ricard, cited in the *Los Angeles Times,* quote reprinted in *Hunger Action Forum,* Vol. 2, No. 3, March 1989, p. 20.

38. Quoted in George J. Church, "The Corporate Crusaders," *Time,* April 28, 1997, p. 56.

39. These definitions are from William Safire, *New Political Dictionary* (New York: Random House, 1993).

40. See, for example, Steve Goldstein (Knight Ridder Washington Bureau), GOP Leaning Too Far to Right, Poll Finds," *Austin American-Statesman,* March 15, 1996, pp. A1 & 4.

41. *Gallup Poll Monthly,* March 1993, p. 34.

42. "Unmasking Religious Right Extremism," American Association of University Women *Outlook,* Summer 1994, pp. 20–25.

43. Discussion of the role of religion in politics and public life warrants more attention than can be provided here. See, for example, Ronald F. Thiemann, *Religion in Public Life: A Dilemma for Democracy* (Washington, DC: Georgetown University Press, 1996); also see sections of Dan Balz and Ronald Brownstein, *Storming the Gates: Protest Politics and Republican Revival* (Boston: Little, Brown, 1996).

44. This discussion of the "poverty lobby" relies on Bill Keller, "Special Treatment No Longer Given Advocates for the Poor," *Congressional Quarterly Weekly,* Vol. 39, No. 16, April 18, 1981, pp. 659–664.

45. Also see Mary Warner (Newhouse News Service), "Labor Renewing Links with Religion," *Austin American-Statesman,* December 28, 1997, p. J1; Kevin Galvin, "AFL-CIO Panel Sets Agenda for 1998," *Austin American-Statesman,* January 31, 1998, p. D3.

46. Rep. Phil Gramm (D-Texas) quoted in Keller, "Special Treatment No Longer Gives Advocates for the Poor," p. 662. Gramm changed parties and is now a Republican U.S. Senator from Texas.

47. Charles Murray, *Losing Ground: American Social Policy, 1950–1980* (New York: Basic Books, 1984).

48. See "Unmasking Religious Right Extremism"; also see materials of People for the American Way, Your Voice Against Intolerance, 2000 M Street, NW, Washington, DC.

49. Federal Election Commission, "PAC Count–1974 to Present," news release, January 12, 1999, http://www.fec.gov/press/paccnt99.htm.

50. Federal Election Commission, "PAC Activity Increases in 1995–96 Election Cycle," press release, April 22, 1997, http://www.fec.gov/press/pacnye96.htm.

51. Federal Election Commission, "Top 50 PAC's—Contributions to Candidates, January 1, 1995–December 31, 1996," http://www.fec.gov/finance/pacnye96.htm.

52. Federal Election Commission, "Major Parties Report Record Amounts in 'Soft Money' Contributions," press release, March 19, 1998, http://www.fec.gov/press/pty97.htm.

53. See Adam Clymer (*The New York Times*), "High Court Rulings Have Eroded Campaign Finance Regulations," *Austin American-Statesman,* June 16, 1996, p. A2; Adam Clymer (*The New York Times*), "Justices Reject Limit on Spending by Parties," *Austin American-Statesman,* June 27, 1996, p. A8; Andrew Mollison, "Some Big Donors Not Averse to Soft-Money Ban," *Austin American-Statesman,* May 31, 1998, p. A9; Walter Shapiro, "The Hard Truth: Soft Money Has Bought This Campaign," *USA Today,* October 4, 1996, p. 9A.

54. Center for Responsive Politics, "Top 50 Soft Money Contributors," http://www.crp.org/crpdocs/bigpicture/top/bp.top50soft.html, includes money from the organizations' treasuries, their political action committees, and their officers, employees, and immediate families.

55. Center for Responsive Politics, "Serious Money: The Top 100 Overall Contributors," http://www.crp.org/crpdocs/bigpicture/top/bp.top100.2.html.

56. Aaron Wildavsky, *The Art and Craft of Policy Analysis* (Boston: Little, Brown, 1979).

CHAPTER

Government and Social Welfare

HISTORICAL PERSPECTIVES ON SOCIAL WELFARE

Social welfare policy as we know it dates back to the beginning of the seventeenth century in Elizabethan England. English colonists who settled in North America brought with them many English welfare traditions. In the colonies, as in England, the earliest sources of welfare aid for the destitute were families, friends, and churches.[1] Later, private charities emerged and local and state governments intervened as a last resort. As the twentieth century brought an increased number of social problems for Americans, the federal government was forced to enact its own social welfare legislation, known as the "New Deal" of the 1930s.

The Great Society programs of the 1960s brought another large-scale attempt on the part of the federal government to alleviate poverty and suffering. But during the 1980s, a different response to hardship in America emerged. Concerned with growing costs and disillusioned with the perceived failure of many public assistance programs, the administration of Republican President Ronald Reagan attempted to limit the federal government's role in social welfare and to increase reliance on state governments and the private sector in providing welfare services. The Bush administration followed a similar path. In 1993 Democrat Bill Clinton assumed the presidency with his own ideas about social welfare. After a long and often bitter debate, in 1996 Congress reached a bipartisan compromise on "welfare reform" which has resulted in a decidedly more conservative approach to public assistance. The following pages contain a brief review of the history of social welfare, a discussion of factors that have contributed to the growth of social welfare programs in the United States, and a consideration of some of the more recent ideas about addressing social welfare problems.

Elizabethan Poor Law

In Europe, the first source of welfare assistance was **mutual aid.** In time of need, the only recourse was this reliance on one another. If a family's food crop failed or the breadwinner became ill and unable to work, brothers, sisters, or neighbors pitched in, knowing that they would receive the same assistance should they need it one day. Later, it became the duty of the church and of wealthy feudal lords to help the needy.[2] During much of the Middle Ages, the emphasis was on doing charitable works as a religious duty.[3] Attitudes toward the poor were benevolent. Those destitute through no fault of their own were treated with dignity and respect and were helped through the hard times.[4]

These early systems of aid were informal, but as the structure of society became more complex, so did the system of providing welfare assistance. The first laws designed to curb poverty were passed in England during the fourteenth and fifteenth centuries. In 1349 the Black Death (bubonic plague) drastically reduced the population of the country. King Edward III responded with the Statute of Laborers to discourage vagrancy and begging; all able-bodied people were ordered to work, and giving alms was forbidden.[5]

Changes in the structure of society eventually pushed the Elizabethan government to develop its own brand of social welfare. The first wave of industrialization in England occurred with a shift from an agrarian economy to an economy based on the wool industry. People left their home communities to seek industrial employment in the cities. The feudal system of life fell apart as this shift was completed. Government was becoming more centralized and played a stronger role in many aspects of society, including social welfare, while the role of the church in welfare was diminishing.[6]

The interplay of new social forces—the reduction of the labor force, the breakdown of the feudal system, and the move toward industrialization—brought about the Elizabethan Poor Law of 1601,[7] the first major event in the Elizabethan government's role in providing social welfare benefits. The law was passed mostly as a means of "controlling" those poor who were unable to locate employment and who might cause disruption.[8] Taxes were levied to finance the new welfare system. The demands placed on recipients were harsh—children whose parents were unable to support them faced apprenticeship, and able-bodied men dared not consider remaining idle.

Distinguishing the "deserving" from the "nondeserving" poor was an important part of the Elizabethan Poor Law. More affluent individuals did not want to be burdened with assisting any but the most needy. The deserving poor were orphaned children and adults who were lame, blind, or unemployed through no fault of their own. The nondeserving poor were vagrants or drunkards—those considered lazy and unwilling to work. **Outdoor relief** was the term used to describe assistance provided to many deserving poor in their own homes. **Indoor relief** was also provided to those unable to care for themselves, but such relief was generally provided in institutions called **almshouses.** The nondeserving poor were sent to **workhouses,** where they were forced to do menial work in return for only the barest of life's necessities.[9]

Stringent residency requirements had to be met by all welfare recipients. Aid was administered by local units of government called **parishes.** Parishes were instructed to provide aid only to people from their own jurisdictions.

Early Relief in the United States

Many aspects of Elizabethan welfare were adopted by American colonists. For example, residency requirements were strictly enforced through the policies of **warning out** and **passing on.**[10] Warning out meant that newcomers were urged to move on to other towns if it appeared that they were not financially responsible. More often, passing on was used to escort the transient poor back to their home communities. These practices continued well into the nineteenth century. In one year alone, 1,800 people were transported from one New York community to another.

Life was austere for the colonists. The business of settling America was a tough job, and the colonists were by no means well off. "Many of them were paupers, vagrants, or convicts shipped out by the English government as indentured servants."[11] Life in the colonies was preferred by many, but sickness or other misfortune could readily place a person in need.

The colonists used four methods to "assist" the needy. "Auctioning" the poor to families that were willing to care for them at the lowest cost was the least popular method. A second method was to place the poor and sick under the supervision of a couple who were willing to care for them at as little cost as possible. The third method, outdoor relief, was provided to most of the needy. The fourth method was the use of almshouses. Many claimed that almshouses were the best method of aid because of the medical care they provided to the sick and elderly. Almshouses in the cities provided a higher level of care than rural almshouses, which were often in deplorable condition and little more than rundown houses operated by a farm family.

The 1800s brought more ideas about what could be accomplished for the poor.[12] The Society for the Prevention of Pauperism and successor groups emerged to help the poor overcome the personal shortcomings that had supposedly led to their condition. In this tradition, the Charity Organization Societies (COS) that developed in the United States in the late 1870s offered a method called "scientific charity." COS workers became the forerunners of today's social workers and their methods developed into today's casework services. Their emphasis was on outdoor relief, but the philosophies of Calvinism, the work ethic, and social Darwinism prevailed. Politicians, welfare administrators, doctors, and charity workers seemed pleased with their progress in assisting the needy during the eighteenth and nineteenth centuries.

The Great Depression and the New Deal

From 1870 to 1920 the United States experienced a period of rapid industrialization and heavy immigration. Private groups such as the COS, settlement houses, and churches and big-city political "machines" and "bosses" provided much of the assistance to the needy. The settlement houses offered many services to those coming to the cities from rural areas and those immigrating from other countries, such as help in finding jobs, counseling, education, and child care. They also prepared people for their roles as citizens in their new communities, and they actively campaigned for social reforms. The political machines operated by trading baskets of food, bushels of coal, and favors for the votes of the poor. To finance this early welfare system, the machine offered city contracts, protection, and privileges to business interests, which in return paid off in cash. Aid was provided in a personal fashion without red tape or delays. Recipients did not feel embarrassed or ashamed, for after all, "they were trading something valuable—their votes—for the assistance they received."[13]

As social problems mounted—increased crowding, unemployment, and poverty in the cities—local and state governments began to take a more active role in welfare. "Mothers' aid" and "mothers' pension" laws were adopted by states to help children in families where the father was deceased or absent. Other state pension programs were established to assist poor aged, blind, and disabled people. This era was one of progressivism, and Progressives were successful in achieving many social welfare and labor reforms.[14] Many states adopted workers' compensation programs to assist those injured on the job. The federal Children's Bureau was established to investigate and improve the lives of children. Women won the right to vote, and laws were passed to better the working conditions of women and children. The Progressives urged a program of social insurance rather than charity. Large-scale federal government involvement in social welfare was not far away.

The Great Depression, one of the bleakest periods in U.S. history, followed the stock market crash in October 1929. Prices dropped dramatically, and unemployment was rampant. By 1932 one of every four people had no job, and one of every six was on welfare. Americans who had always worked no longer had jobs, and they depleted their savings or lost them when banks folded. Many had to give up their homes and farms because they could no longer meet the mortgage payments. Economic catastrophe struck deep into the ranks of the middle classes. Many of the unemployed and homeless slept on steps and park benches because they had nowhere else to go.[15]

The Great Depression dramatically changed American thought about social welfare. The realization that poverty could strike so many forced Americans to consider large-scale economic reform. President Franklin Delano Roosevelt began to elaborate the philosophy of the "New Deal" that would permit the federal government to devote more attention to the public welfare than did the philosophy of "rugged individualism" so popular in the earlier days of the country. The New Deal was not a consistent or unifying plan; instead, it was a series of improvisations that were often adopted suddenly, and some of them were even contradictory. Roosevelt believed that the government should act humanely and compassionately toward those suffering from the Depression. The objectives of the New Deal were "relief, recovery, and reform," and Roosevelt called for "full persistent experimentation. If it fails, admit it frankly and try something else. But above all try something. The millions who are in want will not stand by silently forever while the things to satisfy their needs are in easy reach."[16] Americans came to accept the principle that the entire community has a responsibility for welfare.

The New Deal contained many social welfare provisions. The most important was the Social Security Act of 1935, which remains the cornerstone of social welfare legislation today. The act included social insurance benefits for retired workers administered by the federal government and federal grant-in-aid programs to states to provide public assistance payments for dependent children as well as people who were elderly or blind. Job programs, established through projects such as the Works Progress Administration and the Civilian Conservation Corps, provided a living for many Americans. Other programs included unemployment compensation, employment services, child welfare, public housing, urban aid, and vocational education and rehabilitation.

The Great Society and the War on Poverty

Until the 1950s, there were few notable amendments to the Social Security Act. Dependents of retired workers and survivors of deceased workers did become eligible for social insurance benefits, eligibility requirements were loosened in some programs, and payments were increased, but there were few other changes in the system. Then, beginning in the 1950s, the number of workers covered under Social Security expanded substantially, disabled workers became eligible for social insurance benefits, and the states were able to obtain federal funds to provide public assistance payments to poor people with severe disabilities. Some medical care was also made available to public assistance recipients.

The 1950s and 1960s were unusual times for Americans. Although this was a period of increased prosperity for many, the dichotomy between the "haves" and "have nots" became more apparent. The relative affluence of the times was overshadowed by the nearly 40 million people, many of them members of ethnic minority groups, living in poverty as the decade of the 1960s began. Civil rights and the depressed economic condition of these individuals became the issues of the day. The writings of economist John Kenneth Galbraith directed attention to the existence of poverty in the midst of this affluent culture and influenced President John F. Kennedy to begin acting on the problem. Kennedy initiated a pilot food stamp program and aid to Appalachia and other severely depressed areas.

Following Kennedy's assassination in 1963, President Lyndon Baines Johnson took the lead of his predecessor by "declaring war on poverty" in the Economic Opportunity Act of 1964. The goals of the "war" were to allow ghetto and poor communities to develop their own programs to arrest poverty and to root out inequality in the lives of Americans. Model cities programs, community action agencies, and other devices, such as the Head Start preschool program, were tried as part of the act. Although poverty had declined to 25 million people by 1970, there was a dissatisfaction with many of the more experimental strategies of the War on Poverty, which differed from community to community. Although programs such as Head Start continue to enjoy strong support, the more enduring programs of the "Great Society" of the 1960s were enacted separately from the Economic Opportunity Act. They include the Food Stamp Program to improve the nutrition of low-income people; Medicaid, which provides

ILLUSTRATION 2-1

The Revolution No One Noticed

While Americans were preoccupied with the turmoil of the 1960s—the civil rights movement and the war in Vietnam—a revolution no one noticed was taking place.[a] For many years, the argument for increased attention to social welfare in America had followed clear lines: The United States was spending the largest portion of its budget for defense; programs for people who were poor, sick, aged, or minorities were underfinanced. Social welfare proponents contended that in order to be more responsive to the needs of its citizens, the nation should "change its priorities" and spend more for social programs to reduce poverty and less on wars like that in Vietnam. The argument ended with a call for a change in national priorities.

In a single decade America's national priorities were reversed. In 1965, national defense expenditures accounted for 43 percent of the federal government's budget; social welfare expenditures (social insurance, health, and public assistance) accounted for 24 percent. While the mass media focused on the war in Vietnam and Watergate, a revolution in national policy from "guns to butter" was occurring. By 1975, defense accounted for only 26 percent of the federal budget and social welfare expenditures had grown to 42 percent of the budget. In fiscal year 2000 social welfare expenditures are expected to total 59 percent of the budget compared to about 15 percent for defense. Health programs alone (primarily Medicaid and Medicare) will comprise about 21 percent of the total budget. Social welfare is clearly the major function and major expenditure of the federal government.

Figure 2-1 shows the changing trends in spending for social welfare and defense. Note that defense spending jumped up at the beginnings of the Korean War (1950–1952) and the Vietnam War (1964–1968) and later in the military buildup begun under President Carter and continued under President Reagan. In contrast, social welfare spending rose slowly for many years and then "exploded" in the 1970s after the Great Society programs of the War on Poverty were in place. Social welfare and health spending remained at high levels despite a significant increase in defense spending. This reversal of national priorities occurred during both Democratic and Republican administrations and during the Vietnam War—the nation's longest war. "The mid to late 1960s were quite prosperous years. The unemployment rate fell under 4 percent, real income rose briskly. In the flush of affluence, new programs could be introduced with minimal fiscal strain, even as the Vietnam War expenditures were swelling."[b] In short, ideas that welfare expenditures are not likely to increase during Republican administrations or during times of war turned out to be wrong. America's commitment to social welfare was growing.

Not everyone was comfortable with this change in public spending priorities. There was fear that the nation was sacrificing national defense in order to spend money on social welfare programs that might not work. As the 1980s emerged, a more cautious attitude toward social welfare had developed. Far too many people remained poor in spite of increased welfare spending, and there were some successful attempts to curb these social programs.

continued

ILLUSTRATION 2-1 *(continued)*

FIGURE 2-1

Social Welfare and Defense Priorities (percentage of total federal spending)

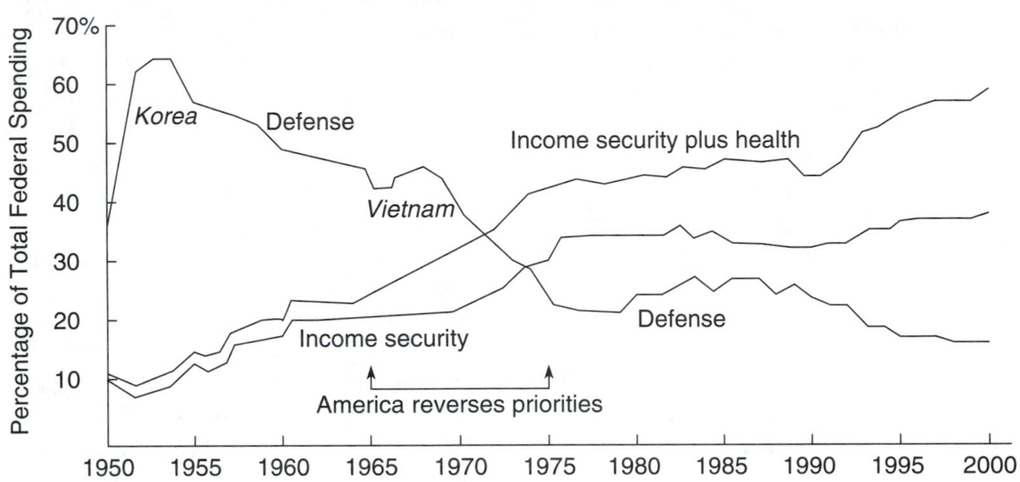

Source: Data for 1950–1996 are from tables found in U.S. Bureau of the Census, *Statistical Abstract of the United States* (Washington, DC: U.S. Government Printing Office) for various years. Remaining data are from Executive Office of the President, Office of Management and Budget, *Budget of the United States Government, Fiscal Year 1999; Fiscal Year 2000* (Washington, D.C.: U.S. Government Printing Office, 1998; 1999). Data for 1999 and 2000 are estimates.

Today there is far more concern—even animosity—about what some forms of welfare spending can accomplish, but the portion of the total federal budget devoted to social welfare continues to grow. As more reductions in military spending have occurred as a result of amazing political changes in various parts of the world—greater democratization in Russia and the other communist bloc countries, the fall of the Berlin Wall between East and West Germany, and the demise of the cold war—pressing social welfare concerns at home have continued to mount, from child poverty and child abuse to immigration, alcohol and drug abuse, and crime. The Medicaid program continues to expand, and the U.S. population continues to live longer, necessitating even more and more varied social services. Even as the country works to reduce the large federal deficit, it will make an even greater commitment to social welfare in the years ahead.

[a]See Aaron Wildavsky, *Speaking Truth to Power: The Art and Craft of Policy Analysis* (Boston: Little, Brown, 1979), especially pp. 86–89 for elaboration on this discussion of "the revolution no one noticed."

[b]Robert D. Plotnick, "Social Welfare Expenditures: How Much Help for the Poor?" *Policy Analysis,* Vol. 5, No. 2, 1979, p. 278.

health care to some poor people; and Medicare, which provides health care to almost all older Americans.

As the 1970s approached, the new presidential administration of Richard Nixon began dismantling the agencies of the War on Poverty. The "welfare rights movement" of the 1960s had raised the nation's consciousness about social welfare needs, and many more people were receiving public assistance. But with so many people added to the rolls, there was also a perception that the public assistance system was now in need of reform. President Nixon, determined to clean up the "welfare mess," attempted another type of reform in the early 1970s—a guaranteed annual income for all poor people. Parts of the plan were adopted, notably the Supplemental Security Income (SSI) program, which provides cash assistance to those who are aged, blind, or disabled and living in poverty. But for the most part, the concept of a guaranteed annual income was rejected by Congress. Some thought it was too much welfare, and others were concerned that the guarantees were too low.

Meanwhile, another type of social welfare movement had arisen as social services designed to address problems in addition to poverty grew increasingly popular in the 1960s and 1970s. Consequently, new legislation was passed to assist abused children, to provide mental health services, and to develop social service programs for elderly Americans. As described in this and the following chapters, during the twentieth century, the United States developed its own unique system of social welfare.[17]

THE EXPANSION OF SOCIAL WELFARE

Since the early 1900s, many factors have contributed to the increase in the number of social welfare programs, the number of people receiving assistance, and the amount spent on social welfare programs. Among these are (1) the rural-to-urban migration, (2) the elimination of residency requirements, (3) the welfare rights movement, (4) cost-of-living adjustments, (5) the aging of America, and (6) increasing numbers of single-parent families.

The Rural-to-Urban Migration

During the late 1800s and early 1900s, America experienced some of its sharpest growing pains as the Industrial Revolution reached its peak. The country changed from a rural, agrarian society to an urban, industrial society. People migrated from poor rural farming communities hoping to find jobs and brighter futures in the cities. People from other countries were also emigrating to American cities, seeking a better life. The dreams of many people were shattered. Those who found jobs were often forced to work long hours for low pay under poor working conditions. Housing was often crowded; sanitation and health problems were common. Those who had come to the cities to "make good" were often far from their families who could have provided financial and psychological support. Social welfare became a growing problem for governments. As the Great Depression unfolded, the cities and states were no longer able to cope with worsening social conditions. The federal government responded to this major economic crisis with emergency aid and temporary work programs, but its most enduring response was the Social Security Act of 1935. The act established the federal government's role in determining social welfare policy and programs.

Residency Requirements Eliminated

One method traditionally used to restrict the number of people eligible for public assistance was **residency requirements.** During Elizabethan and colonial times, the belief was that communities should be responsible for their own poor and needy residents. Financially dependent individuals were not welcome in new communities. As society became more mobile and people moved more frequently to seek jobs and other opportunities, the argument for residency requirements no longer seemed to hold up. Yet states and communities continued to impose these restrictions. Requiring that potential recipients had resided in the city or state for six months or a year, or even requiring that they intended to reside in the city or state, were ways to keep welfare caseloads small. Following a number of court challenges, the U.S. Supreme Court in 1969 declared residency requirements in federally supported welfare programs unconstitutional.[18] As a result, it became easier to qualify for aid, and public assistance caseloads grew.

As public assistance costs continued to escalate through the 1980s and 1990s, some states with General Assistance programs tried to institute procedures to initially pay new arrivals only the amount offered to them in their previous state of residence. Since General Assistance programs rely on state and local funding and receive no federal assistance (see Chapter 5), they are not encumbered by federal regulations. But these restrictions on welfare payments also failed to hold up under legal challenges. The Supreme Court said that such restrictions violated individuals' rights to equal protections under the law and also their right to travel.

In 1996 Congress passed a major revision of the Aid to Families with Dependent Children (AFDC) program. Under the new program, called Temporary Assistance for Needy Families (TANF), states may "treat families who have moved from another state under the cash assistance rules operating in that state, including benefit levels for 12 months."[19] The Supreme Court has already heard challenges to this law. The law's supporters contend that it does not deny anyone aid, it simply provides less aid than would otherwise be available. They also say that the law makes higher benefit states less likely to become "welfare magnets," though there is little evidence to indicate that this would happen.

Welfare Rights

In the 1960s, black and other poor Americans showed their discontent with the welfare system through the "welfare rights movement." It arose in the wake of the civil rights movements, as the poor expressed their dissatisfaction with a political system that had denied them the standard of living that many other Americans enjoyed. These movements were a stormy time in U.S. domestic history, especially from 1964 to 1968, when major cities were rocked by a series of riots. As the number of disturbances increased, so did the number of people applying for public assistance, many with the help of members of the newly formed National Welfare Rights Organization (NWRO). More applications were also being approved for payments.

The welfare rights movement brought changes in the behavior and attitudes of public aid recipients. Frances Fox Piven and Richard Cloward note that "The mood of applicants in welfare waiting rooms had changed. They were no longer as humble, as self-effacing, as pleading; they were more indignant, angrier, more demanding."[20] The mood of welfare administrators and caseworkers also changed. Many practices that had been part of lengthy background investigations ceased. The process of obtaining aid was speeded up, and welfare agencies were not so quick to terminate benefits when recipients did not comply with the rules. "For all practical purposes, welfare operating procedures collapsed; regulations were simply ignored in order to process the hundreds of thousands of families who jammed the welfare waiting rooms."[21]

By 1968 the welfare rights movement was coming to a close. Rioting had dissipated and the NWRO ceased operation. Many goals of the movement had been accomplished—applicants had been informed of their rights; they were being treated better; and a record number were being certified for benefits.

Cost-of-Living Adjustments

Much of the increase in federal social welfare spending since the 1970s is due to congressional approval of **cost-of-living adjustments** (COLAs), also known as **indexing,** designed to keep Social Security, Supplemental Security Income, and Food Stamp Program benefits in line with inflation. Political scientist Aaron Wildavsky reminds us that in the past, Congress had to vote each time Social Security payments were increased, but later Congress decided to automatically adjust most social insurance and public assistance payments annually to reflect increases in the cost of living. Wildavsky commented on the purpose of these automatic adjustments:

> *Such action was not intended to provide greater benefits to recipients, but only to automatically assure them of constant purchasing power. . . . Legislators may see such automatic increases as either favorable or unfavorable. Some may miss the almost yearly opportunity to show their constituents how much they have contributed to the nation's welfare. Others may be happy to continue constant benefits without being seen as wasteful spenders.*[22]

By the early 1980s, COLAs were under attack. Although social welfare payments were being adjusted for cost of living increases, the wages of many workers in the sluggish economy had not kept pace with inflation. Some modifications were made to control COLAs (see Chapter 4 on Social Security and Chapter 7 on the Food Stamp Program), but COLAs continue to be an important concept in social welfare programs. Social insurance and public assistance beneficiaries, especially those who are aged or disabled, would surely wage strong protests if these adjustments were eliminated.

The Graying of America

The growing number of elderly people places increased demands on the social welfare system. Today those over age 65 comprise nearly 13 percent of the U.S. population, compared to 4 percent at the turn of the century. By the year 2020, this figure will approach 17 percent.[23] Improved living conditions and advances in medicine have helped Americans look forward to longer lives than ever before. But in advanced age, people may become increasingly vulnerable and unable to meet all their own needs.

There is general agreement in the United States that older people deserve publicly supported care. The tripling of the proportion of the older population during this century has meant the need for greater planning and more services to ensure that they receive proper treatment. The largest social welfare programs in the United States are Social Security and Medicare (see Chapters 4 and 8, respectively). The vast majority of recipients of these programs are older Americans. Older Americans receive a higher level of social welfare support than any other segment of the population.

Increase in Single-Parent Families

The changing patterns of U.S. family life are among the most controversial issues explaining increased social welfare expenditures. Divorce rates have declined in the last two decades, but family breakup is still common. The number of adults who bear children but never marry has grown tremendously. The increase in pregnancies among teenagers who are unmarried and ill-equipped to care for children has slowed recently but is still cause for national alarm. These social and demographic trends mean that many families today are headed by single parents, primarily women. From 1950 to 1975 the number of female-headed households doubled to over 7 million, and 70 percent of them included children.[24] Female-headed families have an exceptionally high poverty rate. In 1997, 90 percent of the more than 4 million single-parent families in poverty were headed by women.[25] The poverty rate for these female-headed households (41 percent) was more than twice that of single males with children (19 percent). Poverty in two-parent families is substantially lower (7 percent). As a result of the high poverty rates among families headed by women, public assistance programs (primarily TANF, Medicaid, and food stamps) are crucial resources for many families.

FINANCES IN THE WELFARE STATE

Prior to the Great Depression, local and state governments shouldered the major public responsibility for social welfare programs. Today the picture is different. Since 1935 there have been important changes in the way most social welfare programs are established and financed. Although federal, state, and local social expenditures have all increased, the federal government is now the largest welfare spender. Today, about three-quarters of all funds for public assistance, social insurance, health care, and other social welfare services (not counting education) are provided through the federal government. Federal funds account for about 68 percent of public assistance and 82 percent of social insurance spending.[26]

How does the federal government acquire the funds to pay for these programs? The answer, of course, is through the taxes it collects. As shown in Figure 2-2, **individual**

FIGURE 2-2

The Federal Government Dollar, Fiscal Year 2000 Estimates

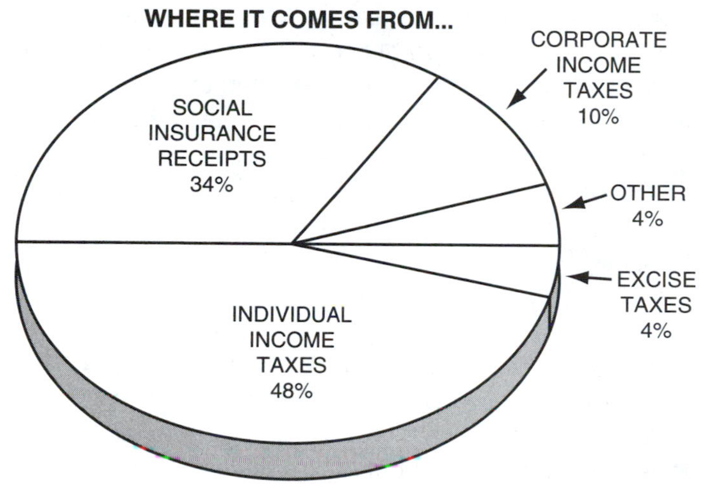

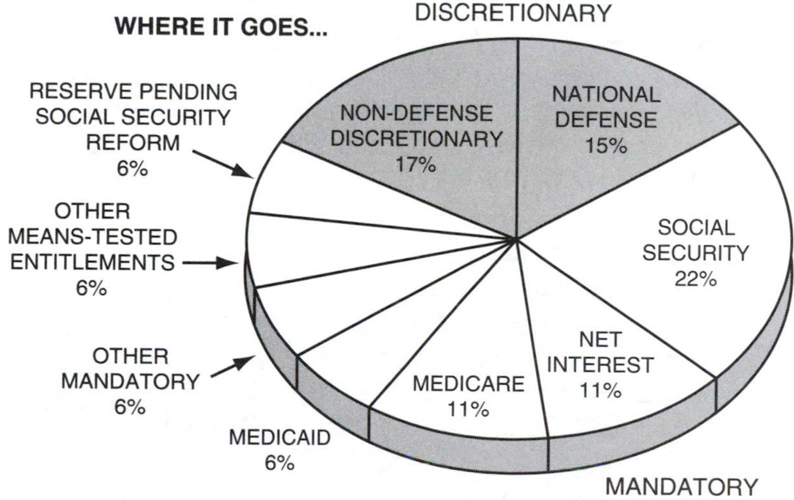

Source: Executive Office of the President, *Budget of the United States Government, Fiscal Year 2000* (Washington, DC: U.S. Government Printing Office, 1999), p. 12.

income taxes are the largest source of federal government revenues (budget receipts). Estimates for fiscal year 2000 indicate that individual income taxes will account for 48 percent of budget receipts. These taxes are channeled to the federal government's **general revenue fund,** which is used for many purposes, among them the financing of public assistance programs. The second major source of budget revenue is the **Social Security tax.** This is a special tax, levied against an individual's income, that is used to finance the social insurance programs (also see Chapter 4). Social insurance receipts will account for an estimated 34 percent of the federal government's revenues in 2000. The federal government also collects revenues through **corporate income taxes, excise taxes** (taxes on products), and other sources. But it is individual Americans who shoulder the major tax burden through personal income taxes and Social Security taxes. Corporate income taxes will account for an estimated 10 percent of government receipts; excise taxes, 4 percent; and other sources, 4 percent.

Although their overall financial role is smaller, the states are important players in social welfare, especially with respect to public assistance payments and social service programs. The states also collect taxes in several ways. Like the federal government, most states levy a personal income tax, although state income taxes are much less than federal income taxes. The **sales tax** is a major mechanism used by states to generate revenue. Some of these taxes are used to provide social welfare services.

At the local level, the **property tax,** largely used to fund public school education, is the major source of revenue. Local governments (cities, counties, and municipalities) provide the smallest share of social welfare services. These governments are mainly concerned with providing other services, such as police and fire protection.

At each level of government, there is always concern about the types of taxes that should be used to generate revenues, who should pay those taxes and how much they should pay, and who should benefit from them. Some taxes are progressive (they tax the rich at higher rates than the poor), and others are regressive (they tax the poor at a higher rate than the rich). The Social Security tax and sales tax are regressive; poorer people end up using a higher percentage of their income to pay for them than richer people. Federal and state income taxes are considered progressive, although they are less progressive than some people think they should be.

Many people believe that there are two distinct groups of citizens in the United States—those that pay taxes and those that receive welfare. But it can be said that "everyone is on welfare" because the government helps all people, some directly through social welfare programs, others through tax incentives.[27] Government-sponsored social welfare programs (public assistance and social insurance) comprise the bulk of help to the poorest citizens. Low-income workers can benefit from the **earned income credit** (EIC). The EIC is a special tax rebate that is paid to these workers through the Internal Revenue Service (IRS). It is a popular way of helping those who earn low wages, because it rewards work and makes use of the regular tax system rather than the public assistance system.

Compared to lower- and upper-income groups, those in the middle-classes pay most of the federal income taxes in this country. But they too get social welfare assistance. Much of the help the middle classes receive comes in the form of **fringe benefit** programs (such as health care and pension plans) offered by employers. Most people don't use the word "welfare" to describe these benefits since they are not provided by government, but workers can also claim federal income tax deductions from their gross personal income for these fringes. In fact, "fringe" is no longer a good word for them, because they comprise a substantial employment and tax benefit. Workers also benefit from such provisions as the **dependent care tax credit.** The primary example is a deduction for working families who pay for child care. This credit is available to most workers, but it is used less frequently by those in low-income brackets, because the costs of child care may be beyond their reach. Some have called for eliminating this credit for upper-income workers in order to increase tax revenues and to concentrate more resources on poorer families. There have also been suggestions for expansion of the dependent care credit to offer more incentives for families to care for their aged and disabled members, rather than rely on public assistance programs like Medicaid that cover the costs of custodial nursing home care for the poor.

The more well-to-do get much of their help directly from the tax system through various "loopholes," deductions, and credits known as **tax expenditures.** Some loopholes (such as certain deductions for real estate investment losses and business-related entertainment) have been narrowed or closed over the years, but others remain. According to the federal government, "tax expenditures are the equivalent of entitlement programs administered by the Internal Revenue Service."[28] Some of these deductions are for the mortgage interest paid on first and second homes and for property taxes and charitable contributions. These deductions are also very important for the middle class, although they generally have less to deduct.

Finally, while businesses pay corporate taxes, they also receive government assistance such as federal contracts, farm subsidies, and various tax deductions. This is called **corporate welfare.** Although some of this help goes to small-business owners who might be struggling to get by, much of it goes to more affluent business owners. Government tax deductions also help to offset the cost of fringe benefits that employers pay to workers.

The amount of government aid that goes to wealthy corporations has so incensed groups like Common Cause that it has focused on exposing the situation through the Stop Corporate Welfare Coalition, composed of both liberal and conservative organizations concerned about government waste.[29] Among the things that it has complained about: "McDonald's has received millions to advertise its fast food products abroad and Sunkist has received $78 million since 1986 to promote its oranges in Asia."[30] In November 1998, *Time* magazine did a four-part series on the costs of corporate welfare largely claiming that rather than create jobs, it results in costs to workers.

Considered in this way, all groups benefit from government assistance. In fact, much of the redistribution of income that results from public policy favors the more rather than the less affluent.

Table 2-1 shows the federal, state, and local tax burden for Americans in various income groups ranging from 19 percent for the poorest group to 42 percent for the very richest. Illustration 2-2 shows that the individual tax burden in the U.S. is less

TABLE 2-1

Percentage of family income for taxes, 1998

Income group	Average earnings	Federal taxes	State/local taxes	Total taxes
Top 1 percent	$659,500	31.9	10.2	42.1
Next 4 percent	160,560	27.3	10.6	37.9
Next 15 percent	87,320	26.1	10.5	36.6
Next 20 percent	56,170	22.9	10.7	33.6
Middle 20 percent	37,290	20.0	11.1	31.1
Fourth 20 percent	22,530	15.1	11.9	27.0
Lowest 20 percent	8,860	5.3	14.1	19.4

Source: Citizens for Tax Justice

than many other industrialized nations, but many other nations enjoy greater income equality than the U.S. and more equal access to costly services such as health care.

There have been many calls to reform the nation's tax collection agency—the dreaded Internal Revenue Service (IRS). Congress has taken steps to ensure that taxpayers' rights are better protected. There have also been many calls to reform the tax system itself. Taxes were a major theme in the 1996 presidential race. Former Senate majority leader and Republican presidential nominee Bob Dole wanted to reduce individual income taxes by 15 percent. Wealthy businessman Steve Forbes, also an early Republican presidential contender, proposed a flat tax. In its purest form a flat tax

ILLUSTRATION 2-2

Intelligence Report: Our Low Taxes

As Americans file their 1040s, it might help to know that our top income-tax rate of 39.6% is *low* compared to that of many other industrialized nations. The highest:

1. Denmark and Netherlands, 60%
2. Finland, 57%
3. France, 56.8%
4. Spain and Sweden, 56%
5. Belgium, 55%
6. Germany, 53%
7. Canada, 52.92%
8. Luxembourg, 51.25%
9. Italy, 51%
10. Austria and Japan, 50%

Source: "Intelligence Report," *Parade Magazine,* April 12, 1998, p. 14. Reprinted with permission from Parade, copyright © 1998.

means that everyone would be taxed at the same rate regardless of income level. There would be no deductions as there are today for interest paid on home loans, high medical expenses, child care, or business entertainment. Flat tax proposals have always been rejected for a number of reasons. For one thing, many people believe that taxes should be progressive. For another, many people don't want to give up their tax deductions. Middle-class people are wed to the deductions for mortgage interest and property taxes. Without these deductions people would find it harder to own a home of their choosing, and the change might cause property values to fall. Some flat tax proposals exempt people with low or even moderate incomes from paying anything at all. Depending on the details of a flat tax, middle-income Americans could actually end up paying more taxes. The process of filing income taxes would, however, be simpler and could possibly result in less tax avoidance and evasion and fewer altercations with the IRS.

Another proposal is to replace the personal income tax with a national sales tax (like the state sales tax, only higher). This is a tax on what one buys rather than on what one earns. Again, the proposal is criticized because of its lack of progressivity. Depending on how it is done, food, prescription drugs, or other necessities might be exempt from taxation. Like the flat tax, a national sales tax might reduce tax avoidance and evasion. More dramatic is that it might do away with the IRS and the need to file returns altogether (cheery thoughts for many). There might be savings from the money the IRS now uses to process and audit returns and prosecute tax cheats, but some systems would need to be put in place to monitor the national sales tax. And unless the country does away with taxes, tax cheating will never be eliminated entirely. Flat tax and national sales tax proposals have appeal despite their many problems, but there is little chance that Congress will do more than tweak the current system from time to time.

THE LEGACY OF "REAGANOMICS"

The number of people served by the various social welfare programs in the United States and the amount of money spent on these programs is impressive, but there has been considerable consternation with many aspects of the system, particularly public assistance. Although helping many, the expansion of social welfare has resulted in a mixture of public policies and programs that are often inconsistent, conflicting, and overlapping. The most severe criticisms of the last few decades are that public assistance programs encourage dependency and are directly to blame for the large number of people who turn to governments for help.

During the 1980s these problems caused disillusionment with the welfare system and eroded many of the liberal ideas and hopes of the two preceding decades. As a result, more conservative philosophies about public assistance gained popularity with the support of the Reagan administration. These philosophies suggested that (1) public spending for these programs should be kept to a minimum; (2) government, especially the federal government, should minimize its role in public assistance; (3) only those in extreme circumstances—the "truly needy"—should receive public assistance; and (4) most assistance should be provided on a short-term basis only.

Changes in a number of programs reflected these ideas. For instance, the rate of spending in the Aid to Families with Dependent Children program was slowed, and eligibility requirements for other programs such as the Food Stamp Program were made more stringent. But this conservative approach to welfare was also blamed for increases in the number of jobless, homeless, and medically needy individuals. As described in the following chapters, social welfare policy remains a struggle between those who support a conservative and selective approach to assist those in need and those who believe in a more generous and universal system of aid.

The Supply Side

Although "Reaganomics" now sounds like ancient history, these ideas have had profound affects on social welfare policy since the early 1980s. A cornerstone of Reaganomics was the belief that past Keynesian policies to reduce unemployment and hold down inflation no longer worked. Keynesian economics is based on the notion that government can boost employment or cut inflation by manipulating the **demand side** of the economy—increasing government spending and expanding the money supply to boost employment, and doing just the opposite to hold down inflation. When Ronald Reagan entered office, he viewed the most important causes of the nation's economic problems—unemployment, inflation, low productivity, and low investment—as being the government itself. According to Reagan, "The federal government through taxes, spending, regulatory, and monetary policies, [had] sacrificed long-term growth and price stability for ephemeral, short-term goals."[31]

Keynesian economics also holds that unemployment and inflation should not occur together—unemployment should reduce income, which in turn would force down prices. But according to government figures, *both* unemployment and inflation remained high during the 1970s. Government efforts to reduce unemployment simply added to inflation; and government efforts to cut inflation simply added to unemployment. Reagan combined the unemployment rate with the inflation rate and called it the **misery index**.

To reduce the misery index, Reagan pursued a package of four sweeping policy directives designed to achieve economic recovery by concentrating on the **supply side** of the economy. These four approaches included (1) budget reform to cut the rate of growth in federal spending, (2) tax reductions on personal income and on business investment, (3) relief from federal regulations that cost industry large amounts of money for small increases in safety, and (4) slower growth of the nation's money supply. Reagan was especially successful in reducing taxes during both his terms.

Although it now seems hard to believe, individual income taxes were once considered unconstitutional.[32] The Sixteenth Amendment to the U.S. Constitution and the Revenue Act of 1913 changed that. In the early days of the federal personal income tax, few households earned enough to pay this levy, but today, most Americans are quite familiar with the annual April 15 filing date. As the federal government's needs for revenue continued to increase, so did taxes. Tax rates have fluctuated over the years, but when President Reagan took office in 1981, he felt that rates were too high (ranging from 14 to 70 percent) and were stifling economic growth.

During his first term, Reagan persuaded Congress to cut personal income taxes for all income groups by 25 percent. He also persuaded Congress to "index" tax rates in the future to eliminate "bracket creep," which occurs when inflation carries taxpayers into higher brackets. Today, taxes are "adjusted" or indexed, so that taxpayers will not carry a heavier burden as inflation rises. During Reagan's second term, he again successfully urged Congress to reform the tax system. The reforms were intended to reduce tax rates and simplify the tax system while eliminating many tax breaks or loopholes. The number of individual tax brackets was reduced from 15 to two primary categories—a 15 and a 28 percent bracket (actually, due to a complicated set of rules, some earners incurred a 33 percent rate). The number of corporate tax brackets was also reduced. Other reforms included increasing the personal income tax exemption; eliminating some real estate tax shelters used primarily by the wealthy; and taxing capital gains (taxes paid on profits from the sale of assets such as real estate and stocks) as ordinary income instead of using lower rates (a move that Reagan did not support). Reagan called it, "the best anti-poverty bill, the best pro-family measure, and the best job-creation program ever to come out of the Congress."[33]

Although most taxpayers welcome lower tax rates, wouldn't large tax cuts reduce governments revenues and increase budget deficits? According to Reaganomics, these problems would not necessarily occur, at least in the long run. Taxes discourage work, productivity, investment, and economic growth. Reduce taxes, and the paradoxical result will be an *increase* in government revenue because more people will work harder and start businesses knowing they can keep a larger share of their earnings. Tax cuts were intended to stimulate economic activity, and although tax rates were lowered, increased economic activity was eventually *supposed* to produce more government revenue.

Reagan's policies were designed to encourage Americans to work, save, and invest. The economy was supposed to grow more rapidly because Americans would keep more of their earnings and purchase more goods. Inflation was supposed to be brought under control by producing more goods rather than by limiting demand. Americans would be encouraged to save a greater proportion of their incomes, and businesses would be encouraged to build new plants and provide more jobs.

Critics of this new "supply side" economics argued that it was really a return to an old and discredited "trickle-down" approach to the economy. Taxes and regulations on businesses and affluent Americans were reduced in the hope that they would reinvest their profits and expand job opportunities for the poor and working classes. In other words, incentives were provided for the wealthy in the hope that benefits would "trickle down" to the poor.[34]

As George Bush campaigned for the presidency and assumed the office after two very popular terms of the Reagan administration, his favorite phrase was "Read my lips—no new taxes." Like Reagan, Bush pressed for a reduction in capital gains taxes. Needless to say, it is the rich rather than poor who most frequently see their incomes boosted by capital gains. Such a reduction was opposed on the grounds that it would further intensify the upper-income tilt of the Reagan tax reforms which had provided the greatest tax relief to wealthier Americans. Bush called for other tax breaks such as tax credits for child care and for adoption, tax incentives for Americans who contribute to personal savings accounts, and "tax-free enterprise zones" to stimulate economic growth in depressed, urban areas.

The growing budget deficit and the inability of Congress and recent presidents to balance the budget caused President Bush to eat his words and consider new taxes. The budget battle that ensued resulted in a series of measures enacted in 1990 that were primarily supported by Democrats in both the House and Senate. The so-called sin tax on alcohol and the gasoline tax—which Bush was most amenable to raising—were increased. Also increased were the "luxury" taxes on items such as expensive cars and boats. The highest personal income tax rate was raised to 31 percent for individuals with annual taxable incomes of more than $125,000 and couples with incomes of more than $200,000, while the 33 percent rate being borne primarily by upper-middle-income earners was reduced to 31 percent. The earned income credit was increased and new credits for health care and parents with newborn children were included. Although Bush did not get the substantial capital gains tax cut he wanted, the highest rate was reduced from 33 to 28 percent. The value of some deductions itemized in computing personal income taxes was reduced, as was the value of the personal income tax exemption for higher-income individuals. The payroll tax that supports Medicare was increased for higher-income earners. In exchange for his tax compromise, Bush got new measures to strengthen spending ceilings to bring the budget into line. Bush's decision to allow new taxes came back to haunt him in the 1992 presidential election, and he later said that his compromise was a mistake.

Helping the "Truly Needy"

President Reagan asserted that his administration would protect the "truly needy" by leaving intact many of the income security programs. He referred to this as preserving the "social safety net," but many of the programs to which he referred were social insurance programs like Social Security and Medicare, which beneficiaries receive regardless of their incomes. Many programs for the poor, such as AFDC and food stamps, were not in his safety net and were targeted for cuts. Federal spending was reduced, and significant numbers of recipients were removed from the rolls.

Reagan was anxious to restructure federal–state relations—specifically to turn over to the states many of the domestic programs of the national government. He believed that this would "end cumbersome administration" and make the programs "more responsive to both the people they are meant to help and the people who pay for them."[35] Critics contended that this would be a step backward in social welfare policy. Many social welfare functions were assumed by the federal government *because* the states failed to respond to the needs of the poor. Even when state governments are well motivated to care for their poor, differences in the economic resources of the states can result in unequal treatment from state to state. The devolution of social welfare was among the most criticized effects of the Reagan administration.

Reagan was unsuccessful in instituting a number of his proposals (such as the federal government assuming full responsibility for Medicaid in exchange for the states taking over the Food Stamp Program and the federal portion of the AFDC program). But the Reagan administration was quite successful in using **block grants** as a means of establishing a **new federalism.**[36] Block grants are federal payments to state or local governments for general functions, such as health, welfare, education, law enforcement, and community development. The money must be spent for the general function of the block grant, but states and communities are free to decide specific uses for the funds. Block grants were intended to reduce the power of "the Washington bureaucrats," to return decision making to state and local governments, and to make federal money available for various purposes with "no strings attached." Block grants developed as a reaction to centralization of power in the Washington bureaucracy. The first major block grants were for law enforcement (the Crime Control and Safe Streets Act of 1968) and later for housing and urban affairs (the Housing and Community Development Act of 1974). The Reagan administration considered block grants preferable to **categorical grants.** (Categorical grants were used to administer AFDC and many smaller programs). They are made for specific purposes after federal agencies review state or local government applications. Categorical grants give states much less flexibility in determining how federal funds channeled to them will be spent.

Block grants may have sounded like a good deal for the states, but they did not always work out that way. When Reagan consolidated many of the smaller social welfare programs into state block grants, the funds allocated were less than the sum previously spent on the individual social welfare programs. The block grants also shifted decision making about specific uses of federal social welfare dollars to state political arenas, where support for social welfare programs is not always as great as it is in Washington. As these changes occurred, much of the politicking and competition over funds also shifted from Washington to state and local levels.

Federal **revenue sharing,** another method of funding social welfare programs, was completely eliminated under the Reagan administration in 1987.[37] Revenue sharing for specific purposes, such as health, housing, and nutrition, began in the 1960s and was targeted for poor communities. In 1972 President Nixon initiated **general revenue sharing.** Most cities eventually became eligible for the funds, and many began using them for services originally paid for by local governments, such as police and fire protection. The argument against federal revenue sharing was that the federal government's huge budget deficit meant that it could no longer afford these payments, while many state budgets were in better shape. Many states have some type of constitutional mandate to balance their budget, but other factors may be stronger motivators in keeping state budgets in check such as the need to maintain good credit ratings with Wall Street in order to borrow money.[38] The federal government does not have these constraints—it has no constitutional mandate to balance the budget, and it can "print money" if the need arises, even though this drives up inflation.

The States as Laboratories

Like Reagan, President Bush encouraged state responsibility for public assistance. But Bush also called for a "kinder and gentler" America, a move perhaps intended to distance his administration from Reagan's harsh stance toward social welfare. Bush referred to the "states as laboratories." The states have long been social welfare labs.[39] The forerunners of the federal–state AFDC program were state and locally supported mothers' aid laws that emerged in the early 1900s. State and local programs for poor, aged, and disabled people also predated federal intervention for these groups. But states were not consistent in their approaches. According to President Bush,

> *Until quite recently a case could be made in many areas of government policy and action that a national approach, with national rules and standards, was warranted. This was so because some states departed widely from national norms in such areas as racial segregation, and some were too poor to accomplish as much as may have been judged appropriate. A lot has changed in the past quarter century.*[40]

Bush encouraged state experimentation by providing federal funds to help support state demonstration projects and by granting waivers that allowed states to deviate from federal rules. For example, waivers have allowed states to try alternatives to institutional care for people who are aged or disabled that would not have been possible under existing rules. State initiatives have also been used to test ideas that may have been too controversial, at least at the time, to gain nationwide support. For example, Wisconsin's "Learnfare" program allowed the state to reduce an AFDC family's benefit if a teenage child dropped out of school, defined as "missing three days of school in a month without a valid excuse." According to President Bush, "some of these experiments are controversial, some may not work, others may prove to cost too much for the benefits produced. That is the nature of 'states as laboratories.' As any scientist knows, the road to success is marked by numerous laboratory failures."[41]

The Privatization of Public Services

Another theme emphasized during the Reagan–Bush years is **privatization.** Privatization has several connotations. In this context it means federal, state, and local governments giving more responsibility to private organizations to deliver services—from postal delivery and space exploration to mass transportation and even social welfare. Consider the following description of the concept:

> *Generally, privatization can be defined as the transfer of government services, assets, and/or enterprises to private sector owners and suppliers, when [they] have the capability of providing better services at lower costs. Privatization replaces monopolies with competition . . . to encourage efficiency, quality, and innovation in the delivery of goods and services.*
>
> *Privatization does not imply the abrogation of government responsibility for any of these services. Rather, it merely recognizes that what matters most is the service provided, not who provides it.*[42]

President Reagan appointed a special commission to explore opportunities for privatization. He also established "private industry councils" under the Job Training and Partnership Act to advise local governments on job opportunities and skills needed to increase employment of disadvantaged individuals (see Chapter 9).

Privatization is really "the American way." In a capitalistic society, entrepreneurs are anxious to turn any opportunities they can into profit-making ventures. Many social welfare services are already provided by the private sector (also see Chapter 10). For example, most child care centers are owned by private for-profit and private nonprofit organizations. Many of the intermediate residential care facilities that serve people with severe developmental disabilities are also privately operated, as are treatment programs for alcoholics, drug addicts, and those with mental health problems.

Perhaps the best example of social welfare services provided through the private sector is health care. Whether purchased by consumers from their own pockets, from coverage obtained through employment, or by the publicly funded Medicare and Medicaid programs, most health care services come from private physicians and other private providers and private hospitals and other privately-owned facilities.

The lines between the private and public sectors are no longer clear. In addition to health care, many other so-called private enterprises rely heavily on government funds. The housing industry, for example, benefits from construction projects funded through the federal government's Department of Housing and Urban Development. Private contractors are able to sell many of their homes through the Federal Housing Administration's home loan and mortgage guarantee programs. Many of the country's community mental health centers (CMHCs) are actually nonprofit corporations originally established with federal funds along with help from state and local governments. As federal funding was reduced, CMHCs turned more to state and local governments, and they face greater pressure to charge clients something for their services and to seek clients who can pay full fees. Many organizations today are really *quasi-public* or *semiprivate*.[43] The United States is truly a "mixed economy," even in the social welfare domain.

The concern is that privatization *has* resulted in federal, state, and local governments abrogating responsibility for social welfare services. Sometimes this has occurred through deregulation.[44] For example, it has been increasingly difficult to assess the impacts of child care services[45] and services for the elderly,[46] because the government has reduced its efforts to collect data and monitor these programs. In other cases, privatization can result in governments spending less for services and subsequent reductions in services.[47] For example, the Bush administration tried to eliminate federal subsidies to Amtrak, but without federal help, Amtrak may find it difficult to offer customers rates competitive with other forms of transportation and to offer service in remote areas. As governments increasingly try to save money, privatization—from fees paid to family preservation programs to aid abusive parents, to charter schools that are administered by private companies, and contracts for the administration of privately operated prisons—is likely to continue. Americans will have to decide whether so many functions that were once the responsibility of the public sector can be carried out to their satisfaction by the private sector.

The Reagan-Bush Finale

So what actually happened after twelve years of Reagan and Bush policies? Although everyone was supposed to benefit from supply-side economics, evidence mounted that the rich got richer and the poor got poorer. The Congressional Budget Office estimated that the lower and middle classes paid a higher net federal tax rate for 1990 than they paid in 1980 prior to tax reform.[48] Although personal income taxes had dropped, other taxes, primarily social insurance taxes, which are more regressive for low-income earners, had increased. As poor Americans saw their income drop in the last decade, their combined federal tax rate increased by 16 percent. At the same time, the richest Americans enjoyed substantial increases in income, because their income tax rates dropped by 5.5 percent. The nonpartisan Citizens for Tax Justice found that only the very poor and the very rich saw tax decreases.[49]

Unemployment and inflation rates had once again abated, but the word *recession* was still being used, and the budget deficit had grown tremendously. Poverty rates were higher than before the Reagan years. Severe cuts in social welfare programs had hurt the poorest Americans, and the underclass had fallen further behind. These groups are largely outside the economic mainstream. Lower taxes had not helped them directly, and cuts in public assistance and social services hurt them the most. An assessment of the Reagan-Bush years may depend on one's own political perspectives, but after twelve consecutive years of Republican presidencies, it seemed that Americans were ready for a change.

THE PRESIDENTIAL YEARS OF BILL CLINTON

The 1992 presidential campaign turned out to be a three-way race between Republican President George Bush, Democratic candidate and governor of Arkansas William Jefferson "Bill" Clinton, and an independent candidate—Texas billionaire businessman H. Ross Perot. Although independent presidential candidates are rarely considered viable opponents, Perot garnered substantial support. But the chances of Perot actually winning were small, and he dropped out before election day so as not to dilute the vote. President Bush failed to make strong showings in the presidential debates, and disillusionment among Americans with the state of the economy and other domestic matters gave way to the election of Bill Clinton. Clinton is the first "baby boomer" (those born post-World War II between 1946 and 1964) and the third youngest president ever elected. Clinton chose Albert "Al" Gore, former senator from Tennessee, also a "boomer," as his vice president. The two set out to accomplish an ambitious set of goals, but among the most important were economic recovery, health care reform, welfare reform, and crime control.

Smoke? Mirrors? Or a Balanced Budget?

Some of the biggest worries of any government are how much it spends and how much it has to spend, but how much do Americans really need to worry about the

national debt? At the end of fiscal year 1998, the **public debt** (the amount the government owed the public from whom it borrowed money to pay for past annual budget deficits) was $3.7 trillion and the **gross federal debt** (the public debt plus the amount of money the federal government had borrowed from itself, largely from government trust funds) was $5.5 trillion.[50] Although both concepts are important, it is public debt that takes the most direct toll on the economy.[51] Intragovernment borrowing raises other important issues, but aren't both these debts just a paper game? Unfortunately, a large national debt is a drag on the economy.

When the federal government spends more than it takes in, it must borrow money by selling U.S. Treasury bonds or bills to the public (or by taking money from its trust funds). The interest that must be paid to the public on these debts drains money that could fuel the economy through expenditures on transportation, education, technology, health, nutrition, or anything else the country believes is desirable. With less money available for investment and for others to borrow, interest rates, and in turn, inflation, are subject to increases, thus inhibiting economic growth. When investment capital is not available in the United States, businesses and even the government may turn to foreign markets, improving the economic situation of these countries at the expense of our own. The government could print more money, but this would drive up inflation even further.

Although some level of federal borrowing may be necessary or even desirable, the gravity of today's federal debt can be difficult to understand. Most of us cannot really comprehend what trillions of dollars mean. One way to put it is that in 1992 the national debt was mounting at a rate of $1 billion a day—a figure clearly too large to be sustained for long. Another way to look at it is that the federal government spent about $4,600 per American in 1993,[52] but it owed about $12,500 per American on the public debt alone. The United States spends 11 percent of its budget on the interest it owes on the federal debt (see Figure 2-2), money that could be spent on more productive purposes. The fiscal health of the U.S. influences virtually all other countries. The deficit was a major issue in the 1992 presidential campaign, and it has received serious attention from Congress, the president, and citizens' groups.

Despite the reputation of Republicans as fiscal conservatives, federal deficits and the accompanying federal debt grew *far* larger during the Reagan and Bush years than under any previous administrations. From 1980 to 1993 federal debt held by the public increased four and a half times.[53] Presidents frequently blame Congress for lack of spending controls. Congress members are under constant pressure from voters who want their favorite programs continued at the same time that they complain about unemployment, inflation, and deficits being too high. Americans may say they want a balanced budget, but we need only look at our own personal spending and borrowing habits to see that many Americans live like the federal government—in debt.

Other factors are also to blame for the debt. Although President Reagan slowed the *rate* of growth in some social welfare programs, the federal government and its budget grew considerably larger each year. At the same time, the income tax reductions that Reagan so skillfully negotiated during his two popular terms in office provided less money for a troubled economy already suffering from what Reagan had dubbed the *misery index*. The theory of supply-side economics—that tax savings to individuals and businesses would in the long run spur economic growth and help everyone—did not materialize as planned.

During the 1992 presidential campaign, independent candidate Perot focused heavily on the debt, calling for "an America that pays its way."[54] Perot was not the usual political candidate. He certainly was not a career politician. His forthright style and the money he commanded, as well as his message, caught the attention of Americans who were perhaps looking for a change from presidential campaign politics as usual. Perot called for cuts in discretionary spending and controls on **entitlement programs** (social insurance and public assistance programs to which anyone who qualifies is legally entitled to receive benefits), a line item budget veto for the president, a strong deficit reduction law, cuts in defense, and more taxes for the rich. America had heard those messages before, but Perot's "infomercials" complete with graphs, charts, and a pointer, seemed to drive home the issue to the U.S. public.

Congress had tried to grapple with the deficit. It took a major step in 1985 with the Balanced Budget and Emergency Deficit Reduction Act, also known as Gramm-Rudman-Hollings after its sponsors, Senators Phil Gramm (R-Texas), Warren Rudman (R-New Hampshire), and Ernest Hollings (D-South Carolina). The act called for across-the-board spending cuts in defense and many domestic programs if Congress failed to meet specific deficit cutting measures. More stringent deficit-cutting measures were enacted in the 1990 Budget Enforcement Act. But all this proved insufficient because some of the provisions were emasculated. Presidents Reagan and Bush both were criticized for never proposing something that resembled a balanced budget, and Congress could not bring itself to enact a balanced budget.

Congress's failure to balance the federal budget led to much talk about a balanced budget amendment to the U.S. Constitution to force its hand. Proponents believed it was the only way to be sure that the government reduced the debt. Former Senate majority leader and President Clinton's opponent in the 1996 presidential race, Bob Dole, wanted to see the measure passed. Opponents felt it would hamstring the federal government in times of war or recession when deficit spending might be necessary. They also argued that the amendment was not necessary because Congress can bring the budget into balance without a constitutional amendment.

An amendment could lead to a legal morass.[55] If Congress failed to enact a balanced budget, the U.S. Supreme Court would have to intervene, and there are questions about whether the Court could really force Congress to do anything. Congress could pass other legislation, take additional spending items "off budget," or devise some other procedure to avoid balancing the budget—not much different from what it has done in the past. In 1996 a balanced budget amendment proved to be a real cliff hanger in Congress, but it and subsequent attempts have failed to be enacted. Instead, Congress and the president have managed to give the illusion of a balanced budget without a constitutional mandate.

During his first presidential campaign, Clinton promised to cut the deficit in half during his four-year term if elected. In fiscal year 1994 President Clinton and Congress were able to accomplish a substantial deficit reduction. There are only three ways to decrease the deficit—raise taxes, decrease spending, or do both. After long hours of negotiation, a compromise was reached that included $241 billion in tax increases and $255 billion in spending cuts. Even though the majority of Congress members then shared the same party as the president, the measures just squeaked by—there was a two-vote majority in the House and Vice President Gore broke the tie in the Senate.[56] No Republicans supported the package.

The spending cuts were achieved by reducing discretionary spending through an extension of the 1990 Budget Enforcement Act and by cutting entitlement programs. The largest entitlement cut came in the form of reductions in the payments made to Medicare providers. Discretionary spending was to be controlled by caps that kept expenditures at 1993 levels until the year 1998. Entitlement spending was subject to "pay-as-you-go" financing, meaning that "any tax cut or entitlement spending increase must be offset by another tax increase or entitlement spending cut."[57]

As the old saying goes, only two things in life are certain, death and taxes. Although taxes are certain, tax policy is not. The deficit was further reduced by raising taxes. Two higher tax brackets were added, bringing the total to five brackets of 15, 28, 31, 36, and 39.6 percent. Other important changes were subjecting *all* the wages workers earn to the Medicare payroll tax and taxing more of the Social Security benefits of higher-income recipients. The highest corporate tax bracket was raised by 1 percent for corporations earning over $10 million (making the highest corporate bracket 35 percent). Tax deductions for some business-related expenses, such as moving and entertainment, were restricted. Gasoline taxes were also increased. Most of the luxury taxes were repealed. On the other side of the ledger, the earned income credit (EIC) was increased for working families with children, a smaller EIC was initiated for low-income workers without children, and deductions for certain equipment purchased by small businesses were increased. The Congressional Budget Office determined that the president would remain true to his pledge not to raise taxes on middle-income Americans—90 percent of the new taxes were projected to fall on those earning $100,000 or more.[58]

As Congress went from Democratic to Republican control, the next years also resulted in serious budget battles with the President. In 1996, a bill that raised the minimum wage also ended up including tax provisions. It lowered some business taxes, gave homemakers the right to shelter money in tax-deferred individual retirement accounts, provided new options for people to save for retirement, and gave tax credits to many people who adopt children. Many federal workers got unexpected vacations when lack of agreement over the 1996 budget led to two shutdowns of many federal government operations. Welfare reform was at the heart of the differences. The president vetoed two major welfare reform bills before an agreement was reached on an overhaul of the public assistance programs (see Chapters 5, 7, and especially Chapter 6).

The next major budgetary event of great importance was the Balanced Budget Act (BBA) of 1997. (Many of the provisions of the act are discussed in more detail later in this book; see especially Chapter 8). Medicare cost containment was central in the BBA. Among the major cuts were curbs on the Medicare payments to be made to doctors, hospitals, and other health care providers as well as to health care plans. The BBA contains efforts to enroll more Medicare and Medicaid beneficiaries in managed care plans, a reduced payment formula for hospitals that serve a large number of poor people, and a stronger plan for dealing with Medicare provider fraud. The BBA extended the previous "pay-as-you-go" budget deficit neutrality requirements through fiscal year 2002, and the act is supposed to make enforcement of budget resolutions mandatory for five years after enactment. There were additions to some programs, notably an effort to insure more low-income children through state Medicaid programs, restoration of some public assistance benefits that had been taken away from immigrants during the 1996 welfare reform, and more money for states to use in helping people go from welfare to work. The budget deficit for fiscal year 1997 was $22 billion, the lowest in three decades.

The budget for fiscal year 1998 also contained many tax provisions passed in the Taxpayer Relief Act of 1997. On the tax hike side, it raised the federal cigarette tax of 24 cents by 10 cents and by 5 more cents in 2002. The bill offered many tax cuts, making it the biggest cut since the Reagan years. Many families got a new tax credit for children up to age 17 (a credit originally proposed in the 1994 Republican Contract with America). By 1999 this credit will be as much as $500 per child. The amount one gets depends on income and family size, but a family can get the credit even if it does not pay income taxes. In general, couples with two children and about $21,000 in income will get the full credit. There are also education tax credits of up to $1,500 for the first two years of college tuition and $1,000 for the third and fourth years and a $2,500 annual student loan interest deduction (these provisions are especially good for those in the middle classes).

Capital gains taxes on investments dropped substantially. Since 1998, the maximum rate has gone from 28 percent to 20 percent for investments held longer than 12 months. The tax-exempt amounts for home sales and inheritance increased substantially (all these items are good for those in the higher-income brackets). Many people pointed out that on balance these breaks would provide more to the rich and middle classes than to the poor. Even though this budgetary package will not increase federal revenues by much, when all the recent budget measures were combined with the effects of a strong economy, the federal budget looked like it would be in balance by 2002.[59]

Will the federal budget be balanced? Not really. The surplus in the Social Security Trust Fund and other mechanisms are still used to mask much of what the government actually owes, but if one believes that a balanced budget is a good thing, then the government is headed in the right direction. Some people think that too much emphasis has been placed on the need to balance the budget, that it is not as detrimental as budget conservatives would have us think. When compared to the gross domestic product, the total governmental debt in the U.S. is about average with many other countries.[60] These individuals also point out that balancing the federal budget is not analogous to balancing the household budget. Unlike you and me, the federal government can print money and manipulate the economy to cover its tracks. But even individuals who do not see much need to fret over the deficit or debt probably agree that people do feel better when the government is not constantly operating in the minus column.

Lest Congress and the President indulge in too much self-congratulatory behavior, a lot of the credit for achieving what looks like a balanced budget goes to the economy which has rebounded nicely in the last few years, thus allowing the government to collect more taxes. The country's budgetary policy and monetary policy (the work of the Federal Reserve Board) are important, but much of the country's economic state depends on things over which none of us has much control (like the performance of the stock market). In light of the country's prosperity and the first balanced budget projections since 1969, efforts to resurrect a balanced budget amendment in the near future seem improbable.

Line by Line

Another budgetary change that came as a surprise was that Congress made Bill Clinton the first president to have limited line item veto power, effective January 1997. The measure was also included in the original Republican Contract with America. It allowed the President to cut particular line items from spending bills rather than veto the whole bill.[61] Governors of 43 states already have line item veto powers. The federal measure pertained to discretionary spending and new spending (not to existing entitlement programs and not to interest on the federal debt). It also permitted the president to veto tax breaks that benefit less than 100 people. Congress did give itself the power to overturn the veto.

The veto provision quickly met with challenges that it is unconstitutional. A federal judge ruled that it violated the separation of powers of the federal government because it gave spending powers to the president that are supposed to be reserved for Congress. Others believe that Congress can legally delegate limited budget authority to the president, that the measure is necessary to cut some of the pork out of the budget, and that the president is not likely to use the measure foolishly (foolishly is, of course, always in the eye of the beholder). *Time* magazine noted that the federal judge's decision would allow James Madison to stop spinning in his grave. But the Supreme Court overturned the federal judge's ruling on a technicality saying that the six Congressmembers who filed the suit could not claim personal injury as they had done. New York Mayor Rudolph Guiliani also filed suit claiming that New York City residents would be injured by a presidential veto that would result in some Medicaid funds being lost to his state (New York raises some of its Medicaid matching funds in a unique way not permitted to other states). In 1998, the Supreme Court agreed that the line item veto as constructed was unconstitutional. A true line item veto would require an amendment to the U.S. Constitution.

Money to Burn?

A balanced budget was projected for 2002, but with the booming economy, the federal government declared a $70 billion surplus earlier, in fiscal year 1998. Even before the surplus was officially declared, there was talk about how to spend it. Some people think the country should take advantage of the opportunity to cut taxes further. Others want to restore some of the benefits eliminated by the 1996 welfare reform law. Many think that both these ideas are ridiculous because the surpluses must be allowed to grow if the country is to keep its promise of Social Security to the generations ahead. Others are scoffing because they see the surplus as a shell game: There is no surplus, not with a large federal debt and borrowing from the Social Security trust funds to mask the deficits that are really there. As part of the fiscal year 1999 budget, Republicans tried unsuccessfully to pass more tax cuts that would have primarily benefited the upper classes. They contended that the cuts would only account for a fraction of the budget surplus in the years ahead, but President Clinton strongly opposed the plan, saying that shoring up Social Security was more important.

Starting to Look Back at the Clinton Years

As we begin to look back at the Clinton years, the strong economy (near full employment and low inflation, the lowest misery index in three decades) seemed to keep the president's popularity high despite the scandals that led to his impeachment. Like most other presidencies, the Clinton administration has seen its share of failures and successes in promoting its social welfare agenda. In addition to economic reform, the president had three major domestic issues on his agenda: health care reform, welfare (public assistance) reform, and crime control.

The sweeping economic stimulus bill the president proposed during his first term, to create nearly a million jobs in a variety of areas from transportation and construction to high technology and social services, failed to pass. Instead the president got a program of enterprise and economic zones for economically depressed areas (see Chapter 9) and later a program to prepare more people for careers in the high-technology fields and more assistance to help adults leave public assistance for work. The strong economy also made for much of its own job creation.

Probably most disappointing to the president was the rejection of his proposed Health Security Act—a plan which would have entitled all Americans to health care coverage (see Chapter 8). The plan failed because many thought it was too much government interference in health care. There has been a series of incremental steps to expand coverage to more individuals, but the number of uninsured has risen faster than the number obtaining insurance.

Bill Clinton pledged to end "welfare as we know it" by turning the welfare office into an employment office and by limiting the time families could spend on welfare. The president finally signed the major 1996 public assistance reform bill even though it had provisions that disturbed him. Among them was cutting most aid to immigrants residing legally in the U.S. Some of these provisions were later modified, but the president lost a number of allies as a result of signing the bill in the first place. Many of these individuals thought the approach was an affront to the nation's children. Public assistance caseloads had begun to drop before the change to TANF due to the healthy economy.

The president did get a major crime bill passed with provisions for more community police, bans on assault weapons, life sentences for three-time felony offenders, more prison funding, more crime prevention funds, and more attention to crimes against women (the Violence Against Women Act of 1994). Crime figures are down, but there is an unprecedented number of people in jails and prisons, many of them as a result of the war on drugs.

As the new Republican-controlled Congress and the president hammered out budget bills that would continue to tame the budget deficits, the strong economy helped budget analysts predict continued surpluses in the years ahead. Though both Republicans and Democrats want to take credit for what seems like a budget in the black, it is difficult to say who or what should get the credit for the country's renewed prosperity. For most Americans it probably only matters that things are better. Others cannot help but point out that substantial poverty remains. They look at the very poorest, those for whom an expanding economy does not seem to make a difference, and they continue to press the public sector to do more for them.

The Big Tasks Ahead

Among the most pressing issues that the country now faces is the health of the Medicare program. Recent budget bills and the strong economy which results in people paying more Social Security taxes have made for an improved short-term financial forecast for Medicare. In the long run, however, Medicare is not on good financial footing. The Social Security retirement trust fund must also be strengthened for the long haul. Not so long ago, the baby boomers' Medicare days seemed far away. Now they are just around the corner. The major challenge for social welfare is to make all facets of the Social Security system strong enough to withstand the boom and to provide for the generations to follow (see Chapter 4).

Another major challenge is ensuring continued job creation and a well-educated workforce to fill these positions. This will keep the economy growing and secure both Medicare solvency and a better standard of living for all the generations. In this regard, the country must prepare its younger generations for the future by seeing that basic services like health care are provided to them, and by seeing that a solid education—from primary and secondary school to vocational education and higher education—is available to them. High school graduation rates are high, but this is not necessarily synonymous with quality education. A broad definition of social welfare services includes education as well as social insurance and public assistance.

The country must also be prepared to address its changing cultural composition (see Chapter 11). The United States is rich in racial and ethnic diversity, but this diversity has also been a source of strife. Among the most recent illustrations of this strife is denying public assistance benefits to immigrants who entered the U.S. legally. Immigrants will continue to play an important role in the economy in the years ahead, especially as more workers are needed to maintain the Social Security system. Equality of opportunity for Americans of all racial and ethnic backgrounds and a fair immigration policy are necessary for the country to sustain its vision of social and economic progress for the future.

Before these goals can be achieved, something else may be in order—restoring faith in government (also see Chapter 1). In 1998, the 105th Congress did not accomplish much as it was preoccupied with the Starr investigation and impeachment hearings. Politicians on both sides of the aisle may need to take stock of their personal and political behavior before they can more effectively return to the business of the country's domestic and foreign agendas.

SUMMARY

The roots of the U.S. welfare system can be traced back to Elizabethan times. Although the United States has developed its own unique brand of social welfare, some of this influence remains apparent.

In the early days of the country, welfare was provided by families, friends, private charities, and churches. But by the late nineteenth and early twentieth centuries, social problems had mounted. State governments began to enact programs for dependent children, the elderly, and people with disabilities. Following the Great Depression, the federal government passed the Social Security Act of 1935 as part of America's New Deal. In the 1960s President Johnson declared "war on poverty" in an attempt to root out the significant poverty that remained in the United States.

During the twentieth century, the expansion of social welfare has occurred for many reasons. Among these are the rural to urban migration, the elimination of residency requirements, the welfare rights movement, and cost of living increases in social welfare programs. The growth of the aged population and the increased number of single-parent families headed by women have also resulted in the need for more social welfare services.

Americans became disillusioned as they spent more on public assistance without the results they had expected. In the 1970s and 1980s America's welfare policies continued to be the focus of political conflict, and a more conservative mood developed. President Reagan was successful in tightening eligibility requirements in most public assistance programs, reducing spending growth in these programs, and consolidating many social programs. Reagan's program for economic recovery was intended to increase the incentive to work and to slow inflation by reducing taxes and slowing the growth of the money supply. Another important aspect of Reagan's plan was to return to the states much of the decision-making power over how public assistance and social service dollars should be spent. Inflation decreased and more people went back to work during the Reagan years, but the number of poor remained high and federal budget deficits increased tremendously.

When George Bush assumed the presidency, he called for "a kinder, gentler America." Bush further encouraged the states to develop innovative solutions to reducing social problems, but he was unable to remain true to his pledge of "no new taxes" in light of mounting federal deficits.

After twelve years of Republican presidents, Democrat Bill Clinton assumed the presidency with ambitious ideas for reducing budget deficits, reforming health care and welfare, and controlling crime. But as Congress turned from Democratic to Republican control, the climate for public assistance became more austere. In 1996 Congress passed a sweeping reform of the public assistance programs.

At the same time, market conditions (like the stock market's stellar performance), a strong monetary policy, and more attention to federal budget controls interacted to make life better for many Americans. Nevertheless, there are still many millions living in poverty for whom this progress has not made a difference. Advocates for the poorest Americans will continue to press the federal government to do more for these individuals.

NOTES

1. For more detailed descriptions of the history of social welfare in the United States, see June Axinn and Herman Levin, *Social Welfare: A History of the American Response to Need,* 3rd ed. (New York: Longman, 1992); Ronald C. Federico, *The Social Welfare Institution: An Introduction,* 3rd ed. (Lexington, MA: Heath, 1980); Blanche D. Coll, *Perspectives in Public Welfare: A History* (Washington, DC: U.S. Department of Health, Education, and Welfare, 1973).

2. See Federico, *The Social Welfare Institution,* p. 52; Coll, *Perspectives in Public Welfare,* pp. 1–2 for an elaboration of the role of the church and feudal landholders in the provision of welfare benefits.

3. Coll, *Perspectives in Public Welfare,* p. 2.

4. Ibid., pp. 2–3.

5. Federico, *The Social Welfare Institution,* p. 104; Coll, *Perspectives in Public Welfare,* p. 4.

6. See Federico, *The Social Welfare Institution,* pp. 52–53 for further elaboration.

7. Ibid.

8. Philip Klein, *From Philanthropy to Social Welfare* (San Francisco: Jossey-Bass, 1968), p. 11, cited in Federico, p. 53.

9. See Federico, *The Social Welfare Institution,* p. 53; and Coll, *Perspectives in Public Welfare,* pp. 5–6 for elaboration on Elizabethan welfare.

10. Much of this section relies on Coll, *Perspectives in Public Welfare,* pp. 17, 20, 21–22, 27–28.

11. Ibid., p. 17.

12. See P. Nelson Reid, "Social Welfare History," in Richard L. Edwards, ed. in chief, *Encyclopedia of Social Work,* 19th ed. (Washington, DC: NASW Press, 1995), pp. 2206–2225.

13. Thomas R. Dye, *Understanding Public Policy,* 4th ed. (Englewood Cliffs, NJ: Prentice Hall, 1981), pp. 116–117.

14. Reid, "American Social Welfare History."

15. Paragraphs describing the Great Depression rely on Thomas R. Dye and L. Harmon Zeigler, *The Irony of Democracy,* 5th ed. (Monterey, CA: Duxbury Press, 1981), pp. 100–101.

16. Cited in Richard Hofstadter, *The American Political Tradition* (New York: Knopf, 1948), p. 316.

17. Reid, "American Social Welfare History."

18. *Shapiro v. Thompson,* 394 U.S. 618; see Frances Fox Piven and Richard A. Cloward, *Regulating the Poor: The Functions of Public Welfare* (New York: Random House, 1971) for an elaboration on residency requirements, especially pp. 306–308.

19. See American Public Human Services Organization (formerly the American Public Welfare Association), "Temporary Assistance for Needy Families (TANF) Block Grants (Title I)," http://www.aphsa.org/reform/tangf.htm, accessed August 22, 1998.

20. This paragraph relies on Frances Fox Piven and Richard A. Cloward, *Poor People's Movements: Why They Succeed, How They Fail* (New York: Vintage Books, 1977); quote is from p. 275.

21. Ibid.

22. Aaron Wildavsky, *Speaking Truth to Power: The Art and Craft of Policy Analysis* (Boston: Little, Brown, 1979), p. 98.

23. Figures from U.S. Bureau of the Census, Current Population Reports, Series P-25-1130, cited in U.S. Bureau of the Census, *Statistical Abstract of the United States: 1997* (Washington, DC: U.S. Government Printing Office, 1997), Table No. 17, p. 17.

24. Robert M. Moroney, *Families, Social Services and Social Policy: The Issue of Shared Responsibility,* DHHS Publication No. (ADM) 80-846 (Washington, DC: Department of Health and Human Services, 1980), p. 43.

25. Joseph Dalaker and Mary Naifeh, *Poverty in the United States: 1997,* Bureau of the Census, Current Population Reports, Consumer Income P 60-201 (Washington, DC: U.S. Government Printing Office, 1998), Table C-3, p. C-9.

26. U.S. Bureau of the Census, *Statistical Abstract of the United States, 1998* (Washington, DC: U.S. Government Printing Office, 1998), Table No. 599, p. 376.

27. Mimi Abramovitz, "Everyone is on Welfare: 'The Role of Redistribution in Social Policy' Revisited," *Social Work,* Vol. 28, No. 6, 1983, pp. 440–445; Richard M. Titmuss, "The Role of Redistribution in Social Policy," *Social Security Bulletin,* Vol. 39, 1965, pp. 14–20.

28. Committee on Ways and Means, U.S. House of Representatives, *Overview of the Federal Tax System,* 1993 edition (Washington, DC: U.S. Government Printing Office, 1993), p. 263.

29. Scott Shepard, "Coalition to Fight 'Corporate Welfare,'" *Austin American-Statesman,* January 29, 1997, p. A3.

30. This quote is from materials urging citizens to join Common Cause, 1250 Connecticut Avenue, NW, Washington, DC 20036; for more information critical of corporate welfare see Michael Moore, *Downsize This!* (New York: Crown Publishers, 1996); web site of the Cato Institute, http://www.cato.org/home.htm; Sara Eckel (Newspaper Enterprise Association), "Welfare That Feeds the Wealthy," *Austin American-Statesman,* October 8, 1996, p. A11; Special Report, "Corporate Welfare," *Time,* November 9, 16, 23, & 30, 1998.

31. President of the United States, *A Program for Economic Recovery* (Washington, DC: U.S. Government Printing Office, February 18, 1981), p. 4.

32. Committee on Ways and Means, *Overview of the Federal Tax System,* 1993 edition, p. 49.

33. Eileen Shanahan, "President Signs Sweeping Overhaul of Tax Law," *Congressional Quarterly,* October 25, 1986, p. 2668.

34. See William Greider, "The Education of David Stockman," *Atlantic Monthly,* December 1981, pp. 27–54.

35. President Ronald Reagan, State of the Union Address, January 26, 1982.

36. For a concise review and bibliography on the issue of federalism, see Kenneth Jost, "The States and Federalism," *Congressional Quarterly Researcher*, September 13, 1996, pp. 795–815.

37. See "The Drive to Kill Revenue Sharing," *Time,* March 11, 1985, pp. 30–31.

38. The remainder of this paragraph relies on Richard Briffault, *Balancing Acts: The Reality Behind State Balanced Budget Requirements* (Washington, DC: Twentieth Century Fund, 1996); also see Robert Greenstein, *The Balanced Budget Constitutional Amendment: An Overview* (Washington, DC: Center for Budget and Policy Priorities, January 28, 1997).

39. For further discussion and illustration of this concept, see David Osborne, *Laboratories of Democracy* (Boston: Harvard Business School Press, 1988).

40. Executive Office of the President, Office of Management and Budget, *Budget of the United States Government, Fiscal Year 1991* (Washington, DC: U.S. Government Printing Office, 1990), p. 171.

41. This paragraph relies on ibid., Section IV, quotes are from p. 176.

42. Executive Office of the President, Office of Management and Budget, *Management of the United States Government, Fiscal Year 1990* (Washington, DC: U.S. Government Printing Office, 1989), p. 3–105.

43. Martin Rein, "The Social Structure of Institutions: Neither Public nor Private," in Sheila B. Kamerman and Alfred J. Kahn, eds., *Privatization and the Welfare State* (Princeton, NJ: Princeton University Press, 1989), pp. 49–71.

44. Marc Bendick, Jr., "Privatizing the Delivery of Social Welfare Services: An Idea to Be Taken Seriously," in Kamerman and Kahn, *Privatization and the Welfare State,* pp. 97–120.

45. Kamerman and Kahn, *Privatization and the Welfare State,* p. 10.

46. Andrew W. Dobelstein with Ann B. Johnson, *Serving Older Adults: Policy, Programs, and Professional Activities* (Englewood Cliffs, NJ: Prentice Hall, 1985), pp. 125–128.

47. Bendick, "Privatizing the Delivery of Social Welfare Services."

48. "Study: Poor Get Poorer as Rich Find Wealth Less Taxing," *Champaign-Urbana News Gazette,* February 17, 1990, p. 5.

49. As reported in Tom Kenworthy, "15 Years of Cuts Said to Enrich the Rich," *Wall Street Journal,* September 13, 1991, p. A23.

50. Executive Office of the President, *Budget of the United States Government, Analytical Perspectives, Fiscal Year 2000* (Washington, DC: U.S. Government Printing Office, 1999), Section 12.

51. Much of this paragraph and the next rely on Executive Office of the President, *Budget of the United States Government, Analytical Perspectives, Fiscal Year 1995* (Washington, DC: U.S. Government Printing Office, 1994), p. 186.

52. Randolph E. Schmid, "Uncle Sam Doles Out More Dollars," *Austin American-Statesman,* April 4, 1994, p. A5.

53. Executive Office of the President, *Budget of the United States Government, Analytical Perspectives, Fiscal Year 1995,* p. 185.

54. Ross Perot, *United We Stand: How We Can Take Back Our Country* (New York: Hyperion, 1992).

55. "Smoke, Mirrors Will Not Yield Balanced Budget," *Austin American-Statesman*, June 9, 1992, p. A12; Michael deCourcy Hines, "Does Chaos Hang in the Balance with a Budget Amendment?" *Austin American-Statesman*, June 11, 1992, p. A14.

56. See James Cullen, "Boll Weevils and Roosting Chickens," *Texas Observer*, April 20, 1993, pp. 4–5.

57. Executive Office of the President *Budget of the United States Government, Fiscal Year 1995* (Washington, DC: U.S. Government Printing Office, 1994), p. 73.

58. Gilbert A. Lewthwaite, "1994 Brings Higher Taxes for Wealthy, Break for Poor," *Austin American-Statesman*, January 1, 1994, pp. A1, 8; Executive Office of the President, *Budget of the United States Government, Fiscal Year 1995*, p. 58.

59. Executive Office of the President, Office of Management and Budget, *Budget of the United States Government, Fiscal Year 1998* (Washington, DC: U.S. Government Printing Office, 1997), p. 306.

60. Century Foundation, *The Basics: Balancing the Budget* (New York: Century Foundation, 1997), http://www.tcf.org/Publications/Basics/Balanced_Budget/index.html.

61. "The Line Item Veto Act After One Year," Congressional Budget Office (CBO) memorandum, April 1998, http://www.cbo.gov/cgi-bin/menu.exe?nodelist=O + cfgfile=/www/bin/cbo2.cfg.

CHAPTER

Defining Poverty: Where to Begin?

WHAT IS POVERTY?

The very first obstacle to a rational approach to reducing poverty in the United States lies in conflict over the definition of the problem. Defining poverty is a *political* activity. Proponents of increased governmental support for social welfare programs frequently make high estimates of the number and percentage of the population that is poor. They view the problem of poverty as a persistent one, even in a generally affluent society. They argue that many millions of Americans suffer from hunger, inadequate housing, remediable illness, hopelessness, and despair. Given the magnitude of the problem, their definition of poverty practically mandates the continuation and expansion of a wide variety of public welfare programs.

In contrast, others minimize the number of poor in the United States. They see poverty as diminishing over time. They view the poor in America today as considerably better off than the middle class of fifty years ago and even wealthy by the standards of most societies in the world. They deny that people need to suffer from hunger or remediable illness if they make use of the public services already available. They believe that there are many opportunities for upward mobility in the United States and that no one need succumb to hopelessness or despair. This definition of the problem minimizes the need for public welfare programs and encourages policymakers to limit the number and size of these programs.

Political conflict over poverty, then, begins with contending definitions of the problem of poverty. In an attempt to influence policymaking, various political interests try to win acceptance for their own definitions of the problem. Political scientist E. E. Schattschneider explained,

> *Political conflict is not like an intercollegiate debate in which the opponents agree in advance on a definition of the issues. As a matter of fact,* the definition of the alternatives is the supreme instrument of power; *the antagonists can rarely agree on what the issues are because power is involved in the definition.*[1]

Although inadequate income has always been a concern during economic depressions, *poverty* has been a *political* issue only for the last forty years. Prior to the 1960s, the problems of the poor were almost always segmented. According to James Sundquist, not until the Kennedy and Johnson administrations did the nation begin to see that these problems were tied together in a single "bedrock" problem—poverty:

> *The measures enacted, and those proposed, were dealing separately with such problems as slum housing, juvenile delinquency, dependency, unemployment, illiteracy, but they were separately inadequate because they were striking only at surface aspects of what seemed to be some kind of bedrock problem, and it was the bedrock problem that had to be identified so that it could be attacked in a concerted, unified, and innovative way. . . . The bedrock problem, in a word, was "poverty." Words and concepts determine programs; once the target was reduced to a single word, the timing became right for a unified program.*[2]

But even political consensus that poverty is a problem does not necessarily mean that everyone defines poverty in the same fashion. The following paragraphs elaborate on five different approaches to the conceptualization of poverty—as deprivation, as inequality, as culture, as exploitation, and as structure.

Poverty as Deprivation

One way to define poverty is as **deprivation**—insufficiency in food, housing, clothing, medical care, and other items required to maintain a decent standard of living. This definition assumes that there is a standard of living below which individuals and families can be considered "deprived." This standard is admittedly arbitrary; no one knows for certain what level of material well-being is necessary to avoid deprivation. But each year the federal government calculates the cash income required for individuals and families to satisfy minimum living needs. These figures are called the **poverty level, poverty line, poverty index,** or **poverty threshold.***

Official calculations of the poverty level were first developed by the Social Security Administration (SSA) in 1964. Economist Mollie Orshansky was the key figure in developing the original poverty levels, and there was great debate over whether her

*__Poverty guidelines__ are simplified versions of the thresholds. While the thresholds are primarily used for statistical purposes, the guidelines are used to determine who qualifies for federally supported public assistance. These figures are similar. In 1999, poverty guidelines for the forty-eight contiguous states were $8,240 for one person and $16,700 for a family of four. The guidelines are usually published every February in the *Federal Register.*

conceptualization was too high or too low.[3] Several revisions have been made in the calculations over the years. For example, since 1981, lower poverty-level figures are no longer used to calculate poverty rates of female-headed households and farm families. Some distinctions based on whether a household is headed by an elderly or nonelderly person are still made.

Originally, the poverty level was derived by estimating a low-cost but nutritious food budget for a household (similar to today's U.S. Department of Agriculture Thrifty Food Plan, described in Chapter 7). This figure was then multiplied by 3, since surveys indicated that about one-third of an average household budget was spent on food. Orshansky recently told *The Wall Street Journal* that her formula was intended only for the aged; nevertheless, it became the government's official definition.[4]

Since 1969, the previous year's poverty levels are simply adjusted to reflect changes in the Consumer Price Index (CPI). There are several variations of the CPI. The measure used today is the CPI for All Urban Consumers (CPI-U). It includes the living costs of more segments of the population than the measure previously used. Even so, the poverty level remains a crude measure of poverty. In 1997 the poverty level for a family of four was $16,400, up from poverty levels of $8,414 in 1980, $3,968 in 1970, and $3,022 in 1960.[5] Poverty levels are also determined for households of varying sizes and compositions as shown in Table 3-1.

The poverty level is an *absolute* measure of poverty because it provides one figure for the number of poor in the country, and individuals and families fall either above or below it. According to this definition, 14.5 percent of Americans were poor in 1994 compared with 13.8 percent in 1995. John Crudele, financial columnist for the *New*

TABLE 3-1

Poverty Threshold by Family Size: 1997[a]

Size of Family Unit			
One person		Four persons	$16,400
Under age 65	$ 8,350	Five persons	$19,380
65 and over	$ 7,698	Six persons	$21,886
Two persons		Seven persons	$24,802
Householder under 65	$10,805	Eight persons	$27,593
Householder 65 and over	$ 9,712	Nine or more persons	$32,566
Three persons	$12,802		

Source: Joseph Dalaker and Mary Naifeh, *Poverty in the United States: 1997,* Bureau of the Census, Current Population Reports, Consumer Income P60-201 (Washington, DC: U.S. Government Printing Office, 1998), p. 1.

[a]Thresholds for each family size vary somewhat by the number of adults and children in the household.

FIGURE 3-1

Number of Poor and Poverty Rate: 1959–1997

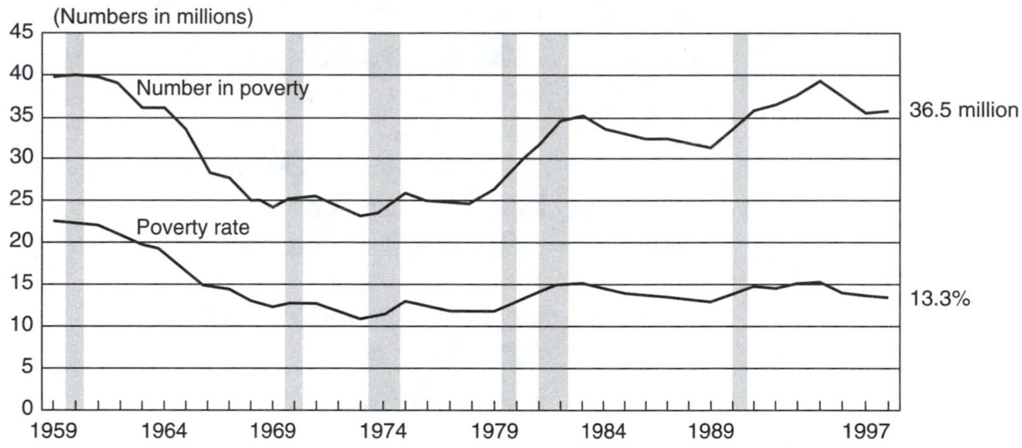

Note: The data points represent the midpoints of the respective years. The latest recessionary period began in July 1990 and ended in March 1991.

Source: U.S. Bureau of the Census, March 1998. Current Population Survey as reported in Joseph Dalaker and Mary Naifeh, *Poverty in the United States: 1997,* U.S. Bureau of the Census, Current Population Reports, Consumer Income P60-201 (Washington, DC: U.S. Government Printing Office, 1998), p. vi.

York Post and frequent critic of how the government counts things, says that while newspapers touted the decline, they did not report that the government surveyed 57,000 people to obtain its 1994 figures but only 50,000 in 1995, making the methodology less reliable. Some of those cut were from areas like Los Angeles that might have made a difference in just how much poverty was found. The 1995 figures were reported in 1996. According to Crudele, poverty "apparently never rises in a presidential election year. . . ."[6]

There were an estimated 35.6 million poor people in the United States in 1997 or about 13.3 percent of the population (see Figures 3-1 and 3-2).* Of all families in the United States, 7.3 million or 10.3 percent of them were poor in 1997 (see Figure 3-3). It would have taken an average of $6,602 to bring each family in poverty to the poverty threshold in 1996.[7] This figure is called the **poverty gap** or the **average income deficit.**

Even if we were to agree that poverty should be defined as deprivation, there are still many problems in establishing an official poverty level based on the federal government's definition as described earlier. First of all, this definition of poverty includes only cash income (such as wages, Social Security and public assistance checks, and

*The margins of error for these estimates are plus or minus 0.9 million people, and plus or minus 0.3 percent, respectively.

FIGURE 3-2

Poverty Rates for Individuals with Selected Characteristics

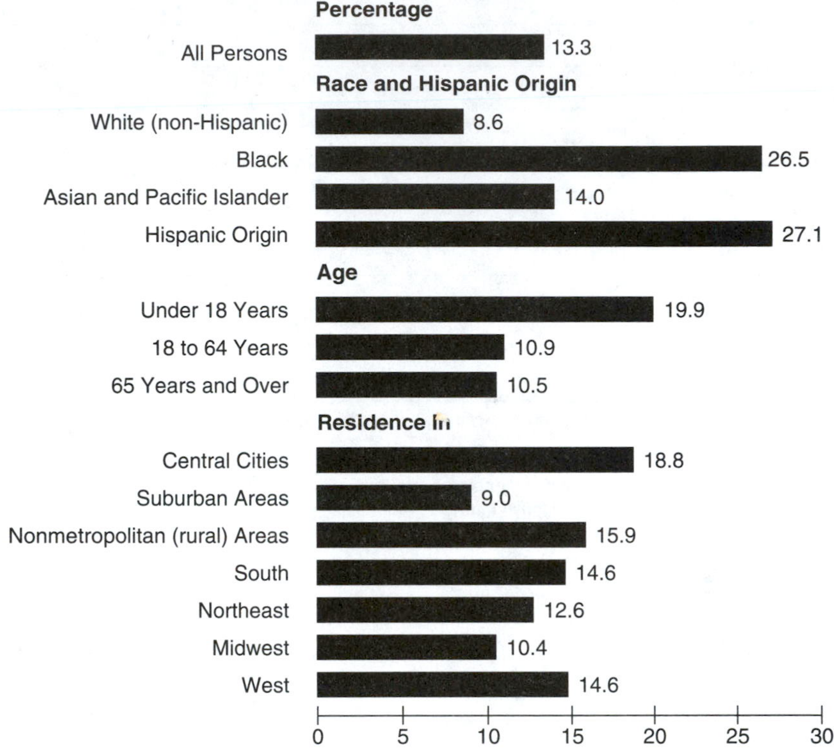

Source: Joseph Dalaker and Mary Naifeh, *Poverty in the United States: 1997,* U.S. Bureau of the Census, Current Population Reports, Consumer Income P60-201 (Washington, DC: U.S. Government Printing Office, 1998), pp. vi & vii.

interest from bank accounts, all *before* taxes) and excludes **in-kind benefits** such as medical care, food stamps, school lunches, and public housing. If these benefits were "costed out" (calculated as cash income), there would be fewer poor people in America than shown in official statistics. Also, many people (poor and nonpoor) apparently underreport their incomes.[8] Taking this into account would further reduce the number of people counted as poor.

There are other problems with this definition of poverty. It does not take into account regional differences in the cost of living, climate, or styles of living. It is unlikely that a family of four can live on $16,400 in New York City, even if it might be possible in Hattiesburg, Mississippi. It does not account for family assets. An older family that has paid off its mortgage does not usually devote as much to hous-

FIGURE 3-3

Poverty Rates for Families with Selected Characteristics

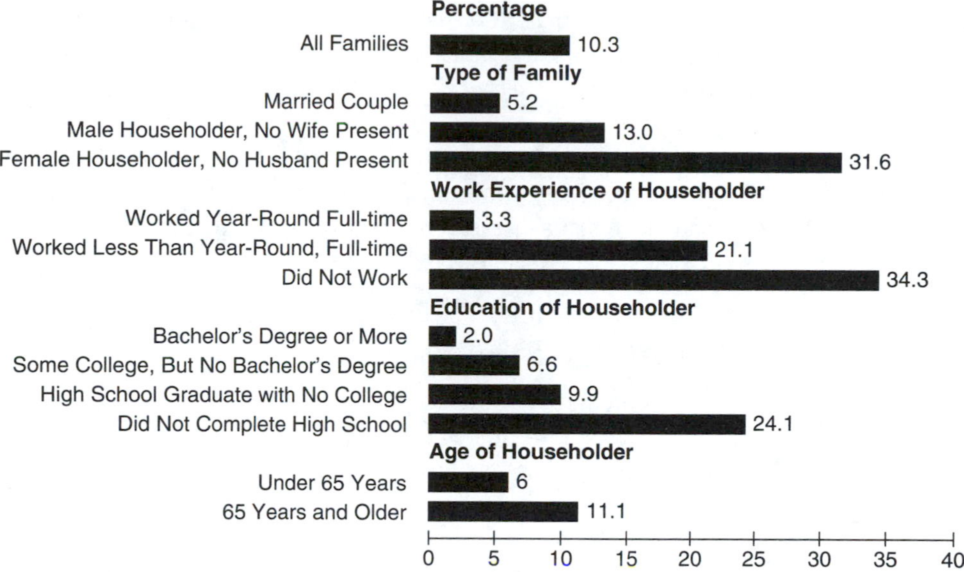

Source: Joseph Dalaker and Mary Naifeh, *Poverty in the United States: 1997,* U.S. Bureau of the Census, Current Population Reports, Consumer Income P60-201 (Washington, DC: U.S. Government Printing Office, 1998), p. vii, 17, and Table 2; Bureau of Labor Statistics and Bureau of the Census, *Annual Demographic Survey,* March Supplement, Table 7, http://ferret.bls.census.gov/macro/031998/pov/8_000.htm.

ing as a young family that rents or has recently purchased a home. It does not recognize differences in the status of individuals or families—for example, whether family members are students or retirees. Some of these people may not consider themselves "poor," although they are counted as poor in official government statistics. This definition also does not recognize the needs of families that may have incomes above the poverty level but have special problems or hardships that drain away income—chronic illnesses, large debts, or other problems. Finally, the estimate that one-third of family income is spent on food is outdated. The high cost of housing, in particular, has changed the composition of the family budget. In 1995, the poorest 20 percent of American families spent 17 percent (nearly one-fifth) of their before-tax income on food while the richest 20 percent spent 12 percent; the national average is 14 percent.[9] Multiplying the family food budget by 5, would yield a considerably higher poverty level. Economist Patricia Ruggles believes that given current consumer spending patterns, the poverty level would have to be increased by at least 50 percent to bring it up to date.[10] Besides considering urban–rural and regional cost-of-living differences, she says that one poverty level may not be enough, depending on our purposes. But as the president of the Urban Institute once said:

> *However contentious, drawing a poverty line is essential. It is a way of knowing how much progress we are making in reducing the numbers of underprivileged in America and, in very practical terms, it is a standard used by federal and state governments to implement programs that aid the poor.*[11]

Of course, we do need some convention for measuring poverty. As another observer noted 30 years ago, "Some arbitrary lines are needed, and these serve well simply because they already exist as a convention. To reopen an argument as to whether they are 'correct' seems a fruitless exercise."[12]

In-Kind Benefits: How Much Are They Worth?

According to the U.S. Bureau of the Census's annual survey, the national poverty rate is about the same as it was a decade ago. In addition to the official definition of income used to calculate poverty, the bureau now defines income seventeen additional ways. Some of these definitions consider income from capital gains (proceeds from the sale of property, stocks, or other assets), health care benefits to workers, in-kind benefits (such as food and housing), and home equity. Although official poverty was 13.3 percent in 1997, using these various definitions, poverty ranged from 10 percent to 21.4 percent.[13]

Several of the alternative definitions of income include in-kind benefits. Since this form of assistance has grown faster than cash benefits, most serious students of social welfare agree that they must be considered if poverty is to be measured more accurately.[14] But in-kind benefits can be difficult to measure, so in 1980 the bureau began conducting research on several approaches to doing this.

Two of these approaches were given extensive consideration in 1987.[15] One is the **market-value approach.** Using this approach, the value of welfare benefits is based on what it would cost a private consumer to purchase the good or service. In some cases, this approach is relatively easy to use. For example, the value of food stamps spent on an item is equal to the amount it would cost any shopper to purchase the same item using cash. Calculating the value of other benefits, such as public housing, is not as easy. Estimates are made, but surveys that equate the value of comparable public and private housing are lacking. Calculating the value of health care benefits is a major headache.[16] It has been said that health care benefits should not be included since they were not used in developing the poverty thresholds and they are not added to the incomes of those above the poverty line. But if health care costs were included for everyone, should we use the cash value of the medical service itself, the value of employer- or government-provided health care benefits, or should out-of-pocket costs only be considered?

A second method used to determine the value of in-kind benefits is the **recipient** or **cash equivalent approach.** This is the cash value that recipients place on the in-kind benefits they receive, which is not always the same as the face value of the item. It is based on the amount of money a poor family or individual not receiving benefits uses to obtain the same goods or services. This approach is difficult to use because individual preferences vary. What is very valuable to one person is not necessarily as valuable to another. For example, a person who is ill would likely place a higher value on medical care than a person who is well. The market value of welfare benefits is considered to be higher than the recipient or cash equivalent value, because it is believed that recipients would prefer cash to in-kind benefits. For example, it is estimated that recipients would trade $1,500 worth of food stamps for $1,440 in cash.

The market and recipient approaches produce relatively similar estimates of annual food benefits for those in poverty (in the 1987 study, $1,605 and $1,519, respectively). But the estimates of housing and medical benefits differ substantially. For example, the market value of housing was $1,786 and of medical benefits was $3,443. For the recipient method, the figures were $952 for housing and $1,010 for medical benefits. In 1987, the market value approach reduced official poverty figures for all people by 5 percent, while the recipient approach reduced poverty rates by 2.5 percent.

We can also consider the effects of cash and in-kind social welfare benefits using the poverty gap. In 1996, the total poverty gap was $196 billion. Social insurance programs reduced it to $107; adding cash public assistance benefits reduced it to $82 billion, in-kind benefits to $63 billion, and federal tax provisions (like the earned income credit) to $60 billion. The number of people in poverty before these government transfer programs was 57 million. The respective reductions with each type of benefit were 39 million, 37 million, 32 million, and 31 million. The poverty rate was 21.5 percent before transfers and the corresponding reduction after transfers were 14.8, 13.7, 12.1, and 11.5 percent. Social insurance programs resulted in a 31 percent decrease in the number of poor; cash public assistance reduced the number of poor by 5.1 percent, in-kind benefits by 7.5 percent, and tax provisions by 3 percent.[17]

In 1992 Congress commissioned a major study of the poverty measure. Most members of the study panel recommended changes to address long-noted problems with the current measure (e.g., adjusting for costs across geographic regions, counting benefits like food stamps). John F. Cogan of the conservative Hoover Institution was the lone dissenter, calling the suggested measure "value judgements made by scientists—with a particular point of view."[19] There is no indication that the government will settle on a method of valuing in-kind benefits or will make other adjustments in its official estimates of poverty anytime soon. And there may be no rush to do since the House Committee on Ways and Means noted that public assistance has had a diminishing impact on reducing poverty in recent years.[18]

Who Are the Poor?

Poverty occurs among all segments of the population and in all areas of the country; however, the incidence of poverty varies among groups (see Figures 3-2, 3-3, and 3-4). In absolute figures, more whites are poor than blacks. Of the 35.6 million people

FIGURE 3-4

Poverty Rates by Age: 1966–1997

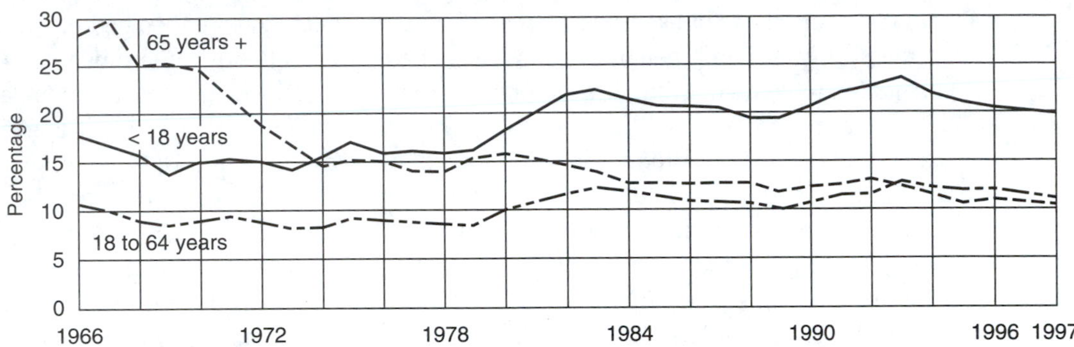

Sources: Leatha Lamison-White, *Poverty in the United States: 1996,* U.S. Bureau of the Census, Current Population Reports, Consumer Income P60-198 (Washington, DC: U.S. Government Printing Office, 1997), p. C-5; Joseph Dalaker and Mary Naifeh, *Poverty in the United States: 1997,* U.S. Bureau of the Census, Current Population Reports, Consumer Income P60-201 (Washington, DC: U.S. Government Printing Office, 1998), p. vi.

counted as poor by government definition in 1997, approximately 16.5 million were white (not of Hispanic origin) while 9.1 million were black.[20] However, the likelihood of blacks experiencing poverty is more than three times greater than it is for whites: *The 1997 poverty rate for the nation's black population was 26.5 percent compared to 8.6 percent for the white (non-Hispanic) population.* In other words, whites outnumber blacks among the poor, but a much larger percentage of the nation's black population is poor. There are 8.3 million poor people of Hispanic origin in the United States (they may be of any race). Their poverty rate is 27.1 percent. Since 1994 the poverty rate for those of Hispanic origin has been higher than that of blacks. From 1996 to 1997, the poverty rate declined significantly for blacks and those of Hispanic origin and stayed the same for whites.

*The primary source of poverty today is families headed by women where no husband is present.** The poverty rate for these female-headed households is 31.6 percent compared to 5.2 percent for families headed by married couples. *For families headed by white women, the rate is 27.7 percent. The rates for families headed by black women and women of Hispanic origin are much higher—39.8 and 47.6 percent, respectively.*

There are approximately 14.1 million poor children under age 18 in the United States, or 19.9 percent of this age group. In 1959 poverty among children was 27.4 percent. By 1969 it had reached a low of 14 percent, much better than we could report

*Additional information on poverty among black and Hispanic Americans and among women is found in Chapter 10.

for 1997. For children of Hispanic origin and black children, the situation is especially bad; *36.8 percent of all children of Hispanic origin and 37.2 percent of all black children in the United States live in poverty, compared to 16.1 percent of white children. Even worse are the poverty figures for children under age 6 residing in female-headed households: 56.9 percent for whites, 67.9 percent for those of Hispanic origin, and 60.8 percent for blacks.*

There is some better news in the official poverty figures. Poverty rates for Americans 65 years of age and older have dropped substantially over the years—from 35.2 percent in 1959 to 24.6 percent in 1970 and 10.5 percent in 1997. The rate for older women is 13.1 percent, compared with 7 percent for older men. Among older Americans, poverty is 26 percent for blacks, 23.8 percent for those of Hispanic origin, and 9 percent for whites. Today, the 10.5 percent poverty rate for those aged 65 and older is not statistically different from the 10.9 rate for those age 18 to 64. However, more older than younger people have incomes that fall just above the poverty level, and remember that official poverty thresholds for elderly households are lower than for younger ones.

Poverty occurs not only in large, urban areas but in rural America as well. In 1996 about 18.8 percent of the residents of central cities were poor, and about 15.9 percent of rural residents were poor. Suburban areas have less poverty (a rate of 9 percent) because those with low incomes are unlikely to find affordable housing there. There is always more poverty in the South than in other regions of the country. About 39 percent of all poor people live in the South, 25 percent live in the West, and in both the Midwest and the Northwest the poverty rate is 18 percent.

An important question we must ask about poverty is whether it is a temporary or transient rather than a persistent, long-lasting problem. Information on this issue comes largely from the University of Michigan's Panel Study of Income Dynamics (PSID), which has tracked 5,000 U.S. families since 1967.[21] Two analyses of PSID data indicate that about 2.6 percent of the total population will be poor for at least eight out of ten years. There is some consolation in the fact that the circumstances of most people who experience poverty will change—although they may lose their jobs, separate, divorce, or become ill, later they may find work, remarry, or get well, thus improving their financial condition. But there are clearly two groups of poor people, those who experience poverty for a relatively short period of time and those who are persistently poor. Other methodologically sensitive studies of "spells of poverty" indicate that persistent poverty is much more serious than once thought. Although the majority still experience poverty for a short time (one or two years), 60 percent of those classified as poor at any given time will experience poverty for seven years or longer.[22] The Survey of Income and Program Participation (SIPP) allows for estimates of the transitions in and out of poverty. These poverty estimates differ somewhat from the official calculations used by the Bureau of the Census, but according to the SIPP, from 1992 to 1993 22.7 million Americans remained poor, 6.5 million entered poverty, and about 6.3 million exited poverty.[23] The chances of escaping poverty diminish over time. The probability is .53 in the first year of a spell, dropping to .36 the second year, and .2 or less by the fifth year.[24] The chances of escaping poverty also vary by demographic characteristics. Households headed by white males are most likely to exit. The chances for families headed by black women are much lower.

Has the percentage of poor in this country changed substantially? Franklin D. Roosevelt said in his second inaugural address in 1937, "I see one-third of a nation ill-housed, ill-clad, ill-nourished." He was probably underestimating poverty; economic historians think that over 50 percent of the nation would have been classified as poor during the Great Depression. Since poverty levels account for the effects of inflation, there is no question that the U.S. political and economic system has succeeded in reducing the proportion of poor (as defined in official government statistics). Poverty declined considerably during the 1960s and reached lows of 11 to 12 percent during the 1970s (see Figure 3-2). But poverty increased in the early 1980s, rising to 15.2 percent by 1983. A sluggish economy that resulted in increased unemployment, along with cuts in some government social welfare programs, explained much of the increase. By 1988 poverty was down to 13 percent, but it increased to 15.1 percent in 1993. Whether economic upturns, different survey approaches, or some combination of the two resulted in reductions in poverty to 13.3 percent in 1997, one thing remains clear, millions of Americans are still poor by government definition.

Poverty as Inequality

Poverty can also be defined as **inequality** in the distribution of income. Unlike the federal government's official definition of poverty, which is tied to an absolute level of deprivation, inequality refers to **relative deprivation**—some people perceive that they have less income or material possessions than most Americans, and they believe they are entitled to more.[25] Even with a fairly substantial income, one may feel a sense of relative deprivation in a very affluent society where commercial advertising portrays the "average American" as having a high level of material well-being.* According to economist Victor Fuchs,

> *By the standards that have prevailed over most of history, and still prevail over large areas of the world, there are very few poor in the United States today. Nevertheless, there are millions of American families who, both in their own eyes and in those of others, are poor. As our nation prospers, our judgment as to what constitutes poverty will inevitably change. When we talk about poverty in America, we are talking about families and individuals who have much less income than most of us. When we talk about reducing or eliminating poverty, we are really talking about changing the distribution of income.*[26]

How can we measure poverty as inequality? One method, used often in cross-national comparisons of poverty, is to calculate poverty as a percentage (perhaps one-

*However, an international study of poverty (cited in Committee on Ways and Means, *1993 Green Book*, pp. 1451, 1453) that includes the United States, Canada, Australia, Sweden, Germany, the Netherlands, France, and the United Kingdom, showed that the United States poverty rate was nearly two to five times higher than these other countries.

half or more) of each country's median income. In the U.S., economists frequently measure the distribution of total personal income across various classes of families. Since relative deprivation is a psychological as well as a social and economic concept, these classes or groups are difficult to establish, but a common method is to divide all American families into five groups—from the lowest one-fifth in personal income to the highest one-fifth. Table 3-2 shows the percentage of total personal income received by each of these groups for selected years since 1936. If perfect income equality existed, then each fifth of U.S. families would receive 20 percent of all family personal income, and it would not even be possible to rank fifths from highest to lowest. But clearly, personal income in the United States is distributed unequally.

The poorest one-fifth of U.S. families now receive less than 5 percent of all family personal income. This group's share of income, like that of the middle class, rose slowly for many years and then declined in recent decades. The opposite situation occurred for the wealthy, defined in Table 3-2 as the highest one-fifth of all Americans in personal income. This group's share of income declined for many years, then rose in recent decades. Those in the top 5 percent of income also lost ground for many years, but lately they too have captured more of the country's wealth.

The income gains made by America's poorest families have been lost. Between 1970 and 1997, the income share of those in the lowest quintile declined by 22 percent while the highest quintile gained 15 percent. Income inequality can also be measured by the *Gini index*, with zero indicating perfect income equality and 1 indicating total inequality. As measured by the *Gini index*, income inequality has grown from .39 in 1970 to .46 in 1997.[27]

Although the hardships of some of the poor are mitigated by in-kind benefits (food stamps, public housing, Medicaid, and similar programs) that are not counted as income, even small reductions in their cash incomes can have serious consequences.

TABLE 3-2

Share of Aggregate Income Received by Each Fifth and Top 5 Percent of Families, Selected Years

Quintiles	1950	1960	1970	1980	1990	1997
Lowest	4.5%	4.8%	5.4%	5.3%	4.6%	4.2%
Second	12.0	12.2	12.2	11.6	10.8	9.9
Third	17.4	17.8	17.6	17.6	16.6	15.7
Fourth	23.4	24.0	23.8	24.4	23.8	23.0
Highest	42.7	41.3	40.9	41.1	44.3	47.2
Total	100.0	100.0	100.0	100.0	100.0	100.0
Top 5 percent	17.3	15.9	15.6	14.6	17.4	20.7

Source: U.S. Bureau of the Census, *Historical Income Tables, Families,* http://www.census.gov/hhes/income/histinc/f02.html.

Those who study income dynamics describe a shrinking middle class and a more economically polarized United States. According to Greg Duncan of the Survey Research Center at the University of Michigan, a "tidal wave of inequality" has been occurring between those with more skills and work experience and those with less of both, and these trends have affected men and women and people of all ethnic groups.[28]

Why Are the Poor, Poor?

Poverty is explained in many ways. We naturally assume that illness, old age, disability, lack of job skills, family instability, discrimination, unemployment, and general economic recessions all contribute to poverty. But how do these problems interact to create poverty?

Perhaps the most popular explanation among economists is the **human capital theory.** This theory explains income variations in a free market economy as a result of differences in productivity. The poor are poor because their economic productivity is low. They do not have the human capital—knowledge, skills, training, education—to sell to employers in a free market. As partial evidence for this theory, we observe that poverty among families headed by a person with less than a high school education is 24 percent, while poverty among families headed by a person who completed high school is 10 percent (see Figure 3-3). For those with some college education, it is 7 percent, and for those with at least a bachelor's degree, it is 2 percent.

Economists recognize that poverty may also result from inadequate demand in the economy as a whole, in a particular segment of the economy, or in a particular region of the nation. A serious recession and widespread unemployment raise the proportion of the population living below the poverty level. Full employment and a healthy economy improve opportunities for marginal workers, but these factors do not directly reduce poverty among people who have no marketable skills.

Absence from the labor force is the largest single source of poverty. This is also demonstrated in Figure 3-3. Thirty-four percent of families in which the household head did not work were poor, compared to 21 percent with a part-time worker, and 3 percent with a full-time worker. A substantial number of the poor are older people and those with severe disabilities who cannot reasonably be expected to be employed. No improvement in the national economy is likely to affect these people directly. They are outside the labor market and, therefore, are largely the concern of government rather than of the private economy. Many of the poor are children, and there is hope of helping them out of poverty by improving the employment opportunities of their parents.

Finally, we must consider poverty that is the direct effect of discrimination against women and particular ethnic groups. It is true that some differences in incomes are a product of educational differences between groups. However, even if we control for education among year-round, full time workers, we can see, for example, that black men and men of Hispanic origin at every educational level earn less than white men (see Table 3-3). If the human capital theory operated freely—without interference in the form of discrimination—then we would not expect differences between blacks

TABLE 3-3

Mean Income of Men Who Worked Year-Round, Full-Time by Race or Ethnicity and Education, 1997

Education	White	Black	Hispanic[a]
Less than 9th grade	$23,651	$20,147	$20,892
9th to 12th grade (no diploma)	30,289	22,133	24,354
High school graduate	35,038	28,128	27,960
Associate degree	42,216	36,388	33,416
Bachelor's degree	58,433	40,388	43,351
Master's degree	73,634	52,920	59,203

Source: Housing and Household Economies Statistics Division of the Bureau of the Census, Table 15, unpublished data.
[a]May be of any race.

and whites and between men and women at the same educational levels. But unfortunately this is not the case.

When in 1776 Thomas Jefferson wrote on behalf of the Second Continental Congress that "all men are created equal . . . ", he was expressing the widespread dislike for hereditary aristocracy—lords and ladies, dukes and duchesses, and queens and kings. The Founding Fathers wrote their belief in equality of law into the U.S. Constitution. But their concern was **equality of opportunity,** not absolute equality. Indeed, the Founding Fathers referred to efforts to equalize income as "leveling," and they were strongly opposed to this notion. Jefferson wrote,

> *To take from one, because it is thought his own industry and that of his fathers has acquired too much, in order to spare to others, who, or whose fathers have not, exercised equal industry and skill, is to violate arbitrarily the first principle of association, the guarantee to everyone the free exercise of his industry and the fruits acquired by it.*[29]

Equality of opportunity requires that artificial obstacles to upward mobility be removed. Distinctions based on race, gender, ethnicity, birth, and religion have no place in a free society. But this is not to say that all people's incomes should be equalized. Andrew Jackson, one of the nation's first democrats, explained,

> *Distinctions in every society will always exist under every just government. Equality of talents, education or wealth cannot be produced by human institutions. In the full enjoyment of the gifts of heaven and the fruits of superior industry, economy, and virtue, every man is entitled to protection by law; but when the laws undertake to add to these national distinctions, to grant titles, gratuities, and exclusive privileges, to make the rich richer . . . then the humble members of society have a right to complain of the injustice of their government.*[30]

But how much equality should we try to achieve? Utopian socialists have argued for a rule of distribution: "From each according to his ability, to each according to his needs." In other words, everyone produces whatever he or she can, and wealth and income are distributed according to the needs of each person. There is no monetary reward for hard work, or skills and talent, or education and training. Since most people's needs are roughly the same, they will each receive roughly the same income. Collective ownership replaces private property. If such a Utopian society ever existed, then near-perfect income equality would be achieved.

But all societies—capitalist and socialist, democratic and authoritarian, traditional and modern—distribute wealth unequally. It is not likely that income differences will ever disappear. Societies reward hard work, skill, talent, education, training, risk taking, and ingenuity. Distributing income equally throughout society threatens the work ethic. The real questions we must confront are how much inequality is necessary or desirable for a society, and conversely, how much inequality can society afford to tolerate? We might argue about the fairness of the current distribution of income (as shown in Table 3-2), but virtually everyone recognizes that a country in which one-fifth of children are growing up in poverty cannot lead to positive outcomes at the individual or societal level.

Of course, when defined as *inequality*, the problem of poverty is not capable of a total solution. Regardless of how well off poor individuals and families may be in absolute standards of living, there will always be a lowest one-fifth of the population receiving something less than 20 percent of all income. We can reduce income inequalities through less drastic political changes than communism or socialism (a more progressive personal income tax or more generous social welfare benefits, for example), but some differences will remain, and to the extent they do, someone will see them as a "problem."

Poverty as Culture

Some argue that poverty is a "way of life" passed on from generation to generation in a self-perpetuating cycle. This **culture of poverty** involves not just a low income but also attitudes of indifference, alienation, and apathy, along with lack of incentives and of self-respect. These attitudes make it difficult for people who are poor to use the opportunities for upward mobility that may be available to them. Increasing the income of poor people may not affect their joblessness, lack of incentives and educational opportunities, unstable family life, incidence of crime, and other social problems.

There are sharp differences between scholars and policymakers over whether or not a culture of poverty exists. The argument resembles the classic exchange between F. Scott Fitzgerald and Ernest Hemingway. When Fitzgerald observed, "The rich are different from you and me," Hemingway retorted, "Yes, they have more money." Observers who believe that they see a distinctive culture among the poor may say, "The poor are different from you and me." But opponents of the culture-of-poverty notion may reply, "Yes, they have less money." But are the poor undereducated, unskilled, poorly motivated, and "delinquent" because they are poor? Or are they poor because they are undereducated, unskilled, poorly motivated, and "delinquent"? This distinction has important policy implications.

One especially controversial view of the culture of poverty is set forth by Harvard professor Edward C. Banfield, who contends that poverty is really a product of "present-orientedness."[31] According to Banfield, individuals caught up in the culture of poverty are unable to plan for the future, to sacrifice immediate gratifications in favor of future ones, or to exercise the discipline required to get ahead. Banfield admits that some people experience poverty because of involuntary unemployment, prolonged illness, death of the breadwinner, or some other misfortune. But even with severe misfortune, he claims, this kind of poverty is not squalid, degrading, or self-perpetuating; it ends once the external cause of it no longer exists. According to Banfield, other people will be poor no matter what their "external" circumstances are. They live in a culture of poverty that continues for generations because they are psychologically unable to plan for the future. Improvements in their circumstances may affect their poverty only superficially. Even increased income is unlikely to change their way of life, for the additional money will be spent quickly on nonessential or frivolous items.

Nicolas Lemann has also described reasons for the culture of poverty that he believes exist in poor inner-city "ghetto" communities that are comprised largely of black residents.[32] He attributes hard-core poverty in these areas to an anthropological cause—the rural southern heritage of many of its residents. As sharecroppers, these individuals were unable to own property, save money, maintain stable family relationships, or obtain an education, and he contends these patterns have carried over to the present day. Opponents of the culture of poverty idea argue that this notion diverts attention from the conditions of poverty that currently foster family instability, present orientedness, and other ways of life of the poor. Social reformers are likely to focus on the condition of poverty as the fundamental cause of the social pathologies that afflict the poor. They note that the idea of a culture of poverty can be applied only to groups who have lived in poverty for several generations. It is not relevant to those who have become poor during their lifetimes because of sickness, accident, or old age. The cultural explanation basically involves parental transmission of values and beliefs, which in turn determines the behavior of future generations. In contrast, the situational explanation of poverty shows how present social conditions and differences in financial resources operate directly to determine behavior. Perhaps the greatest danger in the idea of a culture of poverty is that poverty in this light can be seen as an unbreakable, puncture-proof cycle. This outlook may lead to inaction or at least a relaxation of efforts to ameliorate the conditions of poverty.

If one assumes that the poor are no different from other Americans, then one is led toward policies that emphasize opportunity for individuals as well as changes in their environment. If poor Americans are like other Americans, it is necessary only to provide them with the ordinary means to achieve—for example, job-training programs, good schools, and counseling to make them aware of opportunities that are available to them. The intervention that is required to change their lives, therefore, is one of supplying a means to achieve a level of income that most Americans enjoy.

In contrast, if one believes in the notion of a culture of poverty, it is necessary to devise a strategy to interrupt the transmission of lower-class cultural values from generation to generation. The strategy must try to prevent the socialization of young children into an environment of family instability, lack of motivation, crime and delinquency, and so forth. One drastic means to accomplish this would be to remove children from lower-class homes at a very early age and to raise them in a controlled environment that transmits the values of the conventional culture rather than of the culture of poverty. This was done to some extent in the early part of the century (see Chapter 10). Such a solution is no longer realistic, although certain conservatives have suggested a return to the use of orphanages for children whose parents are unable to provide an adequate upbringing. More acceptable solutions today are special day care centers and preschool programs to remedy cultural deprivation and disadvantage such as Head Start (see Chapter 9). Theoretically, these programs should bring about change in young children through "cultural enrichment."

Poverty as Exploitation

Both Marxist and non-Marxist writers have defined poverty as a form of **exploitation** by the ruling class. Sociologist Herbert Gans contended that poverty serves many functions for the middle and upper classes in America such as providing a cheap source of labor.[33] Gans's implication is that poverty is maintained by ruling classes in order to make their own lives more pleasant. Poverty does not have to exist; it could be eliminated with the cooperation of the middle and upper classes. But it is unlikely that these classes will ever give up anything they believe they have earned through their own hard work, useful skills, or business enterprise. A substantial number of Americans believe that they are insulated from financial disaster and poverty.

Other authors have also written about the class-based nature of poverty. Two of them have called our society the "upside-down welfare state" because "the welfare state is a complicated system in which those who need help the most get the least, and those who need it least get the most."[34] They say that all Americans, rich or poor, benefit from government welfare programs. The poor and near-poor receive government assistance through programs called Temporary Assistance for Needy Families, food stamps, Medicaid, and the earned income credit. The middle classes receive government assistance primarily in the form of home mortgage loans and associated tax deductions and through educational grants. The rich receive government assistance through various income tax deductions, government contracts, and subsidies to business and industry. The difference is that government assistance to the poor is called "welfare," while government assistance to the rich is called "good business"—an investment in the economy and in the nation. In the final analysis, the poor receive only a pittance of all government assistance. Much more government assistance goes to the middle and upper classes.

Social scientists Frances Fox Piven and Richard A. Cloward have also commented on the economic, political, and social utility that the upper classes see in maintaining poverty. In 1971 they published *Regulating the Poor: The Functions of Public Welfare,* in which they claimed that "the key to an understanding of relief-giving is in the functions it serves for the larger economic and political order, for relief is a secondary and supportive institution."[35] Piven and Cloward argued, especially with regard to the AFDC program, that welfare had been used as a device to control the poor in order to maintain social stability. Welfare programs were expanded in times of political unrest as a means of appeasing the poor, and welfare rules and regulations were used as a means of "forcing" the poor into the labor market during times of political stability, especially when there was a need to increase the number of people in the workforce. Piven and Cloward later updated their original ideas when they saw that this cyclical pattern of contraction and expansion of welfare has been replaced by a more permanent set of welfare programs, making people less dependent for their survival on business and industry and fluctuations in the labor market.[36] Piven and Cloward believe in the right to welfare. They have long encouraged Americans to resist cuts in social welfare programs. Of course, the 1996 federal welfare reforms have again put social welfare programs on more shaky footing in another attempt to modify the behavior of the poor (see Chapters 5, 6, and 7). This and other events are reflected in the title of a more recent book by Piven and Cloward called *The Breaking of the American Social Compact*.[37]

If poverty is defined as the exploitation of the poor by a ruling class, then it might be suggested that only a radical restructuring of society to eliminate class differences would solve the problem of poverty. Marxists call for the revolutionary overthrow of capitalist society by workers and farmers and the emergence of a new "classless" society. Presumably, in such a society there would be no ruling class with an interest in exploiting the poor. Of course, in practice, Communist-ruled societies have produced one-party governments that dominate and exploit nearly the entire population (most of these governments have now given way to more democratic governance). There are less radical means to achieving a more egalitarian society. Civil rights legislation is one example. Substantial numbers of people have benefited from such laws, but many people view the remaining class differences as still far too wide.

These perspectives help us to understand that there are indeed class differences in views on poverty. If the upper classes do not deliberately exploit the poor, they sometimes express paternalistic attitudes toward them. Although the upper classes generally have little understanding of the lives of poor people, they believe they "know what's best" for them. Moreover, the upper classes frequently engage in charitable activities and support liberal welfare programs to demonstrate their idealism and "do-goodism," whether the poor are actually helped or not.

Poverty as Structure

Poverty can also be considered by studying the **institutional** and **structural** components of society that foster its continuation. As already mentioned, some poverty can be attributed to the effects of discrimination. The term **institutional discrimination** refers to practices that are deeply embedded in schools, the criminal justice system, and other organizations that serve gatekeeper functions in society. For example, poor school districts generally have fewer resources that can be used to promote educational opportunities for their young citizens than schools in wealthier districts. Such differences have become the bases for court challenges to the ways in which public school education is funded in a number of states. Health care institutions and other service organizations are generally not well organized in poorer communities. Lack of access to health care and other resources also contribute to circumstances that make it more difficult to avoid poverty. Another example of institutional discrimination occurs in the criminal justice system, since jails and prisons are overpopulated with those who are black or of Hispanic origin and poor. Problems of this nature can only be ameliorated by changing the structure of societal institutions that perpetuate them.

The economic structure of the country has also resulted in deep-seated poverty that arises from inadequate demand in a particular sector of the economy or in a particular region of the nation. For example, industrialization and technological development have bypassed large segments of Appalachia, one of the country's poorest areas. The closing of steel mills in large eastern cities and auto plants in midwestern cities also forced workers into poverty. Many workers are able to locate new jobs, but those with few marketable skills are least likely to secure jobs in other segments of the economy; neither are they able to relocate to find employment.

In recent years there has been a concern about a group referred to as the **underclass,** which has been the most severely affected by changes in community and economic structure. Karl Marx used the term *lumpenproletariat* (the proletariat in rags) more than a hundred years ago to describe those who had, in essence, dropped out of society.[38] In the 1960s this concept re-emerged. The term underclass was adopted to describe those who had been unable to weather changes in the country's economic structure and who were not able to obtain jobs in a market that relied increasingly on more highly skilled and educated workers.

Today, the term underclass is used with particular reference to poor, black, ghetto communities characterized by long-term unemployment, long-term welfare dependency, and overall social disorganization, including high levels of street crime.[39] The term is controversial because of its derogatory sound and because it fails to distinguish the diversity among the poor.[40] Regardless, this group is of considerable concern because it is clearly outside the mainstream of the social, economic, and political institutions that are part of the lives of most citizens. Prior to the 1960s these inner-city communities were not as severely depressed as they are today.[41] In the 1940s and 1950s they were home to blacks of all social classes. Fair housing and other antidiscrimination laws had not yet evolved that would allow many middle- and upper-class blacks to move to more affluent city and suburban neighborhoods. Schools, businesses, and other social institutions in these neighborhoods were used by all residents, and the economic exchange in these communities provided jobs for many residents, including those with marginal job skills. But as professional and blue-collar workers were able to find better housing in the suburbs, the most disadvantaged were left behind. According to several authors, community leaders were no longer present to bring stability to these neighborhoods. Their departure also caused a severe decline in economic enterprises. At the same time, the job market in the cities underwent considerable change. Industrial and manufacturing jobs were being replaced by jobs in the financial, technical, and administrative fields, and these were not the kinds of jobs for which most poor inner-city residents were prepared. Jobs in the food and retail industries, which inner-city residents might have been able to fill more readily, were increasing in numbers in the suburbs, but those who needed these jobs the most could not find housing there. It has been said that these structural changes left open a path for social disorganization. As a result, inner-city neighborhoods deteriorated and problems such as unemployment, teen pregnancy, and drug dealing increased.

To remedy this type of severe or persistent poverty, recommendations are that multiple approaches be used; for example, that job training, relocation, and other types of services be coupled with efforts to bring the poor in touch with mainstream society. These solutions sound similar to those suggested to interrupt the culture of poverty. The important distinction is that the notion of a culture of poverty is concerned with changing *personal* characteristics of the poor that prevent them from functioning in the mainstream. Some have referred to this as a "blame the victim" mentality. Poverty viewed as a *structural* issue is quite different. It implies that the solutions to the problem lie in developing new social institutions or modifying existing ones to be more responsive to disadvantaged members of society. This is an important distinction in developing social policies. For example, rather than provide housing for the poor in ghetto communities, a structural approach would be to offer housing in nonghetto communities to allow disadvantaged individuals to avail themselves of greater societal opportunities. Another suggestion to bring young people into the mainstream is a national service requirement for *all* youth. This type of universal program differs substantially from job programs that target only youth from disadvantaged backgrounds. The concept behind such a universal program is that it would provide for better integration of all members of society, but clearly such a requirement would meet with opposition from those who feel that they would not gain by it.

POOR AND HOMELESS: NOT INVISIBLE ANYMORE

In an influential book of the 1960s, *The Other America,* the late Michael Harrington argued that most Americans were blind to the poverty of millions in their own country.[42] Harrington wrote of two nations within the United States—one a nation of comfortable and affluent Americans, the other a nation of the poor—those who suffer deprivation and humiliation because they are without access to adequate education, housing, employment, and health care. Harrington believed that most Americans were blind to poverty because the poor were "invisible"—they did not live, go to school, work, or socialize with the more affluent. Even today, rural poverty can be masked by a beautiful countryside. With mass production of clothing, a poor person may be relatively well dressed but unable to afford decent housing or health care. The elderly poor are invisible because they do not venture far from home. And finally, most poor people are invisible because they have no political power; in fact, they are often the victims of political action.

Since the 1980s, poverty has become more visible, primarily because of increased homelessness. Just how many people are homeless? There are a number of lively accounts of how the estimates were derived.[43] Early estimates ranged from 250,000 in a 1984 study by the Department of Housing and Urban Development (HUD)[44] to suggestions of 3 million in a 1983 report published by the Community for Creative Non-Violence (CCNV).[45] Mitch Snyder, now deceased, was the controversial activist who led the CCNV. Snyder sued HUD over estimates he considered lowball.[46]

Of course, it is difficult to get an accurate count of homeless people when some are sleeping in alleys and under bridges and might rather be left alone. The process has been likened to "fly-fishing with a blindfold."[47] Furthermore, just what constitutes homelessness? Should the definition be reserved for those sleeping on the street? Should it include those in shelters, or should it be broadened to include those "doubled up" with family and friends because they cannot afford their own living quarters?[48] In conjunction with the 1990 national census, the Census Bureau conducted the S (street and shelter)-Night Enumeration using an innovative method of decoys and observers to determine the study's comprehensiveness.[49] The figure derived was 228,000 homeless individuals, an estimate that even conservative Rush Limbaugh thought was too low![50] Among the flaws were serious deficiencies in counting people living on the streets. The Census Bureau does not claim this to be an official count.

In an analysis of homelessness in America, social worker Joel Blau suggests that the best estimates come from the National Alliance to End Homelessness.[51] Using HUD data, the Alliance estimated that 735,000 people are homeless on a given day and that 1.3 to 2 million are homeless at some time during the year.[52] Others indicate that the best available estimate comes from the Urban Institute's 1987 study, which arrived at a figure between 500,000 to 600,000 during a week's time, with more homeless generally found in urban areas.[53] This count has been referred to as the "gold standard" for current homelessness.[54] The 1995 test census is another attempt to determine the prevalence of homelessness at a given point in time by replacing the S-Night approach with one based at soup kitchens and other service sites.[55]

One set of researchers used a telephone survey of a representative sample of U.S. households to study homelessness, which obviously underestimates the problem.[56] They still came up with figures that 12 million people had been literally homeless (e.g., living in an abandoned building or shelter) at some point during their lifetime because they could not afford another arrangement. The figure rose to 28 million when people who had moved in with family or others were included. Those literally homeless often reported deprivation (e.g., lack of food) and victimization (e.g., being robbed or even raped), and they spent considerable time with no place to live. Other recent estimates from various sources indicate that during a year, the number of homeless people is much greater than previously thought, perhaps 2 to 3 million.[57]

Who Are the Homeless?

Most of the poor have some permanent residence. Although the quality of this housing may vary, they do have an address to call home. But some Americans have no address at all. Two groups have comprised most of the homeless population. One is alcoholics and drug addicts. Alcoholic men in particular have long been a significant portion of the homeless population, and now an increase in other types of drug abuse has added to the homeless population.[58] The second group is those with severe mental illness.[59] Deinstitutionalization of people with mental illness beginning in the 1960s, combined with the lack of community-based mental health services, has added to those living on the streets (see also Chapter 10). But today homelessness has a third face—one- and even two-parent families with young children. High housing costs combined with unemployment and low-paying jobs, contribute to families' inability to locate permanent shelter. Spousal violence also adds to the number seeking shelter, and some children are homeless because they have run away as a result of abuse, neglect, or other family problems.[60] Another group of homeless young people have been released from foster care on reaching adulthood without an appropriate transition to independent living.[61]

Most studies indicate that "unaccompanied" men still comprise most of the homeless. Many are veterans, especially Vietnam veterans, and some have criminal histories. With the growth in single-parent homeless families, others suggest that there may now be nearly as many adult women as men in the homeless population. Estimates are that perhaps 15 percent of the homeless population are children, but information on homeless children is particularly sketchy. Families may constitute 25 to 40 percent of all homeless people, perhaps more in some areas, although some researchers believe these estimates are too high. About one-third of homeless people are mentally ill, and about one-third are alcoholics or addicts, with a substantial number having both mental illness and substance abuse problems. The homeless population seems to be younger and more ethnically diverse than in the past.[62]

One couple who have ministered to homeless people suggest that the nation must overcome its "politics of denial" and recognize that alcoholism, drug addiction, and serious mental illness, accompanied by disaffiliation and alienation from family and friends, are the major causes of homelessness today.[63] They point to the population bulge created by the baby boomers and the growth of the underclass as having exacerbated the problem. Others contend that the increase in homelessness is caused by social factors (loosening of family and community ties), economic and structural conditions (unemployment, a more competitive work environment, low wages), and politics (cutbacks in public assistance and social services).[64] They believe that the root of homelessness is the lack of affordable housing, not mental illness or chemical dependency. One point on which everyone seems to agree is that the homeless need good, affordable housing, and that those with mental health and substance abuse problems also need treatment.[65] Martha Burt sums it up this way:

> *It is clear that personal conditions such as poverty, mental illness, alcoholism, physical handicap, and drug addiction increase a person's vulnerability to homelessness; hence a large proportion of homeless people exhibit these characteristics. But many people have had these vulnerabilities in past decades. Only the changes in structural factors can explain why the vulnerabilities led to a much larger homeless population during the 1980s than in earlier times.*[66]

The Salvation Army and church missions have been used by alcoholics and others on "skid row" for years (see Illustration 3-1). Now almost all communities of any size

ILLUSTRATION 3-1

Homeless in Paradise

Coping with homelessness is *hard work,* and often a full-time job in itself. Like any other job, it requires specialized knowledge, as I learned when I asked Mayor Max how he spent his time:

> *On Monday, Wednesday or Saturday, [I'll] get ready to take a shower at the [Rescue] Mission, which is the only place available unless you spent the night at the Salvation Army. . . . [Then I] get something to eat. Depending on what day it is, there are certain places that are open, on certain days or times. You get breakfast at the Mission or Salvation Army if you stay there overnight [but there's a limit of] two nights at the Mission per thirty days, and one night per month at the Salvation Army. . . . When I was first living on the streets, I figured that when I was hungry, I'd go and find a grocery store [dumpster] and see if there's any food, and there was. I learned myself. Nobody ever told me. I was out here for about four days before I found any food, but I found it. And then I, you know, developed a route of the places that had food or the most food that's available.*
>
> *And [then I] look for a job, occasionally on the weekdays. Then, go around, look for aluminum cans, or somebody to get some cash up [for the cans] so I don't run out of cigarettes. Be able to go to a restaurant for coffee once in a while, stuff like that. . . .*
>
> *The Salvation Army will give you [clothes] if it's a real emergency, like if your pants are torn from the cuff to your butt, they'll give you a voucher to go to their thrift store to get one pair of pants. . . . If you talk to the right person, you know I shouldn't use his name, but if you talk to [deleted], if he can see that you're soaking wet, he'll allow you to get a change of clothes. . . . The Mission, when you take showers on Monday, Wednesday, or Saturday, you can get a complete change of clothes, including shoes once a week. . . .*
>
> *During the rainy season, the Mission allows an extra fifteen or twenty people to sleep inside, even if you've used your two days for the month. It's just who gets there first, gets in, and gets a bed out of the rain. And then there's the boxcars, which I've slept in many a night when it was raining 'cause there was nowhere else to go. And, on occasion, I've just gone up to the Amtrak station, under the awnings, and stayed awake all night, until it stopped raining. I've stayed down in the Jungle, . . . under the bridge where we cook, up past the bridge, up the railroad tracks.*

Source: Excerpted from *Homeless in Paradise: A Map of the Terrain* by Rob Rosenthal. Reprinted by permission of Temple University Press.

have shelters for a broader cross-section of the homeless population. Some operate with government assistance, others with private support, or a combination of the two. This humanitarian aid is welcome, but there is a fear that shelters have become substitutes for permanent homes. The addition of families to the ranks of the homeless is perhaps the straw that motivated Congress to pass the Stewart B. McKinney Homeless Assistance Act in 1987. The act provides for emergency shelters, rehabilitation of single-room occupancy dwellings (residential hotels such as those operated by YMCAs), nutrition assistance, health and mental health care, job training, education for homeless children, and other social services. In order to better coordinate these programs, the Department of Housing and Urban Development now uses a continuum-of-care approach, requiring communities to submit funding applications showing how services will be coordinated.[67]

Affordable Housing

There are different views of the causes of homelessness, but there is more agreement that the United States has a serious shortage of affordable housing. The largest item in most household budgets is housing. Whether it is the monthly rent or mortgage payment, housing consumes an increased portion of the personal budget. As far back as the Housing Act of 1949, Congress acknowledged the need for a "decent home and a suitable living environment for every American family." It is difficult for many Americans to realize the American dream—owning a home. It is also difficult for many people to pay the rent. A 1992 study by the Center on Budget and Policy Priorities found that many low-income households use half their income for rent and that in 39 of 44 metropolitan areas studied, housing exceeded the entire grant then received by AFDC families.[68] Using the federal government's definition that housing is affordable if it does not exceed 30 percent of the household budget, in 1994, the nonprofit Low Income Housing Information Service said that "one-third of renters in every state can't afford the prices charged for a one-bedroom apartment."[69] In 1995, HUD reported figures of 43 percent of very low-income renters paying more than half their income for housing.[70] Thirty percent of income is what residents of publicly supported housing are generally expected to contribute to their rent, even though the concept of "shelter poverty" indicates that this formula fails to take into account the various circumstances of individuals and families.[71] Some families may not have enough left for other necessities after they pay 30 percent of their income for housing, while others may be able to pay more than 30 percent. According to the Utah Issues Information Program, the

> *Shelter Poverty model demonstrates the material deprivation of poverty by showing how monthly income and expenses cannot realistically be reconciled by the poor, [yet] they must be paid if the danger of losing housing is to be avoided. As . . . homeless individuals and families will attest, being unhoused is highly disruptive of nearly all other aspects of life and the pathway from homeless to becoming housed once again is a difficult one.*[72]

Federal rental assistance for poor or low-income families, including people who are elderly or disabled, falls under two main categories.[73] The first is public housing. Most peoples' image of public housing is large, high-rise projects, but today this construction tends to be of the lower-density, low-rise type. About 1.3 million households live in public housing; in 1996, their median annual income was $6,420 and they paid an average of $169 for rent each month.[74] The second main category of assistance is subsidized rental programs. Under Section 8 of the 1937 Housing Act, renters receive a certificate or voucher to seek their own housing which can be privately owned or publicly subsidized. About 1.4 million families are being assisted through this program.[75] Waiting lists for these programs are long, and many eligible renters are unable to find qualified housing in the private market. A smaller program allows the government to pay subsidies directly to private owners who rent to low-income tenants. HUD also operates other programs to assist individuals and families in need, some of which focus on assisting groups such as Native Americans. Most HUD-sponsored programs are administered through locally operated housing authorities, and many states and communities offer additional assistance. There are also programs to help people with lower and moderate incomes purchase housing. Considerable federal housing assistance is given to middle- and upper-income households in the form of mortgage assistance and income tax deductions which amount to much more than the money spent on public and subsidized housing.

In order to help more people, President Clinton is seeking funding that will allow an additional 50,000 households to obtain rental assistance vouchers, especially those currently or recently receiving public assistance.[76] The idea is to help them locate housing in areas (mostly suburban) where they can find employment. According to HUD, only one-quarter of public assistance recipients are currently served by subsidized housing programs.

HUD and other governmental programs reach only a small proportion of those who could use help in obtaining safe, affordable, and permanent housing. Unhappy with the number of people living in substandard and unsafe housing, nonprofit groups such as Habitat for Humanity (its most prominent volunteers are former president and first lady Jimmy and Rosalyn Carter) are constructing or "rehabilitating" housing for low-income and poor individuals and families. Many of the beneficiaries contribute "sweat equity"—their own labor—to help build these homes. Most also make modest mortgage payments.

A fortunate circumstance in helping people obtain their own home is that a stronger economy has been accompanied by considerable drops in interest rates in the past two decades. This makes it easier to qualify to purchase a home, since lower interest rates mean lower monthly mortgage payments. In addition to federal mortgage assistance, communities use bond monies to offer low-interest mortgages to low- and moderate-income first-time home buyers. Also being credited with increasing home ownership are the Community Reinvestment Act, which puts more pressure on banks to make loans in low-income communities, and the growth of community development corporations.[77] Another significant piece of legislation is the Cranston-Gonzalez National Affordable Housing Act of 1990 which provides housing block grants to state and local governments for housing assistance such as home ownership programs.[78] In 1997 Secretary of Housing and Urban Development Andrew Cuomo announced that homeownership rates hit 65.7 percent—just slightly more than the previously recorded high of 65.6 percent in 1980.[79] Of course, homeownership is not equally distributed among the population—72 percent of whites are homeowners compared with 51 percent of Hispanics and 45 percent of blacks. Homeownership is higher for male- than female-headed households, and it is higher in the suburbs than in central cities.

The relatively modest amount of assistance provided to low-income people by the Department of Housing and Urban Development may be a result of the many difficulties the agency has faced. Republican Jack Kemp, HUD secretary under the Bush Administration, blamed "government rules and red tape" for declines in homeownership that had occurred at the time,[80] but many of the problems Kemp faced at HUD were in changing the image of an agency tarnished by scandals. There were accusations that prominent Republicans and former HUD officials had raked in millions of dollars in consulting fees in order to steer HUD contracts to particular firms and that private escrow agents siphoned off millions from the sale of foreclosed homes. Kemp worked hard to instill pride in public housing projects, and he even managed to turn ownership of a few projects over to their residents.[81]

When President Clinton appointed former San Antonio mayor Henry Cisneros HUD secretary, Cisneros said "There is no higher priority in our department than helping homeless people."[82] Cisneros worked hard to assist the homeless, to demolish ("blow up" is the term used) decayed public housing and rehabilitate other units under a program called HOPE VI, and to use vouchers to integrate poor people into decent neighborhoods. HUD's budget shrank, however, amid calls to get rid of the financially troubled agency entirely, and eventually, amid his own problems, Cisneros left the agency. HUD's problems have been compounded by some local public housing authorities that have been plagued by poor management. Today, Andrew Cuomo, son of former New York governor Mario Cuomo, heads HUD, but HUD remains a relatively small agency without much political power.[83]

Even if HUD were eliminated, the government would surely assign the task of helping needy people to obtain adequate housing to another agency. This agency would also likely pursue the favored strategies of the day which include seeing that families receiving housing assistance are dispersed throughout neighborhoods rather than concentrated in large public housing complexes, many of which Washington columnist Neal Peirce aptly described as "living hellholes of drugs, crime, and grinding poverty."[84] Merging the current housing assistance programs into a large block grant is another idea that has been proposed. Among the more controversial ideas about transforming public housing is to seek more tenants who earn more and can pay more rent. Such "mixed-income" communities seem desirable, but unless aid is expanded so that the poorest are also helped, those at the bottom rungs of the income ladder might find themselves being helped by homeless shelters rather than housing programs. A writer for *The New Republic* called this strategy "tantamount to making Medicare solvent by denying coverage to the old and the sick."[85]

In 1997 the federal government reported assisting 5.8 million households with rent or homeownership.[86] Housing is so integral to health and general well-being that it seems surprising that it has not been the focus of more attention. Illustration 3-2 shows just how important decent housing is to one woman who grew up in the slums.

ILLUSTRATION 3-2

Pam Jackson's New Apartment

At first glance, Pamela Jackson's apartment looks like any ordinary place. Her living room is functionally appointed with cheap furniture: a black vinyl sofa, matching love seat, glass coffee table, and a TV. Everything appears fairly new. Adjacent to the living room is a perfectly immaculate galley kitchen. In each of two small adjoining rooms, the beds are neatly made. If not for the smattering of framed photographs, a child's drawings, houseplants, and stuffed animals, one might mistake this for a motel suite of above-average cheerfulness. A walk around the two-story redbrick development in which the apartment is situated only exacerbates the pervasive sense of dull normality. Driving around the Chicago suburb of Palatine heightens it further.

But to Pamela Jackson, the apartment represents far more. To her, a clean, safe, affordable place to live still comes as such a surprise that it induces a kind of euphoria when she talks about it, some nine months after moving in. For her, a nondescript apartment in a middle-class neighborhood is the basis of a new life, vastly better than the one she knew before. It is a sanctuary, a safe haven from conditions so degraded that most of us can only imagine them. A slim, bright-eyed woman, wearing a sleeveless denim dress on a hot autumn day, Pam sits on the edge of her sofa and races, tripping over her words as she tries to explain what the apartment means to her: Here there are no crackheads trying to sell secondhand bus transfers for a quarter, no giant rats, random shootings, or playgrounds strewn with broken glass. Instead there's a good suburban school where her daughter is learning to play the clarinet, a parking lot where she walks without fear at night, and a landlord who responds promptly to the complaint of a leaky faucet.

Jackson told me her story when I visited her in 1995. For the first thirty years of her life, she lived in a variety of public housing projects and privately owned slum apartments on Chicago's South Side. At twenty, she got pregnant and gave birth to a daughter, Porshá. Porshá's father, to whom Pam wasn't married, soon left, and she went on public assistance. For the next nine years, she was in and out of work, in and out of apartments, on and off welfare. The father of her daughter sometimes works, she says, but he will quit a job sooner than pay child support.

Poverty and danger turned mother and daughter into refugees in the city. Before moving to Palatine, they lived with the family of Pam's brother at Seventy-sixth and Union, sleeping on a sofa in the living room. Though she had a full-time job at Woolworth's, Pam couldn't afford a place of her own, even in a marginal neighborhood. In the last few years the area where she lived with her brother has gone from bad to intolerable. Seventy-ninth is "the street that never sleeps," Jackson says, with young men standing on the corner dealing drugs "all night, in every kind of weather." After getting off work at ten o'clock, she would have to cross that street to pick up Porshá at her babysitter's. Porshá's school, at Sixty-third and Dulles, was in a similarly menacing precinct, "with people hanging out under the El station, gangs and drug dealers," she says. Parkway Gardens, a blighted housing project, was the school's backyard. "On Sixty-second Street anything can happen," Pam says. Although reconciled to a measure of risk herself, she was afraid for Porshá. "I

continued

ILLUSTRATION 3-2 *(continued)*

wanted some stability in my daughter's life," she says.

When, after a long struggle to get it, Pam moved to her new place in Palatine, the first thing she did was take off all of her clothes. "I never felt I could walk around, you know, free before. My daughter asked, 'Mama, why you walking around without any clothes?' Where I was you just don't have the freedom." They moved in on December 17, 1994. Jackson decided the apartment was her Christmas gift and got a small tree. A few months later, she bought herself a set of living room furniture as a birthday present. . . .

Source: Jacob Weisberg, *In Defense of Government: The Fall and Rise of Public Trust* (New York: Scribner, 1996), pp. 11–13. Jacob Weisberg is Chief Political Correspondent for *Slate* Magazine.

A FUNDAMENTAL SHIFT

This discussion of poverty and homelessness has considered contending definitions of the causes of these problems. In the 1920s the prevailing causes of poverty were attributed to the dominance of business interests and worker exploitation; in the 1930s national economic collapse was the cause, and in the 1960s discrimination (racism and sexism) and lack of opportunity were the prevailing explanations. During each of these eras, the solutions were generally agreed upon. Respectively, they were minimum wages and other fair labor standards; economic recovery, work programs, and a safety net of social insurance and public assistance programs; greater equality of opportunity through civil rights and gender rights legislation and access to nutrition, job training, health care, and early education programs. In the past three decades there have been increasing schisms about the causes of poverty in the United States. Our discussion ends with a contemporary belief that public assistance programs promote poverty and that a philosophy of mandatory work should be adopted that will root out all but some small unavoidable vestige of the problem.

Doesn't Welfare Cause Poverty?

The belief that welfare programs can actually *increase* the number of poor people[87] is certainly not new. Since Elizabethan times, welfare payments have been kept minimal (the principle of **less eligibility**) to discourage potential recipients from choosing welfare over work. The large numbers of people from all social classes who became poor during the Great Depression of the late 1920s and early 1930s made the country realize that poverty could befall almost anyone. Yet many people still believe that welfare should be made an unattractive alternative to earnings. A good deal of attention has been given to the argument that much of today's poverty is a *direct* result of the social policies and programs of the 1960s and 1970s. The argument is presented this way: from 1947 to 1965 the poverty rate was reduced by more than half without massive government social welfare intervention; by the mid-1960s many believed that the poverty that remained was due to lack of opportunities and bad luck.[88] The solution was government intervention to reduce poverty and create more opportunities for the disadvantaged. Welfare spending and the numbers of welfare programs increased, but the number of poor did not decrease. During the 1970s the poverty rate remained at about 12 percent.

The first book to receive widespread attention that claimed welfare was to blame for welfare dependency was George Gilder's *Wealth and Poverty,* published in 1981. Gilder boldly discusses what he calls "the devastating impact of the programs of liberalism on the poor":[89]

> *What actually happened since 1964 was a vast expansion of the welfare rolls that halted in its tracks an ongoing improvement in the lives of the poor, particularly blacks, and left behind—and here I choose my words as carefully as I can—a wreckage of broken lives and families worse than the aftermath of slavery.*[90]

Gilder believes that the expansion of the public assistance system led to an erosion of the work ethic and self-reliance. He contends that as these benefits increase, the value of a *man's* labor to his family decreases, especially if he earns low wages at his job. The welfare system saps his dignity by making him less necessary to his family. This in turn leads to family breakup and to further reliance on welfare. Gilder also criticizes antidiscrimination policies, which he says favor credentials over the drive to succeed. His book contains strong gender biases, because it focuses on the importance on jobs for men over those for women. Using many Horatio Alger-type success stories, Gilder pointed to examples of how poor Americans and immigrants to the United States were able to achieve prosperity through their hard work (the "bootstrap" approach). He is enamored of the advantages that a capitalistic economic system affords to those who are willing to "sacrifice to succeed."

In 1984 Charles Murray made much the same argument in his book *Losing Ground: American Social Policy, 1950–1980.*[91] Using statistical presentations, Murray concludes that there are more poor following the social programs of the Great Society; the underclass has fallen further behind, and social welfare policy is responsible. To make his point, Murray compared three measures of poverty. "Official poverty," as discussed earlier, is the amount of poverty measured by the U.S. government each year. "Net poverty" is official poverty minus the value of in-kind benefits. "Latent poverty" is the number of people who would be poor if they did not receive social insurance and public assistance payments. Murray claims that in-kind benefits have reduced official poverty figures—but not as much as they should considering the amounts of money spent on these programs (e.g., food stamps and Medicaid). Even worse, he believes, is that latent poverty is so much higher than official poverty. In 1980 official poverty was 13 percent. Latent poverty increased after 1968, reaching 22 percent of the population by 1980. The War on Poverty was supposed to make people economically self-sufficient and get them off welfare. The unfortunate situation is that these programs failed to reduce the need for public aid.

Those critical of Murray's work contend that his statistics and analyses can be misleading, because poverty is a complex issue, and many factors must be presented in any discussion of the rising numbers of poor people.[92] For example, bad economic times result in higher unemployment (the lesson of the Great Depression). Lack of preparation for good jobs—not the desire to be on the dole—adds to the ranks of the poor. In hard times it is not surprising that the underclass will be unemployed and require social welfare assistance. Murray ignores many of the approaches to understanding the root causes of poverty suggested in this chapter—structure, exploitation, and discrimination. He blames "the system" for instituting federal welfare programs that have enticed low-income individuals to abandon work and family values.

The thrust of Murray's argument was directed toward public assistance programs like Aid to Families with Dependent Children (AFDC, now TANF), a program that is a small part of the social welfare system (see Chapter 6). Murray used a hypothetical couple named Phyllis and Harold who are unmarried and expecting a baby to describe how the system encourages (1) them to remain unmarried, (2) Phyllis to keep her baby and to go on AFDC rather than work, and (3) Harold to quit his low-paying and unsatisfying job and collect unemployment insurance. Although few would deny the irrationality of many aspects of the current welfare system, Murray went too far in his claims because he used some erroneous premises. For example, he assumed that Harold can easily get unemployment compensation. In fact, unemployment compensation is not available to those who leave their jobs voluntarily and is available only on a short-term basis (see Chapter 4). Murray also implied that welfare officials would not ask Phyllis who the father of her baby is, that she would not be required to comply with the rule that AFDC applicants assist in establishing paternity, and that the state would not at least try to collect child support from Harold (also see Chapter 6). Even more damning is that Murray had little faith that either Phyllis or Harold, both high school graduates in his scenario, would ever get additional education or seek a better life. Many social welfare scholars have discounted much of Murray's arguments "about the effects of welfare or welfare state policies on the poor."[93] It is apparent, however, that Murray and Gilder continue to touch a nerve among the public, many of whom do not get the kind of governmental benefits known as welfare, but who are working hard and still struggle to make ends meet.

From Poverty to Dependency

Murray's view led him to advocate an end to all existing federally-supported public assistance programs for working-age people (AFDC, food stamps, Medicaid, and so on), and leaving the rest of welfare to private charities and state and local governments. Why he favors this solution is unclear, since federal intervention came about as a result of the inability of the local approach to respond to social welfare needs. AFDC or TANF benefits, which are determined by the states, have declined substantially in real dollar terms over the last few decades (see Chapter 6). Turning all public assistance programs back to the states would certainly mean severe cuts in these programs, thereby making welfare even less desirable and more degrading than it is now. But the approaches suggested by Gilder and Murray have had a significant impact on public assistance programs, to an extent that may surprise even these conservatives. Most of us agree that being a productive member of society is important, but there are some public assistance costs to be paid in a highly competitive, technological society, and we continue to struggle with what should be done.

Gilder and Murray have been followed by others writing in the neoconservative vein. In a book published by the Libertarian Cato Institute, Michael Tanner calls the solutions proposed by most neoconservatives insufficiently radical to bring about change. Most conservatives, he believes, think that they can alter the government's approach to achieve their ends. Tanner believes there is no hope at all for government welfare: "Welfare has failed and cannot be reformed. It is time to end it. In its place, the civil society would rely on a reinvigorated network of private charity."[94] Like Marvin Olasky,[95] who inspired Newt Gingrich, Tanner writes about "the bond" or the personal relationship that develops between those in need and those who wish to help—a relationship that the welfare bureaucracy finds difficult to emulate. Private charities can pick and choose whom they want to help, and they can hold those helped accountable for the assistance they receive. Sounding very much like Ronald Reagan and his supply side economic approach (see Chapter 2), Tanner says that high taxes and excessive regulatory policies are standing in the way of job creation and economic growth that provide opportunities for people to rise out of poverty.

Coming from an evangelical Christian perspective, Olasky emphasizes "abstinence and adoption" as keys in reducing welfare. Olasky calls governmental programs "too stingy in what only individuals can give: time, love, and compassion."[96] He makes three suggestions to increase "effective compassion" (1) allow states, rather than the federal government, to levy most of the taxes, and have states give citizens generous tax breaks for philanthropy and volunteerism; (2) allow religious groups to utilize government funding without restricting their religious activity, since change from within, including spiritual change, can help people transcend poverty; (3) allow organizations that help the poor redeem vouchers for the services they provide—but only if they show that the individual being helped has improved.

These ideas will have varying degrees of appeal to Americans, but is it realistic to think that private citizens and organizations can accomplish so much? As we saw in Chapter 1, many people who are well entrenched in serving the poor through the nonprofit and religious sectors do not believe that their organizations, let alone individuals of good will, can do it all, even with the government's support.[97] Rather than decreased dependency, they see increased misery without government involvement in helping the poor.

Americans have not rejected government intervention to reduce poverty. Instead, through their elected officials, they have placed their hopes on "welfare reform." In particular, their bets are on the view expressed by political scientist Lawrence Mead.[98] Mead contends that the welfare state has been too permissive by failing to "set behavioral standards for the poor."[99] Mead rejects notions that low wages, lack of jobs, discrimination, and lack of access to child care and health care are what cause people not to work and to consequently fall into hard core poverty. He believes that liberals have failed the country because they do not give poor people "credit to advance their own interests." With increased public assistance benefits, poor people simply were no longer motivated to work, and poverty became personal, not structural. Complacency developed by thinking of the poor as "victims" rather than "workers." Mead describes the poor as "dutiful but defeated," and he says:

> *To a great extent, nonwork occurs simply because work is not enforced. Overall, I think conservatives have the better of the barriers debate—the chance to get ahead is widely available. But liberals have the more realistic view of the psychology of poverty— the poor do not* believe *they have the opportunity, and this still keeps them from working.*[100]

Mead's analysis is that the poor respond well to structure, including the structure imposed by work programs. He notes that in the debate over poverty, communication between liberals and conservatives has broken down.[101] But conservatives have clearly won the latest round of attempts to address poverty. The following chapters, especially Chapters 6 and 9, show that there has been a strong shift in the wind. As the new millennium dawns, poverty is no longer viewed as a problem of too little income. It is construed as dependency; therefore, poor people must be motivated to be like most Americans who toil at jobs to try to better themselves. "Work, not welfare" is the order of the day. For many people who have devoted themselves to theorizing about poverty and to helping poor people directly, the latest round of welfare reform, particularly the restructuring of AFDC, has been a bitter pill to swallow.

SUMMARY

Defining poverty is a political activity rather than a rational exercise. This chapter included five approaches to defining poverty—as deprivation, as inequality, as culture, as exploitation, and as structure. Americans have not agreed on any best approach for defining this social construct.

If we use the official government poverty level as our arbitrary measure of deprivation, there were nearly 36 million poor people in the United States in 1997, or about 13.3 percent of the population. If we count in-kind welfare benefits as well as cash benefits, the number of poor people is somewhat lower. Since the government began counting around 1960, poverty has declined substantially, but the lows of 11 to 12 percent achieved in the 1970s have yet to be achieved again. Poverty is most frequently found among black and Hispanic Americans and in households headed by women. Although poverty among older Americans has declined, it has increased among children. Homelessness is also a concern.

There will always be differences among people in economic wealth, so it is particularly difficult to define poverty for public policy purposes as inequality. The real concern of society is the inequality that results in squalor. Poverty has many causes. Some people are poor because they lack the resources and opportunities of the nonpoor, and some, such as the elderly, children, and those with disabilities, are not able to work. Discrimination is another source of poverty. Equality of opportunity remains an obstacle to the elimination of poverty in the United States.

The way in which poverty is defined has important implications for strategies to alleviate the problem. Human service professionals have a commitment to increasing opportunities for poor people as a means of reducing poverty. They reject the definition of poverty as culture, believing that disadvantaged people will make use of opportunities if only given the chance.

Increases in the number of poor people may also be defined by structural changes in social institutions such as the economy that leave people without jobs or other adequate means for survival. If this is the case, then solutions should not be directed at individual inadequacies. Educational, economic, and social institutions should be made more responsive to those who are disadvantaged.

Others view poverty as a form of exploitation by the ruling classes. The dominant classes maintain poverty in order to produce a source of cheap labor and to "use" the poor economically, socially, and politically. This definition magnifies class conflict and suggests a restructuring of the social system to reduce poverty.

Several well-publicized books blame the worsened condition of the poor on social welfare policies. Their authors believe that public assistance programs in particular have destroyed incentives to self-sufficiency and undermined the spirit of the poor, making welfare a more attractive alternative than low-paying jobs. Congress and the Clinton administration have moved to "end welfare as we know it." Indications are that poverty rates are decreasing, but reductions seem more closely related to an improved economy than to changes in the welfare system. Time will tell if the neoconservatives are correct. In the meantime, the topics of poverty and dependency, their causes, and their solutions are among the great debates of the American people.

NOTES

1. E. E. Schattschneider, *The Semi-Sovereign People* (New York: Holt, Rinehart, & Winston, 1961), p. 68.

2. James L. Sundquist, *Politics and Policy* (Washington, DC: Brookings Institution, 1968), pp. 111–112.

3. Patricia Ruggles, *Drawing the Line: Alternative Poverty Measures and Their Implications for Public Policy* (Washington, DC: Urban Institute Press, 1990), p. 36.

4. Dana Milbank, "Old Flaws Undermine New Poverty-Level Data," *Wall Street Journal*, October 5, 1995, pp. B1, 8.

5. Joseph Dalaker and Mary Naifeh, *Poverty in the United States: 1997*, Bureau of the Census, Current Population Reports, Consumer Income P60-201 (Washington, DC: U.S. Government Printing Office, 1998), p. A–3.

6 John Crudele (*New York Post*), "Study Showing Rise in Americans' Income Misleading," *Austin American-Statesman*, October 12, 1996, p. D6.

7. Dalaker and Naifeh, *Poverty in the United States: 1997*, p. xii.

8. See U.S. Bureau of the Census, *Measuring the Effect of Benefits and Taxes on Income and Poverty: 1992* Current Population Reports, Series P60-186RD (Washington, DC: U.S. Government Printing Office, 1993), Appendix F.

9. U.S. Bureau of Labor Statistics, "Consumer Expenditure Survey, 1995," ftp://146.142.4.23/pub/special.requests/ce/standard/1995/quintile.txt.

10. Ruggles, *Drawing the Line*, see pp. xiii–xiv, 2, 167.

11. Cited in ibid., p. xiii.

12. Robert A. Levine, *The Poor Ye Need Not Have with You* (Cambridge, MA: MIT Press, 1970), p. 19.

13. Dalaker and Naifeh, *Poverty in the United States: 1997*, pp. C–15.

14. Committee on Ways and Means, U.S. House of Representatives, *Overview of Entitlement Programs, 1993 Green Book* (Washington, DC: U.S. Government Printing Office, 1993), p. 1317.

15. Much of the remainder of this section is based on U.S. Bureau of the Census, *Estimates of Poverty Including the Value of Noncash Benefits: 1987*, technical paper 58 (Washington, DC: U.S. Government Printing Office, August 1988); also see U.S. Bureau of the Census, *Measuring the Effect . . . 1992*.

16. See Committee on Ways and Means, *1993 Green Book,* p. 1318; Committee on Ways and Means, U.S. House of Representatives, *1996 Green Book: Background Material and Data on Programs within the Jurisdiction of the Committee on Ways and Means* (Washington, DC: U.S. Government Printing Office, 1996), p. 1232; Contance F. Ciro and Robert T. Michael, Eds., *Measuring Poverty: A New Approach* (Washington, DC: National Academy Press, 1995). Ruggles, *Drawing the Line,* chapter 7.

17. Committee on Ways and Means, U.S. House of Representatives, *1998 Green Book: Background Material and Data on Programs within the Jurisdiction of the Committee on Ways and Means* (Washington, DC: U.S. Government Printing Office, 1998), pp. 1336, 1341–1343.

18. Committee on Ways and Means, *1993 Green Book,* p. 1319.

19. See Citro and Michael, eds., *Measuring Poverty: A New Approach,* Cogan quote is from p. 386.

20. Poverty figures are from Dalaker and Naifeh, *Poverty in the United States: 1997.*

21. These studies are summarized in Ruggles, *Drawing the Line,* chapter 5.

22. Mary Jo Bane and David T. Elwood, "Slipping into and out of Poverty: The Dynamics of Spells," *The Journal of Human Resources,* Vol. 21, No. 1, 1986, pp. 1–23, especially pp. 11–13. Also see Martha S. Hill, "Some Dynamic Aspects of Poverty," in M. S. Hill, D. H. Hill, and J. N. Morgan, eds., *Five Thousand American Families: Patterns of Economic Progress,* Vol. 9 (Ann Arbor, MI: Institute for Social Research, University of Michigan Press, 1981); Mary Jo Bane, "Household Composition and Poverty," in Sheldon H. Danzinger and Daniel H. Weinberg, eds., *Fighting Poverty: What Works and What Doesn't* (Cambridge, MA: Harvard University Press, 1986), pp. 209–231 and p. 398, note 3; William Julius Wilson and Kathryn Neckerman, "Poverty and Family Structure: The Widening Gap Between Evidence and Public Policy Issues," in Danzinger and Weinberg, especially p. 241; William Julius Wilson, *The Truly Disadvantaged: The Inner City, the Underclass, and Public Policy* (Chicago: University of Chicago Press, 1987), pp. 9–10.

23. T. J. Eller, "Who Stays Poor? Who Doesn't?," *Dynamics of Economic Well-Being: Poverty, 1992–1993,* Current Population Reports, Household Economic Studies, P70-55 (Washington, DC: U.S. Bureau of the Census, June 1996).

24. Ann Huff Stevens, "The Dynamics of Poverty Spells: Updating Bane and Ellwood," *American Economic Review,* Vol. 84, No. 2, 1994, pp. 34–37; also see Eller, "Who Stays Poor? Who Doesn't?"

25. On the subject of relative deprivation, see Edward C. Banfield, *The Unheavenly City Revisited* (Boston: Little, Brown, 1974), especially chapter 6.

26. Victor R. Fuchs, "Redefining Poverty and Redistributing Income," *Public Interest,* No. 8, Summer 1967, p. 91.

27. U.S. Bureau of the Census, *Money Income in the United States: 1996,* Current Population Reports, Consumer Income, P60-200 (Washington, DC: U.S. Government Printing Office, 1998), Table B-3.

28. Testimony of Greg Duncan Before the House Select Committee on Children, Youth and Families, February 1992, based on Greg J. Duncan, Timothy Smeeding, and Willard Rodgers, "W(h)ither the Middle Class: A Dynamic View?" University of Michigan, Survey Research Center, 1991, cited in Committee on Ways and Means, *1993 Green Book,* pp. 1447–1448; also see Greg J. Duncan, Timothy Smeeding, and Willard Rodgers, "Why the Middle Class Is Shrinking," December 1992, cited in Committee on Ways and Means, *1993 Green Book,* pp. 1448–1450.

29. Cited in Richard Hofstadter, *The American Political Tradition* (New York: Knopf, 1948), p. 42.

30. Ibid., p. 45.

31. Edward C. Banfield, *The Unheavenly City* (Boston: Little, Brown, 1968); Banfield, *The Unheavenly City Revisited*; also see William A. Kiskanen, "Welfare and the Culture of Poverty," *Cato Journal,* Vol. 16, No. 1, 1996, pp. 1–15.

32. Nicolas Lemann, "The Origins of the Underclass," *Atlantic Monthly,* June 1986, pp. 31–55 and July 1986, pp. 54–68.

33. Herbert J. Gans, "The Uses of Poverty: The Poor Pay All," *Social Policy,* Vol. 2, No. 2, July–August 1971, pp. 20–24.

34. Thomas H. Walz and Gary Askerooth, *The Upside Down Welfare State* (Minneapolis: Elwood Printing, 1973), p. 5.

35. Frances Fox Piven and Richard A. Cloward, *Regulating the Poor: The Functions of Public Welfare* (New York: Random House, 1971), quote from p. xiii.

36. Frances Fox Piven and Richard A. Cloward, *The New Class War* (New York: Pantheon Books, 1982); on the relationship between social welfare and labor force participation also see John Myles and Jill Quadagno, eds., *States, Labor Markets, and the Future of Old-Age Policy* (Philadelphia: Temple University Press, 1991).

37. Frances Fox Piven and Richard A. Cloward, *The Breaking of the American Social Compact* (New York: The New Press, 1997). Also see Frances Fox Piven and Richard A. Cloward, *Regulating the Poor: The Functions of Public Welfare,* updated ed. (New York: Vintage Books, 1993).

38. This paragraph relies on Michael Harrington, *The New American Poverty* (New York: Penguin Books, 1984).

39. For discussion of the term *underclass,* see Wilson, *The Truly Disadvantaged,* especially p. 7.

40. Ibid.

41. The remainder of this section relies on Wilson, *The Truly Disadvantaged,* and Lemann, "The Origins of the Underclass."

42. This paragraph relies on Michael Harrington, *The Other America: Poverty in the United States* (New York: Macmillan, 1962).

43. See Christopher Hewitt, "Estimating the Number of Homeless: Media Misrepresentation of an Urban Problem," *Journal of Urban Affairs,* Vol. 18, No. 3, 1996, pp. 431–447; Anna Kondratas, "Estimates and Public Policy: The Politics of Numbers," *Housing Policy Debate,* Vol. 2, Issue 3, 1991, pp. 631–647.

44. U.S. Department of Housing and Urban Development, Office of Policy Development and Research, *Report to the Secretary on the Homeless and Emergency Shelters* (Washington, DC: U.S. Department of Housing and Urban Development, 1984).

45. Mary Ellen Hombs and Mitch Snyder, *Homelessness in America: A Forced March to Nowhere* (Washington, DC: Community for Creative Non-Violence, 1983), p. xvi.

46. James D. Wright and Joel A. Devine, "Housing Dynamics of the Homeless: Implications for a Count," *American Journal of Orthopsychiatry,* Vol. 65, No. 3, 1995, pp. 330–329, especially p. 320.

47. Kim Hopper, "Definitional Quandaries and Other Hazards," *American Journal of Orthopsychiatry,* Vol. 65, No. 3, 1995, pp. 340–346, especially p. 340.

48. Robert C. Ellickson, "The Homeless Muddle," *The Public Interest,* No. 99, Spring 1990, pp. 45–60.

49. See James D. Wright, ed., *Evaluation Review,* Vol. 16, No. 4, August 1992 which is devoted to S-Night surveys; and Wright and Devine, "Housing Dynamics of the Homeless: Implications for a Count."

50. Rush Limbaugh, *The Way Things Ought to Be* (New York: Pocket Star Books, 1992).

51. Joel Blau, *The Visible Poor: Homelessness in the United States* (New York: Oxford University Press, 1992), p. 24.

52. Alliance Housing Council, *Housing and Homelessness* (Washington, DC: National Alliance to End Homelessness, 1988), also cited in Institute of Medicine, *Homelessness, Health, and Human Needs* (Washington, DC: National Academy Press, 1988), see pp. 171–172.

53. Martha R. Burt and Barbara E. Cohen, *America's Homeless: Numbers, Characteristics, and Programs That Serve Them* (Washington, DC: Urban Institute, 1989), chapter 2.

54. Ellen Bassuk, "Dilemmas in Counting the Homeless: Introduction," *American Journal of Orthopsychiatry,* Vol. 65, No. 3, 1995, pp. 318–319.

55. Hopper, "Definitional Quandaries and other Hazards in Counting the Homeless."

56. Bruce Link, Jo Phelan, Michaeline Bresnahan, Ann Stueve, Robert Moore, and Ezra Susser, "Lifetime and Five-Year Prevalence of Homelessness in the United States: New Evidence on an Old Debate," *American Journal of Orthopsychiatry,* Vol. 65, No. 3, 1995, pp. 347–354.

57. See Martha Burt, "Critical Factors in Counting the Homeless: An Invited Commentary," *American Journal of Orthopsychiatry,* Vol. 65, No. 3, 1995, pp. 334–339.

58. Gordon Berlin and William McAllister, "Homelessness," in Henry J. Aaron and Charles L. Schultze, eds., *Setting Domestic Priorities: What Can Government Do?* (Washington, DC: Brookings Institution, 1992), p. 64.

59. See, for example, *Outcasts on Main Street* (ADM) 92-1904 (Washington, DC: U.S. Department of Health and Human Services, Interagency Council on the Homeless, and Federal Task Force on Homelessness and Severe Mental Illness, 1992).

60. *A Report on the 1988 National Survey of Shelters for the Homeless* (Washington, DC: U.S. Department of Housing and Urban Development, 1989).

61. Blau, *The Visible Poor,* p. 29.

62. Syntheses of these studies are provided in Blau, *The Visible Poor,* chapter 2; and Berlin and McAllister, "Homelessness"; and are also discussed in Committee on Ways and Means, *1993 Green Book,* pp. 1233–1238; Alice S. Baum and Donald W. Burnes, *A Nation in Denial: The Truth About Homelessness* (Boulder, CO: Westview Press, 1993), chapter 1; Martha R. Burt, *Over the Edge: The Growth of Homelessness in the 1980s* (New York: Russell Sage; 1992).

63. Baum and Burnes, *A Nation in Denial.*

64. See Blau, *The Visible Poor*; Paul Koegel, "Mental Illness Among the Inner City Homeless," *Journal of the California Alliance for the Mentally Ill,* Vol. 1, No. 1, 1989, rev. 1992, pp. 16–17.

65. Koegel, "Mental Illness Among the Inner City Homeless"; Berlin and McAllister, "Homelessness," p. 67; Burt, *Over the Edge,* chapter 2.

66. Burt, *Over the Edge,* p. 226.

67. Office of Community Planning and Development, *1997 Homeless Programs* (Washington, DC: U.S. Department of Housing and Urban Development, 1997).

68. Guy Gugliotta, "Study: Rent Costs Strain Poor in Cities," *Austin American-Statesman,* November 29, 1992, p. A7.

69. "1 in 3 Renters Can't Afford Apartment," *Austin American-Statesman,* April 16, 1994, p. A6.

70. "Why America's Communities Need a Department of Housing and Urban Development," *Issue Brief #10,* June 1995, Washington, DC: U.S. Department of Housing and Urban Development, gopher://huduser.org:73/00/2/briefs/issbr10a.txt.

71. Michael E. Stone, *Shelter Poverty: New Ideas on Affordable Housing* (Philadelphia: Temple University Press, 1993).

72. "Shelter Poverty: A Real-Life Way to Measure Inadequate Incomes," Utah Issues Information Program, Poverty Paper Series, http://www.xmission.com/~ui/shelter.html, accessed December 30, 1997.

73. See Children's Defense Fund, *Homeless Families: Failed Policies and Young Victims* (Washington, DC: Children's Defense Fund, 1991); also see Department of Housing and Urban Development, "Start Here to Find Out About Federal Assistance Programs," http://www.hud.gov/start.html, accessed January 24, 1998.

74. Office of Public & Indian Housing, Public Housing Brief, "Facts You Should Know About Public Housing," Department of Housing and Urban Development, March 1996, http://www.hud.gov/pih/pihpg2.html.

75. Department of Housing and Urban Development, "Section 8 Program Fact Sheet (Rental Vouchers and Rental Certificates)," http://www.hud.gov/start.html, accessed January 24, 1998.

76. This paragraph relies on "Cuomo Welcomes President's Proposal to Use 50,000 Housing Vouchers to Help Families Move from Welfare to Work," press release, HUD No. 98-16, January 21, 1998, http://www.hud.gov/pressrel/pr98-16.html.

77. Neal Peirce, "Community Reinvestment Act: Victory for Smart Regulation," *Austin American-Statesman,* July 8, 1996, p. A7.

78. Committee on Ways and Means, *1996 Green Book,* pp. 915 & 917; Committee on Ways and Means, *1998 Green Book,* pp. 989 & 991–992.

79. The rest of this paragraph relies on "Cuomo Says 1997 Annual Homeownership Rate Hit Record Annual High of 65.7%, Breaking 17-Year Record," press release, HUD No. 98-15, January 21, 1998, http://www.hud.gov/news.html.

80. Advisory Commission on Regulatory Barriers to Affordable Housing, *"Not in My Back Yard": Remov-ing Barriers to Affordable Housing* (Washington, DC: U.S. Department of Housing and Urban Development, 1991).

81. Jeffery L. Katz, "Rooms for Improvement: Can Cisneros Fix HUD?," *Congressional Quarterly,* April 10, 1993, pp. 914–920.

82. "$148 Million More Planned for Disabled, Homeless," *Austin American-Statesman,* April 24, 1993, p. A5.

83. Jonathan Chait, "HUD Sucker Proxy," *The New Republic,* June 23, 1997, pp. 11–12.

84. Neal Peirce, "Clinton Administration Is Redefining Public Housing," *Austin American-Statesman,* May 13, 1996, p. A7.

85. Chait, "HUD Sucker Proxy," p. 12; also see *Special Report,* "Issue: Housing," *Congressional Quarterly,* December 6, 1997, pp. 3017–3018.

86. See Committee on Ways and Means, *1998 Green Book,* p. 994.

87. See, for example, Ellickson, "The Homelessness Muddle."

88. See James Gwartney and Thomas S. McCaleb, *Have Antipoverty Programs Increased Poverty?* (Tallahassee, FL: Florida State University, 1986).

89. George Gilder, *Wealth and Poverty* (New York: Bantam Books, 1981), p. ix.

90. Ibid., p. 13.

91. Charles Murray, *Losing Ground: American Social Policy, 1950–1980* (New York: Basic Books, 1984).

92. Robert Kuttner, "Declaring War on the War on Poverty," *Washington Post,* November 25, 1984, pp. 4, 11. Also see Daniel Patrick Moynihan, "Family and Nation," Godkin Lectures, Harvard University, April 8–9, 1985.

93. See, for example, the critique of the Phyllis and Harold story and the references to other works challenging Murray in Theodore R. Marmor, Jerry Z. Mashaw, and Philip L. Harvey, *America's Misunderstood Welfare State: Persistent Myths, Enduring Realities* (New York: Basic Books, 1990), especially pp. 104–114; quote is from p. 105; also see Rino Patti, Mimi Abramovitz, Steve Burghardt, Michael Fabricant, Martha Haffery, Elizabeth Dane, and Rose Starr, *Gaining Perspective on Losing Ground* (New York: Lois and Samuel Silberman Fund, 1987).

94. Michael Tanner, *The End of Welfare* (Washington, DC: Cato Institute, 1996), quote from p. 148.

95. Marvin Olasky, *The Tragedy of American Compassion* (Washington, DC: Regnery Gateway, 1992); Marvin Olasky, *Renewing American Compassion* (New York: Free Press, 1996).

96. Olasky, *Renewing American Compassion,* p. 152.

97. "Assertion that Charities Can Go It Alone Is Untested and Unreasonable," Twentieth Century Fund report, http://www.epn.org/tcf/julrel.html, accessed January 12, 1998.

98. See Lawrence M. Mead's books, *Beyond Entitlement* (New York: Free Press, 1986); *The New Politics of Poverty* (New York: Basic books, 1992); *The New Paternalism* (Washington, DC: Brookings, 1997).

99. Quotes in this paragraph rely on Mead, *The New Politics of Poverty.*

100. Ibid., p. 134.

101. Lawrence M. Mead, "Conflicting Worlds of Welfare Reform," *First Things,* August/September 1991, pp. 15–17, available at http://www.firstthings.com/ftissues/ft9708/mead.html.

CHAPTER

Preventing Poverty: The Social Insurance Programs

PREVENTING POVERTY THROUGH COMPULSORY SAVINGS

One way to address poverty is to have people insure themselves against its occurrence, much as they insure themselves in the event of death, accident, or property loss. In the social welfare arena, this preventive strategy is called **social insurance.** Social insurance programs compel individuals or their employers to purchase insurance against the possibility of their own indigency, which might result from forces over which they have no control—loss of job, death of a family breadwinner, advanced age, or disability. As statesman Thomas Paine said in 1795, "Were a workman to receive an increase in wages daily he would not save it against old age. . . . Make, then, society the treasurer to guard it for him in a common fund."[1] Social insurance is based on many of the same principles as private insurance—the sharing of risks and the setting aside of money for a "rainy day." Workers and employers pay "premiums" in the form of Social Security taxes, which are recorded by the government under each worker's name and Social Security number. When age, death, disability, or unemployment prevents workers from continuing on the job, they or their dependents are paid from Social Security trust funds. Social insurance offers one relatively simple and rational approach for addressing poverty.

Social insurance differs from another approach to assisting people called **public assistance.** If (1) the beneficiaries of a government program are required to make contributions to it before claiming any of its benefits (or if employers must pay into the program on behalf of their workers) and if (2) the benefits are paid out as legal entitlements regardless of the beneficiaries' personal wealth, then the program is called social insurance. However, if (1) the program is financed out of general tax revenues and if (2) the recipients are required to show that they are poor in order to claim benefits, then the program is called public assistance.

Although the history of helping people in need in the United States began with public assistance approaches, social insurance programs have become the more viable political strategy.[2] Today most Americans are more familiar and more comfortable with the way social insurance programs work. They have come to believe that social insurance is merely enforced savings, and they hope to get back their money during retirement. Although Social Security does not work exactly as many people think it does, one thing is true—Americans feel entitled to receive Social Security because they have paid specific Social Security taxes. Public assistance recipients, in contrast, have never specifically "paid into" a public assistance fund. The assistance they get comes from general tax funds. Although many public assistance recipients have at some time worked and paid into the general revenue fund through income taxes, this is not a requirement of receiving benefits, and there is no public assistance account earmarked with their names. Despite any taxes they may have paid, there is much less perception that they have the right to public assistance. Moreover, while the vast majority of Americans expect to live to see some Social Security benefits returned to them, they do not expect to become public assistance recipients.

The concept of government sponsored social insurance originally appealed to conservatives because it represented a form of thrift. Liberals do not deny the value of thrift, especially in today's political environment. But social insurance appeals to liberals because these programs can also be used to redistribute income from workers to people in economic need—those who are aged, sick, disabled, unemployed, or dependent children. Controversy over the public assistance programs continues (see Chapters 5, 7, 8, and especially Chapter 6). As described in this chapter, controversy over Social Security and other social insurance programs has also mounted.

The Social Security Act

Government old-age insurance, the first social insurance program, was introduced in Germany in 1889 by the conservative regime of Chancellor Otto von Bismarck. The idea spread quickly and most European nations had old-age insurance pension programs before the beginning of World War I in 1914. Private old-age pension plans were begun in the United States by many railroads, utilities, and large manufacturers at the beginning of the twentieth century. The U.S. government began its own Federal Employees Retirement program in 1920. By 1931 seventeen states had adopted some form of compulsory old-age insurance for workers, although eligibility requirements were strict and payments were small.[3]

During the Great Depression, Francis E. Townsend, a California dentist, began a national crusade for very generous old-age pensions of $200 a month to be paid by the government from taxes on banks. The politically popular but very expensive "Townsend Plan" was perceived by government and business leaders as totally unfeasible, even radical, but the combination of economic depression and larger numbers of older people in the population and in the workforce helped to develop pressure for some type of old-age insurance.[4] Despite fears that social insurance would foreshadow a socialist state, during the presidential campaign of 1932, Franklin D. Roosevelt advocated a government insurance plan to protect the unemployed and the aged. This campaign promise and party platform plank actually became law—the Social Security Act (Public Law 74-271), signed by President Roosevelt on August 14, 1935.

One might attribute the Roosevelt administration's political success in gaining acceptance for the Social Security Act to several factors:

1. The weakening of ties among family members and the increasing inability of urban families to care for their aged members.
2. The economic insecurities generated by the Great Depression of the 1930s, including the increasing fear of impoverishment even among the middle class.
3. Political movements on the right (the Townsend Plan, for example) and left (socialism and communism) that threatened the established order.

Roosevelt's skills as a national leader should also be added to these factors. Social Security was presented to the Congress as a *conservative* program that would eventually eliminate the need for public assistance programs. For the first time, Americans would be compelled to protect themselves against poverty.

The Social Security Act of 1935 established the country's basic social welfare policy framework. Although we tend to think of Social Security mostly as retirement benefits, the original act contained social insurance, public assistance, social service, and public health programs. Today, the social insurance programs it provides are

- Federal old-age and survivors insurance (OASI)
- Federal disability insurance (DI)
- Federal health insurance (HI) for older people, called Medicare
- Unemployment compensation (UC) programs in the states

The public assistance programs it includes are

- Federal aid to people who are aged, blind, or disabled under the Supplementary Security Income (SSI) program
- Federal–state aid to families with dependent children under the Temporary Assistance for Needy Families program (formerly Aid to Families with Dependent Children)
- Federal–state medical assistance for the poor, called Medicaid

The social service programs it provides are

- Child welfare
- Maternal and child health
- Additional social services to a number of vulnerable groups

This chapter examines most of the social insurance programs—the old-age, survivors, and disability insurance programs (collectively known as OASDI or OASDHI when Medicare is included), and unemployment compensation. The state-operated workers' compensation programs are also discussed. Subsequent chapters examine the public assistance programs, the health care programs, and social services.

Social Security: The World's Largest Social Welfare Program

Originally, the Social Security program covered only retirement benefits for workers in about half of the labor force; many farm and domestic workers and self-employed people were exempted, as were state and local government employees. This old-age insurance program was financed by employer–employee contributions of 1 percent each on a wage base of $3,000, or a maximum contribution by workers of $30 per year plus a $30 contribution by their employers. It paid for retirement benefits at age 65 at a rate of about $22 per month for a single worker, or $36 per month for a married couple. Benefits were paid as a matter of right, regardless of income, as long as a worker was retired. Thus retired workers were spared the humiliation often associated with public charity. Actually, no taxes were collected until 1937, and no benefits were paid until 1940, to allow the trust fund to accumulate reserves.

Since 1935 there have been scores of amendments to this social insurance legislation. The first major amendments came in 1939 when Congress made dependents and survivors of retired workers and survivors of insured workers who died before age 65 eligible for benefits. In the early 1950s, farmers, domestic workers, and self-employed people were added to the program, bringing the total number of covered workers to over 90 percent of the labor force. In 1954 the "earnings test" for retired workers was liberalized so that those engaged in some employment could earn more without losing Social Security benefits. In 1956 women in the labor force were permitted to retire at age 62 rather than 65 on the condition that they accept 80 percent of the monthly benefit otherwise available at 65; men were allowed to retire at age 62 beginning in 1961. In 1956 disability insurance was approved for totally and permanently disabled workers age 50 and older; benefits for their dependents were added in 1958. Disabled workers younger than age 50 were added to the disability program in 1960. In 1965 Medicare was adopted, and in 1972 Congress enacted COLAs—automatic cost-of-living adjustments (measured by rises in the Consumer Price Index)—to help Social Security payments keep pace with inflation.

Social Security soon became the nation's largest social welfare program. Today, the U.S. Social Security system may rightfully be called the world's largest government program. By 1997, 145 million workers (about 96 percent of the workforce) plus their employers paid Social Security taxes,[5] and nearly 44 million people collected benefits totaling more than $30 billion per month.[6] The public assistance programs pale in comparison to the scope and effects of Social Security.

OASDHI is a completely federal program administered by the Social Security Administration (formerly part of the Department of Health and Human Services and now an independent agency). But it has an important indirect effect on federal, state, and local public assistance programs: by compelling people to insure themselves against the possibility of their own poverty, Social Security has reduced the problems that governments might otherwise face.

The growth of OASDHI in numbers of recipients (beneficiaries), average monthly benefits, and as a percentage of the federal government's total budget is shown in Table 4-1. Social Security taxes are the second largest source of income for the federal government; these tax revenues are exceeded only by the federal personal income tax. The Social Security tax is marked on the paycheck stubs of many workers with the abbreviation FICA, which stands for the Federal Insurance Contributions Act. Self-employed people pay under SECA, the Self-Employed Contributions Act. By 1990, the *combined* maximum annual Social Security contribution for both the employee and the employer had grown to nearly $8,000.

Social Security is considered a regressive tax, because it takes a larger share of the income of middle and lower-income workers than of the affluent. That is because

1. OASDHI taxes are levied only against wages and not against other types of income such as dividends, interest, and rents, which are more frequently sources of income for wealthier Americans.
2. OASDI taxes are levied on a fixed amount of earnings; wages in excess of that amount are not subjected to these taxes.
3. Unlike the federal personal income tax, Social Security taxes make no allowance for situations such as number of dependents or high medical expenses.

TABLE 4-1

Social Security Growth

	1950	1960	1970	1980	1990	1997
Number of OASDI beneficiaries (in millions)	3.5	14.8	26.2	35.6	39.6	43.9
Annual expenditures for OASDI (in billions)	$1	$10.7	$31.9	$120.5	$267.2	$364.5
Average monthly benefit for retired workers (in dollars)	$43.86	$74.04	$118.10	$341.41	$602.56	$747.27[a]
Social insurance taxes (OASDHI) as a percentage of all federal revenue	11.0	15.9	23.0	30.5	36.8	34.2
Medicare expenditures (in billions of dollars)[b]	—	—	$7.1	$35.0	$109.7	$210.4

Sources: Committee on Ways and Means, U.S. House of Representatives, *Overview of Entitlement Programs: 1993 Green Book* (Washington, DC: U.S. Government Printing Office, 1993); Social Security Administration, *Social Security Accountability Report for Fiscal Year 1997,* November 21, 1997, http://www.ssa.gov; Executive Office of the President, *Historical Tables, Budget of the United States Government, Fiscal Year 1999* (Washington, DC: U.S. Government Printing Office, 1998).

[a]1997 figure as of July.

[b]Program began in 1965.

Social Security taxes were not a concern when they amounted to very little, but today, the size of OASDI alone—approximately one-third of the federal government's income and about one-quarter of its expenditures—has an important impact on the overall equity of the country's revenue structure. However, the regressive nature of the Social Security tax on current workers is offset at retirement, because benefits are figured more generously for those who earned less, and because retirees in higher income brackets must now pay taxes on part of their Social Security benefits. What began as a very modest "insurance premium" is now a major expense for both employers and employees.

Even the Best-Laid Plans

The original strategy of the Social Security Act of 1935 was to create a trust fund with a reserve that would be built from the insurance premiums (Social Security taxes) of working people. This trust fund reserve would earn interest, and both the interest and principal would be used in later years to pay benefits. Benefits for insured people would be in proportion to their contributions. General tax revenues would not be used at all. The Social Security system was intended to resemble private, self-financing insurance. But it did not turn out that way.

Roosevelt's planners quickly realized that building the reserve was taking money out of the depressed economy and slowing recovery. The plan to build a large, self-financing reserve was soon abandoned in 1939 under political pressure to pump more money into the economy. And over the years, Congress encountered pressure to increase benefit levels to retirees, even though these retirees never paid enough money into their accounts to cover these benefits. Moreover, benefits under Social Security were no longer proportionate to contributions; they were figured more generously for those whose wages were low than for those whose wages were high. Political pressure to raise benefits while keeping taxes relatively low reduced the trust fund reserve to a minor role in Social Security financing. Social Security taxes were lumped together with all other tax revenue in the federal government's budget. The accounts of workers were simply IOUs—promises to pay—not money specifically set aside in separate accounts for each contributor. COLAs, adopted in 1972, proved to be another very popular feature of the program because of their hedge against inflation, but Social Security ran into trouble. It could no longer cover these regular increases, especially in times of high inflation. Today, Social Security recipients must still have paid into the system to receive benefits, and they are not required to prove that they are needy, but this publicly-sponsored social insurance program is administered much differently from private insurance programs.

Social Security mushroomed into such a large program because Americans came to view these ever increasing benefits as a right. As the number of workers grew and their wages increased during the affluence of the 1950s and 1960s, no one worried much about the program. But during the 1970s and 1980s, the growth in Social Security rolls and payments was accompanied by economic recession.[7] Income from the "pay-as-you-go" Social Security system (about $200 billion per year) matched the outgo in Social Security benefits. The program was on the verge of bankruptcy.

As the problems of Social Security intensified, it became clear that something would have to be done to fix the ailing retirement system. In 1977, for the first time in the program's history, benefits were cut, and taxes were increased again. In 1981 some measures were taken to reduce program spending at President Reagan's request: a minimum benefit was retained for current beneficiaries but was eliminated for many new beneficiaries, and children ages 18 to 22 of deceased, disabled, and retired workers were no longer eligible for benefits. The president established the National Commission on Social Security Reform to tackle Social Security's problems. The commission, also referred to as the Greenspan Commission after its chairperson, Republican economist Alan Greenspan, was comprised of fifteen people with backgrounds in business and industry, politics, labor, and academia.

There were many disagreements about how best to fix Social Security, but Democrats and Republicans alike realized that they would have to put partisan politics aside if a solution was to be achieved. Finally, the commission's report was issued with bipartisan support. Numerous changes were then enacted by Congress in 1983. Among the most important reforms was a delay of the popular cost-of-living adjustment (COLA) and a "stabilizer" that was placed on future COLAs. Along with changes enacted in 1986, the COLA is now provided if there is at least a 0.1 percent increase in the Consumer Price Index for Urban Wage Earners and Clerical Workers (CPI-W); however, if Social Security trust funds fall below certain levels, benefits are indexed according to the CPI-W or the average increase in wages, whichever is lower. Since inflation has varied considerably over the years, so have COLAs. For example, the COLA was 14.3 percent in 1980, 5.4 percent in 1990,[8] and 1.3 percent in 1999.

The 1983 amendments also raised the age at which full retirement benefits can be received. Although about 60 percent of all retirees now opt for early retirement at age 62 rather than waiting to age 65,[9] the age that one may collect full retirement benefits is gradually increasing to age 67. The actual change begins in 2003 and affects those born in 1938 (who will be 65 in 2003) and later. Those born in 1938 will have to be 65 years and 2 months old to receive full benefits, and the regular retirement age will continue to rise in 2-month increments until the new regular retirement age reaches a full 67 years. This will occur in 2027 (if you were born in 1960, you will be 67 in 2027 and among the first Social Security beneficiaries required to be a full 67 years before receiving full retirement benefits). Beneficiaries will still be allowed to retire earlier, at age 62, but the amount of benefits will gradually fall from 80 percent to 70 percent of full retirement benefits by 2027.

Another measure enacted in 1983 to make Social Security more fiscally viable was to reduce so-called windfall benefits. This means that those who receive Social Security and other government pensions (such as military retirement), but who paid into the Social Security system for only a short time, may receive lower Social Security benefits under a new formula. Better news is that by 2008 those who choose to retire after the full retirement age will receive 5 percent more in benefits than they would today. Medicare benefits will still be available at age 65.

More workers were also included under the Social Security system as a result of the 1983 amendments. All new federal employees must participate as well as all members of Congress, the president and the vice president, federal judges, and all employees of nonprofit organizations, among others. Many of these people were formerly included under other systems. For example, federal employees were covered under a separate, more generous retirement system.

The commission made a few changes that primarily benefitted women. For example, divorced spouses may begin collecting benefits at age 62 if their former spouses are eligible but have not yet claimed benefits, and payments to disabled widows and widowers aged 50 to 59 were increased. Other major inequities that many of today's elderly women face were not addressed. Some members of the commission wanted to do more to help women, but there was disagreement about whether the commission should tackle this issue. Many gender inequities remain unresolved today (see Chapter 11 for a further discussion).

Under former provisions, Social Security benefits were not counted as taxable income, but in 1983, and again in 1993 as part of the Clinton administration's deficit reduction plan, this change was instituted. Today, half of Social Security benefits are subject to regular income tax rates if combined income (taxable income plus nontaxable interest) plus one-half of Social Security benefits is between $25,000 and $34,000 for a single person and $32,000 to $44,000 for a couple. Singles whose combined income plus one-half of their Social Security benefits exceeds $34,000 and couples exceeding $44,000 are subject to regular income taxes on 85 percent of their benefits. For years, talk of taxing Social Security benefits was considered "political suicide." Even David Stockman (who later became director of the Office of Management and Budget under the Reagan administration) called it that in his article "The Social Pork Barrel."[10] It is really quite remarkable that some tampering with Social Security benefits is no longer considered the "the third rail" of American politics (touch it and one's political career is over). Taxes on Social Security benefits are returned to the Social Security trust funds. About 25 percent of beneficiaries paid these taxes in 1997, but the taxes were equal to only about 3 percent of OASDI benefits paid.[11]

In 1983 and again in 1996 amendments increased the amount retirees could earn without jeopardizing their Social Security benefits. In 1999, retirees under age 65 could earn $9,600 from employment before beginning to lose Social Security benefits. Additional earnings are "taxed" by 50 percent (that is, beneficiaries lose $1 in benefits for every $2 they earn). Those ages 65 to 69 could earn $15,500 a year without penalty. Earnings over this amount are taxed by one-third. By 2002, the earnings limit for those ages 65 to 69 will jump to $30,000. After 2002, this earnings limit will again be adjusted as it is for retirees younger than age 65 using the same percent as the rise in average wages in the economy. Some people think that the increase to $30,000 is too generous because it is difficult to think of individuals earning this much as being retired. There is no earnings limit for those age 70 and older, and some think that earning restrictions should be eliminated for retirees of all ages. They feel that it is unfair to penalize those who need or want to work, and since taxes are paid on their wages, more money is pumped back into the economy. Eliminating the earnings test is controversial because the Congressional Budget Office reports that it would cost the Social Security program several billion dollars a year.[12] Most of the benefits would go to those who are already better off financially, and this may not seem reasonable when the money is needed to keep Social Security solvent.

Especially important among the 1983 amendments were increases in the Social Security tax rate and taxable wage base. The tax rate was increased gradually until it reached 7.65 percent for both employers and employees in 1990 (a combined rate of 15.3 percent). The tax rate is scheduled to remain constant into the twenty-first century although the percentages to be attributed to the OASI and DI programs will vary slightly over time. In 1998, of the 7.65 percent, 5.35 percent (70 cents of each Social Security tax dollar) went to the OASI program, 0.85 percent (11 cents of each dollar) to the DI program, and 1.45 percent (19 cents of each dollar) to the HI program.[13] Formulas to keep the taxable wage base in line with inflation have also been established. In 1990 the taxable wage base was $51,300, but this was insufficient to finance Medicare, so in 1991 the taxable wage base for the HI part of the program was increased to $125,000. The wage base for HI was increased further in 1992 and 1993, and as of 1994 the HI tax is applied to all earnings. This change to the HI wage base supports the contentions of those who believe that Social Security taxes should be less regressive. The wage base for OASDI is scheduled to grow incrementally with inflation. In 1999 the taxable wage base for OASDI was $72,600. Illustration 4-1 describes how one qualifies for Social Security benefits and how benefits are determined.

Other 1983 reforms, such as the use of more efficient accounting procedures, were also intended to make the Social Security fund solvent without altering the basic structure of the program.[14] The 1983 reforms did a good job of putting Social Security on more stable footing. In the public policy arena, it often takes a crisis before concerted efforts to reduce governmental problems emerge. As Wilbur Cohen wrote of the National Commission on Social Security Reform,

> *After more than a year of deliberation, this fifteen-member panel . . . came forward with the most unusual high-level policy agreement on controversial aspects in Social Security legislation since enactment of the original Social Security Act in 1935. . . . If the Commission's work represented a remarkable achievement in political statesmanship, so did the actions of the Congress in dealing with the legislative package. The bill moved through both houses of Congress in just over ten weeks.*[15]

Cohen was in an excellent position to assess these reform efforts. He had worked with the Committee on Economic Security (which drafted the original Social Security Act), worked for the original Social Security Board, and eventually became Secretary of the Department of Health, Education, and Welfare during the Johnson administration. He died in 1987 while still promoting improvements in social welfare legislation.

Now, more than 15 years since the passage of the 1983 amendments, Social Security is taking in much more than it is paying out (by the beginning of 2007, trust fund assets are expected to be $1.8 trillion![16] But the financial solvency of the trust funds

ILLUSTRATION 4-1

Social Security—Who Qualifies, and How Much Do Beneficiaries Receive?

Approximately 96 percent of workers are now paying into the Social Security system. Employees and employers continue to pay equal amounts toward the employee's OASDHI insurance, and on retirement, workers receive benefits if they have enough *credits* (formerly called *quarters*) to qualify. For example, those born in 1929 or later need forty credits (generally equivalent to ten years of work). In 1999, workers accrue one credit if they earn $740 regardless of how much or how long they worked during the year. The maximum number of credits that can be earned in one year is four (equal to $2,960 in 1999). The amount needed to earn each credit rises gradually each year. At retirement, most workers have far more than the number of credits needed to qualify.

Once it is determined that the worker is qualified to receive Social Security benefits, his or her primary insurance amount (PIA) is calculated. This is the amount that retirees receive if they wait until the full retirement age (currently age 65) to collect benefits. The formula is rather complicated, but it is based on the average amount earned during most of the individual's working years. Workers may retire as early as age 62, but benefits are reduced and calculated as a percent of the PIA. For a person who had *average* earnings, Social Security replaces about 42 percent of earnings. Replacement rates are higher for low-income earners and lower for high-income earners. In any case, payments to retirees are relatively modest—an average of about $780 a month in 1999, although some receive the maximum—now about $1,373 a month.

Insured workers may also be eligible for benefits if they become physically or mentally disabled prior to retirement. The disability must prevent work for at least one year or be expected to result in death. The average monthly payment to disabled workers in 1999 was about $733.

Although there are many complex rules, benefits (calculated as a percentage of the worker's PIA) are often also payable to the dependents of retired and disabled workers and to the survivors of deceased workers. The terms *survivors* and *dependents* refer to spouses and minor children, disabled adult children, and occasionally parents of covered workers. Survivors and dependents must meet certain qualifications, such as age requirements and definitions of disability. For example, a woman age 62 or older who never worked in covered employment, or who worked but earned less than her spouse, is generally entitled to receive an amount that is 50 percent of her retired spouse's benefits. Widows or widowers may receive benefits, generally beginning at age 60 or at age 50 if they are disabled. Widows or widowers caring for children under age 16 can receive benefits at any age, and their children are also entitled to benefits. A lump sum benefit of $255 is also payable on the death of an insured worker to an eligible child or spouse.

Some additional types of benefits are also available. For example, a *special minimum*

continued

ILLUSTRATION 4-1 *(continued)*

benefit may be paid to people who had many years of covered employment but earned low wages. And virtually *all* people 65 years of age and over, whether or not they have ever paid into Social Security, are allowed to participate in Medicare.

Sources: Most of this discussion relies on Committee on Ways and Means, U.S. House of Representatives, *1996 Green Book: Background Material and Data on the Programs Within the Jurisdiction of the Committee on Ways and Means* (Washington, DC: U.S. Government Printing Office, 1996), see Section 1; Social Security Administration, *Social Security: Understanding the Benefits,* SSA Publication No. 05-10024 (Washington, DC: SSA, January 1998); recent figures rely on Social Security Administration, "Fact Sheet, 1999 Social Security Changes," http://www.ssa.gov/press/1999fact.htm.

really depends on what part of OASDHI we are talking about. Each year a board known as the Social Security Trustees (the Secretary of the Treasury, the Secretary of Labor, the Secretary of Health and Human Services, and two members appointed by the President with Senate confirmation to represent the public) determines the health of the trust funds by using optimistic, moderate, and pessimistic assumptions about the country's economic situation. Economic forecasting is always risky because no one can predict with certainty what will happen in the future, but these are the best "guesstimates" we have to help in planning rationally for the future.

In 1998 the Social Security trustees provided the following information based on moderate assumptions.[17] In the short run, from 1998 to 2007, the OASI and DI funds are considered adequate because there will be enough in the funds at the *beginning* of the year to cover the benefits for that year. The same cannot be said for the HI fund; there will not be enough in the fund at the beginning of each year to pay for that year's benefits. The situation for the HI fund gets progressively worse during the 10-year interval due to greater demands on the health care system and the high costs of health care. In fact, the fund is expected to be exhausted (its reserves depleted) by 2008 (had the economy not improved, these reserves would have been depleted sooner). Although money will be coming into the fund, it will be insufficient to cover benefits. This is a serious problem, and we return to HI, or Medicare as it is more often called, in Chapter 8.

The long-term forecast (from 1998 to 2072) for OASDI is also gloomy. In about 2010, the baby boomers will begin retiring; this means that substantially more people will be calling on the system to assist them, but the number of people paying in will not grow as rapidly due to decreases in fertility rates. In 2013, combined OASDI payments are expected to exceed contributions for the first time. In 2019, the DI fund will be exhausted. In 2021, OASDI payments will exceed contributions plus interest income for the first time. In 2032, the combined OASDI funds will be exhausted. In 2034 the OASI trust fund will be exhausted. Since the OASI and DI trust funds are often considered together, the key date is 2032. At the end of the 75-year, long-term forecast, OASI payments will be one and a half times the fund's income. Put another way, as things currently stand, OASDI will be able to pay about three-quarters of benefits in 2032 and about two-thirds of benefits by 2072. For HI, the cost rate will be two and one-quarter times more than its income. Given the current rate of growth, Medicare benefits will eventually exceed OASDI benefits.[18]

No one wants to see the Social Security trust funds depleted. The funds need to be in good actuarial balance (the difference between annual income and out go) for the country to breathe easy. While the year 2032 still seems like a long way off, Americans must give serious consideration to insuring that these funds will be healthy years in advance. The following discussion considers salient issues in preserving Social Security and how the country might go about insuring the security of retirees and people with disabilities as well as their dependents and survivors in the years ahead.

Achieving the Goals of Social Security: Adequacy and Equity

Participation in Social Security is a different experience for younger generations than for older ones. Current workers realize that they are paying a substantial tax to participate. Many Americans, young and old, support the concept of Social Security,[19] but confidence in the program has waned.[20] Surely the Social Security trustees want to scream every time they hear that young people are more likely to believe in UFOs than think they will collect Social Security;[21] nonetheless, the trustees agree that "there has been an alarming erosion of public confidence in the Social Security system."[22]

The current system might not be viewed so pessimistically if (1) today's workers and employers did not view the Social Security tax as overly burdensome (lower-income workers today pay more Social Security taxes than income taxes) and (2) the number of aged people supported by the working population were not increasing so fast. These factors give pause to many younger people who are paying in but unsure of what they might get in return. The fact is that Social Security was never intended to support people fully during their "golden" years. The analogy of a three-legged stool has been used to describe what workers need to retire "comfortably": one leg is Social Security, the second is pension income, and the third is personal savings and investments. Many beneficiaries have at least a small income from sources other than Social Security, but most also receive Social Security retirement benefits that greatly exceed their original investment, and more if Medicare is considered. No wonder the program is so popular among the nearly 45 million current beneficiaries, most of them older people who comprise a very large bloc of the most active voters in the U.S. With such strong support, it has been difficult to consider major changes in the program.

What about today's workers? Will they get their "money's worth" or a fair return on their investment? As shown in Illustration 4-2, a single worker born in 1910 who retired at the full retirement age of 65 in 1975 after earning average wages would have recouped the OASI taxes he or she paid plus interest before the age of 67. A single worker born in 1930 who retired in 1995 at the age of 65 after earning average wages would recoup his or her taxes plus interest just before age 73, while a single worker

ILLUSTRATION 4-2

Will You Reap What You Sow?

The following examples show what individuals might expect to get in Social Security retirement benefits if they retired at the full retirement age in 1975, 1995, and 2015. These hypothetical individuals would have been born in 1910, 1935, and 1949, respectively. It also shows how long it will take them to recoup their contributions and their contributions combined with those of their employer. Figures are also provided for those with a spouse of the same age who never worked outside the home, a situation growing less likely to happen in the years ahead. In the future, more and more spouses will have their own Social Security record on which to draw. The figures are based only on the OASI portion of Social Security taxes and benefits for three broad categories of wage earners: maximum wage earners who paid the full amount of Social Security taxes over their lifetimes, and those considered average and low wage earners. These illustrations do not consider those who need disability benefits earlier in life or those whose survivors draw or will draw on their benefits. In these examples, the base wage year is 1995. In 1995 the OASI tax was assessed on a maximum of $60,600 of earnings. Average wages were $23,900, and low wages were $10,800 for the year. These illustrations also account for the interest earned on the contributions made by the workers and their employees.

Workers who retired in 1975
The wage ceiling was $13,200; average, $8,000; low, $3,600.

		Single workers		Worker and spouse	
		Employee taxes only	Employee and employer taxes	Employee taxes only	Employee and employer taxes
Maximum	**Your monthly benefit:		**$316**		**$475**
	***Your lifetime contribution:	**$7,670**	**$15,339**	**$7,670**	**$15,339**
	Time to recover taxes paid:	**2 yrs.**	**4 yrs., 1 mo.**	**1 yr., 5 mo.**	**2 yrs., 8 mo.**
Average	Your monthly benefit:		**$271**		**$406**
	Your lifetime contribution:	**$5,857**	**$11,714**	**$5,857**	**$11,714**
	Time to recover taxes paid:	**1 yr., 10 mo.**	**3 yrs., 7 mo.**	**1 yr., 3 mo.**	**2 yrs., 5 mo.**
Low	Your monthly benefit:		**$180**		**$270**
	Your lifetime contribution:	**$2,592**	**$5,183**	**$2,592**	**$5,183**
	Time to recover taxes paid:	**1 yr., 3 mo.**	**2 yrs., 7 mo.**	**10 mo.**	**1 yr., 9 mo.**

continued

born in 1949 who retired at age 66 (remember, the full retirement age is rising slowly) in 2015 after earning average wages would not recoup his or her investment until just after age 78. If the taxes that these individuals' employers paid plus interest are added in, then payments for these workers are not recouped until ages 68 years and 7 months, 83 years and 6 months, and 95 years, respectively.

ILLUSTRATION 4-2 *(continued)*

Workers who retired in 1995
The wage ceiling was $60,600; average, $23,900; low, $10,800.

		Single workers		Worker and spouse*	
		Employee taxes only	Employee and employer taxes	Employee taxes only	Employee and employer taxes
Maximum	Your monthly benefit:		**$1,199**		**$1,798**
	Your lifetime contribution:	**$120,100**	**$240,472**	**$120,100**	**$240,472**
	Time to recover taxes paid:	**10 yrs., 6 mo.**	**25 yrs., 7 mo.**	**6 yrs., 7 mo.**	**15 yrs.**
Average	Your monthly benefit:		**$858**		**$1,287**
	Your lifetime contribution:	**$67,564**	**$135,245**	**$67,564**	**$135,245**
	Time to recover taxes paid:	**7 yrs., 11 mo.**	**18 yrs., 6 mo.**	**5 yrs.**	**11 yrs., 1 mo.**
Low	Your monthly benefit:		**$520**		**$780**
	Your lifetime contribution:	**$30,404**	**$60,860**	**$30,404**	**$60,860**
	Time to recover taxes paid:	**5 yrs., 8 mo.**	**12 yrs., 8 mo.**	**3 yrs., 7 mo.**	**7 yrs., 10 mo.**

Workers who will retire in 2015
The projected wage ceiling will be $142,800; average, $59,600; low, $26,800.

		Single workers		Worker and spouse*	
		Employee taxes only	Employee and employer taxes	Employee taxes only	Employee and employer taxes
Maximum	Your monthly benefit:		**$3,283**		**$4,924**
	Your lifetime contribution:	**$557,648**	**$1,116,359**	**$557,648**	**$1,116,359**
	Time to recover taxes paid:	**17 yrs., 6 mo.**	**47 yrs., 1 mo.**	**10 yrs., 11 mo.**	**25 yrs., 4 mo.**
Average	Your monthly benefit:		**$2,074**		**$3,111**
	Your lifetime contribution:	**$258,824**	**$518,102**	**$258,824**	**$518,102**
	Time to recover taxes paid:	**12 yrs., 2 mo.**	**29 yrs.**	**7 yrs., 9 mo.**	**17 yrs., 1 mo.**
Low	Your monthly benefit:		**$1,254**		**$1, 881**
	Your lifetime contribution:	**$116,471**	**$233,146**	**$116,471**	**$233,146**
	Time to recover taxes paid:	**8 yrs., 9 mo.**	**19 yrs., 7 mo.**	**5 yrs., 8 mo.**	**12 yrs., 1 mo.**

Source: Social Security Administration as reported in Patterson Clark, "Will You Get Your Money's Worth?," *The Miami Herald,* August 13, 1995, p. 45. © The Miami Herald/Patterson Clark.

Even if we do live to a ripe old age and collect all we have paid in, it has been argued that we could do far better by placing our investment tax-free in an individual retirement account (IRA) or other private fund. Sam Beard, who writes in a lively way about Social Security, regales in promoting the idea that even minimum-wage workers can become millionaires.[23] He says that due to the principle of compound interest, if you are 20 years old and save $30 a week, tax-free, every week and earn 8 percent interest, you will have $29,000 in 10 years, $110,000 in 20 years, $318,000 after 30 years, $822,000 after 40 years, and after 45 years, as you reach retirement, you will have $1.3 million (actually about $230,000 after controlling for inflation, but still much more than many Americans have in the bank at retirement today). Though this sounds good, many people might not voluntarily save for retirement, and there is no guarantee that people would get an 8 percent return on their investment throughout their working years. Today, many workers take the three-legged stool analogy seriously and try to put away something more than Social Security for retirement, even though this takes another chunk out of current earnings. Others have such a tight cash flow situation that they find this very difficult. Furthermore, about half do not have sufficient private pension income from their former jobs to secure their retirement.[24]

Despite its dilemmas, Social Security has been praised for achieving "a unique blend of adequacy and individual equity," two principles on which the program was founded.[25] It is adequate because it helps many older people escape poverty. It is equitable because those who contributed more get higher benefits, while at the same time the benefits paid are proportionally more generous for those who contributed to the system at the same rate as others but earned smaller wages over their lifetimes.

Social Security is the major source of income for two-thirds of retired Americans.[26] Thirty percent rely on it for at least 90 percent of their income and 36 percent more for at least half of their income. In 1996, Social Security reduced poverty among retired individuals from 61 percent to 16 percent and among couples from 41 percent to 3 percent.[27] In total, about 15 million OASDI recipients are spared poverty through Social Security.[28] The word "social" in Social Security is important because the program has important goals, such as redistribution of income to those less fortunate, that differ from private pension and retirement programs.[29]

Since there is no individual asset-building account for each worker who contributes to Social Security, the adequacy and equity of the program are directly affected by the **dependency ratio**—the ratio of beneficiaries to workers. In 1950 there were 16 workers for each beneficiary; today it takes about three workers to support each beneficiary in the largely "pay-as-you-go" system. As the U.S. population grows older due to lower birthrates and longer life spans, it will take two workers to support one Social Security beneficiary once most of the 75 million baby boomers retire.[30] This is a heavy responsibility to contemplate no matter how much we value adequacy and equity.

Social Security has been described as an "intergenerational compact" in which one generation of workers agrees to help current retirees with the promise of being helped themselves in retirement.[31] This was less of a problem when succeeding generations were much larger than preceding ones. It has been suggested that a key to making everyone feel better about the program is to promote "intergenerational equity," that is, to be as fair as possible to both the old and the young.[32] Largely as a result of OASDHI, the financial status of older people has improved over the years. Some argue that older Americans are now living a better life at the expense of the young. Others bristle at this thought, suggesting that cuts in Social Security benefits do not necessarily mean that more would be done to help younger people. The more salient issue to consider is why the country has been less successful at improving the standard of living of younger Americans than it has for older citizens. (As we will see in Chapter 6, helping younger people is a different political issue than helping older Americans.)

The baby boomers made it possible for many younger individuals to enjoy a very nice standard of living as they were growing up, but will Generation X (and succeeding generations) see the boomers' retirement as a source of consternation? Economist Henry Aaron believes that the fuss about the boomers putting a strain on younger generations is ill founded.[33] After all, the boomers are now paying a substantial tax for their retirement while supporting retirees who are getting back more than their share. Everyone knows that the boomers will not be paid the same rate of return as older generations. The problem of too few workers in the future is not confined to the Social Security system. As Phillip Longman notes, there will also be fewer workers to support all government activities.[34]

Another point of contention is whether the program is operating at unfair expense to members of certain racial and ethnic groups,[35] a growing concern as the country becomes more ethnically diverse. For example, African and Hispanic Americans have shorter life spans than whites. Many African and Hispanic Americans never live to collect retirement benefits, and those who do tend to collect benefits for shorter periods than whites. More members of ethnic minority groups are also employed at jobs requiring physical labor, which take their toll early. Social Security reforms, such as raising the retirement age, place them in an even more untenable position. Furthermore, on the average, these groups (particularly Hispanics) are younger than whites. This places an even greater burden on those who are generally poorer and who will reap fewer retirement benefits to support the growing retirement population that is disproportionately white and more affluent.

Others believe that the program is fair to African and Hispanic Americans. Granted, their life spans are shorter, and they pay a larger portion of their income in Social Security taxes, but they receive disability benefits and their dependents receive survivors' benefits more frequently than whites.[36] Although these factors may not be much consolation, the benefits paid to African and Hispanic Americans proportionate to their wages are also larger in all components of the program. Nearly one-third of today's Social Security recipients are disabled beneficiaries and their dependents and survivors of deceased workers. Without Social Security, many younger people of all racial and ethnic groups might be left with little or no income, since they may not have private disability insurance or large life insurance policies that would guarantee them or their families adequate income in the event of misfortune.

Still another crucial intergenerational aspect of the program is that it protects younger people from having to support their own elderly or disabled parents. Most young people would find it quite difficult to provide much financial support to their parents (although they may help in other ways), and older people do not want to burden their children with this responsibility. Kingson and his colleagues write that "When the program is examined from a long-term perspective, the benefits and costs . . . are shown to be distributed widely across the generations."[37]

Social Security is also a good investment because it is highly portable. It goes with the worker from job to job, a feature still not true of many other pension plans that are tied to a specific job and employer. Portability is important in a mobile society like ours where workers are likely to change jobs several times during their careers. And unlike virtually all current private pensions, Social Security adjusts for inflation.[38]

In addition to adequacy and equity, efficiency is a goal of the Social Security program. Slightly less than one cent per dollar collected is used to administer the program.[39]

Keeping the Wolves from the Door

According to the trustees, a Social Security crisis may not be imminent, but steps should be taken soon in order to make the adjustments needed to fund OASDI for the long haul. As current Social Security Commissioner Kenneth Apfel says, there are no minor changes in Social Security because every change affects millions of people. Solutions for the future are now being seriously considered. In addition to the trustees, an Advisory Council on Social Security is convened every four years to check on the program. The latest group reported in 1996. It concurred with the financial estimates of the trustees, but it did not reach a consensus on how to reform Social Security. Instead it offered three proposals.[40]

One way to increase Social Security's income is to increase the payroll tax once again. Even a one percent increase could result in considerable new revenues. But the tax is already quite high. Advisory Council members agreed that there is little support for raising it in the near future, so they considered other options while trying to remain true to the principles of the program. Members also agreed that the "pay-as-you-go" approach will no longer cut the mustard. The following paragraphs describe the three plans suggested by various contingents of the Advisory Council:

> *The Maintenance of Benefits (MB) Plan involves an increase in income taxes on Social Security benefits, a redirection to the OASDI funds beginning in 2010 of the part of the revenue from taxes on OASDI benefits now going to the Hospital Insurance (HI) Trust Fund, coverage of newly hired state and local government workers not currently covered by Social Security, a payroll tax increase in 2045, and serious consideration of a plan allowing the government to begin investing a portion of trust fund assets directly in common stocks indexed to the broad market.*
>
> *The Individual Accounts (IA) Plan creates individual accounts alongside the Social Security system. It involves an increase in the taxation of benefits, state and local coverage, an acceleration of the already-scheduled increase in the age of eligibility for full benefits up to year 2011 and then an automatic increase in that age tied to longevity, a reduction in the growth of future Social Security benefits structured to affect middle- and high-wage workers the most, and an increase in employees' mandatory contribution to Social Security of 1.6 percent of covered payroll, which would be allocated to individual defined contribution accounts. These individual accounts would be held by the government but with constrained investment choices available to individuals.*

The Personal Security Accounts (PSA) plan creates even larger, fully-funded individual accounts which would replace a portion of Social Security. Workers would direct 5 percentage points of the current payroll tax into a PSA, which would be managed privately and could be invested in a range of financial instruments. The balance of the payroll tax would go to fund a modified retirement program and modified disability and survivor benefits. When fully phased in, the modified retirement program would offer all full-career workers a flat dollar benefit (the equivalent of $140 in 1996, automatically increased to reflect increases in national average wages) plus the proceeds of their PSAs. This plan also would involve a change in benefit taxation, state and local coverage, and acceleration of the age of eligibility for full retirement benefits, increased in future years to reflect increases in longevity, a gradual increase to age 65 for early benefits (although workers could begin withdrawing the proceeds of their PSAs at 62), a reduction in future benefits for disabled workers, a reduction in benefits for women who never worked outside the home, and an increase in benefits for many elderly widows.

What is remarkable about all the plans is the movement from the current method of investing the excess payroll taxes collected in low-yielding but safe government bonds to at least some investments in the private market. Despite the nice ride that the stock market has had recently, it can be very volatile, but Advisory Council members felt that this was the only viable way to increase revenues sufficiently so that younger people would get their money's worth. The IA and PSA plans may boost savings for retirement more than the MB plan, but the three plans are so different that the members could not reach a compromise. The IAs and PSAs are "double-decker" plans that combine a government Social Security account with a private account. These plans have many advocates.[41] The country currently has a double decker plan—Social Security is one tier and means-tested SSI payments, available only to the poor, are the second tier. In these new plans, both tiers require contributions by the individual, whereas today, SSI requires no direct previous contributions (see Chapter 5). There is no plan to do away with SSI for those who need it, but one hope is that better-funded retirement and disability insurance systems will reduce reliance on public assistance. Making government payments only to retirees in financial need is not a serious option, because making Social Security more like public assistance would be an administrative nightmare in attempting to determine eligibility, and it would severely threaten the program's political base of support.[42]

The experience of Chile and other Latin American countries has prompted more serious consideration of privatization through stock market investments.[43] In 1924, Chile became the first Western Hemisphere country to adopt a comprehensive social security system. In 1981, Chile privatized its formerly government-administered social security system under its young minister of labor and social security, José Piñera. Piñera, a Harvard-educated economist, says that his country followed three rules in making the transition: "Do not hurt your grandmother; Give workers a free choice; Do not accumulate more debt for your grandchildren." Piñera's accounts of the new system (see the web site of the Libertarian Cato Institute) suggest that the change has been a booming success—savings and other aspects of economic growth are up and unemployment is down. An important aspect of the Chilean system is that employers contribute nothing. Workers must set aside at least 10 percent of their earnings, based on a set taxable wage base, for their retirement. More than 90 percent of Chileans opted out of the government system and invested in the private system which is run under government rules in order to promote a greater margin of safety.

It is probably too soon to tell if Chile's experience will be as rosy in the long run.[44] There are questions about whether the new social security system or other macroeconomic policy changes are responsible for much of the increased savings and good economic times that Chile has experienced. Early on, several of the biggest private pension fund management companies failed despite strict regulation. And although a minimum benefit is guaranteed by the government for those who have worked and contributed to the system for at least 20 years, there is no guaranteed rate of return on investments. Since the system is relatively new, few have fully retired under it. The Social Security Advisory Council's proposals are not as drastic as Chile's plan, but they all embrace private market investments to some degree, and this constitutes a radical departure from the current Social Security system.

Investing Social Security taxes in the stock market may appeal more to younger generations who are likely to have more experience with mutual funds and common stocks than those who are already retired. Many people are afraid of venturing into the stock market, or they may have read John Crudele, financial columnist for the *New York Post*. In response to the three plans offered by the Advisory Council, Crudele warned that "if Social Security money is invested in the stock market, we can all kiss our retirements good-bye"—a pretty strong statement.[45] The interest in private investments is that they have been yielding a considerably better return than government bonds. Crudele and others say that the real beneficiary of investing Social Security taxes in the stock market will be Wall Street. They believe a problem will arise (at least in the short run) because the federal government does not actually have reserves of Social Security taxes to invest in the market. When Chile began its new program, it had considerable budget surpluses.[46] What the U.S. has instead are the bonds in which it has invested Social Security taxes that are not currently needed to pay benefits. In order to invest in the stock market, the government would have to sell its bonds. This would likely cause interest rates to rise. The government would also have to find another lender to replace the money it is now using from Social Security taxes to fund its activities, probably at a higher interest rate. Crudele says this, in turn, will cause budget deficits to grow again, and interest rates may rise further as investors' confidence in the federal government declines.

According to *The Wall Street Journal*, Britain's foray into partial privatization in 1986, also raises concerns.[47] Britain retained a public pension system for all workers, but higher income workers can invest some of this money. Workers with employer-sponsored pension programs can also invest their own contributions privately. Although many employers no longer contribute to these plans, some workers thought they could recoup the difference and more through private investments. Private companies were supposed to give workers sound advice about whether the new option was in their best interest. Now, reports are that in the switch many workers have lost money, money which the government is making the private insurers repay.

If privatization sounded good at first look, some financial analysts' opinions and some practical experiences give one pause about the prudence of the approach. Alan Greenspan, former chair of the committee that proposed the 1983 Social Security reforms and now Federal Reserve Chairman, said that privatization calls for study but it would not improve things unless Americans save more.[48] Some believe that Social Security has been so successful that there is no need to throw the baby out with the bathwater. Less drastic solutions might do the trick. The Century Foundation criticized the Advisory Council's double-decker plans saying they would destroy the program's adequacy, equity, and efficiency, and it asked Americans to remember that Social Security is an insurance, not an investment, program.[49] Private plans will also be more costly to administer. There is also the issue of how to protect people against unscrupulous investment companies.[50] Any major change such as privatization will require careful planning and will need to be phased in slowly in order to avoid a serious shock to the economy.[51]

Whatever changes are made, the Council felt that current as well as future retirees should share in the consequences. Thus the Council recommended greater taxation of benefits, believing that approach is preferable to increasing the taxable wage base. Increasing the taxable wage base could result in wealthier retirees being entitled to increasingly large Social Security benefits which the system could not afford.

COLAs were another point of discussion. The current method of determining the CPI is said to inflate prices because it simply takes the same market basket of goods and recomputes prices rather than assuming that people will purchase cheaper goods or adjust spending in other ways when faced with higher prices.[52] The Council did not deny that more accurate calculations may be in order, but it warned against adjusting COLAs downward for political reasons. Even a relatively small adjustment in the COLA could produce a substantial savings, but the Council recommend retaining COLAs because they help the neediest recipients (who are often oldest) the most.

The Council recommends reducing benefits paid to retirees' spouses and increasing benefits paid to widows and widowers. This is because widows and widowers need greater benefits when they are alone than when they have a spouse with whom to share expenses. The Council also feels that workers now covered under other arrangements should be brought into the Social Security system. It also believes that people should be encouraged to work longer since many older people remain vital past the current retirement age. The disability insurance (DI) program will be there for those unable to do so.[53] Today, people may be retiring at age 62 or 65 in part because the law arbitrarily sets these age limits and in part because Social Security benefit are figured rather generously.[54] Workers help the economy expand because they pay more taxes, but let's face it, many people look forward to giving up the daily grind.

The Council also recommends changing the Social Security payment formula to include more years of work. This could slightly reduce benefits since earlier years of lower-paid work might be included, but members felt that this procedure ties benefits more closely to work history and may also encourage people to work longer. To make up for any losses to beneficiaries, the Council recommends legislation that will make it easier for small businesses to offer their employees retirement plans. Currently red tape makes small businesses reluctant to offer this benefit.

Just about everyone who writes about Social Security concurs that the time to act is now. The longer the wait, the more difficult it will be to make the necessary changes. Those who will retire in the future should be afforded the opportunity to adjust to whatever plan will be adopted. Public forums on Social Security are taking place around the country. Late in 1998, President Clinton convened a White House conference to address Social Security. Social Security Commissioner Apfel encourages all Americans to join in the great debate about Social Security. It is advice well taken.

UNEMPLOYMENT COMPENSATION

Another major social insurance program—unemployment compensation (UC, also called unemployment insurance)—was part of the original Social Security Act. This program provides some income to recently and involuntarily unemployed people and helps stabilize the economy during recessions. Again, the underlying rationale is to compel employers to contribute to a trust fund that would help employees in the event of job loss. The federal government does this by requiring employers to pay into state-administered unemployment insurance programs that meet federal standards. The federal standards are flexible, and the states have considerable freedom in shaping their own unemployment programs.

In order to receive UC benefits, unemployed workers must apply in person and show that they are willing, able, and ready to work. In practice, this means that unemployed workers must register with the U.S. Employment Service (usually located in the same building as the state unemployment compensation office), actively seek work, and accept a "suitable" job if found. Suitability is generally defined in terms of risks to health, safety, and morals, as well as the individual's physical capabilities; prior education, work experience, and earnings; the likelihood of obtaining employment in one's customary line of work; and distance to the job. But the longer the period of unemployment, the more pressure there is to take whatever is available.[55]

States cannot deny benefits to unemployed workers for refusing to work as strikebreakers or refusing to work for less than prevailing wage in the community, nor can they deny benefits for refusing to take jobs that require union membership. But basic decisions concerning eligibility requirements, the amount of benefits, and the length of time that benefits are paid are largely left to the states. However, in all states, unemployment compensation is temporary, usually a maximum of twenty-six weeks of regular coverage financed by the states, and sometimes thirteen weeks of extended coverage financed by both the federal and state governments. Unemployment compensation is not a protection against long-term or "hard-core" unemployment.

Under the Federal Unemployment Tax Act (FUTA), employers' taxes are placed in a federal unemployment trust fund that contains an account for each state plus accounts for groups such as federal employees. Currently, the federal government requires that employers pay 6.2 percent of the first $7,000 that each employee earns.[56] States with no delinquent federal loans get back 5.4 percent, which is used to pay regular state unemployment claims and half of the claims for the federal-state extended benefits program. The states vary in both the taxable wage base and the tax rate they use to fund their UC programs. The states determine tax rates based on an employer's unemployment (lay off) history; these rates range from zero to 10 percent. In 1995, the estimated tax contributions of employers nationwide averaged 2.2 percent of their taxable payroll with a range from 0.6 percent in South Dakota and North Carolina to 4.9 percent in Pennsylvania. Expressed another way, the average annual tax paid by an employer for a worker earning average wages was $301, with $245 going to the states and the rest to the federal government.

The federal government maintains a fund to bail out any state trust fund that becomes exhausted. In 1997, maximum allowable weekly benefits ranged from $175 in Missouri to $543 in Massachusetts. In 1999, an estimated 8.3 million people will receive an average weekly benefit of $199. Ninety-seven percent of all wage and salary workers have unemployment protection.

But not everyone who is unemployed receives assistance. In 1997, the U.S. Department of Labor estimated that 65 percent of unemployed people did *not* receive benefits. Some of these individuals were "exhaustees" who had used all the benefits to which they were entitled (not a bad name since most people feel exhausted after pounding the pavement looking for work for 26 weeks or more). In 1996, 2.7 million people exhausted all their state benefits. A study of "exhaustees" found that many did not expect to be called back to their previous jobs, and many also had low levels of job skills.[57] Others are unemployed for short periods and either do not qualify or do not bother to apply for benefits. Still others did not earn enough or did not work at their last job long enough to qualify. Some were fired for poor job performance or misconduct or left their jobs voluntarily, including strikers; these situations are not covered by unemployment compensation.

What Is Unemployment, and Who Gets Counted as Unemployed?

Until unemployment compensation insurance was first adopted in 1935, the loss of one's job could have resulted in sheer destitution. Most families depended on the support of one worker—usually the father. If he lost his job, the family's income was immediately reduced to zero. Today many American families benefit from the earnings of more than one worker. Unemployment is still serious, but a second income provides a buffer against economic disaster. Unemployment insurance and food stamps, and other forms of public assistance for those out of work for long periods can also reduce some of the costs of unemployment. These changes have had an important effect on the motivations and expectations of unemployed people. They may now decide to pass up, at least for a while, low-paying or undesirable jobs in the hope of finding better-paying, more satisfying employment.[58]

Considerable fluctuations in unemployment rates have occurred during this century. Nationally, unemployment is now under 5 percent. In fact, in May 1998, unemployment reached a 28-year low of 4.3 percent.[59] This is far better than 1982 and 1983 when unemployment rates exceeded 10 percent in some months, and certainly far below the 20 to 30 percent unemployment rate estimated during the Depression of the 1930s. But it is still more than the 2.5 to 3.5 percent lows achieved during the early 1950s. Of course, there is some unavoidable minimum unemployment. In a large, free economy, hundreds of thousands of people move and change jobs and temporarily find themselves unemployed. This "frictional" unemployment is estimated to be about half of the total unemployment during normal (nonrecession) periods. But others are unemployed for long periods due to poor job skills, ill health, or limited mental capacities, or because they live in areas with few job opportunities. These "structurally" unemployed are estimated to be less than 20 percent of the total unemployed, but they face the greatest challenge in obtaining and maintaining employment.

Determining just who is unemployed has been a real bone of contention.[60] Each month the U.S. Department of Labor estimates the percentage of the workforce that is out of work and actively seeking jobs (state and local unemployment figures are calculated differently). This official unemployment rate is based on a survey of about 50,000 households and includes those 16 years of age and older.[61] The Labor Department is frequently criticized because many of the downtrodden are never counted as unemployed. That is because they have given up even trying to find a job. These "discouraged" workers are excluded from official unemployment statistics, although efforts are made to determine how many people fall into this category. The number of discouraged workers at any one point used to be about one million, but a new, more restrictive definition put the figure at 500,000 during the early 1990s.[62] Now, in better economic times, the figure is about 330,000.[63]

For years, the Labor Department was also criticized because it counted part-time workers as fully employed even if they wanted full-time work. In 1994, the household survey was modified to be more sensitive to this and other issues.[64] For example, in November 1997, 8.2 million workers held more than one job.[65] Their work may equal or exceed the 35 hours that define full-time employment, but they often work at lower wages and do not receive fringe benefits.[66] An excess of part-time employment is an indicator that the economy is not performing as well as the country would like. Part-time employment is now measured because of its importance in setting public policy. To more accurately capture unemployment, attempts have also been made to reduce gender bias. For example, women identified as homemakers are asked whether they are working for pay or are unemployed.[67] And questions are now phrased differently to determine whether laid-off workers expect to return to their jobs or not.[68]

A figure that remains unaccounted for is the number of people who are **underemployed.** Underemployment occurs when people work at jobs for which they are overqualified, but have taken due to need rather than preference. These jobs also tend to pay less than workers may be capable of earning.[69]

Since the workforce continues to grow as the population increases, the number of jobs must also grow each year to keep pace with population growth. Although unemployment rates are now below 5 percent, given prior retrenchment in the steel and auto industries, and current downsizing in even the "high tech" industries, many

Americans are concerned about whether they will have a job tomorrow, and whether that job will be anything like the one they have today.

Some people think that a better way to measure the country's economic health is through the number of current jobs, but the federal government is also criticized for overestimating job growth. And while every presidential administration wants employment and job growth figures to reflect the merits of its economic policy, the opposition is generally out to prove that the current administration's approach is flawed. For example, in 1991 "official" unemployment was 6.7 percent, but using seven alternative means to calculate unemployment, estimates ranged from 1.9 to 10 percent.[70]

How much unemployment is too much? There is an old saying: "When your neighbor is unemployed, it's a recession. When *you* are unemployed, it's a depression." Although most controversy centers on underestimates of unemployment, others believe that these figures are too high. For example, to qualify for programs such as food stamps, able-bodied individuals must sign up with the state employment office in their area. It has been argued that this artificially inflates unemployment, because some public assistance beneficiaries do not really intend to seek work.[71]

In addition to national unemployment, it is important to examine unemployment among subgroups of the population.[72] In good economic times or bad, the unemployment rate for African Americans is at least double that for whites. Hispanic Americans fare somewhat better than African Americans. The teenage (16 to 19 years old) unemployment rate is often three times higher than the rate for the general population. The highest unemployment rate of all is for African American teens. A 40 percent unemployment rate for this group is not uncommon. Unemployment rates for women and men are often quite similar; sometimes women's rates are higher, and sometimes men's rates are higher, but women are concentrated in lower-paying jobs.

The unemployment picture would improve considerably if jobs and unemployed workers were better matched. This could be done in at least two ways. First, more job training and retraining programs could be offered to help workers with limited or outdated skills learn skills that employers are seeking. Efforts such as the Job Training Partnership Act (see Chapter 9) and some aspects of welfare reform (see Chapter 6) are intended to help with this problem. Second, those unable to find employment near their homes could be encouraged or assisted to relocate to areas where jobs are available. Relocation assistance is often provided for higher-paid workers by their employers but not for low-wage earners, who may need this assistance the most.

Future demographic trends may help to ease unemployment. During the 1970s and 1980s, the large population of baby boomers entered the labor market, contributing to unemployment. But as the boomers retire, there will be more room for younger people in the workforce. "These trends will be of special significance to blacks and Hispanics who will comprise much of the future addition to the labor force."[73] They also have important implications for the health of the Social Security system. The preparation of future workers is crucial, because the bulk of new jobs with good salaries and fringe benefits will require a highly skilled workforce. Those without solid qualifications will continue to comprise the ranks of the poor and the unemployed.

Reforming Unemployment Compensation

During the Bush administration there was much haggling about whether to provide extended benefits to unemployed workers once their twenty-six weeks of regular benefits were exhausted. The permanent, extended unemployment benefits program allows for thirteen additional weeks of compensation if certain unemployment levels called "triggers" are met, but the triggers are difficult to activate. President Bush vetoed some extended benefit bills, saying that they violated national deficit reduction targets (they did not include measures that would cover their costs) and that they were not needed because the economy was improving. Four temporary extensions were granted during the Bush years. The states were pleased with these temporary extensions because they were totally federally funded, while the states must share the costs of the permanent, extended benefits program when it kicks in. When the fourth temporary extension expired in October 1993, 60,000 people each week were exhausting their regular benefits. The next extension got temporarily bogged down. Though Congress wanted to extend benefits, the bill became entangled with other matters such as public assistance benefits for immigrants and cutting employees from the federal payroll.[74] Those who supported current public assistance provisions were accused of putting the needs of immigrants over those of Americans. President Clinton signed some temporary measures, with extensions of fewer weeks each time. Given current reductions in unemployment, additional extensions of the temporary program for those who need it will likely be difficult to achieve.

The UC program could be working better. Congress has scurried around during difficult economic times to keep extended benefits going. According to one task force, the program should be made "more reliable for those who depend on it, more responsive to changes in the economy, and more effective in providing relief and helping put people back to work."[75] The task force cited four major problems. First, the program is too complex. Basic benefits are provided, and then there are "triggers" that allow additional benefits to be paid during periods when unemployment is especially high. These triggers and benefit periods change frequently, adding to confusion in the program. Second, the program is too rigid. It can fail to help states and areas with high unemployment. Since unemployment tends to be underestimated, the triggers that would allow extended benefits to be paid may not be set off in states where unemployment is actually high. In addition, if unemployment in a particular area of a state is high, but the overall state unemployment rate does not reach specified levels, the depressed area does not receive additional payments. Third, there are few inducements for workers to seek training that would qualify them for new jobs. Training opportunities are limited, and short-term solutions are used in favor of longer-term gains. The attitude is to take the first job available, whatever it is (a strategy common in this era of welfare reform). Fourth, program financing should be altered. States with the highest unemployment should receive more federal financial assistance rather than face additional financial burdens that can cause their economies to become more depressed when growth is needed most. In order to improve the program, steps should be taken to simplify "triggers" and other regulations, provide more assistance to states and areas with high unemployment, more accurately count the number of unemployed, and provide more inducements for training and job searches that will better match jobs and workers.

Given the small percent of unemployed receiving benefits, other suggestions for reforming UC are to provide benefits to those able to find only part-time work or to those who must leave work to care for a sick child or to flee an abusive partner.[76] Of course, attempts to increase beneficiaries will meet with opposition from employers concerned about a rise in UC tax rates.

WORKERS' COMPENSATION

Workers' compensation is another social insurance program. Federal involvement is limited to those programs which cover federal employees. The first state programs were initiated in Wisconsin and New Jersey in 1911; all states had programs by 1948.[77] Each state's program is operated by its labor department. The programs vary by state, but each provides cash payments and medical benefits to workers who sustain injuries on the job or develop job-related diseases. The intent is to protect employees in the event of "occupational disabilities without regard to fault," not just when employer negligence is involved.[78] But "most [programs] exclude injuries due to the employee's intoxication, willful misconduct, or gross negligence."[79]

Although intended to limit contentious legal cases, workers' compensation claims remain highly litigious because workers must still prove that their injury is work related.[80] Some states view workers' compensation as payments for the discomfort resulting from injury; others see it as payment for future wages lost to injury.[81] Payments are usually calculated as two-thirds or more of the worker's weekly wages at the time of illness, injury, or death, although there are caps on these amounts.[82] Rather than attempt the difficult process of estimating lost wages, administrative and legal expediency has also resulted in the development of schedules that equate particular injuries with a given number of weeks of compensation at the employee's regular wage.[83] The programs help in cases of permanent, long-term disability, but they are especially important, because unlike Social Security, they also help those with short-term disability and longer-term partial disability.[84] Most individuals who receive benefits under the programs recover from their disability.[85] Workers who sustain permanent disabilities are only 1 percent of beneficiaries; their benefits may continue for life, and they may also receive Social Security benefits. Dependents of workers killed in job-related accidents are generally entitled to benefits, and some states provide benefits to widowers as well as widows. The program is mandatory for most private employers in all but three states—South Carolina, Texas, and New Jersey where no employer has asked for an exemption.[86] States vary considerably in how public, nonprofit, religious, and charitable employers are treated.

Most employers insure their workers through a private insurance company; others self-insure, and in some cases, the state insures employers. Employers' premiums are based on the hazardousness of the work involved. Due to the risks involved in some industries, employers may not be able to obtain private coverage and must resort to state operated "high-risk pools." Some states have had difficulties operating their compensation systems because of increased claims, rapidly rising insurance rates, and large program deficits. Originally the programs emerged as state efforts because business people wanted control closer to home, but greater consistency could be achieved through a federal program.[87]

In 1993, 96 million workers were covered by workers' compensation programs.[88] Employers paid $57 billion into the program nationwide, and benefits paid to workers were about $34 billion (the difference in payments and the amount collected is due to the need to pay long-term benefits to some beneficiaries). This translated to a cost of about $597 per covered employee. About 59 percent of benefits were in cash payments and 41 percent in medical benefits. Maximum weekly payments available to those who are disabled vary widely depending on whether they are covered by a federal or state program. For example, the highest payment available to a permanently and totally disabled former federal worker in 1996 was $1,299 compared with a state high of $846 in Iowa and a state low of $264 in Mississippi.

The work-related injury and illness rate for full-time workers in private industry is about 8 out of every 100 workers. The number of workers' compensation claims may continue to rise for at least two reasons: more states are covering illnesses that take longer to manifest and medical advances are leading to the detection of more job-related medical problems (such as repetitive motion–related disorders). However, many states retain time limits on filing claims. The federal government ended its regular collection of workers' compensation data in 1993.[89]

SUMMARY

One strategy for preventing poverty in the United States is social insurance programs. Social insurance helps workers protect themselves and their dependents against poverty, which may result from advanced age, death, disability, or unemployment of a breadwinner. The major social insurance program in the United States is known as Social Security. The Social Security Act of 1935, signed by President Franklin D. Roosevelt, was the first major piece of federal social welfare legislation. This act has been amended many times; today it includes a number of social insurance programs including Old Age, Survivors, Disability, and Health Insurance, collectively called OASDHI or Social Security.

Social Security was originally intended to be a self-financing program, but it developed into a "pay-as-you-go" system because life expectancy increased, and payments were continually raised to keep pace with the cost of living. In order to finance the growing program, the amount of taxable wages increased over the years and the rate at which these wages were taxed also increased. Eventually it looked as if the program would be bankrupt.

In 1981 President Reagan appointed a bipartisan commission to find solutions to the ailing Social Security program. After many disagreements, the commission made a number of recommendations that were adopted by Congress. They included raising the retirement age, increasing the taxable wage base and the Social Security tax rate, taxing part of the Social Security benefits of those with higher incomes, increasing benefits to those who retire later, decreasing benefits to those who retire early, allowing retirees to earn more while losing less in Social Security benefits, and changing the way cost-of-living adjustments are computed if trust funds run low.

Social Security taxes place a considerable strain on current workers. For the time being, the combined OASDI trust funds appear to be on steady footing. In fact, a surplus is now mounting that will be needed to ensure benefits when the "baby boom" generation retires. Careful attention is needed to keep the system afloat as the number of retirees continues to grow in relation to workers. Due to mounting national health care costs, the Medicare or health insurance trust fund is in poor shape. It is being helped by taxing all workers' wages, but it needs immediate attention.

There are many ways Social Security could be reformed to meet the challenges in the century ahead. The payroll tax, the taxable wage base, the retirement age, and taxable benefits could all be increased, and COLAs could be decreased. These methods have all been used before. Today the suggestion getting most attention is privatization, which would allow the government or workers to invest at least part of Social Security contributions in what many believe will be higher-yielding investments in the stock market. This would be a radical departure from the current method of investing surplus Social Security taxes in much safer but low-yielding government bonds. This issue will be hotly debated. Hopefully a bipartisan agreement, as occurred in 1983, will soon put Social Security on secure footing well into the future.

Despite its problems, Social Security has ensured most workers some income in the event of their retirement or disability during their working years. It also insures their dependents in the event of the worker's death. It relieves younger people of much of the burden of supporting their parents and grandparents, and it is a highly portable program that workers take with them from job to job. Social Security is the nation's largest government program and its most effective antipoverty effort. It will remain the country's most important social welfare program for years to come.

Unemployment compensation is another large social insurance program. UC does not help with long-term unemployment. A number of suggestions have been made to reform UC programs so that workers in need can be helped more easily. Workers' compensation, another social insurance program, assists workers who are injured or become ill in work-related situations. Social insurance programs are a preferred alternative for preventing poverty, but particularly important for the years ahead are ensuring a skilled workforce and flexibility in matching workers with job opportunities.

NOTES

1. Thomas Paine, "Agrarian Justice," 1795, available at http://www.mediapro.net/cdadesign/paine/agjst.html; and at Social Security Administration, "Social Security History Page," http://www.ssa.gov/history/quotes.html; also see Bee Moorhead, "Life Savings: Texas Families Could Benefit from Focus on Personal Finances," *Fiscal Notes,* newsletter of the Texas Comptroller of Public Accounts, January/February 1998, pp. 1, 10–12.

2. For further discussion of this point, see Eric R. Kingson and Edward D. Berkowitz, *Social Security and Medicare: A Policy Primer* (Westport, CT: Auburn House, 1993), pp. 29–37.

3. Ibid., p. 33.

4. Joseph A. Pechman, Henry J. Aaron, and Michael K. Taussig, *Social Security: Perspectives for Reform* (Washington, DC: Brookings Institution, 1968).

5. Committee on Ways and Means, U.S. House of Representatives, *1998 Green Book: Background Material and Data on Programs Within the Jurisdiction of the Committee on Ways and Means* (Washington, DC: U.S. Government Printing Office, 1998), pp. 6–7.

6. Social Security Administration, *Accountability Report for Fiscal Year 1997* (Washington, DC: SSA, November 21, 1997), p. iv–v.

7. See Kingson and Berkowitz, *Social Security and Medicare: A Policy Primer,* pp. 48–50.

8. Committee on Ways and Means, U.S. House of Representatives, *1996 Green Book: Background Material and Data on Programs within the jurisdiction of the Committee on Ways and Means* (Washington, D.C.: U.S. Government Printing Office, 1996), p. 38; Social Security Administration, "Calculation of the Cost-of-Living Adjustment," http://www.ssa.gov/search97cgi/97_cgi?action=View&VdkVgwKey = .

9. Committee on Ways and Means, *1996 Green Book,* p. 20.

10. David A. Stockman, "The Social Pork Barrel," *The Public Interest,* No. 39, Spring 1975, pp. 3–30, especially p. 9.

11. Committee on Ways and Means, *1996 Green Book,* pp. 42–43.

12. Committee on Ways and Means, U.S. House of Representatives, *Overview of Entitlement Programs: 1993 Green Book* (Washington, DC: U.S. Government Printing Office, 1993), p. 23.

13. Social Security Administration, *Understanding the Benefits,* SSA Publication No. 05-10024, Washington, DC: SSA, January 1998, p. 4.

14. For a more detailed description of these reforms see "Report of the National Commission on Social Security Reform," *Social Security Bulletin,* Vol. 46, No. 2, 1983, pp. 3–38. For more on House and Senate action, see "Social Security Rescue Plan Swiftly Approved," *1983 Congressional Quarterly Almanac* (Washington, DC: Congressional Quarterly, 1984), pp. 219–226. For a concise consideration of the changes adopted, see Wilbur J. Cohen, "The Future Impact of the Social Security Amendments of 1983," *The Journal/The Institute of Socioeconomic Studies,* Vol. 8, No. 2, 1983, pp. 1–16.

15. Wilbur J. Cohen, *Social Security: The Compromise and Beyond* (Washington, DC: Save Our Security Education Fund, 1983), pp. 4–5.

16. Social Security Administration, *1998 OASDI Trustees Report* available at http://www.ssa.gov/OACT/TR/TR98/trtoc.html.

17. Social Security Administration, *Summary of the 1998 Annual Reports* available at http://www.ssa.gov/OACT/TRSUM/trtsummary.html.

18. "Summary of the 1997 Annual Social Security and Medicare Trust Fund Reports," *Social Security Bulletin,* Vol. 60, No. 2, 1997, pp. 61–67.

19. See Ben Wildavsky, "Poll Watchers Dress Down the Press," *National Journal,* September 13, 1997, p. 1786.

20. Jill Quadango, "Social Security and the Myth of the Entitlement Crisis," *The Gerontologist,* Vol. 36, No. 3, pp. 391–399.

21. Reported by Marshall N. Carter and William G. Shipman, *Promises to Keep: Saving Social Security's Dream* (Washington, DC: Regnery Publishing, 1996) based on a Third Millennium Survey by Frank Lutz and Mark Siegel; also referred to in Sam Beard, "Minimum-Wage Millionaires: The Capitalist Way to Save Social Security," *Policy Review,* No. 73, Summer 1995, http://www.heritage.org/heritage/library.

22. "Summary of the 1997 Annual Social Security and Medicare Trust Fund Reports," p. 67.

23. Beard, "Minimum-Wage Millionaires: The Capitalist Way to Save Social Security."

24. Eugene Steuerle and Jon M. Bakija, "Retooling Social Security for the 21st Century," *Social Security Bulletin,* Vol. 60, No. 2, 1997, pp. 37–60; also see Eugene Steuerle and Jon M. Bakija, *Retooling Social Security for the 21st Century: Right and Wrong Approaches to Reform* (Washington, DC: Urban Institute Press, 1994).

25. Eric R. Kingson, "Misconceptions Distort Social Security Policy Discussions," *Social Work,* Vol. 34, No. 4, 1989, pp. 357–362; Kingson and Berkowitz, *Social Security and Medicare: A Policy Primer;* Gordon Sherman, "Social Security: The Real Story," *National Forum,* The Phi Kappa Phi Journal, Vol. 78, No. 2, 1998, pp. 26–29.

26. Testimony delivered by Social Security Commissioner Kenneth Apfel on February 10, 1998, before the Senate Committee on Aging on the Issue of Social Security Solvency, available at http://www.ssa.gov/policy/solvency_testimony.html; *Austin American-Statesman,* Washington staff, "A Closer Look at Some of the Social Security Proposals," *Austin American-Statesman,* December 6, 1998, p. A14.

27. Executive Office of the President, *Budget of the United States Government, Fiscal Year 1999* (Washington, DC: U.S. Government Printing Office, 1998), p. 229.

28. Testimony delivered by Commissioner Apfel on February 10, 1998, before the Senate Committee on Aging on the Issue of Social Security Solvency.

29. Dorcas R. Hardy, "The Future of Social Security," *Social Security Bulletin,* Vol. 50, No. 8, 1987, p. 7, re-

printed from *Connecticut College Alumni Magazine,* Spring 1987.

30. Jack Anderson, "Why Should I Pay for People Who Don't Need It?" *Parade Magazine,* February 21, 1993, pp. 4–7; Social Security Administration, *Summary of the 1998 Annual Reports.*

31. See Kingson and Berkowitz, *Social Security and Medicare: A Policy Primer,* p. 23; J. Douglas Brown, *Essays on Social Security* (Princeton, NJ: Princeton University Press, 1977), pp. 31–32.

32. Martha N. Ozawa, "Benefits and Taxes Under Social Security: An Issue of Intergenerational Equity," *Social Work,* Vol. 29, No. 2, 1984, pp. 131–137.

33. Henry J. Aaron, "Costs of the Aging Population: Real and Imagined Burdens," in Henry J. Aaron, ed., *Social Security and the Budget: Proceedings of the First Conference of the National Academy of Social Insurance* (Lanham, MD: National Academy of Social Insurance and University Press of America, 1990), pp. 51–61.

34. Philip J. Longman, "Costs of the Aging Population: Financing the Future," in Aaron, *Social Security and the Budget: Proceedings of the First Conference of the National Academy of Social Insurance,* p. 67.

35. This paragraph relies on Robert Gnaizda and Mario Obledo, "1983 Social Security Reforms Unfair to Minorities and the Young," *Gray Panther Network,* Spring 1985, p. 12.

36. This paragraph relies on Kingson, "Misconceptions Distort Social Security Policy Discussions."

37. Eric R. Kingson, Barbara A. Hirshorn, and John M. Cornman, *Ties That Bind: The Interdependency of Generations* (Washington, DC: Seven Locks Press, 1986).

38. See Kingson and Berkowitz, *Social Security and Medicare: A Policy Primer,* p. 78.

39. Testimony delivered by Commissioner Apfel on February 10, 1998, before the Senate Committee on Aging on the Issue of Social Security Solvency.

40. *1994–1996 Advisory Council on Social Security,* Social Security Online, http://www.ssa.gov/policy/adcouncil_intro.html.

41. See, for example, Sam Beard, *Restoring Hope in America: The Social Security Solution* (San Francisco: ICS Press, 1996).

42. Kingson and Berkowitz, *Social Security and Medicare: A Policy Primer,* pp. 82–83.

43. José Piñera, "Empowering Workers: The Privatization of Social Security in Chile," *The Cato Journal,* Vol. 15, No. 2–3, 1995, pp. 155–166, also available at http://www.cato.org/pubs/journal/cj15n2-3-1.htm.

44. Much of this paragraph relies on Barbara E. Kritzer, "Privatizing Social Security: The Chilean Experience," *Social Security Bulletin,* Vol. 59, No. 3, 1996, pp. 45–55.

45. John Crudele (*New York Post*), "Handing Social Security Over to Wall Street Risky," *Austin American-Statesman,* January 11, 1997, p. D3; also see Floyd Norris, "Social Security Shift Could Raise Interest Rates," *Austin American-Statesman,* January 19, 1997, p. A6.

46. Peter G. Peterson, *Will America Grow Up Before It Grows Old?* (New York: Random House, 1996), p. 135.

47. Steve Stecklow and Sara Calian, "Social Security Switch in U.K. is Disastrous; A Caution to the U.S.?", *The Wall Street Journal,* August 10, 1998, p. A1.

48. William M. Welch, "Greenspan Says Social Security in Trouble," *USA Today,* November 21–23, 1997, p. 1A.

49. Twentieth Century Fund (now The Century Foundation), "An Overview of the Major Proposed Reforms," http://www.epn.org/tct/ssfuture.html.

50. See "Social Security Reform Options: Preparing for the 21st Century," Hearing before the Special Committee on Aging, United States Senate, 104th Congress, 2nd session, Serial No. 104-17, September 24, 1996.

51. For additional arguments about both sides of the privatization debate, see the web site at http://policy.com.

52. See Gary Preuss, "Inflation Equation; Inside the Consumer Price Index," *Fiscal Notes,* Newsletter of the Texas Comptroller of Public Accounts, September 1996, pp. 12–13; Steuerle and Bakija, "Retooling Social Security for the 21st Century." These authors agree that cutting COLAs is not a good idea.

53. Steuerle and Bakija, "Retooling Social Security for the 21st Century."

54. Michael Leonisio, "The Economics of Retirement: A Non-technical Guide," *Social Security Bulletin,* Vol. 59, No. 4, 1996, pp. 29–50.

55. Committee on Ways and Means, *1993 Green Book,* p. 497.

56. Figures in this section rely on Committee on Ways and Means, *1996 Green Book,* Section 5, pp. 327–359; Committee on Ways and Means, *1998 Green Book,* Section 4, pp. 327–359; Social Security Administration, *Social Insurance Programs,* July 1997, http://www.ssa.gov/statistics/sspus/unemploy.pdf; Executive Office of the President, *Budget of the United States Government, Fiscal Year 1999,* p. 224.

57. W. Corson and M. Dynarski, *A Study of Unemployment Insurance Recipients and Exhaustees: Findings from a National Survey,* Occasional Paper 90-3 (Washington, DC: U.S. Department of Labor) cited in Committee on Ways and Means, *1998 Green Book,* pp. 342–343.

58. For elaboration of the effects of social welfare programs on labor see Francis Fox Piven and Richard Cloward, *The New Class War* (New York: Pantheon Books, 1982).

59. Unemployment figures can be found at the U.S. Department of Labor web site at http://stats.bls.gov/webapps/legacy/cpsatab4.htm.

60. See, for example, *Counting All the Jobless: Problems with the Official Unemployment Rate,* Hearing before a Subcommittee of the Committee on Government Operations, House of Representatives, 99th Congress, second session, March 20, 1986.

61. Bureau of Labor Statistics, *BLS Handbook of Methods,* Bulletin 2490 (Washington, DC: U.S. Government Printing Office, April 1997), see Chapter 1.

62. U.S. Department of Labor, Bureau of Labor Statistics, *Employment and Earnings,* Vol. 41 (Washington, DC: U.S. Government Printing Office, March 1994), p. 5.

63. Bureau of Labor Statistics, *The Employment Situation: November 1997* (Washington, DC: U.S. Department of Labor, December 5, 1997), http://stats.bls.gov/news.release/empsit.nws.htm.

64. See Sharon Cohany, Anne E. Polivka, and Jennifer M. Rothgeb, "Revisions in the Current Population Survey Effective January 1994," *Employment and Earnings,* Vol. 41 (Washington, DC: U.S. Government Printing Office, February 1994), pp. 13–35.

65. Bureau of Labor Statistics, *The Employment Situation: November 1997.*

66. Most of the remainder of this paragraph relies on "U.S. Job Count Is Revamped," *Austin American-Statesman,* January 14, 1993, p. B1.

67. Earl Golz, "Government Alters Unemployment Data Collection Method," *Austin American-Statesman,* February 5, 1994, p. F1.

68. Robert D. Hershey, Jr., "U.S. Does Poor Job of Counting Jobless," *Austin American-Statesman,* November 17, 1993, pp. A1, 14.

69. Charles Leroux and Stephen Franklin, "Labor Figures Don't Report Entire Unemployment Story," *Austin American-Statesman,* November 14, 1991, p. A21.

70. U.S. Bureau of the Census, *Statistical Abstract of the United States, 1992* (Washington, DC: U.S. Government Printing Office, 1992), p. 401.

71. Kenneth W. Clarkson and Roger E. Meiners, "Government Statistics as a Guide to Economic Policy: Food Stamps and the Spurious Increase in the Unemployment Rates," *Policy Review,* Vol. 1, 1977, pp. 27–51.

72. Unemployment figures for subgroups of the population are available from the Bureau of Labor Statistics at http://146.142.4.24/cgi-bin/surveymost?lf.

73. Executive Office of the President, Office of Management and Budget, *Management of the United States Government, Fiscal Year 1990,* Part 2 (Washington, DC: U.S. Government Printing Office, 1989), p. 4.

74. See, for example, Karen Tumulty, "House Vote Blocks Measure Extending Benefits for Jobless," *Austin American-Statesman,* November 15, 1993, p. A21.

75. Donald J. Pease and William F. Clinger, Jr., "Reform Unemployment Insurance," *Wall Street Journal,* January 29, 1985, p. 26.

76. Scott S. Greenberger, "Panel Backs State Unemployment Revisions," *Austin American-Statesman,* October 15, 1998, p. D2.

77. Edward D. Berkowitz, *Disabled Policy: America's Programs for the Handicapped* (Cambridge, England: Cambridge University Press, 1987), p. 15. Reprinted with the Permission of Cambridge University Press.

78. Committee on Ways and Means, *1996 Green Book,* p. 945.

79. U.S. Department of Health and Human Services, Social Security Administration, *Social Security Handbook 1984,* 8th ed., SSA Publication No. 05-10135 (Washington, DC: U.S. Government Printing Office, July 1984), p. 387.

80. Berkowitz, *Disabled Policy,* pp. 15 & 26.

81. Ibid., p. 26.

82. Committee on Ways and Means, *1998 Green Book,* p. 1022.

83. Berkowitz, *Disabled Policy,* p. 28.

84. Ibid., p. 39.

85. The remainder of this paragraph relies on Committee on Ways and Means, *1993 Green Book,* p. 1702; also see Committee on Ways and Means, U.S. House of Representatives, *Overview of Entitlement Programs: 1994 Green Book* (Washington, DC: U.S. Government Printing Office, 1994), p. 847.

86. Committee on Ways and Means, *1998 Green Book,* p. 1022.

87. Berkowitz, *Disabled Policy,* pp. 15–16.

88. The remainder of this section relies on Committee on Ways and Means, *1996 Green Book,* pp. 945–951; Committee on Ways on Means, *1998 Green Book,* pp. 1020–1027.

89. For additional information on workers' compensation, see Social Security Administration, *Social Insurance Programs,* July 1997, http://www.ssa.gov/statistics/sspus/workcomp.pdf.

CHAPTER

Helping the "Deserving Poor": Aged, Blind, and Disabled

Those who are aged or disabled are among the groups considered the "deserving poor"—groups that society generally feels morally and ethically obliged to aid. Four types of social policy provisions provide this assistance:

1. Social Security disability and retirement benefits for those with sufficient work histories (see Chapter 4)
2. Public assistance for those with little or no income whose conditions prevent them from pursuing gainful employment
3. Social service programs, since virtually all people who are disabled or aged can benefit from a wide range of habilitative, rehabilitative, or social services
4. Civil rights legislation aimed at reducing discrimination in employment, education, and housing, and at providing greater access to public and private facilities

PUBLIC ASSISTANCE FOR THE DESERVING POOR

Prior to the Social Security Act of 1935, many states had public assistance programs to assist the elderly poor. Massachusetts was among the first to appoint a commission to study the problems of the elderly.[1] In 1914 Arizona passed a law establishing a pension program for the aged,[2] and in 1915, the territory of Alaska did the same.[3] By 1935 thirty states already had old-age assistance programs. Eligibility requirements for these state programs were stringent. In addition to financial destitution, recipients generally had to be at least 65 years old, be United States citizens, and meet residency requirements in the location where they applied for benefits. In cases where relatives were capable of supporting an elderly family member, benefits were often denied.

Elderly participants usually had to agree that any assets they had left at the time of their death would be assigned to the state.

People who were blind were also considered "deserving." In fact, eligibility requirements were often more lenient in state pension laws for these individuals than they were for the elderly. By 1935, twenty-seven states had pension programs for people who were blind.[4] Individuals with other disabling conditions were also of concern, but early in the 1900s, policies to assist them varied considerably among states, and many states had no programs at all.

When the original Social Security Act was passed, its most far-reaching provision was the Social Security insurance program for retired workers. Not until 1956 were disabled workers included under social insurance, since many officials had preferred to aid them using public assistance programs.[5] Following the precedent established by many states, the original Social Security Act included three public assistance programs: Aid to Dependent Children (ADC), Old Age Assistance (OAA), and Aid to the Blind (AB). Disability policy continued to lag behind, but in 1950 Aid to the Permanently and Totally Disabled (APTD) was added. OAA, AB, and APTD were called the **adult categorical public assistance programs.**

Although these public assistance programs were federally authorized, each state could decide whether to participate. All states eventually adopted OAA and AB, but several states chose not to participate in APTD. The federal government shared costs with the states and set minimum requirements for participation. Elderly people had to be at least 65 years old to receive federal aid. Those who were blind or otherwise disabled had to be at least 18 years old. The states had primary administrative responsibility and retained a good deal of discretion in determining eligibility requirements (definitions of disability and blindness, terms of residency, and income and asset limitations) and the amount of payments.

State administration of the OAA, AB, and APTD programs had serious ramifications for some beneficiaries. Those who moved to another state might have been denied benefits because they did not meet eligibility requirements in their new state of residence or because they were required to re-establish residency. Benefits were often meager and varied drastically by state. In the OAA program in 1964, West Virginia paid an average monthly benefit of $50, while Wisconsin paid $111.[6] Beneficiaries from poorer states generally received less because their states had less money to operate the program; other states had a tradition of limiting public assistance.

SSI: "Federalizing" Public Assistance

When President Nixon took office in 1972 he wanted to clean up the "welfare mess." Nixon's welfare reform was to provide a minimum income to poor Americans that would replace the AFDC, OAA, AB, and APTD programs and bring an end to the uneven treatment of welfare recipients from state to state. His **guaranteed annual income** proposal, known as the Family Assistance Plan (FAP), was the target of controversy in Congress. Liberals considered it too stingy. Conservatives believed that the reforms provided too much in welfare benefits and would reduce the incentive to work. Senator Daniel P. Moynihan (D-New York), then an adviser to President Nixon and supporter of the FAP, wrote in his book *The Politics of a Guaranteed Annual Income* about the controversy that focused primarily on reform of the AFDC program.[7] AFDC was not reformed, but in the midst of the controversy, the OAA, AB, and APTD programs underwent substantial revisions that were almost unnoticed.[8]

The major change Congress enacted in 1972 was to "federalize" the adult categorical assistance programs under a new program called Supplemental Security Income (SSI), Title XVI of the Social Security Act. Federalizing meant that Congress largely took the programs out of the hands of the states. Beginning in 1974, the states relinquished responsibility for determining basic eligibility requirements and minimum payment levels, and they also turned administration of most aspects of the programs to the federal government. These changes represented the most sweeping reform of the adult categorical assistance programs since APTD was added in 1950. SSI replaced the OAA, AB, and APTD programs by establishing a minimum income for recipients and by standardizing eligibility requirements across all states. Under the change to SSI, no state could pay beneficiaries less than they had previously received, and today most states supplement the minimum payment to at least some recipients.*

How SSI Works

SSI is administered by the Social Security Administration, and since its name sounds like the Social Security program, some people think that these programs are the same. SSI, however, remains a means-tested public assistance program; it is not a social insurance program, as is Social Security. Individuals may receive SSI benefits in addition to Social Security retirement or disability benefits if their income from Social Security and other sources and their assets do not exceed SSI eligibility criteria. Despite its reputation as a guaranteed income for those who cannot earn it themselves, SSI is a "program of last resort"; that is, applicants must claim all other benefits to which they are entitled before they can qualify for SSI.[9] As its name implies, SSI is intended to supplement other income. It is not possible to describe all the details of the SSI program in a few pages, but the following paragraphs provide the basic idea.[10]

U.S. citizens and some immigrants residing legally in the U.S. may qualify for SSI. The minimum age to qualify for SSI to the aged is still 65. Adults (those 18 years or older) are considered disabled if they cannot work because of a "medically determined physical or mental impairment expected to result in death or that has lasted or can be expected to last for a continuous period of at least 12 months." Individuals are considered blind if they have no better than 20/200 vision or tunnel vision of 20 degrees or less in the better eye with a corrective lens. A less stringent definition of visual impairment may be used in the portion of the program for people with disabilities. Children whose disability is similar in severity to that of an adult with the same condition qualify in order to assist their families or others in caring for them.

*Those that pay no supplements are Arkansas, Georgia, Kansas, Mississippi, Tennessee, Texas, West Virginia, and the Northern Mariana Islands.

Residents of public institutions like mental hospitals, nursing homes, or prisons generally cannot receive SSI, but there are exceptions. For example, those residing in institutions for the primary purpose of acquiring vocational or educational training that can help them secure employment may qualify for SSI. Others may qualify if they are living in public facilities with no more than 16 residents, and those in public emergency shelters for homeless people may qualify temporarily. Patients in public medical treatment facilities receive only a $30 monthly SSI payment if Medicaid pays more than half the costs of their care unless the state chooses to offer more.

SSI eligibility requirements restrict the assets and income of recipients. Since 1989 an individual's **countable resources** cannot exceed $2,000 and a couple's cannot exceed $3,000. Countable resources include such items as some types of real estate, savings accounts, and some personal belongings. Several types of resources are not included in determining eligibility. For example, the individual's home and normal household goods are not counted, and allowances are made for the value of a car.

Countable income must also be within certain limits. Since some states supplement payments, the amount of income one may have depends on the state. In 1999, in states with no supplements, an individual who was not working generally could not have more than $520 in monthly income, and couples could not have more than $771. These figures are just $20 more than the federal minimum monthly SSI payment of $500 for an individual and $751 for a couple. For the 37 percent of recipients living independently who receive a state supplement, this adds from $2 to $362 a month.[11] Those who cannot live independently may receive more. In the case of children, their parents' income is usually "deemed" (considered in determining benefits). Allowances are made for the parents' work expenses and the family's living expenses. Countable income includes most earnings from work, Social Security payments, other cash benefits, and interest income. It does not include the value of food stamps or most food, clothing, and shelter provided by nonprofit organizations, but some noncash assistance does count.

Income that is not counted (disregarded) in calculating benefits generally includes the first $20 a month from any source. In order to encourage employment, the first $65 of income from work, plus half of all additional earnings is also disregarded until such point as the individual's countable income exceeds eligibility limits. Certain work- or disability-related expenses for people who are blind or otherwise disabled may also be disregarded in determining payments. These disregards are more generous for those who are blind. Scholarships and grants used for educational expenses are generally disregarded. Recipients who are blind or disabled are also allowed trial work periods while still receiving benefits so they can determine if working is feasible. In 1998, individuals who were working and had no unearned income were eligible for federal SSI payments if their income was no more than $1,073 monthly; for couples the figure was $1,567. There is considerable interest in getting former workers who are now receiving disability payments back to work. Illustration 5-1 shows what happens to an SSI recipient's income when she tries to work.

If an SSI recipient lives in the home of someone who is contributing to his or her support, the SSI payment is reduced by one-third. However, SSI recipients who pay

ILLUSTRATION 5-1

Example of What Happens When You Are Disabled and Work Under SSI

Denni Hunt receives an SSI payment of $500 each month and has Medicaid coverage. This is her only income. She was offered a job in a local fast food restaurant and contacted Social Security to see how this would affect her SSI payment. She was told that Social Security would not count the first $85 of earnings if she had no other income [$20 is automatically disregarded and another $65 is disregarded if the individual works].

Only half of the earnings over $85 would be counted against the SSI payment. Here is how her SSI payment would be affected:

Gross monthly earnings	$215
Subtract the $85 earnings deduction	– 85
	$130
Divide by 2 to get earnings we count	÷ 2
	$ 65
Subtract earnings we count from SSI payment	$500
	– 65
New SSI payment	$435
Add monthly earnings	+ 215
Total income	$650

Note that before she started working, Denni's total income was her SSI check of $500. Now that she's working, she has that extra income in addition to her SSI check ($435), so her total income is $650, even though her SSI payment is slightly reduced.

Denni's pay increased to $367 a month after 18 months. She purchased an electric wheelchair, which cost $52 a month, to help her move better at work. Here's how the work expense deduction helps her:

Gross monthly earnings	$367
Subtract the $85 earnings deduction	– 85
	$282
Subtract work expenses	– 52
	$230
Divide by 2 to get earnings we count	÷ 2
	$115
Subtract earnings we count from SSI payment	$500
	–115
New SSI payment	$385
Add monthly earnings	+ 367
Total income	$752

So, even though her earnings went up by $152 (from $215 to $367), her SSI payment was reduced by only $50 (from $435 to $385) because of the work expense deduction. And her total income now is $752, substantially more than the $500 she had before she started working.

Denni decided that she wanted to get a college degree. Her sister helped her write a PASS which described her plans to work and save money for school. [A PASS is a Plan for Achieving Self-Sufficiency, permitted under SSI, which allows an individual to save a specified amount of money toward a goal such as attending school or starting a business. The PASS

continued

ILLUSTRATION 5-1 *(continued)*

is a formal agreement. The money saved is disregarded in calculating the SSI benefit.] Under the plan, she wanted to save $75 each month for school. Here's how the PASS helps her:

Gross monthly earnings	$367
Subtract the $85 earnings deduction	- 85
	$282
Subtract work expenses	- 52
	$230
Divide by 2 to get earnings we count	÷ 2
	$115
Subtract PASS	- 75
	$ 40

Subtract earnings we count from SSI payment	$500
	- 40
New SSI payment	$460
Add monthly earnings	+ 367
Total income (SSI plus earnings)	$827

Even though her earnings continue as high as they were in the previous example, her SSI checks are increased because we don't have to count the income she is setting aside to go to school. Her total income is now $827 monthly ($367 in earnings plus $460 in SSI).

Source: Social Security Administration, *Social Security: Working While Disabled . . . How We Can Help,* SSA Publication No. 05-10095, January 1997, updated to reflect 1999 SSI payment amount.

their full share of expenses may receive the entire payment. Monthly payments are adjusted each year to keep pace with the cost of living using the same method as for the Social Security insurance programs (see Chapter 4).

Sometimes a person qualifies for benefits under more than one SSI component. For example, an aged person may also be disabled. Since there are additional income exclusions for recipients with disabilities, it may be more advantageous for the individual to qualify as disabled rather than aged. Beneficiaries cannot receive SSI and TANF benefits simultaneously; when an individual qualifies for both programs, a determination should be made as to which provides the greatest benefits. Most SSI recipients are eligible for Medicaid. SSI cases are generally reviewed at least every three years in order to determine if beneficiaries are still eligible. As in other federally funded welfare programs, attempts are made to reduce fraud and error by obtaining income and earnings information from the IRS and the Social Security Administration.

Disability Determination

Those with disabilities are the largest number of SSI recipients. To people unfamiliar with SSI, it may seem like deciding whether or not someone is disabled is a straightforward process, but in many situations it is far from the truth. Once SSI's income and assets tests are met, the more difficult part is deciding whether he or she meets the definition of disabled.[12] The process of **disability determination** is the same in the Social Security Disability Insurance (SSDI) and the SSI programs. It includes five sequential steps. In step 1, applicants currently earning more than $500 per month in gainful employment over and above disability-related work expenses are generally disqualified, even though earned income limits once one is in the program are higher than this. The figure for those who are blind is higher ($1,110 in 1999). Applicants who are not employed or are earning less proceed to step 2 to determine if their condition is "not severe" (does not interfere with work). If it is not, they are disqualified; if it is severe, the applicant moves on to step 3. In this step, a determination is made as to whether the individual's condition meets the criteria described in a document called the *Listing of Impairments* or is of equal severity to these criteria and is expected to last at least 12 months. Cases that do are approved for SSI. Cases that do not are reviewed further in step 4 to determine if the applicant can perform the work he or she did previously. If the determination is that the individual can, the case is denied. If the individual cannot, step 5 is for the government to show whether the applicant can perform any "substantial gainful" work in the national labor force. The applicant's disability, age, education, work history, and skills are considered. Those unable to perform any work are awarded payments, while others are denied. SSI recipients with disabilities may be required to accept vocational rehabilitation services. Cases are reviewed periodically to ensure that the individual continues to qualify for benefits. Reviews are more frequent when the individual's condition is expected to improve. The first review may be as soon as 6 to 18 months after the onset of disability. Following the hew and cry that arose after efforts to trim the welfare rolls during the Reagan years, criteria were established to help ensure that recipients would not be cut from the SSI program unless their medical condition improved or they returned to "substantial work." The Social Security Administration has greatly increased the number of disability reviews it conducts each year.

A disability determination often takes months, not only because medical evidence must be obtained and reviewed, but because of the backlog of cases. In 1996 there were 700,000 pending SSI and SSDI cases.[13] But when an applicant is obviously disabled and in financial need, SSI benefits may be issued prior to a formal decision.

Many SSDI and SSI claims are initially denied. Those who wish to contest a denial or other decisions have recourse to four levels of appeals, culminating with the U.S. district court. Appeals are made frequently. As a result, or perhaps a cause of this litigation, some lawyers specialize and advertise their services in this area. Since many decisions are reversed on appeal, those who believe they are disabled may have to be persistent and patient. In 1997 the average processing time for disability claims appeals was 398 days.[14] President Clinton has promised to reduce the time to 284 days.

SSI Recipients, Payments, and Costs

People who are blind comprise the smallest group of SSI recipients. The number of recipients in this component of the program has been relatively stable over the years due to advances in the prevention and treatment of blindness and to larger numbers of those who are self-supporting. As seen in Table 5-1, about 80,000 people currently receive benefits under this part of the program.

Participation by aged recipients has declined (see Table 5-1), especially considering the rate of growth of older Americans in the general population. In 1950 about 2.8 million people received old-age assistance. Current participation is less than half this number.[15] Declining participation is primarily due to the number of elderly now eligible for Social Security insurance benefits and to corresponding reductions in poverty among the older population. When SSI was enacted, however, it was anticipated that many more elderly would qualify for assistance. Special outreach efforts did help to boost participation, but roughly one-third of poor elderly people do not participate. One group of pollsters asked a sample of elderly people who were poor why they had not applied for SSI. "Twenty percent said they had never heard of SSI. Another 21 percent said they believed they were not eligible. Fourteen percent said they did not need SSI; 6 percent were not willing to accept welfare; and 3 percent said they did not want to deal with the government."[16] The application process may also present difficulties. Nearly three-quarters of older recipients are women, who have both longer life spans and lower incomes than men.

Most SSI growth is the result of large increases in the number of recipients with disabilities. When SSI began, a standard definition of disability was adopted that helped many new recipients join the rolls. More recent growth can be explained by

TABLE 5-1

Number of Adult Public Assistance and SSI Program Recipients for Selected Years (in thousands)

Year	Aged	Blind	Disabled	Total
1940	2,070	73	a	2,143
1950	2,786	97	69	2,952
1960	2,305	107	369	2,781
1970	2,082	81	935	3,098
1980	1,838	79	2,276	4,193
1990	1,484	84	3,320	4,888
1998[b]	1,332	80	5,154	6,566

Sources: U.S. Bureau of the Census, *Historical Statistics of the United States, Colonial Times to 1970* (Washington, DC: U.S. Government Printing Office, 1975), p. 356; Social Security Bulletin, *Annual Statistical Supplement, 1996,* Table 7.A3; Social Security Administration web site at ftp://ftp.ssa.gov/pub/statistics/2a2.

[a]Program did not begin until 1950.

[b]Figures for December 1998.

factors such as laws, regulations, and court decisions that have expanded eligibility; the small number of beneficiaries who leave the rolls to work; and baby boomers reaching the age at which disabilities are increasingly likely.[17] The number of disabled recipients grew from about 369,000 in 1960 to about 5.2 million in 1998. Approximately 28 percent of adult recipients aged 18 to 64 qualify due to mental retardation and 30 percent because of psychiatric disorders; the remainder have a wide range of physical diseases and disorders.[18] Children with disabilities are a fast-growing segment of the program, and the largest group (44 percent) qualify due to mental retardation.[19] Some of this increase is likely the result of prenatal alcohol, drug, and HIV exposure and to premature babies saved through modern technology.[20] More boys than girls receive assistance, and 45 percent of the children are nonwhite.[21]

Average SSI payments to recipients have increased but remain modest. In 1998, elderly recipients received an average of about $277 a month (many also receive some income from Social Security). Beneficiaries who are blind received payments averaging about $390 monthly, and those with other disabilities averaged about $380 monthly (see Table 5-2). In 1997, federal SSI payments constituted about 77 percent of the poverty level for individuals and about 92 percent for couples.[22] When the value of Social Security and food stamp benefits are added, the percentages increase to about 88 percent for individuals and 104 percent for couples.

Under SSI for the aged, costs of payments rose from $2.7 billion in 1980 to about $4.5 billion in 1996 (see Table 5-3). The smaller number of SSI recipients who are blind

TABLE 5-2

Average Monthly Payments for the Adult Public Assistance and SSI Programs for Selected Years

Year	Aged	Blind	Disabled
1940	$ 20.25	$ 25.35	a
1950	43.05	46.00	$ 44.10
1960	58.90	67.45	56.15
1970	77.65	104.35	97.65
1980	131.75	215.70	200.06
1990	218.81	345.17	339.43
1998[b]	277.45	390.19	380.46

Sources: U.S. Bureau of the Census, *Historical Statistics of the United States, Colonial Times to 1970* (Washington, DC: U.S. Government Printing Office, 1975), p. 356; Social Security Bulletin, *Annual Statistical Supplement, 1996,* Table 7.A5; Social Security Administration web site at ftp://ftp.ssa.gov/pub/statistics/2a2.

[a]Program did not begin until 1950.

[b]Figures for December 1998.

TABLE 5-3

Total Federal and State Adult Public Assistance and SSI Payments for Selected Years (in millions of dollars)

Year	Aged	Blind	Disabled	Total
1940	$ 473	$ 22	a	$ 495
1950	1,485	53	$ 8	1,546
1960	1,922	83	287	2,303
1970	1,866	98	1,000	2,964
1980	2,734	190	5,014	7,941
1990	3,736	334	12,521	16,599
1996	4,507	372	23,906	28,792

Sources: U.S. Bureau of the Census, *Historical Statistics of the United States, Colonial Times to 1970* (Washington, DC: U.S. Government Printing Office, 1975), p. 356; Social Security Administration, *Social Security Bulletin, Annual Statistical Supplement, 1997,* Table 7.A4.

[a]Program did not begin until 1950.

means that total payments in this component remain modest; they were $190 million in 1980 and $372 million in 1996. Given the increases in the number of recipients with other disabilities, the most dramatic growth in expenditures has been in this program component. Costs were $5 billion in 1980 and nearly $24 billion in 1996.

SSI Hot Spots

Several contentious issues have arisen in the SSI programs. One concern was the growing percent of SSI recipients who were not citizens. In addition, their SSI benefits were often higher than those of citizens because many had not worked long enough in the U.S. to qualify for any Social Security benefits.[23] As part of the broad package of welfare reforms that Congress passed in 1996, most immigrants legally residing in the U.S. were made ineligible for benefits even if they were already receiving SSI (undocumented immigrants have never been eligible). Exceptions were made for some categories of immigrants such as refugees and asylees (who had fled their countries of origin for political reasons). Also exempt were those who had worked in the U.S. and paid Social Security taxes for 10 years. There were anecdotal reports of elderly immigrants becoming suicidal after learning that they would no longer be entitled to assistance. Cutting immigrants from the program was one of the changes that President Clinton most opposed.

The battle over immigrants in the SSI program was fought again in 1997. The *Congressional Quarterly* called it "the most protracted struggle" in the debates over what should be changed in the 1996 welfare overhaul.[24] Perhaps better economic times helped to quell the backlash. This time, the decision was to allow those who were in the United States as of August 22, 1996 (the day the welfare reform bill was signed) to receive benefits regardless of when they became disabled, even though House Republicans had urged that benefits be available only to those already disabled as of that date. In cases of immigrants with sponsors, the sponsor's income is considered in determining the immigrant's eligibility for several years after entry into the country. The specifics of an applicant's immigrant status are carefully considered to make sure that they fall within the definitional boundaries. In some cases, eligibility for refugees and asylees is restricted to 7 years unless the individual becomes a citizen.

Most SSI hot spots concern people with disabilities other than blindness. A primary example is those with alcoholism and drug addiction. These individuals were required to use a third party (called a "representative payee") to receive their benefits since they are generally considered unable to manage their own money, and they were supposed to be enrolled in treatment programs. Apparently the treatment provision was not well monitored, and resentments toward this group of recipients grew. In addition to the feeling that most could work if they would stop using alcohol or drugs, some believed "that SSI checks were fueling addiction."[25] In 1994 benefits to alcoholics and drug addicts were limited to three years. Then, in 1996 as part of the Republican Contract with America, individuals disabled due to alcohol or drug use were made ineligible for SSI and SSDI. They were also cut from Medicare and Medicaid if their eligibility for these programs was due to their receiving disability payments for alcoholism or drug addiction. If individuals with alcoholism or drug addiction have another disability, they may still qualify for SSI, but they must use a representative payee if they are not capable of managing their benefits and be encouraged to participate in chemical dependency treatment. About half of former SSI recipients with alcohol and drug disabilities are no longer receiving benefits.[26]

Another group that drew the ire of welfare reformers was a less likely target—children. In 1990 the U.S. Supreme Court issued a decision in *Sullivan v. Zebley*.[27] Prior to this decision, children who did not meet the criteria in the Listing of Impairments were disqualified, and some serious childhood conditions were missing from the list. The Zebley decision required that children be afforded the additional functional tests given to adult applicants. According to this ruling, a child was considered impaired if he or she was substantially unable to function as children of the same age are generally expected to do (i.e., unable to engage in "age-appropriate" activities). When the ruling came down, the Social Security Administration had to try locating and reassessing 452,000 children denied benefits as far back as 1980.[28]

Following *Zebley*, the number of children enrolled in SSI more than doubled.[29] But the major increase was due to an expanded category of mental disorders, including mental retardation and attention deficit hyperactivity disorder. Concern was that these children might remain on the rolls throughout their lifetimes. Later, reports emerged of parents coaching children to seem more impaired than they were in an effort to get them on SSI. It was difficult to prove this, but some government-sponsored studies recommended "strengthened" definitions of disability and eligibility criteria. Congress decided to change the definition of disability for children, saying that children must have "marked and severe functional limitations" to qualify. Congress did not write the specifics of the new definition of children's disabilities, allowing Clinton administration staff to craft it. Today, the functional test for children has been eliminated. Children must again meet criteria in the *Listing of Impairments* or have disabilities equal to them.

Groups such as the National Association of Social Workers felt that the Social Security Administration was going too far in weeding out children from the program, particularly with regard to behavioral and mental disabilities.[30] The popular press described families in peril due to the decision,[31] and it publicized figures showing that disqualification rates in some states were much higher than in other states.[32] By late 1997, responding to claims that it had been too zealous in pruning children from rolls, the Social Security Administration announced that it would reconsider its decision in thousands of cases.[33] Earlier in the year, Medicaid benefits were reinstated for children who no longer qualified due to changes in SSI eligibility criteria. Still apparently concerned with the number of children receiving SSI, bills have been introduced to further tighten the definition of childhood disability.

Disability determination and review are also a concern with regard to disabled adults in the program. One GAO report ". . . supports SSA's contention that that there is little chance that a large proportion of beneficiaries will show enough medical improvement to no longer be considered disabled," and suggests that "if SSA is to decrease long-term reliance on these [SSI and SSDI] programs . . . it will need to rely less on assessing medical improvement and more on return-to-work programs."[34]

As recently as 1992, the SSI Modernization Project suggested modifying SSI by increasing benefits and speeding up the disability determination process.[35] About $8 million was awarded to test new outreach methods and to make the application process easier. There are still special efforts to reach groups such as those who are homeless or have AIDS to compensate for barriers to SSI participation. As the decade progressed, however, efforts focused on tightening eligibility. Now, in better economic times, the Clinton administration has proposed raising the SSI gainful employment limit from $500 to $700 per month and allowing those who work to retain their Medicaid benefits.

REHABILITATIVE SERVICES FOR INDIVIDUALS WITH DISABILITIES

Financial assistance through Social Security and SSI can be important resources for elderly people and people with disabilities. Other forms of assistance may also be important. For example, even people with severe mental retardation can benefit from programs of physical and mental stimulation. For those with other disabilities, physical therapy, prosthetic devices, or other services may be needed to carry out day-today activities. Others need special educational programs and learning devices. Still others require vocational education and reeducation.

The Vocational Rehabilitation Program

The first institutions for care of people with disabilities in the United States were established in the early nineteenth century. Training and education programs to assist those living in the community with potential for employment did not emerge until the twentieth century.[36] One of the first of these educational programs began in Massachusetts in 1916.[37] In 1920 Congress passed the Vocational Rehabilitation Act (also called the Smith-Fess Act) to assist vocationally disabled civilians and disabled veterans returning from World War I by providing funds through a federal–state matching formula. The federal and state governments shared costs of the Vocational Rehabilitation (VR) program on a fifty–fifty basis. The program was appealing from conservative and economic viewpoints because rehabilitation is generally less costly than long-term care and income maintenance payments. In fact,

> *People do not regard vocational rehabilitation as a welfare program, and that is one reason for its success. Vocational rehabilitation officials portray rehabilitation as the antithesis of welfare. Where welfare fosters dependence, rehabilitation promotes independence. Welfare represents a net cost to society; vocational rehabilitation is an investment in society's future.*[38]

As the federal government's Rehabilitation Services Administration says, the state VR agencies "assist persons served to become tax-paying citizens and to reduce their reliance on entitlement programs."[39] Although originally intended for those with physical disabilities, in 1943 those with mental illness and mental retardation were included in the VR program, and in the 1960s those with socially handicapping conditions, including adult and juvenile offenders, were included.[40]

Today the federal government provides the majority of funding for VR programs, but each state operates its own program according to federal guidelines and also supplements federal funding. An individual who applies for VR services is evaluated by a doctor or other experts to determine whether a disability exists. Those who have a reasonable chance of becoming employed or re-employed qualify for services.

Each applicant accepted for services is assigned a VR counselor who works with the consumer (client) in developing an individualized written rehabilitation plan, which may include guidance, medical services, education, financial assistance, and job placement services. Although this sounds like a rational way to optimize services, available funds cannot be stretched to meet all the needs of all those who are eligible. Consumers' needs must be prioritized. In addition, because each state administers its own program, people with the same or similar disabilities may receive different types and amounts of services depending on the state in which they live.

There are other provisions for employment of people with disabilities The state employment offices have a legal responsibility to assist those with disabilities. Individuals may also qualify under the Job Training Partnership Act (see Chapter 9) or other programs.

Creaming

In its earlier days critics charged the Vocational Rehabilitation program with a practice called **creaming.** Creaming means accepting applicants who can achieve rehabilitation most easily. Although the goal of the VR program is rehabilitation, it seems that most of the program's early clients were young, white males whose disabilities were neither chronic nor severe.[41]

> *In 1938 the federal [vocational rehabilitation] office captured the policy that lay behind the selection of the vocational rehabilitation case load when it told the states that eligibility does not necessarily imply feasibility. Anyone over 18 was technically eligible for rehabilitation, but such factors as advanced age, extreme disability, bad attitude of mind, or low social status limited feasibility.*[42]

This did not set well with potential consumers, and pressure developed to serve those with more severe disabilities.[43] This was realized with the 1973 amendments to the Vocational Rehabilitation Act. Clients are also supposed to have discretion in choosing services and employment goals. However, the rehabilitation counselor retains considerable control of the process since each works with a limited budget and pressure remains to close cases successfully. In most cases, a client must be employed for ninety consecutive days in order for the counselor to claim a successful case closure.

VR and other employment programs for those with disabilities have not achieved all their intended successes. With about 200,000 individuals placed in jobs each year, they "have never made a noticeable impact on the employment rate nationwide."[44] The number of new applications processed by state VR agencies has actually declined over the years. In 1975, 800,000 applications were processed. In 1997, the figure was 617,000.[45] After dwindling, the percent of applicants accepted into the program increased to 79 percent in 1997. In 1975, a total of 1.4 million clients were served by state VR agencies. Fewer than 1 million were served during the 1980s and early 1990s. In 1997, the number served grew again to nearly 1.3 million. Nearly 80 percent of clients now have severe disabilities. About 61 percent of clients are successfully rehabilitated. The rehabilitation rate is similar for clients with severe disabilities. Federal and state funding for the VR program was $1.1 billion in 1980, $1.9 billion in 1990, and $3 billion in 1997.

Several reasons for the decline in the numbers of consumers served have been suggested, including funding limitations and the shift from consumers with less severe to more severe disabilities.[46] VR has never achieved the status of an entitlement program. Not everyone who wants or needs assistance may be served, and for those who are served, counselors may not be able to procure all the funds and services needed.

Although VR is a modest effort compared to the public assistance and social insurance programs for people with disabilities, it remains the nation's largest rehabilitation program.

THE ERA OF CIVIL RIGHTS FOR PEOPLE WITH DISABILITIES

If vocational rehabilitation constitutes one wave of a more enlightened public response to disability, and income maintenance through public assistance and social insurance programs a second, then the third and most recent wave is surely civil rights reform.[47]

> *The disability rights perspective views people with disabilities as a minority group that has been subject to discrimination and unfair treatment—in legal terms, a class of people. It stands in contrast to a charitable perspective which views people with disabilities as unfortunate and deserving of pity and care. Likewise, it stands in contrast to a medical model, which views people with disabilities as needing to be "cured." It also stands in contrast to a rehabilitation perspective, which views people with disabilities as needing experts and professionals who can provide services to enhance the functioning of the individual.*[48]

The various aspects of the disability rights movement are considered in this section.

From Deinstitutionalization to Normalization and Inclusion

One of the first responses of modern society to those with severe physical and mental disabilities was "indoor" relief—the "warehousing" of these individuals in large institutions. Treatment in these places was frequently deplorable. Even with efforts to see that patients or residents had some decent level of care, beliefs mounted that one should not be subjected to a life in an institution. The movement toward **deinstitutionalization** eventually gained judicial backing when, in 1972, the U.S. Supreme Court ruled in the case of *Wyatt v. Stickney* that "No persons shall be admitted to the institution unless prior determination shall have been made that residence in the institution is the least restrictive habilitation setting."[49] Subsequent court decisions have reaffirmed this right, such as *City of Cleburne, Texas v. Cleburne Living Center* in 1985, which supported the rights of people with mental retardation to reside in the community. Today the goal of deinstitutionalization has been taken further to include the desire for **normalization** and **independent living.**

The concept of normalization apparently emerged in Scandinavia, particularly in Denmark as part of its 1959 Mental Retardation Act.[50] It was adopted in other countries and has been broadened to include those with other disabilities. Normalization means that regardless of the severity of people's disabilities, they should have the opportunity to live like other citizens.[51] Their homes should be located in regular residential communities and resemble other homes in the community, and they should have opportunities for shopping, recreation, and other everyday activities.[52] They should also have the right to occupy the same social roles—spouses, parents, workers, etc.—as others.[53]

Although it seems logical from humanistic, cost savings, and civil rights perspectives, people with disabilities continue to face obstacles to normalization. These obstacles include negative attitudes from the general public, employers, and even human service professionals who underestimate their abilities; architectural and other barriers that continue to prohibit or restrict the use of buildings; and public transportation and other facilities and programs that still provide minimal assistance and foster dependence rather than promote integration.[54] You might think that people with mental retardation or other disabilities would have won the right to live wherever they choose a long time ago, but they (and those who serve them) continue to be thwarted in their efforts to establish community residences. Neighborhood residents frequently cite deed restrictions, declining property values, and safety issues as reasons for "not in my backyard." A different view "is that constitutionally, these people have a right to live anywhere they want."[55]

The Independent Living Movement

Along with deinstitutionalization and normalization has come the movement for independent living. An important part of this movement are **independent living centers** (ILCs), which are "private non-profit self-help organization[s] that provide a range of basic services that help people with disabilities live independently in the community."[56] Advancements in educational techniques, technology, and medicine have made it possible for many more people to live independently. Equally important is that people with disabilities have begun to force the issue of their civil rights. ILCs developed through local efforts and represent the empowerment of those with disabilities via their own self-help movement. A prototype is the Center for Independent Living in Berkeley, California. The centers break with the professional model of care in that those with disabilities are in charge. They teach others with disabilities how to get all the services to which they are entitled such as social insurance, public assistance, rehabilitation, education, attendant care (also called personal assistance services), and other services that will allow them to live as independently as they can and wish. Illustration 5-2, from an outspoken publication called *The Disability Rag*, now *The Ragged Edge*, shows just how important attendant care services are. The group called ADAPT—American Disabled for Attendant Programs Today—was formed to focus on the need for these services. According to ADAPT's home page on the World Wide Web, "There's no place like home, and we mean real homes, not nursing homes."[57]

A New Bill of Rights for People with Disabilities

Most everyone in the United States and in many other countries is familiar with the international symbol of access for people with disabilities of a person in a wheelchair. Persistent political efforts by individuals with disabilities, their families, and other advocates have resulted in legislation requiring increased access for those with

ILLUSTRATION 5-2

What Is Reasonable Accommodation for People with Disabilities?

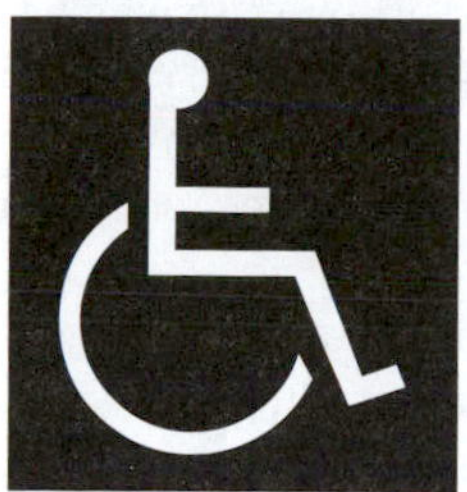

International Symbol of Access for People with Disabilities

When disability activist Judy Heumann* taught school years ago, she said, "I had to go to court just to get my teaching credentials." To even suggest she needed help going to the toilet "would've been the kiss of death.

"I had to ask people all the time 'if I could get a favor' from them—if they could please help me go to the bathroom.

"The issue, to me on a personal level, is a very frightening situation. These are the realities of your life—having to always worry about if you can have something to drink when you're out; if you're going to have a bladder infection, what's going to happen if you have to 'go' and you're not at home with an attendant."

This country is "squeamish" about the idea of attendant service when it comes to using the toilet, Heumann said. "I don't know why it is, but people think you have to have a nurse to pull your pants down."

Even disabled people have this squeamishness.

"Even people who need the service don't articulate what they need specifically enough," she said. As a result, both business and the administration have only an arm's-length understanding about what "personal assistance" entails. They recognize only that it involves "touching a disabled person."

It's no wonder, Heumann says that she increasingly hears "medical evidence" at meetings that older people with polio or cerebral palsy are now experiencing bladder problems. It's not from their disabilities, she said—it's from "never being allowed to go to the bathroom."

That's why it's crucial that explicit mention of things like using the restroom be in Americans with Disabilities Act regulations, says Heumann. It's "to show that business has to do it, has to provide it, to begin to allow disabled people to say up-front that they can need this service and not feel embarrassed about it."

Just a few weeks ago, Heumann said, she heard from a woman who'd just been hired in a job that required traveling. "But she hadn't told them in the interview that she'd need assistance because she said she was afraid she wouldn't have gotten the job.

"Now she's afraid that if she does tell them she needs assistance when she travels, they'll change the job and won't let her do the traveling—which she really wants to do."

By defining "reasonable accommodation" as interpreters and readers but not personal attendant services, Heumann points out, regulators are saying that personal assistance is fundamentally a different service. The disability movement has always argued that readers, interpreters and personal assistance all constitute "personal services."

*Judy Heumann is now U.S. Assistant Secretary for Special Education and Rehabilitative Services.

continued

ILLUSTRATION 5-2 *(continued)*

The deaf community really pushed the issue of interpreters; but the community of people who needed attendants didn't push the issue during the law's passage, said Heumann.

"Everybody is always very embarrassed about the issue. People just don't talk about having to go to the bathroom."

Even people within the movement consider anything more than the minimum of attendant time as "maid service." One disability activist she knew criticized someone who had an attendant cook Thanksgiving dinner for a dozen guests. He didn't consider this an "appropriate" use of an attendant.

"But why not?" argues Heumann. "If the woman weren't disabled, she'd be able to cook that Thanksgiving dinner herself. Since she is disabled, why is it wrong to have someone do it for her?

"We can have attendant services minimally—we can go to the bathroom when we get up and maybe once during the day," says Heumann. "It's OK to need a reader at meetings—but it's not OK to need one too much." Heumann quarrels with this acceptance of minimal service.

It's becoming more acceptable to have interpreters at meetings and performances—even when there's no assurance a deaf person is actually in the room at any one moment, she says. She lauds this expansion. "Interpreter services should not just be provided at meetings. People should have interpreters available whenever they need them."

So should anyone else who needs assistance. "Why in the world can't a big concert have someone available to help you eat a sandwich or use the restroom? I mean, what's the big deal?"

Heumann offered an analogy. "If there were no restrooms in public facilities, then I'd say OK, then nobody can use the toilet. But can you imagine going to any public event and not being able ever to use a restroom? No? Disabled people have to do it all the time."

Having to go to the bathroom is "the great unspoken issue of our movement," according to Heumann.

So, she said, she talks about it every chance she gets; particularly when she gives speeches. "I talk about how the denial of the right to go to the bathroom is a denial of the most basic right people have. Everyone has that right—unless you need assistance."

At one speech, to a group of pre-med students, Heumann told the class she felt she had a basic human right to be able to drink something when she was thirsty. "This one guy said that if I needed money from the government to be able to go to the bathroom then I didn't, in fact, have the right to drink something whenever I wanted it." Her questioner, it turned out, had had a disability.

Source: Mary Johnson, "The Great Unspoken Issue of Our Movement," *The Disability Rag*, July/August 1991, pp. 11–12.

disabilities. For example, the Architectural Barriers Act of 1968 includes specifications aimed at making buildings accessible and safe for those who are blind, deaf, using wheelchairs, or who have other disabilities. It requires that all buildings constructed in whole or in part with federal funds and buildings owned or leased by federal agencies have ramps, elevators, and other barrier-free access. Although it sounds as if the law would carry a considerable price tag, estimates are that the cost to the builder is "one-tenth of one percent of the total cost of a new building."[58] The results of the legislation are far from adequate. Many buildings today continue to fall short of the standards for restrooms, parking lots, doors, and warning signals. Locating suitable housing is particularly difficult for people with some types of disabilities. For example, those using wheelchairs find that few apartments or houses have accessible entrances, sufficiently wide doorways, or appliances that can be easily reached.

One of the most important pieces of civil rights legislation for people with disabilities is Title V of the Rehabilitation Act of 1973. Under this act,

1. Federal agencies must have affirmative action programs to hire and promote qualified people with disabilities.
2. The Architectural and Transportation Barriers Compliance Board was established to enforce the 1968 Architectural Barriers Act. Its activities have been expanded to include communication barriers.
3. All businesses, universities, foundations, and other institutions holding contracts with the U.S. government must have affirmative action programs to hire and promote qualified people with disabilities.
4. Discrimination against qualified people with disabilities—employees, students, and consumers of health care and other services—in all public and private institutions receiving federal assistance is prohibited.

This act was the first to provide specific protections for people with disabilities in programs receiving federal funding. "Even though the Act was passed in 1973, implementing regulations were not issued until 1977—and then only after extensive demonstrations by people with disabilities throughout the country."[59] There are offices of civil rights in the U.S. Department of Education and the U.S. Department of Health and Human Services that have responsibility for enforcing federal laws that prohibit discrimination against people with disabilities.

But no piece of legislation, court decision, or administrative ruling holds more significance for people with disabilities than the Americans with Disabilities Act, passed with overwhelming support by Congress in 1990 and with strong backing from the Bush administration. The definition of disability in this bill is the same as that in parts of the Rehabilitation Act and in amendments to the Fair Housing Act. An individual with a disability is one who has "a physical or mental impairment that substantially limits one or more major life activities, a record of such an impairment, or being regarded as having such an impairment." The act goes much farther in requiring private sector compliance than any previous legislation. For example, retail establishments such as restaurants, hotels, and theaters must be made accessible. In debates over the bill, businesses argued that not only were the costs to adopt the new measures unrealistic and outrageously expensive, but that they were also unclear and potentially unsafe. For example, in testimony to the Senate, a representative of the National Association of Theater Owners argued against allowing patrons in wheelchairs to sit wherever they want, because "it is not only reasonable, but it is essential from a safety standpoint that wheelchair patrons be seated near an exit."[60]

The act also broadened prohibitions on employment discrimination for businesses with fifteen or more employees (including Congress but not federal agencies!). It includes bans against discrimination in hiring, firing, compensation, advancement, and training, and also requires employers to make "reasonable accommodations" for those with disabilities unless this would cause "undue hardship." Reasonable accommodations may include providing readers or interpreters, modifying buildings, adjusting work schedules, and purchasing needed devices. Undue hardship is defined as "requiring significant expense." Just how far must employers go to make "reasonable" efforts, and how much is a "significant" expense? According to the U.S. Chamber of Commerce, "this language is an invitation to litigation,"[61] and it has indeed spawned many lawsuits. Some social welfare theorists complained that the ADA "was legislation on the cheap, mandating new responsibilities for private employers without offering any new financial assistance either to the employers or to the disabled people themselves."[62]

Telecommunications provisions of the ADA require that telephone companies provide relay services for customers with hearing and speech impairments. In the area of transportation, all new buses and trains must be made accessible to wheelchair users, but old vehicles were exempted. Amtrak, the federally subsidized rail system, has taken steps to assure that all new cars have facilities for passengers with disabilities. Representative Steny Hoyer (D-Maryland), the bill's chief sponsor, called the bill an "Emancipation Proclamation" for those with disabilities.

Implementation of the ADA has not moved fast enough for many proponents. For example, large numbers of people with disabilities remained unemployed. As a result, the disability rights movement has become increasingly strident with a series of lawsuits aimed at promoting compliance by businesses, universities, and other facilities as well as demonstrations at public and private facilities, including the Department of Health and Human Services, state capitol buildings, and local establishments such as restaurants. Demonstrators often subject themselves to arrest. Part of the importance of the ADA is that it is applicable across the United States, but some states already have more stringent legislation. "For example California's Fair Employment and Housing Act provides for compensatory and punitive damages where the ADA does not."[63] Primary authority for enforcing the ADA lies with the U.S. Department of Justice (DOT). Most cases of noncompliance that are pursued are resolved out of court, but disability activists have complained that the DOJ is not aggressive enough in pursuing cases. *Mouth* magazine, which calls itself the "voice of the disability nation," published a double issue in 1998 highly critical of the DOJ, saying that the agency has taken only one ADA case to full trial. Instead, its 40 attorneys prefer to "educate, negotiate, mediate."[64]

Airlines are not included in the ADA because they are covered under the 1986 Air Carrier Access Act, which prohibits airlines from discriminating against travelers with disabilities. Directives issued in 1990 by the U.S. Department of Transportation state that if an airline requires that an individual with a disability be escorted, the escort must be allowed to fly free.[65] Another directive is that many planes must have moveable armrests and that wide-body planes must have an accessible lavatory. In addition, people with disabilities must be allowed to select any seat, except where this might be a safety hazard. The National Federation of the Blind was outraged by even this restriction. Not surprisingly, the Air Transport Association (composed of airlines) expressed concerns that implementation of these new provisions would be excessively costly.

Many more policy issues involve the civil rights of citizens with disabilities. The right to obtain as well as to refuse treatment and to informed consent, guardianship, fair treatment if accused of a crime, and voting rights and zoning restrictions on community residences are some that remain on the public agenda.[66]

Additional issues confront advocates of the rights of people with mental retardation. There have been outcries against a U.S. Supreme Court decision that allows states to execute death row inmates who are mentally retarded, and against a decision by the Iowa Supreme Court that once again gives courts in that state the power to decide whether mentally retarded people can be sterilized. The institutionalization of people with mental retardation has been particularly vexing because they are often denied the same rights as mentally ill people to have their cases reviewed for discharge.

DISABILITY POLICY FOR CHILDREN

Many of the advancements in assisting people with developmental disabilities (DD) stem from efforts in the 1960s.[67] Advocates gained a valuable ally in President John F. Kennedy, who had a sister with mental retardation. The original, federal definition of developmental disabilities appeared in the Developmental Disabilities and Facilities Construction Act of 1970 and was expanded in the Developmental Disabilities Assistance and Bill of Rights Act of 1975. In 1987 the Rehabilitation Comprehensive Services and Developmental Disabilities Amendments eliminated specific diagnostic categories such as mental retardation, cerebral palsy, epilepsy, and autism in favor of a broader definition of developmental disability. Amendments during the 1980s and 1990s continue to foster the evolution of a more acceptable definition. The current definition is found in the Developmental Disabilities Assistance and Bill of Rights Act Amendments of 1994.

> *Developmental disability means a severe, chronic disability of an individual 5 years or older that is attributable to a mental or physical impairment or a combination of mental and physical impairments; is manifested before the individual reaches age 22; is likely to continue indefinitely; results in substantial functional limitations in three or more of the following areas of major life activity: self-care, receptive and expressive language, learning, mobility, self-direction, capacity for independent living, and economic self-sufficiency; and reflects the individual's need for a combination and sequence of special, interdisciplinary, or generic services, supports, or other assistance that is of lifelong or extended duration and are individually planned and coordinated; except that such term, when applied to infants and young children means individuals from birth to age 5, inclusive, who have substantial developmental delay or specific congenital or*

acquired conditions with a high probability of resulting in developmental disabilities if services are not provided.

Individuals with developmental disabilities, their families, and professionals in the field are pleased that this definition is more functionally oriented, less stigmatizing, and does not restrict services to only those with specific diagnoses. Concern is that the definition may leave too much room for interpretation and prevent people with less severe disabilities from receiving services that could substantially improve the quality of their lives. In addition, an argument can be made that age 22 is an arbitrary cutoff point adopted for administrative expediency as much as for developing a rational definition.

Federal legislation that has amended the definition of developmental disabilities has also expanded the array of services to which people with such disabilities are entitled. In addition, every state has either a separate commission or a special unit in its Vocational Rehabilitation office to serve those who are blind, and a number of schools provide education and training at the kindergarten through twelfth-grade levels specifically to children who are blind. At the federal level, the Deafness and Communicative Disorders Branch of the Rehabilitation Services Administration provides consultation to the states in developing services for those who are deaf or have other communication disorders. It also works on developing technological devices to assist people with disabilities. Designated, publicly funded schools throughout the country provide residential programs for children who are deaf from infancy through high school. In 1972 the Economic Opportunity Act was amended to include a goal that 10 percent of Head Start enrollees be children with disabilities.

Among the often controversial issues faced by children with disabilities and their families and communities is **inclusion,** also known as **mainstreaming.** Inclusion allows children with disabilities to receive their education in regular public school programs whenever possible. The Education for All Handicapped Children Act of 1975, P.L. 94-142, renamed the Individuals with Disabilities Education Act (IDEA) in 1990, states that every child with a disability is entitled to an "appropriate elementary and secondary education." If a child must be placed in a private school by the local education authority in order to obtain an appropriate education, this service must be provided at no cost to the child's family. Other services, including transportation and special devices, must also be provided. Through the act, many more children with disabilities are receiving a publicly financed education.

Inclusion has been hailed as a sensible and effective way to ensure that children with physical and mental disabilities are afforded full opportunities to learn and to interact with other children. It allows for the integration of these children into the mainstream of society and prepares them to be part of the community. Inclusion also allows other children to view this experience as normal. Children who are mainstreamed may attend some special classes, and their teachers in regular classrooms are assisted in developing educational programs to meet the needs of these students.

Inclusion has met with more conflicts as the number of children to be accommodated has grown.[68] School systems, especially smaller and poorer ones, feel the financial strain of providing all the necessary services. An individual education plan must be developed for each child. Parents have the right to participate in this planning, but not all do. There is also the possibility that even the best designed educational plans will not be carried out because of lack of time and resources. Teachers who want to be helpful may have large classes and heavy workloads that prevent individualized instruction. Although the federal government assists the states and communities with block grants to fund the act, children's advocates have complained that Congress has appropriated only about 7 percent of the costs of educating children with disabilities when the 1975 law says it is supposed to cover 40 percent.[69] In 1997 IDEA was reauthorized with various amendments, including provisions to expand mediation services when parents and schools disagree on what a child needs and will get.

BUILDING A BETTER POLICY ON DISABILITY

A Fair Definition

There are many types of disabilities. Amputations, arthritis, blindness, bone problems, brain injuries, burns, cancer, cerebral palsy, cleft lip and palate, deafness, diabetes, disfigurement, emotional disturbances, epilepsy, heart disease, mental retardation, mongolism, multiple sclerosis, muscular atrophy, muteness, paralysis, respiratory disorders, stroke, and stuttering are just some.[70] In addition to classifying these conditions as disabilities, they may also be classified in terms of degree of impairment.[71] For instance, those with visual impairments may have varying degrees of sight. Some people have disabilities so severe that they can perform few activities of daily living, yet others function quite well, even with severe disabilities. The traditional definition of disability is health-related problems that prevent an individual from working.[72] A more contemporary definition is limitations on any role or task a person usually performs in society, especially if these limitations exist for a long period of time.[73] According to the independent federal agency called the National Council on Disability, 54 million Americans have some type of physical or mental disability.[74]

The definitions of disability in various federal and state laws are not always consistent, and whether or not to include some conditions has been problematic. During the 1980s, controversies erupted over the human immunodeficiency virus (HIV) and acquired immune deficiency syndrome (AIDS). Several decisions supported the interpretation that these conditions are included under various federal laws.[75] For example, in 1988 the U.S. Department of Justice reversed an earlier opinion it had issued and stated that those with HIV as well as those who have developed AIDS are covered under the Rehabilitation Act. The U.S. Supreme Court ruled in 1996 that this same interpretation applies to the ADA.

A former ruling by the U.S. attorney general called alcoholism and drug addiction physical or mental impairments that are handicapping conditions if they limit one or more of life's major activities.[76] But as noted earlier in this chapter, they are no longer sufficient conditions for receiving SSDI and SSI. Alcohol and drug disorders are also not treated like other disabilities in the ADA. The ADA does prohibit discrimination against alcoholics and illegal drug users in receiving medical services. But the ADA generally excludes those with "current psychoactive substance use disorders" (which in the American Psychiatric Association's *Diagnostic and Statistical Manual of Mental Disorders,* 4th ed., includes alcohol and other drug abuse and dependence) from employment protections. Employment protections are, however, extended to people with these disorders who no longer use such substances, and they may apply to individuals with other disabilities even if they use illegal drugs. As one person in the chemical dependency field wrote, "controversies over passage of the ADA reflect ambivalence about whether to view alcoholism/addiction as a 'real' disability."[77] Like other social problems, disability is a social construction, "a social judgment,"[78] and these constructions are subject to change. Illustration 5-3 is based on the Equal Employment Opportunity Commission's efforts to help employers decide when to accommodate employees who have the various constructs called mental illnesses.

A Fair Policy[79]

Most of us admire people with severe disabilities who succeed against tremendous odds, even if they don't want to be viewed in this way and feel they are just doing what they have to do. And at the risk of sounding harsh, we may wonder why others do not try harder. We may also be perplexed by the Social Security Administration's decisions to award disability benefits to one individual and to deny another with a seemingly greater disability. No definition written on paper can really capture the abilities or the limitations of a person with a disability, but disability determination personnel are expected to weigh the evidence and make these decisions every day about individuals whom they generally have never seen. Is it the right of people with disabilities to receive social welfare benefits, or is it their obligation to make whatever contributions they can? Does society prefer to pay benefits to people with disabilities rather than do what is necessary to include people with disabilities in the mainstream of U.S. life? Is our goal to make people with disabilities fit the workplace and other social institutions, or is it to make society accommodate people with disabilities?

In his extensive considerations of disability policy, historian Edward Berkowitz claims that the structure of financial assistance programs (including those administered by the Veterans Administration for service-related disabilities) encourages people to drop out of the workforce rather than seek rehabilitation.[80] From the start, there was controversy over whether SSDI would stifle rehabilitation.

The goals of the different waves of disability policy—financial assistance, rehabilitation programs, and civil rights—are often at odds with each other.[81] In fact, the growth of SSDI and SSI seems paradoxical given medical, technological, and civil rights advances that are supposed to make it easier for people with disabilities to function in the workplace. Discrimination against people with disabilities explains some of the irony, but the structure of the financial assistance programs also factors into the equation. Berkowitz estimates that only 2 percent of the money spent for those with disabilities goes to rehabilitation programs.[82] To summarize some of these public policy

ILLUSTRATION 5-3

Guidance from the EEOC in Implementing the Americans with Disabilities Act in Cases of Psychiatric Impairment

Some of the examples offered by the Equal Employment Opportunity Commission to help employers implement the Americans with Disabilities Act of 1990 in cases of psychiatric disabilities are found below.

Example: An employee was distressed by the end of a romantic relationship. Although he continued his daily routine, he sometimes became agitated at work. He was most distressed for about a month during and immediately after the breakup. He sought counseling and his mood improved within weeks. His counselor gave him a diagnosis of "adjustment disorder" and stated that he was not expected to experience any long-term problems associated with this event. While he has an impairment (adjustment disorder), his impairment was short term, did not significantly restrict major life activities during that time, and was not expected to have permanent or long-term effects. This employee does not have a disability for purposes of the ADA.

Example: An employee with a psychiatric disability works in a warehouse loading boxes onto pallets for shipment. He has no customer contact and does not come into regular contact with other employees. Over the course of several weeks, he has come to work appearing increasingly disheveled. His clothes are ill-fitting and often have tears in them. He also has become increasingly antisocial. Co-workers have complained that when they try to engage him in casual conversation, he walks away or gives a curt reply. When he has to talk to a co-worker, he is abrupt and rude. His work, however, has not suffered. The employer's company handbook states that employees should be courteous to each other. When told that he is being disciplined for his appearance and treatment of co-workers, the employee explains that his appearance and demeanor have deteriorated because of his disability which was exacerbated during this time period.

The dress code and co-worker courtesy are not job-related for the position in question and consistent with business necessity because this employee has no customer contact and does not come into regular contact with other employees. Therefore, rigid application of these rules to this employee would violate the ADA.

Example: A reference librarian frequently loses her temper at work, disrupting the library atmosphere by shouting at patrons and co-workers. After receiving a suspension as the second step in uniform, progressive discipline, she discloses her disability, states that it causes her behavior, and requests a leave of absence for treatment. The employer may discipline her because she violated a conduct standard—a rule prohibiting disruptive behavior towards patrons and co-workers—that is job-related for the position in question and consistent with business necessity. The employer, however, must grant her request for a leave of absence as a reasonable accommodation, barring undue hardship, to enable her to meet this conduct standard in the future.

Source: Excerpted from Equal Employment Opportunity Commission, *EEOC Enforcement Guidance on the Americans with Disabilities Act and Psychiatric Disabilities* (Washington, DC: The Commission, March 25, 1997).

dilemmas, in the SSDI and SSI programs, one is either disabled or not, and evidence indicates that there are insufficient incentives to encourage people to work as much as they can. When earnings are minimal and may jeopardize health care and other benefits, forgoing employment and selecting social insurance or public assistance may be a rational choice. Research shows that the higher the level of disability payments, the more people apply for them.[83] Of course, without adequate payments, people may be forced to do some sort of work even if it jeopardizes their health. One study found that most disability insurance beneficiaries studied worked due to "financial need and worked without attributing their decision to an improvement in their health."[84] The first job they took after receiving benefits "had less exertion, fewer hours, and lower pay" than their previous job. Another study found that only 12 percent of those who are not working when they begin receiving SSDI start a job and that half leave the job while still receiving SSDI. Most report leaving due to health concerns such as inability to keep up with the work, inability to do the same type of work they did previously, or the work was making their health worse.[85]

Originally there was to have been a strong link between the federal disability payment programs and vocational rehabilitation, but this never materialized to the degree intended. Limited funding prevented the VR programs from keeping up with the demand for services, and practices such as creaming also prevented applicants from obtaining services. Coupled with incentives to remain unemployed and a lack of incentives to work, the success of the rehabilitation approach has been limited. Estimates are that nearly half of those receiving disability payments are unable to work due to advanced age or short life expectancy.[86] For others there may be potential for at least some work contribution if only the contribution that each person is able to make would be valued as such. The most likely candidates for a return to work are younger and have greater motivation, education, and work experience. Current thinking is that returning to work sooner rather than later is preferable. One researcher found that beneficiaries who received physical therapy were more likely to start working and to remain employed, while those who received job placement services were also more likely to start working but were also more likely to terminate employment.[87] Others have called for investing in the types of assistive technology that will maximize each person's potential despite public and private health care providers' reluctance to pay for it.[88] But like other programs, rehabilitation and related services probably work best for those who see them as the best among their alternatives.

Berkowitz believes that rehabilitation efforts have "reached a low ebb."[89] Public policy decisions always involve trade-offs. Some people view decisions favoring cash benefits as the best alternative. Others may want to tip the scales in favor of rehabilitative services. Still others advocate for greater balance between the two.

Given the many and often contradictory disability policies and programs, Berkowitz recommends a congressional oversight committee and a federal agency dedicated to bringing together the many experts needed to see disability as a whole. The oversight committee would address the national budget for disability and serve as the conduit for disability policy. He suggests expanding the scope of the National Council on Disability so it could do more to insure that public policy "recognizes the capabilities" of those with disabilities. Berkowitz also recommends flexible policies that provide the supports needed by those who can and want to remain in the labor force and that help others retire with dignity and a decent standard of living.[90] Given that old programs will not completely yield to new, he recommends making it easier for people to qualify for SSI (something not likely to happen). Since SSDI and SSI use the same definition of disability, those who do not qualify for SSDI are also ineligible for SSI, and have nowhere else to turn. He advocates the creation of "independence initiatives," which individuals could use to purchase attendant care or to make environmental modifications, and "independent living block grants" to localities to establish ILCs. Two other crucial provisions he addresses are the guarantee of health care and the "vigorous enforcement" of civil rights protections.

GENERAL ASSISTANCE: THE STATE AND COMMUNITY RESPONSE TO WELFARE

Most of the major social welfare programs discussed thus far are totally or partly the responsibility of the federal government. But some social welfare programs are developed, administered, and financed by state and local governments, independent of the federal government. The term used to describe many of these programs is General Assistance (GA). General Assistance predated the New Deal, when local and state governments were the major suppliers of public assistance. Although the New Deal and subsequent developments at the federal level created many important social welfare programs, they do not include many needy people who were covered under the original General Assistance programs.[91] General Assistance exists today because the United States continues to use a fragmented approach to meeting social welfare needs. Some poor people do not meet the criteria for *any* of the major federal or federal–state welfare programs. They may not be aged or disabled, at least not according to federal standards; they may not have dependent children; they may not be entitled to unemployment benefits, or they may have exhausted them. They may need immediate assistance, unable to wait for federal benefits, which may take thirty days or more to begin. In other words, to qualify for social welfare assistance, simply being "needy" is not always enough.

Although most Americans have heard of the AFDC (now TANF), Food Stamp, and Medicaid programs, General Assistance is not as well known. In some places it is referred to as "county welfare," "county aid," or "general relief." General Assistance programs are administered differently from state to state and even from one locality to another within the same state. The types and amounts of services also vary considerably, as do the types of recipients served. In some cases, the state government is entirely responsible for the General Assistance program. It determines the policies and procedures for General Assistance, and state workers accept applications and provide assistance to recipients. In other areas, the state may set policies and determine eligibility requirements, but General Assistance is administered by city and county governments. In these cases, the state may provide all the funding, or the state and local governments may share funding responsibilities. Other states have no involvement in General Assistance. Local governments are free to establish programs if they desire. If not, no General Assistance is available.

General Assistance has many uses. Historically the program has aided people who receive little or nothing from other social welfare programs and who need help, especially in emergencies. TANF and SSI beneficiaries are usually ineligible for GA except while waiting for these public assistance payments to begin. In some areas the emphasis is on helping poor people cover medical expenses. Other uses have been to assist the elderly and people with disabilities, especially before improvements in the SSI program, and also to help the unemployed and those who earn very little.[92]

Some programs provide cash assistance; others rely on in-kind assistance such as medical care, and some use a combination of the two. A report on General Assistance commissioned by the federal government described it as

> *an important component of the income assistance system . . . serving as the ultimate "safety net" for low-income individuals and families who are not eligible for federally-supported assistance programs. . . . Eligibility criteria vary from strict disability requirements . . . to broad income requirements with no categorical restrictions. Benefit levels vary from small one-time payments to regular payments virtually identical to AFDC [now TANF] or SSI. Forms of assistance vary from bus tickets or firewood to vendor payments to vouchers to cash. Some jurisdictions have one comprehensive GA program, and some have several special programs. . . . Some have strict work requirements or workfare programs, and some have no special work provisions. . . . Compounding all this variation is the fact that GA program characteristics . . . are unusually sensitive to budget pressures . . . and change much more frequently than any other part of the welfare system.*[93]

Following passage of the Social Security Act, General Assistance expenditures decreased sharply from almost $1.5 million in 1935 to about $450,000 in 1936.[94] Although annual expenditures have fluctuated over the years, estimates indicate that in 1996 about $2.9 billion was spent and about 767,000 people were served each month.[95] Broad descriptions of the General Assistance (GA) program should be interpreted cautiously, because there are no federal regulations requiring reporting, "recordkeeping is notoriously lax,"[96] and information is difficult to obtain.[97] It has been suggested that counties do not collect or report GA data because they fear that the information might be used to mount legal challenges to the amount of aid provided and the way it is provided.[98]

The most recent comprehensive study of GA programs was conducted by the Urban Institute in 1996.[99] Among the 50 states and the District of Columbia, 25 operate programs with uniform eligibility rules and payments that are state-funded. Eight others mandate programs statewide but rules, benefits, and/or funding may vary by locality. Eighteen states have no statewide program. In nine of them, some localities have a program. The remaining nine have no viable entity that can be identified as GA although some emergency aid may be available. Table 5-4 contains some information on GA programs. According to the Urban Institute, there has been an erosion of GA

TABLE 5-4

General Assistance Programs at a Glance, by Number of States, Summer, 1996

Availability of GA Programs	
States with GA Programs	42
Program throughout entire state	33
Program in only portion of the state	9
States with no GA Program	9
Populations Served by GA Programs	
Disabled, elderly, and/or unemployable individuals	42
Children and/or families with children	31
Employable individuals without children	16
Form of GA Benefits	
Cash	28
Vendor Payments/Vouchers	11
Mix of Cash and Vendor Payments/Vouchers	3
Maximum Cash Benefits as a Percentage of Poverty (individual recipients)	
Average	39%
Low (Missouri)	12%
High (Nebraska)	100%
Duration of GA Benefits	
No time limits	18
Time limits for a portion of beneficiaries	15
Time limits for all beneficiaries	9

Source: Cori E. Uccello, Heather R. McCallum, and L. Jerome Gallagher, State General Assistance Programs 1996 (Washington, DC: Urban Institute, 1996), p. 1–4.

benefits and the populations served. Some programs have dropped able-bodied unemployed adults without children and Pennsylvania also dropped those with children. Arizona and Rhode Island dropped pregnant women. Most states provide benefits only to those whose income is 55 percent or less of the poverty level. A study of California's General Assistance Program found that it was serving mostly "individuals who, handicapped by mental disability, recent incarceration, or recent refugee status, lack the capacity for self-support and generally do not have access to the rehabilitative services needed to develop that capacity."[100] Recent accounts indicate that state GA is being cut back at the same time that the federal government has chosen a policy of devolution and restricted eligibility for public assistance.

FEDERALISM AND SOCIAL WELFARE

American **federalism**—the constitutional division of power between the national government and the states—directly affects the administration and financing of social welfare programs. The major public assistance programs (TANF, SSI, Medicaid, food stamps, and General Assistance) are administered and funded in different ways. TANF and Medicaid are joint ventures of the federal and state governments, which share in funding the programs. The federal government sets administrative guidelines but the states play a major role in determining eligibility requirements and benefits. There are, however, important differences in the intergovernmental arrangements in these two programs. While Medicaid remains an open-ended entitlement program available to all who qualify, TANF (formerly AFDC) is now structured as a block grant program with capped federal funding, regardless of how many families meet eligibility requirements. Under TANF, states have considerably more discretion over program rules than they did under the AFDC entitlement program (see Chapter 6).

Food stamps and SSI are primarily programs of the federal government. The federal government assumes full responsibility for eligibility requirements and benefit levels in the Food Stamp Program. In the SSI program the federal government finances minimum benefits and establishes basic eligibility requirements, but most states make some effort to supplement federal SSI benefits for at least some categories of recipients. SSI checks are generally mailed directly to recipients by the Social Security Administration, while food stamps are generally distributed through state and local welfare offices. General Assistance is a highly discretionary type of program and is the major public assistance program funded and administered by state and/or local governments with no federal participation. Most social service programs, like mental health and child welfare, are jointly funded by the federal and state governments, with the level of involvement in funding and administration by the federal government and the states varying substantially depending on the specific program.

For many years following the New Deal, the trend was toward greater centralization or federalization of social welfare programs. But during the Reagan presidency, debate over the appropriate approach to federalism in social welfare took on new vigor. Reagan wanted to turn over to the states many of the domestic programs of the national government. Reagan had some successes in achieving this goal, primarily collapsing a number of small programs into several block grants. His successor, George Bush, continued the effort by allowing some states to experiment with reforms in AFDC and other programs, a practice expanded during the Clinton administration. Clinton did want to institute national health insurance (see Chapter 8), but even his plan called for a certain amount of state discretion in administering the program. Some people believe that public assistance and social service programs should be the responsibility of state governments—government closer to home. Others believe that only greater federal involvement can assure fair treatment of those in need. Disagreement over the role of federalism in social welfare programs and over the virtues of centralized versus decentralized social welfare programs have led the United

States to use many different combinations of federal, state, and local involvement to address human needs. Determining the appropriate roles of the federal, state, and local governments remains an important social welfare issue.

SUMMARY

Four types of social welfare provisions are available to people who are aged or disabled: social insurance, public assistance, social and rehabilitative services, and civil rights legislation. The major public assistance program available to these individuals is the Supplemental Security Income (SSI) program. Despite problems such as delays in determining eligibility, SSI has been one of the major improvements in providing social welfare benefits to Americans since the original Social Security Act became law in 1935.

An important social service program for people with disabilities is the Vocational Rehabilitation (VR) program. VR is a limited program because not everyone who is disabled is entitled to assistance. The primary criterion for participation is the individual's potential for returning to work. For years, the VR program was accused of creaming—taking on clients who are most easy to rehabilitate and rejecting others—but in recent years the program has focused on clients with more severe disabilities.

Individuals with physical and mental disabilities face a number of obstacles in achieving independence. Laws which emerged in the 1960s and 1970s were important steps in recognizing the rights of people with disabilities. The most important achievement of this period was Title V of the Rehabilitation Act of 1973, which makes it illegal for programs and agencies that receive federal funds to discriminate against people with disabilities in employment, education, and use of services.

Another significant piece of legislation was the Developmental Disabilities Assistance and Bill of Rights Act of 1975. As a result of this act, an array of services are available to those whose disability was manifested before age 22. The Individuals with Disabilities Education Act guarantees all children, regardless of their disability, a free, publicly funded education. Under this act, children are supposed to be "mainstreamed"—placed in regular schools and classrooms whenever possible. In theory, mainstreaming is a widely accepted concept, but it has resulted in controversies when teachers and other school personnel with heavy workloads have not had the time to invest in these children's educations. No piece of legislation has been more encouraging for promoting the inclusion of citizens with disabilities than the Americans with Disabilities Act of 1990 with its expanded provisions to prevent discrimination in public and private accommodations, employment, communications, and travel.

Despite civil rights advances that might lead to greater employment of people with disabilities, SSI and Social Security Disability Insurance rolls have soared. This is largely because the social welfare policies that affect people with disabilities are contradictory. Most publicly funded assistance for people with disabilities comes in the form of much needed cash payments. What is lacking are rehabilitative services, attendant care services, and other services that promote inclusion, independence, and meaningful activity.

An important public assistance program for some individuals with limited financial resources is General Assistance. GA programs are funded and administered by state or local governments with no federal government involvement. These programs vary considerably across states and communities with respect to eligibility criteria and payment levels. GA may be a form of unemployment relief or a means for assisting those who do not qualify for other welfare programs. Some states and communities have no GA program at all.

The United States lacks a consensus about the best methods for funding and administering welfare programs. Although some believe that the federal government is best suited to perform these functions because of its large revenue base and its equal treatment of recipients regardless of the state in which they live, others feel that welfare decisions should be made closer to the people and are rightfully a concern of the states. Americans use many arrangements for delivering social welfare services because they cannot agree on which are best.

NOTES

1. John G. Turnbull, C. Arthur Williams, Jr., and Earl F. Cheit, *Economic and Social Security* (New York: Ronald Press, 1967), p. 83.

2. Ibid.

3. The remainder of this paragraph relies on Robert J. Myers, *Social Security* (Bryn Mawr, PA: McCahan Foundation, 1975), pp. 400–401.

4. This paragraph relies on ibid., p. 401.

5. See Edward D. Berkowitz, *Disabled Policy: America's Programs for the Handicapped* (Cambridge, England: Cambridge University Press, 1987), p. 58. Reprinted with the permission of Cambridge University Press.

6. U.S. Bureau of the Census, *Statistical Abstract of the United States: 1965* (Washington, DC: U.S. Government Printing Office, 1965), p. 309.

7. Daniel P. Moynihan, *The Politics of a Guaranteed Income* (New York: Random House, 1973).

8. Robert A. Diamond, ed., *Future of Social Programs* (Washington, DC: Congressional Quarterly, August, 1973), p. 15.

9. Committee on Ways and Means, U.S. House of Representatives, *Overview of Entitlement Programs, 1993 Green Book* (Washington, DC: U.S. Government Printing Office, 1993), p. 818.

10. Much of the information in this section relies on *Social Security Handbook*, 13th ed. (Washington, DC: Social Security Administration, 1997), SSA Publication No. 65-008; also see Committee on Ways and Means, U.S. House of Representatives, *1998 Green Book: Background Material and Data on Programs Within the Jurisdiction of the Committee on Ways and Means* (Washington, DC: U.S. Government Printing Office, 1998), Section 3, pp. 261–326.

11. Committee on Ways and Means, *1998 Green Book*, p. 288.

12. Discussion of the steps in disability determination is based on Cille Kennedy and Ronald W. Manderscheid, "SSDI and SSI Disability Beneficiaries with Mental Disorders," *Mental Health, United States, 1992* (Rockville, MD: National Institute of Mental Health, 1992), chapter 5, pp. 219–230; updated with information from Committee on Ways and Means, *1998 Green Book*, pp. 42–43.

13. See Committee on Ways and Means, *1998 Green Book*, p. 51

14. The remainder of this paragraph relies on Executive Office of the President, *Budget of the United States Government, Fiscal Year 1999* (Washington, DC: U.S. Government Printing Office, 1998), p. 232.

15. For information on SSI participation by the elderly, see the Social Security web site at ftp://ftp.ssa.gov/pub/statistics/2a5; Committee on Ways and Means, *1998 Green Book*, pp. 297, 299 & 306–309.

16. "Supplemental Security Income (SSI): Current Program Characteristics and Alternatives for Reform," A Background Paper by the Subcommittee on Retirement Income and Employment of the Select Committee on Aging, House of Representatives (100th Congress, August 1988), p. 11. Also see John A. Menefee, Bea Edwards, and Sylvester Schieber, "Analysis of Nonparticipation in the

SSI Program," *Social Security Bulletin,* Vol. 44, No. 6, 1981, pp. 3–21.

17. Committee on Ways and Means, U.S. House of Representatives, *1996 Green Book: Background Material and Data on Programs Within the Jurisdiction of the Committee on Ways and Means* (Washington, DC: U.S. Government Printing Office, 1996), p. 305; Executive Office of the President, *Budget of the United States Government Fiscal Year 1999* (Washington, DC: U.S. Government Printing Office, 1998), p. 232.

18. Committee on Ways and Means, *1998 Green Book,* pp. 294 & 297.

19. Committee on Ways and Means, *1993 Green Book,* p. 839; also see Social Security Administration news release, "SSA will review 45,000 cases of children who had SSI disability benefits ceased, offer second chance for appeal to all," December 17, 1997, http://www.ssa.gov/press/childhood_press.html.

20. "More Children Get Disability Benefits," *Austin American-Statesman,* March 9, 1993, p. A5.

21. Committee on Ways and Means, *1998 Green Book,* p. 299.

22. The remainder of this paragraph relies on ibid., pp. 291–293.

23. See ibid., pp. 1388–1392.

24. "Issue: Welfare," *Congressional Quarterly,* December 6, 1997, p. 3013.

25. Melanie Conklin, "Out in the Cold: Washington Shows Drug Addicts the Door," *The Progressive,* Vol. 61, No. 3, March 1997, pp. 25–27.

26. Some of this paragraph relies on Committee on Ways and Means, *1998 Green Book,* pp. 302–304.

27. For a further description of the Zebley decision see Committee on Ways and Means, *1996 Green Book,* pp. 262–263.

28. Committee on Ways and Means, *1993 Green Book,* pp. 852–853.

29. See Committee on Ways and Means, *1996 Green Book,* pp. 297–298; *1998 Green Book,* pp. 301–302.

30. "Impact of New SSI Rules for Children Decried," *NASW News,* May 1997, p. 5.

31. Adam Cohen, "Are the Cuts Unkind?" *Time,* July 14, 1997, p. 50.

32. Molly Ivins, "Welfare Reform Punishes Children with Disabilities," *Austin American-Statesman,* November 12, 1997, p. A17.

33. Robert Pear (*New York Times*), "Government Will Review Benefit Cutoffs," *Austin American-Statesman,* December 18, 1997, p. A2; Social Security Administration news release, "SSA will review 45,000 cases of children who had SSI disability benefits ceased, offer second chance for appeal to all."

34. U.S. General Accounting Office, "Social Security Disability: Improvement Needed to Continuing Disability Review Process," Abstracts of GAO Reports and Testimony, HEHS-97-1, October 16, 1996, http://www.gao.gov/AIndexFY97/subject/Supple1.htm; also see U.S. General Accounting Office, *Supplemental Security Income: SSA Is Taking Steps to Review Recipients' Disability Status,* HEHS-97-17, October 1996, http://www.gao.gov/AIndexFY97/subject/Supple1.htm.

35. Supplemental Security Income Modernization Project, *Final Report of the Experts* (Baltimore, MD: Social Security Administration, August 1992); also see Committee on Ways and Means, *1993 Green Book,* p. 862.

36. For a history of programs and policies addressing disability, see Richard K. Scotch, *From Good Will to Civil Rights: Transforming Federal Disability Policy* (Philadelphia: Temple University Press, 1984); Berkowitz, *Disabled Policy.*

37. Edward D. Berkowitz, "The American Disability System in Historical Perspective," in Edward D. Berkowitz, ed., *Disability Policies and Government Programs* (New York: Holt, Rinehart, & Winston, 1979), p. 43.

38. Berkowitz, *Disabled Policy,* p. 164.

39. Rehabilitation Services Administration, "Basic Vocational Rehabilitation Services," http://www.ed.gov/offices/OSERS/RSA/PGMS/bvrs.html, accessed June 17, 1998.

40. Scotch, *From Good Will to Civil Rights.*

41. Berkowitz, "The American Disability System in HIstorical Perspective," p. 45.

42. FBVE, "Administration of the Vocational Rehabilitation Program," Bulletin 113, rev. under imprint of the Department of Interior, Office of Education (Washington, DC: U.S. Government Printing Office, 1938), cited in ibid.

43. Berkowitz, *Disabled Policy,* pp. 176 & 177.

44. National Council on Disability, *Achieving Independence: The Challenge for the 21st Century* (Washington, DC: The Council, July 26, 1996), p. 63; on the effects of the vocational rehabilitation approach, also see Berkowitz, *Disabled Policy*; Eric Kingson and Edward D. Berkowitz, *Social Security and Medicare: A Policy Primer* (Westport, CT: Auburn House, 1993), pp. 144–146.

45. Figures in this paragraph rely on U.S. Bureau of the Census, *Statistical Abstract of the United States, 1989* (Washington, DC: U.S. Government Printing Office, 1989), p. 360; *1992,* p. 367; *1998,* p. 388.

46. This paragraph relies on Berkowitz, *Disabled Policy,* pp. 175, 180, & 183.

47. Ibid., p. 186.

48. National Council on Disability, *Achieving Independence: The Challenge for the 21st Century,* pp. 19–20.

49. *Wyatt v. Stickney,* 3195 U.S.3 (1972).

50. Eric Emerson, "What Is Normalisation?" in Hilary Brown and Helen Smith, eds., *Normalisation: A Reader for the Nineties* (London: Tavistock/Routledge, 1992), pp. 1–18.

51. Bengt Nirje, "The Normalization Principle," in R. Kugel and A. Shearer, eds., *Changing Patterns in Residential Services for the Mentally Retarded,* rev. ed. (Washington, DC: President's Commission on Mental Retardation, 1976), p. 231.

52. Ibid.; Wolf Wolfensberger, ed., *The Principle of Normalization in Human Services* (Toronto: National Institute on Mental Retardation, 1972).

53. For a discussion of the various conceptions of normalization, see Brown and Smith, *Normalisation,* especially Emerson's chapter, "What Is Normalisation?"

54. Roberta Nelson, *Creating Community Acceptance for Handicapped People* (Springfield, IL: Charles C. Thomas, 1978), pp. 12–22.

55. Linden Thorn cited in Pat Harbolt, "The Fight Against Community Programs," *Access: A Human Services Magazine,* Vol. 4, No. 4, February/March 1981, Florida Department of Health and Human Services, pp. 14–18. Also see Denise Gamino, "Neighborhood Fights Home for Mentally Retarded," *Austin American-Statesman,* February 2, 1994, p. A7.

56. World Institute on Disability, *Just Like Everyone Else* (Oakland, CA: World Institute on Disability, 1992), p. 9.

57. ADAPT's home page address is http://www.adapt.org.

58. Shirley Cohen, *Special People: A Brighter Future for Everyone with Physical, Mental, and Emotional Disabilities* (Englewood Cliffs, NJ: Prentice Hall, 1977), p. 132.

59. World Institute on Disability, *Just Like Everyone Else,* p. 13.

60. Testimony of Malcolm C. Green, Chairman, National Association of Theater Owners, presented on May 10, 1989, before the Senate Subcommittee on the Handicapped on S.933, the "Americans with Disabilities Act," *Congressional Digest,* December 1989, Vol. 68, p. 309.

61. Testimony of Zachary Fasman, U.S. Chamber of Commerce, presented on May 9, 1989, before the Senate Committee on Labor and Human Resources on S.933, the "Americans with Disabilities Act," *Congressional Digest,* December 1989, Vol. 68, p. 299.

62. Kingson and Berkowitz, *Social Security and Medicare: A Policy Primer,* p. 148.

63. World Institute on Disability, *Just like Everyone Else,* p. 13.

64. *Mouth,* March–April 1998, quote from p. 8.

65. "U.S. Officials Order Changes to Aid Disabled Air Travelers," *Champaign-Urbana News-Gazette,* March 3, 1990, p. A6.

66. For an extensive consideration of these issues and others, see Bruce Dennis Sales, D. Matthew Powell, Richard Van Duizend, and associates, *Disabled Persons and the Law: State and Legislative Issues* (New York: Plenum Press, 1982).

67. This paragraph relies on Kevin DeWeaver, "Developmental Disabilities: Striving Toward Inclusion," in Diana M. DiNitto, C. Aaron McNeece, and contributors, *Social Work: Issues and Opportunities in a Challenging Profession* (Boston: Allyn and Bacon, 1997), pp. 149–167.

68. Sam Allis, "The Struggle to Pay for Special Ed," *Time,* November 4, 1996, pp. 82–83; "Inclusion Isn't Working," *Austin American-Statesman,* April 8, 1996, p. A8.

69. Allis, "The Struggle to Pay for Special Ed."

70. This list is from Jane Mullins and Suzanne Wolfe, *Special People Behind the Eight-Ball: An Annotated Bibliography of Literature Classified by Handicapping Conditions* (Johnstown, PA: Mafex Associates, 1975).

71. Saad Z. Nagi, "The Concept and Measurement of Disability" in Edward D. Berkowitz, ed., *Disability Policies and Government Programs* (New York: Holt, Rinehart, & Winston, 1979), p. 2; Cohen, *Special People,* p. 8.

72. Monroe Berkowitz, William G. Johnson, and Edward H. Murphy, *Public Policy Toward Disability* (New York: Holt, Rinehart, & Winston, 1976), p. 7.

73. Berkowitz, "The American Disability System in Historical Perspective," p. 43.

74. See home page of the National Council on Disability, http://www.ncd.gov, accessed June 18, 1998.

75. See "AIDS: Covered Indirectly," *Congressional Quarterly Weekly Report,* May 13, 1989, p. 1123.

76. See HEW Task Force on Public Awareness and the Disabled, "It's a New Day for Disabled People," *American Education,* Vol. 13, December 1977, pp. 17–18, 20–21.

77. John de Miranda, "The Common Ground: Alcoholism, Addiction and Disability," *Addiction & Recovery,* August 1990, pp. 42–45.

78. Berkowitz, *Disabled Policy,* p. 3.

79. Much of this section relies on Berkowitz, *Disabled Policy,* pp. 161, 184, 188, 226, 227, 234, 236, 237, & 239; Kingson and Berkowitz, *Social Security and Medicare: A Policy Primer,* especially chapter 8.

80. See Berkowitz, *Disabled Policy,* p. 184.

81. Much of this paragraph relies on Kingson and Berkowitz, *Social Security and Medicare: A Policy Primer,* especially chapter 8.

82. Ibid., p. 138.

83. Ibid., p. 149.

84. Evan S. Schechter, "Work While Receiving Disability Insurance Benefits: Additional Findings from the New Beneficiary Followup Survey," *Social Security Bulletin,* Vol. 60, No. 1, 1997, pp. 3–17.

85. John C. Hennessey, "Job Patterns of Disabled Beneficiaries," *Social Security Bulletin,* Vol. 59, No. 4, 1996, pp. 3–11.

86. The first part of this paragraph relies on *Stranded on Disability: Federal Disability Programs Failing Disabled Workers,* Hearing before the Special Committee on Aging, United States Senate, 104th Congress, 2nd session, Washington, DC, June 5, 1996, Serial No. 104-14, pp. 4–6.

87. John C. Hennessey, "Factors Affecting the Work Efforts of Disabled-Worker Beneficiaries," *Social Security Bulletin,* Vol. 60, No. 3, 1997, pp. 3–20.

88. See Statement of Edward A. Eckenhoff, President, National Rehabilitation Hospital, in *Problems in the Social Security Disability Programs; The Disabling of America?,* Hearing before the Special Committee on Aging of the United States Senate, 104th Congress, 1st session, Washington, DC, March 2, 1995, Serial No. 104-1, pp. 88–93.

89. Berkowitz, *Disabled Policy,* p. 8.

90. Kingson and Berkowitz, *Social Security and Medicare: A Policy Primer,* p. 149.

91. James Patterson, *Congressional Conservatism and the New Deal* (Lexington, MA: Lexington Books, 1981), p. 63, cited in Hugh Helco, "The Political Foundations of Antipoverty Policy" in Sheldon H. Danzinger and Daniel H. Weinberg, eds., *Fighting Poverty: What Works and What Doesn't* (Cambridge, MA: Harvard University Press, 1986), p. 315.

92. For a discussion of how General Assistance has been used, see Duncan M. MacIntyre, *Public Assistance: Too Much or Too Little?* (Ithaca, NY: New York State School of Industrial and Labor Relations, Cornell University, 1964), p. 51.

93. Urban Systems Research & Engineering, *Characteristics of General Assistance Programs 1982* (Washington, DC: U.S. Department of Health and Human Services, May 1983), pp. 1–2.

94. U.S. Bureau of the Census, *Statistical Abstract of the United States: 1943* (Washington, DC: U.S. Government Printing Office, 1943), p. 193.

95. U.S. Bureau of the Census, *Statistical Abstract of the United States: 1998* (Washington, DC: U.S. Government Printing Office, 1998), Table 605, p. 379.

96. Joel F. Handler and Michael Sosin, *Last Resorts, Emergency Assistance and Special Needs Programs in Public Welfare* (New York: Academic Press, 1983), p. 81.

97. Urban Systems Research & Engineering, *Characteristics of General Assistance Programs 1982.*

98. Ailee Moon and Leonard Schneiderman, *Assessing the Growth of California's General Assistance Program* (Berkeley, CA: California Policy Seminar, 1995), http://www.sen.ca.gov/ftp/sen/committee/STANDING/HEALTH/_home/rear02.htm.

99. Cori E. Uccello, Heather R. McCallum, and L. Jerome Gallagher, *State General Assistance Programs 1996* (Washington, DC: Urban Institute, 1996), http://newfederalism.urban.org/pdf/sgap96.pdf; Cori E. Uccello and L. Jerome Gallagher, *General Assistance Programs: The State-Based Part of the Safety Net* (Washington, DC: Urban Institute, 1997), http://newfederalism.urban.org/pdf/anf_4.pdf.

100. Moon and Schneiderman, *Assessing the Growth of California's General Assistance Program.*

CHAPTER 6

Ending Welfare as We Knew It: Temporary Assistance for Needy Families

FROM MOTHERS' AID TO AFDC

The family is the primary social unit, yet the United States has no broad policy that considers the economic, health, social, and psychological needs of families. Instead, a variety of programs address these needs. Since the early twentieth century, three main programs have assisted with financial difficulties faced by poor families with children. The first was state and local mothers' aid programs. Then came federal assistance under the Aid to Dependent Children program, later called Aid to Families with Dependent Children (AFDC). Congress passed legislation in 1996 that transformed AFDC into a block grant—Temporary Assistance for Needy Families (TANF). All of these programs have provided cash assistance so that children can continue to be cared for in their own homes. Today, one-fifth of children in the United States live in poverty. If there is any segment of society for whom people have compassion, it is children, who are completely dependent on others to meet their needs. Why then have these public assistance programs been mired in a sea of controversy? As we shall see, the conflict centers on the parents of poor children and whether these parents participate in the labor force and provide financial support to their children.

Mothers' Aid

In the early twentieth century, the states began formalizing laws to help children whose parents lacked the financial means to care for their physical needs. Local governments often provided the funds for these programs. The programs were intended to help children whose fathers were deceased; sometimes assistance was also provided to children whose fathers were disabled or absent through divorce or desertion. These early programs were called *mothers' aid* or *mothers' pensions.*[1]

Aid to Dependent Children

The federal government stepped in to share responsibility for dependent children in 1935, when the Aid to Dependent Children (ADC) program was included as part of the original Social Security Act. ADC was conceived of as a short-term device to assist financially needy children. The program was intended to diminish and eventually become outmoded as more and more families came to qualify for assistance under the social insurance programs of the Social Security Act.[2] According to Senator Daniel P. Moynihan (D-New York), the "typical beneficiary" was supposed to be "a West Virginia mother whose husband had been killed in a mine accident."[3] But the emphasis of the early ADC program was not on providing aid for widows; it was on providing help to mothers on behalf of their children.

Keeping the Family Together

The ADC program grew slowly for many years with only minor changes made in some aspects of the program. Not until 1950 were the needs of the parent in an ADC family considered, and they too became eligible for assistance. Other improvements were also made. Medical services, paid in part by the federal government, became available to recipients. In 1958 a formula was developed so that states with lower per capita incomes received more federal assistance for their ADC programs than wealthier states.

But other parts of the program were becoming sore spots. One of the most stinging accusations leveled against ADC was that it contributed to fathers deserting their families. Although this argument was difficult to prove,[4] we can see how it arose. Under ADC, families with an able-bodied father residing at home were not eligible for benefits. In some cases, unemployed fathers qualified for other assistance—unemployment compensation, workers' compensation, Social Security Disability Insurance, or Aid to the Permanently and Totally Disabled. But it was quite likely that the father did not qualify for any of these programs or had exhausted his benefits. Consequently, an unemployed, able-bodied father who could not find work did not qualify for ADC and could not support his family. However, if he deserted, the family could become eligible for ADC assistance. It is not known how many fathers left so their families could receive aid. Parents may be absent for many reasons. They may be separated from their spouses because of incompatibility, or they may be in mental hospitals, nursing homes, or prisons. But the fact remained that when an able-bodied but unemployed father was at home, the family could not receive ADC.

To address this problem, two changes were made in ADC. First, in 1961 a new component called the ADC-Unemployed Parent (UP) program was enacted. This antirecession measure made it possible for children to receive aid because of a parent's unemployment.[5] Second, in 1962 the program's name was changed to Aid to Families with Dependent Children (AFDC) to emphasize the family unit. More importantly, a second adult was considered eligible for aid in states with AFDC-UP programs and in cases where one of the child's parents was incapacitated.

In 1967 the AFDC-UP program was changed to the AFDC-Unemployed Father program, but in 1979 the U.S. Supreme Court ruled that it was unconstitutional to provide benefits to unemployed fathers but not to unemployed mothers. Thus the program was changed back to AFDC-UP. Only half of the states voluntarily enacted AFDC-UP programs, and the number of fathers who received aid remained small. In 1988, the Family Support Act made some significant changes in AFDC. Among them, it required all states to have an AFDC-UP program. Despite the commotion over it, relatively few families were added to the rolls.[6] This was probably because many states' eligibility requirements remained quite strict, and AFDC-UP programs had to favor parents who were recently unemployed, while excluding the "hard core" unemployed.

In retrospect, it may seem unfair to have excluded families with able-bodied unemployed parents from the ADC and AFDC programs. But for all the concern about welfare causing family breakup, a 1977 review of studies failed to show that AFDC-UP programs were associated with increased marital stability; in fact, evidence pointed in the opposite direction.[7] Although some data did show greater marital instability in states with higher AFDC payments, there was "little support" for higher payments "being a powerful destabilizer."[8] A decade later, researchers concluded that "the impacts of welfare on family structure are very modest. Comparisons of changes in family structure over time with changes in the welfare system and of differences in family structures across states both suggest that welfare has minimal effects on family structure."[9] Changes in family dynamics and family composition had occurred among all segments of the population and seemed to be a more reasonable explanation for the composition of families receiving AFDC. In the 1990s the evidence was the same: "While it is true that the system does provide adverse incentives for the formation of two-parent families, the empirical studies show conclusively that the magnitude of these disincentive effects is very small, such that our welfare system cannot explain the high rates of [female] headship and illegitimacy."[10]

Man-in-the-House Rules

Even if public assistance is not the root cause of family instability, the number of able-bodied parents who receive benefits continues to fuel debate in a public concerned with the morality of welfare recipients. The work ethic, firmly entrenched in American culture, suggests that those capable of self-support should not be entitled to public aid. In the early days of ADC and AFDC, this belief was reflected in "man-in-the-house rules." It was clear that only in specific circumstances could able-bodied fathers be present while the family collected AFDC benefits. These concerns also carried over into welfare mothers' relationships with other men. The thought of welfare mothers allowing able-bodied men to spend time in their homes presented a threat to those who wanted to ensure that payments went only to the "right" people. The AFDC check was intended for the children and their mother, and in some cases, the children's father. It was considered immoral and illegal for the mother to allow anyone else to benefit from the welfare check. "Midnight raids"—home visits to welfare mothers late at night—were sometimes conducted to ensure that no adult males resided in

AFDC households, because these men could be considered "substitute fathers" responsible for the family's financial support. Although welfare "cheating" continues to be a concern (see Chapter 7), midnight raids are now eschewed by most professionals. More sophisticated means, often electronic checks of state and federal records, are generally used to monitor recipients' compliance with program rules.

TRYING TO MAKE PARENTS PAY

In 1968 the U.S. Supreme Court determined that man-in-the house rules could not be used as a method for "flatly denying" children public assistance. The emphasis today has shifted to methods of making legally recognized fathers and mothers support their children. Congress's first attempt to intervene in child support came in 1950. Subsequent and also largely futile efforts to improve child support collections followed in the 1960s.[11] Not until 1975 did Congress make more concerted efforts to locate absent parents, establish paternity, and obtain child support through Part D of Title IV of the Social Security Act (called the IV-D program).[12] This action was prompted by the growing number of children receiving AFDC who were born to parents who were not married to each other and whose absent parent was contributing little or nothing to their support. Rising divorce rates were also contributing to nonsupport.

Because states were not collecting enough, and because their efforts were still considered too lax, the Child Support Enforcement (CSE) Amendments of 1984 toughened the methods that states could use to collect overdue support payments. Sentiments regarding the measure were so strong that the bill passed both houses of Congress unanimously. Parents whose payments are in arrears (usually 30 days late or more) may be subject to warning notices, reports to credit agencies, wage garnishment, civil and criminal charges, interception of federal and state income tax refunds, property liens, seizure and sale of property, and requirements that they post a bond. Unemployment checks can also be tapped. Even so, these measures prompted only a small amount of arrearage collections (in 1991 only 8 percent of the $21 billion owed was recovered).[13]

In addition to AFDC families, the 1984 amendments extended child support enforcement assistance to all families in which children were not receiving financial support from their noncustodial parent. Today, this provision applies to families who are not receiving TANF. Although there is often more to be collected for non-TANF families, criticism is that this provision detracts from efforts to secure support for the nation's poorest children. Some of those who believe that the emphasis should be on families receiving public assistance bluntly state that it is these families who are costing the taxpayers money. Because states are backlogged with cases, private companies have organized to increase child support collections. Generally they take a percentage of whatever is recovered in back due support. The public CSE programs must charge an application fee not to exceed $25 to non-TANF families (the fee can be assessed to the noncustodial parent).

In about one-third of child support cases, the child's parents do not reside in the same state.[14] When a child's parents reside in different states, the states are supposed to cooperate in securing child support. These cases are often more difficult to pursue, because not all states use the same approach at reciprocity, and local courts exercise considerable autonomy in handling cases. There are several methods of enforcing support across state lines. One is "long arm of the law" statutes, which allow the state in which the child resides to "reach out and grab" the noncompliant parent. To improve interstate support all states eventually passed some form of the Uniform Reciprocal Enforcement of Support Act, but it was apparently "uniform in name only."[15] As part of the Personal Responsibility and Work Opportunity Reconciliation Act of 1996, all states were required to adopt the model Uniform Interstate Family Support Act (UIFSA) by 1998. UIFSA limits control of child support to a single state and should bring about better interstate enforcement.[16] Hopes are that a beefed-up federal locator service will also boost collections. The Welfare Reform Act of 1996 also established a National Directory of New Hires. The names of newly employed workers submitted by employers are traced to see if these individuals are in arrears on child support. The 1996 law and earlier provisions put a great deal of emphasis on automated systems to promote CSE collections.

Despite increased enforcement, by 1991 44 percent of families with an absent father did not have a child support order.[17] In one third of these cases the custodial mother did not pursue an award. Other reasons for no award were inability to locate the father, or the father's inability to pay. In 1993, 40 percent had no order. According to some researchers, many mothers do not pursue an award because it is "not worth it."[18] The feeling is that they have more to gain (or little to lose) financially and emotionally by maintaining informal relationships with the noncustodial parent rather than tangling with the child support bureaucracy. As a practical matter in TANF cases, the federal and state governments generally take all the father pays to recover TANF payments, so the family does not gain financially by working with the CSE agency. In other cases the custodial parent does not seek an award because she fears the noncustodial parent or feels he will be a bad influence on the child.

Of all families due support in 1991, about half received the full amount due, about a quarter received partial payment, and about a quarter received no payment.[19] The average amount due was $3,321, and the average amount received was $2,227. Studies indicate that many fathers can pay more than they are asked to contribute.[20] Mothers who have less than a bachelor's degree, were never married, are black or of Hispanic origin, or are poor are least likely to have orders. Although the percentage of women who actually collect payments is similar regardless of demographic characteristics, women with the aforementioned characteristics collect less.

In 1993, child support paternities were established in just 45 percent of 1.2 million births to unwed mothers,[21] still far short of the goals that the CSE program had hoped to achieve. To increase the number of supporting fathers, mothers or other caretakers receiving AFDC were required to assist with paternity determination as they are under the TANF program. Those who refuse to cooperate can lose at least 25 percent of the family's TANF grant or be terminated from the program. The federal government allows states to excuse the child's mother or other caretaker from this requirement if it is not in the child's best interest. Federal law now allows states to determine when this is not required. Typically exemptions have been made if the noncustodial parent is abusive. Sometimes the child support collection is sufficient to remove the family from the public assistance rolls, but in 1991 about 24 percent of custodial parents due child support were in poverty, and this figure would not have changed significantly even if all the child support payments due them had been made.[22] States were required to send the first $50 a month collected in child support to the AFDC family without a reduction in AFDC benefits, but they no longer have to do this under TANF. Most states wasted no time in revoking this "$50 pass through" when TANF became effective.[23]

The Office of Child Support Enforcement, established in 1975, is the federal entity responsible for overseeing the IV-D program and assisting states with their programs. The federal government pays 66 percent of most costs of operating state IV–D programs; it pays 90 percent of the costs of blood tests for paternity determination and 80 to 90 percent of the costs of automated tracking systems.[24] The states must share the collections they make in TANF cases with the federal government in order to defray some of the federal costs of TANF. In order to promote collection efforts, the federal government makes incentive payments to states of at least 6 percent of their collections regardless of how much they collect and as much as 10 percent for states with better ratios of collection to administrative costs. States vary considerably in their ratios of expenditures to collections. After criticisms that the 6 percent incentive did nothing to encourage efficiency and that non-TANF cases were detracting from collecting in TANF cases, the non-TANF incentives were capped. Today, the incentive for non-TANF cases cannot exceed 115 percent of the incentive for TANF cases.

States that fail to comply with federal CSE regulations may be subject to reduced TANF grants. To further rectify problems with the incentive system, the Secretary of Health and Human Services was required to make recommendations to Congress. Her plan would reward program performance based on five key indicators: paternities established, support orders established, collection on current and past due support, and cost effectiveness. The secretary has proposed that incentives be based on the amount states collect, but with no cap on collections in non-TANF cases. Congress may soon act on these recommendations.[25]

One way that the federal government is trying to boost collections is to require states to adopt "a simple civil process for voluntarily acknowledging paternity," including efforts to have fathers acknowledge paternity at the hospital when their child is born.[26] One study suggested that the highest rates of paternity determinations are made in counties where fathers have more than one opportunity to acknowledge paternity voluntarily, rather than in counties that handle all cases through the courts.[27] Counties that provide multiple opportunities generally assign the cases of cooperative fathers to the welfare agency and reserve the courts for contested cases.

Many noncustodial parents pay their child support voluntarily. Some pay directly to the custodial parent, although today payments are commonly made through a local government office. To further ensure that payments are made, the norm is now to require employers to withhold money directly from the noncustodial parent's paycheck. Since 1994, all states must use this method when a new support order is initiated (there are exceptions), whether or not the state's CSE agency is involved.

When an absent, nonsupporting parent cannot be located with information from the custodial parent, additional efforts are supposed to be made. To do this, each state operates a parent locator service with information from its tax, motor vehicle registration, unemployment compensation records, and similar sources. There is also the Federal Parent Locator Service with access to Social Security, IRS, veterans, and other national databases. Since many paternity cases are not acknowledged voluntarily, the states resort to blood typing, DNA evidence, or other tests.[28]

States must also establish guidelines to determine the amount of child support noncustodial parents should pay. In most cases, states must now also pursue health care coverage for the child. There are basically three approaches used to determine the amount of support owed.[29] The *income shares* method, used in 31 states, is based on both parents' income. It rests on the assumption that children should receive the same share of their parents' income as if the family lived together. A percentage of the parents' combined income is used to determine the amount of support required. The higher the parents' income, the lower the percent they are assessed, but the total amount rises as income increases. The amount owed is apportioned between the parents based on their incomes. The actual child support award is the amount assessed the noncustodial parent. A second approach, *percentage of income,* also assumes that children should share in their parents income, but it is based on the noncustodial parent's income and the number of children. The 15 states that use this approach differ in the percent assessed. Wisconsin, for example, assesses 17 percent for one child, rising to 34 percent for five or more children. A basic difference between the two approaches is that the percentage of income approach is based on a flat rate, while with the income shares approach, the percent of income contributed declines as the noncustodial parent's income increases. Some people believe the income shares approach is inequitable because the child should have the same right to the noncustodial parent's income even if that income rises. Others believe the percentage of income approach is inequitable because it disregards what the custodial parent can afford to contribute. *Melson-Delaware* is a third approach. Used in only three states, it begins with setting aside an amount deemed necessary for each parent to meet his or her subsistence needs. Next, a primary support amount is determined for each child and is apportioned between the parents. If the parents have additional income, a percentage of it is also allocated to the children. Massachusetts and the District of Columbia use variants of the three approaches. These procedures can produce very different amounts for the same family from state to state. For families in poverty, the approaches used to determine payments take their very low income into account and are more complex.[30] Review and modification of child support orders are important to ensure that they remain adequate and equitable. Since court procedures are especially costly, time consuming, complex, and arduous, administrative processes often seem preferable in establishing child support orders.[31] Even so, the courts may afford greater protections and remedies to parents.

The number of paternity determinations and amount of support collected has increased, but the system is still not working well. States continue to be criticized for dragging their feet in pursuing delinquent parents. In 1995, the national paternity determination rate for CSE programs was 41 percent, ranging from 80 percent in Wisconsin to 4 percent in the District of Columbia.[32] In that year, the federal and state governments spent almost $3 billion to collect $10.8 billion in child support. About 294,000 families left AFDC due to child support collections. In 1996, the rate of paternity determinations increased to 50 percent. About $3 billion was spent to collect $12 billion in support (about $9 billion was for non-AFDC families and $3 billion for AFDC families); nearly 16 percent of AFDC payments were recouped due to CSE programs; 5.8 million parents were located, and 717,000 paternities and over 1 million support orders were established.[33] Data for 1997 indicate that the number of cases with collections increased to 4.2 million, up 48 percent since 1992. Total collections were $13.4 billion. In all 1.3 million paternities were established, two and a half times the 1992 figure.[34]

Although most states' CSE programs are coming out ahead, the federal government continues to lose money. In 1998, its net cost was $1.2 billion.[35] Much of this resulted from the non-TANF cases that were pursued and the federal financial assistance given to states for their CSE programs. There are other ways to look at these costs. It has been pointed out that these costs do not consider welfare cost avoidance. One study estimated that in 1991 for every $5 collected in support for non-AFDC cases, $1 of welfare payments was avoided, a welfare savings of $1 billion.[36] On the other hand, some people believe that CSE costs are understated because figures are not adjusted for the number of paternities that would have been established and payments that would have been made without CSE programs. One estimate is that only 25 percent of collections in AFDC cases were a direct result of CSE.[37]

The Committee on Ways and Means reports that over the years, CSE performance has not changed much. Compared to 1978, awards made in 1993 still amounted to only 60 percent of cases; the number of the families that received any payment increased only 2 percent, while the number that received full payment decreased by 6 percent.[38] More is being collected, but this is apparently due to the influx of cases, especially cases not previously under CSE purview in which payments would have been made anyway. Perhaps the 50 or so changes made to the nation's CSE program by the 1996 welfare reform legislation will help to improve this picture. The states must now work toward establishing paternity in 90 percent of cases, a pretty tall order given that many states have not come near this figure.

If there is something more positive to be said about government intervention in child support, perhaps it is that no dollar estimate can capture the social and psychological benefits to families that may occur when parents pay support, or the symbolic benefits that the public feels from knowing that justice has been served.[39] States have gotten tougher. Some were revoking drivers', business, and recreational licenses of parents who fail to pay support even before the Personal Responsibility Act included this provision. Some communities print the names or pictures of nonsupporting parents in local newspapers and others use Internet web sites for this purpose.

President Clinton supports posting pictures of the worst offenders in post offices. Some communities conduct stings or roundups of "deadbeat" parents as they are often called, and some judges don't hesitate to send parents to jail when they repeatedly fail to pay. At the same time, noncustodial fathers have organized to focus attention on their rights. Some fathers are concerned that they are paying child support when they have little recourse if the child's mother refuses visitation or spends the child support unwisely. Fathers with joint custody and visitation rights are more likely to pay support[40] so there is considerable reason to focus on arrangements that are fair to both parents. Recognizing this, the federal government has provided some funding for all states to promote access and visitation. Illustration 6-1 provides some interesting information about the ways mothers and fathers view CSE.

Despite a less-than-stellar history, hope remains that child support can be increased. The federal government is funding demonstration programs to determine what might be helpful. These include collaborations among child support enforcement, Head Start, and child care programs and looking at ways of making CSE programs responsive to low-income noncustodial fathers in order to encourage more responsible parenting. Washington state has received permission to use some of its federal CSE funds to implement "Devoted Dads," a program to promote the financial and emotional involvement of parents, especially young fathers, in their childrens' lives.[41]

There are other ways to help children obtain support. Irwin Garfinkel and his colleagues discuss a child support assurance (rather than enforcement) system.

> *Under this system, child support awards would be set by a nationally legislated formula based on a percentage of the noncustodial parent's income, and payments would be deducted from the absent parent's earnings, just like Social Security deductions. The federal government guarantees a minimum level of child support*—an assured benefit—*just like minimum benefits in old age and unemployment insurance.*[42]

Garfinkel believes that an assured benefit would increase the number of families receiving government subsidies but that it would actually reduce "the size of government and administrative costs" because of the time and expense it takes to administer public assistance programs as opposed to a more universal child assurance program.[43] No matter how reasonable this approach sounds, it is unlikely that Garfinkel or anyone else will convince the Republican-controlled Congress that his plan has either fiscal or moral utility. Even liberals would have a difficult time defending it in the current political climate. It is a far cry from the plan set out by Congress in the Personal Responsibility and Work Opportunity Reconciliation Act of 1996.

WELFARE AND WORK

The original ADC program was designed when the preference was for mothers to stay home to care for their children. Requiring mothers to work or forcing fathers to pay child support had not yet entered the equation. But demographic, social, and economic

ILLUSTRATION 6-1

What Mothers and Fathers Think About Child Support Enforcement

The custodial mothers and noncustodial fathers who are most clients of Child Support Enforcement (CSE) programs have much to say about CSE. Although not necessarily representative of all families involved in CSE, the following excerpts provide some impressions of those who have been involved in the Parents' Fair Share Demonstration Program or similar programs designed to help unemployed, noncustodial parents increase their abilities to support their children.

WHAT SOME MOTHERS HAVE TO SAY[a]

IMPRESSIONS OF THE CHILD SUPPORT SYSTEM

Most of the people I spoke to felt that the Office of Child Support was more a part of the problem than of the solution. There was no one who had not had at least some contact with the Office of Child Support, which the residents of Baltimore City referred to simply as "downtown." While everyone I spoke to endorsed the principle of child support, they were generally disgusted with the way the current system operates. In the focus group, Beebee Evers seemed to sum up the feelings of everyone around the table when she declared: "The system sucks. . . . It really does because . . . the guys go down there and still don't pay anything." Her comment prompted a round of complaints about downtown.

"EVERYTHING GETS LOST IN THE MAIL."

The most frequent criticism of child support was that the system does not work. After a round of disparaging comments in the focus group about the way things work downtown, I remarked: "I hear a lot of you saying you don't have much faith in the system here." The responses were similar:

Angie: Not at all.

Amy: That's no joke.

Lydia: "We mailed it off two weeks ago."

Amy: "You should have had it, and I don't know what happened."

Lydia: And then when they lose a check, and you got to go down there and look through all these checks. . . . I don't know how many checks that I haven't received.

Complaints about the inefficiency of the system were rampant. In both the focus group and interviews, I was regaled with stories about the system's inability to collect payments. Beebee describes the former partner of one of her friends:

Now he works for the city. Why can't they just snatch him up real quick and fast? I don't think that they are doing anything about it. I really don't. . . .

"THEY GIVE UP ON THE FATHERS THAT DON'T PAY."

As the comments above indicate, most women thought that the system was not really interested in pursuing the men who held out. Other women bitterly protested that men who

continued

ILLUSTRATION 6-1 *(continued)*

defied the system generally got away with it. Several reported that attempts to garnish their child's father's wages only backfired. They claimed the men responded by quitting their jobs when they were told that they would have to pay back child support. In the focus group, the women reported that the child support system succeeded in scaring the men, but there was little follow through. "Don't scare them," Amy said, "do it. The only way that it would probably have helped Jordon is just stop scaring him, just throw him in jail, period." She wanted downtown to be tougher. A few other women shared her view that if the system were tougher, there might be more compliance.

Others in the group had their doubts that tougher enforcement was possible or even that it would be a deterrent in their families. Wanda, for example, claimed that Lionnel would just defy attempts at getting tough. In any event, even if he were thrown in jail, it would not help her kids. It seemed that some women despaired of getting any cooperation from resistant fathers who had little to lose by refusing to comply.

And the men I spoke to—both those who paid and those who did not—were not any more sanguine about getting the system to operate more effectively. Some favored tougher sanctions. Others thought that approach would not work. But almost all agreed that the system was too impersonal to be responsive to people's needs. Ricky, with a mixture of concern and scorn, described how he had been discouraged from paying child support by the bureaucratic rules. He, like other fathers, preferred to pay child support directly or "under the table," believing that the money was more likely to reach his children. The practice of paying outside the system was common. Vernon told me that he simply took care of his child's expenses without a formal agreement.

"THE MONEY DOESN'T GET TO THE CHILDREN, ANYWAY."

Ricky's view that paying into the system does not work to the child's benefit was held by other informants. Several women who had received cash assistance described how child support payments were used to pay back the welfare system:

> *They sent me a letter [and] told me that they would continue on taking his taxes until the full amount [for back assistance] is paid up.*

This procedure of linking child support to the repayment of welfare had the effect of making both the father and mother feel that the money that came into the system was not going to support their children. For some men, this was a further excuse to evade payments; for some women, the low payoff from the system discouraged them from cooperating in efforts to locate the father. For both men and women, it reinforced the impression that downtown was more of an interference than a source of assistance. They were convinced that the system was not designed to help them out.

WHAT SOME FATHERS HAVE TO SAY[b]

PAYING: THEORY VERSUS REALITY

Their current lack of income is only one of the reasons that many of the men interviewed are not fulfilling their child support obligations. These reasons were seldom explicitly stated in terms of "I don't pay because. . . ." However,

continued

ILLUSTRATION 6-1 *(continued)*

the fathers talked about the child support system, and sometimes the mothers of their children, in ways that often sounded like: "If I had the money and it were up to me, I might not pay because. . . ."

PROVIDING VERSUS PAYING THROUGH THE SYSTEM

For some, there is a crucial distinction between complying with the formal child support system and making direct payments to the mothers and/or buying things for their children. While Milt B. claimed to be a lavish provider for his son, he was not doing all of it through the formal child support system and, in fact, he objected strongly to the legal mechanisms for child support, which he thought were unnecessary for fathers who were in contact with their children: "It's another thing to pay the [child support enforcement agency] and see your kid, too. I see my kid every day." After describing the expensive clothes and other items that he had provided, Milt B. volunteered—even bragged—that he was doing this outside the system:

> *I don't give the [child support enforcement agency] all my goddamn money. No way. . . . What I can't see is why you want to pay them. I can see you owe a hospital bill or something like that, right? Whyn't you just send the money to the hospital bill? You give the [child support enforcement agency] money, your wife don't get the money for three weeks later.*

"MAKE ME"

Clark S. had a different explanation for his defiance of the system. He told a complicated tale of the child support enforcement agency's failure to take his money:

> *They screwed up at first. [Everyone laughs.] They did, seriously. When they first told me they was going to start garnishing my check, I had left the first job I was working at. So now all this paperwork done, they found out where I was working at, I talked to the man and worked out my payments. Now they sent me some more paperwork, but from the previous job that I had, not from the job I was at then. So they messed me up. 'Cause they could have been taking money. I was at the job four years . . . They didn't do anything. And I wasn't gonna say: "Well, hell, come and take care of this" 'cause that's money I had to survive on.*

As Clark S. explained it, when the child support enforcement agency finally caught up to him, he lost his job, and he blamed the child support system for his accumulated debt. . . .

Two other men in the group reported situations that could easily have been the result of years of noncompliance with the child support system. Robert D., a soft-spoken man who had difficulty getting into the discussion, made his statement several times before he was recognized: "I owe $14,000." At one time, he had had $18,000 in child support arrears and he was intrigued by a rumored (but nonexistent) method of discharging child support debts: "They have a new thing they bringing out, you can go to the penitentiary and stay two years, and you don't have to pay no more child support." Robert D. was 37 years old, with a child age 20; his "baby" was 15.

Roger J., who was on his third time through the job-finding workshop, was about $8,000 in arrears on child support, and his

continued

ILLUSTRATION 6-1 *(continued)*

noncompliance had interrupted his life considerably:

> *I'm just getting tired of getting locked up every so often, every eight months or so. I don't have no bad record, no record at all. But I just keep getting locked up for child support, that's the main thing. . . .*

THE SYSTEM: "THAT'S NOT RIGHT"

The local child support enforcement agency came in for a lot of criticism from the men involved in this group. It sometimes seemed to be the source of all their troubles, and certainly was the source of a great deal of pressure in their lives. As Robert D. put it: "Yeah, [the child support system] that's the number one racket." John D., who estimated his child support arrears at $600, said that "it's hectic"—trying to keep up child support payments, pay off past child support debts, and have money for themselves and/or their new families. "That's what's killing us," he said.

[a]Frank F. Furstenberg, Jr., "Daddies and Fathers: Men Who Do for Their Children and Men Who Don't," in Frank F. Furstenberg, Jr., Kay E. Sherwood, and Mercer L. Sullivan, Parents' Fair Share Demonstration, *Caring and Paying: What Fathers and Mothers Say About Child Support* (New York: Manpower Demonstration Research Corporation, July 1992), pp. 34–56. These excerpts are from mothers in the Baltimore area and are found on pp. 51–53. Copyright © 1992 by the Manpower Demonstration Research Corporation and used with their permission.

[b]Kay E. Sherwood, "Child Support Obligations: What Fathers Say About Paying," in Frank F. Furstenberg, Jr., Kay E. Sherwood, and Mercer L. Sullivan, Parents' Fair Share Demonstration, *Caring and Paying: What Fathers and Mothers Say About Child Support* (New York: Manpower Demonstration Research Corporation, July 1992), pp. 57–76. These excerpts are from fathers in the Grand Rapids, Michigan, area and are found on pp. 61–62. Copyright © 1992 by the Manpower Demonstration Research Corporation and used with their permission.

changes caused the program to evolve in ways that no one had anticipated. As the 1960s emerged, the focus was no longer on providing financial support alone as a means of alleviating poverty; "rehabilitating" people to help them escape poverty through greater opportunities became the order of the day. But as AFDC rolls continued to grow, Americans became increasingly unhappy about providing public assistance to those who seem capable of working. The focus shifted again, this time to decreasing welfare dependency through more incentives and tougher requirements to work.

Rehabilitation for Work

The first large-scale approach at rehabilitating people in order to break their ties with public assistance came in the 1962 social service amendments to the Social Security Act. This approach was designed to reduce poverty by treating personal and social problems that stood in the way of financial independence.[44] Services included counseling, vocational training, child management training, family-planning services, and legal services. States found a bonus in providing social services to public assistance recipients—for every dollar they spent, the federal government matched it with three more dollars, far more lucrative than the reimbursement formula for AFDC cash payments. To ensure the success of the social service amendments, worker caseloads were to be small—no more than sixty clients. But states were criticized for claiming federal matching funds for many services they were already providing to clients,[45] and it was difficult to find enough qualified social workers to provide services.[46] What had sounded good in theory could often not be put into practice.

Job Training and WIN

When social services were introduced as a way to help welfare recipients achieve financial independence, the AFDC caseworker was responsible for seeing that the family got its benefit check and its social services. In fact, AFDC mothers may have feared that if they did not accept social services, benefits might be terminated. At the same time, social workers complained that the time spent determining eligibility left little time to provide social services.[47]

In 1967 Congress separated payments from social services. A payments worker became responsible for matters related to the welfare check, while another worker was responsible for providing social services. This was the era of welfare rights, and this new approach recognized that poverty may be attributable to a variety of causes—some of them purely economic; not all poor families needed rehabilitation through social services. Families who wished to receive social services were still entitled and encouraged to do so. Social workers could devote more time to these cases.

Enthusiasm for the rehabilitation approach faded rapidly as welfare rolls continued to grow. A new strategy was needed, and the one chosen was tougher. Amendments passed in 1967 also emphasized work, and both "carrot" and "stick" measures were employed to achieve this purpose.[48] The "stick" included work requirements for unemployed fathers on AFDC, as well as for mothers and some teenagers. The "carrot" was the Work Incentive Now (WIN) program, established by Congress to train recipients for work and to help them locate employment. (The original name was the Work Incentive Program but the acronym WIP obviously could not be used.) The federal government threatened to deny AFDC matching funds to states that paid benefits to able-bodied recipients who refused to work or receive job training.

Other measures were also taken to encourage recipients to work. According to the "thirty plus one-third rule," welfare payments were not reduced for the first $30 of earned income, and one-third of all additional income was disregarded in determining eligibility until the limit on earnings was reached. Day care services were supposed to be provided for WIN participants, but in many cases, shortages of licensed facilities prevented placing children while their mothers worked or trained for jobs.

AFDC rolls were still climbing. Strategies aimed at encouraging welfare recipients to work once again failed to produce the results that rational planners had intended. Perhaps these failures had to do with the fact that participants did not earn enough in marginal, low-wage jobs to make work a rational alternative after deducting work-related expenses (clothes, transportation, and child care). Short-term training programs generally do not enable recipients to substantially increase their earnings.[49] Some find that in order to survive they must rely on a combination of "a little work and a little welfare." In fact sociologist Roberta Spalter-Roth and economist Heidi Hartmann found that 40 percent of AFDC mothers had rather substantial work effort over a two-year period, and that these women either combined paid work and welfare benefits or cycled between work and welfare.[50] These researchers believe that "combining work and welfare" could be a promising strategy for raising families receiving public assistance out of poverty—*if* current policies are revised to "make work pay" such as increasing the minimum wage and guaranteeing health care benefits. As economist Gary Burtless puts it, "The truth is that lifting welfare recipients out of poverty requires both work programs *and* generous transfer benefits."[51]

Workfare

The next approach to emerge was workfare—mandatory employment in return for welfare payments. This concept is actually as old as the hills. In its most punitive forms, the workhouses of the Elizabethan period and similar institutions in the United States fit under the rubric of workfare.[52] The concept has carried over into present-day welfare programs. As more women with young children have joined the labor force, the argument has been that mothers receiving public assistance should do the same. Feminist Barbara Ehrenreich calls this line of thinking illogical, arguing that just because it is the trend does not mean it is right. She adds that "We are being asked to believe that pushing destitute mothers into the work force (in some versions of workfare, for no other compensation than the welfare payments they would have received anyway) is consistent with women's striving toward self-determination."[53] Another set of views on workfare can be summed up this way: after nearly four hundred years of various forms of these programs, both experience and empirical evidence indicate they have failed to improve the job skills of participants; they have failed to reduce the costs of welfare; they do not discourage malingering because the number of malingerers is already negligible; and welfare recipients who can would gladly take jobs if decent ones were available.[54] But as we shall see, workfare programs have received increasing public and political support.

There was some evidence that work programs could work. For example, in the 1980s the Massachusetts Employment and Training Program, called ET, got good reviews (albeit at a time when the state's unemployment rate was quite low and recipients could be more easily placed in jobs). ET was a voluntary program and participants could choose between career counseling, education and training, on-the-job training, and job placement. Those in training got day care services for a year and Medicaid benefits for fifteen months. Would a mandatory approach to work programs produce the same success?[55] Early controlled studies funded primarily by the Ford Foundation and conducted by the nonprofit Manpower Demonstration Research Corporation (MDRC) suggested that it might be possible. A multisite study primarily involving the states of Arkansas, Virginia, and West Virginia and the cities of Baltimore and San Diego during the WIN program era showed that

1. Workfare was "successful" for AFDC mothers, but not necessarily AFDC fathers; mothers' employment rates increased and so did their earnings.
2. There were welfare cost savings, but participants did not necessarily net substantially more than they would have from welfare alone.
3. Participants without recent work histories made greater gains than those with recent work histories.
4. Participants generally worked at entry-level jobs and did not substantially increase their work skills.
5. Participants and employers were generally pleased with the program, although participants felt they were underpaid and that the employer benefited most.[56]

The sites used different approaches, but most relied on job search assistance and thirteen weeks mandatory employment. No one model proved superior.

Another question raised was whether longer and more intensive efforts could improve results. So, MDRC studied a long-term mandatory workfare program—the Saturation Work Initiative Model (SWIM) in San Diego—and also found higher employment rates and earnings for experimental group participants; there were also welfare cost savings.[57] But again, net income for the experimental group did not change much—"gains in earnings were largely offset by reductions in government transfer payments." Participants spent the first two weeks in a job search workshop. Those who did not find jobs "were assigned to three months unpaid work experience" and "bi-weekly job club sessions" that provide links to social services in the community.

MDRC also published a study of the longer-term effects of the federally funded SWIM program and three of the state-initiated programs described above that were created under WIN.[58] Again the states included were Virginia and Arkansas and the cities were Baltimore and San Diego. The programs in Virginia and Arkansas were the lower cost, lower service intensity models, with costs per recipient of $430 and $118, respectively. In Baltimore and San Diego the costs were $953 and $920, respectively; these programs were more likely to include training and education services for participants. Most of the participants were women. The data cover a five-year period, two to three years longer than previous studies, in order to determine if the modest gains made by enrollees grew over time. The positive results were that the programs made cost-efficient use of their limited resources; employment among AFDC recipients increased and short-term AFDC receipt was reduced; the portion of AFDC participants' incomes from earnings increased; two of the four programs also resulted in public savings (San Diego and Arkansas) and one likely broke even (Virginia). Less positive was that participants in two of the programs had little or no net gain in income and only one site (Baltimore) showed clear indication of increased job pay; long-term AFDC receipt was not effected in two programs and in the other two reductions were "modest at best." All programs achieved some positive results, but the impacts were not consistent across the four programs. For example, Baltimore participants had the largest increase in earnings but this program was the only one that did not show public savings. The MDRC concluded that:

> *A complex mix of job search, unpaid work assignments, and various kinds of basic and remedial education and occupational training may be necessary for achieving a larger impact within a given program budget. The effectiveness of such services may hinge on the proper combination of program structure, rewards and sanctions, and support services and work incentives.*

The JOBS Program

The evidence to support traditional work programs may have been weak, but the country was not about to give up on work requirements, and so Congress enacted what it considered a better approach—the Job Opportunities and Basic Skills (JOBS) program. As part of the Family Support Act of 1988, JOBS was intended to be "a new social contract between government and welfare recipients," changing the AFDC program from a cash assistance program to a jobs and independence program.[59] It replaced WIN and was to be coordinated with the programs of the Job Training Partnership Act (discussed in Chapter 9). JOBS offered basic education; job skills and readiness training; job development, search, and placement; supportive services; on-the-job training; and community work experience "in areas where it was feasible."[60] Participants' needs such as education and child care were to be considered, as well as their work experience and employability. Most states assigned "case managers" to see that clients received services and that they participated in JOBS.

One parent in AFDC-UP families was generally required to work a minimum of sixteen hours per week in a public- or private-sector job. States had to require single parents with children 3 years of age and older to participate in JOBS, *if* state resources were available; and states could require this of parents with children as young as 1 year if they wished. Federal matching funds for JOBS were set at $1.3 billion for fiscal year 1995 and $1 billion annually thereafter. States could draw 90 percent match for many services, but many did not draw their full allotment, claiming that state budgets were too tight.

The states differed dramatically in the percentage of recipients they claim were eligible for JOBS. For example, in 1991, Kansas, Maryland, and Hawaii reported that 6 percent of their AFDC recipients were required to participate, while Colorado reported 69 percent and Nebraska, 73 percent. The national average was 15 percent. By 1995, states were required to have 20 percent of eligible adults in single-parent families participating in JOBS activities. The national average participation rate was 27 percent of eligibles. In the AFDC-UP program, 38 percent of eligible parents were participating while the requirement was 50 percent with state rates ranging from 6 percent in Hawaii to 80 percent in Kentucky.[61] More than 40 percent of JOBS participants were from 5 states.

Under JOBS, teen parents without high school educations were not required to work, but they were to attend school as a condition of receiving AFDC payments. Many of the Family Support Act provisions were targeted at young parents in the hope of preventing them from joining the ranks of people who are long-term, structurally unemployed and welfare dependent.

The 1988 act required states to provide child care if an AFDC parent was employed or attending training. The federal government supported this effort with unlimited matching funds at the same rate as for AFDC payments. Child care was also to be provided to families that were not receiving AFDC but would be at risk of doing so without child care. In order to make work more attractive, the amount of earnings disregarded in determining AFDC payments was increased. Another important incentive to maintain employment was the extension of health care benefits.

The JOBS program tried to recodify the "welfare problem" from poverty—being poor and lacking opportunity—to dependency—not having a job and the need for greater incentives to self-sufficiency.[62] But did the supposedly intensified efforts under JOBS work better than previous efforts? The MDRC studied two JOBS program approaches over a two-year period.[63] One approach was called labor force attachment (short-term approaches to get participants to work quickly); the other was the human capital development approach (which focused on delaying work entry in favor of building job skills over a longer time period). The attachment approach produced a 24 percent increase in the number working, increased by 16 percent the number leaving AFDC, and raised earnings 26 percent. Still, 57 percent of the treatment group remained on AFDC and the *average* earnings were just $285 a month. The control group earned $226 a month on average and 66 percent stayed on AFDC. Perhaps because the two-year follow-up period was relatively short, the human capital approach did not produce consistent increases in earnings or employment. There was, however, a 14 percent AFDC cost savings. The General Accounting Office (GAO) used another approach to study JOBS.[64] It surveyed a representative sample of 453 JOBS administrators, most of whom estimated that less than half of "job-ready" participants were employed. For the most part, the administrators reported that subsidized jobs and work experience programs were not used to assist participants. The GAO concluded that the programs lacked a strong employment focus.

MDRC has focused considerable energy on studying one of the most highly regarded JOBS programs, California's Greater Avenues for Independence (GAIN) program.[65] GAIN was important because it emphasized basic education for those who lacked it. Participation was required for those who wanted to receive AFDC benefits. After three years, single parents in the experimental group earned a total of $1,414 or 22 percent more than the control group, and they received 8 percent less in AFDC benefits than controls. More than half (53 percent) of experimentals were still receiving AFDC at the end of the three-year period compared to 56 percent of controls. Results were weaker for single parents than for heads of two-parent families. In some of the six counties studied results were more impressive than in others. Most impressive was Riverside County in which experimentals earned 49 percent more than controls, and AFDC payments made to experimentals were 15 percent less than for controls. Comparison of program costs with savings from reduced welfare spending and taxes participants paid on their earnings showed that the Riverside program produced $2.84 for every $1 invested in the program.

After reviewing results of many MDRC studies, it is not surprising that Senator Daniel Patrick Moynihan dubbed Judith Gueron, head of the MDRC, "Our Lady of Modest but Positive Results."[66] For those who wish to delve further into the results of welfare-to-work programs and the complexities of interpreting them, see Dan Bloom's *After AFDC*.[67]

WHY THE FUSS ABOUT AFDC?

Public assistance is a "hot button" topic (see Illustration 6-2). As armchair quarterbacks, we can now review events that spawned the welfare reform of 1996.

Recipients and Costs

The number of ADC and AFDC recipients grew from 1.2 million individuals (349,000 families) in 1940 to 8.5 million individuals (2.2 million families) in 1970, and 11.5 million individuals (4 million families) in 1990 (see Figure 6-1).[68] Since some of this increase can be attributed to general population growth, a fairer way to view the situation

FIGURE 6-1

AFDC Recipients, 1950–1998[a] and Total Benefits, 1950–1996[b]

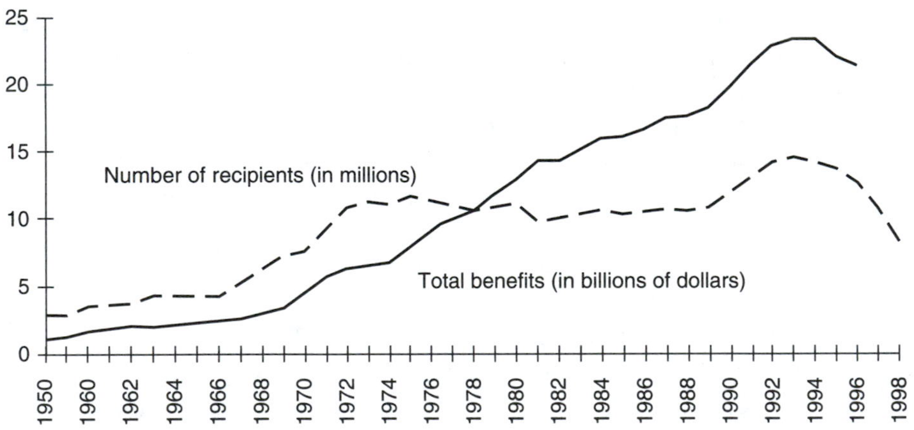

Sources: Social Security Administration, *Social Security Bulletin, Annual Statistical Supplement, 1997* (Washington, DC: Social Security Administration, 1997), http://www.ssa.gov/statistics/supp97/pdf/t9g1.pdf; Administration for Children and Families, Temporary Assistance for Needy Families (TANF), 1936–1998, http://www.acf.dhhs.gov/news/tables.htm.

[a]Recipient figure for 1998 as of June.

[b]Benefit figures for 1997 and 1998 are not available.

ILLUSTRATION 6-2

Why Mother Slapped Me

by Ann Withorn

In our hot southern kitchen, as always, mother washed dishes. I dried while Sister Barbara put away.

I was a senior in high school, taking "Problems in American Democracy," finding out about a new issue every week that needed to be fixed, in time for Mr. Morrow's standard Friday paper. . . .

That week we were studying poverty. Usually, I avoided discussing politics with Mother. She was so sure of her beliefs, and we would fight so easily about so much. But this time I assumed, given the childhood poverty which had shaped her life, that we could have a discussion.

Wrong.

She was adamant that people who took welfare were lazy, and just didn't want to work hard like she and my father did. "Good people can find jobs if they aren't so picky. Women who have made their bed must lie in it," she insisted.

No radical yet, but I was always willing to react to that tone of dismissal in her voice, heard in so many criticisms of me: "Good girls who try to look pretty, and go to church, and don't read so much will be fine. They won't turn out weird like you."

So I took the bait. "But Mother, I thought you would be more sympathetic. After all, you grew up on welfare."

Mother was not a hitter. Words were her weapons. So when the slap in my face came it was almost an involuntary spasm, accompanied by words hissed between closed teeth. "Don't you *ever* say that again. My family did *not* grow up on welfare. Your grandfather was ill, in the hospital, and received veterans benefits. We earned what we received from the government because he fought in the war. We were *never* on welfare." Then she left, yet another night when my "disrespect" left me with the washing *and* the drying of the dishes.

In our household of denial, the incident would never be discussed again. I was left alone to ponder how my grandmother's poverty—caused by Pop's mental illness after tough service in World War I, followed by his life-long hospitalization beginning when Mother was five—was so different from welfare. The Veteran's Administration never sent enough money, and the checks sometimes just did not come. Grandmother had to live, with three kids, in rummy apartments, share space with questionable relatives, and never have enough. People would look down on her; even her cousins would taunt that her children's father was a "crazy man." Why wasn't that like welfare?

I still wonder and still cannot discuss welfare with Mother.

But I can talk and teach and continually try to figure out why it is that welfare is such a hot zone for people. . . .

Once, on a bus, I sat behind two men who were talking about "welfare queens." Both agreed that it was pathetic that the government was giving them money to do nothing, raise criminals, and get fat. But as they talked, their voices got louder, echoing my mother's deep fury. "Who do they think they are?" one

continued

ILLUSTRATION 6-2 *(continued)*

man almost shouted to his friend as he left the bus, "having babies with no fathers, expecting *me* to pay for them?"

It has even affected me. An old friend was in my kitchen, trying to express his doubts to me about whether welfare is good for the Black community where he works. Somehow the idea that I have to defend women on welfare even in my own home, with my own friends, makes me furious. I yelled that he didn't know what he was talking about, how I wouldn't listen to such ignorance in my own kitchen.

I don't usually do this. But I, too, find it hard not to take welfare as a personal issue. When I hear people say cruel things about women on welfare, I want to jump up and scream about how they do not know Debby or Mary or Juanita (or my grandmother?). They work so hard, with so little, and manage so well, or sometimes not so well, in spite of stresses and pressures undiscussed by any "Problems in American Democracy" class.

Over the years of studying poverty, I have come to see that talking about welfare is not about public policy, about how much money should be or can be spent to provide basic economic security to families with children in an uncertain economy. It is about deeply based assumptions about how we view women, and work, and the meaning of the compromises we are supposed to make in this life. . . .

[It] is extremely dangerous to deny the reality to which welfare is such a meager response. Many families *do* fail women who can't survive with bodies and souls intact if they remain either with birth families or with the fathers of their children. Most jobs fail single mothers because they cannot provide the income, benefits, and flexibility they need to raise their children. So welfare, which also fails women, still becomes the best solution. At the cost of continued poverty, disrespect, and bureaucratic indignity, it provides at least time and some flexibility to face, and not deny, the life that one has.

Welfare is so personal because, if we think about it, we cannot escape thinking about how insecure jobs are within this capitalist economy and how so many families are not the source of love and support we wish them to be. It also suggests that there could be another way. . . .

Right now, almost the whole society is trying to slap down women on welfare, telling them, with a societal hiss stronger than any mother could conjure up: "Don't you *ever* say we could have chosen assistance rather than stay in bad marriages; don't you claim that we could have done anything besides take two jobs, never seeing our children and making ourselves sick; don't you *ever* say it because then nothing we've endured makes any sense."

Somehow I knew then, and I know even more clearly now, that even if I have to do the dishes and dry, and get slapped sometimes, it is better to try to say what has to be said, to make such claims, to cry out loud.

Source: Ann Withorn, "Why Mother Slapped Me," in Diane Dujohn and Ann Withorn, eds., *For Crying Out Loud: Women's Poverty in the United States* (Cambridge, MA: South End Press, 1996), pp. 13–16 is to consider AFDC recipients as a percentage of the population. In 1950 recipients were 1.5 percent of the population; by 1970 they were over 4 percent.[69] At the peak number of 14.2 million individuals in 1994, recipients were 5.5 percent of the population. Perhaps this was a smaller percentage of the population than some people thought, yet the perception was that too many people were relying on AFDC.

AFDC costs had also grown over time. In 1940 AFDC benefits totaled $134 million; in 1970 they were $4.9 billion,[70] and by 1990, the total bill for AFDC benefits was $19.1 billion (see Figure 6-1).[71] Even after controlling for inflation, costs had spiraled. But AFDC was only a very small part of governments' budget. At its peak enrollment in 1994, less than 1 (.9) percent of all federal, state, and local expenditures went to the program.[72] Still, many people thought that a substantial number of adult recipients could work and that the public was needlessly providing benefits to many families.

Though total program costs were rising, benefits per family were always very modest. In 1970, the average monthly cash payment to an AFDC family was $178; by 1992 the average had increased to $388. Using the Consumer Price Index, $178 in 1970 was equivalent to $644 in 1992, indicating a 40 percent drop in the average AFDC payment.[73] Prior to "welfare reform" in 1996, the maximum payment had dropped by 51 percent in purchasing power.[74] Within the contiguous states in 1996, maximum benefits for a three-person family ranged from a low of $120 per month in Mississippi to $703 in Suffolk County, New York,[75] a substantial difference even considering variations in the cost of living.

How did states decide what to offer in benefits? They generally started out in a rational manner by calculating a standard of need that considered what it would cost families of various sizes to meet basic food, shelter, clothing, and other needs. The Center for Budget and Policy Priorities found that the most common methods of determining need were adoption of the federal government's poverty guidelines; a "market basket" approach in which living expenses were calculated for the area; and use of Bureau of Labor Statistics figures for a modest standard of living.[76] Other methods were also used, but in some states need was not really determined. For example, in a few states the legislature determined the standard based on available funding, and another handful had used the same standard for so long that the method used to determine it could not be recalled!

States were then supposed to consider as eligible families whose gross income did not exceed 185 percent of need as long as their net income (after allowable deductions) did not exceed the standard of need. However, payment standards could be set below the standard of need, and only families with net incomes less than the payment standard were actually offered assistance. In 1996, most jurisdictions paid less than the need standard, and 16 also had a maximum benefit that was less than its payment standard.[78] For example, in Alabama, the need standard for a parent and two children was $673 a month, but both its payment standard and maximum benefit were $164. In California, the needs standard and payment standard were $730 but its maximum payment was $607. In Wyoming, the need standard was $674, the payment standard was $590, and the maximum benefit was $360.

These examples might seem more rational if we consider that families receiving public assistance usually get other benefits like food stamps that help to meet their survival needs. Under TANF (and previously under AFDC) families in states with lower payments receive more in food stamp benefits than families in states with higher TANF payments. This is because TANF benefits are considered in calculating food stamp benefits (but food stamps do not count against TANF benefits). Under the AFDC program, benefits on average accounted for 36 percent of the poverty guidelines, but state variations were striking. In Mississippi, the poorest state in the nation, the maximum AFDC payment of $120 for a family of four accounted for only 11 percent of the federal poverty line. Suffolk County, New York, is a much wealthier jurisdiction with a much higher cost of living; its $703 payment accounted for 65 percent of the federal poverty line. Food stamps brought families to 40 percent of the poverty line in Mississippi and to 86 percent in Suffolk County. When the value of food stamps was added, the national average was 65 percent of the poverty line.

According to the Center for Budget and Policy Priorities, reports that welfare pays better than work rely on inflated estimates of benefits that assume that all recipients receive housing assistance, which few get. Now that states have more flexibility under TANF—for example, states can use the cash they would have given recipients to subsidize jobs for them—only the future will tell what the trend in payments will be. Currently, "most states have retained the same basic benefit levels that existed under AFDC, but all states have added provisions that lower or exclude benefits for certain groups of recipients." [79]

More Fact and Fiction in AFDC[80]

One AFDC myth concerned the size of families receiving assistance. Most families were not as large as people thought. About three-quarters had one or two children; only 10 percent had four or more children. Most of the children were quite young. In 1995, 45 percent were under age six and 82 percent were under age 12, requiring supervision that may have prevented a parent from working. Some people say that pointing out that most AFDC families contain few children is needlessly apologetic, that there should be no need to apologize for having more than one or two children.[81] Of course, this position has become increasingly unpopular given that many families make the decision how many children to have based on how many they think they can afford.

Similar numbers of blacks and whites received AFDC. Although it is true that blacks have been overrepresented in the program because they are much smaller percentage of the population, they also have higher poverty and unemployment rates than whites, which may cause them to seek assistance. In 1995, blacks were 37 percent of AFDC recipients and whites were 36 percent. Hispanics had grown to 21 percent of AFDC recipients as they became an increasingly larger portion of the U.S. population. They are also overrepresented in the program. Asians were 3 percent of those receiving AFDC and Native Americans were 1 percent.

In 1995, 80 percent of mothers receiving AFDC were ages 20 to 39, and 14 percent were age 40 and older. Less than one-tenth of a percent of AFDC mothers were ages

15 to 17, and just 6 percent were ages 18 to 19, but teen parents are at risk for long-term welfare receipt.[82] About 55 percent of AFDC mothers were adolescents when they had their first child, compared with 31 percent of women not receiving AFDC.[83] The education of mothers in AFDC families was known for only 54 percent of recipients, but among this group, 22 percent had less than a high school education, 24 percent had a high school degree, and 8 percent had at least some college education.

Although people may think that most AFDC families lived in housing paid for by the government, only 23 percent lived in public or subsidized housing. Most (64 percent) rented private housing. Another 4 percent lived in housing they owned or were buying and 9 percent lived in group or free housing. Most AFDC families received Medicaid and food stamps. They were automatically eligible for Medicaid (most TANF recipients also received Medicaid) and although virtually all were also eligible for food stamps, 10 percent were not receiving them in 1995.

The vast majority of adult recipients have been single mothers. In 1995, only 11 percent of AFDC families had a father in the home. In nearly 60 percent of cases the parents had never married, and in another 25 percent the parents were separated or divorced. One analysis found that among AFDC mothers, 68 percent were not married when their first child was born, compared to 27 percent of mothers not receiving AFDC.[84] The number of children receiving AFDC whose parents had never married gnawed away at some people. In only 2 percent of cases was a parent deceased, and in only 4 percent of cases was a parent considered incapacitated (disabled). In 8 percent of cases, the reason for receiving AFDC was a parent's unemployment.

One often-cited research study showed that becoming a female head of household with children was by far the most frequent reason that women applied for AFDC, and another study showed that changes in family structure (primarily getting married) was most often the way off of AFDC, followed by working for pay.[85] These findings were based on annual data. When monthly data were used, a different picture emerged.[86] Many more exits were due to work effort and far fewer to changes in family structure. A more recent study which tracked women beginning at age 21 or younger showed that having a baby was the most frequent cause of welfare receipt.[87]

Despite all the attempts at getting AFDC mothers to work, few were working in 1995. Four percent worked full time and 5 percent worked part time. Only 12 percent were receiving training. Of course, those who had obtained decent jobs were no longer receiving AFDC and are not reflected in the counts. Fathers were only a small percent of AFDC recipients, but of them, 5 percent were working full time and 7 percent, part time; 13 percent were in training, and 18 percent were considered unemployed. Many adults were exempt from work requirements primarily due to their caretaking roles. Smaller numbers were exempt because of age or poor health or because they lived in remote areas with little hope for employment. Just 10 percent of families had income from work, and the number with earnings had declined over time. Studies that show that substantially more AFDC mothers had some recent earnings may be based on different reporting periods and data collection methods.[88] In addition, in an effort to survive, some mothers apparently just do not report their earnings (see Illustration 6-3).

ILLUSTRATION 6-3

The Unreported Work of Mothers Receiving Public Assistance

This excerpt is from a larger study of how poor women make ends meet.

Because of the high tax the welfare system imposed on reported work, *welfare-reliant* mothers who chose to work seldom reported their jobs. The proportion of welfare-reliant mothers who told us they had engaged in some unreported work during the preceding twelve months to supplement their incomes was quite high, roughly four in ten. Those who did such work earned $229 in a typical month.

For welfare-reliant mothers who were busy piecing together enough money to keep their families together each month, choosing unreported over reported work made a great deal of sense. This is clear from a brief review of the federal welfare rules at the time, which applied to all the states we studied. During the first four months of a mother's employment, states were required to deduct or "disregard" the first $30 of her earnings, a standard monthly deduction of $120, and a third of all additional earnings when calculating a mother's cash welfare benefits. For the next eight months, states were supposed to disregard the $30 and the $120 deductions but subtract all other earnings from the mother's welfare check. After the first year, states disregarded only $90 of earned income each month. . . .

Welfare recipients found unreported jobs in a variety of ways. Some took a formal sector job under a false social security number, some worked only a short amount of time using their own social security number (to avoid being reported to the Department of Labor), and some simply reversed two numbers of their own social security number on their employee documentation—a trick that easily fooled employers. Others colluded with employers to receive their pay in cash, an arrangement some employers liked because it saved them money too. Many employers requiring temporary, contract, or irregular labor preferred not to list these jobs on their official payrolls in order to avoid paying into unemployment and workers' compensation programs.

Typically, employers who offered off-the-books work also took advantage of the welfare-reliant mothers' need to hide their employment by offering them wages below the legal minimum. One woman who found work at a local restaurant told us,

> *This new restaurant opened up. But they said since they'd just started, they couldn't pay more than $2 an hour, Then the boss said, "Why don't you just stay on welfare, then I'll pay you under the table."*

Many believed they could avoid detection, even using their own social security number, by working only two or three months at a time. In most cases, this strategy worked, apparently because these employers did not list their short-term employees on their quarterly report. One woman told us,

> *I worked at a grocery store for a month and a restaurant for a month and I worked at a pizza place for two months, so maybe about four months total I worked last year. That way they can't catch you.*

Most mothers felt guilty about not reporting such work. One mother told us,

> *I wish I could report my job, I really do. But then I just couldn't make it right now, not*

continued

ILLUSTRATION 6-3 *(continued)*

> *until I get a raise or some overtime. I dream about the day when I can go in and tell my caseworker, "I don't need your assistance. I got a job." I dream about the day I can kiss welfare goodbye.*

Welfare-reliant mothers who took jobs in the informal economy felt far less guilty about failing to report such work to their caseworkers than those who worked under false identities in formal sector jobs. Since they did not see these as "real" jobs, and since they were virtually undetectable, most mothers found it inconceivable that any mother would report these earnings to the caseworker. The urban economies of all four sites provided various forms of unreported work in the informal economy, such as housecleaning, babysitting, laundry, yard work, house painting, apartment-building maintenance, operating neighborhood taxis, cooking meals for others, and sewing.

These occupations provided crucial supplemental income for welfare recipients, though earnings were very unpredictable. One mother told us,

> *I'm pretty resourceful. Where I live we have a pretty big garage, and I collect junk, trash pick—the ultimate trash picker—and I go to garage sales. I have my friends picking up stuff in alleys and at garage sales for me too. They're all like, "Oh, let's grab this for her!" whenever they see some old crap. Then on the weekends, I'll get this friend of mine to help me load his pickup and we get a table at the flea market for about $50. Some weekends I'll make $200 or $300 on old junk I might have paid $20 total for, but that's not all the time.*

Another recipient ran her own lottery. She purchased counterfeit bus passes each month and sold $1 chances to win a $60 bus pass. She determined the winner according to the last two digits of the winning state lottery number on the last day of each month. Though she paid roughly $30 each for the passes (legitimate passes cost $60), she still netted a profit of over $200 in a typical month. When the city police began cracking down on users of counterfeit passes, she started purchasing $20 or $30 items from pawn shops to sell chances on and netted roughly the same profit.

Unreported work was not limited to welfare recipients but was an important income-generating strategy for *wage-reliant mothers* as well. In our coding scheme, supplemental unreported work included all earnings that workers did not report to the IRS or to any means-tested program. Those who worked at such jobs earned an average of $207 a month.

Working mothers were motivated to hide side-income to maintain eligibility for food stamps, housing subsidies, Medicaid, and student aid, as well as to avoid paying additional income taxes. Those receiving means-tested benefits had the strongest motivation to hide earned income, because reductions in such benefits constituted an extra "tax" on additional earnings. Not surprisingly, workers receiving these subsidies were far less likely to engage in supplemental reported work and somewhat more likely to take on an unreported job than nonbeneficiaries were. For those receiving means-tested benefits, hiding work was nearly as risky as it was for welfare-reliant mothers, because if they were caught they had to reimburse the program that had "overpaid" them.

Source: Kathryn Edin and Laura Lein, *Making Ends Meet,* © 1997 Russell Sage Foundation. New York, New York. Used by permission of the Russell Sage Foundation.

Most families received AFDC for a relatively short time. In 1994, the median length of stay was 23 months. In 1995, 34 percent had received AFDC for no more than 12 months; 17 percent had been in the program from 13 months to two years. An additional 28 percent had received payments for 25 months to five years, and the remaining 20 percent had received assistance for more than five years. Data showed that 43 percent of current enrollees had a previous period on AFDC. The data on length of stay or "spells" of AFDC deserve closer examination. An update of a widely cited 1983 report using annual data shows that of people *starting* their first spell of AFDC, 30 percent would receive assistance for one to two years, 20 percent for three to four years, 19 percent for five to seven years, and 30 percent for eight or more years, but at any one point, 65 percent would have received AFDC for eight or more years.[89]

A more recent analysis of welfare spells relies on monthly data. It showed that 35 percent of those entering AFDC for the first time would receive assistance for more than five years, that 76 percent in the midst of a spell would receive AFDC for more than five years, and that 48 percent of those in the program had already received AFDC for more than five years.[90] Projections were that those just entering the program would receive benefits for an average of six years, and that those currently in the midst of a spell would receive benefits for an average of thirteen years. Evidence indicates that while most families will receive aid for a relatively limited period, the majority at any one time are long-term participants who use most of the program's resources.[91] The longer-term AFDC recipients had less than a high school education, had never been married, had not worked recently, were younger than age 24, were Hispanic or black, had a child younger than age 3, and had at least three children.[92]

Another important issue in the welfare reform movement is whether growing up in an AFDC family produced another generation of families on public assistance. An analysis by the House Committee on Ways and Means using 1984 data indicated that 58 percent of daughters from families who received welfare later received some welfare as adults, compared to 27 percent of daughters from non-AFDC families.[93] However, most of the 58 percent were not "highly" dependent on welfare. Conversely, 42 percent of daughters from welfare families later received no welfare, compared with 73 percent of daughters from nonwelfare families. A later study was more optimistic: 37 percent of daughters whose parents received AFDC also received AFDC, compared with 9 percent of daughters whose families had not received AFDC.[94] Among the highly dependent AFDC families (defined by number of years receiving AFDC), only 20 percent of daughters became highly dependent compared with 16 percent of those from moderately dependent AFDC families and 3 percent from families that received no AFDC. A 1991 review of studies concluded that while there was consistently strong correlational evidence of intergenerational transmission among daughters (only one study looked at sons), it is impossible to tell if there is a causative relationship because the studies do not control for other background variables that might also affect welfare receipt.[95] For example, welfare receipt is associated with fewer parental resources and exposure to more disadvantaged neighborhoods and schools that may be more defining factors in welfare receipt than having received welfare alone.[96] One researcher compared daughters who grew up in families that received AFDC with daughters from families that were eligible but did not participate in AFDC.[97] The daughters in families receiving AFDC were more likely to have had a child by the study's end (53 percent versus 33 percent for the households not receiving AFDC), and they were more likely to receive AFDC (56 percent versus 33 percent), but the researcher also indicates that factors such as low family income when growing up contribute to a woman's welfare receipt even if her family did not receive welfare.

AN END TO WELFARE AS WE KNEW IT

There have long been ideas for reforming the social welfare system. Some of them would constitute a radical departure from AFDC and TANF.

Nonwelfare Approaches

Early proposals for "fixing" welfare called for a *guaranteed annual income* or a *negative income tax.* These may be called universal or "nonwelfare approaches"[98] because they suggest using systems like the Internal Revenue Service (IRS) that are part of the lives of virtually all Americans—rich or poor. Milton Friedman's negative income tax plan and President Nixon's Family Assistance Plan (FAP) are among the best examples of these ideas. A negative income tax could be used to guarantee everyone a minimum standard of living and encourage recipients to work by allowing them to keep a portion of their earnings without severe reductions in benefits.

Each negative income tax (NIT) or guaranteed annual income plan has its own set of procedures and requirements, but let us consider one example of how such a plan might work. Say that the guaranteed annual income for a family of four is set at $16,000, with an earnings deduction of 50 percent. A family with no income would receive $16,000. A family with earnings of $4,000 would receive a payment of $14,000, for a total income of $18,000. A family earning $16,000 would receive a payment of $8,000, for a total income of $24,000, and a family earning $32,000, the breakeven point, would receive no payment. Since this plan is a logical extension of the income tax system already in place in the United States, everyone would continue to file an income tax return as they do today. Most citizens would continue to pay taxes, but those at the lower end of the income scale would receive payments or negative income taxes. Checks could be mailed through the U.S. Treasury Department as income tax refunds are today. Since welfare applications, means tests, and other eligibility procedures would be eliminated, much of the welfare bureaucracy would be reduced.

But the United States has no practical experience with a guaranteed income or NIT. It is possible that near-poor people would qualify for benefits and prefer accepting that guarantee. This is probably the greatest concern working against such a proposal. Planners would need to estimate how many people might qualify for payments at various levels, but policymakers might end up basing their decision about payments levels on what they believe the country can afford rather than what seems to be a fair standard of living. The Nixon FAP, introduced in 1970, was designed to address many problems of the welfare system: disincentives to work, discouragement of family life, inequities among the states, and discrimination against the working poor. "However, the FAP failed in Congress because of the combined opposition of those who felt it was too much welfare and those who felt it was not enough."[99]

One tax measure that is available to low-income workers through the IRS is the earned income credit (EIC). The EIC has been available to workers with children since 1975. The amount of the credit has increased in recent years. In 1998, the maximum amount for a family with one or more children was $3,656.Workers with one child could claim at least part of the credit if their income was less than $26,473. With two or more children, income had to be less than $30,095. The amount workers receive is based on their earnings. Those expecting to receive it can get part in advance by asking their employer to include it in their regular paychecks. Since 1994, a smaller credit has been available to low-income workers without children. This approach to helping low-income households is popular with many people because it rewards work.

Many other industrialized countries use nonwelfare approaches to support young families with children.[100] Several European countries have universal benefit programs that are far more generous than the United States offers. Norway has provided benefits to *all* families with children younger than age 16—one and two parent, rich and poor—with additional supplements for single parents. France has also had a universal family allowance policy with additional benefits for young families and single-parent families; the benefits are considered generous enough so that mothers of young children can choose to work or remain at home. Sweden and the Federal Republic of Germany have also employed universal children's allowances. Even in Great Britain, where a means-tested public assistance approach is used, mothers have not been pressured to work outside the home until the youngest child is 16 years old. But many countries are facing budget problems, and some are rethinking their approaches to social welfare.[101] Universal benefit programs could be discussed at far greater length, but they are clearly not among the alternatives on the U.S. agenda.

Still another nonwelfare approach—an assets and investment approach that would complement current welfare programs—has been advocated by social worker Michael Sheradden. This approach, already available to the middle and upper classes, allows for accumulation of wealth through government-sponsored home mortgage loans and government and private retirement programs (also see Chapter 2). Under the former AFDC program and most current public assistance programs, recipients who accumulated even small amounts of cash or other assets were disqualified from assistance. But without assets, Sheradden argues, it is unlikely they will be able to leave welfare behind; assets make people part of the social mainstream, and assets make them feel differently about the future. How could such a system be accomplished for low-income people? One suggestion is individual development accounts that

> *would be optional, earnings-bearing, tax-benefited accounts in the name of each individual, initiated as early as birth and restricted to designated purposes [such as education, home ownership, or self-employment]. . . . The federal government would match or otherwise subsidize deposits for the poor, and there would be potential for*

creative financing from the private sector and account holders themselves [such as stocks, bonds, or money market funds].[102]

Under demonstration programs, the state of Iowa began allowing AFDC families to accumulate $2,000 in assets, and in Wyoming the amount was $2,500. Other AFDC demonstration or waiver programs allowed mothers to accumulate assets such as computers or sewing equipment to develop their own businesses or to retain more of their earnings without reducing benefits. The SSI program (see Chapter 5) already afforded people with disabilities the opportunity to own equipment that helps them function in the workplace and makes less severe the reductions in payments once earnings begin.

There are other forms of the asset accumulation approach. Businessman Eugene Lang's I Have a Dream Foundation and similar programs guarantee college tuition to children from poor families who complete high school. The Corporation for Enterprise Development is a nonprofit organization interested in investment strategies that encourage entrepreneurship and self-employment as a route to self-sufficiency. Other countries have publicly funded entrepreneurship programs. The best example is France's Chomeur Createur (Unemployed Entrepreneur) program, which entitles "unemployed people or those who have never worked . . . to unemployment benefits to set up a new business or even to buy an existing business."[103] The results are reportedly impressive. Great Britain has a similar program, in which unemployed people can receive payments to start businesses, although participants must raise some capital themselves. Another approach which has been used primarily in underdeveloped countries is "microcredit." This strategy makes use of banks or other lending institutions which assist individuals or groups of individuals with easier to access credit that is used to support business ventures.[104] Often the loan is secured by the group which promises to repay it if any individual defaults. Of course, these programs are not without problems, and the United States has its own version of help to entrepreneurs, such as loans through the Small Business Administration.

The March to TANF Begins

The current era of welfare reform began during the Reagan administration. President Reagan wanted "to determine welfare needs more accurately, improve program administration, reduce fraud and abuse, and decrease federal and state costs."[105] In order to do so, various changes were made in the AFDC program, such as counting stepparents' income in determining eligibility, capping deductions for work-related expenses such as child care, and limiting the "thirty plus one-third" rule to four months. About 500,000 families were removed from the program,[106] with researchers at the University of Michigan's Institute for Social Research and those at the General Accounting Office finding that many children had been plunged deeper into poverty.[107]

Perhaps President Bush's most notable contribution to welfare reform was to encourage more state innovation in the AFDC program. But what looked like a positive innovation to some was considered punitive by others. For instance, under Wisconsin's

Learnfare program, working families could keep more of their pay without losing AFDC benefits, but if a teenage child dropped out of school, "defined as missing three days of school in a month without a valid excuse," the family faced a reduction in benefits.[108] In Wisconsin and New Jersey, women who had another child while receiving AFDC were denied additional payments. In Michigan, AFDC recipients who did not go to work or school or contribute volunteer service faced being docked $100 in benefits a month. Another Wisconsin initiative, referred to as "Bridefare," encouraged young women to marry by allowing them to keep some benefits. Much more drastic measures were suggested by Charles Murray (also see Chapter 3), who believes that the federal government should end virtually all its involvement in public assistance as a deterrent to out-of-wedlock births and welfare dependency, and that for some children, orphanages might be preferable to their home environments. The Republican party articulated many of its ideas about welfare reform in its Contract with America. Momentum had built to do something more about "welfare."

Enter the Clinton Administration

When Bill Clinton first campaigned for the presidency, he pledged to "end welfare as we know it," and he appointed a task force of "welfare experts" to help him keep his promise. He wanted to increase incentives to self-sufficiency through education and training, raise the earned income credit, and provide "seamless" child care and health care benefits. He also wanted to "make work pay" by increasing asset limitations and earnings disregards and permitting individual development accounts. Other parts of his proposal included improving paternity establishment and child support collections and promoting contacts between children and their noncustodial parents. The president also wanted to launch a national campaign to curb teen pregnancy. Bill Clinton agreed with many conservatives that welfare payments should be limited to two years and that "welfare should not be a way of life."[109]

There was considerable concern about whether there would be enough jobs for all those who would have to work in lieu of receiving assistance and what would happen to those who might not find employment. Since JOBS had put only a portion of recipients to work, the assumption was that many employment strategies would be needed to end welfare. Suggestions included subsidized private employment, paying groups to place recipients in private-sector jobs, federal public works program like those used during the Great Depression, and placing recipients in public-sector jobs in the community. Unions were concerned that any large-scale job efforts would displace those already working in low-wage employment. Predictions were that it would be difficult to do better than JOBS unless substantial amounts were allocated for training and education.

While Congress hammered out its plan, the states were moving ahead with welfare reform. The Wisconsin legislature declared that it wanted to withdraw completely from the AFDC program by the end of the decade. It had already begun implementing a two-year moratorium on AFDC payments through its experiment called "Work, Not Welfare." Florida began a demonstration to hire welfare recipients and provide a minimum-wage job to those who did not locate work after two years on AFDC. By the time Congress and the president agreed on a welfare reform plan, about 40 states had already obtained waivers from the federal government so they could make changes to their AFDC programs that fell outside the current rules.

Has Welfare as We Know It Ended?

Although an improved economy had already caused AFDC rolls to drop, conservatives and many others thought that the program still needed a radical restructuring. Congress twice delivered comprehensive welfare reform bills to President Clinton which he vetoed believing they were too punitive. Then, on the third try, the president relented and signed the Personal Responsibility and Work Opportunity Reconciliation Act of 1996 even though he disliked some of its components. Some of the nation's best known welfare experts and the president's closest welfare advisers, Mary Jo Bane, David Ellwood, and Peter Edelman, quit in protest over the bill's signing fearing it was too harsh. Many advocates for the poor criticized the president for selling out. In a description of the politics of the 1996 welfare reform, Ellwood wrote that the president's sound bites ("ending welfare as we know it" and "two years and you're off") were not intended to mean that no more help would be available but that the Republican takeover of Congress led welfare reform on a "remarkable political journey."[110] In a statement about the political expediency of president Clinton's signing of the bill, one columnist wrote that his "decision to sign the sweeping welfare reform bill will give him the biggest social policy accomplishment of his presidency, even though the Republican Congress wrote it and liberal Democrats hate it."[111] The bill's most dramatic change was the end of the 61-year-old entitlement program known as AFDC and the birth of a block grant program called Temporary Assistance for Needy Families (TANF).

The new TANF program, authorized through fiscal year 2002, is actually composed of two block grants.[112] One is the family assistance block grant, used to provide cash to families, to help families go to work, and to avert out-of-wedlock pregnancies. The money can also be used to encourage parents to establish or maintain two-parent families. This block grant combines the functions of the former AFDC and JOBS programs but caps funding for them. The other block grant is for child care to help families leave the public assistance rolls or avoid receiving public assistance without concern about their children's supervision. This block grant consolidates several government-supported child care programs and increases funding for them. In order to continue receiving federal funds, states had to replace AFDC with TANF by July 1, 1997. Each state has almost free rein in defining those that will be included and those groups that will be excluded from TANF. Federal funds cannot, however, be used to pay TANF benefits to most immigrants legally residing in the United States during their first five years in the country. After the five years, states can continue to exclude immigrants who have not become citizens.

Under TANF, most families may receive cash assistance for no more than five years, while under AFDC, families were eligible until their youngest child was 18 years old.

All able-bodied adults who have received public assistance for two years are expected to work toward self-sufficiency. This is a more stringent requirement than in previous incarnations of AFDC. Some states had already moved in this direction. States may exempt 20 percent of their caseload from the five-year limit. Exemptions are determined by the state and may be granted in situations where family violence or disabilities may make it difficult for the adult head to care for the family without assistance.

The family assistance block grant is fixed at $16.4 billion per year through fiscal year 2002. This is slightly more than what was spent for AFDC and JOBS in fiscal year 1995. The child care block grant increases funds previously spent for child care with $14 billion in entitlement funds and $6 billion in discretionary funds available through 2002. Although the change to TANF received much of the attention in the welfare reform package, most federal savings will come from the Supplemental Security Income program (see Chapter 5) and the Food Stamp Program (see Chapter 7). These programs are mostly the responsibility of the federal government while TANF is more heavily financed by the states.

To receive its entire TANF allotment, a state must spend at least 75 percent of what it expended on AFDC in 1994. States which fail to meet federally established work participation rates in a given year must spend at least 80 percent of their 1994 expenditures the following year. States which experience more than average population growth or receive less than the national average amount of federal welfare funds for each poor resident are eligible for supplemental TANF funds through fiscal year 2001 (a total of $800 million is available). States which automatically qualified for these funds because of the low federal welfare funds they acquire for poor people are Alabama, Arkansas, Louisiana, Mississippi, and Texas. States which already qualify because of population growth are Alaska, Arizona, Colorado, Idaho, Nevada, and Utah.

As of 1999, states with "high-performing" TANF programs are eligible for bonuses. The award criteria include job entry, job retention, and earning gains. There are also other stakes involved. Up to five states with the greatest reductions in out-of-wedlock births *and* greatest reductions in abortions will get a bonus payment. Finally, states undergoing recession (measured by high unemployment and increased food stamp caseloads) can tap a $2 billion contingency fund if they have spent more than 100 percent of their 1994 AFDC levels on TANF.

After two years, or less if the state stipulates, adults must "engage in work" (as defined to some extent by each state) or be terminated from the program. The federal government calculates work participation rates based on the number of adults who are involved in the following activities: unsubsidized or subsidized private or public employment; work experience; community service; on-the-job training; job search and job readiness activities (usually counted for only several weeks or somewhat longer if the state has a high unemployment rate); vocational education (which cannot be counted for more than one year); caring for children of TANF parents who are doing community service; job skills training; education directly related to employment (for high school dropouts only); working on a high school diploma or GED (for high school dropouts only).

Most single parents not participating in job skills or education programs were required to put in 20 hours a week at one of the work activities in 1998 and 25 hours in 1999. In 2000 the number of hours is 30 where it is currently intended to remain. Single parents with children under age 6 are not required to do more than 20 hours a week. In two-parent families, one adult must work 35 hours weekly. If they receive federally funded child care, the other parent is supposed to work 20 hours per week unless that parent is disabled or caring for a child with disability. Parents who fail to work all the expected hours can be docked at least a portion of their benefits.

The highest work priorities are for parents in two-parent families and single parents whose children are in school, especially those who have older children. The states can use TANF funds to create a job in lieu of making cash payment to recipients. They can also require parents who have received aid for two months and are not otherwise working to perform community service, but states may exempt parents with a child under age 1 from all work requirements.

The federal government required states to see that 25 percent of all TANF families had an adult working in 1997 with an increase of 5 percent each year so that by 2002, 50 percent must be working. For each percentage point that a state reduces its TANF rolls, its work participation rate is decreased by 1 percent, provided that the reduced rolls were not due to stiffer eligibility requirements. In 1997 and 1998, at least one parent in 75 percent of two-parent families had to be working. In 1999 this rate was 90 percent. There are penalties for states that do not get enough people to work. The penalty is 5 percent of TANF funds after the first year of failure. Each subsequent year of failure results in an additional 2 percent penalty up to a maximum yearly penalty of 21 percent.

States which do not comply with TANF expenditure levels or fail to limit families to five years face losing part of their block grant, and they must use state funds to replace the amount lost. The Secretary of the Department of Health and Human Services can waive penalties if states take corrective action. If a state's TANF program results in an increase of 5 percent or more in its child poverty rate, it must implement a plan to reduce this poverty if it wants to continue to receive TANF funds.

States can set a shorter time limit than five years for receiving benefits. If families need longer-term benefits, states can use their 20 percent exemption from the five-year rule to assist them, and they can use part of their Social Services Block Grant (see Chapter 10) to provide non-cash assistance such as vouchers to needy families who reach the time limit. They can also use their own funds to assist families for longer periods if they wish.

Families cut from TANF due to increased earnings may retain Medicaid benefits for 12 months (6 months of full benefits and 6 months of subsidized benefits) if their income is no more than 185 percent of the poverty level. There is a four-month Medicaid extension for families who leave TANF due to increased child support. Some families that would have been eligible for cash assistance under AFDC rules but do not qualify under TANF may also be entitled to receive Medicaid.

To discourage out-of-wedlock births, states may eliminate all cash payments to unmarried teen parents. States that offer payments must require that the teen parent live with an adult and attend school. States can also choose to enforce a "family cap" by denying payments for a child born while the family is receiving TANF. The Personal Responsibility Act emphasizes reducing out-of-wedlock births. In addition to the limits placed on benefits for teenage parents and the bonuses for states that reduce illegitimacy, the act provides funds for abstinence education and urges states to consider methods of reducing teen pregnancy through prevention programs, statutory rape laws, and other strategies.

There are other ways states can limit TANF payments. They can pay recipients moving from other states no more than they received in their previous state of residence for a period of 12 months (this provision is being challenged). They can also test recipients for illegal drug use and penalize those who test positive. Unless a state "opts out" by passing a new law, convicted drug offenders can be barred from the program forever. Though their children can receive benefits, there is less to go around for the whole family.

Other provisions allow states to contract with religious and private organizations to deliver public assistance services. This provision is controversial among those who feel that religion and public service functions may not mix well, and those who feel that governments should not abrogate their public responsibilities to enterprises that might be motivated by profit. More positive is that states may use TANF funds to establish individual development accounts for beneficiaries for specific purposes.

According to HHS Secretary Donna Shalala, welfare reform picked the right time to come along.[113] As the economy hummed, AFDC caseloads started dropping well before the 1996 welfare reform legislation was enacted. By 1997, caseloads dropped below 11 million for the first time since 1970; by June of 1998, there were 8.4 million recipients or 3.1 percent of the population, a rate not experienced since the late 1960s.[114] Some states like Wisconsin with aggressive work-to-welfare efforts had already seen more than a 40 percent decline in recipients (only Hawaii had not seen a decline). Governor Tommy Thompson has made Wisconsin the premier welfare reform state. Wisconsin has used many demonstrations, including requiring people to spend 60 hours looking for work (what is called a diversion measure) in order to get assistance and reducing assistance for every hour of training or work missed.[115] Reports were that some applicants were deterred from even applying when they heard about new program requirements. Among the more punitive measures some states are reportedly using is cutting food stamp benefits along with TANF benefits when parents don't comply with program rules. The new law requires fewer safeguards such as appeal processes when applicants and recipients feel they have been treated unfairly. The president's Council of Economic Advisors estimated that 40 percent of the reduction in welfare caseloads was due to a stronger economy, that nearly one-third was due to state innovations (many of which preceded the 1996 law in the form of waivers), and the rest to other factors such as an increased earned income credit, stronger child support enforcement, and more child care funding.[116]

States have actually been earning money from welfare reform because they get a fixed amount from the federal government rather than an amount based on each recipient served. Their allocation is based on what they spent in 1994 when caseloads were at an all-time high. States have also gained because as welfare caseloads drop, the percent of the TANF population required to work also drops. What are states doing with their welfare savings? Some, like Wisconsin, are apparently investing in those left on the TANF rolls. The *Congressional Quarterly* notes that Wisconsin is spending about $15,000 per recipient in an effort to achieve self sufficiency.[117] Other states are being criticized for not putting the money back into the program. Although there are requirements on what states must spend to draw down their full TANF allotment, states can use any surpluses as they please. In Texas, for example, a good deal of the surplus was reportedly used to supplant funds that the state would have spent on job programs, child care, and child protective services. Instead of expanding these programs, the savings was returned to the state's General Revenue fund.[118]

Is TANF really an end to welfare as we knew it? As the country transforms its antipoverty strategy from providing income to reducing dependency (also see Chapter 3), states are apparently trying to turn their welfare offices into employment offices. For recipients who are not successful in obtaining employment, there are some ways that states can avoid cutting off people in need. States can exempt 20 percent of recipients from the five-year limit, and there are the supplemental and contingency funds for states in particular circumstances. Much of this sounds good now, but the Center for Budget and Policy Priorities and the Congressional Budget Office are not so optimistic. They believe that if the past is a good guide, the additional funding is not nearly enough to cover the needs that a recession would bring, and eventually, there will be another recession.[119] According to David Ellwood:

> *States cannot and will not do the impossible, but they will do the possible. The possible is to cut people off, to offer less service, to provide less child care for the working poor not on welfare. Because the block grant will reduce federally required state spending and eliminate federal laws regarding eligibility, some states will find it much easier to cut people off than to move them to work. And so the race to the bottom will begin. Even governors and legislators who want to focus on work-based reform may find it too costly if nearby states threaten to dump their poor by simply cutting benefits.*[120]

States might want to put any surpluses aside for a rainy day, because a future increase in caseloads could put a great strain on TANF programs, not only in making payments to recipients, but also in meeting work requirements that will rise steeply should caseloads increase.[121]

Recipients now working are those most likely to have found work on their own anyway. Many left in the program have the most serious obstacles to employment. Indications are that the decline in caseloads has already leveled off. Some states had difficulty meeting JOBS quotas, and many did not draw down their full JOBS funding allotment. Many states have had trouble putting 75 percent of two-parent TANF families to work. The 25 percent of all parents who were required to be working in 1997 was an easier goal to achieve because declining caseloads reduced this percentage for many states.[122] Some states have not yet invested what it may take to help those with serious obstacles to employment like drug addiction get jobs. For those with less severe problems, getting a job may not be that difficult in these good times, but keeping it may be when a child is sick or other problems arise.

Child care is another issue. Though a substantial amount of money was allocated, the Center for Budget and Policy Priorities argues that the new law does not increase child care funding, largely because it caps funds rather than offering an open-ended entitlement. The Congressional Budget Office predicted that as early as 1999 child care funding would be inadequate to meet program requirements.[123] The General Accounting Office (GAO) added that many areas would face child care deficits from the beginning due to lack of available, affordable, and adequate slots.[124]

Many effects of welfare reform remain to be seen because TANF has not been around long enough for most recipients to hit the time limits. Most terminations so far have come from failure to comply with program rules.[125] The GAO reported on 18,000 terminations, mostly in Iowa, Massachusetts, and Wisconsin. The largest group did not comply with work requirements, primarily because they wanted to be at home with their children or they did not want to perform community service or accept a low-paying job. More than 80 percent had an identifiable source of support or had returned to the program, but significant numbers had also lost food stamp and Medicaid benefits in the process. One problem that will arise is states' ability to determine who has reached the maximum time on TANF because their client tracking systems have not been designed to do this. Since time on welfare in other states must be included in the total, tracking is especially difficult.

Some media reports indicate that the dire predictions about welfare reform have yet to be seen, but reports from late 1998 from the U.S. Conference of Mayors and the National Coalition for the Homeless suggest a relationship between welfare reform and homelessness.[126] The Department of Health and Human Services has issued its first annual report to Congress on TANF.[127] The report generally paints a positive picture of the early effects. Perhaps it must since TANF is new government policy. Though much of the data are incomplete, the report emphasizes reductions in TANF rolls and increases in the numbers working, concluding that "In most states, state policy and spending choices have reflected a focus on work rather than a race to the bottom."

The state of Florida is conducting a controlled experiment on its time-limited Family Transition Program (FTP) in which most families can receive benefits for only two years in a five-year period. Participants receive social services and financial incentives to encourage employment.[128] After 15 months, 46 percent of the experimental group was employed compared to 40 percent of the control group. During the last 3 months, experimentals earned $169 (24 percent) more than controls. Due to the financial incentives, such as larger earning disregards, FTP had not increased the rate at which participants are leaving the family assistance program. Increased earnings have led to a 9-percent reduction in food stamp benefits received, but earnings have not been great enough to remove families from the food stamp program. Some people have been terminated from FTP, but few have reached the time limits. The study's authors are considering various hypotheses about how time limits will affect people's behavior. One hypothesis is that time limits will cause parents to find work fast so they can save their months on welfare for a rainier day.[129] An alternative hypothesis is that they will not secure employment until termination is imminent. The researchers are also interested in different approaches to moving people from welfare to work. Are recipients better off if they seek work quickly with the hope of gaining education and training during the course of employment? This approach would stop the welfare clock in case people need TANF later. Or will they fare better if they seek education and training while receiving TANF in order to prepare themselves for a better job once their time on welfare ends?

Surely recipients will learn the system well enough to use what is available to their best advantage, but an important question remains: Even if families leave the welfare rolls for work, will they escape poverty? Thus far, the Urban Institute has some encouraging news on this point.[130] In a 12 state study, it found that:

- As a family moved from no work to part-time, minimum wage work, its income rose an average of 51 percent, ranging from 38 percent in Washington State to 108 percent in Mississippi.
- Moving from part-time to full-time work raised a family's income by an average of 20 percent.
- Moving from full-time minimum wage work to full-time work at $9.00 raised a family's income by an average of 16 percent.
- The earned income credit plays an important role in helping low-income families increase their incomes by working.
- Child care subsidies and the assurance of continued Medicaid assistance are important incentives to work.

The federal government is also implementing studies to determine the impact of welfare reform. States have substantial reporting requirements, and the Survey of Income and Program Participation (also see Chapter 3) is being expanded to determine the extent to which families leave welfare, the types of jobs TANF recipients obtain, the effects of the reforms on children and on out-of-wedlock births, and information on spells of welfare receipt. The Urban Institute's massive initiative called "Assessing the New Federalism" is tracking the effects of the devolution. Some states are devolving welfare further by passing some responsibilities to county governments.[131] The Urban Institute reports that

- Most states are offering the same level of cash benefits. Three states and the District of Columbia decreased payments while five states increased them.
- Thirty states increased the earnings recipients can keep and still receive cash assistance. Eight states lowered the earnings that can be kept starting with the first month of work, and 12 states and the District of Columbia are maintaining previous policies.
- Forty-five states have adopted time limits that cut off aid for the whole family; 24 states and the District of Columbia are using the federal maximum of five years of welfare receipt, and 20 states allow benefits to be cut off sooner than five years.
- Thirty-five states have new policies that make it easier for two-parent families to qualify for benefits.

- Many states have stiffened penalties for noncompliance with work requirements. Fourteen states have provisions for eliminating the entire family's benefit after the first noncompliance incident, and 7 states call for lifetime sanctions for repeated noncompliance.
- In 22 states, potential recipients may receive cash payments for emergency needs or to become self-sufficient if they agree not to apply for other assistance for a specified time.
- Twenty-two states have a full or partial family cap (many had adopted them prior to TANF). All but three states have permission to implement caps.[132]

The Center on Hunger and Poverty at Tufts University developed a scale to determine whether states' policies under TANF and other aspects of welfare reform will be better or worse for recipients. According to this scale, recipients are faring better with states' asset development and child care policies than they are with other aspects of welfare reform such as eligibility requirements, benefit levels, work requirements and sanctions.[133]

The 1998 federal budget added some sweeteners to welfare reform. Many of them support the president's plea to "hire a welfare recipient." The Welfare to Work Jobs Challenge adds $3 billion to encourage communities to help recipients go to work through job creation, job placement, job retention, subsidies to employers, and support services to help long-term welfare recipients maintain employment. A tax credit for employers was also added. Employers will receive 35 percent of the first $10,000 paid in wages to a new hire who has been a long-term welfare recipient and 50 percent of the first $10,000 in wages the second year.

Is welfare reform a cruel hoax on the nation's children and their parents, as some would like us to believe, or is it the way public assistance for families should have been conducted all along, as others believe? Since the five-year time limit is still down the road, it is not clear what states will do if or when they find themselves with a substantial number of families still in need. So far, Michigan seems to be the only state pledging to help people who don't find work as long as they comply with program rules. Surely a country with the resources of the United States will not abandon children whose parents cannot or do not support them, whether or not their parents have played by the rules.

SUMMARY

No social welfare program has been as controversial as Aid to Families with Dependent Children. Its forerunners—mothers' aid and Aid to Dependent Children, were not topics of much concern. As AFDC caseloads rose due to divorce, desertion, and especially out-of-wedlock births and the lack of noncustodial fathers paying child support, concerns mounted that AFDC needed a major overhaul. There was a series of attempts to get mothers as well as the few fathers receiving AFDC to become self-sufficient through work, but none made more than a very modest dent in the program. Stronger enforcement of child support has also not been the kind of success that politicians and the public had hoped.

AFDC was an entitlement program. Very poor families headed by single parents, and some headed by two parents in which a parent was unemployed or disabled, were eligible for AFDC as long as there was a minor child in the home. Many families received AFDC for a short time or vacillated between work and AFDC, but there was a group of recipients who never managed to shake free from the program. These highly welfare-reliant families used much of the program's resources and were the major target of concern. Liberals and conservatives alike hoped that they would be able to deter what came to be known as a cycle of dependence on public assistance.

During the Bush administration states began experimenting with welfare reform. Liberals thought that many of these ideas were ill-considered. Yet state applications to the federal government for waivers to deviate from AFDC program rules multiplied. While Congress and the president haggled over welfare reform, the states were busy changing the face of welfare. President Clinton vetoed two major welfare overhauls passed by the Republican-dominated Congress, but he signed a third bill which effectively "ended welfare as we knew it." It changed AFDC from an open-ended entitlement program to a block grant program called Temporary Assistance for Needy Families, with fixed amounts sent to the states and more freedom for the states to do with welfare as they wish. The president had grave reservations about the bill, but many of his concerns related to Supplemental Security Income and food stamps, not to AFDC. Among the bill's many components are rather stiff requirements about how many TANF recipients must go to work or face losing benefits after two years. The maximum lifetime period that a family can receive benefits is five years.

The welfare rolls had begun dropping before Congress and the president agreed on the welfare reform plan. A healthy economy had put some people to work, and some believe that changes that states had made in their programs also contributed to declining rolls. The true tests of the effectiveness of TANF are yet to come. Will the states be able to meet the employment targets? What happens when the economy takes a turn for the worse? What happens when the easiest to employ are working and those with the most serious obstacles to employment are left? What will states do with families who need help and reach the two- and five-year limits? Will children and their parents be allowed to do without? Will those who leave welfare for work escape poverty? Advocates for the poor are keeping close tabs and will be reporting to Congress, the states, and the public on the outcomes.

NOTES

1. For a history of mothers' aid, see Linda Gordon, *Women, the State, and Welfare* (Madison, WI: University of Wisconsin Press, 1990); Linda Gordon, *Pitied but Not Entitled: Single Mothers and the History of Welfare* (New York: The Free Press, 1994).

2. Laurence E. Lynn, Jr., "A Decade of Policy Developments in the Income-Maintenance System," in Robert H. Haveman, ed., *A Decade of Federal Antipoverty Programs: Achievements, Failures, and Lessons* (New York: Academic Press, 1977), p. 60; Martin Rein, *Social*

Policy: Issues of Choice and Change (New York: Random House, 1970), p. 311.

3. Quoted in Lynn, "A Decade of Policy Developments in the Income-Maintenance System," p. 73.

4. Gilbert Y. Steiner, *The State of Welfare* (Washington, DC: Brookings Institution, 1971), p. 81.

5. See Committee on Ways and Means, U.S. House of Representatives, *Overview of Entitlement Programs, 1993 Green Book* (Washington, DC: U.S. Government Printing Office, 1993), p. 623.

6. Ibid., p. 733.

7. John Bishop, *Jobs, Cash Transfers, and Marital Instability: A Review of the Evidence,* Institute for Research on Poverty, University of Wisconsin, Madison, written testimony to the Welfare Reform Subcommittee of the Committees on Agriculture, Education and Labor, and Ways and Means of the U.S. House of Representatives, October 14, 1977, p. 9.

8. Ibid., p. 8.

9. David T. Elwood and Lawrence H. Summers, "Poverty in America: Is Welfare the Answer or the Problem?" in Sheldon H. Danzinger and Daniel H. Weinberg, eds., *Fighting Poverty: What Works and What Doesn't* (Cambridge, MA: Harvard University Press, 1986), pp. 92–93.

10. Hilary Williamson Hoynes, *Work, Welfare, and Family Structure: What Have We Learned?,* Working Paper 5644 (Cambridge, MA: National Bureau of Economic Research, July 1996), p. 36.

11. See Alfred J. Kahn and Sheila B. Kamerman, *Child Support: From Debt Collection to Social Policy* (Newbury Park, CA: Sage, 1988).

12. Much of this section relies on Committee on Ways and Means, U.S. House of Representatives, *1996 Green Book: Background Material and Data on Programs Within the Jurisdiction of the Committee on Ways and Means* (Washington, DC: U.S. Government Printing Office, 1996), Section 9.

13. Committee on Ways and Means, *1993 Green Book,* p. 776.

14. Administration for Children and Families, *Temporary Assistance for Needy Families (TANF) Program, First Annual Report to Congress* (Washington, DC: Department of Health and Human Services, August 1998), http://www.acf.dhhs.gov/news/welfare/congress/index.htm.

15. Committee on Ways and Means, *1996 Green Book,* p. 558–559; also see Committee on Ways and Means, *1993 Green Book,* Section 8, for a discussion of interstate child support enforcement.

16. Committee on Ways and Means, U.S. House of Representatives, *1998 Green Book: Background Material and Data on Programs Within the Jurisdiction of the Committee on Ways and Means* (Washington, DC: U.S. Government Printing Office, 1998), p. 586.

17. Most of the remainder of this paragraph is based on U.S. Bureau of the Census, *Child Support for Custodial Mothers and Fathers: 1991,* Current Population Series P60-187 (Washington, DC: U.S. Government Printing Office, 1995); also see U.S. Bureau of the Census, *Statistical Abstract of the United States: 1997* (Washington, DC: U.S. Government Printing Office, 1997), p. 565.

18. Janice H. Laakso, "Child Support Policy: Some Critical Issues and the Implications for Social Work," The University of Texas at Austin, School of Social Work, January 26, 1998.

19. U.S. Bureau of the Census, *Child Support for Custodial Mothers and Fathers: 1991,* Current Population Series P60-187.

20. Committee on Ways and Means, *1996 Green Book,* p. 784.

21. See ibid., pp. 618–619.

22. U.S. Bureau of the Census, *Child Support for Custodial Mothers and Fathers: 1991.*

23. Office of Child Support Enforcement, "$50 Pass-Through," December 1997, http://www.acf.dhhs.gov/programs/cse/new/csr9712.htm 9712d.

24. This paragraph relies on Committee on Ways and Means, *1996 Green Book,* Section 9.

25. *Child Support Enforcement: A Clinton Administration Priority,* January 9, 1998, Administration for Children and Families Press Office, http://www.hhs.gov/cgi-bin/waisgate?WAISdoc10 = 39759890 + 3 + 0 + 0 + WAISaction = retrieve.

26. Committee on Ways and Means, *1996 Green Book,* p. 539.

27. Freya L. Sonenstein, Pamela A. Holcomb, and Kristen S. Seefeldt, *Promising Approaches to Improving Paternity Establishment Rates at the Local Level* (Washington, DC: Urban Institute, February 1993), cited in Committee on Ways and Means, *1993 Green Book,* pp. 756–757.

28. Committee on Ways and Means, *1996 Green Book,* p. 540.

29. See Committee on Ways and Means, *1996 Green Book,* pp. 542–544; Irwin Garfinkel, Marygold S. Melli, and John G. Robertson, "Child Support Orders: A Perspective on Reform," *The Future of Children,* Vol. 4, No. 1, Spring 1994, pp. 84–119.

30. Garfinkel, et al., "Child Support Orders: A Perspective on Reform."

31. Committee on Ways and Means, *1996 Green Book,* p. 541.

32. *Child Support Enforcement: A Clinton Administration Priority.*

33. Data for 1996 rely on Committee on Ways and Means, *1998 Green Book,* pp. 548–549.

34. Administration for Children and Families, *Temporary Assistance for Needy Families (TANF) Program.*

35. Executive Office of the President, *Budget of the United States Government, Fiscal Year 2000* (Washington, DC: U.S. Government Printing Office, 1999), p. 248.

36. Committee on Ways and Means, *1993 Green Book,* p. 782.

37. Ibid., p. 785.

38. Committee on Ways and Means, *1998 Green Book,* pp. 607–609.

39. Committee on Ways and Means, *1993 Green Book,* p. 777.

40. U.S. Bureau of the Census, *Child Support for Custodial Mothers and Fathers: 1991.*

41. *Child Support Enforcement: A Clinton Administration Priority.*

42. Garfinkel, et al., "Child Support Orders: A Perspective on Reform," p. 93.

43. Irwin Garfinkel, *Assuring Child Support* (New York: Russell Sage Foundation, 1992).

44. Steiner, *The State of Welfare,* p. 36; Lynn, "A Decade of Policy Developments in the Income-Maintenance Programs," pp. 62–63.

45. Donald Brieland, Lela B. Costin, Charles R. Atherton, and contributors, *Contemporary Social Work: An Introduction to Social Work and Social Welfare* (New York: McGraw-Hill, 1975), p. 100; Steiner, *The State of Welfare,* p. 37.

46. Steiner, *The State of Welfare,* p. 37.

47. Andrew W. Dobelstein with Ann B. Johnson, *Serving Older Adults: Policy, Programs, and Professional Activities* (Englewood Cliffs, NJ: Prentice Hall, 1985), p. 126.

48. Lynn, "A Decade of Developments in the Income-Maintenance System," p. 74.

49. For further discussion of this point, see Sheldon H. Danzinger, Robert H. Haveman, and Robert D. Plotnick, "Antipoverty Policy: Effects on the Poor and the Nonpoor," in Danzinger and Weinberg, *Fighting Poverty,* pp. 50–77.

50. Roberta M. Spalter-Roth, Heidi I. Hartmann, and Linda Andrews, *Combining Work and Welfare: An Alternative Anti-Poverty Strategy* (Washington, DC: Institute for Women's Policy Research, 1992); Heidi Hartmann, Roberta Spalter-Roth, and Jacqueline Chu, "Poverty Alleviation and Single-Mother Families," *National Forum,* Vol. 76, No. 3, 1996, pp. 24–27.

51. Gary Burtless, "When Work Doesn't Work: Employment Programs for Welfare Recipients," *Brookings Review,* Vol. 10, Spring 1992, p. 29.

52. Leonard Goodwin, "Can Workfare Work?" *Public Welfare,* Vol. 39, Fall 1981, pp. 19–25.

53. Barbara Ehrenreich, "A Step Back to the Workhouse?" *Ms.,* Vol. 16, November 1987, pp. 40–42; quote is from p. 40.

54. Goodwin, "Can Workfare Work?".

55. Ellen Goodman, "Volunteer Workfare Program Proves Worth," *Austin American-Statesman,* March 5, 1985, p. A11.

56. Judith M. Gueron, *Reforming Welfare with Work* (New York: Ford Foundation, 1987).

57. Gayle Hamilton and Daniel Friedlander, *Final Report on the Saturation Work Initiative Model in San Diego* (Washington, DC: Manpower Demonstration Research Corporation, November 1989), quotes are from pp. x and vii.

58. This paragraph relies on Daniel Friedlander and Gary Burtless, *Five Years After: The Long-Term Effects of Welfare-to-Work Programs* (New York: Russell Sage Foundation, 1995), quote from p. 35.

59. Jan L. Hagen and Irene Lurie, "How 10 States Implemented Jobs," *Public Welfare,* Vol. 50, Summer 1992, p. 13.

60. Much of this section relies on Committee on Ways and Means, *1993 Green Book,* Section 7, especially pp. 624–644.

61. Committee on Ways and Means, *1998 Green Book,* pp. 476, 481, & 482–488.

62. Robert B. Husdon, personal communication.

63. Stephen Freedman and Daniel Friedlander, *The JOBS Evaluation: Early Findings on Program Impacts in Three Sites, Executive Summary* (New York: Manpower Demonstration Research Corporation, 1995); also cited in Committee on Ways and Means, *1996 Green Book,* p. 428.

64. U.S. General Accounting Office, *Welfare to Work: Most AFDC Training Programs Not Emphasizing Job Placements* (GAO/HEHS-95-113), (Washington, DC: GAO, May 1995).

65. James Riccio, Daniel Friedlander, and Stephen Freedman, *GAIN: Benefits, Costs, and Three-Year Impacts of a Welfare-to-Work Program* (New York: Manpower Research Development Corporation, 1994).

66. Peter Passell, "Like a New Drug, Social Programs Are Put to the Test," *New York Times,* March 9, 1993, pp. C1, 10.

67. Dan Bloom, *After AFDC: Welfare to Work, Choices and Challenges for States* (New York: Manpower Demonstration Research Corporation, 1997).

68. Administration for Children and Families, Department of Health and Human Services, "Temporary Assistance for Needy Families (TANF), 1936–1998," May 1998, http://www.acf.dhhs.gov/news/tables.htm.

69. Administration for Children and Families, U.S. Department of Health and Human Services, "Aid to Families with Dependent Children (AFDC), Temporary Assistance for Needy Families (TANF), 1960–1998," August 1998, http://www.acf.dhhs.gov/news/tables.htm.

70. Social Security Administration, *Social Security Bulletin, Annual Statistical Supplement, 1991* (Washington,

DC: U.S. Department of Health and Human Services, 1992), p. 305.

71. Committee on Ways and Means, *1996 Green Book*, p. 459.

72. See U.S. Bureau of the Census, *Statistical Abstract of the United States: 1997* (Washington, DC: U.S. Government Printing Office, 1997), Table 477, p. 299.

73. Committee on Ways and Means, *1993 Green Book*, p. 615.

74. Committee on Ways and Means, *1996 Green Book*, p. 442.

75. Ibid., pp. 435 & 437.

76. This description of methods used to determine standards of need is based on Center for Budget and Policy Priorities, *Enough to Live On* (Washington, DC), cited in "Study Faults State AFDC 'Need Standards,'" *NASW News*, Vol. 38, July 1993, p. 11.

77. This paragraph and the next rely on Committee on Ways and Means, *1996 Green Book*, pp. 436–438, 451–453.

78. Center for Budget and Policy Priorities, "The Cato Institute Report on Welfare Benefits: Do Cato's California Numbers Add Up?" (Washington, DC, March 7, 1996), http://epn.org/cbpp/cbcato/html.

79. Center on Hunger and Poverty, *Are States Improving the Lives of Poor Families?: A Scale Measure of State Welfare Policies* (Medford, MA: Tufts University, February 1998), pp. 13 & 23; also see Committee on Ways and Means, *1998 Green Book*, p. 524.

80. Unless otherwise noted, the information in this section relies on Department of Health and Human Services, Administration for Children and Families, "Characteristics and Financial Circumstances of AFDC Recipients, FY 1995," December 31, 1996, http://www.acf.dhhs.gov/programs/ofa/content.htm; or on information for fiscal year 1994 from Department of Health and Human Services, Administration for Children and Families, as noted in Committee on Ways and Means, *1996 Green Book*, pp. 473–474.

81. Milwaukee Welfare Warriors, "Apologies Don't Help," in Diane Dujon and Ann Withorn, eds., *For Crying Out Loud: Women's Poverty in the United States* (Boston: South End Press, 1996), pp. 367–368.

82. Committee on Ways and Means, *1993 Green Book*, p. 725.

83. Nicholas Zill, Tabulation of unpublished data from the *Survey of Income and Program Participation* (Rockville, MD: Westat, Inc., 1996), cited in Committee on Ways and Means, *1996 Green Book*, p. 516.

84. Ibid.

85. Mary Jo Bane and David T. Ellwood, *Beginnings* (1983) and David T. Ellwood, *Endings* (1985), cited in Committee on Ways and Means, *1993 Green Book*, pp. 724–725; Mary Jo Bane and David T. Ellwood, *The Dynamics of Dependence: The Routes to Self-Sufficiency* (Cambridge: Urban Systems Research and Engineering, 1983), Department of Health and Human Services, Contract No. HHS-100-82-0038, cited in Committee on Ways and Means, *1996 Green Book*, pp. 503–504.

86. LaDonna A. Pavetti, *The Dynamics of Welfare and Work: Exploring the Process by Which Women Work Their Way Off Welfare,"* unpublished doctoral dissertation, Harvard University, cited in Committee on Ways and Means, *1996 Green Book*, p. 503.

87. J. Cao, *Welfare Recipiency and Welfare Recidivism: An Analysis of the NLS Data*, Discussion Paper No. 1081-96 (Madison: University of Wisconsin, Institute for Research on Poverty, 1996), cited in Committee on Ways and Means, *1996 Green Book*, p. 504.

88. Spalter-Roth et al., *Combining Work and Welfare*.

89. Mary Jo Bane and David T. Elwood, *The Dynamics of Dependence: The Routes to Self-Sufficiency*, Committee on Ways and Means, *1996 Green Book*, pp. 505–506.

90. LaDonna A. Pavetti, "Questions and Answers on Welfare Dynamics" (Washington, DC: Urban Institute, 1995), paper presented at a research meeting on welfare dynamics, cited in Committee on Ways and Means, *1996 Green Book*, pp. 506–507.

91. Bane and Elwood, *The Dynamics of Dependence*.

92. Pavetti, "Questions and Answers on Welfare Dynamics."

93. Reanalysis by the Committee on Ways and Means staff, based on data from Martha S. Hill and Michael Ponza, "Does Welfare Dependency Beget Dependency?" (Ann Arbor, MI: University of Michigan, Institute for Social Research, mimeo, Fall 1984), cited in Committee on Ways and Means, *1993 Green Book*, p. 723.

94. Greg J. Duncan, Martha S. Hill, and Saul D. Hoffman, "Welfare Dependence Across Generations," *Science*, Vol. 239, January 1988, pp. 467–471.

95. Robert Moffitt, *Incentive Effects of the U.S. Welfare System: A Review*, Special Report No. 48 (Madison: University of Wisconsin, Institute for Research on Poverty, 1991).

96. Ibid; also see Committee on Ways and Means, *1996 Green Book*, p. 510.

97. Peter Gottschalk, "The Intergenerational Transmission of Welfare Participation: Facts and Possible Causes," *Journal of Policy Analysis and Management*, Vol. 11, No. 2, 1992, pp. 254–272.

98. This phrase is from William Raspberry, "The Non-Welfare Approach to Aid Poor," *Austin American-Statesman*, February 26, 1988, p. A12.

99. Thomas R. Dye, *Understanding Public Policy*, 3rd ed. (Englewood Cliffs, NJ: Prentice Hall, 1978), p. 131.

100. This paragraph relies on Sheila B. Kamerman and Alfred J. Kahn, *Mothers Alone: Strategies for a Time*

of Change (Dover, MA: Auburn House, 1988); also see Linda Hantrais, "Comparing Family Policy in Britain, France, and Germany," *Journal of Social Policy,* Vol. 23, No. 2, 1994, pp. 135–160; Jami Curley and Michael Sherradden, *The History and Status of Children's Allowances: Policy Background for Children's Savings Accounts* (St. Louis: Center for Social Development, Washington University, January 1998).

101. Tom Buerkle, "Britain Sets Out on Welfare Overhaul," *International Herald Tribune,* March 27, 1998, p. 5.

102. Michael Sherraden, *Assets and the Poor: A New American Welfare Policy* (Armonk, NY: Sharpe, 1991), quote from p. 297; also see Karen Edwards and Michael Sherraden, *Individual Development Accounts: Emergence of an Asset-Based Policy Innovation* (St. Louis: Center for Social Development, Washington University, November 1994).

103. Much of this paragraph relies on Robert E. Friedman, *The Safety Net as Ladder: Transfer Payments and Economic Development* (Washington, DC: Council of State Policy & Planning Agencies, 1988), quote from p. 101; also see Robert L. Woodson, Sr., "Welfare Reform: A Message from the 'Receiving End,' " *National Forum,* Vol. 76, No. 3, 1996, pp. 15–19.

104. United Nations, "Microcredit Warning," *Development Update,* No.25, September–October 1998, http://www.un.org/News/devupdate/.

105. Executive Office of the President, Office of Management and Budget, *A Program for Economic Recovery* (Washington, DC: U.S. Government Printing Office, 1981), p. 1-11.

106. John L. Palmer and Isabel V. Sawhill, eds., *The Reagan Record* (Cambridge, MA: Ballinger, 1984), p. 364.

107. "AFDC Cuts Hurt," *ISR Newsletter,* University of Michigan, Spring–Summer 1984, p. 3.

108. Executive Office of the President, *Budget of the United States Government, Fiscal Year 1991* (Washington, DC: U.S. Government Printing Office, 1990) p. 176.

109. Much of this section relies on Jeffrey L. Katz, "Clinton's Welfare Reform Plan to Be Out in Fall, Aides Say," *Congressional Quarterly,* Vol. 51, July 10, 1993, p. 1813; National Association of Social Workers, "Policy Recommendations of the Clinton Administration's Working Group on Welfare Reform, Family Support and Independence" (Washington, DC: May 6, 1994); also see Executive Office of the President, Office of Management and Budget, *Budget of the United States Government, Fiscal Year 1995* (Washington, DC: U.S. Government Printing Office, 1994).

110. David T. Ellwood, "Welfare Reform as I Knew It: When Bad Things Happen to Good Policies," *The American Prospect,* No. 26, May–June 1996, pp. 21–29, http://epn.org/prospect/26/26ellw.html.

111. Robert A. Rankin, "Clinton Steers to the Middle, and Traditional Welfare Falls," *Austin American-Statesman,* August 4, 1996, pp. D1, 6.

112. This account of the new TANF program is largely based on Committee on Ways and Means, *1996 Green Book,* Appendix L; also see American Public Welfare Association, "Temporary Assistance for Needy Families (TANF) Block Grants (Title 1)," http://www.apwa.org/reform/tanf.htm; David A. Super, Sharon Parrott, Susan Steinmetz, and Cindy Mann, "The New Welfare Law" (Washington, DC: Center on Budget and Policy Priorities, August 13, 1996), http://epn.org/cbpp/wcpmfbl2.html.

113. Jason DeParle, "A Sharp Decrease in Welfare Cases Is Gaining Speed," *New York Times,* February 2, 1997, p. A1.

114. Administration for Children and Families, "Temporary Assistance for Needy Families (TANF) 1936–1996."

115. DeParle, "A Sharp Decrease in Welfare Cases Is Gaining Speed."

116. See "The Personal Responsibility and Work Opportunity Reconciliation Act of 1996," Department of Health and Human Services Press Release, August 12, 1997.

117. Jeffrey L. Katz, "Thompson's Welfare Revolution," *Congressional Quarterly,* October 25, 1997, p. 2608.

118. The Center for Public Policy Priorities, *The Policy Page,* An Update on State and Federal Action, August 1, 1997, available from the Center, 900 Lydia St., Austin, TX 78702, www.cppp.org.

119. Super, et al., "The New Welfare Law."

120. Ellwood, "Welfare Reform as I Knew It: When Bad Things Happen to Good Policies."

121. Gordon Mermin and C. Eugene Steuerle, "The Impact of TANF on State Budgets" (Washington, DC: Urban Institute, November 1997).

122. Robert Pear (*New York Times*), "States Satisfying Welfare-to-Work Plan of '96 Reforms," *Austin American-Statesman,* December 30, 1998, p. A4.

123. Much of this paragraph relies on Super, et al., "The New Welfare Law."

124. General Accounting Office, "Welfare Reform: Implications of Increased Work Participation for Child Care," May 29, 1997, http://www.gao.gov/AlndesFY97/abstracts/he97075.htm.

125. General Accounting Office, "Welfare Reform: States' Early Experiences with Benefit Termination," May 5, 1997, http://www.gao.gov/AlndexFY97/abstracts/he97074.htm.

126. Leslie Miller (Associated Press), "Welfare Reform Compounding Homelessness This Christmas," *Austin American-Statesman,* December 18, 1998, p. A28.

127. Administration for Children and Families, *Temporary Assistance for Needy Families, First Annual Report to Congress.*

128. Dan Bloom, James J. Kemple, and Robin Rogers-Dillon, *The Family Transition Program: Implementation and Early Impacts of Florida's Initial Time-Limited Welfare*

Program (New York: Manpower Demonstration Research Corporation, May 1997).

129. Also see Sheila Zedlewski and Linda Giannarelli, "Diversity among State Welfare Programs: Implications for Reform" (Washington, DC: Urban Institute, January 1997), p. 7.

130. Gregory Acs, Norma Coe, Keith Watson, and Robert I. Lerman, *Does Work Pay? An Analysis of the Work Incentives under TANF* (Washington, DC: The Urban Institute, July 1998), http://newfederalism.urban.org/pdf/occa9.pdf.

131. Richard Wolf, "Welfare Gets Closer to Home," *USA Today,* May 9, 1997, p. 3A; L. Jerome Gallagher, Megan Gallagher, Kevin Perese, Susan Schrieber, and Keith Watson, *One Year After Federal Welfare Reform: A Description of State Temporary Assistance for Needy Families (TANF) Decisions as of October 1997* (Washington, DC: The Urban Institute, May 1998).

132. Gallagher, et al., *One Year After Federal Welfare Reform;* "TANF—One Year Later—The Carrot and the Stick," *New Federalism: Policy Research and Resources,* a newsletter of the Urban Institute, Issue 3, June 1998, p. 2.

133. Center on Hunger and Poverty, *Are States Improving the Lives of Poor families?: A Scale Measure of State Welfare Policies* (Medford, MA: Tufts University, February 1998).

CHAPTER

Fighting Hunger: Nutrition Policy and Programs in the United States

MALNUTRITION AMID PLENTY

Whether it is Ethiopia, Somalia, Rwanda, Bosnia, or another country in desperate straits, the media continue to portray the dire consequences of starvation. The number of deaths attributable to hunger has declined, but it is still frightening to know that each day 24,000 people around the world die hunger-related deaths and that most of these deaths are among young children.[1] UNICEF, a United Nations organization dedicated to children's well-being, reports that "malnutrition contributes to over 16 million child deaths each year, 55 percent of the nearly 12 million deaths among children under five in developing countries."[2] Americans shocked by famines around the world have responded with an outpouring of aid. Although the planet has the capacity to feed everyone adequately, wars, political strife, and red tape, as well as extensive poverty in many areas, have prevented an end to world hunger. And recent reports raise questions about whether world food production can keep pace with a world population that is expected to exceed 8 billion by 2025.[3]

More Americans than one may think suffer from **malnutrition.** Malnutrition is "any condition caused by excess or deficient energy or nutrient intake or by an imbalance of nutrients."[4] **Overnutrition** is the term for this excess and **undernutrition** the term for this deficiency. The irony of malnutrition in the United States is that much of it is overnutrition. According to the first *Surgeon General's Report on Nutrition and Health,* "for most of us the more likely problem has become one of overeating—too many calories for our activity levels and an imbalance in the nutrients consumed along with them."[5] The report acknowledges that undernutrition is a problem for certain Americans. Anemias and other nutritional deficiencies cause approximately 3 deaths per 100,000 population in the United States.[6]

Increased attention to the dietary health of Americans resulted in the national Nutrition Monitoring and Related Research Act of 1990, which strengthened the federal government's ongoing data collection efforts. Among the findings of the *Third Report on Nutrition Monitoring* were that:

- Food intakes of vitamins A, E, and B6 and of zinc and copper were below recommended levels for most age, gender, race, and ethnic groups. Calcium intakes from food were deficient in many groups, including black children, nearly all adolescents, all adult women, black men ages 20 to 59, and all males age 60 and older. Certain groups also had insufficient iron, magnesium, and folate intakes.
- Although low-income adolescents and adults had lower intakes of vitamins and minerals than those from higher-income groups, their levels were not more likely to fall below recommended standards. Low-income children did not have lower intakes than other children.
- Nine to 13 percent of low-income Americans reported that they sometimes or often did not have enough food to eat. Mexican Americans and non-Hispanic blacks more often reported that they did not have enough to eat than did whites.
- For particular subgroups of the population, low income continues to be a substantial risk factor in nutrition-related health problems such as anemia, high-serum total cholesterol, hypertension, and being overweight.[7]

Among low-income groups, patterns of eating are of particular concern.[8] For example, poor people may eat adequately at the beginning of the month, but when limited earnings or public assistance payments run out near the end of the month, eating habits may change. Or the poor may have to decide between buying more food or paying other bills.[9] Children may get their main source of nutrition from school meals, but receive inadequate nutrition at home. The poor elderly may have difficulty getting to the store or may not have teeth with which to chew food. Homeless people often have no regular means for obtaining meals.

In a country like the United States, how should hunger be defined? One suggestion is that individuals "should be considered malnourished if for economic or other reasons beyond their control, they experience repetitive periods of hunger, even though their total intake of nutrients is sufficient to protect them from symptoms of deficiency disease."[10] There is still no widely agreed-on definition of hunger in the United States. To rectify this problem, some nutrition advocates suggest that hunger should be redefined by using a policy goal of **food security.** According to this goal, all Americans should "have access to nutritionally adequate food from normal food channels,"[11] such as grocery stores and restaurants or directly from farmers or their own gardens. Everyone recognizes that trash bins and garbage cans are not normal food sources. Community soup kitchens and food pantries could also be considered non-normal food sources. Yet they are used by substantial numbers of Americans each day. The United States Department of Agriculture (USDA) has attempted to measure food insecurity. Using a definition of "limited or uncertain access to food" and based on data from 1995, it estimated that 12 million U.S. households experienced food insecurity, with 4 million experiencing moderate or severe hunger.[12]

SETTING NUTRITIONAL POLICY

Prior to the 1930s, states and communities used their own methods to feed their "deserving poor," but with the advent of the Great Depression more and more people were unable to obtain enough to eat. Scores stood in bread lines or waited at soup kitchens to obtain their only means of survival. Despite the effort, these methods of feeding the hungry were clearly inadequate for meeting the country's needs.

Commodity Food Distribution

By 1930 farmers had successfully encouraged the federal government to stabilize farm prices by buying their surplus agricultural commodities. The U.S. Department of Agriculture (USDA) and the Federal Emergency Relief Administration were authorized to purchase the commodities, and in 1933 the Federal Surplus Relief Corporation was established to aid in the process. This action was intended to help farmers, but rather than let these products go to waste, the new agricultural policy provided an opportunity for distributing large amounts of food to poor people. Unfortunately, recipients continued to face long waits in commissary lines to receive whatever foods were available, and at least some public officials were concerned that this method of food distribution only added to the degradation of the poor.[13] In addition, perishable foods were difficult to preserve. A better method of providing food was needed.

As a solution, in 1939 the nation attempted its first food stamp program in some parts of the country, this time with added encouragement from grocery store operators.[14] Participants could purchase from $1 to $1.50 of orange stamps per person, which could be exchanged for any type of food at regular retail grocery stores.[15] For each dollar of orange stamps purchased, they received fifty cents worth of blue stamps free. Blue stamps could be exchanged only for designated surplus foods. The new program provided farmers a market for their surplus foods, preserved normal channels of trade through grocery stores, and gave recipients greater food choices.[16] The program's drawbacks were (1) it was available only to public assistance recipients and not to others in need, (2) many eligible individuals could not afford the purchase requirements, and (3) there was criticism that products other than surplus foods were being purchased with the blue stamps.

The country's first food stamp program ended in 1943, largely because of the increased demand for agricultural surpluses created by World War II. Given this demand, it seems ironic that the country abandoned the use of food stamps in regular grocery stores and returned to commodity distribution. The new commodity program, called the Needy Family Program, made use of surplus farm goods as well as products purchased specifically for the program.[17] This new program did little to rectify problems such as large containers of food that were inconvenient to use, not easily preserved, and sometimes not very appealing. Interest in a better method remained strong, and new food stamp program bills were introduced in every session of Congress.[18]

A New Food Stamp Program

Not until 1961, under the administration of President John F. Kennedy, was a new food stamp program pilot-tested in several areas of the country.[19] Evidence that the approach resulted in recipients purchasing more foods and those of higher nutritional quality helped to spur passage of the Food Stamp Act of 1964.[20] However, communities were still free to use commodity distribution.

The new Food Stamp Program was also the responsibility of the USDA, but each state determined eligibility criteria, and state and local welfare agencies certified eligible recipients and provided them with the stamps. Eligibility criteria were usually the same as for the state's other public assistance benefits. Recipients were then given an allotment of stamps (also called *coupons*) determined by the federal government according to household size. The federal government also determined how much recipients were charged for the stamps based on their income. The stamps, like paper money, came in various denominations and were exchanged at their face value for food products in regular retail grocery establishments that chose to participate in the program. The difference between the amount recipients paid and the total value of the stamps was called the **bonus value.**

Politics Discovers Hunger

Despite the 1964 Food Stamp Act, the extent of hunger in America was exposed in several ways during the 1960s. Particularly poignant is Nick Kotz's description of the visit of Senators Robert F. Kennedy and Joseph Clark in 1967 to the filthy shack in Cleveland, Mississippi, where Annie White and her six children lived.[21] The senators' trip was at the request of Marian Wright Edelman (now head of the Children's Defense Fund), and they were stunned at what they saw. One of the children, a girl about 2 years old, had a swollen stomach and was so listless that Senator Kennedy was never able to get her to respond to his cajoling. White said she could not afford to buy food stamps, and all the family had to eat at that time was the last rice and biscuits from its surplus commodity allotment. A study by the Citizen's Board of Inquiry into Hunger and Malnutrition in the United States called *Hunger U.S.A.* (supported by the Field Foundation of Chicago's Marshall Field department store) and a CBS television documentary also helped the country to "discover hunger."

In 1968 Congress responded by establishing the U.S. Senate Select Committee on Nutrition and Human Needs, chaired by Senator George McGovern. In 1969 President Richard M. Nixon called a White House Conference on Food, Nutrition, and Health, and the USDA established the Food and Nutrition Service (from 1994 through 1997 it was known as the Food and Consumer Service) to administer its federal food assistance programs.[22]

As described in the 1964 Food Stamp Act, the program was to be broader than previous efforts. States were to make stamps available not only public assistance recipients, but also to low-income or near-poor people unable to afford an adequate diet. However, as the change from commodity foods to food stamps took place, participation dropped precipitously. "In theory," says Kotz, "the food stamp plan *sounded* simple and workable, and should have been an enormous improvement over commodity distribution," but what really happened was "extortion":

> *It was no accident that the stamp payment formula produced the outcries "We can't afford the stamps" and "The stamps run out after two weeks." Following their congressional leaders' twin desires of helping the farmers but not providing welfare to the poor, Agricultural Department bureaucrats had designed a Food Stamp program so conservative that reformers called the plan "Scrooge stamps."*[23]

Political activism by groups such as the Poor People's Campaign helped to spur reforms in the program.[24] Amendments passed in 1971 during the Nixon administration required that the program provide a "nutritionally adequate diet." Benefits were increased and eligibility criteria and application procedures were standardized so that applicants would be treated similarly, regardless of where they lived. Participants could not be charged more than 30 percent of their income for the stamps, based on the estimate that low-income families devoted 30 percent of their income to food (as noted in Chapter 3, the poverty level is based on a calculation whereby the minimum amount needed by a family to acquire an adequate diet is multiplied by three). Unemployed adult recipients capable of holding jobs became responsible for registering for work and accepting employment if a "suitable" job could be found. In determining eligibility, income deductions for work-related expenses, housing, and medical expenses were introduced. Stamps were provided free to the poorest participants, and benefits were to be automatically adjusted (indexed) each year for changes in food costs.

More changes came in 1973. All communities had to adopt food stamps as their official nutrition program, and coupon allotments were to be indexed for inflation twice a year. The most troublesome requirements of the program were that recipients had to buy their stamps, and they had to buy all the stamps to which they were entitled at one time. In 1974 this requirement was modified so that a portion of the stamps could be purchased. A series of lawsuits resulted in a 1975 court order to increase outreach efforts to make potentially eligible people aware of the program.

Eliminating the Purchase Requirement

Despite the benefits that were supposed to have been reaped, the Food Stamp Program had not necessarily made eating better or easier for the poor. Purchase requirements were just too high. The most significant program change came in 1977 during the Carter administration when the purchase requirement was eliminated. Recipients no longer had to put up cash to receive food stamps—they were simply given the bonus value of the stamps to which they were entitled. The USDA estimated that in the Southeast, the Mountain Plains, and the Southwest participation rose by about 30 percent.[25] These areas include many of the poorer, largely rural states.

But not all the news in 1977 was good for those in need. National poverty guidelines were adopted as the income eligibility standard, so that those with net incomes greater than these amounts could no longer participate. Income deductions were also tightened; benefits were reduced more rapidly as income rose (by 30 cents for every dollar of income), and requirements for student participation were made tougher. Thus, at the same time that elimination of the purchase requirement helped add needy people to the roles, others were being disqualified.

Politics Rediscovers Hunger

The decade of the 1980s began with additional tightening of the Food Stamp Program and disagreement about the extent of hunger in America. In 1980, cost of living adjustments were changed from twice to once a year. The Reagan administration also had an impact on the Food Stamp Program. Reagan felt that the program had grown too large during the 1970s by allowing families with greater than poverty-level incomes to participate and that the result was "to divert the Food Stamp Program away from its original purpose toward a generalized income transfer program, regardless of nutritional need."[26] The elimination of the purchase requirement had indeed contributed to making food stamps more like an income maintenance program,[27] an effect that others thought was important and long overdue.

In 1981 and 1982 the philosophies of the Reagan administration resulted in expenditure cuts and eligibility restrictions in the Food Stamp Program. Changes included further tightening of income deductions and income limitations, calculating family income partly on past income rather than on current income alone, prohibiting the use of federal funds to conduct outreach, and monitoring the program more closely to reduce fraud and error. Program participation began to drop (see Figure 7-1).

New charges emerged that hunger was on the rise due to Reagan's social program cuts and also to rising unemployment. Concerned that reports of hunger were exaggerated,[28] Reagan appointed the President's Task Force on Food Assistance. Its general conclusion, published in 1984, was that undernutrition was not a serious problem in the United States. Social action groups lambasted the report,[29] and leading nutrition experts charged that "Despite their almost total lack of qualifications, the task force members did manage to find that hunger has reappeared in America. But because of their ineptitude, they were unable to qualify its extent, or to discern the presence of chronic malnutrition."[30] Meanwhile, the Food Research and Action Center (FRAC) publicized results of its own work indicating that infant mortality had increased in some areas of the country due to nutritional deficiencies; the Citizens' Commission on Hunger in New England also concluded that malnutrition and hunger again confronted America, and the Physician Task Force on Hunger in America identified 150 "hunger counties" in which substantial numbers of poor people were not receiv-

FIGURE 7-1

Food Stamp Program, Bonus Value of Stamps and Number of Average Monthly Participants, 1964–1997

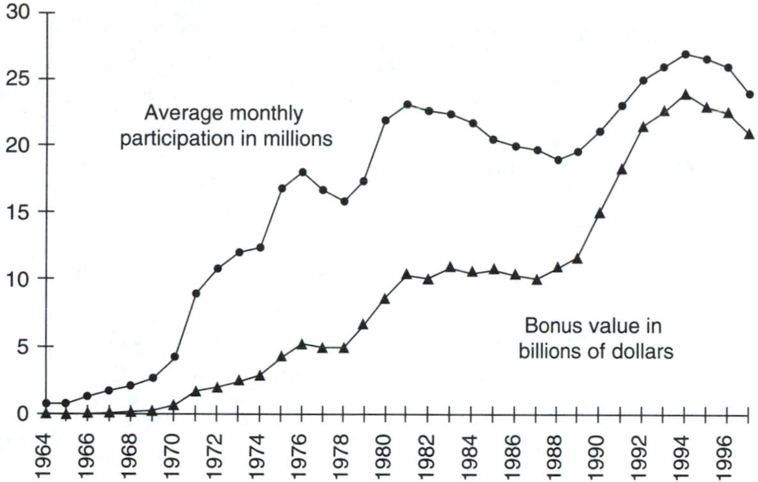

Sources: Social Security Administration, *Social Security Bulletin, Annual Statistical Supplement, 1997* (Washington, DC: Social Security Administration, 1997), p. 359; Food and Consumer Service, *Explanatory Notes to Accompany Administration's Budget Request for FNS in 1999,* http://www.usda.gov/library/expla98.doc; USDA Nutrition Program Facts, "Food Stamp Program," http://www.usda.gov/fcs/stamps/fspfor~1.htm.

ing food stamps.[31] The Reagan task force recommended replacing the Food Stamp Program with a block grant, monitoring spending more closely, and beefing up efforts to detect fraud and abuse, while the other groups encouraged increased food stamp spending, making it easier to obtain and use benefits, and establishment of a bipartisan commission to put an end to the country's hunger.

By the mid 1980s, much of the new food stamp legislation was kinder to recipients. In 1985 the Food Security Act reauthorized the Food Stamp Program and eased some requirements. AFDC and SSI recipients were declared automatically eligible, and states that charged a sales tax on food could no longer tax food stamp purchases. But states were also required to establish a Food Stamp Employment and Training (E&T) program by 1987 in order to reduce Food Stamp Program participation.

The Food Stamp Program was expanded in 1986 and 1987 with provisions such as making it easier for homeless people to participate. For example, no fixed address is required, and homeless individuals may use their stamps to purchase low-cost meals in participating restaurants.[32] The 1988 Hunger Prevention Act increased food stamp allotments, further increased access to the program, reinstated the use of federal funds for states' outreach efforts (although outreach activities are optional), and made life easier for the states by setting more realistic error tolerance rates.

In 1990 the Mickey Leland Memorial Domestic Hunger Relief Act, named after the late representative from Texas, reauthorized the Food Stamp Program through 1995. Leland's efforts to bring attention to the problem of world hunger were well known, and he chaired the House Select Committee on Hunger. The committee's efforts were highly respected, but it had only an advisory role, and the House abolished it in 1993 despite strong outcries. A USDA-sponsored hunger forum was held in 1993 to help the Clinton administration set its nutrition agenda. People with various interests in food programs, including food stamp participants, testified at the forum. During this period, Congress increased income deductions and disregards. The 1996 farm bill reauthorized the Food Stamp Program through 1997, but bigger changes were in store.

TIGHTENING FOOD STAMPS' BELT: THE WELFARE REFORM OF 1996[33]

In keeping with the country's mood to do something about the Aid to Families with Dependent Children program (see Chapter 6), national welfare reform legislation entitled the Personal Responsibility and Work Opportunity Reconciliation Act (PRWORA) of 1996 made substantial changes in the Food Stamp Program. The program was saved from being converted into a block grant which might have resulted in a cap on the number of eligible people who could be assisted, but many eligibility rules were made more stringent. For example, in determining whether households meet financial eligibility criteria, the standard income deduction (intended to cover some basic living expenses) is frozen indefinitely rather than adjusted annually as had been the practice. Annual adjustments to the excess shelter deduction (designed to assist people with high housing costs) will rise between 1997 and 2001 but are capped beyond that. A cap of $4,650 has also been placed on the allowable value of a vehicle.

What does all this mean for those who rely on food stamp benefits? Some will no longer qualify. There have been various analyses about the effects for those who are able to maintain eligibility. The Center for Budget and Policy Priorities says that by 2002, these households will have been hit with a 20 percent reduction in their food stamp benefits, from an average of 80 cents provided per person per meal to 66 cents.[34] The Center also says that half of the food stamp cuts will be borne by those with incomes of less than half of the poverty line, calculating these cuts at a total per household of $656 in 1998 and $790 by 2002.

The act severely limits the number of legally admitted immigrants who are entitled to receive food stamp benefits. Only a few categories of legally admitted residents continue to qualify, such as certain refugees and asylees. Although President Clinton signed the welfare reform bill, his administration hoped to reverse some of its most onerous provisions, including those that are particularly detrimental to non-citizens residing legally in the United States. Many states are using their own funds to assist at least some elderly, disabled, and child recipients whose benefits were ended.

The act makes it easier for states to operate Food Stamp Employment and Training programs, but it contains stiffer work requirements for recipients. For example, unless exempt due to reasons such as physical or mental disability, able-bodied adults (ages 18 to 50) without dependents (ABAWDs as they are referred to by the USDA) who do not meet work or other job program requirements can receive food stamps for only three months in a 3-year period. They may regain eligibility by working or participating in a work program for 80 hours in a 30-day period. Furthermore, in lieu of giving a household its food stamp allotment, the states may use the funds to subsidize a job for a household member participating in a work supplementation or support program. Other welfare reform provisions "delete lack of adequate child care as an explicit good cause exemption for refusal to meet work requirements" and establish minimum disqualification periods for those who fail to meet work or workfare requirements of the Food Stamp Program. (States can request exemptions from work requirements in areas where unemployment is over 10 percent or there is otherwise an insufficient number of jobs to accommodate food stamp participants. States also have the option of exempting 15 percent of those covered under the new work rule.) Food stamp rolls continue to drop during the current period of economic prosperity, but concern remains that those who do not have dependents and who cannot find work where they live will unjustly be denied a benefit to which they were once entitled.

The PRWORA eliminates some provisions that standardized the operation of food stamp offices across the country. For instance, there is no longer a requirement for a uniform national application. Some protections for applicants and participants are no longer mandatory, such as waiving office interviews for elderly and disabled applicants. States are no longer required to assist applicants in obtaining necessary information or completing applications. Protections for participants have taken a beating in reforming welfare. The PRWORA did reauthorize the Food Stamp Program through fiscal year 2002.

The reforms contained in the act are couched in conservative rhetoric that promises a reduction in welfare dependency and an increase in self-sufficiency by raising expectations about the work performance of public assistance recipients and by denying benefits to immigrants. Social welfare program advocates believe that the consequences will be severe for many poor households that need financial assistance in securing an adequate diet. The effect may be to place more reliance on other government-sponsored nutrition programs as well as greater reliance on nonprofit and church-related programs. Despite the improved economy, the U.S. Conference of Mayors reported a sharp increase in the number of emergency requests for food assistance after the last round of cuts became effective.[35]

FOOD STAMP PROGRAM OPERATIONS[36]

The Food Stamp Program currently operates in all fifty states, the District of Columbia, Guam, and the U.S. Virgin Islands. Once recipients are certified eligible, they pick up their stamps or coupons each month at a designated bank or post office, although some recipients receive their stamps by mail, and many now receive them through electronic transfer systems. Recipients then use their stamps or electronic benefits to purchase food at regular retail stores. The only cash that recipients who use stamps may receive is change of less than one dollar that results from a food purchase. Those using electronic benefits receive no cash.

Determining Eligibility

Means testing is the basis for determining food stamp eligibility. Eligibility determination is complicated and is done by "household units." In fact, it takes more than five pages of small print in the *Federal Register* to spell out what constitutes a food stamp household![37] At the risk of oversimplification, a food stamp household generally consists of an individual or a group of individuals who live together and prepare meals together, whether or not they are members of the same family. Some eligibility requirements are more generous for households that have a member who is elderly or disabled. For example, most households are limited to $2,000 in countable assets (such as bank accounts), but households in which one member is at least 60 years old may have $3,000 in countable assets. A household's home, personal effects, business assets, and certain other items are not considered countable assets, and exemptions are made for the value of an automobile.

For households with at least one person age 60 or older or a disabled member, there is no limit on gross income. For other households, gross income (which includes most cash received such as earnings and public assistance* and social insurance payments) cannot exceed 130 percent of federal poverty guidelines (in fiscal year 1999, $1,783 a month for a family of four, except in Hawaii and Alaska, where poverty guidelines are somewhat higher). Certain cash income is excluded (disregarded) in calculating gross income such as child support paid, federal educational aid, income earned by children attending school, and income tax refunds. Net income for *all* households cannot exceed 100 percent of poverty guidelines ($1,371 a month for a family of four in fiscal year 1999). In determining net income, certain amounts of money are also disregarded in order to cover at least some of the households' living expenses.** A flat amount of income of $134 a month is automatically disregarded (except in Alaska, Hawaii, and Guam, where it is higher, and in the Virgin Islands, where it is lower). In cases where one or more family members are working, 20 percent of all earned income is disregarded. There is also a deduction for the costs of caring for a child or other dependent while household members work or participate in training or education. The maximum allowable deduction is $200 per month for each child under age 2 and $175 for each other dependent. This deduction is, however, used by only about 2 percent of households because many households are too poor to pay for this type of care.[38]

*Note, however, that the value of food stamps is not counted in determining eligibility for most other public assistance programs such as TANF and SSI.

**Using federal poverty guidelines to determine whether a household meets the *net* income criteria for eligibility is somewhat more generous than it seems, because federal poverty guidelines are actually measures of gross income rather than net income. See James C. Ohls and Harold Beebout, *The Food Stamp Program: Design Tradeoffs, Policy, and Impacts* (Washington, DC: Urban Institute, 1993), p. 33.

Another income disregard, the excess shelter deduction, is used by many more households. It is calculated by determining the amount of the household's housing costs (mortgage or rent, utilities, property taxes, and insurance) that exceeds 50 percent of their remaining income after all other disregards or deductions are made. For households with elderly or disabled members, there is no cap on this deduction, but for other households the maximum deduction in 1999 was $275 per month (again, higher in Alaska, Hawaii, and Guam and lower in the Virgin Islands). Another income deduction for those who are elderly or disabled includes all but $35 of the medical expenses that they pay themselves. States also have the option of disregarding the first $50 of child support payments a household receives if the state pays the additional amount of the food stamp benefit that results from doing so.

Individuals who fall into certain additional categories may qualify for the Food Stamp Program. They include victims of natural disasters and people living in some types of not-for-profit facilities such as alcoholics and drug addicts in halfway houses, homeless people living in shelters, women and children in battered women's shelters, and people who are disabled or elderly and residing in group homes. Native Americans living on or near reservations may participate in the Food Distribution Program on Indian Reservations (a commodity program) as an alternative to the Food Stamp Program if they wish. Some people are expressly excluded from participation in the Food Stamp Program, such as most people living in large institutions, those who have quit a job without good cause, strikers, and undocumented individuals living in the U.S. In addition to most immigrants residing legally in the U.S., the 1996 federal welfare reform legislation added another category of ineligibles: those convicted of federal or state felony drug offenses. States can exclude others such as those disqualified from other public assistance programs, individuals who do not cooperate with child support enforcement, and those in arrears on child support.

In 1982, a block grant replaced the Food Stamp Program in the U.S. territory of Puerto Rico in an effort to control error, abuse, and rapidly rising costs.[39] By that time, 56 percent of Puerto Rico's population was receiving food stamps, while agricultural production had declined.[40] Some of Puerto Rico's grant funds are used to strengthen agricultural production. Recipients now receive benefits by check. American Samoa recently began a nutrition program for elderly and disabled people. Under separate legislation, a block grant is also provided to the U.S. territory of the Northern Mariana Islands; participants receive coupons that the Islands print themselves, and 25 percent must be used for native products. In the territories, income eligibility limits are only about half of what is allowed in the forty-eight contiguous states.

Participants and Costs

In March 1994 average monthly Food Stamp Program participation reached an all-time high, just short of 28 million individuals, nearly 11 percent of the U.S. population.[41] Increased participation was partly due to growth in the U.S. population, but as shown in Figure 7-1, the number of participants has fluctuated over the years. These fluctuations reflect a variety of factors, primarily economic recession and unemployment[42] as well as tightening and loosening of eligibility requirements during the program's history.

By November 1998 the number of food stamp particpants had dropped below 19 million.[43] Declining participation is due mostly to improvements in the economy. Making most legally-admitted immigrants ineligible has also contributed and dropping able-bodied adults who are not working may also be having an effect. Recipiency rates vary by state. Naturally, poorer states have the highest rates.

The USDA periodically compiles descriptions of households that receive food stamps. In 1996, 60 percent of households contained children, 20 percent had a member who was disabled, and 16 percent had an elderly member.[44] Just over half (51 percent) of participants were children and 7 percent were age 60 or older. Women recipients outnumbered men two to one. The average food stamp household had two or three members, and the average monthly income per household was $528. Of all recipients, 41 percent were white, 34 percent African American, and 19 percent Hispanic. In addition, 91 percent of households had poverty level incomes. The gross income of households with children was 54 percent of the poverty level, and for households without children, it was 60 percent. Almost 23 percent of households had some earned income. Most food stamp households receive other forms of public assistance or social insurance benefits. About 37 percent received AFDC (now TANF), 24 percent receive SSI, 19 percent receive Social Security or veterans benefits, and 6 percent receive General Assistance.

The states share most administrative costs of the Food Stamp Program equally with the federal government, but the federal government bears all costs of the value of the food stamps as well as the costs of printing, distributing, and redeeming the stamps through the nation's Federal Reserve System.[45] The total bonus value of food stamps increased from $4.4 billion in 1975 to $10.7 billion in 1985, and $22.5 billion in 1996 (see Figure 7-1). Total federal costs (including administration) were $24.3 billion in 1996 with more than $60 million in benefits provided every day.[46] Appropriations were $26.3 billion in 1997 but $25.1 billion for 1998 as participation declined.[47]

Despite the changes in 1996, the Food Stamp Program remains available to a broader cross-section of the population than any other public assistance program. It can still be described as the nation's only noncategorical public assistance program—although recipients must be poor to qualify, they need not be aged, disabled, or have dependent children. The program tends to reach those in greatest need, but about 26 percent of eligible individuals (31 percent of eligible households) were not participating in 1994.[48] Almost all eligible households with incomes of less than half the poverty line participated, compared with about 76 percent of those whose income was between 50 and 100 percent of the poverty line. Participation for other subgroups varies substantially; although 86 percent of eligible children were enrolled, only one-third of eligible elderly participated. Almost all eligible single-parent households participated compared to 78 percent of two-parent households. Participation rates were 92 percent for eligible African Americans compared to 61 percent for Hispanics, and 59 percent for whites. Estimates are that enrollees use 82 percent of the benefits that would be available to the total pool of eligibles.

Reasons cited for nonparticipation include the stigma of receiving welfare benefits, lack of knowledge of the program, and inability to reach a food stamp office to apply.[49] To this list, the General Accounting Office adds "limited office hours, unnecessary screening forms, failure to help applicants obtain necessary documents . . . and failure to consider applicants for expedited benefits [which must be processed within 5 days]."[50] Ernie's story, found in Illustration 7-1, describes several of these problems. In other cases, people do not realize they are eligible, they do not think they need the benefits, the amount of benefits to be received is small and may not be worth the hassle, or mistakes by workers lead people to believe they are not eligible.[51] Ohls and Beebout suggest that administrative requirements may be less burdensome than some people realize, but in some localities, they seem to be a greater obstacle to participation than stigma.[52]

Nonprofit groups like Second Harvest try to fill the gaps in providing food assistance through food gleaning efforts which have grown substantially in the United States. There is certainly a lot to be gleaned. "A July 1997 USDA study shows that 96 billion pounds of food—over one quarter—of the 356 billion pounds of goods produced for human consumption is lost at the retail and food service levels."[53] The USDA has its own food gleaning program, and Congress passed the Bill Emerson Good Samaritan Food Donation Act of 1996 to limit the liability of those who donate and distribute the food.

NUTRITION PROGRAMS FOR YOUNGER, OLDER, AND DISABLED AMERICANS

In addition to the Food Stamp Program which reaches a broad cross section of those in need, a number of other nutrition programs target specific segments of the population.

Meals for School Children[54]

The first federal legislation to help schools serve lunches to students was passed during the Great Depression in 1933. In 1946, The National School Lunch Act, signed by President Harry Truman, established permanent legislation to provide children from low-income families free or low-cost hot lunches. The federal government, through the USDA's Food and Nutrition Service, provides cash assistance and food commodities to state departments of education to operate the National School Lunch Program. These departments then distribute the funds and food to participating public and private nonprofit schools. Children whose family income is not more than 130 percent of the poverty line receive free lunches, and reduced-price lunches are available to those with family incomes between 130 and 185 percent of the poverty level. Schools cannot charge more than 40 cents for reduced-price lunches, but they determine the amount that children from families with incomes greater than 185 percent of poverty guidelines are charged for full-cost meals.

ILLUSTRATION 7-1

A Client's View of the Food Stamp Program

Ernie[a] applied for food stamps in a Rustbelt state a month after one of the local factories had laid off two thousand employees. The administration of the program in this state was handled through county welfare offices. Even though the county paid for none of the direct costs of the food stamps, the county commission had been grumbling about not receiving adequate reimbursement from the state for its administrative costs. One organization of welfare clients had charged that county officials were engaged in a purposeful "slow down" of the eligibility process, hoping to deter prospective clients from applying for food stamps.

The day before, Ernie had called the county welfare office and inquired about the procedures for applying for food stamps. The first dozen or so times he had gotten a busy signal. Finally, a secretary answered and told him in a matter-of-fact voice that he should come to the welfare office the next morning as early as possible in order to complete an application. Ernie asked whether he would need to bring any type of documentation with him, and he was told only that the procedures would be fully explained by the social worker when he completed the application.

The next morning, Ernie arrived at the county welfare office at 7:45 A.M. to find that there was no available parking within at least six blocks and that there was already a line stretching out the door and around three sides of the block. (The day was December 8, the temperature was just about freezing, and a light drizzle was falling.) Most of the other people in line were women with small children. One woman had four preschool children with her. She spent most of her time holding them, changing diapers and feeding the two smaller children, and trying to keep the two older ones from wandering into the street.

Around 10:00 A.M., Ernie finally made it into the building. He really didn't mind waiting the next forty-five minutes; after all, it was warmer inside. Just before 11:00 A.M., he completed his application and handed it to the secretary. She studied it for a moment and then asked, "Where are our supporting documents?" When Ernie asked for an explanation, she said, "You know, rent receipts, medical bills, stuff like that."

Ernie was puzzled (and very angry) about not being given this information on the phone the previous day, but there was nothing he could do except go home and gather this documentation. He returned again the next morning, and the line was somewhat shorter. By 10:30 A.M., he had reached the secretary's desk and handed her his application and a fistful of documents. She indicated that this would, indeed, be adequate and invited him to sit in the waiting room to see the social worker.

At 1:30 P.M., Ernie had his first meeting with the social worker who reviewed his application and documents and informed him that he did not meet the eligibility requirements because he had refused employment the week before. (Ernie had turned down a job offer that would have required him to relocate to a community approximately sixty miles away. His reason was simple: He didn't have the money to move his family.) Unlike many food stamp applicants, Ernie didn't take this social worker's opinion as the final word.

continued

ILLUSTRATION 7-1 *(continued)*

He asked to see her supervisor and was given an appointment the following week.

Ernie brought photocopies of the legislation governing the Food Stamp Program to the next meeting, as well as copies of the state's and county's administrative guidelines for program operation and eligibility determination. He had done this on the advice of one of his friends, a union shop steward who had helped several others denied benefits by county welfare officials. He also let the supervisor know that he knew thoroughly the procedures for appeal and that he intended to take this case "all the way to the county commission." After a five-minute meeting, she approved Ernie's application.

The secretary issued Ernie a card certifying his eligibility, and then he received his next surprise. He happened to live in a state where food stamp distribution was handled by private banks. Applicants were certified by the county welfare office and then sent across the street to the bank to pick up their stamps.

The first thing that Ernie noticed upon entering the bank was a sign with large red lettering stating: "All Food Stamp Clients Must See Cashier No. 3." He could tell from the size of the lines which cashier was distributing food stamps. He also noticed that the bank's other customers seemed to resent the presence of food stamp clients. Some cast sidelong glances; others openly verbalized their hostility.

Ernie's next surprise came when he and his wife went to the supermarket to purchase groceries with their food stamps, but that's a completely different story. . . .

Source: Reprinted from Diana M. DiNitto and C. Aaron NcNeece, *Social Work: Issues and Opportunities in a Challenging Profession* (Englewood Cliffs, NJ: Prentice Hall, 1990), pp. 229-230.

[a]Ernie is a pseudonym; nevertheless, he was a real client.

In the 1998–1999 school year, the federal government reimbursed most schools about $1.94 for each free meal, $1.54 for each reduced-price meal, and 18 cents for each full-price meal.[55] States can also select from a number of "entitlement" commodities that are worth 15 cents per meal. Additional "bonus" commodities are provided as they become available. Approximately 95,000 schools (almost all public schools and many private) participate in the School Lunch Program. Participation now averages about 26 million youngsters each day. In 1996, 49 percent of children participating received their lunch free and 8 percent at reduced price.[56] In 1997, 2.2 billion free lunches and 351 million reduced-price lunches were served.[57] The 1997 program appropriations were $5.2 billion with $700 million in entitlement commodities. Appropriations for 1998 were considerably less, $4.2 billion, although some funds were carried over from 1997.

Controversy over the lunch program has centered on whether the aid goes to children who need it most.[58] For example, schools that did not have kitchens, generally those in poor districts, were not allowed to participate. Catered meals could have been used by these schools, but school lunch administrators had been known to lobby against earmarking funds for free meals to poor children for fear that private caterers would take their jobs.[59] They contended that they could adequately provide for these children with general school lunch aid, although criticisms were that they provided free lunches to only half of eligible children. When some schools on Indian reservations were still not allowed to participate due to lack of equipment, the Physician Task Force on Hunger charged that the federal government had enough of the necessary equipment in storage to solve the problem.[60] The Reagan administration was successful in tightening income eligibility criteria and in reducing subsidies for the School Lunch Program, but it was not successful in deducting the value of school meals from a household's food stamp allotment or in eliminating the subsidies for full-price meals. According to the Committee on Ways and Means, more than 90 percent of federal school lunch aid now goes to pay for the meals of children in low-income families due to the much larger subsidies for free and reduced-price lunches.[61]

More recent concerns are that school lunches and breakfasts were too high in fat, cholesterol, and sodium, and did not meet the Dietary Guidelines for Americans (the federal government's own nutrition standards). The USDA has been developing more healthful school meals and offering students more choices, including those that are appealing to children and reflect ethnic preferences of the locality.[62] More fresh fruits and vegetables are being served, and the USDA is developing new low-fat products like cheese and turkey sausage. Lunch programs have the option of offering rather than automatically serving children foods in order to reduce waste.

The Healthy Meals for Healthy Americans Act of 1994 made it easier for some institutions and individuals to participate in the country's child nutrition programs. It also requires that school meals meet national dietary guidelines. Schools now select from five approaches to menu planning, and the USDA provides educational assistance to children and school meal personnel to improve food choices. The idea of serving all school meals free is being tested as a result of the legislation. This makes for less work and expense in determining who qualifies for meals, allows staff more time for meal planning, and reduces stigma associated with public assistance.[63]

Smaller in scope than the lunch program is the School Breakfast Program. This additional boost to child nutrition was established under the Child Nutrition Act of 1966. It uses the same eligibility criteria as the lunch program. Schools cannot charge more than 30 cents for a reduced-price breakfast, but they determine the price of full-cost breakfasts.[64] The regular subsidy for a free breakfast during the 1998–1999 school was $1.07, 77 cents for a reduced-price breakfast, and 20 cents for a full-price breakfast (subsidies are higher in Alaska and Hawaii). Schools with a "severe need designation," due to large numbers of children who receive free and reduced-price lunches and higher-than-average meal preparation costs, receive up to 20 cents more for each free and reduced-price breakfast served. In 1996, 80 percent of children participating received their breakfasts free and 6 percent at reduced price, making it a program that clearly targets low-income children.[65]

All schools with subsidized lunch programs may operate a breakfast program. In 1989, Congress mandated that states do more to make school districts aware of the breakfast program and provided grants to help start programs. Despite knowledge that a nutritious breakfast can improve attention and learning,[66] reluctance to start programs may have been due to the extra administrative responsibilities and personnel costs involved in adding this program to the school day. Today about 69,000 schools, or 73 percent of those with lunch programs, participate in the breakfast program. Daily participation averaged 6.8 million children in early 1998. This is a substantial increase from the 4.1 million children who participated in 1990, but only one in four children who eat a school lunch eat a school breakfast. The 1996 welfare reform legislation eliminated funds for starting and expanding breakfast programs. Federal appropriations for the breakfast program were $1.3 billion in 1998.

Since 1954 the Special Milk Program, which provided a market for surplus dairy products, has served millions of children. Today this program is restricted to schools and child-care facilities not participating in the school lunch and breakfast programs because these programs include milk. About 140 million half-pints of milk were provided with a federal appropriation of $19.2 million in 1997.[67] The 1998 appropriation was $18.2 million. Schools may provide milk free to all children, provide it free only to poor children, or charge all children, but the program must be operated on a nonprofit basis. During the 1997–1998 year, schools were reimbursed 12.5 cents for each half-pint of milk sold, and they were reimbursed at the net purchase price for milk provided free. Nearly 8,000 schools and residential care institutions participated as well as 1,400 summer camps and other programs.

Another program serving children is the Summer Food Service Program (SFSP).[68] Since 1968 it has provided free lunches to children in poor communities during summer vacations. More than 2 million children benefited in 1997. Appropriations were $250 million in 1997 and $272 million in 1998. Concerns are that eligible children in communities serving meals are not taking part in the SFSP due to families' lack of knowledge about the program,[69] and that many communities are not participating. People over age 18 with physical and mental disabilities who participate in school programs may also be served by the SFSP.

WIC

Among the most highly regarded, federally supported nutrition programs is the Special Supplemental Nutrition (formerly Food) Program for Women, Infants and Children, commonly called WIC.[70] Established in 1972, it is intended to improve the nutrition of low-income women who are pregnant or postpartum, infants, and children up to age 5 who are certified to be at "nutritional risk" according to federal guidelines. Risks include priority medical conditions such as anemia or a history of pregnancy complications; they may also include inadequate diet. Participants must also meet state residency requirements and receive AFDC, food stamps, or Medicaid, or meet other state-determined income limitations (usually income that does not exceed 185 percent of poverty guidelines). WIC is administered by the USDA in conjunction with state health departments, Indian tribal organizations, and local agencies operating at more than 8,000 sites. About 46,000 merchants participate.

Participants receive WIC coupons that allow them to purchase "food packages," usually in regular grocery stores. The food packages are specified according to the recipient's age and nutritional needs and contain nutritious food such as infant formula, dairy products, cereals, and juices. When possible, WIC participants are encouraged to breastfeed their babies. Since WIC's bill for infant formula is high, states negotiate rebates with formula manufacturers to reduce costs, but scandals have risen over price fixing by manufacturers. Perhaps this is because $620 million was spent on infant formula in 1996 after subtracting rebates of $1.2 billion. In 1996, the food cost of the average WIC package was a little more than $31 a month, and the average monthly costs of nutritional risk assessments and administration were $11 a month.[71] Recipients also receive nutrition education and referrals to other health and social services. Efforts have been made to increase attention to alcohol and drug education and to screening for alcohol and drug abuse among participants.[72]

The relationship between adequate nutrition in pregnancy and lower infant mortality and morbidity rates is clear. In addition, proper nutrition during childhood is crucial in promoting normal development and in preventing life-threatening illnesses and problems that may affect health throughout the life cycle. According to the Physician Task Force on Hunger, studies of the impact of WIC on pregnancy outcomes all show positive results.[73] One study showed that WIC participation was associated with "a 21% decrease in low-birth-weight infants, a major decrease in neonatal mortality, and a 45% reduction in the number of women with inadequate or no prenatal care."[74] Another study demonstrated that "participation in WIC is associated with a statistically significant reduction in the poorer outcomes of pregnancy; in particular, with 23% fewer low-birth-weight and very-low-birth-weight infants, fewer small-for-gestational-age infants, fewer premature infants, and fewer infant deaths."[75] Other researchers note that when compared with their siblings who did not receive WIC, children whose diet had been supplemented by WIC participation "showed significant enhancement of most intellectual and behavioral measures in the current home and school setting, including IQ, attention span, visual-motor synthesis, and school grade-point average."[76] A national evaluation of the WIC program confirms many positive findings.[77] Others take a more qualified approach in their praise of WIC, saying that its real benefits may be in getting women earlier prenatal care.[78] WIC is also associated with reduced Medicaid costs.[79]

Despite the benefits associated with WIC, it has never been made an entitlement program. Funds are divided among the states using a need formula, and states give preference to recipients at greatest nutritional risk. When an agency reaches maximum participation, a priority system is used to fill vacancies; at the top of the list are pregnant and breastfeeding women and infants with a nutrition-related medical condition. In 1982 the program served 2.2 million women and children at a federal cost of $948 million.[80] Fiscal year 1997 appropriations were $3.6 billion with about 7.4 million participants.[81] In 1998, appropriations increased to $3.9 billion. Estimates are that the program now reaches 60 percent of those who are eligible, including 98 percent of infants. Many individuals and organizations have called for funding that will allow all eligible women, infants, and children to participate. Instead, 1996 federal welfare reforms eliminate requirements that the USDA "promote" the WIC program through public service announcements and other activities.

The Farmers' Market Nutrition Program (FMNP), begun in 1992, now provides additional coupons to those receiving WIC benefits so they can purchase fresh produce. It is also intended to increase use of farmers' markets. It operates in a relatively small number of communities, but federal appropriations have increased from $6.8 million in 1997 to $12 million in 1998. To support farmers in their own area, states may specify the foods that can be purchased.

Nutrition for Older Adults

Many of the nutrition benefits for older people are provided through programs established in 1972 amendments to the Older Americans Act of 1965 (see Chapter 10). Under this act the Administration on Aging provides funds to states which in turn channel these monies to local programs in order to serve meals for older Americans at "congregate sites" such as community centers and churches and to deliver meals to home-bound people who are older or disabled. The Older Americans Act also provides supportive services such as shopping assistance and nutrition education. The USDA participates in the meal programs by providing cash and some commodities. Individuals age 60 or over and their spouses of any age are eligible. Native American tribes may set lower minimum age requirements. There is no means test and no set price for meals, but cash donations or food stamp payments are welcome. Each meal must generally provide one-third of the RDAs.

The program for home-bound people is known as "Meals on Wheels." In many communities volunteers give their own lunch hours one or more times a week to deliver meals. In addition to improved nutrition, the positive spillover effects of these nutrition programs are support of independent living, social contacts with other members of the community, and the opportunity for referral should an older or disabled person need additional assistance. In 1995, 242 million meals were provided to 3.4 million older people.[82] Funding for the nutrition programs for the elderly was $610 million in 1997. About half the meals are served at congregate sites and half are delivered. Considerably more money to support these programs comes from state, local, and private sources. Many communities have waiting lists for the home-delivered meals. Some elderly and disabled people are also allowed to use their food stamps to purchase low-cost meals in restaurants.*

More Nutrition Programs

Other nutrition programs include the Child and Adult Care Food program, which provides meals and snacks year round to preschool children in day care facilities, to children served in homeless shelters, and to adults with disabilities who participate in day

*Apart from some recipients who are elderly, disabled, or homeless, other food stamp participants cannot use their coupons to purchase meals in restaurants. The food stamp benefits of residents of approved not-for-profit facilities are used to offset the costs of their meals.

care programs. In addition to public and not-for-profit facilities, for-profit facilities may be eligible if they serve a substantial number of low-income participants. Participants may receive meals free or be charged, depending on their income. Fiscal year 1998 appropriations were $1.5 billion. In early 1998, 2.6 million children and 58,000 adults were being served.[83]

The Commodity Supplemental Food Program (CSFP) operates in some states to serve low income pregnant and breastfeeding women, infants, and children as well as poor older Americans. To qualify, women, infants, and children must be participating in another public assistance program. Elderly people cannot have incomes that exceed 130 percent of the poverty level. The states have considerable discretion in determining eligibility and operating the program. In some areas this program is used instead of WIC coupons. In 1997, the CSFP provided commodity foods to 370,000 individuals each month; federal appropriations for 1998 were about $96 million.[84] The Emergency Food Assistance program (TEFAP), introduced under the Reagan administration originally as a temporary measure, allows states to obtain surplus foods as they become available. The program was established to reduce federal food inventories and storage costs and to help needy people.[85] States determine eligibility criteria. Due to changes which reduced subsidies in the federal agricultural price-support programs, the USDA is acquiring less surplus food; therefore, TEFAP has been allowed to purchase nonsurplus products to assist those in need. The amount each state receives depends on the size of its low–income and unemployed population. The foods may go directly to people in need or to organizations that feed them. Participants in other nutrition programs may also be eligible for TEFAP. Appropriations in 1998 were $100 million for food purchases and $45 million to state and local governments to run their programs. The former Soup Kitchens/Food Banks Program was combined with TEFAP, continuing to allow states to distribute additional foods provided by the USDA to organizations that help needy individuals. The USDA also operates a commodity program to help people following natural disasters.

NUTRITIONAL POLITICS

Both the Senate and the House of Representatives have a committee and subcommittee with primary responsibility for nutrition legislation. In the Senate they are the Committee on Agriculture, Nutrition, and Forestry and its Subcommittee on Research Nutrition, and General Legislation. In the House, the Agriculture Committee and its Subcommittee on Department Operations, Nutrition, and Foreign Agriculture are the major entities. Advocacy groups, particularly the Food Research and Action Center (FRAC) and the Center on Budget and Policy Priorities, are also key players in nutrition legislation. In their 1993 account of the Food Stamp Program, economists Ohls and Beebout note that food stamp legislation is primarily influenced by about thirty people who have the most intimate knowledge of the program; furthermore, food stamp legislation tends to be very detailed, with little discretion left to administrators, because of the importance legislators attach to this program.[86]

Despite the blows to nutrition programs dealt by the 1996 welfare reform legislation, food assistance tends to generate a strong emotional response that has generally resulted in expanded aid. As nutrition advocates work to reverse the most onerous provisions of the 1996 reforms, there are some enduring issues of political significance that also deserve consideration in our discussion of nutrition legislation. They are the form that nutritional benefits should take; the adequacy of food stamp benefits (see Illustration 7-2); and waste, abuse, and fraud in the Food Stamp Program. Also of interest is who should administer nutrition programs.

Rendering the Cash versus In-Kind Debate Obsolete with EBT

Public assistance benefits fall along a continuum from in-kind to cash. Commodity food distribution uses the in-kind strategy, because participants are given specific food products. Cash benefits (in the form of checks) are used in programs such as AFDC and SSI. Food stamps are often referred to as in-kind benefits, but they actually fall in the middle of the continuum, representing a compromise between those who prefer to deliver nutrition benefits using cash and those who prefer to do so using commodities.[87]

Advocates of the commodity approach, generally those with conservative viewpoints, contend that this method assures that nutritious food will be provided to participants (though it does not assure that the food will be consumed). They believe the cash approach is flawed because it does not ensure that food will be purchased by recipients; the money can be diverted to meet other needs of recipients. Commodity proponents also argue that food stamps do not ensure that nutritious foods will be purchased. While they may concede that food stamps are generally used to purchase food, they are concerned that stamps have resulted in an illegal market (referred to as "trafficking") and can be used to purchase just about anything anyone wants.

Advocates of cash benefits say that commodities rob people of their dignity because they do not allow them the food choices that other citizens have. They believe that most recipients are responsible people who use cash benefits wisely and that stamps or even the new electronic benefit cards unnecessarily embarrass or stigmatize participants in grocery stores. In addition, neither stamps nor electronic benefits can be used to purchase cleaning supplies, paper goods, and other necessities* that account for approximately 25 cents of every dollar spent in grocery stores by other shoppers.[88] Since many food stamp recipients also receive TANF or SSI, advocates of cash benefits point to the administrative savings that would accrue from simply adding the value of food stamps to the public assistance checks already being sent to them.

Whether cash or stamps really make a difference has been the subject of empirical investigation in studies undertaken by the USDA. In a "cash-out" demonstration in Alabama, there was no statistically significant difference in recipients' food expenditures or in the nutrient value of food they purchased when the two methods

*In addition to food products, stamps can be used to purchase seeds and plants to grow food for personal consumption, and in remote areas of Alaska hunting and fishing equipment may be purchased with food stamps.

ILLUSTRATION 7-2

The Thrifty Food Plan—How Much Is It Worth?

Food stamp benefits used to be based on the USDA's Economy Food Plan (EFP), but in the 1975 case of *Rodway v. USDA*, the U.S. Supreme Court found the EFP inadequate to meet nutritional needs. Today, food stamp benefits are calculated using the Thrifty Food Plan (TFP), the most economical of the USDA's four plans, which also include the Low-, Moderate-, and Liberal-Cost Plans.[a] Each plan has the same nutritional value and is based on the Recommended Daily Allowances (RDAs) for nutrients published by the National Academy of Sciences as well as typical food selections of households in each of the four income groups. There is a wide variation in the monthly dollar value of these four meal plans. In June 1998, they were from lowest to highest, $419.00, $538.20, $671.20, and $809.00.[b]

Using the TFP, the maximum food stamp benefit is determined for a prototype family of two adults, ages 20 to 50 and two children, one age 6 to 8, and the other, age 9 to 11. This allotment is then adjusted for households of different sizes and economies of scale (larger households can buy in larger quantities and make more efficient use of food products). The monthly food stamp allotment for a family of four on the U.S. mainland with no countable income in 1999 was $419, or about $1.13 per person per meal for a typical thirty-one day month. As countable income rises, 30 percent of it is deducted from the maximum allowable payment of $419. For example, a family of four with $400 of countable income received a monthly food stamp allotment of $299. The true deduction actually amounts to about 20 to 25 percent of income because of disregards (the amounts not counted in determining eligibility).[c] Food stamp allotments are higher in Hawaii, Alaska, Guam, and the Virgin Islands due to higher food costs in those locations. Nutrition benefits are also higher in the Mariana Islands, but in Puerto Rico, where benefits are now paid in cash, the maximum payments are lower.

The RDAs and the TFP are useful in determining benefit levels, but they do not solve all the problems of obtaining an adequate diet. For example, the TFP has been criticized for falling short of the RDAs needed for some nutrients. The RDAs are based on healthy people, not those with special health and dietary needs; they are guidelines and provide neither the minimum requirements nor optimal levels of nutrient intake for all persons; they are averages, and trying to meet all of them every day is "difficult and unnecessary."[d] But all food stamp households receive benefits based on the TFP for the prototype family regardless of whether they contain members (such as teenagers) who might require greater food consumption or those (perhaps older members) who may consume less. Benefits could be calculated to more precisely reflect the composition of various households, but the tradeoff might be to increase administrative costs.[e] The TFP was improved in 1983, but the House Committee on Agriculture still had to fend off criticisms stating that "although not ideal, it theoretically provides the basis of a nutritionally adequate diet."[f] The committee also noted that many Americans fail to eat properly even with the necessary resources.

continued

ILLUSTRATION 7-2 *(continued)*

The USDA concedes that the TFP "relies heavily on economical foods such as dry beans, flour, bread, and cereals. It includes smaller amounts of meat, poultry, and fish than families typically use. The Low-Cost and Moderate-Cost food plans are suitable for most American families. They also allow for more variety and less home preparation of food."[g] The USDA contends that it could develop plans that cost even less than the TFP, "but they would be very monotonous and less like families' food consumption practices and preferences."[h] The Physician Task Force on Hunger believes that the TFP "was never intended to meet family nutrition requirements," asserting that

> *The Department [of Agriculture] has never determined that this computerized plan represents an adequate expenditure level to achieve desirable nutrition levels. . . . The thrifty food plan is an example of bureaucracy gone awry. A federal expenditure level was set, and a computer was programmed to design a food plan equal to that level—irrespective of human need.*[i]

Beginning in 1990, stamp allotments were increased to 103 percent of the TFP, but 1996 federal welfare reform legislation returned allotments to 100 percent of the TFP. The USDA provides menus and other information to help food stamp recipients keep their food purchase within budget. But regardless of the adequacy of the TFP, virtually everyone would agree that it takes a very careful shopper to stretch food stamps benefits over an entire month. One study found that households that followed TFP menus spent an average of 3.5 hours per day preparing meals, compared with less than 2 hours for other households.[j] Other factors also affect the ability of an individual or family to use its food stamp benefits as efficiently as possible. For example, some food spoilage is inevitable. And benefits are indexed for inflation each October based on food prices in the previous June. These adjustments are made after the costs of food have increased so the lag has some negative effect on the amount of food that can be purchased. Since the TFP is based on average food prices, it also disadvantages those who live in areas where food prices are higher, as well as those who cannot shop in stores offering the best buys. The USDA's Center for Nutrition Policy and Promotion is currently updating the TFP. This update is sure to receive careful scrutiny from nutrition program advocates.

There are some interesting interactions between the Food Stamp and Medicaid programs (both in-kind types of programs) and the cash public assistance programs that affect beneficiaries' standard of living. Analyses indicated that food stamps and Medicaid had been used to substitute for increased AFDC payments to recipients.[k] Food stamps also help to equalize TANF and SSI payments across state lines. Since public assistance recipients in states with lower TANF and SSI payments have less countable income, they receive more in food stamp benefits. Food stamps may serve to ease the consciences of state lawmakers as they have allowed the real value of cash public assistance benefits to decline in recent decades. Furthermore, most food stamp households have incomes that remain well below federal poverty guidelines, even if the cash value of food stamps is taken into account.[l]

continued

ILLUSTRATION 7-2 *(continued)*

[a]For a discussion of the Thrifty Food Plan see James C. Ohls and Harold Beebout, *The Food Stamp Program: Design Tradeoffs, Policy, and Impacts* (Washington, DC: Urban Institute Press, 1993), chapter 2.

[b]USDA, "Official USDA Food Plans: Cost of Food at Home at Four Levels, U.S. Average, June 1998," http://www.usda.gov/cnpp.

[c]Committee on Ways and Means, U.S. House of Representatives, *1998 Green Book: Background Material and Data on Programs within the Jurisdiction of the Committee on Ways and Means* (Washington, DC: U.S. Government Printing Office, 1998), p. 923.

[d]Eleanor Noss Whitney and Sharon Rady Rolfes, *Understanding Nutrition* (Minneapolis/St. Paul: West Publishing, 1993), p. 14.

[e]Ohls and Beebout, *The Food Stamp Program*, p. 36.

[f]Subcommittee on Domestic Marketing, Consumer Relations and Nutrition, Committee on Agriculture, U.S. House of Representatives, *A Review of the Thrifty Food Plan and Its Use in the Food Stamp Program*, April 1985, p. viii.

[g]USDA, Human Nutrition Information Service, *Home and Garden Bulletin*, Number 183, rev. September 1984, p. 3.

[h]Brenda Shuler, "Making Food Dollars Count," *Food and Nutrition*, Vol. 13, No. 3, 1983, pp. 16–19.

[i]Physician Task Force on Hunger in America, *Hunger in America: The Growing Epidemic* (Middletown, CT: Wesleyan University Press, 1985), pp. 106 & 134; also see David Hosansky, "Allotments Cook Up Controversy," *Congressional Quarterly Weekly Report*, November 4, 1995, p. 3363.

[j]Subcommittee on Domestic Marketing, Consumer Relations and Nutrition, *A Review of the Thrifty Food Plan*; also see Hosansky, "Allotments Cook Up Controversy."

[k]Robert Moffitt, "Has State Redistribution Policy Grown More Conservative?," *National Tax Journal*, June 1990, pp. 123-142.

[l]Ohls and Beebout, *The Food Stamp Program*, p. 71.

were compared.[89] In a similar study in San Diego, there were rather small but statistically significant differences; for example, the energy value of food consumed was 5 percent greater for recipients using stamps rather than cash.[90] An earlier demonstration showed little or no difference in nutrient intake among elderly people who received stamps and those who received cash.[91] In Puerto Rico the switch from stamps to cash did not result in changes in participants' food expenditures or diet quality.[92] Although a number of previous analyses using econometric modeling do show greater food expenditures using stamps,[93] more recent statistical modeling "suggests that the loss of food expenditures associated with a cash-only program may be less than previously imagined."[94] Some evidence indicates that nutrition education might be more important in improving diet quality.[95]

Although there is little evidence to suggest that the bulk of cash benefits would not be used to purchase food, and neither cash, nor stamps, nor electronic benefits can ensure that recipients will purchase nutritious foods, the USDA has no plans to convert the Food Stamp Program to a cash benefit program.[96] Apparently ignoring the research findings as well as the savings to be accrued, the USDA concluded that there were "no advantages to cashing out, and stated that "because the Food Stamp Program was designed as a nutrition assistance program, . . . many people . . . were concerned that cash-out would not ensure that food stamp benefits will be used to buy food."[97] The 1996 federal welfare reform legislation prohibits waivers to cash out food stamps, but some demonstrations are continuing in which the value of food stamps is combined with SSI or TANF benefits. The older welfare programs, AFDC, now TANF, and SSI (and its forerunners) are cash benefit programs, but the preference among policymakers during the last few decades has not been cash benefits. The major, newer welfare programs, Food Stamps and Medicaid, lie more in the realm of in-kind benefits. At the beginning of the 1960s, about 90 percent of welfare benefits were paid in cash; only 10 percent were in kind; by the 1980s, 70 percent were in kind; only 30 percent were distributed in cash.[98] Since recipients prefer cash to in-kind benefits, cashing-out might add to the rolls a substantial number of eligible people who are not participating in the program.[99] But it is apparent that in-kind benefits are integral to the political support of the Food Stamp Program and that a cash-out might result in far less support, lower benefits,[100] and perhaps even stricter eligibility requirements. Some people would prefer to see all the cash benefit programs converted to in-kind benefits because of the control they afford.

Cash versus in kind still provides for a satisfying debate among those who care to argue these issues, but the advent of electronic benefit transfer (EBT) has really rendered the debate moot. EBT has emerged as the most politically feasible way to provide public assistance benefits.[101] EBT operates on the same principles as a debit card. The welfare agency places the amount of the individual's benefits in an account. In the grocery store checkout line, the recipient's EBT card is "swiped" through a reader or "point-of-sale" terminal, and recipients punch in their personal identification number (PIN). The cost of the purchase is deducted immediately from the recipient's account.

In 1984, Reading, Pennsylvania, was the first location to test EBT for food stamp benefits. Maryland was the first to use EBT statewide. Beneficiaries there use EBT to access their food stamp benefits as well as their TANF, Child Support Enforcement, and General Relief benefits. The majority of states now use EBT in all or part of their service areas.[102] All states must complete the transition to EBT by 2002. A task force of federal agencies is working to ease the transition among agencies and to reduce costs. EBT is widely regarded as a useful alternative to food stamps. The USDA reports that food stamp participants prefer EBT. They do not have to make a special trip to pick up their food stamps, and the card may be less conspicuous when paying for grocery purchases. Recipients apparently have adapted to EBT. The electronic system also eliminates the need to print stamps; although cards must be made and distributed, they need not be issued each month. In late 1997, the USDA reported that the Food Stamp Program issued 2.5 billion coupons annually which were handled by 210,000 retailers, who made 2 million deposits each month in 30,000 banks which then had to make more than 40,000 food stamp deposits each month in Federal Reserve District Banks. Coupons have to be "counted at each step, making the accounting enormously complex and labor intensive. EBT eliminates much of the paper handling involved . . . and automates the accounting process."[103] Retailers are automatically paid at the end of each business day.

EBT provides additional security features. For example, a lost or stolen card is more difficult for someone else to use than cash, a check, or stamps, because the PIN is supposed to be known only by the recipient. Electronic benefits are also more difficult to use in underground markets than food stamps because the electronic record of each transaction makes it easier to identify improper use of benefits. EBT may eliminate the reputation of food stamps as the "second U.S. currency," a reference to the use of food stamps in trafficking. In Texas, one of the first states to implement EBT, the state comptroller credited EBT with reducing food stamp rolls and fraud. The comptroller reported that "food stamp sales [at retail stores] rose by $4.5 million from one month to the next, even though comparable benefits were issued for both months."[104]

Proponents of EBT also point to the cost savings for recipients and governments. Since cash benefits like TANF and SSI are issued in the form of checks and not dollars, recipients must cash their checks. Many low-income individuals cannot afford to maintain checking accounts, and in some cases they may have to pay a substantial fee to cash a check. It also costs the federal government less to do an electronic benefit transfer (about 4 cents) than to issue a check (about 30 cents).

A major drawback has been the startup costs in changing to an EBT system, but recent demonstrations show that EBT can reduce administrative costs. In order to keep EBT costs in line, the federal government has encouraged "piggybacking." This involves combining EBT with commercial, electronic funds transfer systems (for example, automated teller machines) already widely available, rather than separate EBT systems used only for public assistance benefits. Grocery retailers have also been concerned about the costs of converting to EBT, for example, making EBT available in all checkout lanes in order to see that food stamp users are treated equitably. Over time, the costs for all involved are supposed to diminish. States now implementing a new system must operate on a "cost-neutral" basis (it cannot cost more than the coupon system).

Another snag that EBT encountered was Regulation E of the Electronic Funds Transfer Act.[105] The act requires that institutions such as banks using electronic transfers issue all users a monthly statement of their accounts. If applied to public assistance benefits, the costs of EBT would increase considerably. The Federal Reserve Board temporarily allowed states testing EBT an exemption from the part of Regulation E that would have held them liable for lost or stolen benefits in excess of $50, if recipients report the missing EBT card within two business days. Lost or stolen food stamp benefits are not replaced, and states were concerned about their liability as well as fraud if Regulation E were imposed on benefits distributed electronically.[106] The 1996 federal welfare reform exempts states from complying with the regulation.

EBT holds the promise of combining added efficiency with greater assurances that benefits will be used for food purchases. Most current systems are "online," requiring hookup to a central computer. "Smart cards," which use offline technology, have been used in Montgomery County, Ohio. A computer chip with all necessary information is embedded in the smart card. Wyoming has also tried an offline system in some areas for WIC and food stamps. Once the entire country converts to EBT, the Food Stamp Program will need a new name.

In 1977 social scientist Jodie Allen wrote that the Food Stamp Program "should not be viewed as an alternative to broader reform of our tax and transfer programs" and noted that Americans who need food assistance but are able to work would prefer lower taxes, lower inflation, and jobs to direct food assistance.[107] For years, political debates about food stamps and other nutrition programs focused more narrowly on whether cash or stamps are preferable, rather than placing these discussions in the broader context of welfare reform. In 1996, the Food Stamp Program was placed in this broader context. It was just not the context that welfare advocates had in mind.

How Much Fraud, Abuse, and Error in Welfare?

If programs like food stamps reached precisely the target groups for whom they were intended, then there would be no concern about fraud, abuse, and error. But it is impossible for large, bureaucratically administered programs to achieve such a feat. Although everyone agrees that these problems exist, there is substantial disagreement over their extent. Some indicate that only a tiny percentage of applicants and recipients—less than 1 percent—are reported for purposely cheating social welfare programs, and that even a smaller number are prosecuted.[108] But others have gone so far as to say that "[W]hile official rates are 3 to 5 percent, professionals frequently estimate that 30 to 50 percent of [former] AFDC cases involve[d] some fraud."[109]

Regardless of who is right about the extent of fraud and cheating, one does hear of creative ways to do it. For example, some recipients have sold stamps for less than face value to merchants who then redeem them at face value, or recipients have sold stamps at less than face value to others who then use them to purchase groceries. These illegal practices may have been attempts at outright deceit or a desperate attempt to get cash for a necessary purpose. A different type of example results from high nursing home costs. It involves older people transferring their assets to their children in order to gain eligibility for long-term care through Medicaid without depleting their savings. Another example that one occasionally hears of is people applying for duplicate benefits by using more than one name or applying in different states. The media like to dramatize the most blatant examples of fraud and abuse. The widely read *Reader's Digest* once published an article entitled "Time to Crack Down on Food-Stamp Fraud," which said "in Kentucky undercover policemen discover that federal food stamps are being traded for automobiles, drugs, and automatic weapons."[110] One newspaper story declared that, "Food stamps are being bartered for everything from crack to birdbaths in the poverty pockets of Dallas."[111] Another newspaper article caught this reader's eye with the headline: "Thousands of Dead People Remain on Food Stamp Lists."[112] For 1993, the USDA estimated that food stamp trafficking amounted to $800 million or 3.7 percent of benefits issued. In 1996, one-quarter of erroneous food stamp payments were estimated to have been fraudulent, amounting to less than 2 percent of benefits.[113]

The emphasis on detecting fraud has greatly increased. The USDA conducts sting operations or "sweeps" at grocery stores by having people pose as clerks or food stamp recipients in order to find those who engage in illegal practices. Computer detection is also widely used.[114] For example, in order to determine whether a person is underreporting income when applying for or renewing benefits, welfare departments use computer matching to check Internal Revenue Service, Social Security, unemployment insurance, and other agencies' files.

Computer-assisted methods are also used to audit health care vendors' charges to determine if they might be perpetrating fraud. EBT systems also help, but they are not fail-proof. There are reports of hackers breaking into EBT systems and of consumers asking vendors to ring up phony purchases (instead of purchasing groceries, the customer takes cash and the clerk gets a cut of it).

Among the newest attempts at rooting out fraud is finger imaging, a form of biometrics. A fingerprint is taken at the time of application similar to what states are doing when people apply for or renew a driver's license. Early results suggest that it may initially deter eligible applicants from applying, perhaps due to fear or discomfort with the new system, but some of these individuals eventually comply so that they can receive benefits.[115] One recent study of a finger imaging demonstration project failed to uncover anyone receiving duplicate benefits; furthermore, no savings were incurred that could be attributed to the system, indicating the demonstration project did not deter fraudulent activity.[116] The 1996 federal welfare reform legislation increases penalties for vendors and program participants who engage in illegal food stamp activities. Individuals convicted of food stamp trafficking of $500 or more are permanently barred from program participation, not to mention other legal penalties they may face.

Much of the emphasis on rooting out fraud, abuse, and error is now directed toward those who supply goods and services to public assistance and social insurance recipients. Food stamps used to be the program that was most likely to make media headlines over fraud. Today government health care programs, especially Medicare, seem to take first place with accusations that vendors (doctors, clinics, medical supply stores) charge for services that are not needed, overcharge for what was received, or even charge for services never received. Senate hearings carry titles like *Gaming the Health Care System*[117] and *Milking Medicaid and Medicare.*[118] A recent *Miami Herald* headline was equally provocative: "Medicare Audit: Fraud Still Rampant," citing a government report of 11 percent of Medicare funds being spent for all the wrong reasons, although there was no indication of how much was actually fraud and how much was due to error.[119]

Efforts to deter and detect fraud are euphemistically called "promoting integrity."[120] These efforts also include promoting competition so that the government can get the best price for items like prescription drugs. Reducing errors is equally important because the rules, regulations, and eligibility requirements of social welfare programs are so complex and change often. Estimates are that about half of all errors are made by clients and the other half by program personnel—the caseworkers and administrators who process applications, determine eligibility, and calculate the amount of payments clients receive.[121] Client mistakes can involve misremembering information or misinterpreting questions. Staff errors may be a result of inadequate job training, failure to understand or even know some of the rules governing the program, the large number of cases processed per worker, the volume of paperwork involved, miscalculations, and other unintentional or careless mistakes.

As a result of concerns about fraud, abuse, and error, the federal government uses **quality control** procedures. Quality control originated in business and industry. In industry, it refers to taking a sample of products—for example, cars—and checking or testing them to ensure that they perform properly. In social welfare, quality control involves taking a sample of cases to ensure that recipients are eligible and that they are receiving neither too much nor too little in benefits. It is also used to ensure that people have not been incorrectly denied benefits. Sampling is based on scientific techniques so that the cases reviewed are representative of the larger client population. In the Food Stamp Program alone, over 90,000 cases are reviewed every year.[122]

The federal government sets quality control standards, and state welfare agencies review food stamp and Medicaid cases by conducting field investigations, including interviewing clients and verifying records such as rent receipts and paychecks. Federal personnel conduct the SSI quality control studies, because it is largely a federally administered program. Although some error is bound to occur in programs as large as these, the federal government believes that only a certain amount of error is tolerable. Quality control has been a major bone of contention for state governments, which are liable for fines if their error rate exceeds federally determined limits.

One indication of how difficult it is to comply is that by 1987, only three states had kept food stamp error rates to acceptable levels for any period of time. States bitterly complained that the 5 percent allowable error rate in the Food Stamp Program at that time was unrealistic.[123] Even a miscalculation of a dollar can place a case in the overpayment or noneligible category. The General Accounting Office urged the states to recoup overpayments from recipients,[124] but the states called for modifications in the quality control system.[125] The differences of opinion led to continuing appeals. In 1990, the federal government forgave state quality control penalties for the years 1983 to 1985,[126] and in 1993 the USDA and twenty-four states resolved a dispute over fraud and errors in the Food Stamp Program for the years 1986 to 1991, with the states agreeing to pay some fines.[127] In 1988, the federal government decided that a flat 5 percent error tolerance rate was too stringent. The tolerance level was liberalized, resulting in a rate of 10.8 percent in 1989.[128] It was modified again in 1993 so that states are subject to sanction if their combined overpayment and underpayment rates exceed the national weighted average.[129] The higher the error rate, the higher the percent assessed. In 1996, the combined national food stamp error tolerance rate was 9.2 percent, 6.9 percent for overpayments and 2.3 for underpayments.[130] The rate for improper denials and terminations in 1994 was 3.8 percent. States with rates lower than 6 percent are provided financial rewards in the form of additional administrative funding for their program, and states with higher rates are expected to do better. States' error rates vary widely; in 1996 they ranged from 3.5 percent in South Dakota to 14 percent in Virginia. In 1996, 24 states exceeded acceptable error rates and 6 states were rewarded for error rates lower than 6 percent. Prior to 1996, the lowest recorded national overpayment rate was 7 percent in 1991. Underpayment rates have been relatively constant. The Committee on Ways and Means reported that only $10 million of the $1 billion in sanctions assessed to the states through 1995 was collected by the federal government. Rather than continue squabbling over sanctions, the usual procedure today seems more rational—states are allowed to invest sanction amounts in improving program administration.

Methods of improving program administration include identification of the sources of errors. In the Food Stamp Program, the cases most prone to error include larger households with earned income, while one-person households with no earned income are less error-prone.[131] This suggests that efforts to reduce error should focus on cases in which error is most likely to occur.

Congress also forgave millions of dollars in AFDC penalties through an "amnesty" provision and relaxed some rules used to calculate AFDC errors.[132] In fiscal year 1991, the AFDC error tolerance rate was increased from 3 to 4 percent or the national average AFDC error rate, whichever was higher, based on overpayments. In 1991, AFDC overpayments were estimated at $1 billion or a national error rate of 4.96 percent, the lowest ever recorded.[133] Under the Omnibus Budget and Reconciliation Act of 1989, all sanctions for years prior to 1991 were waived. In 1994, state AFDC overpayment error rates ranged from 2.52 percent in Hawaii to 14.41 percent in Florida with an average of 6.11 percent. Erroneous payments were reported at $1.4 billion of the nearly $23 billion made in payments.[134] Underpayment rates ranged from .11 percent to 2.97 percent amounting to $207 million. Welfare reform legislation has changed many things. Under the TANF block grant program (see Chapter 6), the federal government no longer requires the states to calculate error rates. Some states continue to calculate them as a way of monitoring the program because they believe it is important in their stewardship role.[135] The Medicaid tolerance rate is 3 percent. Rather than the usual quality control study, states with lower rates can utilize their quality control funds to conduct pilot studies that will help them further reduce Medicaid errors. For example, a state may decide to study spousal impoverishment (cases in which one spouse is in a nursing home receiving Medicaid and the other spouse remains at home). Determining eligibility in these cases can be very complex (see Chapter 8).

Although the savings from reduced error may offset the costs of quality control[136] without substantial net savings, these efforts may serve more to appease critics than to reduce public assistance costs. Even in most cases of ineligibles receiving benefits or of overpayment to eligible recipients, these households are not financially well off. Government officials have been criticized for focusing on overpayments and on keeping ineligibles off the rolls rather than showing more concern for those unjustly denied benefits. Warnings about misreporting information on welfare applications and notices posted in some welfare offices have been called intimidation tactics designed to keep people from applying at all.[137] The government has also been criticized for paying excessive attention to sniffing out errors in public assistance without equal attention to other programs (recall the effects of deregulation and the resulting collapse of many savings and loan institutions and scandals in the securities industry). And it is unlikely that fraud and error in public welfare would ever match the money lost in tax avoidance and evasion by the nonpoor.[138] As one economist concluded in a major book on social welfare, most individuals "are simply unaware of how little waste, fraud, and abuse there is in the public welfare system."[139]

Who Should Administer Nutrition Programs?

The early surplus commodity distribution programs begun in the 1930s were closely tied to federal agricultural policy. Without the extensive federal system of public assistance programs now available, it seemed logical to place these programs under the legislative auspices of the agriculture committees of Congress and under the administrative auspices of the USDA. The government's commodity distribution programs enjoyed strong support from the powerful farm lobby, the American Farm Bureau Federation, and the nation's farmers. The Food Stamp Program also had the strong support of farmers and of organizations that viewed it as a means of increasing the demand for farm goods. Members of Congress from rural districts saw the program as a way to support the agricultural interests of their constituents, and those from urban areas saw it as way to help their constituents while simultaneously gaining rural allies in Congress.[140] By the 1970s, the Food Stamp Program had outgrown all other USDA programs; however, agricultural markets were also changing. By 1980, nearly half of all U.S. farm products were sold in international markets. Agricultural interests came to recognize that the Food Stamp Program was not directly linked to farm prices; the stamps were used for a wide variety of packaged foods sold at retail stores. The Food Stamp Program's ties to the agricultural industry had begun to weaken.

Although many of today's nutrition programs continue to make use of surplus farm products, it might be argued that it would be more efficient for the U.S. Department of Health and Human Services, which is responsible for most other welfare programs, to administer nutrition programs. This seems even more reasonable given the recent move toward EBT with its opportunities to combine access to welfare benefits from different programs. In most areas, applications for TANF, Medicaid, and food stamps can already be made simultaneously. In addition, the USDA now purchases a substantial amount of nonsurplus products to support the school lunch, WIC, and other programs. The USDA has come under sharp criticism for some of its business practices, such as continuing to fail to comply with an executive order issued by President Reagan that denies contracts to businesses that rig bids or engage in other abuses of government.[141] But it is unlikely that any of the nutrition programs, which constitute a very substantial part of the USDA, would be willingly relinquished to another department. As has been noted, "the Food Stamp Program can maintain a unique identity that distinguishes it from other cash welfare programs run by different agencies."[142] Without this identity, support for the program might be considerably weaker.[143] In light of recent welfare reforms and other pressing social welfare concerns, like Medicare solvency, moving nutrition programs to another department does not seem to be on the federal government's agenda.

SUMMARY

One irony of nutrition problems in the United States is that many of them have to do with receiving too many calories from nonnutritious foods. An important health goal for the country is to encourage a more nutritious diet among all segments of the population. More ironic is that some poor Americans lack the resources to obtain an adequate diet in a country that could easily feed everyone in need. The early commodity distribution program and the current Food Stamp Program have contributed to improvements in the nutrition of poorer Americans, but it can be difficult to stretch food stamp benefits over the course of a month. Federal welfare reforms of 1996 have hurt the Food Stamp Program. Still, it reaches a broader cross section of Americans than any other public assistance program. A number of other federally supported and state and locally operated nutrition programs target children and their mothers and aged and disabled people. Most of these programs also reach large numbers of recipients, though it is still surprising to see the number of eligible people who are not being helped. Some people reject government aid, but in many cases, inadequate funding, administrative barriers, and inadequate outreach are to blame. The form nutrition benefits should take remains an issue in nutrition programs, though the use of electronic benefits seems to have quelled the issue in the Food Stamp Program. Using some methods may increase the likelihood that more food will be consumed, but no feasible method can ensure that recipients will improve the quality of their diets. To achieve this goal, nutrition education and greater availability of appealing, nutritious foods may be the keys to improving Americans' nutritional well-being.

NOTES

1. The Hunger Project, "Decline in the Number of Hunger Related Deaths," January 1997, http://www.thp.org/thp/reports/decline.htm.

2. UNICEF, *The State of the World's Children 1998, Fact Sheets,* http://www.unicef.org/sowc98/fs01.htm, accessed January 4, 1998.

3. Curt Anderson, "By 2025, Population Growth May Outpace Food Production," *Austin-American Statesman,* December 11, 1997, p. A21; David Briscoe, "Scientists Fret Over Future of Global Food Supply," *Austin American-Statesman,* October 28, 1996, p. A10; Special Report, "Earth's Bounty: Will It Be Enough?" *Austin American-Statesman,* December 8, 1996, Section K.

4. Eleanor Noss Whitney and Sharon Rady Rolfes, *Understanding Nutrition* (Minneapolis/St. Paul: West Publishing, 1993), p. 15.

5. U.S. Department of Health and Human Services, Public Health Service, *The Surgeon General's Report on Nutrition and Health,* DHHS (PHS) Publication No. 88-50211 (Washington, DC: U.S. Government Printing Office, 1988), p. 1.

6. Centers for Disease Control and Prevention, "Births and Deaths, United States, 1996," *Monthly Vital Statistics Report,* Vol. 46, No. 1, Supplement 2, September 11, 1997, Table 11.

7. Life Sciences Research Office, Federation of American Societies for Experimental Biology, *Third Report on Nutrition Monitoring in the United States,* Vol. 1 (Washington, DC: U.S. Government Printing Office, 1995).

8. Much of this paragraph relies on Barbara Bode, Stanley Gershoff, and Michael Latham, "Defining Hunger Among the Poor," in Catherine Lerza and Michael Jacobson, eds., *Food for People, Not for Profit* (New York: Ballantine, 1975), pp. 300–302.

9. Also see Shannon Johnson, "Starvation Is a Concern for Millions of Elderly," *Austin American-Statesman,* November 16, 1993, pp. A1, 6.

10. Bode et al., "Defining Hunger Among the Poor," p. 301 (quote edited slightly).

11. The remainder of this paragraph relies on Hearing Before the Select Committee on Hunger, House of Representatives, 101st Congress, *Food Security and Methods of Assessing Hunger in the United States,* March 23, 1989; quote is from p. 9.

12. "Vice President Gore and Agriculture Secretary Glickman Kick Off First-Ever National Food Recovery and Gleaning Summit; Issue National Call to Action," USDA Press Release No. 0316.97, http://www.usda.gov/fcs/library/0316.htm, accessed June 4, 1998.

13. Lucy Komisar, *Down and Out in the USA: A History of Social Welfare* (New York: New Viewpoints, 1974), p. 51.

14. Maurice MacDonald, *Food, Stamps, and Income Maintenance* (New York: Academic Press, 1977).

15. Joan Higgins, "Feeding America's Poor," in Alice L. Tobias and Patricia J. Thompson, eds., *Issues in Nutrition for the 1980s: An Ecological Perspective* (Monterey, CA: Wadsworth Health Science Division, 1980), pp. 271–275.

16. The remainder of this paragraph relies on Kenneth W. Clarkson, *Food Stamps and Nutrition* (Washington, DC: American Enterprise Institute for Public Policy Research, 1975); American Enterprise Institute for Public Policy Research, *Food Stamp Reform* (Washington, DC: The Institute, May 25, 1977).

17. James C. Ohls and Harold Beebout, *The Food Stamp Program: Design Tradeoffs, Policy, and Impacts* (Washington, DC: Urban Institute Press, 1993), p. 14.

18. Clarkson, *Food Stamps and Nutrition;* MacDonald, *Food, Stamps, and Income Maintenance.*

19. The history of the Food Stamp Program is described in a number of sources; see, for example, MacDonald, *Food, Stamps, and Income Maintenance*; Ellen M. Wells, "Food Stamp Program," in Anne Minahan, ed., *Encyclopedia of Social Work,* 18th ed. (Silver Spring, MD: National Association of Social Workers, 1987), pp. 628–634; Safety Net Reexamined Policy Research Project, *The Social Safety Net Reexamined: FDR to Reagan* (Austin, TX: Board of Regents, University of Texas, 1989), chapter 2; Social Security Administration, *Social Security Bulletin, Annual Statistical Supplement, 1991* (Washington, DC: U.S. Government Printing Office, 1991), pp. 95–97.

20. Clarkson, *Food Stamps and Nutrition;* MacDonald, *Food, Stamps, and Income Maintenance.*

21. This paragraph relies on Nick Kotz, *Let Them Eat Promises: The Politics of Hunger in America* (Englewood Cliffs, NJ: Prentice-Hall).

22. U.S. Department of Health and Human Services, Public Health Service, *Surgeon General's Report on Nutrition and Health.*

23. Kotz, *Let Them Eat Promises,* pp. 52–53.

24. Ibid.

25. U.S. Department of Agriculture, "Food Stamp Changes Help the Rural Poor," *Food and Nutrition,* Vol. 10 (February 1980), p. 2.

26. President of the United States, *America's New Beginning: A Program for Economic Recovery* (Washington, DC: U.S. Government Printing Office, February 18, 1981), p. 1.

27. Wells, "Food Stamp Program."

28. Mary Cohn, ed., "Hunger Reports Prompt Food Aid Expansion," *1983 Congressional Quarterly Almanac* (Washington, DC, 1983), pp. 412–416.

29. "Report on Hunger Overlooks Role of Cuts," *NASW News,* Vol. 49, No. 2 (February 1984), p. 19.

30. Jean Mayer and Jeanne Goldberg, "New Report Documents Hunger in America," *Tallahassee Democrat,* March 29, 1984, p. 16E.

31. Physician Task Force on Hunger in America, *Hunger in America: The Growing Epidemic* (Middletown, CT: Wesleyan University Press, 1985), chapter 7.

32. See Food and Nutrition Service, "Help for Homeless People," *Nutrition Program Facts* (Alexandria, VA: U.S. Department of Agriculture, April 1994).

33. This section relies on Food and Consumer Service, *Summary of Food Stamp Provisions, Personal Responsibility and Work Opportunity Reconciliation Act of 1996* (Alexandria, VA: USDA, 1996), http://www.usda.gov/fcs/fs.htm.

34. Center for Budget and Policy Priorities, "The Depth of the Food Stamp Cuts in the Final Welfare Bill," http://epn.org/cbpp/food.html.

35. See "Hunger in the U.S." at the Food Research and Action Center website, http://www.frac.org/html/federal_food_programs/, accessed June 3, 1998; Jennifer Loven, "Food-Stamp Cuts Adding to Needy, Aid Groups Say," *Austin American-Statesman,* January 15, 1997, p. A4.

36. For information on operation of the Food Stamp Program, see the United States Department of Agriculture web site at http://www.usda.gov; Committee on Ways and Means, U.S. House of Representatives, *1998 Green Book: Background Material and Data on Programs Within the Jursidiction of the Committee of Ways and Means* (Washington, DC: U.S. Government Printing Office, 1998), pp. 923–949; Food and Consumer Service, *Summary of Food Stamp Provisions, Personal Responsibility and Work Opportunity Reconciliation Act of 1996.*

37. Ohls and Beebout, *The Food Stamp Program,* p. 23.

38. Ibid., p. 29.

39. Wells, "Food Stamp Program"; U.S. Department of Agriculture, *Food Assistance Programs* (Alexandria, VA: USDA, 1992).

40. Food and Nutrition Service, "The Nutrition Assistance Programs in Puerto Rico and the Northern Marianas," *Food Program Facts* (Alexandria, VA: U.S. Department of Agriculture, May 1993).

41. USDA, "Nutrition Program Facts, Food Stamp Program," October 1997, http://www.usda.gov/fcs/stamps/fspfac~2.htm.

42. See Ohls and Beebout, *The Food Stamp Program,* p. 65.

43. Andrew C. Revkin, "Food Stamp Use Drops; Some Fear Needy Aren't Seeking Aid," *Austin American-Statesman,* February 25, 1999, p. A6.

44. "Special Analysis: Characteristics of Food Stamp Households," information from the USDA available at the website of the Food Research and Action Center, http://www.frac.org/html/news/fscharacteristics.html, accessed June 3,1998; The full report by Scott Cody, *Characteristics of Food Stamp Households, Fiscal Year 1996* (Washington, DC: Mathematics Policy Research, 1998) can be found at http://www.usda/gov/fcs/oae/chrctr96.pdf.

45. See Committee on Ways and Means, *1998 Green Book,* p. 924.

46. USDA, "Some Food Stamp Facts," http://www.usda.gvo/fcs/stamps/fsfacts.htm, accessed January 2, 1998.

47. USDA, "Nutrition Program Facts: Food Stamp Program."

48. Committee on Ways and Means, *1998 Green Book,* pp. 940–941.

49. Physician Task Force on Hunger, *Hunger in America, Unfed America '85, A Report of Hunger Watch U.S.A. Surveys* (Washington, DC: Bread for the World Educational Fund, 1985).

50. Cited in Hunger Project, *Hunger Action Forum,* Vol. 2, No. 1, 1989, p. 2.

51. Also see Ohls and Beebout, *The Food Stamp Program,* pp. 56–57 for a discussion of nonparticipation.

52. Ibid, pp. 58–59.

53. USDA, "Nutrition Program Facts, USDA Food Recovery and Gleaning Initiative," May 1998, http://www.usda.gov/fcs/ogapi/foodre~1.htm.

54. See USDA, "Nutrition Program Facts, National School Lunch Program," October 1997, http://www.usda.gov/fcs/cnp/school~2.htm; July 1998, http://www.usda.gov/cgi-bin/waisgate? WAISdocID = 4016941 52 + 7 + 0 + 0&.

55. USDA, "Nutrition Program Facts, National School Lunch Program," July 1998.

56. Figures from the USDA, Food and Consumer Service, cited in Committee on Ways and Means, *1998 Green Book,* p. 999.

57. U.S. Bureau of the Census, *Statistical Abstract of the United States, 1998* (Washington, DC: U.S. Government Printing Office, 1998), Table 630, p. 391.

58. Dorothy James, *Poverty, Politics and Change* (Englewood Cliffs, NJ: Prentice Hall, 1972), pp. 58–59.

59. Kotz, *Let Them Eat Promises,* p. 59.

60. Physician Task Force on Hunger in America, *Hunger in America.*

61. Committee on Ways and Means, U.S. House of Representatives, *1996 Green Book: Background Material and Data on Programs Within the Jurisdiction of the Committee on Ways and Means* (Washington: DC: U.S. Government Printing Office, 1996), p. 924.

62. See Food and Nutrition Service, *Food & Nutrition,* Vol. 19, No. 3, 1989; Food and Nutrition Service, "Nutrition Education and Training," *Nutrition Program Facts* (Alexandria, VA: U.S. Department of Agriculture, April 1994); *USDA, Budget Summary, Fiscal Year 1999,* "Food, Nutrition and Consumer Services," http://www.usda.gov/agency/obpa/Budget-Summary/1999/text.html.#fns.

63. See "Meals for All," *Fiscal Notes,* newsletter of the Texas Comptroller of Public Accounts, February 1997, p. 5.

64. Much of the information in this section relies on USDA, "School Breakfast Program," September 1997, http://www.usda.gov/fcs/cnp/breakf ~ 1.htm; USDA, "Time for School Breakfast: The Facts," March 2, 1998, http://www.usda.gov/fcs/ogapi/FACTS4.htm; USDA, "Nutrition Program Facts: The School Breakfast Program," July 1998, http://www.usda.gov/fcs/ogapi/breakf ~ 3.htm.

65. Figures from the USDA, Food and Consumer Service, cited in Committee on Ways and Means, *1998 Green Book,* p. 1000.

66. For a summary of this research, see USDA, Food and Nutrition Service, "Time for School Breakfast: The Research," http://www.usda.gov/fcs/ogapi/research.htm, March 2, 1998.

67. USDA, "Nutrition Program Facts: Special Milk Program," December 1997, http://www.usda.gov/fcs/cnp/specia ~ 2.htm.

68. USDA, "Nutrition Program Facts: The Summer Food Service Program," October 1997, http://www.usda.gov/fcs/cnp/sfspfa ~ 2.htm and July 1998, http://www.usda.gov/fcs/ogapi/sfspun ~ 1.htm.

69. "Kids Missing Free Summer Meals, Study Finds," *Austin American-Statesman,* February 24, 1994, p. A11.

70. Much of this section relies on USDA, *Nutrition Program Facts, WIC: The Special Supplemental Nutrition Program for Women, Infants, and Children,* September 1997, http://www.usda.gov/fcs/wic/wicfac ~ 2.htm; February 1998, http://www.usda.gov/fcs/ogapi/wicunf ~ 1.htm.

71. Food and Consumer Service, *1997 Explanatory Statement* (Alexandria, VA: USDA, 1997); also see Committee on Ways and Means, *1998 Green Book,* p. 1001.

72. *Federal Register,* Vol. 58, No. 37, February 26, 1993, pp. 11497–11507.

73. These studies are summarized in Physician Task Force on Hunger in America, *Hunger in America.*

74. Milton Kotelchuk, Testimony Concerning the Special Supplemental Food Program for Women, Infants, and Children, Subcommittee on Agriculture, Nutrition and Forestry, April 6, 1983, cited in Physician Task Force on Hunger in America, *Hunger in America,* p. 100.

75. Ibid.

76. Lou E. Hicks, Rose A. Langham, and Jean Takenaka, "Cognitive and Health Measures Following Early Nutritional Supplementation: A Sibling Study," *American Journal of Public Health,* Vol. 72, No. 10, 1982, p. 1110.

77. David Rush, *The National WIC Evaluation, An Evaluation of the Special Supplemental Food Program for Women, Infants and Children* (North Carolina: Research Triangle Institute, 1987).

78. See Victor Fuchs, *How We Live: An Economic Perspective on Americans from Birth to Death* (Cambridge, MA: Harvard University Press, 1983).

79. See Physician Task Force on Hunger in America, *Hunger in America*; Barbara Devaney, Linda Bilheimer, and Jennifer Shore, "Medicaid Costs and Birth Outcomes: The Effects of Prenatal WIC Participation and the Use of Prenatal Care," *Journal of Policy Analysis and Management,* Vol. 11, No. 4, 1992, pp. 573–592; and Lucinda R. Kahler, Robert M. O'Shea, Linda C. Duffy, and Germaine M. Buck, "Factors Associated with Rates of Participation in WIC by Eligible Pregnant Women," *Public Health Reports,* Vol. 107, No. 1, 1992, pp. 60–65.

80. Committee on Ways and Means, *1998 Green Book,* p. 1002.

81. The remainder of this section relies on USDA, *Nutrition Program Facts, WIC: The Special Supplemental Nutrition Program for Women, Infants, and Children,* September 1997, http://www.usda.gov/fcs/wic/wicfac ~ 2.htm.

82. See *Developments in Aging: 1996, Vol. 1, Report of the Special Committee on Aging,* United States Senate, (Washington, DC: U.S. Government Printing Office, 1997), see especially pp. 273–278; also see USDA, Food and Consumer Service, "Nutrition Program Facts, Nutrition Program for the Elderly," May 1998, http://www.usda.gov/cgi–bin/waisgate?WAISdocID = 4384713105 + 15 + 0 + 0&; Administration on Aging, "The Elderly Nutrition Program," http://www.aoa.dhhs.gov/factsheets/enp.html, accessed January 10, 1999.

83. Much of this paragraph relies on USDA, "Nutrition Program Facts, Child and Adult Care Food Program," December 1997, http://www.usda.gov/fcs/cnp/cacfpf ~ /.htm; July 1998, http://www.usda.gov/fcs/ogapi/cacfp6 ~ 2.htm.

84. Food and Consumer Service, *1997 Explanatory Statement;* USDA, "Nutrition Program Facts: Commodity Supplemental Food Program," May 1998, http://www.usda.gov/cgi–bin/waisgate?WAISdocID = 418387939 + 16 + 0 + 0&.

85. USDA, Food and Consumer Service, "Nutrition Program Facts: The Emergency Food Assistance Program (TEFAP)," October 1997, http://www.usda.gov/fcs/food/tefapf ~ 2.htm; May 1998; http://www.usda.gov/cgi–bin/waisgate?WAISdocID = 4408313227 + 17 + 0 + 0&.

86. This paragraph and part of the next rely on Ohls and Beebout, *The Food Stamp Program,* see pp. 129, 130, 156, 165.

87. MacDonald, *Food, Stamps, and Income Maintenance.*

88. U.S. Department of Agriculture, Human Nutrition Service, "Your Money's Worth in Foods," *Home and Garden Bulletin,* No. 183 (rev. September 1984), p. 5.

89. Thomas M. Fraker, Alberto P. Martini, James C. Ohls, Michael Ponza, and Elizabeth A. Quinn, *The Evaluation of the Alabama Food Stamp Cash-Out Demonstration: Recipient Impacts* (Princeton, NJ, and Washington, DC: Mathematica Policy Research, September 1992).

90. James C. Ohls, Thomas M. Fraker, Alberto P. Martini, and Michael Ponza, *The Effects of Cash-Out on Food Use by Food Stamp Program Participants in San Diego* (Princeton, NJ, and Washington, DC: Mathematica Policy Research, December 1992).

91. J. S. Butler, James C. Ohls, and Barbara Posner, "The Effect of the Food Stamp Program on the Nutrient Intake of the Eligible Elderly," *Journal of Human Resources,* Vol. 20, No. 3 (1985): 405–420.

92. Barbara Devaney and Thomas Fraker, "Cashing Out Food Stamps: Impacts on Food Expenditures and Diet Quality," *Journal of Policy Analysis and Management,* Vol. 5, No. 4, 1986, pp. 725–741.

93. See, for example, Ben Senauer and Nathan Young, "The Impact of Food Stamps on Food Expenditures: Rejection of the Traditional Model," *American Journal of Agricultural Economics,* Vol. *68,* No. 1, 1986, pp. 37–43; for a review of this literature, also see J. William Levedahl, "The Role of Functional Form in Estimating the Effect of a Cash-only Food Stamp Program," *Journal of Agricultural Economics Research,* Vol. 43, No. 2, 1991, pp.11–19.

94. Levedahl, "The Role of Functional Form . . ." p. 18.

95. Clarkson, *Food Stamps and Nutrition;* Butler et al., "The Effect of the Food Stamp Program . . .".

96. See U.S. Department of Agriculture, *Food Assistance Programs, 1992,* p. 63.

97. USDA, "Nutrition Program Facts: Food Stamp Program," October 1997, http:www.usda.gov/fcs/stamps/fspfac ~ 2htm.

98. Gary Burtless, "Public Spending for the Poor: Trends, Prospects, and Economic Limits," in Sheldon H. Danzinger and Daniel H. Weinberg, eds., *Fighting Poverty: What Works and What Doesn't* (Cambridge, MA: Harvard University Press, 1986), pp. 23–24.

99. Levedahl, "The Role of Functional Form . . .".

100. Ohls and Beebout, *The Food Stamp Program*, pp. 48, 162.

101. This section relies on USDA, "Nutrition Program Facts: Electronic Benefit Transfer," September 1997, http://www.usda.gov/fcs/stamps/ebtfac~2.htm; Food and Nutrition Service, *Food & Nutrition*, Vol. 20, No. 2, 1991; U.S. Department of Agriculture, *Food Assistance Programs, 1992;* Food and Nutrition Service, "Electronic Benefit Transfer," *Nutrition Program Facts* (Alexandria, VA: U.S. Department of Agriculture, April 1994).

102. USDA, "Food Stamp Program Electronic Benefit Transfer (EBT)," May 1998, http: www.usda.gov/fcs/stamps/ebthlts.htm.

103. USDA, "Nutrition Program Facts: Electronic Benefit Transfer," http://www.usda.gov/fcs/stamps/ebtfac ~ 2.htm, accessed January 2, 1998.

104. "Lone Star Card Helps Shrink Food Stamp Rolls," *Fiscal Notes*, Texas Comptroller of Public Accounts, March 1996, p. 3.

105. *Impact of Regulation E of the Electronic Funds Transfer Act on the Food Stamp Electronic Benefits Transfer Delivery Systems*, Hearing Before the Subcommittee on Domestic Marketing, Consumer Relations, and Nutrition of the Committee on Agriculture, House of Representatives, 102nd Congress, 2nd session, Serial No. 102-69, March 25, 1992.

106. Diane Thomas and Greg Martin, "State EBT Program Will Debut This Fall," *Fiscal Notes* (Publication of the Texas Comptroller of Public Accounts), March 1994, p. 3.

107. Jodie T. Allen, "The Food Stamp Program: Its History and Reform," *Public Welfare*, Vol. 51, No. 1, 1993, pp. 25–26, 46; first published in 1977.

108. Department of Health, Education and Welfare, "Welfare Myths vs. Facts," pamphlet SRS-72-02009, cited in Ronald C. Federico, *The Social Welfare Institution: An Introduction*, 3rd ed. (Lexington, MA: Heath, 1980), p. 83.

109. Gary W. Hutton, "Welfare Fraud and the Police," *The Police Chief*, November 1979, p. 46, cited in Gary W. Hutton, *Welfare Fraud Investigation* (Springfield, IL: Thomas, 1985), p. 21.

110. Randy Fitzgerald, "Time to Crack Down on Food-Stamp Fraud," *Readers' Digest*, February 1983, p. 138.

111. "Stamps for Food Traded for Drugs," *Austin American-Statesman*, June 6, 1989; p. B3.

112. Larry Lipman, "Thousands of Dead People Remain on Food Stamp Lists," *Austin American-Statesman*, March 11, 1998, p. A2.

113. Committee on Ways and Means, *1996 Green Book*, p. 872; *1998 Green Book*, pp. 939–940.

114. See, for example, David Greenberg and Douglas Wolf with Jennifer Pfiester, *Using Computers to Combat Welfare Fraud: The Operation and Effectiveness of Wage Matching* (New York: Greenwood Press, 1986).

115. Tod Newcombe, "Finger Imaging Points to Welfare Savings," *Government Technology*, Vol. 9, No. 4, 1996, pp. 14–15.

116. "UT Austin Researchers Determine Welfare Reform Project Did Not Reduce, Deter Fraud," *On Campus*, November 11, 1997, p. 3.

117. *Gaming the Health Care System: Trends in Health Care Fraud*, Hearing before the Special Committee on Aging, United States Senate, 104th Congress, March 21, 1995, Serial No. 104–2.

118. *Health Care Fraud: Milking Medicare and Medicaid*, Hearing before the Special Committee on Aging, United States Senate, 104th Congress, November 2, 1995, Serial No. 104–8.

119. "Medicare Audit: Fraud Still Rampant," (AP), *The Miami Herald*, April 25, 1998, p. 4A.

120. See Executive Office of the President, *Budget of the United States Government, Fiscal Year 1999* (Washington, DC: U.S. Government Printing Office), p. 72.

121. Committee on Ways and Means, *1998 Green Book*, p. 939.

122. Ibid., p. 936.

123. See *Quality Control and Fiscal Sanctions in the Food Stamp Program*, Joint Hearing Before the Subcommittee on Domestic Marketing, Consumer Relations, and Nutrition of the Committee on Agriculture, House of Representatives, and the Subcommittee on Nutrition and Investigations of the Committee on Agriculture, Nutrition, and Forestry, United States Senate, 100th Congress, 1st Session, 1987, pp. 6–7.

124. General Accounting Office, *Benefit Overpayments: Recoveries Could Be Increased in the Food Stamp and AFDC Programs*, GAO/RCED-86-17 (Washington, DC: 1986).

125. See, for example, Dennis P. Affhalter and Fredrica D. Kramer, eds., *Rethinking Quality Control: A New System for the Food Stamp Program* (Washington, DC: National Academy Press, 1987).

126. U.S. Department of Agriculture, *Food Assistance Programs, 1992.*

127. Robert Greene, "Texas, 23 Other States Settle Federal Food Stamp Dispute," *Austin American-Statesman*, January 27, 1993, p. A15.

128. Committee on Ways and Means, *1993 Green Book*, p. 1598.

129. See Committee on Ways and Means, *1996 Green Book*, pp. 869–872.

130. The remainder of this paragraph relies on Committee on Ways and Means, *1998 Green Book,* pp. 937–938.

131. Charles L. Usher and Dean F. Duncan, III, "Integrating Analysis and Mangement to Control Errors in the Food Stamp Program," *Public Productivity Review,* Vol. 9, No. 1, 1985, pp. 49–61.

132. See Committee on Ways and Means, *1993 Green Book,* pp. 1588–1601.

133. Jennifer Dixon, "States Overpaid $1 Billion for Aid to Families in 1991," *Austin American-Statesman,* April 12, 1994, p. A9; also see Committee on Ways and Means, *1996 Green Book,* pp. 495 & 498.

134. Committee on Ways and Means, *1998 Green Book,* pp. 465–472.

135. Personal communication with Suzette Ashworth of the Texas Department of Human Services, June 4, 1998.

136. Usher and Duncan, "Integrating Analysis and Management. . . ."

137. Physician Task Force on Hunger in America, *Hunger in America.*

138. "New Federal Task Force to Hunt Down Tax Cheats," *Austin American-Statesman,* April 21, 1994, p. A16.

139. Edward M. Gramlich, "The Main Themes," in Sheldon H. Danzinger and Daniel H. Weinberg, eds., *Fighting Poverty: What Works and What Doesn't* (Cambridge, MA: Harvard University Press, 1986), p. 346.

140. Ohls and Beebout, *The Food Stamp Program,* pp. 128–129.

141. "Agriculture Agency a Holdout, Needs to Comply with Reforms," *Austin American-Statesman,* October 6, 1993, p. A6.

142. Levedahl, "The Role of Functional Form. . . ," p. 18.

143. Ohls and Beebout, *The Food Stamp Program,* p. 162.

CHAPTER

Improving Health Care: Treating the Nation's Ills

GOOD HEALTH OR MEDICAL ATTENTION?

Health policy in the United States exemplifies many of the problems of rational policymaking. Political issues intervene at every stage of decision-making—in defining the goals of health policy, in identifying alternative courses of action, in assessing their potential costs, and in selecting policy alternatives that maximize the quality and accessibility of health care while containing costs.

Health care is a basic human need. Most everyone agrees that no one should suffer or die for lack of financial resources to obtain medical attention. But how much are Americans willing and able to pay for health care? If health care is a *scarce resource,* then how do we decide who will get what care and how? As we shall see, these are largely *political* questions that do not lend themselves easily to rational planning.

Health care is an issue that affects *all* of us directly, but unlike other industrialized nations, the United States has no national health insurance program. For years, Congress debated the issue of subsidizing health care for poor people and older persons and made only modest gains in covering these vulnerable populations. Then in 1965, as part of the programs of the Great Society, major health care programs were established for both groups. These programs were important for several reasons:

1. The poor and the aged, on the average, require more medical attention than the general population; indeed, "the incidence of many chronic conditions is directly related to age and inversely related to family income."[1]

2. Even though an ounce of prevention may be worth a pound of cure, preventive health care for many poor people is infrequent. In addition to health risks facing the poor, even minor costs can delay treatment until health problems develop into major crises. Health problems are a major contributor to unemployment and poverty.

3. The health care delivery system (facilities and personnel) is particularly disorganized and inadequate in poor communities—both inner cities and rural areas.

But even with these programs, millions of Americans are uninsured because they do not fit any of the categories for government sponsored medical assistance; they do not receive privately sponsored coverage through their employer; and they cannot afford to pay for premiums out of their own pockets. Before the 1940s, few people had private health insurance.[2] When they needed medical care, they arranged payment with their local doctor or hospital. But with greater sophistication of medical practice and technology came rapidly increasingly health care costs. Health care is among the most pressing social welfare issues in the United States. The cost of health care for *all* citizens is so high that policymakers can no longer be concerned about how to provide health care for the poor and elderly alone. Politicians, health care providers, employers, and citizens are concerned about health care for the entire nation.

The first obstacle to a rational approach to health policy is deciding on our goal. Is health policy a question of *good health*—that is, whether we live at all, how well we live, and how long we live? Or are we striving for *good medical care*—that is, frequent and inexpensive visits to doctors, well-equipped and accessible hospitals, and equal access to medical attention by *all* citizens?

Good medical care does not necessarily mean good health. Good health is related to many factors over which medical personnel and facilities have no control—heredity (the health of one's parents and grandparents), lifestyle (smoking, eating, drinking, exercise, stress), and the physical environment (sewage disposal, water quality, conditions of work, and so forth). Of course, doctors can set broken bones, stop infections with drugs, and remove swollen appendixes. Anyone suffering from health problems certainly wants the careful attention of a skilled physician and the best of medical facilities. But in the long run, infant mortality, sickness and disease, and life span are affected surprisingly little by the quality of medical care.[3] If you want to live a long, healthy life, choose parents who have lived long, healthy lives, and then do all the things your mother always told you to do: don't smoke, don't drink too much, get lots of exercise and rest, don't overeat, relax, and don't worry.

Historically, most of the reductions in infant mortality (deaths during the first year of life) and adult death rates, in the United States and throughout the world, have resulted from improved public health and sanitation—including immunization against smallpox, clean public water supplies, sanitary sewage disposal, improved diets and nutrition, and improved standards of living. Many of today's leading causes of death, including heart disease, cancer, stroke, emphysema and other pulmonary disease, accidents, diabetes, cirrhosis of the liver, suicides, and acquired immune deficiency syndrome (AIDS), are closely linked to heredity, lifestyle, or personal habits.

There have been major declines in the "crude" death rate (the number of deaths per 100,000 people) and the age-adjusted death rate (which accounts for changes in the age composition of the population) in the past century. Preliminary data for 1997 indicate another drop in the crude U.S. death rate and a record low age-adjusted death rate.[4] This record low was 487.9 deaths per 100,000 population. Life expectancy reached an all-time high of just over 76.2 years. Infant mortality declined to 7.1 deaths per 1,000 live births. There were decreases in mortality from the two largest killers—heart disease and cancer—which account for more than half of all deaths in the U.S. Decreases also occurred in most of the other 15 leading causes of death, most notably in deaths due to HIV infection. Yet Americans have a lower life expectancy than those in many other industrialized countries (ranking nineteenth for women and twentieth for men out of 29 countries) and higher infant mortality (ranking twenty-third).[5] Despite the availability of the most advanced health care in the world, Americans are not the healthiest of peoples.

HEALTH CARE POLICY TODAY

Federal health care policy is now largely composed of two programs: Medicare and Medicaid. Medicare is a social insurance program operated by the federal government that covers virtually all people age 65 years and older as well as some younger people with long-term disabilities. Medicaid is a public assistance program that provides health care benefits to certain poor people; it is a shared responsibility of the federal and state governments. At the federal level, both programs fall under the auspices of the U.S. Department of Health and Human Services and its Health Care Financing Administration (HCFA). This chapter focuses on Medicaid and Medicare as well as health care concerns for the general population. Several other important federally funded health care programs that are not discussed in detail but deserve mention. One of them is operated by the Department of Veterans Affairs; another is operated by the Defense Health Program for active duty military and their dependents. Also important is the federally funded Indian Health Service which serve members of the many Indian tribes in the U.S.

Medicaid: Health Care for Some of the Poor[6]

Black, Hispanic, and poor Americans have greater health problems than do white and more affluent Americans. Although adult and infant death rates for all segments of the population have declined over time, they remain much higher for the poor and for blacks. A case in point is the infant mortality rate (deaths per 1,000 live births), which is considered to be especially sensitive to the adequacy of health care, and is frequently used as a general indicator of well-being. In 1997 the preliminary black infant death rate was 13.8, still 2.3 times higher than the white infant death rate of 6.0; this gap has actually widened since the mid 1970s.[7] These and other health statistics clearly indicate that all Americans do not enjoy the same good health.

Interest in national health care for the poor dates back to the turn of the century, when Progressive era reform groups first proposed a national health insurance plan. Opposition from the American Medical Association (AMA) forced President Franklin D. Roosevelt to drop the idea of including health insurance in the original Social Security legislation for fear that it would endanger passage of the entire bill.[8]

Every year from 1935 to 1965, major health insurance bills were introduced in Congress. All failed, in large part because of the opposition the AMA was able to arouse. National health insurance became a major issue in the Truman administration in the late 1940s, but the medical establishment continually succeeded in branding national health insurance as "socialized medicine." Proposals for national health insurance generally tried to "socialize" health insurance but did *not* call for government ownership of hospitals and employment of physicians as in Great Britain. Even so, fear of government interference in medical practice and opposition from the medical community succeeded in defeating major government health programs for thirty years.

In 1950 the federal government did authorize states to use federal–state public assistance funds for medical care for poor, aged, blind, and disabled people (see Chapter 5) and poor families with dependent children (see Chapter 6). And in 1957 the Kerr-Mills Act began a separate federal and state matching program for hospital care for the elderly and the poor, but not all the states participated.

Then, in 1965, important changes were made in the Social Security Act to provide health care to poor and aged people. Medicaid, the program for poor Americans, was established under Title XIX of the act. Medicaid, a combined federal and state program, replaced and expanded earlier medical assistance under the Kerr-Mills Act. All the states eventually adopted a Medicaid program, although Arizona held out until 1982. Medicaid rapidly grew to be the federal government's most expensive public assistance program. The costs of Medicaid now exceed the costs of any other "welfare" program—including the SSI, TANF, and Food Stamp programs. In 1970, total Medicaid costs were about $5 billion; by 1990 they had risen to about $72 billion, and in 1998 the total bill was estimated at about $185 billion.[9] The federal government pays about 57 percent of Medicaid costs (from general tax revenues); in 1998 this share was about $104 billion. The states use their own general tax revenues to fund Medicaid, and they are under constant pressure to raise more revenue to pay their share and to draw down as much federal matching funds as possible. States may receive 50 to 83 percent of total Medicaid services expenditures from the federal government, with poorer states (as determined by per capita income) receiving the most. This percentage is calculated annually. The U.S. territories are reimbursed at 50 percent for services. All jurisdictions are reimbursed at 50 percent for their administrative costs for most services rendered.[10]

The states exercise broad control over many aspects of Medicaid policy. For example, they determine reimbursement rates for Medicaid services. Since 1989, federal guidelines say that reimbursement rates must be sufficiently adequate so that services will be as available to Medicaid recipients as they are to the general population in the area. But this does not mean that providers are anxious to accept Medicaid payments. Many physicians do not participate because of the paperwork involved and because reimbursement rates remain quite low compared to what the market will bear.

Like SSI and food stamps, Medicaid is an entitlement program; everyone who qualifies must be served if they wish. Although states determine many eligibility requirements (such as income and asset limitations), they must cover certain categories of people. Prior to welfare reform in 1996 (see Chapter 6), states were required to cover all those receiving AFDC. There is no automatic link between Medicaid and TANF, but in general, states must cover all those who meet AFDC financial eligibility criteria in place in their state on July 16, 1996.[11] (There are some options that states can use to limit or increase their previous AFDC income and resource standards if they wish.) States can terminate Medicaid benefits to adults who do not meet TANF work requirements. States must continue to cover most SSI recipients. Should SSI recipients earn enough to make them ineligible for SSI, or when TANF recipients earn enough or get sufficient income from child or spousal support to make them ineligible for TANF, they are entitled to continue to receive benefits for certain lengths of time so that their Medicaid benefits are not abruptly ended.

States must also cover pregnant women and children under age 6 with incomes up to 133 percent of the official poverty level. These women are entitled only to pregnancy-related services under Medicaid, but the children receive all Medicaid benefits. All children born after September 30, 1983, whose family's income is less than the poverty level are also eligible until their nineteenth birthday. Medicaid must also cover a few other categories of poor children such as those living in certain types of institutions.

Through their Medicaid programs, states must also pay Medicare premiums, coinsurance, and deductibles for "qualified Medicare beneficiaries" (QMBs). QMBs are Medicare beneficiaries (aged or disabled) with incomes below 100 percent of the federal poverty level and resources less than twice the amount allowed by SSI. States are also required to provide more limited assistance by paying Part B Medicare premiums (supplemental medical insurance largely for outpatient care) for those who would be QMBs except that their income is between 100 and 135 percent of the poverty level. States must also pay a portion of Part B premiums for those with incomes of 135 to 175 percent of poverty. In addition, states must use Medicaid funds to pay Part A Medicare premiums (hospital insurance) for those who previously received Medicare and Social Security Disability Insurance but have returned to work, as long as their income is not more than 200 percent of the poverty level and their resources do not exceed twice the SSI standard.

States can cover more groups if they wish. They can cover pregnant women and infants (under one year old) with incomes greater than 133 percent but not more than 185 percent of the poverty level. They can also offer full Medicaid benefits to QMBs, and they can extend coverage to people in institutions or those at home who require similar care. Other groups that states can cover under Medicaid include additional low-income people who are aged, blind, or otherwise disabled.

In addition, 35 states, the District of Columbia, and 4 U.S. territories provide Medicaid to people who fall under a category that the federal government calls "medically needy." This category includes individuals and families who are similar to other groups covered by Medicaid except that their income and assets exceed eligibility requirements. The states have some discretion in defining the groups considered medically needy, but if a state provides a medically needy program, it must include all children under age 18 who would qualify under a required Medicaid category as well as pregnant women who would qualify under a mandatory or optional category, if their income and resources were lower. Of course, there are caps on allowable financial resources.

Many legally admitted immigrants are ineligible for Medicaid. Those admitted after August 22, 1996 cannot receive Medicaid for 5 years, though permanent residents who have earned 40 work credits under Social Security (see Chapter 4) can. Those in the U.S. before the August date can qualify. Also eligible for 7 years after entry are those admitted as asylees or refugees. In addition, immigrants with past or current U.S. military service and their dependents may qualify. States will be able to decide whether to include legally admitted immigrants with 5 years of residence since August 22, 1996.

Without intimate knowledge of a state's Medicaid program, it would be difficult to say exactly who qualifies and who does not. Even in states with the most generous Medicaid programs, many poor people do not fit any of the eligibility categories and therefore have no claim to Medicaid. This is especially true for poor, able-bodied adults with no dependent children. In 1996, less than half (about 45 percent) of those officially poor by government standards received Medicaid.

The federal government requires the states to provide the following services to those categorically eligible for Medicaid: inpatient and outpatient hospital care; physicians' services; laboratory and x-ray services; nursing home services for those over age 21; home health care (for those entitled to nursing home care); family-planning services and supplies; nurse midwife services; early and periodic screening, diagnosis, and treatment (EPSDT) services for those under age 21; and family and pediatric nurse practitioner services. States can limit many services (e.g., the number of days of hospital care or the number of visits to physicians), but they cannot limit certain services to children. Medicaid participants are afforded some protections. For example, they usually must be offered some choice in selecting health care providers.

States may offer other benefits to Medicaid beneficiaries such as prescription drugs, eyeglasses, psychiatric services to those under age 21 or over age 65, or special services to elderly people with disabilities or to people with developmental disabilities. Many states offer at least some optional services. For example, in 1996, at least 31 states and territories offered clinic services, transportation, prescription drugs, prostheses, and rehabilitative services. At least 25 also offered psychical therapy, optometrists' services, podiatrist services, dental services and dentures, eyeglasses, skilled nursing care for those under age 21, case management services, speech and hearing services, and emergency hospital care.[12] The federal government reimburses optional services at the same rate as required services.

Medicaid services are provided in kind. Patients receive services from physicians and other health care providers, and these providers are directly reimbursed by the government. No prior contributions are required by the beneficiaries. A number of states do use some type of program cost sharing, such as requiring recipients to pay small deductibles or copayments for services, but they cannot impose cost sharing requirements on services for children under age 18, or for emergency, pregnancy, and family-planning services. No copayments are charged to people in custodial nursing facilities and intermediate-care facilities, because virtually all their income already goes toward their care. States also cannot charge fees for health maintenance organization (HMO) services to categorically eligible recipients.

In 1997, about 33 million people (12 percent of the U.S. population) were enrolled in Medicaid programs. Medicaid is the country's largest purchaser of maternity care, and one-fourth of the nation's children are enrolled in the program. Medicaid also pays for nearly two-thirds of the nursing home care for those who are older or disabled. About two-thirds of Medicaid funds (61 percent) go to help older and disabled people, a population which constitutes less than one-third of Medicaid recipients. Other adults (mostly parents receiving TANF) and children are more than two-thirds of beneficiaries, but they use less than one-third of Medicaid funds.[13] In 1995, Medicaid services cost an average of $8,868 for each aged person, $8,842 for each disabled recipient, $9,256 for each blind recipient, $1,777 for each adult AFDC recipient, and $1,047 for each AFDC child recipient.[14] The higher costs for elderly and disabled recipients result because more of them reside in nursing homes or other institutional facilities.

Due to Congressional action and state initiatives, Medicaid is constantly changing. Much of the description of the Medicaid program presented here is fast becoming dated. States have been obtaining waivers allowing them to operate their programs using managed care arrangements like HMOs and to enroll more people than would qualify under traditional Medicaid programs. Among the more ambitious goals of these arrangements is to allow all low-income people with no other access to insurance to enroll in the state's Medicaid system. The 1997 Balanced Budget Act allows states to enroll most Medicaid beneficiaries in managed care plans without a waiver.

In addition to Medicaid, block grants are also used to provide medical care, primarily to low-income people. The Maternal and Child Health Services Block Grant provides medical care to additional low-income pregnant women and young children. The Preventive Health and Health Services (PHHS) Block Grant provides funds for a variety of services.[15] States have most often used the money to fund educational services and risk reduction programs, such as smoking cessation programs and nutrition advice; to treat those with specific health problems, such as hypertension and tuberculosis; and to provide some emergency medical services and rodent control programs. The PHHS Block Grant is also used to prevent sex offenses and to provide treatment to survivors of sex offenses. States and communities also search for creative ways to stretch their health care dollars, but many people remain without a regular source of health care and without a way to pay for health care bills.

Medicare: Health Care for Older Americans

Social welfare policy has done more to meet the income and health care needs of older Americans than any other group. Older Americans have higher incomes and fewer live in poverty than ever before, but the aging process is associated with an increased incidence of acute illnesses and chronic conditions. Older Americans have more restricted activity days and days in bed and in hospitals than the general population.[16] Prior to Medicare, less than half of elderly people had any health insurance. Even with

Medicare, the health care needs of older Americans contribute to their incurring more out-of-pocket costs for health care than other Americans. In 1995, households with a member 65 to 75 years of age spent $2,618 out-of-pocket and those with a member 75 years and older spent $2,683 compared to $1,487 for younger households.[17]

Medicare was established in 1965 as Title XVIII of the Social Security Act to help meet the medical needs of the country's growing older population. Most Medicare beneficiaries are people aged 65 or older receiving Social Security retirement benefits (or who would be eligible for Social Security if they retired). Since Medicare is a social insurance program, eligibility is generally tied to prior contributions, not current income; however, Medicare is also available to older persons who do not qualify for Social Security. Some younger people also qualify for Medicare. Most younger beneficiaries are former workers who have been receiving Social Security Disability Insurance (SSDI) for at least two years. The program also covers a special category of people—those with end-stage renal disease (kidney failure). As part of the Social Security system, Medicare compels employers and employees to pay into the program during working years in order for workers to enjoy the benefits of health insurance after retirement or long-term disability.

The Medicare program has two basic parts—**hospital insurance (HI)** called Part A and **supplemental medical insurance (SMI)** called Part B.[18] Part A pays for beneficiaries' hospital care, skilled nursing care following a hospital stay, some home health care, and hospice care, and is financed by a portion of the overall Social Security payroll tax (also see Chapter 4). This compulsory 1.45 percent tax is now levied on *all* the wages of current workers. Older people who do not qualify for Social Security may participate in Part A by paying premiums (in 1999 either $170 or $309 monthly depending on the individual's work history). Under Part A, beneficiaries using services must pay a deductible ($768 in 1999), after which Medicare pays for the remainder of the first sixty days in the hospital and a portion of additional days. For days 61 through 90 in 1999, the patient's coinsurance payment is $192 per day, with the federal government paying the remainder, and for days 91 to 150, the coinsurance payment is $384 a day (these 60 days are reserves that can only be used once in a lifetime). If more hospital days are needed, the patient must assume all the costs.

Part B, supplemental medical insurance, is a voluntary component that covers physician and other outpatient medical services. Medicare Part A beneficiaries who wish to participate in Part B are assessed premiums. In 1999, monthly Part B premiums were $45.50. This cost is so low compared to private insurance that almost all Part A participants are enrolled in Part B. Even those age 65 and older who are not insured under Part A can participate in Part B. In addition to physician services, Part B includes a range of other outpatient services such as diagnostic tests. Part B premiums can be deducted automatically from Social Security checks. Part B beneficiaries must pay for the first $100 of services themselves each year, after which Medicare pays 80 percent of most services and the patient pays the remaining 20 percent. Home health services are included under Part B for those not participating in Part A and do not require deductibles or coinsurance payments. Some home health services included under Part A are being transferred to Part B. Since Part B premiums cover only about

25 percent of the costs of covered services, general revenue funds are also used to fund this component.

Both Parts A and B require patients to pay an initial charge in order to discourage unnecessary medical care and to recover some program costs. Medicare does *not* pay for custodial nursing home care, most dental care (including dentures), private-duty nursing, eyeglasses and eye examinations, most prescription drugs, routine physician examinations, and hearing tests and hearing devices.

About 33 million older individuals and 5 million disabled younger people were eligible for Medicare in 1998. Federal Medicare spending was nearly $157 billion (a little more than 10 percent of all federal outlays) in 1995 and it is expected to be $252 billion in 2003 (about 13 percent of the federal budget) with about $160 billion going to Part A and $92 billion to Part B.[19] This is a huge increase from the $3.4 billion Medicare cost in 1965 and the $32 billion it cost in 1980. Despite the increase in the amount of wages subject to taxes, there is a constant concern about the Medicare trust fund's ability to keep up with health care costs. This concern is growing as the baby boom generation gets closer to claiming its Medicare benefits.

Covering Medigaps

A serious problem with the health care system in the United States is the inadequate coverage provided by most types of health insurance—both public and private. Private health insurance plans often fail to cover all medical needs. They may limit payments to the first thirty or sixty days of hospital care; place caps on the dollar amounts paid to hospitals and physicians for a patient during her or his lifetime; exclude various diagnostic tests, outpatient care, office visits; and so on. Moreover, private insurance often will not cover people initially found to be in poor health, who need insurance the most. Perhaps the most serious concern about private insurance is that it frequently fails to cover "catastrophic" medical costs—costs that can easily run into the tens and even hundreds of thousands of dollars for serious, long-term illnesses. If such a catastrophe occurred, most people would lose everything they owned.

The Medicare program also has some serious gaps referred to as **medigaps.** The most notable medigaps are prescription drugs, long-term custodial care, and the costs of catastrophic illnesses. In 1988, Congress attempted to close some of these gaps—primarily long hospital stays and high prescription drug costs—when it passed the Medicare Catastrophic Coverage Act. The added coverage was to be financed by a "surtax" on the incomes of Medicare recipients—$22.50 for each $150 dollars of federal income tax an individual or couple paid—and an additional $4 a month for SMI. The maximum surtax was set at $800. But one year after it took effect, Congress repealed the law. In a nutshell, many older Americans were *not* willing to pay that much more for the increased coverage, and they successfully pressured Congress to repeal the law. The surtax was a major miscalculation in health care policy.

The act would have helped poorer older Americans with serious health problems the most, but many individuals who would have paid the surtax already had supplemental policies that cover some medigaps. Of course, some policies cover medigaps better than others. Unscrupulous individuals have taken advantage of older Americans' fears of impoverishment from illness by selling them policies that sound good but do not cover the gaps. Congress has intervened with legislation to regulate the sale of these policies. Since 1992, medigap carriers must offer 10 levels of policies from A to J. At any given level, the same types of benefits are supposed to be offered (for example, all policies at level A should have the same benefits). Level A offers the fewest benefits and costs the least, and level J offers the most benefits at the highest cost. This structure makes it easier to compare policies across carriers, but costs and coverage still vary widely depending on several factors, including the state in which the policy is purchased. Florida residents reportedly pay the most.[20]

The Medicaid program covers many of the gaps for the poorest elderly. Most older people have some type of medigap coverage through private or public means.[21] Given the costs of private policies, more older people are turning to HMOs. Medicare HMOs cover many medigaps without an increase over regular Medicare premiums and without the need to file insurance claims. Nevertheless, there are some concerns that Medicare HMOs may be short-changing older people. Some HMOs are not anxious to accept older patients or have dropped them because they use larger amounts of expensive care than many younger health care consumers.

Long-term care services are a major medigap. These services are needed when people cannot dress, bathe, or perform other activities of daily living such as shopping or money management. Most people who need long-term care are older, but younger people with disabilities may also require such services. Long-term care includes nursing home care and home health care. Nursing home care is provided at three levels—skilled, intermediate, and custodial. Skilled is the highest level and the only type reimbursed by Medicare. It is generally needed for a short time, for example, following some surgeries. Supplemental Medicare policies also generally do not cover intermediate and custodial nursing home care, yet this type of care is often needed.

Home health care includes a variety of services provided in the individual's own home or sometimes in homelike community-based programs. Home health is the fastest growing Medicare service.[22] Medicare covers some in-home care, but it does not cover care needed on a twenty-four-hour basis. Most (perhaps more than 70 percent) in-home care is actually provided informally by family, friends, and other nonpaid caregivers.[23] About 75 percent of informal caregivers are wives and daughters of the person in need, and 35 percent are elderly themselves.[24] This care can take emotional and financial tolls on family members. Caregivers may "reduce their work hours, take time off without pay, or quit jobs because of elder care responsibilities."[25]

When an individual needs long-term care that is not covered by Medicare and not supplied by informal caregivers, there are generally two options. One is for patients to pay for it themselves. The problem is that nursing home care is expensive. Even a modest facility is beyond the financial reach of many people. In 1996 the average annual cost of nursing home care was between $36,000 and $50,000.[26] Many people enter a nursing home with some funds, but savings can easily be depleted if they stay very long. Often there is a spouse at home who also has living expenses to pay.

The second way long-term care is covered is by Medicaid. To qualify for nursing home care under Medicaid, a person must be poor by state Medicaid standards. Eligibility for Medicaid-paid nursing home care varies considerably by state. Until recently, when there was a spouse at home, both the nursing home patient and the spouse had to deplete their assets to qualify. Now, under Medicaid impoverishment provisions passed in 1988, the spouse of a Medicaid nursing home patient is allowed to keep considerably more assets and income. The federal government sets a minimum and a maximum, and each state then determines exactly how much it will allow. States may recoup Medicaid payments by taking proceeds from the sale of nursing home patients' homes or other parts of their estate after their deaths though little has actually been recovered in this way. There has been considerable attention to the issue of older people transferring assets ("Medicaid estate planning" as it has been called) in order to qualify for nursing home care at public expense. An individual's eligibility may be delayed if assets were transferred or sold for less than fair market value in the three years prior to application.

Without greater governmental participation, one option individuals have for paying for long-term care is private insurance.[27] These policies may cover nursing home and home health care. According to the Health Insurance Association of America, "for policies paying $100 a day for nursing home care and $50 a day for home health care with inflation protection and a 20-day deductible period, average annual premiums in December 1994 [were] $1,950 when purchased at the age of 65 and $6,314 when purchased at the age of 79."[28] The premiums alone could fast put a dent in one's savings. Fewer than 3 percent of Americans have long-term care insurance.[29] Insurers are proceeding cautiously with long-term care coverage because this is still uncharted territory. Policies are generally written to limit the insurers' liability through caps on the amount of coverage per day of care. Without inflation adjustments, coverage can prove to be quite inadequate. In addition, people with certain conditions may be excluded from coverage. One thing that would help is to broaden the base of purchasers to spread the risk (as in other types of insurance policies), perhaps using group policies offered through employers. Another approach is to offer policies based on the amount of assets an individual wishes to protect. For example, a person could buy $50,000 worth of lifetime coverage rather than a policy that would pay a certain number of dollars a day for a specified number of years (say $80 a day for 4 years), thereby lowering the insurer's liability and the individual's premiums.

In the hope of encouraging more people to buy long-term care insurance, some states are experimenting with a plan that allows those who purchase long-term insurance to protect a fixed amount of assets while still allowing them to participate in Medicaid once assets in excess of this amount are depleted. For example, if a person buys coverage to protect $50,000 of assets, once the insurer pays out $50,000 for the individual's long-term care, the individual would be allowed to participate in Medicaid as long as they have no more than $50,000 in assets. Linking private and public insurance in this way is a novel idea that might save Medicaid dollars by delaying the time when a person qualifies for long-term care under Medicaid, but it is too soon to predict the results. Few employers offer long-term policies and even fewer contribute to the costs, but this is another approach to helping people pay for long-term care. The earlier one begins paying, the lower the annual costs, but over a worker's lifetime, those costs mount. Employers who offer this coverage might also offer coverage for spouses, parents, and parents-in-law of employees.

Another type of private coverage available to those with resources is to purchase a unit such as an apartment in a facility for senior citizens, and to pay a fixed amount per month for its upkeep and maintenance. Lifetime care, including nursing home care, is then assured for the individual or couple on the condition that the dwelling becomes the property of the facility at the time of their death. As the life span increases, more Americans are giving thought to these alternatives.

What is the country's need for long-term care? In 1994, about one-quarter of the elderly or 7.3 million needed at least some assistance with daily living needs.[30] Three-quarters were living in the community and the rest in nursing homes. The need for long-term care is growing rapidly. The greatest need is among those age 85 and older who are the fastest growing segment of the older population. By 2020, 10 to 14 million may need care and by 2060 as many as 14 to 24 million.[31]

In 1996, public and private nursing home expenditures were $78 billion and total home health care expenditures were $30 billion.[32] Nursing home care was about 8 percent of all personal health care expenditures. Public funds (primarily Medicaid) paid for 62 percent of nursing home care. The remainder came from private sources, and nearly all of it (82 percent) came directly from consumers' pockets. Private insurance paid for only 5 percent of nursing home care. About 59 percent of home health care costs were paid by public programs, primarily Medicare. The remainder was paid from private sources with 20 percent of all home care costs paid out-of-pocket.

Nearly three-quarters of public long-term care expenditures go to nursing home care. More could be done to help older people in their own homes by shifting the balance of funding to in-home care. To give older people more choices the federal government now allows tax deductions for long-term care insurance premiums for those who itemize, and it has made long-term care expenses that exceed 7.5 percent of income tax deductible like other medical expenses. More could also be done to help families keep their older and disabled members at home by providing tax breaks for family caretakers and by providing more governmentally supported services like respite services for them. A review of many studies found that home-based care may actually not result in cost savings because elderly persons cared for at home may enter hospitals more frequently than those in institutions; on the other hand, evidence of satisfaction with home and community-based care by elderly people, their caregivers, service providers, and policymakers may be reason enough to pursue these options.[33] Concerns about funding long-term care and the options available to provide this care mount with each passing year as the population ages. The baby boom generation will make a substantial contribution to this increase, and since women outlive men, they will continue to be the majority of nursing home residents.

WHAT AILS MEDICINE?

Have changes in national policy made a difference in the health of Americans, especially poor Americans? There is no doubt that *access* to medical care has improved with Medicaid and Medicare. By the 1970s, the poor were actually seeing doctors about 20 percent more often than the nonpoor, and their rates of hospitalization were also greater.[34] This may not be as surprising as it seems, because the poor are more likely to be ill or disabled. Other evidence indicates that once individuals' health status is controlled, the poor receive less health care.[35] Not surprisingly, the uninsured use health care less than those with public or private insurance.

Despite a general increase in access to health care, there has not been a concomitant improvement in health. Evidence from the early 1970s on this point was particularly bleak—there seemed to be *no* relationship between increased health care expenditures and improved health for vulnerable groups.[36] The poor continue to have higher infant mortality rates, higher death rates due to specific causes, and shorter average life spans than the nonpoor. Improvements in general health statistics were just as great prior to the enactment of Medicaid and Medicare as they have been since these programs were enacted. Increased expenditures to improve the health of the country have fallen considerably short of expectations.

Also consider the contrasts posed by the states of Utah and Nevada. These states have similar climates, rates of urbanization, and numbers of physicians and hospital beds, and their residents have similar income and educational levels. Utah has enjoyed one of the highest levels of health in the nation—lower death rates, fewer days lost to sickness, and longer life spans. Why are the statistics for Nevada so much worse? According to Victor Fuchs,

> *The answer almost surely lies in the different lifestyles of . . . the two states. Utah is inhabited primarily by Mormons . . . who do not use tobacco or alcohol and in general lead stable, quiet lives. Nevada . . . has high rates of cigarette and alcohol consumption and very high indexes of marital and geographic instability.*[37]

Channeling more funds to help Americans adopt healthier lifestyles might be one of the best uses of health care dollars. The greatest benefits to health and reductions in health care costs would accrue if people would stop smoking, something that apparently is easier said than done.

It has been argued that what America needs is a national health plan, but the need may not really be for more health care. Indeed, some Americans may be receiving too much medicine. Although the number of hospital beds has decreased from 6 per 1,000 population in 1980 to 4 in 1996,[38] "physician supply has grown rapidly over the past three decades," exceeding general population growth.[39] The need in health care today is for a rational means of distributing a scarce resource—medical care—in an efficient fashion to improve the nation's health. We cannot really hope to provide *all* the health care that *everyone* wants.

The Nation's Health Care Bill

Most people would expect a highly developed society to invest a substantial amount in health care. The United States does just that, exceeding spending in all other developed nations. Table 8-1 provides information on health care spending from all sources in several countries. No other country comes close to the $3,708 per person the United States spent on health care in 1996. The closest is Germany at $2,222 followed by Canada at $2,002. The United States also spends more on health care as a percent of gross domestic product (GDP) than other countries. At 14.2 percent in 1996, it exceeded Germany's 10.5 percent and France's 9.6 percent. But less than half of the U.S. population enjoys the benefits of *publicly* sponsored hospital insurance, while in the other countries shown in Table 8-1, over 90 percent of the population is covered. In addition, Americans make less than half the visits to doctors as those in Japan and Germany.[40] The United States and South Africa are the only industrialized countries that do not have some form of national health insurance.

TABLE 8-1

Health Care Expenditures Per Capita and as a Percentage of Gross Domestic Product (GDP), and Percentage of Population with Public Health Insurance for Selected Countries

Country	Per Capita Expenditure in U.S. Dollars (1996)	Expenditures as Percent of GDP (1996)	Percent of Population with Publicly Mandated Hospital Insurance (1995)
Australia	$1,776	8.4%	100
Canada	2,002	9.2	100
Finland	1,389	7.5	100
France	1,978	9.6	99.5
Germany	2,222	10.5	92.2
Ireland	923	4.9	100
Italy	1,520	7.6	100
Japan	1,581[a]	7.2[a]	100
Norway	1,937	7.9	100
Spain	1,131	7.6[a]	99.3
Sweden	1,405	7.2[a]	100
Switzerland	2,412[a]	9.8[a]	99.5
United Kingdom	1,304	6.9	100
United States	3,708	14.2	46

Source: "OECD Health Data 1960/1995: 1997 Edition. Copyright OECD, 1997."

[a]Data are for 1995

It would be much easier to offer health care benefits to all Americans if medical costs were not so high. National health care expenditures have risen rapidly in the United States. In 1965, prior to Medicare and Medicaid, the country's total (public and private) health care bill was $42 billion; in 1990 it was $698 billion, and in 1997 health care expenditures were $1.1 trillion (see Table 8-2). Figure 8-1 shows that for every dollar spent on health care, private insurance paid 32 cents, governmental expenditures accounted for 46 cents, and out-of-pocket payments were 17 cents.

Several factors have contributed to the escalation of medical costs:

1. "Third-party financing," including the expansion of private insurance and the Medicaid and Medicare programs, has contributed to these rapidly increasing health costs. All have increased demand for health care.

2. The growing number of older people has also contributed, since those over age 65 use more health care services than the rest of the population.

TABLE 8-2

U.S. National Health Care Expenditures, 1997 (in billions of dollars)[a]

Expenditures	
Health services and supplies	$1,058
Personal health care	969
Hospital care	371
Physicians' services	218
Dentists' services	51
Other professional services	62
Home health care	32
Drugs and other medical nondurables	109
Vision products and other medical durables	14
Nursing home care	83
Other health services	30
Net cost of insurance and administration	50
Government public health activities	38
Medical research	18
Medical facilities and construction	17
Total	$1,092 billion

Source: Health Care Financing Administration, Office of the Actuary, National Health Statistics Group, http://www.hcfa.gov/stats/nhe%2Dproj/default.htm.

[a]Numbers may not add up to totals due to rounding.

FIGURE 8-1

Where the Nation's Health Care Dollar Came From: 1997

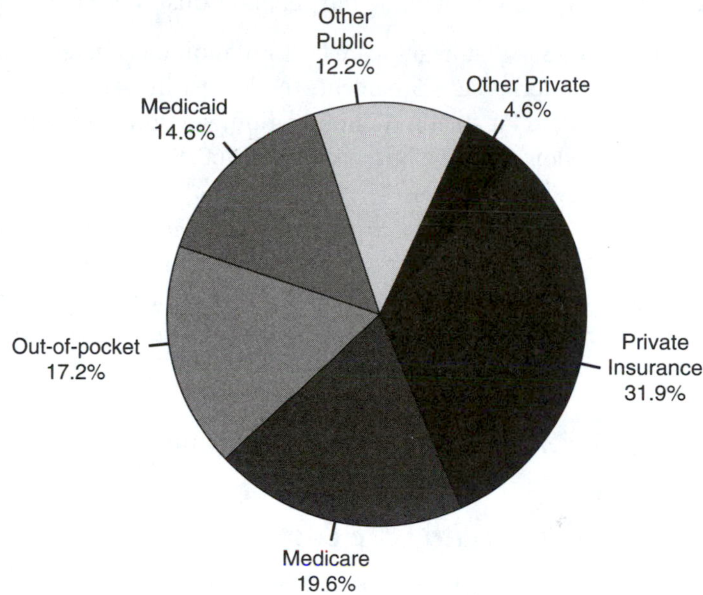

Source: Health Care Financing Administration, Office of the Actuary, National Health Statistics Group, http://www.hcfa.gov/stats/nhe%2Dproj/default.htm.

3. Advances in medical technology are also contributors. Amazing improvements have occurred in the diagnosis and treatment of many illnesses—including heart disease and cancer—which not long ago were invariably considered fatal. Equipment such as CAT scanners and magnetic resonance imaging and techniques such as organ transplants and other extraordinary means of sustaining life also add to costs. The technology that continues to be developed has allowed for increased survival rates of the tiniest infants and people with the most serious ailments.

4. There has been a vast expansion of medical facilities, including hospital beds that are expensive to maintain.* Medicaid funding has spawned many new nursing home facilities and resulted in many more people being placed in them.

5. The threat of malpractice suits results in doctors ordering more tests, even if their utility is questionable. Patients generally want all the best services available, and so do their physicians. Given the number of malpractice suits with large

*The reverse is true for some rural areas that may not even have a doctor, let alone a hospital. Some rural hospitals have closed because of rising health care costs.

awards, the cost of malpractice insurance increases. These costs are also passed on to consumers.

6. Health care cost inflation is also to blame. In 1982 alone, health care cost inflation was 11 percent while the general Consumer Price Index rose 3.9 percent.[41]

Better news is that health care cost inflation has abated in recent years. Using CPI figures, in 1996 it was 3.5 percent, the lowest in 24 years,[42] and using figures from the Health Care Financing Administration, spending grew by 4.4 percent from 1995 to 1996, the lowest rate of growth since 1960.[43]

> *Several factors contributed to . . . [this] slowdown . . . : the continuing . . . migration of workers out of high-cost indemnity plans and into lower-cost managed care alternatives; increased competition among managed care plans; and attempts by health care providers to temporarily hold down price increases in the hopes of heading off government health-care reforms.*[44]

There is concern about how much longer this downward trend can continue.

Holding Down Public Health Care Costs

In the 1980s, the escalating public health care bill eventually caused the federal government to take measures to curb health care costs. Since Medicaid reimbursement rates are so low, the initial target of these efforts was the Medicare program. The major vehicles enacted were *diagnosis-related groups* (DRGs) and *Medicare assignment.*

In 1983 Congress adopted its controversial DRG system. Prior to this, there were some restrictions on what Medicare would reimburse hospitals, but generally hospitals were reimbursed for the reasonable costs incurred in treating a patient. This was a retrospective (after-the-fact) method of paying for hospital care. Despite strong opposition, the DRGs introduced a prospective reimbursement method in which the federal government specifies in advance what it will pay hospitals for the treatment of 487 different illnesses, or diagnosis-related groups. A reimbursement formula was devised to include the average cost of treating a Medicare patient in the hospital, the average cost of treating the particular DRG, whether the hospital is in a large urban area or other area, and hospital wages in the area compared to the national average hospital wage. Greater reimbursement is provided for very costly cases, to hospitals that serve a large number of low-income patients or are the only providers in the area, and to regional referral centers and cancer treatment centers. Anyone who takes time to read the rules will be dazzled by the complexity of the DRG system. When a hospital spends more to treat a patient, it must absorb the additional costs, but when the hospital spends less than the DRG allows, it can keep the difference. Participating hospitals are not allowed to charge Medicare patients more than the DRG. Obviously, the purpose of DRGs is to make hospitals more cost efficient, and immediate drops in hospital stays along with cost savings were seen.

Containment of physicians' charges was more difficult to achieve. Medicare traditionally paid physicians what was "usual, customary, and reasonable" in their community. Opposition from physicians and the AMA to controlling fees was a formidable obstacle to overcome.[45] Cost control provisions have included freezes on the amount that "participating" physicians can charge Medicare patients. Participating physicians agree to accept Medicare reimbursement as payment in full, while "nonparticipating" physicians may charge patients in addition to the amount covered by Medicare. Each year the U.S. Department of Health and Human Services determines the fees that will be paid to physicians under the Medicare program. Incentives used to increase the number of participating physicians include higher payments, prompter reimbursement, and distribution of participating physician directories.

In 1989, Congress reckoned further with the AMA by instituting three major changes to control physicians' fees, largely borrowed from the Canadian national health care system. The first was "expenditure targets." If total Medicare costs are within the year's target, the increase in physicians' fees for the next year is larger than if the target is not met. If the target is not met, the excess costs are taken from the next year's budget. The second change limited "balance billing," which occurs when physicians charge the patient for the difference between their usual charge and what Medicare pays. Since 1993, nonparticipating physicians cannot charge Medicare patients more than 115 percent of Medicare's allowable charges, and they are reimbursed at 95 percent of the amount received by participating physicians. Participating physicians cannot charge Medicaid patients more than the amount Medicare reimburses. The third change was to pay physicians according to a fee schedule for about 7,000 different services beginning in 1992.

In spite of Congress's attempts to hold down expenditures, the government's share of health care costs increased substantially during the 1990s relative to that paid by the private sector and by households.[46] Most troubling was that the Medicare trust fund was headed for exhaustion in 2001 even though Congress had taken measures to control costs and to raise more funds by levying the Medicare tax on all workers' earned income. As Congress searched for ways to bring the federal budget into balance, health care became a prime target, a target that Congress hit as part of the Balanced Budget Act of 1997.

The Balanced Budget Act or BBA made cost savings changes in Medicaid and Medicare, but most savings will come from Medicare, projected to be $115 billion over five years compared to about $15 billion in Medicaid. Most of the Medicare savings will be from smaller increases in payment updates to hospitals and doctors. Facilities that are exempt from the DRG system (rehabilitation facilities, long-term care facilities, psychiatric hospitals, children's hospitals, cancer centers, and hospice facilities) will also face reduced payment updates. Likewise, home health agencies, skilled nursing facilities, and outpatient services are seeing their future payments reduced. Managed care plans serving Medicare beneficiaries also face lower payments.

The act repeals the Boren amendment which required states to make "reasonable and adequate" payments to hospitals and nursing homes. This gives states more flexibility, but it is particularly controversial because Medicaid nursing home reimbursement rates are already very low in many places. If states choose to reduce their payment rates further, there may be an inadequate number of beds to serve Medicaid beneficiaries or a reduction in the quality of care.[47]

Also controversial has been the savings to be gained from disproportionate share hospital (DSH) payments. In the past, hospitals and physicians have made up for the costs of providing services to those who could not pay their bills by shifting these costs to third-party payers (government programs and private health insurers) and to patients who could afford the bills. Today, this is increasingly difficult to do because of public and private cost-containment strategies. DSHs serve many Medicaid enrollees and many poor people who have no health insurance. Disproportionate share payments have been made to compensate hospitals for this service. DSH payments became a sore spot for the federal government because states were taxing these hospitals, running the taxes through the state treasury, using the taxes to draw down federal DSH payments, and then returning the taxes and the DSH payments to the hospitals.[48] Some states use this leveraging far more than others. The BBA and previous legislation passed during the 1990s limit the DSH payments that can be drawn down. These measures are intended to save the government money through more efficient health care delivery.

Medicare beneficiaries will also be paying more under the BBA. For example, Part B premiums will rise faster than they have in the past and are expected to be $105 a month in 2007. Some of this increase will occur as more home health care is switched from Part A to Part B along with additional premiums to cover the rising demand for this care. Between now and 2007, projections are that the traditional, fee-for-service Medicare program covering hospitals and physicians will absorb 51 percent of the BBA savings, managed care plans will absorb 24 percent, beneficiaries, 20 percent, and other measures, 5 percent.[49] Prior to the BBA, the Medicare Part A trust fund faced imminent exhaustion. With savings from the BBA and a strong economy, it now looks like Medicare will stay afloat until 2015. But then, the baby boomers will begin receiving their Medicare cards. Long-range Medicare solvency is a serious issue. The National Bipartisan Commission on the Future of Medicare, appointed by President Clinton and other Democratic as well as Republican leaders, was deeply divided over how to rescue Medicare and failed to agree on a set of recommendations. But one cannot help but think that workers are going to be asked to pay higher taxes, retirees are going to be asked to pay more of their health care, and health care providers are going to be paid reduced fees. Some have suggested raising Medicare eligibility to age 67 (consistent with receiving full Social Security retirement benefits as described in Chapter 4). Others have suggested raising the age for full Social Security retirement benefits and Medicare eligibility to age 70.

Like business and industry, the BBA also plans to achieve savings through greater use of managed care and other health care options for poor and older people. It has been suggested that "new choices under the BBA deserve very close attention to determine which are in fact leading to lower program costs and greater beneficiary choices, and which may cause access and quality problems."[50] For example, in order to encourage managed care plans to operate in rural areas, they will be paid more than traditional Medicare service providers in the same area, thus providing different incentive effects for the two types of providers. There will also be a leveling of payments made to managed care plans in different parts of the country. While this may encourage plans to operate in areas where payments have been low, it may dampen incentives for plans to operate in areas where payments will be reduced. Many of these changes may sound rather academic to the average person because they affect health care providers more directly than consumers, but they have important ramifications for almost everyone.

The private sector is also vitally concerned about health care costs. Even though most businesses require employees to contribute some portion of the costs of their health care plan, providing health care benefits is an important cost of doing business. In 1995, private business spent $249 billion on health care ($184 billion went to private health insurance premiums and most of the rest to the Medicare trust fund).[51]

In this era of managed health care, whether one has a public or private health care plan, what is on consumers' minds is how managed care affects them. We now turn to a discussion of this important issue.

Is Managed Care Hazardous to Your Health?

It used to be simple. When you needed health care, you went to a doctor, paid the fee on the spot, or negotiated payment arrangements with the physician. Doctors even came to the home when a family member was ill. Now consumers complain that a glossary is needed just to figure out what type of arrangement they should select to obtain health care, even before they see a physician. Until the 1940s, most health care was paid for out of pocket as the need arose. Then companies such as Blue Cross and Blue Shield developed, offering the public health insurance; a monthly premium entitles the consumer to reimbursement for many health care services. Workers generally obtain their health insurance through their employer's group plan, because these plans are less expensive than individually-purchased plans. As both the demand for health care services and health care costs grew, the country's entrepreneurial spirit led to the development of various arrangements for obtaining health care benefits.

Among the first alternative arrangements that became widely available to Americans were **health maintenance organizations** (HMOs). The concept of HMOs was supported by the federal government, which in 1973 passed a Health Maintenance Organization Act that provided federal assistance for the development of HMOs. HMOs are membership organizations. Some hire doctors and other health professionals at fixed salaries to serve dues-paying members, often in a clinic-type setting (now known as group HMOs). Many now contract with private physicians who treat patients in their own offices (known as **individual practice associations** or IPA HMOs). In IPA HMOs, there is often a capitation fee through which doctors are paid a set annual fee for each patient enrolled regardless of how much health care patients use. IPA HMOs can provide a greater choice of physicians than a clinic setting.

Both types of HMOs typically provide comprehensive health care for enrollees. Members pay a regular fee (the fee may be somewhat higher than the premium for traditional, private health insurance) that entitles them to hospital care and physicians' services at little or no extra costs (unlike traditional insurance, which pays a percentage of the bills after a deductible is met). Like traditional health insurance, HMOs vary in the services they offer. Some cover treatment for alcohol and drug disorders, prescription drugs, and eyeglasses; others do not. Many HMOs do require modest copayments to defer a portion of costs and deter unnecessary visits.

Advocates tout HMOs as being less costly than fee-for-service medical care, because physicians have no incentive to overtreat patients. Moreover, HMOs are supposed to emphasize preventive medicine, and therefore attempt to treat medical problems before they become serious illnesses. Another attractive feature is that HMOs do away with the need to pay for services and then to file claims for reimbursement.

HMOs rapidly grew in popularity from 235 in 1980 to 651 in 1997.[52] Some were operating in the red (pun intended) and have gone out of business. Others have merged or been bought out by competitors. As HMOs are bought and sold, enrollees may be covered by one HMO today and another one tomorrow, one not necessarily of their choosing. The number of Americans who obtain their employer-sponsored health care benefits through HMOs continues to increase. Although many larger employers offer their employees a selection of health care plans from which to choose, some, especially smaller companies, may offer a single HMO.

The HMO concept was soon followed by **preferred provider organizations** (PPOs). Again the motive was cost containment. Under PPOs, employers or their insurance carriers reimburse a higher percentage of services—for example, hospital care—if employees use designated hospitals or other providers. Employees can use other services but their reimbursement level is lower (for example, 80 percent as opposed to 90 percent for preferred providers). PPOs developed as a result of competition among health care providers who want to keep their patient counts high and are willing to negotiate their fees to do so.

Some large employers are choosing **self-insurance** in which companies directly cover employees' health care costs rather than contract with an insurance company. Under this option, companies may place more limits on the type and amount of services available to employees. These companies generally hire staff who shop for the best health care buys and monitor employees' use of services to keep costs down.

Still another option is **point-of-service** (POS) plans. These plans blend features of HMOs and PPOs. Each enrollee has a primary care physician, but patients can still be reimbursed when they see specialists without approval of their primary care physician if they are willing to pay more for the service. Furthermore, in almost all cases now, hospital stays and other extensive treatment, except in dire emergencies, must be preapproved by the health carrier regardless of the type of plan.

Various permutations and combinations of these health care options continue to emerge. If you have a choice of health care plans, which do you choose? To make the best decision, consumers must study the options carefully even though few people really want to read the fine print. If you want greater choice in selecting physicians, traditional insurance (fast becoming a thing of the past) or a preferred provider option may be the best choice. If an individual has high prescription drug costs, it is important to determine whether an HMO or another type of plan will provide better coverage. Families with young children generally need a series of routine care services, and HMOs usually cover them without a deductible. If you hate paperwork and see a doctor fairly frequently, an HMO might also be a good bet. Becoming an informed consumer is increasingly the best defense in the health care arena.

There is no doubt that managed care has reined in health care inflation. And in many ways, HMOs are an attractive alternative to traditional insurance: after all, they limit out-of-pocket expenses and paperwork. HMOs also receive their share of complaints. One initial complaint from patients was that they did not always see the same doctor when they came for care. Now, HMOs generally assign a primary care physician to patients; often the patient selects from a list of available physicians.

Other complaints about HMOs have been more persistent and have been the targets of federal and state policymakers. For example, the services of specialists are generally covered by the HMO only if a referral is made by the patient's primary care physician. Complaints from patients who did not always agree with their HMO's decisions in these matters has led to greater flexibility in seeking care from specialists. The high costs of health care have sometimes led to charges that HMOs are limiting care in order to cut costs (you may have heard horror stories about treatment denied). Some HMOs offer bonuses to physicians who keep costs down or penalize those who don't. These practices sound disturbing, but they have been defended by some as ways to reduce unnecessary rather than necessary care. In 1996, the federal government issued rules telling HMOs serving Medicaid and Medicare participants that they cannot make payments to physicians as a reward for limiting treatment to a patient. The rules also make physicians responsible for carrying insurance to cover losses they might incur treating HMO patients so they will be less likely to limit care.

Other concerns about managed care organizations have arisen when people were discharged too quickly from hospitals. When insurers told new mothers to leave the hospital almost immediately after delivery, Congress passed a law in 1996 requiring health plans to allow mothers to stay at least 48 hours when the delivery is natural and up to four days for a Cesarean delivery. This is one example of the vexing problem of who makes the decisions about patient care and who is responsible if something goes wrong. HMOs claim that they should not be liable for medical decisions because they pay for health care but do not make medical decisions. Others argue that HMOs have a tremendous influence on patient care decisions because they determine which services will be covered.

And then there are the problems of "loyalty oaths" and "gag rules" that limit what doctors can tell their patients about HMO practices such as treatments not covered by their plans.[53] The federal government also issued rules telling HMOs to stop limiting what doctors can tell patients about treatment options. HMOs say they have already done this, but the AMA contends this is not so.[54] Another problem is "medlining"—not signing up doctors who specialize in treating serious health problems or locating HMO clinics only in areas with more affluent populations.[55]

States have begun to address the problems posed by managed care. Texas and Missouri passed laws allowing patients to sue HMOs for malpractice. In Minnesota, all managed care plans must be nonprofit.[56] Congress may soon join efforts to hold HMOs more accountable. In order to provide greater protection for those with more serious or chronic health care problems, some plans pay HMOs at different rates depending on whether they see patients who have more or less health problems (a risk approach).

Not so long ago, patients would never have dreamed that they would need to be protected from the health care system, but times have changed. President Clinton appointed an advisory commission to suggest patient protection legislation and to draft a patients' bill of rights (see Illustration 8-1).

Like the private sector, the public sector is increasingly turning to managed care. The state of Arizona has used managed care since it inaugurated its Medicaid program, called the Arizona Health Care Cost Containment System, in 1982, and Tennessee adopted its own managed care system called TennCare. Now states are increasingly enrolling Medicaid participants in HMOs and other managed care plans. From 1991 to 1997, managed care enrollment increased from 10 to 48 percent of Medicaid caseloads.[57]

Managed care faces some special challenges in the public sector.[58] A third of Medicaid participants are people who have physical or mental disabilities or are older. They often require more health care than the general population and are less attractive to HMOs. Some states continue to use **primary care case management** to serve these consumers in which case managers coordinate beneficiaries' care for a small fee, but the actual health care services are paid on a fee-for-service basis. Due in part to difficulty in attracting HMO providers, states have tended to shy away from enrolling individuals who are aged or disabled in Medicaid managed care plans. Instead they have concentrated on enrolling children and nondisabled adults (often the parents in AFDC, now TANF, families). But even with this healthier clientele, Medicaid funding per patient remains low, thus posing problems in getting managed care plans to cover this population.

Under the traditional Medicaid program, the federal government required states to give enrollees a choice of health care providers. Many states have obtained waivers allowing them to enroll Medicaid beneficiaries in managed care plans while restricting their choice of providers and waiving other Medicaid program requirements. Though enrollee choice is restricted, the states have been able to use this arrangement to include more low-income people in their Medicaid programs. The Balanced Budget Act of 1997 goes even further by allowing states to require many Medicaid beneficiaries to enroll in managed care plans without a waiver to restrict their choices.

Managed care is also affecting Medicare. The percentage of Medicare recipients enrolled in HMOs is relatively small (13 percent in 1997)[59] but predicted to grow considerably as older people try to reduce escalating out-of-pocket health costs. Medicare HMOs often cover some medigaps because their profits must be used to provide benefits to patients. In order to give older people a wider range of health plan options, Medicare + Choice (also called Medicare Part C) has been added to Medicare. It continues to allow Medicare beneficiaries to enroll in HMOs, the only so-called "private plan" that has been available to Medicare participants. Under the Balanced Budget Act of 1997, participants can now select from several other options, including two additional managed care options. One is preferred provider organizations and the other

ILLUSTRATION 8-1

A Proposed Consumer Bill of Rights and Responsibilities

1. Consumers have the right to receive accurate, easily understood information and some require assistance in making informed health care decisions about their health plan, professionals, and facilities.
2. Consumers have the right to a choice of health care providers that is sufficient to ensure access to appropriate high-quality health care.
3. Consumers have the right to access emergency health care services when and where the need arises. Health plans should provide payment when a consumer presents to an emergency department with acute symptoms of sufficient severity—including severe pain—such that a "prudent layperson" could reasonably expect the absence of medical attention to result in placing that consumer's health in serious jeopardy, serious impairment to bodily functions, or serious dysfunction of any bodily organ or part.
4. Consumers have the right and responsibility to fully participate in all decisions related to their health care. Consumers who are unable to fully participate in treatment decisions have the right to be represented by parents, guardians, family members, or other conservators.
5. Consumers have the right to considerate, respectful care from all members of the health care system at all times and under all circumstances. An environment of mutual respect is essential to maintain a quality health care system.
6. Consumers have the right to communicate with health care providers in confidence and to have the confidentiality of their individually identifiable health care information protected. Consumers also have the right to review and copy their own medical records and request amendments to their records.
7. All consumers have the right to a fair and efficient process for resolving differences with their health plans, health care providers, and the institutions that serve them, including a rigorous system of internal review and an independent system of external review.
8. In a health system that protects consumers' rights, it is reasonable to expect and encourage consumers to assume reasonable responsibilities. Greater individual involvement by consumers in their care increases the likelihood of achieving the best outcomes and helps support a quality improvement, cost-conscious environment.

Source: President's Advisory Commission on Consumer Protection and Quality in the Health Care Industry, "Consumer Bill of Rights and Responsibilities," July 19, 1998, http://www.hcqualitycommission.gov/cborr/.

is **provider sponsored organizations** (PSOs) in which doctors and hospitals group together to offer medical services. PSOs are similar to HMOs except that HMOs are run by insurance companies, and PSOs are run by medical providers themselves. Whether or not managed care is good for one's health, selecting a plan, understanding the benefits, and cashing in on them is causing Americans stress.

THE POLITICS OF HEALTH CARE FOR ALL

Most Americans have some type of health care coverage. According to the Census Bureau, in 1997, 70 percent of Americans had private health insurance of some type (mostly sponsored through their employer) for at least part of the year; 13 percent had Medicare, 11 percent had Medicaid, and 3 percent had military coverage (some were covered by more than one plan).[60] Estimates of the insured vary,[61] but Census Bureau figures show that more than 43 million individuals (16 percent of the population) were without health insurance for all of 1997. Despite a booming economy and record low unemployment, these figures are higher than for 1996. The poor are far more likely to be uninsured than the general population. Their uninsured rate was 32 percent. Those ages 18 to 24 are much more likely to be without insurance (30 percent) than any other age group, while those aged 65 and over are most likely to have insurance (only 1 percent have no coverage). Hispanics were the ethnic group least likely to have health insurance. The portion of the child population without health insurance has risen over time despite Medicaid's expansion. It is a shame that the U.S. lags so far behind most other industrialized countries in providing health care coverage to the population. This is largely because health care coverage is the responsibility of private citizens, unlike many other countries in which the government plays a larger role in seeing that everyone is covered (see Table 8-1).

When the term *national health insurance* is used, most people think of the type of socialized medicine practiced in Great Britain in which physicians and other health care providers are employees of the federal government and the government owns and controls hospitals and other medical facilities. The Canadian system is much different; physicians and hospitals are part of the private sector, but the government sees that all citizens have health care coverage. Canada adopted universal hospital insurance in 1958 and universal physician insurance in 1968. Care is considered quite good and the system is reported to function more efficiently by centralizing services and equipment.[62] Physicians maintain substantial incomes under the Canadian plan. In Britain and Canada, health care is rationed in part by time rather than money. Patients may have to wait hours to see a doctor and months to undergo nonemergency surgeries. It is those who are willing and able to wait rather than pay who are served. There is some dissatisfaction with these systems, and in Great Britain, some private practice by physicians has been permitted for patients willing and able to pay. But it is very doubtful that any country used to universal health care coverage would opt for a system like that in the United States. It is equally doubtful that the United States will ever adopt a system like Britain's, because the free enterprise system prevails, and physicians are powerful enough to resist that much government control.

In the 1930s President Franklin D. Roosevelt backed off from the idea of national health insurance when he feared it might endanger passage of the original Social Security Act. The AMA, already an important political force, contended the plan would not work without the support of the nation's physicians. President Harry S. Truman pushed hard for national health insurance, but it was again branded as socialized medicine by the medical community and defeated. President Lyndon Johnson chose a narrower approach—health care for the poor and for the aged, and he succeeded in adding Medicare and Medicaid to the Social Security Act in 1965. President Bush advocated tax credits and tax deductions to help people pay for health care premiums. For many years, Senator Edward M. "Ted" Kennedy (Democrat-Massachusetts) has pushed for national health insurance. Among his early proposals was a plan called Health Care for All Americans, which would have required all Americans to have health insurance. A National Health Board would have overseen the program. Taxes would have been collected from workers and employers and allocated to private insurance companies to process claims. Those without jobs would have been insured through a special fund. Everyone would have been entitled to comprehensive health care. The government would have set physicians' fees and hospital charges, and Congress would have determined the national health insurance budget each year. Separate Medicare and Medicaid programs would not be needed.

In his more recent attempts at universal coverage, Kennedy has noted that the costs are about equal to government aid to the savings and loan industry, and costs to business would be no more than the alcohol and tobacco industries' advertising bills. Scores of other plans have been offered, but to date all attempts at national health care have failed. Even much more limited plans have been rejected. For example, Theodore Marmor, a national health care expert, proposed "Kiddie Care," a plan to provide basic health care at reasonable costs to the nation's children that would protect against long-term and debilitating illnesses.[63] It never got serious consideration.

The Failed Health Security Act

During his first race for the presidency, Bill Clinton's number one campaign promise was national health insurance. The president appointed Hillary Rodham Clinton to chair the large task force that helped devise the plan. The 1,300-page plan, called the Health Security Act, was submitted to Congress on September 22, 1993. Advocates hoped that it would be a major step in reducing poverty, and that it would keep national health costs in check with expenditure controls and provide the opportunity for all Americans to get preventive and early treatment.

The plan would have worked in the following way.[64] All citizens and legal immigrants would get a "health security card" guaranteeing them comprehensive benefits, including preventive care, for life. Services would include inpatient and outpatient medical care, prescription drugs, vision and dental care, long-term care, and mental health and substance abuse treatment. No one could be denied coverage, and coverage would be continuous regardless of employment. Workers would have more flexibility to seek better jobs because they would be assured of health benefits, and families receiving public assistance would not have to worry about losing health benefits if they go to work. Standard benefit claim forms for health services would be used, unlike the myriad forms used by the hundreds of insurers in the U.S. today, each with different eligibility and reimbursement requirements.

Competition was a main theme of the Clinton plan. Participants would have bought into large purchasing pools, called **health care alliances,** in order to get the best value for their health care dollar. Each alliance would have offered a choice of plans. According to the act's proponents, most people with coverage would not have paid more while getting an equally comprehensive benefit package. In fact, they might not have noticed much difference from the way they now obtain health care. Almost everyone would have shared in the costs of health insurance. Employers would have been required to pay 80 percent of the average premium for the standard benefit package. Workers would pay the rest.

Health plans used by the alliances would not have been allowed to refuse anyone and would have been required to provide everyone the full range of services at the same community rate. The alliances would have paid higher rates to plans that enroll higher-risk individuals. Premium targets would have been set to protect against cost inflation. A National Health Board would have established the targets for each alliance. Plans accepted by alliances would have been required to meet the target, and if below the target, the state in which the alliance operated would have been able to keep some of the savings.

Poor individuals would have received premium discounts or would not have been charged. Medicaid would have covered premiums for eligible individuals such as public assistance recipients who would also receive discounts on coinsurance payments. But everyone would have been served by an alliance. Medicare would have remained, but individuals could have chosen Medicare or a regional alliance. Prescription drug benefits would have been added to Medicare. A federal–state long-term care benefit including home- and community-based services for people with disabilities, regardless of age and income, would have been initiated.

It was anticipated that about three-quarters of funding for the Health Security Act would come from current sources—employers, individuals, and families—with additional funding from cost-savings measures in Medicare and Medicaid. The health care programs of the Departments of Veterans Affairs and Defense and the Federal Employees Health Benefit Program would be coordinated with the new plan. A substantial increase in cigarette taxes was also suggested to raise revenues. The act would have taken a stab at lowering malpractice costs by requiring the use of dispute resolution practices as a first step, limiting the percentage lawyers can take of awards, and requiring evidence of wrongdoing *before* a lawsuit is filed. As one academic wrote:

> *The president's proposal . . . [was] not a clean, simple design tailored to a single dominant philosophy as are, for example, the Canadian and German health systems. True to American tradition, it . . . [was] a complex compromise that has been bent and twisted onto the Procrustean bed of a pluralistic set of ethical precepts and of an equally pluralistic set of narrow economic interests pursued by politically powerful groups.*[65]

In the wake of the president's bill came dozens of competing proposals.[66] Many of a more liberal ilk advocated greater government regulation, including a single-payer system. Instead of alliances and competition among plans, they wanted the federal government to collect all funds used to pay for health care and to pay all claims. They wanted to eliminate the two-tier system of health care in America in which the rich receive better treatment and the poor get second-class treatment. But the fear was that without competition, there would be no incentive for efficiency; instead the demand for services, even unnecessary services, would increase, creating another morass. (Actually, Clinton's proposal did permit states to use a single-payer system, as long as they allowed for competition among health care plans.)

At the other end of the spectrum were those who felt that the Clinton plan was too much government regulation. They were concerned that many health care decisions would be made by bureaucrats rather than between doctor and patient. They believed that the alliances in the Clinton proposal were too large, and they preferred to increase competition with a larger number of smaller alliances. These conservatives wanted to leave far more to the competition that flows from natural market forces, and they wanted to take a much more incremental approach. For example, Senator Phil Gramm (Republican-Texas) called for government tax credits and subsidies to help poor people obtain coverage, but his approach did not require that everyone be covered, nor did it specify any minimum set of benefits that must be made available to those who are insured. His proposal also did not require businesses to contribute to employees' health care coverage. Some of the strongest opposition to the Clinton plan came from those who believe that employer mandates would threaten the survival of small or low-income-producing enterprises. Other proposals required that employers make insurance plans available but also did not require that employers contribute to employees' premiums. Proposals such as Gramm's might help some people gain access to health care, but they were a far cry from universal coverage.

The Clinton plan was actually a mix of government intervention and free-market enterprise. Of course, some say, "Don't fix it if it's not broken," meaning that 84 percent of Americans already have some type of health care coverage. They want to focus only on those who have no coverage. But this largely ignores controlling costs and making insurance continuous. Clinton's plan did maintain the most common structure for obtaining coverage—through employment. The AMA and the Health Insurance Association of America saw the handwriting on the wall and joined the call for universal health insurance. Several years ago the AMA endorsed mandatory employer-supported health care, but these organizations criticized aspects of Clinton's plan, especially spending controls.[67]

As noted by two editors of the scholarly journal *Health Affairs,*

> *One need look no further than America's previous failures to reform the health system to recognize that it is a complex undertaking. The challenge is daunting because it must attract broad political support in a nation that has never achieved consensus on an overriding social ethic (universal coverage) to which all other worthwhile goals in health care must take second place. . . . The result of this ambivalence—open espousal of a lofty goal, but open hostility to the only means of achieving that goal—has led to the perennial stalemate that is the hallmark of congressional wrangling over universal health insurance.*[68]

Millions were spent to support the president's plan, and millions more were spent to defeat it.[69] We can assume the President Clinton took office with the hope that he would go down in history as the president who instituted national health insurance. The ray of hope for national health insurance quickly faded as Republicans and Democrats reverted to incremental means to increase the insured population.

Expanding Health Care Coverage the Incremental Way

Even before Congress considered President Clinton's plan for national health insurance and the many other proposals offered by Congressmembers, the states had moved ahead to do something about the uninsured at their doorsteps. As mentioned earlier, Arizona and Tennessee had already adopted managed care systems for low-income residents. Hawaii was requiring employers to insure most of the workforce. Minnesota's Health-Right had extended insurance to low-income residents without coverage, charging them on a sliding-scale basis. Florida adopted a plan of eleven regional Community Health Care Purchasing Alliances to help small businesses and self-employed people obtain coverage. Some of the states had obtained federal waivers to serve low-income people who had no health care coverage and were not eligible for Medicaid by allowing them to "buy into" Medicaid through premium payments. Some state plans were especially controversial. Oregon's, for instance, extended coverage to more people while simultaneously rationing services to participants. California voters rejected two attempts to create a state health insurance program, but the state did create the Health Insurance Plan of California. At no cost to taxpayers, employers can participate through voluntary purchasing pools which allow employees to choose from multiple plans. The premiums employees pay are used to finance the program along with employers' required minimum contribution set at half the cost of the least expensive plan for each employee.[70]

Congress had, of course, both required and encouraged the states to expand their Medicaid programs to more groups over the years. As part of the Consolidated Omnibus Budget Reconciliation Act (COBRA) of 1985, Congress also allowed many former employees to keep their insurance coverage for a specified time after leaving their job if they could afford to pay the premiums themselves. Then in 1996, three years after President Clinton unveiled his national health plan, Congress passed the Health Insurance Portability and Accountability Act, also known as the Kassebaum-Kennedy bill. It contained many provisions to increase health care coverage in a not so easy to digest 500 pages. The law's complexity has made for a lot of confusion about what it does and how it is to be implemented. It provides more opportunity for employees to get health insurance when they change jobs even if they have a pre-existing condition, but there may be a waiting period if the employee did not have insurance coverage which included the condition for 12 months at their last job. Other caveats may also affect one's ability to get insurance under the act. For example, employees with a break of 63 or more days without insurance coverage may be excluded for 12 months before being able to obtain insurance through their new job, and nothing in the law requires a company to provide insurance to employees.

The Kassebaum-Kennedy bill increases health insurance tax deductions for self-employed individuals, provides tax benefits for those who pay or whose employer pays for long-term care insurance, and contains viatical provisions. The viatical provisions allow people with chronic or terminal conditions who have life insurance policies to sell these policies without paying federal taxes on the proceeds. They can then use this money to pay medical, living, or other expenses prior to their death.

The portability and accountability law also allows for **medical savings account** (MSA) demonstration programs (also called medical IRAs after the individual retirement accounts that many people have as described in Chapter 4). Some insurance companies offer these accounts, but they have not had the tax advantages available under the demonstration programs, so few people participated. Under the demonstrations, a number of self-employed persons and employees of small companies whose employers make this option available can make tax-deductible contributions to MSAs. The MSAs are coupled with insurance policies that have a high deductible but can be used in the event of illness or injury that results in large medical costs.[71] Money in the accounts can be used to pay for medical care up to the amount of the deductible (under the demonstrations the deductible is set at $1,500 to $2,250 for an individual and $3,000 to $4,500 for a family). Any money left at the end of the year is carried over and interest is paid on the contributions. The money is tax-free until age 65; even then it will not usually be taxed if used to pay for medical care. There are penalties for early withdrawal. The demonstrations will determine if MSAs promote savings and reduce health care costs or if workers prefer not to tie up their money this way. The employees are also free to select whatever health care they want rather than the more restricted options with which today's employees must often contend. Provisions of the portability and accountability law were phased in through 1998.

MSAs are also being tested in the Medicare program as part of the 1997 Balanced Budget Act. The BBA includes so many options that Medicare beneficiaries can use to obtain health care that confusion prevails as the country's senior citizens and the rest of us try to navigate this new territory. Medicare participants can conduct business as usual under traditional fee-for-service Medicare, but many companies will present attractive-sounding alternatives to them. Many may be good options offering more comprehensive services with less out-of-pocket costs. Others may limit beneficiaries' costs but will restrict or limit the care to which they are entitled. There is a phase-in period during which Medicare recipients can change plans on a monthly basis as they can do today, but beginning in 2002, enrollment and disenrollment periods will be more restricted. Demonstrations are also being conducted to integrate acute and long-term care and Medicare and Medicaid benefits under managed care arrangements to see if a comprehensive set of services can be provided in a more rational manner.[72] The BBA also expanded the preventive health care services that must be available to Medicare patients such as mammographies and prostate cancer screening.

President Clinton wants to expand health care coverage by allowing people as young as age 55 to buy into Medicare. This would help individuals who have lost their jobs and thus their health care coverage and younger retirees without access to coverage. Others feel that Medicare's precarious financial condition makes this imprudent.

Another federal initiative contained in the BBA is the State Children's Health Insurance Program (CHIP) established as Title XXI of the Social Security Act. Given the federal funds allocated, CHIP has the potential to extend insurance coverage to 5 to 6 million uninsured children in low-income families, including working families. The states can extend coverage to children whose family income is up to 200 percent of the poverty line. States must submit a proposal to the federal government to obtain CHIP block grant funds. They can cover CHIP-eligible children by expanding their Medicaid program, creating a new program, or using a combination of approaches. An Urban Institute analysis reveals some perverse features of Medicaid and CHIP.[73] First, estimates are that 1.6 to 4.5 million eligible children are not participating in Medicaid and are ineligible for CHIP because states cannot use CHIP funds to cover Medicaid-eligible children. Once Medicaid-eligible children are eliminated from the number of uninsured, the Urban Institute believes that nationwide, about 3.2 million children are CHIP-eligible, rather than the 5 or 6 million that could potentially be covered with the federal funds that have been allocated. Second, states get a bigger federal return for covering the higher-income children eligible under CHIP than they do for covering poorer Medicaid-eligible children. Third, CHIP's funding formula reimburses states based on the number of uninsured children. This penalizes states which have already made more progress in insuring low-income children. Fourth, all states will get more federal funds per dollar they invest in CHIP than they do under Medicaid, but states with higher per-capita incomes end up with a higher percentage increase than states with lower per-capita incomes. This may give the lower-income states less financial incentive to increase the number of children covered. Fifth, concerns are that some employers that now provide insurance to low-income working families may no longer cover children in these families if they know that CHIP will pick them up. It will certainly be interesting to see what happens to the number of uninsured children with CHIP in place, but it seems that it would be easier to provide universal access for children through some form of kiddie care.

The BBA requires states to restore Medicaid to children who lost their SSI coverage as a result of a more stringent definition of disability now applied in child cases (also see Chapter 5). States may also provide 12 months of continuous coverage to children once they become Medicaid participants even if their circumstances change.

The BBA addressed issues in addition to access to health care, particularly under Medicare, such as confidentiality protections and efforts to prevent fraud and abuse by health care providers. Democrats and Republicans are continuing to put their own stamp on new health care bills and are arguing about issues such as how much leeway patients should have to sue managed care companies and health care providers. The country is taking a decidedly more incremental approach to seeing that more Americans have health care coverage, but a number of political pundits have commented that piece by piece, the Clinton plan is being enacted through state and federal legislation and through the private sector's embrace of managed care.[74]

HEALTH CARE—SOME ETHICAL DILEMMAS

Bioethical dilemmas like health care rationing are also social welfare concerns. Since there are limits to the amount of health care that can be provided, what factors should be considered in rationing? For example, should we forgo life support for the very old in favor of more preventive health care for children? This is an extremely difficult question, and there is no consensus on how health care should be ranked or rationed. In fact, some people insist that spending 14 percent or more of the country's GDP should not be an issue at all; the country should avoid rationing services. But health care *is* rationed by a number of factors—whether an individual has third-party coverage or can otherwise afford care; whether those who are ill present themselves for treatment; and whether the medical community responds to the need rather than refusing to treat or "dumping" indigent patients. Desperate parents have tried to influence rationing decisions by using television to plead for a transplant donor for their terminally ill child when they felt that existing networks were not moving fast enough. Without a substantial amount of money up front, transplants are out of reach for many patients. Some Medicaid programs no longer pay for transplants.

Other dilemmas include the "right to die"—who should be able to make such decisions and under what circumstances? Patients have asked the courts to permit them to remove life-sustaining devices such as respirators, but there is no consistent response to this issue, and state laws on the subject are generally unclear. **Living wills** can help to clarify an individual's wishes when death is imminent. Another document called a **durable power of attorney** can also clarify one's wishes and transfer legal powers to another to make medical decisions. For example, terminally ill individuals may request that they not be resuscitated (another term for this practice is **passive euthanasia**), or they may request that certain methods be used to sustain their life. The Patient Self-Determination Act of 1991 requires that many medical facilities receiving Medicare or Medicaid funds provide information to patients about advance directives. Estimates are that only about 15 percent of people have these directives.[75]

Even individuals with advance directives cannot be assured that their wishes will be carried out, because family members, medical professionals, or the courts might not know an individual's wishes, or they may see the situation differently. For example, in 1990, the U.S. Supreme Court reviewed the case of the Cruzans, a couple that wanted to stop feeding their unresponsive adult daughter, who was severely injured in a car crash. They believed it was their daughter's wish not to live in a vegetative state. The state of Missouri refused to comply with the parents' wishes on the grounds that it had no such instructions from the patient and that her treatment was not causing pain. The Court upheld the state's position, stating there was not "clear and convincing" proof of the patient's wishes. The decision was the Court's first in a right-to-die case. The implications of the decisions are that patients do have a constitutional right to reject medical treatment if their desires are made clear, but that states have considerable authority in determining how this right will be upheld. Most states allow family members more authority in making decisions on behalf of patients in vegetative states than is permitted in Missouri. Later, when presented with additional evidence, a Missouri probate judge allowed the feedings to stop. Ms. Cruzan died shortly after.

Another reason that the question of the proper limits of life are being debated is because life spans continue to increase. Several years ago, one governor gained national attention when he suggested that the elderly have a "duty to die." Medical technology may be able to sustain people, regardless of the quality of life, and the capabilities of medical technology continue to increase, making it even more difficult to decide between sustaining life and allowing death to occur. Recently identified diseases also present challenges. In one case an elderly Florida man was found guilty of murder and imprisoned after he shot to death his wife, who had Alzheimer's disease. He said he could no longer bear to see her suffer.

Many people would empathize with the families in these situations, but medical personnel must uphold their own codes of ethics and obey state laws. Those who do believe in the individual's right to determine when life should end point to the Netherlands, which permits physicians greater latitude in helping patients with voluntary, active euthanasia in which the physician administers or prescribes drugs to promote death.[76] Although active euthanasia is technically illegal, it has been practiced in the Netherlands for some time and seldom results in serious legal repercussions if the physician follows guidelines developed as a result of judicial decisions made in the 1970s. For example, the patient must make the request, the physician must have known the patient previously, and the physician is not compelled to honor the request. The Dutch parliament was deeply divided on the morality of the issue, but in 1993 it supported the practice.[77] The Dutch policy is among "the world's most liberal policies for mercy killings."[78] It requires consultation with a second physician to ensure that all requirements are satisfied, and prison terms may be imposed for violations. Those opposed to the law believe that condoning the practice promotes the idea of social Darwinism (survival of the fittest) and will open the door to use in inappropriate cases. In 1995, the Northern Territory of Australia passed the world's first explicit voluntary euthanasia law. A few people used it to end their lives before the Australian Parliament overturned it.

In the United States, the Oregon legislature passed a law in 1994 which allowed doctors to assist patients with lethal doses of medication. The law requires that an individual be mentally competent, have less than six months to live, make a written request that is witnessed, drink a cocktail of drugs rather than be administered an injection, and wait 15 days to be given the cocktail. Two physicians must concur, and a physician must discuss alternatives with the patient. In 1995, a federal judge ruled the law unconstitutional to prevent error, abuse, and discrimination. In 1996, the Ninth Circuit Court of Appeals overturned a Washington state law making it a felony to assist in a person's death by ruling that a mentally competent person who is terminally ill has a constitutional right to commit suicide with a doctor's help. In 1996 a federal appeals court found New York's law against physician assisted suicide unconstitutionally discriminatory. Unlike the Washington decision, it did not find a constitutional right to assisted suicide based on the Fourteenth Amendment's guarantees of liberty and privacy. Instead it said that while those on life support can hasten death by turning off machines which sustain their life, others in terminal situations have no such recourse, thus violating the Constitution's equal protection clause.

The U.S. Supreme Court agreed to hear appeals of the Washington and New York cases, a surprising move in that the high court usually tries to avoid the issue. In June 1997, it concluded that there is no constitutional right to physician assisted suicide. The ruling allows states to ban physician assisted suicides but does not stop states from allowing them in narrowly defined cases. The high court refused to hear an appeal of the Oregon law, but in November 1997 the issue was again put to Oregon voters. By a 20 percent margin, Oregonians affirmed approval of access to physician assisted suicide. Oregon is the only U.S. state with such a law. The Drug Enforcement Administration tried to block the Oregon law by threatening to revoke the narcotics licenses of physicians who participate in suicides of terminally ill people. Attorney General Janet Reno informed the DEA that the issue was not in its purview.

Retired pathologist Dr. Jack Kevorkian devoted himself to the cause by assisting in suicides of ill individuals (or at least in helping them end their suffering). Kevorkian was prosecuted in a few of these cases and was acquitted each time. A Michigan ban on assisted suicide and an attempt to invoke unwritten common law failed to stop him. Neither did the time he spent in jail. In late 1998, Kevorkian was charged and later convicted after a tape he provided to "60 Minutes" aired showing him give a man with Lou Gehrig's disease a lethal injection.

The Hemlock Society is one organization interested in the "right of the terminally ill person to choose voluntary euthanasia."[79] On the other side of the issue, the AMA opposes physician assisted suicide, and the National Right to Life Committee works to block efforts that support the right to die. Physician assisted death has been likened to the issue of abortion, not only on constitutional grounds, but also on the makeup of the groups that have rallied around the issue and the fervor with which they have pursued their positions. Ethical, moral, and legal questions have been raised. Among them is the issue of discrimination. Many refer to it as a slippery slope bound to go further than most intend. For example, some fear that assisted suicide laws may turn into a duty to die because in the United States a terminal illness as well as a chronic, long-term illness can bankrupt a family (unlike other countries where national health insurance protects families from financial disaster due to medical conditions). There is also a belief that in many cases, patients' requests to end their lives are due to inadequate medical attention such as lack of sufficient pain medication and other palliative care that can ease suffering. In this case, the answer may lie in better education of medical professionals. Others contend that doctors fear repercussions for prescribing sufficient doses of potentially addictive pain-relieving narcotic medications. The Assisted Suicide Funding Restriction Act of 1997 expresses the opinion of Congress and President Clinton by making it illegal to use federal funds to support physician assisted suicide.

SUMMARY

Health care for aged and poor Americans has been on the social welfare policy agenda since the early twentieth century. Major federal health-care proposals were introduced for fifty years before Medicaid and Medicare were adopted. The medical establishment worked to delay large-scale federal government involvement in medical assistance by branding it socialized medicine.

Medicaid is a public assistance program operated jointly by the federal and state governments. Most TANF and SSI recipients receive Medicaid. Other medically indigent people may also qualify, but Medicaid insures less than half of all poor Americans. Medicare is a social insurance program financed by the government through payroll taxes. It serves the nation's aged population as well as many former workers under age 65 with long-term disabilities.

Health care makes up an increasing amount of public and private expenditures. Health maintenance organizations and other managed care arrangements are attempts at keeping these costs under control. Managed care is the major theme in providing health care coverage to Americans today.

Many of the leading causes of death for those in all income brackets are related to heredity and lifestyle issues rather than lack of medical care. The United States spends more for health care than other industrialized nations, yet fewer Americans have health insurance, and U.S. adult and infant mortality rates exceed those of most of these countries. Black, Hispanic, and poor Americans continue to experience worse health outcomes than the general population.

President Clinton wanted to create a national health care program to ensure that all Americans have continuous health care coverage. The plan would have relied heavily on fees paid by employers, but employees would have shared costs and other enrollees would also have paid some premiums. The major opposition came from those who thought it was too much government interference in health care, but others advocated greater government involvement through a single-payer system like Canada's.

What has occurred instead is a decidedly more incremental approach to expanding health care coverage. Some states are including more low-income people in their Medicaid programs, and some have put more pressure on employers to provide health care benefits to employees. Congress has passed legislation that helps more people keep their insurance if they leave their job, but it does not require employers to provide health care benefits. The Balanced Budget Act of (BBA) 1997 extends health care coverage to more low-income children and gives states more flexibility to use managed care to cover Medicaid-eligible individuals.

Much of the savings in the BBA comes from controlling costs in the Medicare program. The act also offers Medicare beneficiaries greater choice in obtaining benefits, but it could prove to be a minefield as older Americans and those with disabilities navigate this new territory. Between the BBA and an improved economy, Medicare is supposed to be solvent until 2015. The National Bipartisan Commission on the Future of Medicare failed to agree on recommendations that would keep Medicare solvent into the retirement of the baby boom generation and so the search for a long-term solution continues.

NOTES

1. Committee on Ways and Means, U.S. House of Representatives, *Overview of Entitlement Programs: 1993 Green Book* (Washington, DC: U.S. Government Printing Office, 1993), p. 226; also see Robert Sapolsky, "How the Other Half Heals," *Discover,* April 1998, pp. 46, 50–52.

2. For an extensive consideration of the history of health care, including health insurance, see Paul Starr, *The Social Transformation of American Medicine* (New York: Basic Books, 1982).

3. Although this point may seem arguable, the research literature is extensive. See, for example, Victor R. Fuchs, *Who Shall Live? Health, Economics, and Social Choice* (New York: Basic Books, 1974); Victor R. Fuchs, "The Clinton Plan: A Researcher Examines Reform," *Health Affairs,* Vol. 13, No. 1, Spring I, 1994, pp. 102–114; Nathan Glazer, "Paradoxes of Health Care," *Public Interest,* No. 22, Winter 1971, pp. 62–77; Leon R. Kass, "Regarding the End of Medicine and the Pursuit of Health," *Public Interest,* No. 40, Summer 1975, pp. 11–42.

4. These data rely on Centers for Disease Control and Prevention, National Center for Health Statistics, *Monthly Vital Statistics Report,* Vol. 46, No. 12, Supplement 2, September 4, 1998.

5. *OECD Heath Data 97* (Paris: Organization for Economic Cooperation and Development, 1997), http://www.oecd.org/publications/figures/health.html; also see Gerard F. Anderson, "In Search of Value: An International Comparison of Cost, Access, and Outcomes," *Health Affairs,* Vol. 16, No. 6, 1997, pp. 163–171.

6. Much of this section relies on Committee on Ways and Means, U.S. House of Representatives, *1996 Green Book: Background Material and Data on Programs Within the Jurisdiction of the Committee on Ways and Means* (Washington, DC: U.S. Government Printing Office, 1996), pp. 879–914; Committee on Ways and Means, U.S. House of Representatives, *1998 Green Book: Background Material and Data on Programs Within the Jurisdiction of the Committee on Ways and Means* (Washington, DC: U.S. Government Printing Office, 1998), pp. 950–988.

7. See Centers for Disease Control and Prevention, National Center for Health Statistics, *Monthly Vital Statistic Report,* Vol. 46, No. 12, Supplement 2, September 4, 1998, and Vol. 45, No. 11 (S)2, June 12, 1997.

8. For a discussion of the political history of health care in the United States, see Theodore R. Marmor, *Political Analysis and American Medical Care* (Cambridge, England: Cambridge University Press, 1983), especially Chapter 7.

9. See Committee on Ways and Means, *1998 Green Book,* pp. 968–969.

10. Ibid., p. 958.

11. See Comparison of PRIOR LAW and the PERSONAL RESPONSIBILITY AND WORK OPPORTUNITY RECONCILIATION ACT OF 1996 (P.L. 104–193), Department of Health and Human Services, http://www.hhs.gov/policy/policy2html, accessed February 9, 1998.

12. For a more complete listing of optional services and the number of states providing them see Committee on Ways and Means, *1998 Green Book,* p. 988.

13. Executive Office of the President, *Budget of the United States Government, Fiscal Year 1999* (Washington, DC: U.S. Government Printing Office, 1998), p. 214.

14. See Committee on Ways and Means, *1998 Green Book,* pp. 985–987.

15. Centers for Disease Control, *Preventive Health and Health Services Block Grant* (Washington, DC: U.S. Department of Health and Human Services, 1991); also see *Catalog of Federal Domestic Assistance,* 93.991: Preventive Health and Health Services Block Grant, http://aspe.os.dhhs.gov/cfda/p93991.htm, accessed August 2, 1998.

16. U.S. Bureau of the Census, *Statistical Abstract of the United States, 1998* (Washington, DC: U.S. Government Printing Office, 1998), Table No. 200, p. 144.

17. U.S. Bureau of Labor Statistics, "Health Expenditures and the Aging Population," *Issues in Labor Statistics,* Summary 97-12, November 1997, http://stats.bls.gov/pdf/opbils15.pdf.

18. Each year the Health Care Financing Administration distributes a Medicare handbook to all beneficiaries describing program benefits.

19. Executive Office of the President, *Budget of the United States Government, Fiscal Year 1998,* pp. 186–187; *Budget of the United States Government, Fiscal Year 1999,* p. 221.

20. John Hendren (Associated Press), "'Medigap' Rates Vary Widely by State," *Austin American-Statesman,* July 8, 1997, p. D3.

21. Committee on Ways and Means, *1996 Green Book,* p. 979.

22. Committee on Ways and Means, *1998 Green Book,* p. 137.

23. Committee on Ways and Means, *1993 Green Book* pp. 243, 257; also see Lynn Osterkamp, "Family Caregivers: America's Primary Long-Term Care Resource," *Aging,* No. 358, 1988, pp. 3–5.

24. See The Pepper Commission, U.S. Bipartisan Commission on Comprehensive Health Care, *A Call for Action, Final Report* (Washington, DC: U.S. Government Printing Office, September 1990), especially pp. 93–100; Robyn Stone, Gail Lee Cafferata, and Judith Sangl, "Caregivers of the Frail Elderly: A National Profile,"

Gerontologist, Vol. 27, No. 5, October 1987, pp. 616–626; Committee on Ways and Means, *1996 Green Book,* p. 984.

25. The Pepper Commission, *A Call for Action, Final Report,* p. 94.

26. "Financing of Long-Term Care," The Nursing Home Information Site, http://angelfire.com/tn/Nursing Home/finance.html, accessed January 15, 1999.

27. Much of this paragraph and the next rely on Committee on Ways and Means, *1996 Green Book,* pp. 989–992.

28. See Committee on Ways and Means, *1996 Green Book,* p. 990.

29. See statement of Senator William Cohen in *Planning Ahead: Future Directions in Private Financing of Long-Term Care,* Hearing before the Special Committee on Aging, United States Senate, 104th Congress, 1st session, Serial No. 104–4 (Washington, DC, May 11, 1995), p. 2.

30. Committee on Ways and Means, *1996 Green Book,* p. 984

31. U.S. General Accounting Office, *Long-Term Care: Diverse, Growing Population Includes Millions of Americans of All Ages* (Washington, DC: Author, November 1994), (GAO/HEHS 95–26), cited in Committee on Ways and Means, *1996 Green Book,* p. 984.

32. Figures are from Health Care Financing Administration, Office of the Actuary, National Health Statistics Group, http://www.hcfa.gov/stats/nhe%2Dproj/default.htm.

33. William G. Weissert, Cynthia Matthews Cready, and James E. Pawelak, "The Past and Future of Home- and Community-Based Long-Term Care," *The Milbank Quarterly,* Vol. 66, No. 2, 1988, pp. 309–386.

34. See Ronald W. Wilson and Elijah L. White, "Changes in Morbidity, Disability and Utilization Differentials Between the Poor and the Nonpoor; Data from the Health Interview Survey: 1964 and 1973," paper presented at the 102nd Annual Meeting of the American Public Health Association, October 21, 1974, cited in Dorothy P. Rice and Douglas Wilson, "The American Medical Economy: Problems and Perspectives," *Journal of Health Politics, Policy and Law,* Vol. 1, Summer 1976, pp. 151–172; Theodore R. Marmor, "Rethinking National Health Insurance," *Public Interest,* No. 46, Winter 1977, pp. 73–95. For a critique of the argument that access to health care is greater for the poor than the nonpoor, see Catherine Kohler Riessman, "The Use of Health Services by the Poor: Are There Any Promising Models?" *Social Policy,* Vol. 14, No. 4, 1984, pp. 30–40.

35. The remainder of this paragraph relies on Paul Starr, "Health Care for the Poor: The Past Twenty Years," in Sheldon H. Danzinger and Daniel H. Weinberg, eds., *Fighting Poverty: What Works and What Doesn't* (Cambridge, MA: Harvard University Press, 1986), pp. 106–137.

36. Ibid.

37. Fuchs, *Who Shall Live?,* p. 53.

38. U.S. Bureau of the Census, *Statistical Abstract of the United States, 1998,* Table No. 200, p. 134.

39. The remainder of this paragraph relies on Committee on Ways and Means, *1993 Green Book,* pp. 289, 292.

40. Material from the Single Payer Coalition, June 1992, reprinted by the National Association of Social Workers, 750 First Street, NE, Suite 700, Washington, DC 20002-4241.

41. Mary Cohn, ed., "Major Changes Made in Medicare Program," *1983 Congressional Quarterly Almanac* (Washington, DC, 1983), pp. 391–394.

42. U.S. Bureau of the Census, *Statistical Abstract of the United States, 1997,* Table No. 752, p. 487.

43. Katharine R. Levit et al., "National Health Care Expenditures, 1996," *Health Care Financing Review,* Vol. 19, No. 1, 1997, pp. 161–200.

44. Information from the Foster-Higgins consulting firm reported in Patricia Lamiell, "Health Benefit Costs Are Reported up 8%," *Austin American-Statesman,* February 15, 1994, p. E1; also see Jon Gabel and Derek Liston, *Trends in Health Insurance: HMOs Experience Lower Rates of Increase than Other Plans* (Washington, DC: KPMG Peat Marwick, December 1993).

45. Starr, "Health Care for the Poor . . . ," pp. 109–110.

46. Cathy A. Cowan and Bradley R. Braden, "Business, Households, and Government: Health Care Spending, 1995," *Health Care Financing Review,* Vol. 18, No. 3, 1997, pp. 195–206.

47. Joshua M. Wiener and David G. Stevenson, *Long-Term Care for the Elderly and State Health Policy* (Washington, DC: Urban Institute, 1997).

48. David Liska, *Medicaid: Overview of a Complex Program* (Washington, DC: Urban Institute, May 1997).

49. Marilyn Moon, Barbara Gage, and Alison Evans, "An Examination of Key Provisions in the Balanced Budget Act of 1997" (The Commonwealth Fund, September 1997), http://www.cmwf.org/medfutur/moon246.html.

50. Moon et al., "An Examination of Key Provisions in the Balanced Budget Act of 1997."

51. Figures from the Health Care Financing Administration, Office of the Actuary: Data from the Office of National Health Statistics, cited in Cowan and Braden, "Business, Households, and Government. . . ," p. 196.

52. Interstudy, Minneapolis, MN, *The Interstudy Competitive Edge,* annual cited in U.S. Bureau of the Census, *Statistical Abstract of the United States, 1998,* Table No. 187, p. 128.

53. Paul Gray, "Gagging the Doctors," *Time,* January 8, 1996, p. 50.

54. Robert Pear (*The New York Times*), "Doctors in HMOs Ordered Not to Limit Patient Advice," *Austin American-Statesman*, December 7, 1996, p. A22.

55. David S. Hilzenrath, "The Life Savers' Dilemma," *The Washington Post*, January 17, 1998, pp. D1, 2.

56. George J. Church, "Backlash Against HMOs," *Time*, April 14, 1997, p. 37.

57. Health Care Financing Administration, "National Summary of Medicaid Managed Care Programs and Enrollment," June 30, 1997, http://www.hcfa.gov/medicaid/trends97.htm.

58. Much of this paragraph relies on Stephen Zuckerman, Alison Evans, and John Holahan, *Questions for States as They Turn to Medicaid Managed Care* (Washington, DC: Urban Institute, 1997); also see Committee on Ways and Means, *1998 Green Book*, p. 960.

59. Executive Office of the President, *Budget of the U.S. Government*, Fiscal Year 1999, p. 219.

60. U.S. Bureau of the Census, "Health Insurance Coverage: 1997," April 3, 1998, http://www.census.gov/hhes/hlthin97.html.

61. See Kimball Lewis, Marilyn Ellwood, and John L. Czajka, *Counting the Uninsured: A Review of the Literature* (Washington, DC: Urban Institute, 1998).

62. George Anders, "Canada Hospitals Provide Care as Good as in U.S. at Lower Costs, Studies Show," *Wall Street Journal*, March 18, 1993, p. B5.

63. Theodore R. Marmor, "The Politics of National Health Insurance: Analysis and Prescription," *Policy Analysis*, Vol. 3, No. 1, 1977, pp. 25–48.

64. This account relies on Executive Office of the President, *Budget of the United States Government, Fiscal Year 1995*, chapter 4.

65. Uwe E. Reinhardt, "The Clinton Plan: A Salute to American Pluralism," *Health Affairs*, Vol. 13, No. 1, Spring I, 1994, p. 116.

66. See Walter A. Zelman, "The Rationale Behind the Clinton Health Care Reform Plan," *Health Affairs*, Vol. 13, No. 1, Spring I, 1994, pp. 9–29.

67. "Can Anything Resist Hillary Clinton? Time Will Tell," *New York Times*, October 3, 1993, section 3, p. 2; Robert Pear, "Insurers End Opposition to Health Reform," *Austin American-Statesman*, December 3, 1992, pp. A1, 17.

68. Uwe E. Reinhardt and John K. Iglehart, "From the Editor, The Policy Makers' Dilemma," *Health Affairs*, Vol. 13, No. 1, Spring I, 1994, pp. 5–6.

69. Peter T. Kilborn, "Unions Commit $10 Million to Push Health Plan," *Austin American-Statesman*, February 22, 1994, p. A2; Jim Dinkard, "Health Care Reform Lobbying Costing Millions," *Austin American-Statesman*, April 25, 1994, p. A2.

70. "California Quake, Golden State's Trials Offer Lessons for State Policy Makers," *Fiscal Notes*, publication of the Texas State Comptroller, February 1996, p. 10.

71. See Margaret O. Kirk (*The New York Times*), "A New Trend in Health Care," *Austin American-Statesman*, February 23, 1997, p. J4; National Association of Social Workers, "Government Relations Update" (Washington, DC: NASW, October 4, 1996).

72. Rosalie A. Kane and Mary Olsen Baker, *Managed Care Issues and Themes: What Next for the Aging Network* (Minneapolis: University of Minnesota and National Academy for State Health Policy, July 1996); Robert L. Mollica and Trish Riley, *Managed Care, Medicaid & the Elderly: Five State Case Studies* (Minneapolis: University of Minnesota and National Academy for State Health Policy, 1996).

73. Frank Ullman, Brian Bruen, and John Holahan, *The State Children's Health Insurance Program: A Look at the Numbers* (Washington, DC: Urban Institute, March 1998).

74. See, for example, Jonathan Chait, "Reform Placebo," *The New Republic*, January 19, 1998, pp. 15–16.

75. Henry Glick, Marie E. Cowart, and J. Donald Smith, "Advance Medical Directives in Hospitals and Nursing Homes: Limited Success for the Federal Patient Self-Determination Act," *Viewpoints on Aging*, newsletter of the Pepper Institute on Aging and Public Policy, Vol. II, September 1995, Florida State University.

76. Alan L. Otten, "Fateful Decision: In the Netherlands, The Very Ill Have Option of Euthanasia," *Wall Street Journal*, August 21, 1987, pp. 1, 6.

77. Tamara Jones, "Dutch Set Euthanasia Guidelines," *Austin American-Statesman*, February 10, 1993, p. A12; on the case of the Netherlands and on assisted suicide and euthanasia in general, see Michael M. Uhlmann, ed., *Last Rights?: Assisted Suicide and Euthanasia Debated* (Washington, DC: Ethics and Public Policy Center, 1998).

78. Jones, "Dutch Set Euthanasia Guidelines."

79. Derek Humphry, *Final Exit* (New York: Dell, 1991), p. 201.

CHAPTER

Changing Paradigms in the Poverty Wars: Victories, Defeats, and Stalemates

American confidence in government's ability to solve problems was once so boundless that President Lyndon Johnson was moved to declare in 1964, "This administration today, here and now, declares unconditional war on poverty in America." And later, when signing the Economic Opportunity Act of 1964, he added, "Today for the first time in the history of the human race, a great nation is able to make and is willing to make a commitment to eradicate poverty among its people."[1] Ten years later, Congress abolished the Office of Economic Opportunity. Although poverty declined during the 1960s, many thought that the effects of the "war" itself had been minimal, and throughout the 1970s, 25 million people remained poor. The government had passed a law, created a new bureaucracy, and spent $25 billion dollars. But according to many critics, nothing much had happened.

An especially scathing critique of the social welfare policies of the 1960s and 1970s is that they spawned more poverty (also see Chapter 3). The federal government was accused of creating additional misery through antipoverty programs that actually encouraged welfare dependency instead of self-sufficiency.[2] Today some of the programs, and just about all the enthusiasm, of the War on Poverty have gone by the wayside. Programs such as Head Start do continue to thrive. Other important programs that were not contained in the Economic Opportunity Act but were part of this era called the Great Society have grown in importance. In particular, it would be difficult to imagine U.S. social welfare policy without food stamps (see Chapter 7) and Medicaid and Medicare (see Chapter 8). Nonetheless, as described in Chapter 3, the paradigm in the wars against poverty has changed. The New Deal of the 1930s, the first major war on poverty in the U.S., was a war of moderates with its centerpiece of social insurance and dabs of public assistance. The war on poverty of the 1960s and 1970s was waged by liberals. The war itself tried to employ a curative strategy with aid to depressed and disadvantaged communities and efforts to make people self-sufficient through work and education programs, but there was also a vast expansion of public assistance during this time. The strategy of the war on poverty embedded in the 1996 federal welfare reform legislation is one of conservatives. It ups the ante on work requirements and cuts off aid for failure to comply. As Americans wait to see if getting tougher is the key to reducing poverty, this chapter looks back on the victories, defeats, and stalemates of the Great Society and discusses current work-related strategies that are supposed to help reduce poverty as the twenty-first century dawns.

THE CURATIVE STRATEGY IN THE 1960s WAR ON POVERTY

The War on Poverty was an attempt to apply a **curative** strategy to the problems of the poor. In contrast to the **preventive** strategy of social insurance, which compels people to save money to relieve economic problems that are likely to result from old age, death, disability, sickness, and unemployment, and in contrast to the **alleviative** strategy of public assistance, which attempts only to ease the hardships of poverty, the curative strategy stresses efforts to help the poor become self-supporting by bringing about changes in these individuals and in their environment. The curative strategy of the War on Poverty was supposed to break the cycle of poverty and allow economically disadvantaged Americans to move into the country's working classes and eventually its middle classes. The strategy was "rehabilitation and not relief." The Economic Opportunity Act of 1964, the centerpiece of the War on Poverty, was to "strike at the causes, not just the consequences, of poverty."

The first curative antipoverty policies originated under President John F. Kennedy. Kennedy had read socialist Michael Harrington's *The Other America*—a sensitive description of continuing poverty that most Americans did not notice (see also Chapter 3).[3] Kennedy, the Harvard-educated son of a multimillionaire business investor, was visibly shocked when, during his 1960 presidential campaign, he saw the wooden shacks of West Virginia's barren mountains. And Kennedy's economic advisor, John Kenneth Galbraith, had in 1958 written another influential book, *The Affluent Society,* which called attention to poverty in the midst of a generally affluent society.[4] Galbraith distinguished between **case poverty** and **area poverty.** Case poverty was largely a product of some personal characteristic of the poor—old age, illiteracy, inadequate education, lack of job skills, poor health, race—which prevented them from participating in the nation's prosperity. Area poverty was a product of economic deficiency relating to a particular sector of the nation, such as West Virginia and much of the rest of Appalachia. "Pockets of poverty" or "depressed areas" developed because of technological change or a lack of industrialization—for instance, decline in the coal industry, the exhaustion of iron ore mines, and the squeezing out of small farmers from the agricultural market. Area poverty has also resulted from declines in the automobile, steel, and petroleum industries in areas that came to be called the country's "rust belt," and in deteriorated inner city neighborhoods as economic enterprise moved to the suburbs. Illustration 9-1 provides a history of three approaches to helping revitalize depressed communities.

ILLUSTRATION 9-1

Community Development: A Foundation Perspective

by John Foster-Bey

Foundation experience with community development probably began in the 1960s with the Ford Foundation's Gray Areas Programs and Mobilization for Youth, both of which became prototypes, or models, for the War on Poverty. At that time, the War on Poverty started what was called the community action approach, a new concept that ran into problems with the political establishments in most cities almost immediately. This was the natural result of the War on Poverty's funding of many groups at the neighborhood level to challenge city hall to do things differently. By the late 1960s, community action programs had evolved into the economic development model exemplified by community development corporations (CDCs).

One surprising thing about community development is that despite a twenty-year history, there is not really a precise definition of the field. Definitions have tended to encompass the activities of a variety of locally based actors attempting to improve the social and economic functioning of a particular place. Given its roots in the War on Poverty, most people have primarily focused on improving the conditions of poor people and places. They work to stem the resource leakage that can destroy the local economy by ensuring that businesses are controlled by local organizations. An additional area of community development organization (CDO) intervention is an attempt to improve the community's social foundations. The Bedford-Stuyvesant Restoration Corporation is generally thought of as the first of these groups. Though they are funded by the government as well, funding from foundations is important, because it comes with fewer restrictions, allowing for greater latitude and local discretion in its use, than government funds. Early CDCs were large, multifunctional organizations that employed many community people.

The first wave of CDOs were replaced in the 1980s by "lean and mean" groups, focused on one or two activities, such as housing and commercial real estate development. These groups abandoned the involvement in direct business activities and social development that characterized the older wave, because of the loss of federal support for their activities. Public support dwindled as the neighborhoods of the CDCs continued to decline. Concerned that the government funding streams were inadequate, the foundation community decided to encourage the private sector to support community development. To attain the support of business, quantitative documentation of the success of the CDCs was needed. So, in the early 1980s, the Ford Foundation tried to move the field forward by creating a national financial intermediary called the Local Initiative Support Corporation (LISC). LISC focused on providing financial capital and raising money from the for-profit sector and foundations. Since the 1980s, foundations and the private sector, as well as the government, have focused a large share of their support on funding CDCS. There are probably about three thousand CDCs nationally, mostly single-purpose entities, focusing primarily on brick and mortar projects. These

continued

ILLUSTRATION 9-1 *(continued)*

CDCs form an infrastructure for neighborhood revitalization and are funded mainly by foundations and other philanthropic giving, with a substantial contribution from the public sector as well.

The second major category in the field is community empowerment and organizing, which also has roots in the community action work early in the War on Poverty. It owes much of its current work to activists such as Saul Alinsky, and his Industrial Areas Foundation in Chicago. Their core belief is that people in poor places are poor because they lack the power to force the system to respond to their needs and concerns. The response, then, is to form organizations that will press for their interests with these powerful establishments. By this means, there would be some redistribution of resources, and poor places would be improved because more services would be delivered there. In this context, community organizing is both confrontational and consensus building or collaborative. Many CDCs actually started as this type of community organization. Because of this, there is often an interesting tension between these two branches of community revitalization work. This part of the field is not well funded, with most support coming from small, socially progressive foundations, and from funding by church-based philanthropy, such as the Campaign for Human Development.

The third category is neighborhood-based social development, or human capital development. The roots of these efforts are again the War on Poverty, but also the settlement house movement that began in the early part of this century. In this model, the poor must become acculturated to the values and norms of the mainstream in order to improve their skills and ability to succeed. Social services and social programs help to meet and address immediate needs and problems, but they also provide the opportunity to develop skills, attitudes, and values necessary for success. This strategy resulted in an array of programs delivered at the neighborhood level. Much of the funding for these programs comes from community and family foundations and from corporate giving, including the United Way.

The last category is an emerging one: the comprehensive, or community-building approach, a new interpretation of another War on Poverty strategy, Model Cities. Model Cities sought to collaborate and coordinate programs and sectors to encourage a multifrontal attack on poverty in particular poor places, and to coordinate a whole range of services to do that. This strategy emphasizes more collaboration and less confrontation. While many consider the Model Cities program to have failed from an operational and political point of view, the comprehensive approach grew out of a recognition that, despite some notable success with the spheres of activity discussed above, conditions in poor communities were not improving. This strategy represents a merging and synergy among the three strategies, and a tailoring of them to local needs. Foundations and CDCs are currently experimenting with the comprehensive approach. Almost all of these have been difficult to initiate and to evaluate.

Community development is still struggling to achieve its promise, even as the national economy has become more global. As the economy and social structure of most metropolitan areas has changed, the field, and the foundations which have supported it, are now faced with an enormous challenge. One of the major areas of concern is whether revitalizing

continued

ILLUSTRATION 9-1 *(continued)*

poor places is still relevant. If so, how can it be reconciled with institutional changes now taking place? All of the data now suggest that we can no longer look at cities, and neighborhoods within cities, as self-contained units. With population growing much more rapidly outside than inside center cities, it may not be possible to revitalize poor communities by focusing on place-based strategies alone. Several of us in the foundation community have begun to explore other approaches that are less dependent on local, or even metropolitan, approaches. This exploration arises from a growing interest in providing economic opportunity for the poor, based on the premise that what is at the root of the problems in poor places may be the lack of opportunity for steady income and upward mobility for poor individuals and families.

William Julius Wilson, now at Harvard, has talked about healthy communities as being places that are organized around work and production, a sharp contrast to the conditions in most poor places now. The hypothesis is that given access to economic opportunity, poor people will have the wherewithal to find or create their own healthy communities. The only way to get rid of poor places and poverty is to ensure that poor people become fully functioning participants in the mainstream economy. The economy is not neighborhood-based. In order to improve economic opportunities for poor people, we have to build bridges between poor places and the regional and metropolitan economy. While few foundations have clearly articulated a program strategy premised on supporting regional approaches, some of the early work around employment and economic opportunity is opening this area up for much wider scrutiny. For example, some of us have been exploring ways to increase access for poor job seekers to the entry-level jobs being created in many suburbs, in a process known as reverse commuting, or worker mobility. Funders also have a growing interest in finding ways to connect employment programs for the poor to private employers. Several years ago, a colleague and I at the Ford Foundation started looking at what we called sector development employment projects, which were an approach to try to link employment programs for the poor with targeted industries such as health care, manufacturing, or printing, which may have opportunities, but not be located near poor communities. At this point, there are several such projects.

Foundations have begun to think more about the issue of concentrated poverty in relation to the housing field. Some of us have started to question whether some of the early work we supported may have contributed to poverty concentration by focusing affordable housing in already low-income communities. As a result, we are talking about how to create mixed-income communities, which in the past we might have considered tantamount to gentrification. We're also beginning to look at ways to more equitably distribute low-income housing around metropolitan regions, rather than concentrating it in poor neighborhoods. Does this mean that foundations have decided to move away from the traditional community development field for what may seem greener pastures? I don't think so. Most funders continue to support traditional CDCS, although I do think there's a shift toward a comprehensive, or community-building approach. Foundations are only beginning to examine whether these two approaches may be in conflict, or whether there may be a way of creating a more synergistic strategy.

continued

ILLUSTRATION 9-1 *(continued)*

Current social, economic and political factors that are determining the ways metropolitan areas are developing may force foundations, city governments, and community practitioners to slightly restate a popular saying: Rather than think globally and act locally, we may have to think locally and act regionally if we want to see real improvement for poor people. If community development is not placed within a regional or metropolitan framework, it will only achieve modest results at best, and at worst may be an utter failure. Likewise, if the focus on the needs and concerns of the poor, which should be the hallmark of a good community development approach, is not integrated into regional approaches, the potential benefits of regionalism will continue to elude the poor, and the conditions in the core cities will only get worse.

Source: Institute on Race & Poverty, "Linking Regional and Local Strategies to Create Healthy Communities," Conference April 12–13, 1996.

The initial forays in the War on Poverty begun in the Kennedy administration included the fight against area poverty. The Area Redevelopment Act of 1961, for example, authorized federal grants and loans to governments and businesses in designated "depressed areas" to promote economic activity. This program was later revised in the Public Works and Economic Development Act (EDA) of 1965. Over the years, the EDA has come under criticism. Some call it a trickle-down approach to alleviating poverty, with most benefits going to business and not the poor. Republicans have also called it a pork barrel program to aid Democrats in getting reelected. The Reagan administration tried to abolish the Economic Development Administration (EDA), contending that "There is no evidence that these programs have resulted in net job creation nationwide. EDA does not target assistance to those in need, but instead serves narrow and specialized local and regional political interests at the Nation's expense."[5] Congress has continued to support the EDA, part of the U.S. Department of Commerce, albeit with modest appropriations in the vicinity of $400 million annually.[6] The agency defends its work, saying that "EDA programs pay for themselves by helping create jobs and generating tax revenues in distressed communities."[7] Another program, the Community Development Block Grant (CDBG), begun in 1974, also provides funds to local Community Development Corporations to aid depressed areas with economic development and a variety of other neighborhood revitalization activities.[8] Current CDBG appropriations are about $5 billion annually.[9] The CDBG is administered by the Department of Housing and Urban Development. The EDA and CDBG are just two federal efforts to address area poverty.

The fight against case poverty began with the Manpower Development and Training Act (MDTA) of 1962—the first large-scale, federally funded job training program. Eventually, MDTA was absorbed into the Comprehensive Employment and Training

Act of 1973 and later into the Reagan administration's Job Training Partnership Act of 1982. These programs are addressed later in this chapter.

LBJ AND THE ECONOMIC OPPORTUNITY ACT

When Lyndon B. Johnson assumed the presidency in 1963 after the assassination of President Kennedy, he saw an opportunity to distinguish his administration and to carry forward the traditions of Franklin D. Roosevelt. Johnson, a former public school teacher, believed that government work and training efforts, particularly those directed at youth, could break the cycle of poverty by giving people the basic skills to improve their employability and make them self-sufficient adults. In order to do this, he championed the Economic Opportunity Act.

The multitude of programs created by the Economic Opportunity Act were to be coordinated in Washington by a new, independent federal bureaucracy—the Office of Economic Opportunity (OEO). OEO was given money and authority to support varied and highly experimental techniques for combating poverty in both urban and rural communities. As evidence of its priority, OEO's first director was Sargent Shriver, brother-in-law of the late President Kennedy and later Democratic vice-presidential candidate with George McGovern in 1972. OEO was encouraged to bypass local and state governments and to establish new programs throughout the nation, with the poor participating in their governance. OEO was generally not given authority to make direct, cash grants to the poor as relief or public assistance. Most OEO programs were aimed, whether accurately or inaccurately, at curing the causes of poverty rather than alleviating its symptoms.

Community Action

The core of the Economic Opportunity Act was grassroots **community action programs** to be carried on at the local level by public or private nonprofit agencies, with federal financial assistance. Communities were urged to form community action agencies composed of representatives of government, private organizations, and, most importantly, the poor themselves. OEO was originally intended to support antipoverty programs devised by the local community action agency. Projects could include literacy training, health services, legal aid, neighborhood service centers, vocational training, childhood development activities, or other innovative ideas. The act also envisioned that the community action agencies would help organize poor people so that they could become participating members of the community and could avail themselves of the many programs designed to serve them. Finally, the act attempted to coordinate federal and state programs for the poor in each community.

Community action programs were to be "developed, conducted, and administered with the maximum feasible participation of the residents of the areas and members of the groups served." This was perhaps the most controversial phrase in the act. The more militant members of the OEO administration frequently cited this phrase as authority to "mobilize" the poor "to have immediate and irreversible impact on their communities." This language implied that the poor were to be organized as a political force by government antipoverty warriors using federal funds. Needless to say, neither Congress nor the Johnson administration really intended to create rival political organizations that would compete for power with local governments.

The typical community action agency was governed by a board consisting of public officials (perhaps the mayor, a county commissioner, a school board member, and a public health officer), prominent public citizens (from business, labor, civil rights, religious, and civic affairs organizations), and representatives of the poor (in some cases selected in agency-sponsored elections, but more often hand-picked by ministers, social workers, civil rights leaders, and other prominent community figures). A staff was hired, including a full-time director, paid from an OEO grant. A target area was defined—a low-income area of the county or the ghetto of a city. Neighborhood centers were established in the target area, perhaps with counselors, employment assistance, a recreation hall, a child care center, and a health clinic. Staff also did **outreach**—assisting the poor in contacting the school system, the welfare department, employment agencies, the public housing authority, and so on. Frequently, the centers and the antipoverty workers who staffed them acted as advocates for the poor and as intermediaries between the poor and public agencies.

Youth Education

Community action agencies also devised specific antipoverty projects for submission to OEO's Washington offices for funding. The most popular of these projects was Operation Head Start—usually a cooperative program between the community action agency and the local school district. Preschool children from poor families were given six to eight weeks of special summer preparation before entering kindergarten or first grade. The idea was to give these children a "head start" on formal schooling. Congress (and the public) was favorably disposed toward this program and favored it in later OEO budget appropriations. In addition to education, Head Start emphasized social skills, nutrition, health and mental health services, and parental participation. A program called Follow Through was added in 1967 to continue comprehensive Head Start efforts for poor children through the third grade, and Upward Bound provided educational counseling.

Other youth-oriented OEO programs were also attempts to break the cycle of poverty at an early age. The Job Corps was designed to provide education, vocational training, and work experience in rural conservation camps for unemployable youth between the ages of 16 and 22 (today participants are ages 14 to 24). Job Corps trainees were to be "hard core" unemployables who could benefit from training away from their home environment—breaking habits and associations that were obstacles to employment while learning reading, arithmetic, and self-health care, as well as auto mechanics, clerical work, and other skills. The Neighborhood Youth Corps was designed to provide work, counseling, and on-the-job training for young people in or out of school who were living at home. The Neighborhood Youth Corps was to serve young people who were more employable than those expected in the Job Corps. The Work-Study program helped students from low-income families remain in high school or college by providing them with federally paid, part-time employment in conjunction with cooperating public or private agencies.

Legal Services

Still another antipoverty project was legal services to assist the poor with rent disputes, contracts, welfare rules, minor police actions, housing regulations, and so on. The idea was that the poor seldom have access to legal counsel and are frequently taken advantage of because they do not know their rights. Antipoverty lawyers using federal funds have brought suits against city welfare departments, housing authorities, public health agencies, and other government bodies. Congress amended the Economic Opportunity Act in 1967 to ensure that funds would not be used to assist defendants in criminal cases.

In order to protect legal services from political pressure, President Nixon proposed making it an independent corporation. In 1974, a separate Legal Services Corporation (LSC) was established, financed with federal tax dollars and governed by an eleven-member board. No more than six members may be from the same political party. LSC programs also receive funding from other public and private sources. Despite efforts to insulate it, the LSC has been a political hot potato. Conservatives have long argued that it is ridiculous to have a government-funded agency to sue other government agencies and that the LSC has gotten into issues well beyond its appropriate purview.[10] Particularly controversial have been the LSC's "lobbying" activities and its involvement in class action suits (on behalf of groups of people). Defenders counter with claims that the poor deserve legal representation and that most LSC cases involve issues of survival (e.g., child support, family violence, divorce, separation, eviction, housing discrimination, income maintenance, consumer finance, employment, health, safety, education, farm foreclosures). LSC attorneys are paid very modest salaries; they serve clients at a fraction of the cost of private attorneys; and they utilize the services of private attorneys who assist *pro bono*. Defenders also note that the country's private attorneys have failed to provide anywhere near the free legal services needed by those who have no access to legal assistance.

Congressional authorization for the LSC actually expired in 1980, but annual Congressional appropriations continue to keep the agency alive.[11] Controversy over the LSC reached a boiling point during the Reagan administration. None of Reagan's twenty-five appointments to the LSC board was approved by Congress, because all were viewed as hostile to the agency's mission. In order to circumvent the approval process, Reagan made nineteen board appointments while the Senate was in recess. The Senate retaliated by limiting the board's power to cut funds to LSC programs until such time as it confirmed the president's nominees. President Bush continued to make recess appointments.

Better news for the LSC came with the election of President Bill Clinton, who is an attorney as is his wife, Hillary Rodham Clinton, a past chair of the LSC board. But Congress remains deeply divided over the role, scope, and even existence of the agency.[12] As amended in 1977, the Legal Services Act limits lobbying, class action, and political activities and prohibits assistance in cases involving nontherapeutic abortions and school desegregation. Congress continued to tack on prohibitions to the agency's activities. For example, in 1991, it prohibited the use of federal funds in any cases involving abortions or undocumented immigrants. LSC advocates contended that since these new restrictions were not contained in the LSC act itself, non-federal funds the agency receives could be used to conduct these activities. Legislation enacted in 1996 contained nineteen restrictions, including a ban on participation in any class action suits and in partisan activities related to redistricting. This legislation also prohibits LSC lawyers from pursuing cases involving these nineteen restrictions even if non-federal funds are used. By the time of the 1996 act, LSC lawyers had already severely restricted their involvement in class action suits. In that same year, a New York state judge ruled it unconstitutional for Congress to tell the LSC how to spend non-federal funds, yet as long as Republicans are in control, LSC lawyers fear that pursuing class action suits will ensure the death of the agency.[13]

In fiscal year 1995, Congress increased LSC appropriations to $400 million but in both 1997 and 1998 only $283 million was appropriated. There have also been recommendations to turn legal services into state block grants. Over time about 200 legal services office have closed[14] with about 300 remaining.[15]

More Office of Economic Opportunity Projects

Other antipoverty projects funded by OEO included family-planning programs (advice and devices to facilitate family planning by the poor), homemaker services (advice and services on how to stretch low family budgets), and additional job training programs (such as special outreach to bring the hard-core unemployed into established workforce programs). There were also programs to help small businesses and to provide direct economic assistance to residents of rural areas. Finally, there was Volunteers in Service to America (VISTA). VISTA, which continues to operate, was modeled after the popular Peace Corps idea, but volunteers work in domestic, poverty-impacted areas rather than in foreign countries. Many of the volunteers are young people who want to serve their country.

The Great Society

The Economic Opportunity Act established many programs, but the act was only a portion of the Great Society. President Johnson's plan included a number of other programs. Among the most important are

- *The Elementary and Secondary Education Act of 1965.* This was the first major, general federal aid-to-education program. It included federal funds to "poverty-impacted" school districts and remains the largest source of federal aid to education.

- *The Food Stamp Program.* This nutrition program was an important step in the development of major in-kind benefit programs. It continues as a major source of relief to a broad cross section of poor people (see Chapter 7).
- *Medicare.* This health insurance program was created as an amendment to the Social Security Act. It covers virtually all the aged in the United States, as well as many younger former workers with long-term disabilities (see Chapter 8).
- *Medicaid.* This amendment to the Social Security Act remains the major federal health care program for certain groups of poor people (see Chapter 8).
- *Job Training.* This array of programs expanded the Manpower Development and Training Act and has evolved into other job and training programs.
- *The Public Works and Economic Development Act of 1965* and *the Appalachia Regional Development Act of 1965.* These efforts encouraged economic development in distressed areas.

POLITICS OVERTAKES THE WAR ON POVERTY

The reasons for the OEO's demise are complex. OEO programs were often the scene of great confusion. Personnel were young, middle-class, inexperienced, and idealistic, and there was a high turnover among administrators. Aside from Head Start, there were no clear-cut program direction for most community action agencies. Many of the poor believed that the program was going to provide them with money; they never really understood or accepted that community action agencies provided other services—community organization, outreach, counselling, training, and similar assistance. Many community action agencies duplicated, and even competed with, existing welfare and social service agencies. Some community action agencies organized the poor to challenge local government agencies. As a result, more than a few local governments called on the Johnson administration and Congress to curb community action agencies that were using federal funds to "undermine" existing programs and organizations. There were frequent charges of mismanagement and corruption, particularly at the local level. Some community action agencies became entangled in the politics of race; some big-city agencies were charged with excluding whites; and in some rural areas, whites believed that poverty agencies were "for blacks only."

Perhaps the failures of the War on Poverty can be explained by lack of knowledge about how to *cure* poverty. In retrospect, it seems naive to believe that local agencies could have found their own cures for eliminating or even reducing poverty.

Can poverty be cured? Opinions are frequently conflicting. For example, some social commentators point to evaluation studies of Job Corps programs indicating that after completing the program, enrollees had income increases ranging from less than $200 to no more than about $500 a year, and they conclude that "the programs were seldom disasters; they simply failed to help many people get and hold jobs that they would not have gotten and held anyway."[16] In contrast, government officials who reviewed the same evidence stated, "While there are always uncertainties, the size of this increment provides reasonable certainty that the Job Corps investment in human resources is profitable."[17] In a more global assessment of the job creation and training programs of the 1960s and 1970s, researchers concluded that

> *[I]t is women and the economically disadvantaged who have benefited. . . . In most cases the resulting employment and earnings gains . . . have been modest, in part because it is not easy to solve the employment difficulties of the hard-to-employ and in part because the resources devoted to any one individual are fairly modest. There is some indication that programs providing intensive (and extensive) investment in each participant, such as the Jobs Corps and Supported Work Demonstration, have, at least for some groups of the disadvantaged, more than paid for themselves from a society-wide point of view.*[18]

Whether one believes that the War on Poverty was a victory or a defeat,[19] OEO became an unpopular stepchild of the Johnson administration even before LBJ left office, so the demise of the OEO programs cannot be attributed to political partisanship—that is, to the election of a Republican administration under Richard Nixon. Nor can the demise of the poverty program be attributed to the Vietnam War—since both "wars" were escalated and later de-escalated at the same time.

The Nixon administration "reorganized" OEO in 1973, transferring the Job Corps, the Neighborhood Youth Corps, and other job training programs under new legislation, called the Comprehensive Employment and Training Act (CETA), to the U.S. Department of Labor. Head Start had already been transferred to the U.S. Department of Health, Education and Welfare (HEW). The Work-Study and Upward Bound programs were also transferred to HEW (which is now two departments—the Department of Education and the Department of Health and Human Services). VISTA became part of a larger federal volunteer program called ACTION. The Ford Administration abolished the OEO in 1974. It turned over a greatly reduced community action program to an independent (and now defunct) Community Services Administration, and it turned over legal services to the independent Legal Services Corporation. Today community action organizations receive help from the Community Services Block Grant (CSBG), another Great Society program. States use the funds to support about 900 nonprofit community action agencies, but the CSBG has had a precarious existence in recent years due to claims that it duplicates the Social Services Block Grant and other federal programs. The Reagan administration tried to abolish the CSBG saying that much of it goes to administrative costs and that community action agencies have been around long enough to administer their programs without these funds.[20] But Congress has continued to fund the CSBG, and the program has had the support of the Clinton administration. Current funding is about $490 million annually, a figure that exceeds appropriations of the early 1990s.[21]

It has been argued that the War on Poverty was never funded at a level that would make a substantial impact. OEO funds were spread over hundreds of communities. Such relatively small amounts could never offset the numerous, deep-seated causes of deprivation. The War on Poverty raised the expectations of the poor, but it never tried to cope with poverty on a scale comparable to the size of the problem. Often the outcome was only to increase frustration.

In an obvious reference to public policies affecting the poor and blacks in America, in 1968, Aaron Wildavsky wrote,

> *A recipe for violence: Promise a lot; deliver a little. Lead people to believe they will be much better off, but let there be no dramatic improvement. Try a variety of small programs, each interesting but marginal in impact and severely underfinanced. Avoid any attempted solution remotely comparable in size to the dimensions of the problem you are trying to solve. Have middle-class civil servants hire upper-class student radicals to use lower-class Negroes as a battering ram against the existing local political systems; then complain that people are going around disrupting things and chastise local politicians for not cooperating with those out to do them in. Get some poor people involved in local decision-making, only to discover that there is not enough at stake to be worth bothering about. Feel guilty about what has happened to black people; tell them you are surprised they have not revolted before; express shock and dismay when they follow your advice. Go in for a little force, just enough to anger, not enough to discourage. Feel guilty again; say you are surprised that worse has not happened. Alternate with a little suppression. Mix well, apply a match, and run.*[22]

It would be difficult to find a better summary of the unintended consequences of the many public programs of the 1960s. The quote also speaks to a more recent event—the 1992 Los Angeles riots that erupted in the wake of the acquittal of white police officers in the beating of Rodney King, an African American stopped for speeding. The rioting renewed the verbiage about a return to community and a revitalization of communities that sounds much like the idea of community action that the creators of the Economic Opportunity Act envisioned. Though as one commentator noted, many middle-class Americans were more concerned about restoring law and order than were with "coming up with money for the urban poor."[23]

WHY HASN'T HEAD START "CURED" POVERTY?

When the Economic Opportunity Act first authorized the creation of local community action programs, responsibility for devising antipoverty projects was to be vested in local participants. But some local officials balked at giving poor people a substantial role in the programs and refused to participate. Within one year, the Johnson administration and the Washington Office of Economic Opportunity decided that Head Start programs were the most desirable antipoverty projects and could reduce opposition to participation.[24] OEO earmarked a substantial portion of funds for Head Start programs. Helping to prepare disadvantaged children for school was certainly more appealing to the middle classes than programs that provided free legal aid for the poor, helped them get on welfare rolls, or organized them to fight city hall. Nearly all the nation's community action agencies operated a Head Start program, and by the late 1960s over one-half million children were enrolled throughout the country. Some communities expanded Head Start to full-time programs and also provided children with health services and improved daily diets. Head Start became OEO's showcase program.

Politics, Evaluation, and Head Start

Head Start was very popular, but were these programs really making a difference? Understandably, Head Start officials within the OEO were discomforted by the thought of a formal evaluation of their program. They argued that educational success was not the only goal of the program, that child health and nutrition and parental involvement were equally important goals. After much internal debate, Sargent Shriver ordered an evaluative study, and in 1968 a contract was given to Westinghouse Learning Corporation and Ohio University to perform the research.

When Richard Nixon assumed the presidency in January 1969, hints of negative findings had already filtered up to the White House. In his first comments on the poverty program, Nixon alluded to studies showing the long-term effects of Head Start as "extremely weak." This teaser prompted the press and Congress to call for the release of the Westinghouse Report. OEO claimed that the results were still "too preliminary" to be revealed. However, after a congressional committee investigation and considerable political pressure, OEO released the report.[25]

The report stated that the researchers had randomly selected 104 Head Start projects across the country. Seventy percent were summer projects, and 30 percent were full-year projects. Children who had gone on from these programs to the first, second, and third grades in local schools (the experimental group) were matched on socioeconomic background with children in the same grades who had not attended Head Start (the control group). The children were given a series of established tests covering various aspects of cognitive and affective development. The parents of both groups of children were also matched on achievement and motivation.

The unhappy results can be summarized as follows: summer programs did not produce improvements in cognitive and affective development that could be detected into the early elementary grades, and full-year programs produced only marginally effective gains for certain subgroups, mainly black children in central cities. However, parents of Head Start children strongly approved of the program.[26]

Head Start officials reacted predictably in condemning the report. Liberals attacked the report believing that President Nixon would use it to justify major OEO cutbacks. The *New York Times* reported the findings under the headline "Head Start Report Held 'Full of Holes.' " It warned that "Congress or the Administration will seize the report's generally negative conclusions as an excuse to downgrade or discard the Head Start Program"[27] (not unreasonable in light of the findings, but politically unacceptable to the liberal community). Academicians moved to the defense of the War on Poverty by attacking methodological aspects of the study. In short, scientific assessment of Head Start was drowned in a sea of political controversy.

Years Later

It is difficult for educators and the social welfare establishment to believe that education, especially intensive preschool education, does not have a lasting effect on the lives of children. The prestigious Carnegie Foundation decided to fund research in Ypsilanti, Michigan, at the Perry Preschool, that would keep tabs on disadvantaged youngsters from preschool to young adulthood. In 1980 a report was released on an eighteen-year study of the progress of a relatively small sample of 123 low-IQ children, fifty-eight of whom (the experimental group) were given a special Head Start-type education at ages 3 and 4 and continued to receive weekly visits throughout later schooling.[28] The others (the control group) received no such special educational help. Both groups came from low socioeconomic backgrounds; half their families were headed by a single parent, and half received welfare. Because the sample was small and local, researchers were able to track the children's progress to age 19.

Initial results were disappointing. Most gains made by the children with preschool education disappeared by the time they had completed second grade (a phenomenon now called "fade out"[29]). As children in the experimental group progressed through grade school, junior high school, and high school, their grades were not better than those of the children in the control group, although they did score slightly higher (by about 8 percent) on reading, mathematics, and language achievement tests. More importantly, only 19 percent of those in the experimental group ended up in special classes for slow learners, compared to 39 percent of the control group. The former preschoolers also showed fewer delinquent tendencies and held more after-school jobs. The key to this success appeared to be a better attitude toward school and learning among those with preschool education. Finally, the former preschoolers were more likely to finish high school and to find jobs and were less likely to be involved in crime and to end up on welfare than the control group.

According to many people, a Head Start-type experience is a bargain to society because it reduces the later need for social welfare programs.[30] Some claim that Head Start benefits exceed per pupil costs at least seven times over.[31] But even academics and researchers who support Head Start are concerned about naive acceptance of this claim. They note that the sevenfold benefit is unsubstantiated and that evaluations of model programs like the Perry Preschool Project (which spent far more per child than does the average Head Start program) indicate what *can* be achieved, not necessarily what *is* being achieved.[32] They further note that there are many positive short-term results of the programs, but that long-term benefits are far more modest than the public has been led to believe. They conclude that much more innovation is needed to help the children of current generations.

The Head Start children of today face more serious social problems.[33] They often have only one parent to support them, and they live in environments where substance abuse, poor education, violence, unemployment, and teen pregnancy are common. They also come from diverse cultures with various languages spoken in the home, providing additional challenges to the staff who operate programs. Since each program is locally managed, there is concern about the quality of the Head Start programs.[34] But Head Start continues to garner political support. President Reagan included it in his social safety net.[35] President Bush proposed substantial increases for Head Start, but he stopped short of Congress's desire to increase funding to allow all eligible children to participate.[36] By 1993, the more than 700,000 children participating[37] were still less than half of all eligible children, despite substantial funding increases over the years.[38] In 1997 more than 1,400 organizations offered Head Start programs to about 800,000 children.[39] More than 13 million children and their families have been served since the program's inception.[40] The programs are now primarily half-day sessions offered throughout the school year to 3- and 4-year-olds. About one-third of the staff are parents of current or former Head Start enrollees.[41] In 1998 Head Start appropriations were nearly $4.4 billion,[42] up from $2.8 billion in 1993.[43] Nearly 900,000 children were expected to participate, with President Clinton hoping to reach 1 million participants by 2002.[44] Among the other efforts to help young children develop is Early Start for children up to age 3. This program also focuses on helping adults better fulfill their roles as parents.

Can government-funded preschool programs have a substantial long-term impact in the life of an individual? According to two people who have studied Head Start over the years,

> *Head Start is not a panacea for poverty, and attempts to posture it as such will lead to an inevitable fall. Clearly, it will be unwise to strengthen our national investment in Project Head Start if this investment is not accompanied by the continuation, improvement, and expansion of the other services and institutions that affect Head Start children and families.*[45]

No politician would seriously threaten the Head Start program, but a series of posters from the U.S. Department of Labor promoting welfare to work (WtW as it is known) programs better captures the spirit of the latest war on poverty. One poster shows a small child asking "Mommy, will we always be on welfare?", and another encourages parents to be good role models for their children by going to work. Thus this chapter turns to work initiatives as a remedy for poverty.

FUELING EMPLOYMENT: MAKE-WORK VERSUS THE REAL THING

The Nixon Administration proposed the Comprehensive Employment and Training Act of 1973 (CETA) to accomplish two major goals:

1. Consolidate job programs from the Manpower Development and Training Act of 1962; the Economic Opportunity Act of 1964, including community action programs featuring job training, the Job Corps, and the Neighborhood Youth Corps; and the Job Opportunities in the Business Sector program.
2. Decentralize these programs, giving control to local governments.

The U.S. Department of Labor was given overall responsibility for consolidating these job-training programs and distributing funds to city, county, and state governments, which served as **prime sponsors** for the programs.

Initially, CETA was directed at the structurally unemployed—the long-term, "hard core" unemployed who have few job skills, little experience, and perhaps other barriers to employment. But later, particularly in response to the economic recession of 1974–1975, Congress included people affected by "cyclical" unemployment—temporary unemployment caused by depressed economic conditions. In order to expand the target group, Congress forced the Nixon and Ford administrations to accept more public-service jobs through CETA than either administration requested.

CETA provided job training for over 3.5 million people per year. Programs included classroom training, on-the-job experience, and public-service employment. Prime sponsor local governments contracted with private community-based organizations (CBOs) to help recruit poor and minority trainees, provide initial classroom training, and place individuals in public-service jobs.

As it turned out, a major share of CETA funds was used by cities to pay individuals to work in regular municipal jobs. CETA offered local governments the possibility of substantially lowering their labor costs by substituting federally paid CETA workers for regular employees. In addition, CETA enabled many local governments to shift regular employees (e.g., police, firefighters, refuse collectors) to the CETA budget. Instead of creating new jobs, a substantial portion of CETA money simply funded a continuation of existing jobs. Obvious substitution occurred when a government laid off employees and then rehired them in their old jobs with CETA funds. Although CETA regulations officially prohibited substitution, estimates were that about half of all CETA jobs were formerly paid for by local governments. Others argued that substitution was not wasteful if municipal employees were going to lose their jobs without CETA assistance. It allowed cities facing financial stress to cut back on their own spending without laying off large numbers of their employees.

But CETA funds were not all targeted to those who needed the assistance most—the economically disadvantaged and long-term, hard-core unemployed. One estimate was that only one-third of all CETA workers came from families receiving public assistance. Prime sponsors tended to skim off the most skilled of the unemployed. Nonetheless, according to federal figures, about 40 percent of the participants were minorities, about 45 percent had less than a high school education, 39 percent were age 21 or younger, and 73 percent were classified as "low income."[46]

The Humphrey-Hawkins Act of 1978 "guaranteed" jobs to every "able and willing" adult American. The ambitious language of the act reflects the leadership of its sponsor, the late Senator Hubert H. Humphrey (D-Minnesota). The act viewed the federal government as "the employer of last resort" and pledged to create public-service jobs and put the unemployed to work on public projects. Lowering the unemployment rate to 3 percent was to be a national goal. But the Humphrey-Hawkins Act is more symbolic of liberal concerns than it is a real national commitment. Of course, pressure on Congress and the president to expand funding for public-service jobs increases during recessions, but it is unlikely that the national unemployment rate will ever be reduced to 3 percent (even in the very strong economic times being experienced now). Despite rhetoric about putting every able-bodied public assistance recipient to work, even if work means community service, Congress is more concerned with the creation of what has been called "real," permanent, private-sector jobs.

The Job Training Partnership Act

In order to address the criticisms, the Reagan administration allowed CETA legislation to expire and replaced it with the Job Training Partnership Act (JTPA) of 1982. JTPA was coauthored by the unlikely team of Senator Edward Kennedy (Democrat-Massachusetts) and former Republican Vice President Dan Quayle while he was an Indiana senator. Funds are provided to states in the form of block grants, and the focus is on helping low-income individuals. The tune of JTPA's goals is familiar: to increase employment and earnings and thereby reduce poverty and welfare dependency among unemployed and underemployed people by providing them with skill training, job search assistance, counselling, and related services. Since JTPA is intended to meet the employment needs of local communities, about 600 Private Industry Councils have been established composed of volunteers from the business sector with knowledge of job skills needed in their communities. The councils give advice to job training centers established by state and local governments with federal funds.

Has JTPA worked? Early evidence, which compared program results with federal performance standards, showed that the number of adults who obtained jobs exceeded the federal standard and that placement costs for adults and youths were lower than the standard.[47] These positive results contrasted with findings that adult participants earned less than the federal standard and that fewer youth participants attained employment competencies, entered training programs, returned to school, and completed school than the standards stipulated. The report also indicated that creaming remained a concern. In 1995, 38 percent of youth who participated in the year-round JTPA program became employed at an average hourly rate of $5.80. Of adult participants leaving JTPA, 63 percent were employed, and they earned an average of $7.26 an hour,[48] a figure substantially higher than the minimum wage.

Although some of these results sound encouraging, they are based on federally determined performance standards; they do not compare JTPA participants with similar individuals who did not participate in JTPA. A later study of about 17,000 adult and youth JTPA applicants provides information eighteen months and 30 months after they made application to the program.[49] Sixteen sites across the country participated. Although the sites were not chosen randomly, they represent a cross section of programs, and applicants were assigned randomly to control and treatment groups. The results for adults (those ages 22 and older) at 18 months can be summarized as follows:

1. The earnings of adult women who were assigned to the JTPA services group increased by an average of $539 or 7.2 percent more than the control group (those not assigned to JTPA services), and employment among the women assigned to JTPA was 2.1 percent higher. The gains in earnings were due to increases in both hours worked and hourly wages. These results were statistically significant.

2. The adult men assigned to receive JTPA services did about as well as the women assigned to JTPA. Their earnings increased by $550, and they had 2.8 percent greater employment than the control group men, but their improvements did not differ statistically from those of the men in the control group.

It is important to note other points about this study. For example, many applicants who were assigned to the JTPA group never actually enrolled in the services, although they are included in the results. The impacts just noted were greater for those people who actually enrolled than for each assignee. Those in the on-the-job training (OJT) and job search assistance group showed the greatest increases in performance over controls. However, subjects were assigned to services based on staff assessments and recommendations. They were not randomly assigned to services. People who received OJT and job search services tended to be the most employable of the applicants. It cannot be determined if these services would have similar effects on less employable adult applicants. Evidence showed that employment barriers (welfare receipt and limited education and work experience) negatively affected adult employment rates. The greatest difference between adult assignees and controls was found among those with fewer employment barriers.

The youth in the study (ages 16 to 21) were not in school at the time of assignment. Over the eighteen-month period, the results for youth indicated that

3. The female youth assigned to receive JTPA services earned $182 less than their female controls. This difference was not statistically significant, and there was also no difference in their employment rates. Many of the young women assigned to JTPA services earned less because they were participating in classroom education rather than paid employment.

4. Findings were the worst for male youth. Although there was no difference in employment rates, the male youths assigned to JTPA services earned $854 (7.9 percent) *less* than their controls, a statistically significant difference. The lack of improvement in males assigned to JTPA services was attributed to the prior arrest record of 25 percent of this group. JTPA assignees with arrest records earned far less than controls (a statistically significant difference); assignees without arrest records also earned less, but this difference was not statistically significant.

There were no differences in youths' outcomes with respect to the services they received or employment barriers. An important positive finding is that significantly more female and male youth in the JTPA services group received a high school diploma or General Equivalency Diploma (GED) certificate than the control group.

Results after 30 months were similar. The researchers concluded "that JTPA works reasonably well for adults," with $1.50 returned in earnings for every $1.00 invested in the program.[50] JTPA participation, however, had little effect on the AFDC benefits received by female members of the treatment group, and food stamp benefits were not affected for men or women. OJT and job search assistance seemed to be particularly successful for the AFDC mothers who received these services. The findings for youth continued to be disappointing. The males in the experimental group still had less earnings than controls, and the females had only small earnings gains that were not statistically significant compared to controls. For both groups of youths, JTPA produced net social *costs*. The researchers also considered subgroups of youths and could not find any group that had earnings gains from JTPA participation. Studies of more intensive services for youth have also not shown positive effects on youth's earnings.

Apparently, a different employment strategy is needed for young people, yet little information is available about what this would be. The researchers suggest rigorous evaluations of strategies such as programs to keep youth from dropping out of school and school-to-work approaches.

Today a special summer JTPA program for economically disadvantaged youths ages 14 to 21 includes remedial education, classroom and on-the-job training, and work experience for which the youths earn the minimum wage. The substantial expenditure of $1 billion for this program in the summer of 1992 included a large additional appropriation made in the wake of the Los Angeles riots; 782,000 youths were served.[51] In fiscal year 1997, $871 million was appropriated and an estimated 530,000 youths were served. The Job Corps, now a part of JTPA, cost $1.2 billion in 1997 with 64,300 new enrollees.[52] There are 111 Job Corps centers around the country. In program year 1995, 75 percent of Job Corps enrollees had "positive terminations" from the program—65 percent entered employment and 10 percent continued their education. Enrollees spent an average of 6.9 months in the program.

The Economic Dislocation and Worker Adjustment Assistance Act expands services available under the JTPA to assist workers affected by major layoffs and plant closures. The act took effect in 1989 and is intended to provide rapid assistance when layoffs and closures occur. Farmers, self-employed people, and long-term unemployed individuals may also qualify. Services include retraining. About $2.2 billion were allocated to the adult JTPA programs in 1997.[53]

Progress Towards One-Stop Shopping at the U.S. Employment Service

One problem with putting more Americans to work is that the labor market does not always coordinate available jobs with unemployed workers. This is particularly true in the case of unskilled and semiskilled workers. In 1933 the U.S. Employment Service (USES) was established under the Wagner-Peyser Act to help the millions of Depression-era unemployed find jobs.[54] Today the USES consists of about 2,000 state-operated employment offices throughout the nation.[55] Employment offices are funded from federal unemployment insurance taxes paid by employers on their employees' wages. The federal government distributes these funds to states using two criteria—the state's share of the labor force and its share of unemployed workers. State USES offices received about 6 million job listings in 1996 and placed about 3.2 million workers.[56]

The USES serves both employers and unemployed workers. It accepts job listings from private and public employers, and it accepts job applications from individuals seeking employment. State employment offices are also supposed to coordinate their efforts with federal and state job initiatives such as JTPA programs in their communities. For both employers and job seekers, these are "free" job services. Most state unemployment insurance programs require recipients to register with USES, and recipients must actively seek employment in their field (see Chapter 4).

In many cases, food stamps and other welfare benefits are distributed to adults on the condition that they register with the USES, whether or not there is a real likelihood that they will be employed. As part of welfare reform, the Clinton administration pledged to "make the welfare office look more like an employment office" and to "make work pay." In order to do this, President Clinton, like President Bush, endorsed the idea of "one-stop shopping"—multiservice centers that would consolidate what has been called the "crazy quilt" of "150 federal job programs run by twenty four-agencies."[57] The federal government has helped a number of states implement these one-stop service centers which help people who are out of work with their unemployment compensation claims, job training, job search, and other employment-related services at a single location, but Congress is having difficulties working out a plan to coordinate its own crazy federal quilt of programs. Although both Republicans and Democrats support the "one stop" concept, turf battles over consolidating programs and issues such as requirements that states would have to meet have bogged down a compromise.[58] Meeting work requirements under the new Temporary Assistance for Needy Families program (see Chapter 6) and the current Food Stamp Program (see Chapter 7) demand much more cooperation between public welfare and employment offices and a variety of other strategies as well.

During his first term, President Clinton convened a seven-nation summit to discuss unemployment. With the passage of the North American Free Trade Agreement (NAFTA) and similar legislation affecting many countries, U.S. employment strategies must include a global perspective. Working in a fast-food restaurant or a movie theater can help young people earn money and learn good work habits, but more Americans must be educated for higher-paying jobs to meet the financial demands of supporting themselves and their families. Congress failed to pass the $16 billion economic stimulus package that President Clinton proposed during his first term. Republicans balked at what they considered more pork during a time when the budget deficit had soared and the economy was moving back on track. Among the Clinton administration's most recent plans is a multimillion-dollar initiative to fill the many job vacancies in computer programming and related high-technology jobs. Funds have been allocated for training low-income and laid-off workers to fill these jobs and to develop an Internet site to match workers and jobs. Efforts will also be made to make "high-tech" careers sound attractive and attainable. At least at these jobs workers can expect to earn a decent wage, afford reliable transportation, and perhaps receive benefits like health insurance.

Should the Minimum Wage Get Another Raise?

Laws establishing minimum wages for workers are an accepted strategy in fighting poverty. The federal Fair Labor Standards Act of 1938 was intended to guarantee a wage that would sustain a decent standard of living for all workers. The minimum wage began at 25 cents per hour (see Table 9-1). The labor act also established a forty-hour work week; employees can work longer, but for hourly-wage workers, overtime usually requires additional pay. Over 90 percent of nonsupervisory personnel are covered by the law, with certain exceptions in retail trade, services, and agriculture.

Many believe that the minimum wage is the most direct and comprehensive way to increase the earnings of the working poor, but if only one person in a household is

TABLE 9-1

The Minimum Wage Since It Was Established in 1938 by the Fair Labor Standards Act

1938	$0.25	1975	$2.10
1939	0.30	1976	2.30
1945	0.40	1978	2.65
1950	0.75	1979	2.90
1956	1.00	1980	3.10
1961	1.15	1981	3.35
1963	1.25	1990	3.80
1967	1.40	1991	4.25
1968	1.60	1996	4.75
1974	2.00	1997 to present	5.15

Source: U.S. Department of Labor, http://www.dol.gov/dol/esa/public/minwage/main.htm.

employed, minimum-wage earnings may fall well below the official poverty level. For example, the poverty threshold (see Chapter 3), for a family of three is about $13,000, while a full time worker earning the federal minimum wage earns a gross salary of $10,300. Certainly, a high minimum wage helps the person who has a job, particularly an unskilled or semiskilled worker who is most likely to be affected by minimum-wage levels. The need for a living or livable wage has been argued consistently. Concerns prevail, however, that increases in the minimum wage increase unemployment by discouraging employers from hiring additional workers who have limited skills and whose labor may not be "worth" the minimum wage. Research shows that past increases in the minimum wage have not resulted in any substantial job loss.[59]

Those who might be excluded from jobs by a higher minimum wage are teenagers, whom some feel have not yet acquired the skills to make their labor commensurate with the minimum wage. A higher minimum wage might induce employers such as fast-food chains, movie theaters, and retail stores to reduce their teenage help to cut costs. At a lower minimum wage, more teens might be expected to find work. The teenage unemployment rate is about three times the adult rate. Some economists claim that youth unemployment is partly a result of the minimum wage, but there is no consensus about whether a reduction or elimination of the minimum for teens would substantially reduce youth unemployment.

One approach to encouraging teenage employment is a "subminimum" or "training wage" that allows employers to pay teenagers less during their first few months of employment. This idea was seriously considered during the Reagan administration. Although the Fair Labor Standards Act was not amended during Reagan's terms, the minimum wage was one of the first major domestic battles of the Bush administration. Bush and Congress favored raising the minimum wage, but they could not agree on how much of a raise was justified. Eleven states had already adopted minimum wage laws that exceeded the federal level, and in other areas employers were paying more than the minimum.[60] Congress agreed on $4.55, but President Bush stood firm on $4.25, the figure ultimately adopted. More controversial was Bush's insistence on a training wage of $3.40 for all workers in their first six months on the job. Congress vehemently opposed this training wage, claiming it would hurt those adult workers who earn the least and change jobs often in order to remain employed. The agreement finally reached included a temporary training wage for teenage workers of $3.35 in 1990 and $3.61 from 1991 to 1993. Employers could pay 16- to 19-year-olds the training wage for the first 90 days of employment if the teenager had not worked before and could extend it for another 90 days if the employer had a training program.

President Clinton favored another increase in the minimum wage, but with health care and welfare reform legislation on the table, it was not until 1996 that a serious effort to give the minimum wage another hike was mounted in Congress. By this time the minimum wage was reported to be at a near 40-year low in purchasing power. In 1996, 5 million Americans 16 years and older who were paid on an hourly basis earned the minimum wage or less; nearly one-third were 16 to 19 years old and half of them were 25 years or older.[61] Proponents of a higher wage argued that it was needed to "make work pay," especially to encourage more people to leave welfare for work. They also argued that the pay of CEOs and other high-end workers had risen much more rapidly than for workers at the low end of the pay scale and that Congress has been far more generous in voting itself pay raises. One argument against the increase was that higher-wage workers would also demand a raise. All these raises would increase employers' costs and result in lost jobs, higher prices to consumers, or both.

There was much political maneuvering over the issue. Democrats tried unsuccessfully to tack the minimum wage measure on to a Republican-favored bill to increase the government's borrowing authority and on an immigration bill. Then Senate Majority Leader Bob Dole, who had voted for raising the minimum wage in the past, wanted to package the new minimum wage bill with other Republican-supported economic measures. President Clinton said he would veto the bill if it included an amendment to exempt new hires and businesses that make less than $500,000 a year. In the end, the bill that was passed raised the minimum to $4.75 initially and then to $5.15 in July 1997. A subminimum wage for those under age 20 in their first 90 days with an employer was set at $4.25 per hour. The additional costs to businesses were cushioned because the bill also included various tax breaks for them. Citing a lack of negative consequences from these recent hikes in the minimum wage, President Clinton and labor advocates want another increase.

There are other ways to raise the wages of the working poor. Some think that the earned income credit (EIC) is a better mechanism. The EIC was raised substantially when President Clinton took office (see Chapters 2 and 6). Other ideas include indexing the minimum wage to inflation or setting it at half of the national average wage, which in May of 1998 was about $12.70 for nonsupervisory employees in private industry.[62] These latter methods are more than Congress would probably entertain.

The minimum wage should be an important consideration in welfare reform as more public assistance recipients are pushed into the workforce. But the emphasis is more on shaping their behavior though work requirements or the "new paternalism" as it has been called.[63] The approach is reflected in the names of states' "WtW" programs such as "Wisconsin Works" and Michigan's "Work First." It is also reflected in the new names of public assistance agencies such as Michigan's Family Independence Agency. President Clinton has issued pleas to "hire a welfare recipient." One way this is being made attractive to business and industry is through tax breaks known as "corporate welfare" (see Chapter 2). Additional employment strategies are the enterprise and empowerment zones described next.

Enterprise and Empowerment Zones

One effort to revitalize communities is called **enterprise zones,** or more recently, **empowerment zones.** Their purpose is to encourage businesses to locate in economically depressed areas in order to boost employment and the local economy and increase community services. One newspaper editorial referred to these zones as "mini tax havens" because of the financial incentives they provide to employers.[64] Enterprise zones have been adopted by state and local governments and were first introduced to Congress about twenty years ago, but Congress was slow to give the approach financial support because of the loss in federal tax revenue. The 1992 Los Angeles riots made Congress rethink its non–decisions. The same editorial called these zones a good idea, but only if the businesses that benefited from them were expected to meet some reasonable goals for hiring disadvantaged residents. Republicans have been strong supporters of this approach because of the business incentives they entail.[65]

In 1993 Congress created funding for nine empowerment zones or EZs (six in urban and three in rural areas) and 95 enterprise communities or ECs (65 in urban and 30 in rural areas), opening competition for $3.5 billion in federal funding. Each empowerment zone selected got tax incentives including as much as $20 million in tax-exempt bonds. For each area resident a business in the zone hires, it can deduct up to $3,000 (20 percent of the first $15,000 of the employee's income) and some training expenses from its taxes. Each urban empowerment zone also got a $100 million social service block grant (for services such as child development, drug treatment, and job training), and each rural zone got $40 million; the enterprise communities received about $3 million each for these purposes. Zone applicants were required to submit a plan for supplementing the federal funding with state and local resources.

In a 1994 *New York Times* article Nicholas Lemann recounted the Great Society effort to revitalize economically depressed cities, noting that such a transformation never occurred and that conditions in inner cities had become worse.[66] Many people are looking to see if federal involvement is making a difference this time as shown in Illustration 9-2. After some delays, Congress appropriated the necessary funds for a second round of EZs and ECs in 1999.

ILLUSTRATION 9-2

Report Card on Empowerment Zones

U.S. urban centers continue to seek effective means of spurring reinvestment and development. The creation of empowerment zones, along with other economic development tools, can assist cities in moving toward their economic goals. An improved local economy, with increased jobs, property valuation, and overall economic activity that expand municipal resources to fund services and infrastructure improvements, can positively impact rating factors over the long term. City administrators and planners point to the leveraging of federal funds and local incentives as a means to stimulate local economies.

Due to the sustained growth in the national and regional economies, the fiscal health of many cities is stronger than in a number of years. While this is a positive and promising trend, a number of underlying challenges remain. During the 1970s and 1980s, a number of cities saw a decline in their ability to provide services because of an erosion in their economic base. Many cities experienced economic dislocation, income declines, declining populations, and lagging job growth that impeded their ability to provide services and attain balanced operations. While much of urban America is on the rebound, many challenges still remain as the new century approaches.

Empowerment zones are designated and designed to stimulate investment, create jobs, expand businesses, and provide support for the community. This concept, in conjunction with broad economic development plans, has been used to stimulate the economy of major urban cities that experienced various degrees of economic decline. In 1994, 72 urban and 33 rural areas were designated as recipients of $1.5 billion in performance grants and $2.5 billion in tax incentives to help stimulate investment in their economies. The June 1997 HUD report, "State of the Cities," calls for an increase in urban empowerment zones to 87. Empowerment zones are intended to work in conjunction with local programs to combine grants, tax incentives and investments to lure new businesses, expand and support existing businesses.

Initially, the federal government chose seven cities—Chicago; Detroit; Baltimore; Philadelphia; Atlanta; Camden, N.J.; and New York—based on proposals submitted to HUD. Since their designations, these cities have had varying degrees of success getting their programs up and running. Problems that slowed or stalled success of the projects included lack of partnerships between community groups and business, and failure to coordinate services available at all levels of government.

URBAN CHALLENGES: JOBS, WEALTH, MIDDLE CLASS MIGRATION

Economic and human resources are necessary to jump-start areas struggling under an eroding economic base, high unemployment, and limited access to financing for infrastructure and other capital projects.

The strength of the U.S. economy over the past several years resulted in a national unemployment rate under 5% and has had a beneficial effect on urban economies. However, the areas with the most vibrant economic growth continue to be in suburban areas, which attracted and created higher-paying professional

continued

ILLUSTRATION 9-2 *(continued)*

jobs as well as lower-paying service and retail jobs.

A significant issue for many urban centers is the transportation to locations where newly created employment opportunities exist. Without a reliable system of transportation, many city residents will not attain the benefits of these opportunities.

Population losses have affected urban centers for the past several decades. Only 21 of the 30 largest cities recorded population gains since 1970. While the U.S. population grew by 4.5 million during the 1970–1990 period, only 20% chose to reside in urban centers. In general, real median family income fell in many of the nation's largest 50 cities.

As the taxpayer base shrinks in urban areas, so do the resources available to fund school districts, repair and maintain infrastructure, and provide cultural and recreational services. Often, city resources are allocated to spruce up decaying downtown areas in order to attract businesses, while surrounding neighborhoods remain neglected.

Empowerment zones are part of a decade-long program that seeks to:

- Leverage private sector investment by using federal and local funding.
- Plan for revitalizing cities by using a federal and local effort that spans multiple years.
- Establish measures for determining progress against established goals, and
- Create cities that form the core of metropolitan regions.

When successful, such efforts can contribute to the improvement of a local economy and lead to an improvement in an issuer's credit rating. For example, Standard & Poor's recently raised Detroit's unlimited tax GO rating to 'BBB+' from 'BBB' and the city's limited tax GO rate to 'BBB' from 'BBB-'. Reversing the trend of a deteriorating economy and financial position is a long-term goal best supported as part of a multi-government effort.

John Fargnoli 212-208-1826
LaVerne Thomas 212-208-1284

DETROIT'S TURNAROUND

In 1994, the federal government designated an 18.4-square mile section as an empowerment zone in Detroit, making the city eligible for $100 million in grants and $250 million in federal tax credits. The Detroit empowerment zone brings together a strong coalition of financial support including a business investment of $43.8 billion.

Ford, Chrysler and General Motors agreed to purchase parts and services from small businesses that locate in the empowerment zone. General Motors alone has earmarked $1 billion in contracts for its suppliers that relocate to the empowerment zone. Since the inception of the empowerment zone, 2,752 jobs have been created and 500 will result from the supplier arrangement. Tax incentives allow companies to take a $3,000 credit for each worker hired. Local banks pledged $1 billion over 10 years for business and home mortgages.

A decidedly pro-business attitude has also helped to re-establish Detroit as a partner with suburban communities to tackle metropolitan economic development. Since 1994, the city's jobless rate declined to 8.7% from 11% as the size of the labor force remained the same and crime rate fell. A

continued

ILLUSTRATION 9-2 *(continued)*

one-stop capital shop and computerized Jobnet employment data bank is scheduled to be operational in the near term, further aiding the city to expand employment opportunities to its citizens.

Kenneth A Gear 212-208-8421

BALTIMORE FOCUSES ON SMALL- AND MEDIUM-SIZED COMPANIES

Baltimore's economic development efforts focus on attracting and retaining small- and medium-sized companies that are increasingly and collectively fueling job growth nationally. Baltimore's use of empowerment zones is one of several tools used to create jobs and improve urban areas. The city targeted life science, warehouse distribution, tourism, and not-for-profit companies as part of economic development. Planning goals include the creation of 8,885 jobs by 2004, representing 3% of the labor force and annual payroll of $151 million, or 1% of city 1995 income. In addition, $225 million in tax credits are available to employers in the empowerment zones. To address the out-migration of the middle class, Baltimore, in partnership with FNMA, created several programs that provide up to $5,000 toward the purchase of a home in an empowerment zone or within the city.

Part of the draw of doing business in a major urban area is ease of product and service distribution and, for employees, the ease of commuting. When 500 employees of Sylvan Learning Systems moved into downtown Baltimore, it marked a departure from the 20-year trend of businesses moving to suburban areas. In order to compete with lower property tax rates, affordable and available housing, cities such as Baltimore developed strategies to compete with suburban towns and cities. Successfully luring Sylvan to the 20-acre Inner Harbor East meant a $32 million facility investment and city housing for many of its employees.

Chesapeake Biological Laboratories Inc. (CBL) provides another example of the federal, state and local coalitions that can bring business back to aging cities. The relocation will create jobs and property tax revenue and play a small role in diversifying the taxpayer base. CBL will receive tax credits, a local loan and state debt financing secured with a bank LOC.

Jodi Hecht 212-208-1727

Source: Standard & Poor's Credit Week Municipal, December 22, 1997, pp. 9–11.

There are other ideas for boosting employment of disadvantaged individuals. For example, "targeted jobs credits" give employers located in various segments of the economy a tax break for hiring economically disadvantaged workers, but the Clinton administration is unconvinced that by themselves these work, because the new employees would likely have been hired anyway. Apprenticeship programs for youth are another alternative, especially for young people who do not go on to college, and there is interest in doing more to help non–college-bound students make the transition to employment with the necessary vocational education and skills.[67]

BUILDING COMMUNITIES THROUGH SERVICE

In 1995, Robert Putnam published an essay entitled "Bowling Alone: America's Declining Social Capital," in which he lamented Americans' lack of "civic engagement" and "passive reliance on the state."[68] (Putnam's cites many examples, the most whimsical being that while more Americans are bowling than ever before, many fewer are bowling in leagues, and many more bowl than vote.) There is a great deal of interest in how to foster a deeper sense of community. One way is through community service as exemplified through a pet program of President Clinton's called AmeriCorps.

AmeriCorps provides various options for Americans 18 years and older to earn money for college or vocational education in exchange for service within the United States. AmeriCorps has subsumed the former VISTA program in a program now called AmeriCorps*VISTA. It also includes AmeriCorps*State and National Direct (members are sponsored by nonprofit organizations) and AmeriCorps*National Civilian Community Corps (participants, ages 18 to 24, live together in one of several designated communities to provide service).

When the President first proposed AmeriCorps, many members of Congress as well as the public gave it a very warm reception. There were some partisan detractors who thought the plan far too ambitious. They felt that the program did not target poor and low-income individuals and that national student loan programs and private initiatives were already available to assist with further education. They also worried that the president's plan would create yet another large federal bureaucracy. In addition to initiating AmeriCorps, the president wanted to change the privately administered student loan program into a federally administered program that would save millions of dollars. Needless to say, the banking industry balked at the potential loss to it in interest payments. The debate turned into a filibuster in the Senate.

What emerged was a diluted version of the Clinton plan, the National and Community Service Trust Act of 1993, which established the Corporation for National Service to administer AmeriCorps. AmeriCorps participants can earn $4,725 for a year of community service (they may serve for two years), which they can use to pay for tuition or student loans. Service may be done before, during, or after their education. They also get a stipend or living allowance of at least $7,400 a year while serving full-time (1,700 hours of work in a nine- to twelve-month period). Part-time work is also permissible for half the stipend. Volunteers serve in educational, public safety, environmental, health, and social welfare positions. They get health care benefits and, if needed, child care benefits. There is no maximum age limit and no financial eligibility requirements to participate. Opponents who have tried to strip AmeriCorps's funding contend that voluntary efforts should not be paid efforts.[69]

As plans were made to accept the first AmeriCorps volunteers, competition for the individual slots and competition among agencies hoping to administer the program locally mounted. The president also got a direct, federal student loan demonstration program enacted with the compromise that it be phased in and provide 60 percent of all new loans by the 1998–1999 school year.[70]

In addition to AmeriCorps, the Corporation for National Service oversees the Senior Corps, which includes the Foster Grandparent Program, the Retired Senior Volunteer Program, the Senior Companion Program, and most recently, the Seniors for Schools initiative, all designed to encourage Americans ages 55 and older to serve their communities. Another of the Corporation's programs is Learn and Serve America which encourages community service by elementary, secondary, and college students. America Reads is an initiative to utilize volunteers from existing Corporation programs and other efforts to see that all children are reading independently by the end of the third grade. The Corporation also administers the National Service Scholarship Program which helps high school students earn $1,000 college scholarships as a reward for outstanding community service.

SUMMARY

Since the New Deal of the 1930s the paradigms of the wars on poverty have changed. The curative strategy of the War on Poverty in the 1960s and 1970s was an attempt to eradicate many of America's social problems, but a decade later 25 million Americans remained poor. The War on Poverty sounded like a creative approach to remedying many social ills, but it was plagued by problems such as inexperienced staff and experimental programs without clear goals. Case studies of Head Start programs, the Comprehensive Employment and Training Act (CETA), and the Legal Services Corporation all illustrate how politics interferes with rational approaches to policymaking. The Office of Economic Opportunity was abolished in 1974. Its remaining programs were transferred to other federal departments.

Despite criticisms of the War on Poverty, many OEO-originated programs such as Head Start and the Legal Services Corporation survive. Although CETA has been replaced with the Job Training Partnership Act, employment and training programs to reduce welfare dependency play a key role in the current social welfare agenda. JTPA and similar programs seem to have at least some positive effects. Other programs that emerged from additional legislation of the Great Society, such as the Food Stamp, Medicare, and Medicaid programs, continue to help millions of people.

The Reagan years witnessed considerable hostility to the ideas of the Great Society. Many programs remained at the status quo during the Bush years. Democratic President Bill Clinton took office with his own set of ideas about how to fight poverty and revitalize communities. President Clinton has been successful in raising the minimum wage and in establishing a program of empowerment zones and enterprise communities. He has encouraged community service and careers in high-tech fields.

Today the cure for poverty, or dependency as the problem is framed, lies in demanding work behavior, but the current federal minimum wage does not ensure an escape from poverty. An improved economy is helping as Americans work to revitalize depressed areas and to renew what many feel is a lost sense of community. In the meantime, there is no getting around the need for a better prepared work force as good jobs require higher levels of skills and global competition mounts. We will have to wait and see if round three of the poverty wars can take another bite out of poverty.

NOTES

1. Cited in Daniel Patrick Moynihan, *Maximum Feasible Misunderstanding* (New York: Free Press, 1969), pp. 3–4; see this book for an account of the early history of the War on Poverty.

2. For an extensive elaboration of this argument, see Charles Murray, *Losing Ground: American Social Policy, 1950–1980* (New York: Basic Books, 1984).

3. Michael Harrington, *The Other America: Poverty in the United States* (New York: Macmillan, 1962).

4. John Kenneth Galbraith, *The Affluent Society* (Boston: Houghton Mifflin, 1958).

5. Executive Office of the President, *Budget of the United States Government, Fiscal Year 1990* (Washington, DC: U.S. Government Printing Office, 1989), pp. 2–26.

6. Executive Office of the President, *Budget of the United States Government, Fiscal Year 1999* (Washington, DC: U.S. Government Printing Office, 1998), p. 273.

7. See Economic Development Administration, "1998 Fact Sheet," March 1998, http://www.doc.gov/eda/1998fct2.htm#EDAlegi.

8. See U.S. Department of Housing and Urban Development, "Community and Economic Development," October 28, 1997, http://www.hud.gov/sec1.htm.

9. Executive Office of the President, *Budget of the United States Government, Fiscal Year 1999*, p. 272.

10. See Bill Keller, "Special Treatment No Longer Given Advocates for the Poor," *Congressional Quarterly*, Vol. 39, No. 16, April 18, 1981, pp. 659–664.

11. This paragraph relies on David Masci, "As New Legal Aid Law Is Written, Old Battles Will Be Refought," *Congressional Quarterly*, Vol. 52, No. 3, January 22, 1994, pp. 123–125; Steven Pressman, "Reagan's Recess Appointments Rankle Hill," *Congressional Quarterly*, Vol. 42, No. 28, July 14, 1984, pp. 1698–1699.

12. Histories of the LSC are found in Henry Cohen, "The Legal Services Corporation," Congressional Research Services Report for Congress, May 7, 1996; Karen Spar, "Legal Services Corporation: Basic Facts and Current Status," Congressional Research Services Report for Congress, May 10, 1996.

13. For stories on the LSC and the judge's ruling on class actions, see Don Van Natta, Jr., "Legal Services Wins Suit for the Poor," *New York Times*, December 27, 1996, pp. B1, 8; Don Van Natta, Jr., "Lawyers Split on Impact of Ruling on Suits for Poor," *New York Times*, December 29, 1996, metro section, p. 27.

14. ABA [American Bar Association] Testimony by Doreen D. Dodson, 105th Congress, Testimony #4, April 17, 1997 (Chicago, IL: American Bar Association).

15. Spar, "Legal Services Corporation: Basic Facts and Current Status," pp. 2, 3.

16. Murray, *Losing Ground: American Social Policy, 1950–1980*, p. 37.

17. This is a quote from Robert Taggart, Office of Youth Programs, U.S. Department of Labor, in the introduction to Charles Mallar, Stuart Kerachsky, Craig Thornton, Michael Donihue, Carol Jones, David Long, Emmanuel Noggoh, and Jennifer Schore, *The Lasting Impacts of Job Corps Participation, Youth Knowledge Development Report 3.4* (Washington, DC: U.S. Department of Labor, May 1980), p. ii.

18. Laurie J. Bassi and Orley Ashenfelter, "The Effect of Direct Job Creation and Training Programs on Low-Skilled Workers," in Sheldon H. Danzinger and Daniel H. Weinberg, eds., *Fighting Poverty: What Works and What Doesn't* (Cambridge, MA: Harvard University Press, 1986), p. 149.

19. *War on Poverty—Victory or Defeat*, Hearing Before the Subcommittee on Monetary and Fiscal Policy of the Joint Economic Committee, Congress of the United States, 99th Congress, 1st Session, June 20, 1985.

20. Executive Office of the President, Office of Management and Budget, *Major Policy Initiatives, Fiscal Year 1990* (Washington, DC: U.S. Government Printing Office, 1989), pp. 122–123.

21. See Jill Zuckman, Jeffrey L. Katz, and Thomas H. Moore, "Low-Income Programs," *Congressional Quarterly, Special Report*, Vol. 51, Supplement to No. 49, December 11, 1993, p. 104; "Fiscal 1998 Labor-HHS-Education Spending," *Congressional Quarterly*, November 15, 1997, p. 2857.

22. Aaron Wildavsky, "The Empty Headed Blues: Black Rebellion and White Reactions," *Public Interest*, No. 11, Spring 1968, pp. 3–4.

23. Bob Greene (Tribune Media Services), "Middle-Class Demands for Police Likely to Be Legacy of L.A. Riots," *Austin American-Statesman*, May 12, 1992, p. A10.

24. Edward Zigler, Sally J. Styfco, and Elizabeth Gilman, "The National Head Start Program for Disadvantaged Preschoolers," in Edward Zigler and Sally J. Styfco, eds., *Head Start and Beyond: A National Plan for Extended Childhood Intervention* (New Haven, CT: Yale University Press, 1993), pp. 1–41.

25. Westinghouse Learning Corporation, Ohio University, *The Impact of Head Start* (Washington, DC: Office of Economic Opportunity, 1969).

26. For additional information on an early study, see David P. Weikart, Dennis J. Deloria, Sarah A. Lawser, and Ronal Wiegerink, *Longitudinal Results of the Ypsilanti Perry Preschool Project* (Ypsilanti, MI: High/Scope Educational Research Foundation, August 1970).

27. See James E. Anderson, *Public Policy-Making* (New York: Holt, Rinehart, & Winston, 1975), p. 150.

28. These results are summarized in *Newsweek,* December 22, 1980, p. 54. Also see the series of monographs of the High/Scope Educational Research Foundation, Ypsilanti, Michigan, reporting the results of studies of the Perry Preschool Project.

29. See Deborah A. Phillips and Natasha J. Cabrera, eds., *Beyond the Blueprint: Directions for Research on Head Start's Families* (Washington, DC: National Academy Press, 1996). An extensive annotated bibliography on Head Start and related preschool program research is available from the Department of Health and Human Services and can be found at http://www.acf.dhhs.gov.cgi-bin/hs/text_field_search.

30. For additional information on evaluations of early education programs, see Nathan Glazer, "Education and Training Programs and Poverty," in Danzinger and Weinberg, *Fighting Poverty: What Works and What Doesn't,* pp. 153–179; Zigler, Styfco, and Gilman, "The National Head Start Program for Disadvantaged Preschoolers."

31. See Ann Crittenden, "A Head Start Pays Off in the End," *Wall Street Journal,* November 29, 1984, p. 32.

32. See Zigler, Styfco, and Gilman, "The National Head Start Program for Disadvantaged Preschoolers."

33. The challenges faced by Head Start programs are summarized in Valora Washington and Ura Jean Oyemade Bailey, *Project Head Start: Models and Strategies for the Twenty-First Century* (New York: Garland, 1995).

34. Zigler, Styfco, and Gilman, "The National Head Start Program for Disadvantaged Preschoolers"; Zuckman, et al., "Low Income Programs"; Washington and Bailey, *Project Head Start: Models and Strategies for the Twenty-First Century.*

35. Washington and Bailey, *Project Head Start: Models and Strategies for the Twenty-First Century.*

36. Julie Rovner, "Full Funding for Head Start Approved by Senate Panel," *Congressional Quarterly,* June 30, 1990, p. 2072.

37. Committee on Ways and Means, U.S. House of Representatives, *Overview of Entitlement Programs: 1993 Green Book* (Washington, DC: U.S. Government Printing Office, 1993), p. 1691.

38. Zuckman, et al., "Low-Income Programs," p. 104.

39. Administration on Children and Families, Head Start Bureau, "Head Start Frequently Asked Questions," October 23, 1997, http://www.acf.dhhs.gov/programs/hsb/faq.htm.

40. "Head Start . . . how and why it works," prepared by the U.S. Department of Health and Human Services, Administration for Children and Families, can be found on the web site of the Santa Clara County, CA Office of Education at http://www.sccoe.k12.ca.us/child/highscop.htm.

41. L. Brush, A. Gaidurgis, and C. Best, *Indices of Head Start Program Quality* (Washington, DC: Administration for Children, Youth and Families, 1993) cited in Washington and Bailey, *Project Head Start: Models and Strategies for the Twenty-First Century,* p. 62.

42. "Fiscal 1998 Labor-HHS-Education Spending, *Congressional Quarterly,* November 15, 1997, p. 2857.

43. Committee on Ways and Means, *1993 Green Book,* p. 1691.

44. Executive Office of the President, *Budget of the United States Government, Fiscal Year 1998* (Washington, DC: U.S. Government Printing Office, 1997), p. 58.

45. Washington and Bailey, *Project Head Start: Models and Strategies for the Twenty-First Century,* p. 141; also see John Hood, "Caveat Emptor: The Head Start Scam," *Policy Analysis,* No. 187, December 18, 1992, http://www.cato.org/pubs/pas/pa-187.html; William Julius Wilson, *When Work Disappears* (New York: Alfred A. Knopf, 1996), p. xv.

46. Executive Office of the President, *Budget of the United States Government, Fiscal Year 1982* (Washington, DC: U.S. Government Printing Office, 1981) p. 220.

47. Grinker Associates, *An Independent Sector Assessment of the Job Training Partnership Act, Final Report, Program Year 1985* (New York: Author, 1986).

48. Committee on Ways and Means, U.S. House of Representatives, *1998 Green Book: Background Material and Data on Programs Within the Jurisdiction of the Committee on Ways and Means* (Washington, DC: U.S. Government Printing Office, 1998), pp. 1003–1004.

49. Howard S. Bloom, Larry L. Orr, George Cave, Stephen H. Bell, and Fred Doolittle, *The National JTPA Study: Title II-A Impacts on Earnings and Employment at 18 Months* (Bethesda, MD: Abt Associates, 1993).

50. Larry L. Orr, Howard S. Bloom, Stephen H. Bell, Fred Doolittle, Winston Lin, and George Cave, *Does Training for the Disadvantaged Work? Evidence from the National JTPA Study* (Washington, DC: Urban Institute Press, 1996).

51. See Committee on Ways and Means, *1998 Green Book,* pp. 1006–1008.

52. Data in the remainder of this paragraph rely on Committee on Ways and Means, *1998 Green Book,* pp. 933–934.

53. Executive Office of the President, *Budget of the United States Government, Fiscal Year 1998,* p. 66.

54. See Henry P. Guzda, "The U.S. Employment Service at 50: It Too Had to Wait Its Turn," *Monthly Labor Review,* Vol. 106, No. 6, June 1983, pp. 12–19.

55. U.S. Department of Labor Program Highlights, "Employment Service," Fact Sheet No. ETA 90-1, http://www.doleta.gov/uses/proghigh.htm, accessed June 22, 1998.

56. U.S. Bureau of the Census, *Statistical Abstract of the United States: 1998* (Washington, DC: U.S. Government Printing Office, 1998), Table 684, p. 426.

57. "Clinton Proposes Changes in Unemployment, Training," *Austin American-Statesman,* March 10, 1994, p. A2.

58. "Issue: Job Training Programs," *Congressional Quarterly,* December 6, 1997, pp. 3015–3016; Mary Agnes Carey, "Senate Jobs Bill Heads to Floor; Enactment Unlikely This Year," *Congressional Quarterly,* September 27, 1997, p. 2320.

59. "Statement of Robert B. Reich Secretary of Labor Before the Joint Economic Committee," Congressional Testimony, February 22, 1995, http://www.dol.gov/search97cgi/s97-cgi.exe.

60. Charles Green, "Senate Sends Minimum Wage Bill to Bush," *Austin American-Statesman,* November 9, 1989, p. A4.

61. U.S. Bureau of Labor Statistics, unpublished data, cited in U.S. Bureau of the Census, *Statistical Abstract of the United States: 1997,* Table 675, p. 433.

62. U.S. Bureau of Labor Statistics, "Nonfarm Payroll Statistics from the Current Employment Statistics (National) Home Page," June 22, 1998, http://146.142.4.24/cgi-bin/surveymost.

63. Lawrence M. Mead, ed., *The New Paternalism: Supervisory Approaches to Poverty* (Washington, DC: Brookings Institution, 1997).

64. This paragraph relies on "Done Right, Enterprise Zones Can Benefit All," *Austin American-Statesman,* June 21, 1992, p. D2.

65. Also see "Issue: Enterprise Zones," *Congressional Quarterly,* Special Report, Vol. 51, December 11, 1993, p. 3391.

66. Nicholas Lemann, "The Myth of Community Development," *New York Times Magazine,* January 9, 1994, p. 27.

67. Jill Zuckman, "Hill Gives Friendly Greeting to School-to-Work Plan," *Congressional Quarterly,* August 7, 1993, p. 2163; Executive Office of the President, *Budget of the United States Government, Fiscal Year 1999,* p. 210.

68. Robert Putnam, "Bowling Alone: America's Declining Social Capital," *Journal of Democracy,* January 1995, pp. 65–78.

69. "Clinton Seeking 5-Year Extension for AmeriCorps," *Austin American-Statesman,* November 30, 1997, p. A8.

70. "Direct Student Loans," *Congressional Quarterly,* Special Report, Vol. 51, December 11, 1993, pp. 3394–3395.

CHAPTER

Providing Social Services: Help for Children, the Elderly, and People with Mental Illness

SOCIAL SERVICES IN THE UNITED STATES

Social welfare programs are often equated with programs for the poor, but there are many social services that people may need regardless of their income and social status. Developing a list of all the social services available in the United States is nearly impossible, but it would include a number of services for individuals, families, and also communities.[1] Among the services for individuals are those that target children, including community youth centers, child protective services, foster home care, adoption assistance, and voluntary guidance programs such as Big Brothers and Big Sisters of America. Other services are for individuals who are disabled or elderly, such as transportation, homemaker and chore services, opportunities for socialization at senior citizen centers or other community programs, adult protective services, and long-term care. Social services may also benefit families. Services aimed at family units include family planning; marital and family counseling; day care and after-school care for children; assessments for courts and schools; family preservation and renunificiation services when abuse or neglect has occurred; and respite care to provide relief to caretakers of older or disabled family members. Still other services are called **community organization** because they involve mobilizing groups such as community residents concerned about drugs and crime, mothers receiving welfare, migrant workers, newly arrived immigrants, tenants, individuals with disabilities and their families, and even gang members, to achieve beneficial goals for themselves and their communities.

Some services, such as education, counseling, and rehabilitation, are offered in several types of settings—churches, schools, general hospitals, workplaces, community mental health centers, outpatient treatment centers for alcoholics and drug abusers, and residential facilities such as juvenile detention centers, psychiatric hospitals, and community residences and state schools for those with mental or physical disabilities. To this growing list of services we can add information, referral, advocacy, and consumer services of various types, and there are many more. During their lifetimes, virtually all Americans will use some type of social services.

Who Provides Social Services?

Social services are provided by five types of organizations: (1) public agencies; (2) private not-for-profit corporations; (3) private for-profit corporations; (4) self-help groups, and (5) religious organizations. Services such as day care may be provided by all these types of organizations. Other services, such as child and adult protection, are provided only by public agencies or their designees, because these agencies have the legal right to intervene in cases of neglect or abuse.

Public agencies are established by law and are operated by federal, state, or local governments. The U.S. Department of Health and Human Services (DHHS) is the major federal agency responsible for social welfare services. Some states also have large umbrella agencies for the many departments that deliver the states' social services. In other states, several separate agencies administer the various social welfare programs. Many counties and cities also operate social welfare agencies.

Private not-for-profit corporations, also called **voluntary** agencies, are governed by boards of directors or trustees. These agencies may receive funds from endowments and donations; client fees; other community organizations such as the United Way; or local, state, and federal governments in the form of grants, contracts, or fees for service. Private not-for-profit agencies provide a multitude of services, such as day care for children, mental health services, and nursing home care. Many of these agencies charge fees to clients on a sliding scale, based on the client's ability to pay for the services. Other not-for-profit agencies, such as rape crisis centers, generally do not charge their clients. Some not-for-profit corporations act as advocates for their clientele by informing policymakers and the public of their clients' needs. The Arc (formerly the Association for Retarded Citizens of the United States) and its local affiliates, the Child Welfare League of America, and the National Council on Alcoholism and Drug Dependence are private not-for-profit organizations.

Private profit-making organizations are also called **proprietary agencies.** They too provide services like child care, nursing home care, and mental health care, but generally charge their clients for services at the current market rate. Government agencies sometimes purchase services from private agencies, because the government may not directly provide a service needed by a client and cannot obtain it from a not-for-profit agency more economically. A great deal of Medicaid funds are used to purchase long-term care from proprietary nursing homes.

Self-help groups also provide social services but generally do not rely on governmental funding at all. Their structure is less formal than other social service agencies. Alcoholics Anonymous (AA), the best known self-help group, was founded in 1935 and helps people with drinking problems. The only requirement for membership is the desire to stop drinking. The group relies solely on its members for financial support. The self-help category also includes **cooperatives** where people band together to share child care, to purchase groceries more economically, or achieve another mutual goal. Other self-help organizations have emerged to assist people with mental disorders and their families, including the National Alliance for the Mentally Ill and Recovery, Inc. Some of these groups may be organized as not-for-profit corporations, but their focus is on mutual aid provided by those who share a common problem, rather than reliance on professional service providers.

Finally, religious organizations have a long history of providing social services. Although their services are generally provided by the clergy or lay members of a particular religious sect, they may be available to people regardless of their personal religious beliefs. Among the services religious groups offer are child care, crisis pregnancy counseling, adoption, mental health counseling, food and shelter for people who are homeless or poor, and outreach to those who are incarcerated.

These different types of agencies can allow consumers more choice when it comes to selecting services. However, Chapter 2 discussed a blurring of the sectors as governments pursue policies of privatization. In addition, more privately operated social service organizations have come to accept public funds in order to fill service gaps and sustain their missions. Many alternative service organizations originally emerged because the public sector was not providing needed services (such as rape crisis or substance abuse services) or it was not sensitive to the concerns of particular clientele (such as women or lesbians and gay men). One effect public monies can have is to subvert the original intent of these alternative agencies, because they must now conform to the expectations of these funders.[2] In other words, the various types of social service agencies may look more and more alike.

The Development of Social Services

Before the 1900s, social services were provided by family members, neighbors, church groups, private charitable organizations, and local governments in the form of indoor and outdoor relief (see Chapter 2). In fact, the Charity Organization Societies of the late 1800s, which helped poor people, preferred to provide social services rather than financial aid. During the first half of the twentieth century, the federal and state governements largely provided cash and in-kind assistance to destitute people. Although child welfare services were part of the original Social Security Act of 1935, most social services remained outside federal purview until 1956 when Congress amended the Social Security Act to provide social services to families on relief.[3]

More social service amendments were added to the Social Security Act in 1962 and 1967 (also see Chapter 6). The rationale was to rehabilitate poor people, help them overcome their personal problems, and thereby reduce their dependence on welfare. The federal government began giving the states three dollars for every dollar the states spent on social services, with virtually no limit on spending. The federal government's willingness to subsidize social services was a boon to the states that were willing to increase the social services available to clients. But the costs of social services increased so fast—from $282 million in 1967 to $1.7 billion in 1973[4]—that Congress decided to take action. In 1976 Title XX was added to the Social Security Act to place a ceiling on expenditures and to ensure that the majority of federally funded social services went to the poor.

In 1981, the Reagan administration convinced Congress to replace Title XX with the Social Services Block Grant. The goals of the block grant are to increase economic self-support and self-sufficiency, reduce abuse and neglect of children and adults, reduce inappropriate institutional care, and secure institutional care when needed. The grant is based on the premises that economic and social needs are interrelated and that states know best what services their residents need. State matching requirements were eliminated, and block grant funds are now allocated to states on the basis of population. But under the block grant, federal contributions to social services have decreased considerably. After accounting for inflation, figures show a 67 percent spending reduction from 1977 to 1997.[5] States initially reacted to the cuts by appropriating more state money for social services.[6] Most funds do go to assist low-income clients, and states are most likely to use their block grant funds for child welfare and related family services as well as adult protective services.[7] Federal expenditures for the Title XX Social Services Block Grant are capped at about $2.4 billion through fiscal year 2002 and at $2.8 billion thereafter.

Since the Reagan era, block grants have become the federal government's primary tool for supporting social services. In addition to the Title XX Social Services Block Grant, the Preventive Health and Health Services Block Grant, the Maternal and Child Health Services Block Grant, the Substance Abuse Prevention and Treatment Block Grant, the Community Mental Health Services Block Grant, the Low-Income Home Energy Assistance Block Grant, the Developmental Disabilities Assistance and Bill of Rights Act, the Older Americans Act, and many other pieces of federal, state, and local legislation also provide social service funding.

A significant development in social welfare is the recognition that those who are not poor can also benefit from social services. The growth of private social service agencies that cater to middle- and upper-class groups is an indication that many Americans need social services. People with problems of mental illness, alcohol and other drug abuse, child abuse and neglect, and the frailties that may accompany old age are among those who have received increased attention from social service providers since the 1960s. Social welfare policies that affect these groups are discussed in the following pages.

SOCIAL SERVICES FOR PEOPLE WITH ADM PROBLEMS

Among the many obstacles to rationalism in providing alcohol, drug abuse, and mental health (ADM) services is a lack of consensus about how to define these problems, how to identify the number in need, how to determine the services best suited to remedying these problems, and assuring that those in need have access to services.

Defining the Problems

Mental health professionals have long debated the best way to define mental illnesses,[8] but as laypeople we may conceptualize mental health and mental illness as two ends of a continuum. At one extreme are people who behave in an acceptable manner. At the other extreme are people with psychoses who are unable to cope with reality and cannot function within the community. Depression is a common mental health problem that can range from mild and temporary to so severe that an individual may become dysfunctional and even suicidal. The American Psychiatric Association publishes a manual for mental health professionals called the *Diagnostic and Statistical Manual of Mental Disorders* (*DSM*) that describes dozens of mental health and alcohol and drug problems. Even this guide is controversial, because it drives the way mental health professionals are paid for their services, and it promotes labeling and categorizing people even when they may not specifically fit these categories, or when labeling may be counterproductive for the individual.[9]

All people experience emotional stress at some time in their lives. Most do not need professional help. Time and the care and concern of family and friends is generally sufficient to see them through these difficult times. Today more emphasis is placed on preventing mental health problems and treating them before they become severe. Mental health professionals, particularly in the private sector, are as likely to see family members with temporary adjustment problems to divorce or the loss of a loved one, as they are to see those who are severely depressed, suicidal, or schizophrenic.

Many people who need professional assistance seek treatment voluntarily, but many Americans cannot locate affordable or free services. Others with severe mental illness may not recognize their need for treatment, and in these cases, state and local policies stipulate the conditions under which an individual may be judged mentally ill and in need of treatment. Involuntary admission to a psychiatric hospital is generally reserved for people who psychiatrists believe are dangerous to themselves or others and who may not perceive the need for treatment. Involuntary commitment laws are controversial because there can be a fine line between involuntary hospitalization and civil rights infringements.

Defining mental disorders, alcoholism, and other drug problems is also difficult because there is no proof of the cause of many of these problems. The disease or biological model of chemical dependency has been useful in reducing stigma and promoting treatment, but this model is just one of several that has been used to describe alcohol and other drug problems.[10] Psychological and sociocultural theories often seem just as convincing in explaining these conditions.

Estimating Problems and Services

Despite disagreements about definitions, governmental bodies do estimate the numbers of people who experience mental illness and substance abuse. According to a major national survey based on psychiatric interviews, 48 percent of those ages 15 to 54 have had at least one psychiatric disorder during their lifetimes, and almost 30 percent reported at least one disorder in the last year.[11] The most common diagnoses were major depression, alcohol dependence, and certain phobias. Among those with a lifetime addictive disorder, 41 to 66 percent also had a mental disorder, and among those with at least one mental disorder, 51 percent had an addictive disorder.[12] There is a special concern about the population with severe mental illness, generally defined as those having a mental disorder and serious impairment within the last year.[13] Using this definition, 5.4 percent of the population had serious mental illness, with 2.6 percent meeting an even more stringent definition referred to as serious and persistent mental illness. Data also indicate that 9 to 13 percent of children ages 9 to 17 have serious emotional disturbance.[14]

Twenty-seven percent of Americans had a substance abuse or dependence diagnosis in their lifetimes, and 11 percent in the last year. In 1996, there were nearly 488,000 drug-related hospital emergency room episodes nationwide, fewer than the 518,000 reported in 1995.[15] Alcohol and other drug use among young people continues to be a concern. According to the 1997 National Household Survey on Drug Abuse, 4.8 million young people ages 12–20 reported that they had engaged in binge drinking (they drank 5 or more drinks on at least one occasion in the last month), and 2 million were heavy drinkers (they drank 5 or more drinks per occasion on 5 or more days in the past month). Among youths ages 12–17, 11 percent used an illicit drug in the past month (the rate was 5.3 percent in 1992). An estimated 1.1 million Americans used hallucinogens for the first time, 675,000 Americans used cocaine for the first time, and 171,000 used heroin for the first time. Although the overall number of cocaine users did not change significantly from 1996 to 1997, the number of heroin users grew, with the initiation rate for youth at a 30-year high. In addition, "more than half of all youth ages 12–17 reported that marijuana was easy to obtain. About 21 percent reported that heroin was easy to obtain. Fifteen percent of youth reported being approached by someone selling drugs during the 30 day period prior to the interview."[16] There is also concern that the alcohol and other drug problems of older Americans are underestimated.

Since a substantial percentage of the population have mental or substance use disorders, service providers are particularly anxious to find successful treatment approaches. But only a small portion receive assistance. Evidence shows that "only four of every ten respondents with a lifetime history of at least one disorder ever obtained professional help, only one in four obtained treatment in the mental health specialty sector, and about one in twelve were treated in substance abuse facilities."[17] Among those who experienced problems in the last year, "only one in five obtained any professional treatment, one in nine obtained treatment in the mental health specialty sector, and one in twenty-five were treated in substance abuse facilities."[18] These data are consistent with previous studies that show that most people with diagnosable disorders get no treatment at all. Each year the federal agency called the Substance Abuse and Mental Health Services Administration (SAMHSA) attempts to count the number of clients receiving substance abuse services in public, private nonprofit, and private for-profit facilities on a particular day as an estimate of the number of clients in treatment.[19] Of 13,562 facilities contacted, 10,641 responded. On October 1, 1996, these facilities reported that approximately 940,000 individuals were receiving specialty treatment for substance use disorders. The vast majority (88 percent) were receiving outpatient services.

Achieving Treatment Parity

Mental and substance disorders exact a high price from society. In 1990, these costs were estimated at $314 billion (50 percent from lost productivity from injury, illness, and premature death, 28 percent due to health care and treatment costs, and 22 percent due to crime and criminal justice costs).[20] Any U.S. family that has not been touched by these problems is indeed lucky. No wonder these problems rate high on the public's list of the nation's ills. Treatment advocates want to increase access to services and promote more adequate and earlier treatment. Many believe that these goals could be achieved through a national health care plan (see Chapter 8) that includes the same coverage for these problems as for other health problems.

One step in this direction is the federal Mental Health Parity Act of 1996 which generally prevents employers with more than 50 employees who offer health plans that include mental health coverage from imposing more restrictive annual or lifetime dollar limits on these services than they do on medical or surgical care. A closer look shows that the act does not solve the parity problem. It does not require an employer to offer mental health coverage; it does not pertain to those with less than 50 employees; it exempts employers if the costs of compliance are at least 1 percent of the health plan's annual costs; it does not prevent plans from limiting the number of visits covered or requiring copayments or deductibles; and care can be limited to that deemed "medically necessary."[21] Furthermore, the act does not include care for substance disorders. State laws also affect parity, and some achieve greater parity than the federal act. For instance, "while parity in Maryland means coverage for all mental disorders and substance abuse treatment, parity in New Hampshire refers to treatment coverage for specific biologically based severe mental disorders."[22] The Congressional Budget Office estimated that the costs of mental health parity to the private sector would be 4 percent of health insurance premiums.[23] Other reports point to the positive experience that some insurers have had following compliance with their state's parity law.[24]

Despite a substantial "offset" literature demonstrating cost savings,[25] not to mention the humanitarian benefits of mental health care, true parity may be a long way off. This is especially true of alcohol and drug problems which receive a much more ambivalent reception from politicians and the public than do mental health problems like depression. The physician president of the Washington Business Group on Health Care is more optimistic. She believes that "one of the messages conveyed by the recently enacted mental health law is that arbitrary benefit limits to control use of mental health and substance abuse services soon will be unacceptable."[26] Meanwhile, many people with medical coverage have limited mental health and substance abuse coverage or have no coverage at all.

The differences between the public and private tiers of the health care system (also see Chapter 8) is even more pronounced in the mental health and chemical dependency treatment delivery systems. Private insurance coverage for mental illness emerged in the 1950s, and separate coverage for substance use disorders began in the 1970s.[27] But we should not forget that the public sector often offers clients a broader range of services than the private sector. For example, public mental health services may offer housing, child care, and other supportive services for clients and their families at low or no cost that the private sector may not offer at all, even if one can afford to pay for these services.[28]

Finding Better Prevention and Treatment Approaches

People with mental illness were once thought to be possessed by the devil and were hidden away from public view, but by the nineteenth century treatment began to take different forms.[29] Phillipe Pinel, a French physician, introduced "moral treatment," which consisted of caring for patients with kindness and consideration, providing the opportunity for discussion of personal problems, and encouraging an active orientation to life. This was a far more humane approach to treating mental illness, but it was not the treatment offered to most patients. Institutionalization or incarceration were the typical methods for dealing with mental illness. Dorothea Dix, a social reformer during the mid-1800s, sought to improve the plight of severely mistreated mental patients. Dix succeeded in improving conditions within mental institutions, but with increasing numbers of people being labeled mentally ill, institutions grew larger and less capable of helping patients.

The Industrial Revolution increased many social problems, including mental illness. People came to the cities seeking jobs and wealth; instead many found overcrowding, joblessness, and misery. Coping with urban problems was difficult, and new arrivals were often without the support of family and friends. Immigrants from other countries also flocked to the cities. Those who did not acculturate or assimilate quickly into U.S. society were often labeled deviant or mentally ill.[30] City dwellers, overwhelmed with problems, had little tolerance for behavior they considered abnormal. This increased the number of people sent to mental institutions.

Apart from state institutions, there was little in the way of social policies and public programs for people with mental illness. Following Dix's efforts, Clifford Beers introduced the "mental hygiene movement" in the early twentieth century. In 1909 he founded the National Mental Health Association. Beers knew well the dehumanizing conditions of mental institutions; he himself had been a patient. His efforts to expose the inhumane conditions of the institutions, like Dix's, resulted in better care, but the custodial and institutional philosophies of mental health treatment continued.

During World War II, a large number of young men were needed for military service. Part of the screening procedure for new recruits was a psychiatric examination. The number of young men rejected as unfit for military service or later discharged for psychiatric reasons was alarming. Although these psychiatric screening procedures have been criticized, the identification of so many young men with mental problems brought renewed concern for mental health. This concern was reflected in the Mental Health Act of 1946. The act established the National Institute of Mental Health (NIMH), with its focus on training, education, and research.

In the 1950s another important event occurred—the development of improved psychotherapeutic drugs that reduced many of the troubling symptoms (such as hallucinations) that patients experienced. This allowed hospital staffs to reduce restrictions placed on patients and made patients more acceptable to the community. Psychotropic medications can have serious side effects, and the appropriate use of drug therapy has been debated,[31] but it is evident that they have reduced the need for hospitalization for many patients. New and better drugs are being developed all the time, but they are often costly, thus prohibiting more people from obtaining them.

The use of psychotherapeutic drugs helped to lay the groundwork for the Community Mental Health Act of 1963. The act was a key element of an emerging community mental health movement. It emphasized more federal involvement in community-based care, better coordination between hospitals and community services, improved services to people with serious mental illness, a reduction in state hospital treatment, an increase in community treatment consistent with deinstitutionalization and normalization (also see Chapter 5), education and prevention services, and greater use of paraprofessional staff.

Community Mental Health Centers

The Mental Retardation Facilities and Community Mental Health Centers Construction Act of 1963, often called the Community Mental Health Act, mandated that community mental health centers (CMHCs) provide five essential services: inpatient care, outpatient care, emergency services, partial hospitalization (day care), and consultation and education. In 1975 more essential services were mandated, including special programs for children and the elderly, aftercare and halfway house services for patients discharged from mental health hospitals, and screening services to courts and related agencies to identify those in need of treatment. In 1977 NIMH began the Community Support Program which established federal-state partnerships to encourage long-term care for those with serious mental illness.

In the 1970s, a number of studies evaluated the success of community mental health centers.[32] The General Accounting Office discussed the positive effects of CMHC programs, including an increase in the availability of community care. In another report, the Senate Committee on Labor and Public Welfare also discussed the positive results achieved by community-based care. Some reports were not as complimentary. A 1974 report by Ralph Nader stated that CMHCs had not reduced the number of people admitted to state mental hospitals and accused psychiatrists of benefiting unfairly from the programs and of neglecting services to the poor.

To improve services, the Mental Health Systems Act of 1980 continued many provisions of the Community Mental Health Act and included recommendations of the President's Commission on Mental Health, appointed by Jimmy Carter in 1977 and headed by First Lady Rosalyn Carter. There were provisions for special groups, including people with serious mental illness, severely disturbed children and adolescents, and others who were unserved or underserved. The act was rescinded in 1981 shortly after President Ronald Reagan took office and attention was directed back to the states.[33] Today, CMHCs are no longer required to provide the essential services formerly identified, and federal funds are channeled through block grants. Each state must now develop a State Comprehensive Mental Health Services Plan. These three-year plans cover services to people with serious mental illness, homeless people with mental illness, and children with severe disturbances. NIMH recommends one or more of the following services for them: residential services (e.g., short-term crisis stabilization units and supported housing options); client and family support (e.g., counseling, medication services, and emergency screening); psychosocial habilitation or rehabilitation (for developing vocational, social, and independent living skills); case management (e.g., coordination of multiple services needed by clients and outreach). Special initiatives such as the PATH and ACCESS programs are efforts to prevent or remedy homelessness among people with mental illness.

A major study of the effectiveness of mental health services conducted by the National Association of Social Workers found that short-term treatment tends to produce better outcomes than long-term treatment.[34] The news that short-term services are of benefit is certainly encouraging in this era of managed care when health plans are authorizing less treatment for mental as well as physical illnesses. Unfortunately, this has also meant that patients may get outpatient care when professionals think they need inpatient care or less intensive services when more intensive services seem warranted.[35]

A War on Drugs or on Drug Addicts?

Concerted federal efforts to assist alcoholics did not occur until passage of the Comprehensive Alcohol Abuse Prevention, Treatment, and Rehabilitation Act of 1970. The act established the National Institute on Alcohol Abuse and Alcoholism (NIAAA). This was soon followed by the establishment of the National Institute on Drug Abuse (NIDA). These actions were the first major governmental attempts to recognize alcohol and drug dependence as treatable illnesses.

When Ronald Reagan collapsed funding for alcohol, drug abuse, and mental health services under a single block grant, the federal funds available to states were reduced. Critics continue to contend that this fiscal austerity has contributed both to homelessness among people with mental and substance disorders and to their inability to obtain treatment and other social services. Today, community mental health centers and substance abuse treatment programs are under increasing pressure to focus services on those with the most serious problems.

The nation's growing concerns about drug abuse did prompt the Reagan administration to establish the Office of Substance Abuse Prevention, with a focus on communities' efforts to halt drug use among their younger members. First Lady Nancy Reagan joined the effort, although her "Just Say No to Drugs" campaign, directed at children, was often criticized as being too simplistic to strike at the many causes of drug use and abuse. AIDS added to the concern about drug abuse with President Reagan's Commission on the Human Immunodeficiency Virus Epidemic calling for "treatment on demand" for drug abusers to help prevent the spread of HIV.[36]

Since the Reagan years, the theme of drug abuse prevention has been that of a "war on drugs." In 1986 and 1988 Congress passed omnibus drug abuse legislation to further arm this war.[37] The 1988 Anti-Drug Abuse Act established the Office of National Drug Control Policy (ONDCP), headed by a cabinet-level "drug czar" in the Executive Office of the President. The emphasis has been on interdiction (stopping the flow of drugs into the United States) and on stiffer legal penalties for drug-related crimes (including the possiblity of the death penalty when a murder is involved). These provisions are said to strike at the *supply side* of the drug problem. Prevention, education, and treatment efforts were also included in the act in an attempt to influence the *demand side* of the drug problem. There are numerous other provisions in the 1988 act, including those for drug-free workplaces and eviction of public housing residents who engage in or permit drug use on or near the premises.

But even the most casual observer will probably agree that the law enforcement approach has not substantially stemmed drug trafficking. No matter how many tons of drugs are seized, the enticement provided by the lucrative drug trade causes more to be produced. Many people in the United States and elsewhere are lured into this underground economy. The country's prisons are bulging at the seams with inmates convicted of drug-related crimes. Drug crimes are the single greatest contributor to the phenomenal increase in incarceration in the United States. According to the ONDCP, "The increase in drug offenders accounts for nearly three-quarters of the growth in the federal prison population between 1985 and 1995, while the number of inmates in state prisons for drug-law violations increased by 478 percent over the same period."[38] Prisons are responding with more drug treatment, and there are now prisons devoted entirely to rehabilitating drug offenders.

In 1985, while President Reagan was in office, 82 percent of the federal budget for drug control went to law enforcement efforts and 18 percent to treatment, education, and prevention.[39] Under the Bush administration, treatment, education, and prevention garnered 30 percent, but social service advocates remained concerned that too little of Congress's efforts were aimed at these services. The Clinton administration has directed slightly more (about one-third) of the federal drug control budget to these demand reduction efforts with the remainder being used for law enforcement, interdiction, and other supply-side interventions.[40]

The legalization of drugs through controlled sales would provide quite a different approach to addressing the nation's drug problem, but this viewpoint apparently does not represent the tenor of the country.[41] Congress expressly added a subtitle to the 1988 Anti Drug Abuse Act stating its view against legalization. Former U.S. Surgeon General Joycelyn Elders came in for considerable public criticism when she suggested at least studying the possibility of legalization. President Clinton, who appointed Elders and whose family has experienced alcohol and drug problems firsthand, does not share this position. Drug courts and deferred adjudication for some drug offenders contingent on rehabilitation are being used in more communities. These approaches do represent a willingness to consider some forms of decriminalization as drug problems continue to mount.

Relapse rates for those with alcohol and drug problems, even those who receive help from treatment programs or self-help programs like AA and Narcotics Anonymous, continue to be high. While we hope for approaches that will keep more people "clean and sober," something else seems warranted. Alternatives such as needle exchange programs for injection drug users are designed to save lives by stopping the transmission of HIV. But these programs have met with serious opposition, including a federal funding ban, despite evidence that they reduce transmissions and do not encourage new users (see Illustration 10-1). A number of these "harm reduction" programs operate underground or with unofficial sanction from community authorities since many people see their value even if it is difficult to get offical approval for them. Long-established methadone maintenance programs are known to reduce crime and help heroin addicts maintain more stable lives. However, they remain so controversial (a case in point is New York City Mayor Rudolph Giuliani's strong public stance against them) that there is little chance that heroin substitution programs operating in some countries would be seriously considered in the U.S. Despite Americans' voracious appetite for drugs and our lack of knowledge of the causes of abuse and dependence, the definitions of illicit drugs and the penalties for their possession and distribution (as contained in the federal Controlled Substances Act and other legislation) speak volumes about Americans' approach to "the drug problem."

THE RIGHTS OF MENTAL HEALTH SERVICE CONSUMERS

People with mental illness and chemical dependency problems are often unable to recognize their need for treatment. They may be subjected to involuntary hospitalization for short periods of time for observation and assessment, and if found in need of mandatory care, ordered by the courts to remain in treatment. For those currently experiencing severe and acute problems, treatment provided on an outpatient basis or in community facilities may not be sufficient. Community programs may not be equipped to assist these individuals (now referred to as mental health consumers), or specialized facilities may not exist in a community.

Inpatient treatment may be deemed a necessity by professionals, but it restricts an individual from moving about in the community and participating in normal, daily activities. These restrictions on one's liberties mean that great care should be taken to prevent unnecessary confinement. Although the U.S. Constitution is necessarily concerned with protecting individual liberties, the states have primary responsibility for providing mental health services, and it is often courts at the state level that have intervened to offer civil rights protections.

Until the mid 1880s, involuntarily commitment was mostly done through informal procedures rather than state statute; then, in 1845, "the Massachusetts Supreme Court established the precedent that individuals could be restrained only if dangerous to themselves or others and only if restraint would be conducive to their restoration."[42] But in practice patients had few means to contest their confinement. Some remained

ILLUSTRATION 10-1

Needle-Exchange Programmes in the USA: Time to Act Now

One in three of the more than 570,000 AIDS cases reported in the USA since the beginning of the epidemic has been caused, directly or indirectly, by injection drug misuse. Although HIV-infection rates among homosexual men have fallen, rates due to intravenous drug misuse have soared and about half of new HIV infections now can be traced to that source. Those affected are not only the drug misusers infected by contaminated needles but their sexual partners (most of whom have been poor, black, and Hispanic women) and the children of women infected by drug misuse or sexual contact with infected drug misusers. Injection drug misuse is now the leading primary cause of paediatric AIDS.

Yet, despite this epidemic, the USA remains one of the few industrialised countries that refuses to provide easy access to sterile syringes. Of the 100 or so US needle-exchange programmes most are small and underfunded, and some are illegal. Most US states still have laws on drug paraphernalia or syringe prescription that make it a crime to give a drug misuser a clean needle.

The Clinton Administration now has an opportunity to address this problem. In 1997 the US Congress banned the use of Federal funds for needle-exchange programmes until March 31, 1998, but after that date the legislation allows funding if the Secretary of Health and Human Services determines that exchange programmes are effective in preventing the spread of HIV and do not encourage the use of illegal drugs. But with the deadline fast approaching, the Secretary of Health and Human Services, Donna Shalala, has yet to make an official determination, causing AIDS activists to wonder whether the Administration will refuse to endorse needle-exchange programmes out of fear that the step will open the President to the charge that he is "soft on drugs".

If this is true, it would be a remarkably callous decision for the Administration to make. Yet, given the weight of the scientific evidence supporting the efficacy of needle-exchange schemes, it is hard to attribute the reluctance to back such programmes to anything other than political considerations. Study after study has found that needle-exchange programmes reduce the risk of HIV infection. In 1993, a study on needle-exchange programmes by the Centers for Disease Control and Prevention and the University of California, San Francisco, concluded that "the time has arrived for federal, state, and local governments to remove the legal and administrative barriers to increased needle availability and to facilitate the expansion of needle exchange programmes in the "US". In 1995, the National Academy of Science's Institute of Medicine, an independent organisation set up by Congress for advice on scientific and technical matters, concluded that needle-exchange programmes were effective and did not encourage illegal drug use. In 1997 an independent consensus panel convened by the National Institutes of Health found that "an impressive body of evidence suggests powerful effects from needle-exchange programmes . . . there is no longer doubt that these programs work".

Just last month, the President's Advisory Council on HIV/AIDS issued a report urging the Administration to move immediately to end the ban on Federal funding for needle exchanges. "The debate at this time should no longer be if, but how, needle exchange

continued

ILLUSTRATION 10-1 *(continued)*

programs should be established", wrote the council's chairman, R. Scott Hitt. And the debate is not academic. A study published in *The Lancet* last year by Peter Lurie and Ernest Drucker, who used conservative estimates of interventions that give injection drug misusers access to sterile injection equipment, concluded that if the USA had adopted such programmes in 1987, it could have prevented between 4394 and 9666 HIV infections. Moreover, they found that if current policies are not changed, an additional 5150–11329 preventable HIV infections could occur by the year 2000 in the USA. Who will stop these preventable infections? The Clinton Administration should act now. Delay is costing lives.

Note: As of the publication of this book, neither the Clinton administration nor Congress has moved to fund needle-exchange programs, and there is no indication that they will.

Source: The Lancet, "Needle-exchange programmes in the USA: Time to act now," Vol. 351, January 10, 1998, p. 75.

hospitalized for decades, even if their placement was no longer necessary or they had been placed inappropriately (such as those confined because they were mentally retarded, not mentally ill). In 1960, California's Lanterman-Petric-Short Act, and in 1972, Wisconsin's *Lessard v. Schmidt* decision, restricted the grounds for involuntary commitment and established stringent due process procedures. Soon after, in 1975, the U.S. Supreme Court ruled in Florida's Donaldson case, reinforcing the view that it is unjust to confine patients who are not dangerous in psychiatric institutions when they are not provided treatment and they can survive on their own. In 1980, Congress passed the Civil Rights of Institutionalized Persons Act to protect people held in state and local institutions.

Today, consumers in mental health hospitals and drug treatment facilities must be informed of their rights both to obtain and to refuse treatment. Those who cannot read must have this information explained to them. Despite these legal protections, major obstacles continue to prevent consumers from receiving the best treatment in these facilities. As David Mechanic, an authority on mental health policy, has noted "the welfare of patients depends more on excellent systems of care than on legal definitions."[43] Mental health consumers should always be treated in a way that respects their individual dignity, but this manner of treatment is contingent on the quality and resources of the treatment facility and of its staff. Facilities, especially public and not-for-profit ones, are often crowded. Some are located in remote areas where it may be difficult to recruit and retain qualified staff. Yet decisions about a consumer's day-to-day activities are largely staff decisions. Consumers may have little influence in choosing these activities, short of refusing to participate. Moreover, when mental health consumers refuse to participate, they are often considered to be uncooperative and resistant to treatment. This may serve to prolong their stay in the hospital.

Mental health consumers have the right to know the reason for their admission and what must happen before release will be granted. They must be provided legal representation and access to mental health laws. Consumers should be afforded privacy when they have visitors, and visits should not be denied unless there is reason to believe that they might be harmful to the consumer or others. Unfortunately, when hospitals are located far from the consumer's home, it is more difficult for family to maintain ties and for the consumer to visit family on short leaves from the hospital. These leaves can aid in reintegration into the community.

Liberty or Neglect?

Thomas Szasz, in his well-known book *The Myth of Mental Illness,* called psychiatric illnesses "stigmatizing labels, phrased to resemble medical diagnoses and applied to persons whose behavior annoys or offends others."[44] Szasz took the position of the true libertarian in denouncing all involuntary treatment as "crimes against humanity." Most people do not share this position; every community contains individuals whom other members of society feel are in need of protection. But it is sometimes difficult to know when intervention is necessary. Mechanic's assessment is that except for previous dangerous behavior, the conditions that qualify as dangerous to self or others have not been clearly identified.[45]

During the late 1980s, the well-publicized story of Joyce Brown of New York City, a 40-year-old woman who had worked as a secretary, typified the dilemma of deciding who requires societal protection.[46] Brown was confined to Bellevue (psychiatric) Hospital against her will. According to media accounts, Brown's behavior would probably seem unusual to most of us. She relieved herself on the sidewalk, shouted obscenities, burned money, slept on a steam grate, and wore filthy clothing. Brown had been hospitalized previously, and her sisters said that her abusive behavior caused them to ask her to vacate their home. But controversy erupted over whether Brown should have been hospitalized involuntarily. During a court appearance to determine whether she should remain in the hospital, the judge decided that Brown did not appear to present a danger, and he blamed the lack of decent housing for her predicament. The judge's ruling was later reversed by an appellate court, but this court would not allow the city to medicate Brown against her will, and she was released. Brown did well for a period, working and even lecturing on the matter, but later reports indicated that she had returned to the streets.

New York City is generally thought to have a higher tolerance for deviant behavior than many other cities, but its former mayor Ed Koch came in for criticism from some camps for his decision that freezing weather meant homeless people would be given shelter, even against their will. In his essay "When Liberty Really Means Neglect," Charles Krauthammer gave serious consideration to Koch's position and the dilemmas posed by citizens like Joyce Brown. According to Krauthammer,

> *Why not make compassion an all-weather policy? Danger should not be the only warrant for giving someone, even an unwilling someone, shelter and care. Degradation—*

a life of eating garbage, of sleeping on grates, of recurrent illness and oppressive hallucinations—should suffice. . . .

Liberty counts for much, but not enough to turn away from those who are hopelessly overwhelmed by the demands of modern life. To permit those who would flounder in the slowest lane to fend for themselves on very mean streets is an act not of social liberality but of neglect bordering on cruelty.[47]

Too Much Access or Too Little?

As more people acquired private insurance coverage for mental health care, and others qualified for Medicare and Medicaid, the private sector saw an opportunity to attract consumers to more appealing treatment facilities in middle-class communities. The private sector offered expensive inpatient services that could be accessed very easily, perhaps too easily.

These programs began to market their services aggressively and made special appeals to parents who were worried about the behavior of their adolescent children.[48] Although the growth of the private mental health sector has helped to "normalize" the idea of receiving mental health services, these facilities gained noteriety in 1991 when newspapers carried accounts of their alleged wrongdoing. Some hospitals were accused of paying fees for consumer referrals (considered taboo by most mental health professionals), hospitalizing people who did not necessarily require inpatient care, providing little treatment, and keeping consumers until their insurance ran out and then "dumping" them (discharging them without follow-up care or transferring them to other facilities). There is considerable evidence of patient dumping.[49]

Concerns filtered from several states to Washington, D.C., where the matter was also investigated. As expected, there were outcries by consumers and former employees about these practices and denials of misconduct by hospital administrators. Some industry officials did agree that abuses had occurred, and testimony to Congress did cause legislators to recommend greater oversight of these facilities. In Texas, where the outcry began, additional steps were taken to ensure that facilities inform consumers and their families of their rights and to make it illegal to accept "finder's fees." More stringent rules were adopted requiring physician justification of admissions and face-to-face assessments within seventy-two hours of admission.[50] The attorney general of Texas also ruled that state agencies have the power to conduct inspections of private psychiatric facilities at random or as the result of a complaint.

From Deinstitutionalization to Recriminalization

"Treatment in the least restrictive manner" means that it is not appropriate to confine someone in a hospital when a community facility can meet the individual's needs. Hospitals may compound consumers' problems by making them "institutionalized." Consumers are generally required to get up at certain times and to eat at certain times; their meals are prepared for them and their clothes washed for them; they may be told when to bathe and when to take their medication. As a result, they become increasingly dependent on others. When they return to their homes and communities, they may not have the skills to live independently.

Deinstitutionalization, with its reliance on community-based treatment, is certainly a theoretically humane concept, but as a public policy it has presented its own long-standing problems. The discharge of large numbers of patients from state institutions to their home communities frequently resulted in added stress for both patients and communities, and families were often not equipped to care for mentally ill members who needed frequent supervision or special services. There have never been enough community facilities to provide the care that is needed.

Zoning laws that require communities to incorporate provisions for these facilities served as one approach for integrating community mental health services, although there was concern that this may have the unintended effect of creating "social service ghettos." Educating neighbors before consumers move in and gaining their support was also recommended, despite the position that these people should be able to live wherever they want.[51] Another approach has been "transinstitutionalization"—moving patients to other types of residential facilities such as nursing homes.[52]

Today, occasional battles over locating residential or outpatient facilities still ensue, but many communities have taken a different attitude. *Parade* magazine reports that in a representative survey of 2,503 people, "72 percent say they would be willing to have a small, supervised group home for the mentally ill in their own community."[53] Residential facilities, even prisons, are being sought by a number of communities because they mean employment and economic revitalization in depressed areas. Residents who vehemently oppose them at first calm down when negative incidents fail to occur and the facility becomes a community fixture.

"Deinstitutionalization" is now old news, a fact of life for communities. Many younger people with serious mental illness have never been institutionalized for any appreciable period of time. Communities have come to believe that there will never be an adequate number of treatment facilities, due to inadequate funding and a growing number of people in need of care. By default, they have adopted other means for responding to mental health care. Although Joyce Brown was sent to a psychiatric hospital, many other people with mental illness are now once again "served" through the criminal justice system.[54] Although their crimes may be petty—vagrancy or trespassing—their mental health problems may be severe, and they are left on the streets until some problem results in a justification for jailing.[55] Without care, some deteriorate to the point that they become involved in more serious incidents.

Mental illness and drug dependence are major concerns of law enforcement agencies and correctional facilities. Estimates are that 6 to 14 percent of inmates currently have severe mental illness, that 82 percent have had a mental disorder during their lives, and that nearly 75 percent may have substance disorders; the co-occurrence of mental and substance disorders among this population is especially high.[56] It may be naive to assume that increasing mental health and substance abuse services will alleviate jail and prison overcrowding in a "tough on crime" society, but a rational approach to addressing these problems must certainly consider why so many people with mental illness and chemical dependency problems are now "treated" by the criminal justice system.

Is there hope for the public mental health system's mission to help those with severe mental illness? In Illustration 10-2, noted psychiatrist E. Fuller Torrey, whose own sister has schizophrenia, makes suggestions for improving care. Although you may or may not agree with his approach, it provides a basis for discussion of how the country might improve its response to mental illness.

CHILD WELFARE POLICY

Americans place a high value on privacy, and governmental interference in the private matters of the home is generally considered an unwelcome intrusion. As a result, the United States has no official national family policy. Instead, a number of federal, state, and local laws govern various aspects of family relations. This section focuses on one area of family relations—child welfare, especially child abuse and neglect.

Discovering Child Abuse

Following the tradition of English common law, children in colonial America were considered chattels—the possessions of their parents.[57] Parents who severely punished their children, even beat them, were not defying community standards or breaking the law; they were merely making sure their children obeyed. Eventually case law allowed for criminal prosecution of parents in very severe cases, but in reality little was done to protect children. Children in need of care were subject to the same demeaning forms of social welfare as adults—often almshouses or poorhouses, and they were also subject to indenture. This tradition prevailed in America until the Industrial Revolution brought an abundance of new social problems. Among them were the conditions of urban cities, which were often overcrowded and unsanitary and where hunger and disease were not uncommon. During this period it was thought that children from poor homes might be better raised in separate institutions. Institutions such as the New York House of Refuge were established for neglected, abandoned, and delinquent youth. But the emphasis was not on protecting children from parents who harmed or neglected them. It was thought that institutional placement would help reverse the trend of poverty by teaching children proper social values and good work habits. Some organizations, like the Children's Aid Society founded by Charles Loring Brace in 1853 and the Children's Home Society founded by Martin Van Buren Van Arsdale in 1883, decided that children would best be served in rural areas, and they sent thousand of them to live and work with families, generally Christian families, away from the cities and their own families.

In 1874 the famous case of Mary Ellen brought public attention to the plight of severely mistreated children. The folklore surrounding the little girl's plight is that the laws protecting animals were stronger than those protecting children, and so Henry Bergh of the New York Society for the Prevention of Cruelty to Animals (NYSPCA)

ILLUSTRATION 10-2

What to Do About Helping People with Severe Mental Illness

Until research provides more definitive answers regarding causes and treatments, we will continue to be faced with providing psychiatric services for an estimated 5.6 million people who are mentally ill. As I have emphasized . . . , we know how to provide services that are high-quality, humane, and cost-effective, but for a variety of reasons we do not do so. The following summary highlights my major recommendations . . . for achieving such services.

1. *The economic solution: Single responsibility funding.* Cost-shifting between federal and state, and state and local governments is the single largest cause of the mental illness crisis.
   a. Single responsibility funding is the proposed solution. The states would be given authority for planning and for financing services, although the funds may be derived from federal and local as well as state taxes. The states would also be held accountable for treatment outcomes, and this would continue to be true even if the states subcontract for the services with county or city governments or with private sector providers.
   b. Block grants of federal funds to the states are consistent with single responsibility funding as long as the states are required to spend those funds on the target population and treatment outcomes are being measured.
   c. The measurement of treatment outcomes is mandatory for solving the present crisis. If treatment outcomes are being measured, then performance contracting becomes possible.
   d. We do not yet know the optimal system of financial incentives for ensuring quality services for people who are mentally ill. Therefore, it is appropriate to encourage state and local governments to try different arrangements, using public, private, nonprofit, and for-profit resources, as long as treatment outcomes are being measured and the outcomes of the various financial arrangements are being assessed. At the same time, the dismal record to date of the for-profit sector in providing services for individuals with severe mental illnesses should be acknowledged and makes it more likely that definitive solutions will come from the nonprofit sector.
2. *The legal solution: Recognition of the need for involuntary treatment.* Since approximately half of all persons with severe mental illnesses have impaired insight because of their illnesses and therefore do not recognize their need for treatment, a substantial number of the mentally ill will have to be treated involuntarily if they are going to be treated at all. The failure to do so is a major contributor to this crisis.
   a. Involuntary commitment laws for hospitalization and treatment should be based not only on dangerousness to self or others, but also on the need for treatment. As measures of insight improve and scales with good inter-rater reliability are developed, a measure of insight should also be included in commitment criteria.
   b. In assessing a mentally ill person's need for involuntary treatment, the person's

continued

ILLUSTRATION 10-2 *(continued)*

past history should always be considered. Special attention should be directed to the person's history of violent behavior, alcohol and drug abuse, and noncompliance with medication since these are known to be the major predictors of future violent behavior.

c. Conditional release, guardianships, and outpatient commitment should be available and used for mentally ill persons who are in need of involuntary treatment and who can live successfully in the community as long as they take their medication.

d. Interstate reciprocity should be established and enforced for mentally ill persons who are involuntarily committed to treatment in one state.

e. The federally funded Protection and Advocacy program should be abolished.

f. For mentally ill persons who also abuse alcohol or drugs, SSI, SSDI, and VA* benefits should be paid directly to a representative payee who is directly connected to the person's treatment program. The person's benefits should become part of the treatment plan to reduce the person's alcohol or drug abuse. The benefits would therefore change from being part of the problem to being part of the solution.

g. SSI, SSDI, and VA benefits for mentally ill persons should be standardized. Consideration should also be given to establishing two levels of disability—partial and total—to encourage people to work who are capable of doing so.

h. A small percentage of the mentally ill are not capable of living in the community because of the severity of their symptoms, their propensity toward violent behavior, their concurrent alcohol or drug abuse, or their nonresponsiveness to all available medication. It should be acknowledged that long-term hospitalization is both appropriate and necessary for these patients.

3. *The ideological solution: Divorce mental illness from mental health.* The continuum concept, which has dominated twentieth-century thinking about mental disorders, is an important cause of the mental illness crisis. Severe mental illnesses are *not* merely one end of a mental health continuum. It is therefore necessary to return to the nineteenth-century idea that these illnesses are in a different category from problems of mental health. A divorce of mental illness from mental health could be accomplished by the following:

   a. A National Brain Research Institute should be formed by a merger of the National Institute of Mental Health and the National Institute of Neurological Disorders and Stroke.

   b. State departments of mental health should be abolished. People with severe mental illnesses should be the responsibility of the state department of health and should receive services in the same clinics as do patients with other neurological disorders.

   c. In medical schools, the departments of psychiatry and neurology should merge. The joint department would train neuropsychiatrists who would be specialists in neurological disorders, mental illnesses, and other nonsurgical disorders of the brain.

   d. Since medical resources are finite, a system of prioritization should be

continued

ILLUSTRATION 10-2 *(continued)*

established in which severe mental illnesses are prioritized along with other medical disorders. A combination of criteria could be used, including structural and functional brain abnormalities, functional impairment, likelihood of benefit from treatment, economic cost-benefit, social cost-benefit, and fairness.

e. Since severe mental illnesses would no longer be part of a mental health spectrum, they should no longer be politicized.

*SSI is Supplemental Security Income, SSDI is Social Security Disability Insurance, and VA stands for Veterans Administration.

Source: E. Fuller Torrey, *Out of the Shadows: Confronting America's Mental Illness Crisis,* excerpted from pp. 196–199.

decided to plead her case on the basis that the child was a member of the animal kingdom. Historical records do reflect Mr. Bergh's intervention, but apparently as a private citizen who presented the girl as a child in need of protection, not as a member of the animal kingdom.[58] The story, however, has become woven into the history of child welfare and did raise public consciousness about child abuse (see Illustration 10-3).

Despite efforts of the settlement houses and eventually the Charity Organization Societies to focus on services to the family unit, the prevailing philosophy in the early twentieth century remained removing children from their homes rather than rehabilitating parents. The establishment of juvenile courts during this period did little to change this, but as the century progressed, more concern was expressed for the children themselves. Orphanages and foster homes became the preferred alternatives for child placement. New state mothers' aid programs provided some financial means to children in their natural homes, and slowly, child welfare philosophy in the twentieth century came to reflect "the great discovery . . . that the best place for normal children was in their own homes."[59] Still, abusive parents were not themselves the targets of social policies or social programs, and the public largely condoned parents' use of physical force on their children.

According to Stephen Pfohl, it was not the social reformers, nor the juvenile court authorities, nor the public at large who finally "discovered" child abuse.[60] It was pediatric radiologists who identified the problem or "syndrome," gave it legitimacy, and aroused public concern. Beginning in 1946, the work of pediatric radiologist John Caffey led to the identification of parents as the cause of many of the bone fractures seen in children. Although emergency room and family physicians (not radiologists) were the first to come into contact with abused children, at least four factors prevented them from recognizing the problem: (1) child abuse was not a traditional diagnosis; (2) doctors may have found it difficult to believe that parents would perpetrate such acts;

ILLUSTRATION 10-3

Little Mary Ellen

Before 1875, U.S. authorities had no legal means to interfere in cases of battered children. The laws were changed with the help of the Society for the Prevention of Cruelty to Animals (SPCA).

A 9-year-old named Mary Ellen became the exemplar of the battered children's plight. Indentured to Francis and Mary Connolly (and rumored to be the daughter of Mary's ex-husband), the girl was whipped daily, stabbed with scissors and tied to a bed. Neighbors reported the situation to Etta Wheeler, a church worker, in 1874. When Wheeler found that there was no lawful way to rescue the child from her brutal guardians, she went to Henry Bergh of the SPCA for help.

Under the premise that the child was a member of the animal kingdom, the SPCA obtained a writ of habeas corpus to remove Mary Ellen from her home. On April 9, 1874, she was carried into the New York Supreme Court, where her case was tried. She was pitifully thin, with a scissor wound on her cheek. Mrs. Connolly was sentenced to a year in prison. Mary Ellen was given a new home. The following April, the New York Society for the Prevention of Cruelty to Children (NYSPCC) was incorporated.

Before-and-after photos of Mary Ellen (as a pathetic waif upon her rescue and as a healthy child a year later) still hang at the New York SPCA, framed with Mrs. Connolly's scissors.

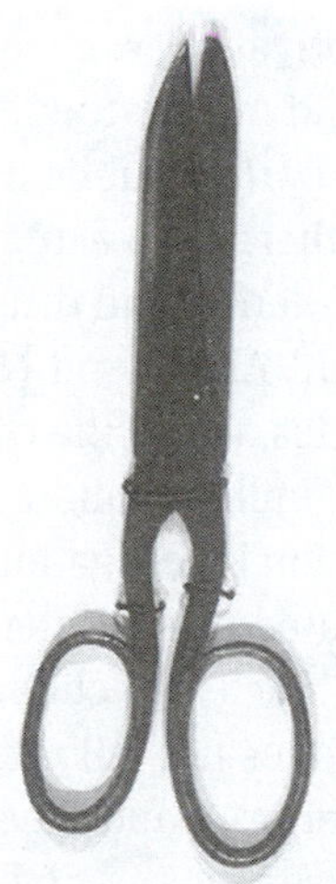

ASPCA's before and after photos of Mary Ellen, with scissors used to punish her.

Source: Reprinted with permission from Irving Wallace, David Wallechinsky, and Amy Wallace, "Significa," *Parade* magazine. Photos courtesy of ASPCA Archives.

(3) if the family, rather than just the child, was the doctor's patient, reporting abuse may have constituted a violation of patient confidentiality; and (4) physicians may have been unwilling to report criminal behavior because of the time-consuming nature of criminal cases and their dislike for serving as witnesses in legal proceedings. Pediatric radiologists exposed child abuse because they did not deal directly with the child and the family. Issues regarding confidentiality and court proceedings were not their primary concerns. Their "discovery" also elevated the position of radiologists, who held lower status since they did not provide direct patient care.

To keep child abuse under the purview of the medical profession, it had to be viewed as a medical rather than a social or legal problem. In 1962, Dr. Henry Kempe and his associates labeled child abuse with the medical terminology "the battered-child syndrome," which legitimized its recognition by physicians.[61] Magazines, newspapers, and television programs, such as *Ben Casey* and *Dr. Kildare*, publicized the problem. Between 1963 and 1967 every state passed child abuse reporting legislation. Today, child abuse legislation is aimed more at rehabilitating parents than punishing them. Most cases are reported to social welfare rather than law enforcement agencies.

Extent of Child Maltreatment

Child maltreatment consists of both abuse and neglect. Abuse occurs when severe harm is inflicted on a child such as broken bones or burns, but it can also be emotional or sexual. Neglect occurs when a parent or caretaker fails to provide a child with the essentials needed to live adequately, including proper schooling, or it may result from psychological deprivation, such as isolating the child from others. Between 1986 and 1995, reports of child maltreatment increased by 42 percent.[62] The number of reports has grown due in part to public awareness of these problems. Child welfare authorities also believe there is an actual increase in the incidence of abuse due to factors such as poverty, violence, and drug (especially crack cocaine) use.

In 1996, the National Child Abuse and Neglect Data System (NCANDS) showed that protective service agencies across the country received 3 million reports of suspected abuse or neglect of 2 million children (a rate of 44 per 1,000 children in the population).[63] Of the 1.6 million investigations conducted, in only 34 percent of cases was maltreatment substantiated or indicated. In total, 970,000 children were found to have been maltreated (15 per 1,000 children). Sometimes reports are not investigated because the situation does not fall under the state's rules for investigation, or the case is not given a high priority and the state lacks the resources to follow up on every report. Investigated cases may not be substantiated because abuse or neglect cannot be verified or a report was made in error. Substantiation rates vary considerably by state.

Data on the types of maltreatment in substantiated cases have been relatively consistent over time. In 1996, NCANDS shows that 52 percent of cases constituted neglect; 24 percent, physical abuse; 12 percent, sexual abuse; 6 percent, emotional abuse; 3 percent, medical neglect; and 16 percent, other types of maltreatment such as abandonment or congenital drug addiction (some children are counted in more than one category). About 7 percent of abused and neglected children are less than 1 year old; 32 percent are ages 1 to 5; 40 percent are ages 6 to 12; and 21 percent are age 13 or older. Fatalities are more likely to occur among younger children. Girls are 52 percent of abuse and neglect cases. White children are 53 percent; African-American children, 27 percent; children of Hispanic origin, 11 percent; Native American and Native Alaskan children, 2 percent; and children of Asian and Pacific Islander origin, 1 percent of cases. For African American and Native American children, these rates are twice as high as their representation in the population. The vast majority of perpetrators are the children's caretakers (the child's parents in 77 percent of cases and other relatives in 11 percent). In only 2 percent of cases are the perpetrators day care staff, foster parents, or the staff at residential facilities. Perpetrators in 10 percent of cases are not in caretaker roles or their relationship to the child is not known.

The figures on child abuse and neglect reported above are based on states' reports. Because states differ in their definitions of problems and the procedures they use to screen calls and investigate cases, there are inconsistencies or gaps in the picture these data present. In addition, a few states generally do not report their figures. Another approach now being used to collect data is a community-based national incidence study. According to this study, 1.5 million children experienced "demonstrable harm" due to abuse or neglect in 1993 compared to only 869,000 substantiated cases gleaned from state reports.[64] Also troubling is that the community-based study showed a fourfold increase in serious injuries from about 142,000 in 1986 to 565,000 in 1993. A Gallup poll based on parents' own reports puts the figure even higher, at over 3 million cases of physical abuse each year.[65] Taken together, the various studies indicate that while the majority of reports to child welfare authorities go unsubstantiated, a large number of cases of concern are not even reported or detected.

Of all the things the government counts, abused and neglected children would seem among the most important. It has taken about 20 years, but two systems intended to provide better data on children involved in the protective services system and the services they receive, along with requirements for states to participate in reporting, are now being instituted. One is the Adoption and Foster Care Analysis and Reporting System (AFCARS) and the other is the Statewide Automated Child Welfare Information Systems (SACWIS).

Services for Abused and Neglected Children

The federal government's initial concern about the welfare of children began with the first White House Conference on Children in 1909 and the establishment of the Children's Bureau in 1912. The bureau addressed a broad range of child welfare issues, from health and child labor to delinquency and orphaned children. Under Title V of the original Social Security Act, the bureau was directed to cooperate with the states to develop child welfare services. Services were expanded, primarily during the 1960s. The AFDC-Foster Care program was established in 1961 to provide out-of-home care to poor children after the state of Louisiana dumped 22,000 black children from the AFDC program because it considered their own homes "unsuitable" to the children's well-being, a move which led to the growth of the foster care system. Child welfare services originally included under Title V of the Social Security Act were expanded under Title IV-B in 1967. In 1974 Congress passed the Child Abuse Prevention and Treatment Act and established the National Center on Child Abuse and Neglect. In addition to assisting the states, the center conducts child abuse and neglect research. In 1975, Title XX allowed more child welfare services to be provided. The Title XX Social Services Block Grant has become another important source of child welfare service funding.

The most significant recent development in the child welfare arena is the Adoption Assistance and Child Welfare Act of 1980, also known as the "permanency planning law." Amendments to the law were made by the Adoption and Safe Families Act of 1997. The 1980 law was a reaction to scathing indictments of the child welfare system, particularly the number of children who had been removed from their homes and who had become *lost* in the child welfare system. The law was intended to prevent the *drift* of so many children into foster care for long periods.[66] Federal policy had unwittingly encouraged the removal of children from their homes by providing much more funding for foster care and much less for in-home services. Some blamed the high levels of foster care utilization on a broadened definition of when intervention was needed—from "risk of harm to the child" to "vague notions of parental fitness of the child's best interest."[67] The 1980 and 1997 laws recognize children's rights to a permanent home. Financial penalties can be imposed on states that do not comply with the act. The components of these laws are Titles IV-B and IV-E of the Social Security Act which are supposed to work in concert with each other.

The purposes of IV-B, Child Welfare Services and Promoting Safe and Stable Families Program (formerly the Family Preservation and Support Services Program), are

1. Protecting and promoting the welfare of all children, including handicapped, homeless, dependent, or neglected children.
2. Preventing or remedying, or assisting in the solution of problems that may result in the neglect, abuse, exploitation, or delinquency of children.
3. Preventing the unnecessary separation of children from families by identifying family problems, assisting families in resolving their problems, and preventing breakup of the family where the prevention of child removal is desirable and possible.
4. Restoring to their families those children who have been removed, by the provision of services to the children and the families.
5. Placing children in suitable adoptive homes, in cases where restoration to the biological family is not possible or appropriate.
6. Assuring adequate care of children away from their homes, in cases where the child cannot be returned home or cannot be placed for adoption.

Under IV-B, states must have written plans for every child and each case must be reviewed at least every 6 months. As a result of the 1997 amendments, within 12 months of placement (it was 18 months under the 1980 law), each case must have a permanency planning hearing to determine whether the child will be returned home, placed for adoption, or referred for another permanent living arrangement. With some exceptions, states must begin procedures to terminate parental rights if a child has been in foster care 15 of the past 22 months. Although states must make "reasonable efforts" to prevent foster care placement and to reunite children with their parents, there is no federal definition of reasonable efforts. States' interpretations vary.[68] The U.S. Supreme Court decision in *Suter v. Artist M.* failed to support the right to sue a state official or agency if reasonable efforts are not made. A panel of child welfare experts convened at Congressional request studied reasonable efforts to keep families together. The panel concluded that despite the lack of a federal definition, reasonable efforts provisions had positive impacts and that existing federal requirements should be enforced.[69] Some panel members felt that a set of federally mandated services to promote reasonable efforts is unecessary because of the successes already achieved. They felt that this specificity should come from the local level, contrary to recommendations of the Child Welfare League of America.[70]

Title IV-E, Foster Care and Adoption Assistance Programs, now provide foster care services for children who would have been eligible for AFDC and adoption assistance for children with special needs (for example, older children, those with physical and mental disabilities, and sibling groups). It includes continued Medicaid eligibility for these children and grants to adoptive parents to encourage adoption. IV-E also provides services to help foster children make a better transition to independent living once they reach adulthood. Many former foster children were experiencing difficulties because they had not finished high school; had no work experience; had mental, alcohol, or drug problems; or became pregnant at a young age.[71]

Although the federal government has increased its role in remedying abuse and neglect, there is no single definition of these problems, and no single piece of legislation that uniformly addresses them throughout the nation. Child abuse and neglect statutes remain the prerogative of the states. Available model legislation often serves as the basis for state statutes, but it is still difficult to achieve consensus on definitions. Even if there were agreement on definitions, the best strategies for intervention are often unclear, and funding to provide all needed services is clearly inadequate. A good many child welfare services are provided by not-for-profit agencies and foundations devoted to improving the lives of children.

The Congressional Budget Office predicts substantial increases in the need for federally assisted foster care and adoptions.[72] IV-E foster care caseloads are expected to increase from 282,000 children in 1997 to 341,000 by 2002. If so, federal costs, which have already increased dramatically, will rise again from an estimated $3.3 billion in 1997 to $4.7 billion by 2002. The federal match for these services is the same as each state receives for Medicaid (the national average is 57 percent). California and New York account for nearly half of IV-E foster care expenditures. In 1995, there were nearly 6 children per 1,000 in family (non-relative) foster care in New York and about 3 per 1,000 in California.[73] States' basic monthly reimbursement rates for children in foster care also vary widely; for example, a 9-year-old child was allotted $586 in the state of Connecticut in 1994, compared to $202 in West Virginia, but most states or counties supplement their rates with additional payments. IV-E adoption assistance caseloads are estimated to rise from 141,000 in 1997 to 229,000 in 2002 with costs of

$562 million in 1997 and $1.1 billion in 2002. States' adoption assistance payments also vary. Data on the number of children nationwide in substitute care are lacking because reporting has been voluntary and inconsistent; however, an estimated 716,000 children received some type of substitute care in 1995. Not all children in need of placement are victims of abuse or neglect. Some are orphans; other have parents who are too ill to care for them or are incarcerated.

Although New York state reports the highest foster care placement rate in the nation, Illinois has by far the highest rate of children in all forms of substitute care at 17 per 1,000 children. The state with the lowest overall rate of children in substitute care is Idaho at 3 per 1,000 children. Any conclusions to be drawn from the varying rates should be made carefully. A low rate is not necessarily good and a high rate is not necessarily bad. Placements are affected by many factors, such as policies about removing children from their homes, the resources states allocate for care, the types of services they fund most heavily, and the extent of parents' problems. At any rate, the 1997 amendments to the permanency planning law are intended to speed up the process by which children are placed for adoption and to provide financial incentives in the form of bonus payments for each adoption the state makes over previous levels ($4,000 for each regular foster care adoption and $6,000 for each special needs adoption).

Federal allotments for IV-B child welfare services are expected to be about $292 million annually through 2002.[74] Funds are allocated to states based on their population under age 21 and their per capita income. The new family preservation program (Promoting Safe and Stable Families) has been authorized through 2001. Its funding is set to increase from $275 million in 1999 to $305 million in 2001.[75] In 1990 the American Public Welfare Association estimated that federal funds constituted about 43 percent of all public child welfare expenditures with the remaining 57 percent coming primarily from the states.[76]

Interest in family preservation has resulted in a number of studies to determine its efficacy. A 1987 review of permanency planning programs revealed that children reunited with their biological parents were as likely to return to foster care as were children prior to permanency planning legislation, and adjustment of children in permanent placements seemed no better than for those in temporary placement.[77] More encouraging was that the programs produced a "somewhat higher rate of adoption from foster care" and that these adoptions tended to be stable. Assessments indicate that intensive family preservation services improve family functioning and that out-of-home placements may be substantially reduced initially, but they apparently increase over time.[78] The Homebuilders program, which originated in Tacoma, Washington, is an intensive family preservation model in which services are available to families 24 hours a day for several weeks in order to prevent the removal of children to foster care.[79] Several other intensive family preservation models have also been used in various parts of the country. In a recent review, Cameron and Vanderwood found few outcome studies specifically on the Homebuilders model.[80] They called the outcomes from other intensive family preservation programs inconsistent and found that placements increased over time, suggesting the need for followup services or for modifying criteria for "graduating" families from services. Child welfare advocates have long asserted that the goals of family preservation are derailed because only minimal services (usually education and surveillance) are provided to most families.[81] The National Association of Social Workers said that the $65 million increase allocated for family preservation over three years through the Promoting Safe and Stable Families Program "makes no significant investment in reunification services or needed training of child welfare and court staff."[82]

For some child advocates like the Children's Defense Fund, child abuse and neglect result from the lack of a broad pro-family policy which sees that every family with young children has the basic resources it needs. For them, public assistance reform (see Chapter 6) is not doing child welfare any favors. For others, these problems are rooted in the wanton acts of parents or the difficulties of those severely impaired by mental or substance use disorders. In theory, keeping families together is a laudable goal, but does the theory sometimes go too far? In a statement critical of child protective services (CPS) in Texas, a spokesperson for an advocacy group called Justice for Children said: "CPS has adopted the unproven social theory that it is more important to 'save the home for the child' than to 'save the child from the home'" and that "CPS is making unreasonable efforts to keep unhealthy families together, causing further risk to the child and jeopardizing the criminal case against the abuser."[83] Another child welfare worker said, "The problem with permanency planning for some children is that it creates impermanence. For most of its history as a policy, permanency planning has emphasized outcome over process, location over relation, legal ties over family ties."[84] The 1997 Adoption and Safe Families Act responds to these criticisms by specifying conditions under which reasonable efforts to reunite children with their family need *not* be made, such as when the parent has abandoned the child, or perpetrated serious physical harm or sexual abuse on the child, or when the parent's rights to a sibling of the child have been terminated. In these cases, termination of parental rights can begin almost immediately so that the child can be freed for adoption.

Problems with the System

There are apparently overwhelming problems in the delivery of child welfare services. With greater demands for services, state child protective service agencies cannot respond to the numbers of children and parents in need, so they have resorted to prioritizing cases. The more serious cases get the attention while others may not get addressed unless, or until, they become as serious. Citizens who report cases to child abuse hotlines and later find that little has been done are, not surprisingly, angry. The public is particularly outraged when a child is not removed from the home and is later severely injured or dies as a result of abuse or neglect. Of course, there are also reports of parents whose children were taken away without an appropriate investigation of the situation. "Social workers" often take the blame in these situations because it is they who investigate the cases. Actually, many staff members are not professionally qualified and may lack the education necessary to do the job.[85] High caseloads, low pay, and stressful working conditions that result in staff burnout and turnover are also blamed for problems in the child welfare delivery system.[86] The threat of lawsuits also hangs over child welfare workers' heads. But in 1989 the U.S. Supreme Court ruled six to three that public employees could not be held liable for failure to protect citizens from harm by other private citizens. The case involved the Winnebago County, Wisconsin, department of social services and Joshua DeShaney, who suffered severe, permanent brain damage as a result of abuse by his father after the department failed to remove him from his home. Many child advocates were shocked by this decision.

In 1994 the U.S. Supreme Court again granted protections to social workers by saying that they are immune from being sued even if their accusations against parents are wrong.[87] The high court's ruling stemmed from a Kentucky case in which the 6th U.S. Court of Appeals stated that social workers should "not [be] deterred from vigorously performing their jobs as they might if they feared personal liability." They can be sued, however, if they violate the "clearly established" civil rights of citizens. Although child welfare personnel might breathe a sigh of relief at these decisions, the troubling question of how to prevent child welfare tragedies remains, and the threat of criminal as well as civil prosecution is still a possibility for child welfare workers and administrators. Given the current state of affairs, communities should probably be thankful that people are willing to take jobs in the child welfare system. There appears to be support for granting them limited immunity from legal prosecution in fulfilling their responsibilities.[88]

Removing children from their homes even temporarily can be traumatizing for the child, and finding an appropriate placement may be difficult. The number of foster homes is never sufficient, and sometimes abuse is repeated in these homes. To ensure that as many children remain in their own homes as possible, it has become more common to remove the abuser from the home rather than the child. Children often see their own removal from home as a punishment rather than protection, and they can become quite fearful about their future. When a parent is removed, children are also likely to need help in understanding that they are not to blame.

Child abuse and neglect generally do not remedy themselves. Intervention and treatment are needed by all family members. Child protection agencies and the courts usually mandate that parents who have perpetrated abuse get professional help, but there are often long waits for services at community mental health and family guidance agencies, and private treatment is costly.

Finding adoptive homes for children who are permanently removed from their families can also be difficult. Many people are interested in adopting, but the preference is often for healthy, white infants. Children in foster care generally do not fit this description. Many are older, of ethnic minority backgrounds, and enter care with behavioral, developmental, medical, or other problems, and many of them live in a number of foster homes before they reach adulthood. There has been controversy over the placement of black, Hispanic, and Native American children in white homes.[89] The practice has been called "cultural genocide" and critics contend that non-whites who wish to adopt have been treated unfairly by social service agencies. Others believe that given the disproportionate numbers of ethnic minority children in foster care, transracial and transcultural adoptions can ensure more children a permanent home. Although the Small Business Job Protection Act of 1996 seems unrelated to adoptions, a provision in it prohibits agencies receiving federal funding from denying or delaying opportunities for adoptions or foster care placements on the basis of the prospective parents' or child's race or ethnicity.

Another approach to substitute care is "kinship care." Kinship care was once eschewed because it left the child unavailable for adoption or might result in more harm to the child due to continued contact with the abusive parent. But kinship care has grown in use because it leaves the child in the context of his or her own family and it helps address the shortage of foster and adoptive families. Some rules prohibiting children's relatives from obtaining foster care payments have been removed, thus making this arrangement more financially viable for many family members who want to care for the child.

Americans may be less shocked these days by accounts of child neglect and abuse, but they are still outraged when a child dies as a result of abuse. We can assume that the growing number of reports to child protection agencies means that many people are trying to get help to these children, although Jonathan Kozol suggests that many are willing to do so only at arm's length.[90]

As attention to child maltreatment has increased, many new child welfare issues have swept the country. The legal rights of children are among these issues. Children caught up in the child welfare system generally have *guardian ad litems* or court-appointed special advocates to help protect their interests, but often their rights seem subordinate to those of their parents and the state. Before she became First Lady, attorney Hillary Rodham Clinton already had a long history as a child welfare advocate. She was criticized by some for her view that circumstances may warrant allowing children to sue their parents for inadequate care. In 1992, a Florida court decided to hear the case of Gregory Kingsley. Gregory, who took the name Shawn Russ, won his case—the first in which a child was allowed to bring his own legal action for termination of parental rights.

In another case which gained national attention, *Home Alone* became more than a movie when two young sisters were allegedly left at home unsupervised while their parents went on vacation. With all the resources available in the United States, it is amazing that more unwanted pregnancies are not prevented and that parents and communities are not better prepared to provide children with the care they need. The 1996 welfare reform act passed by Congress places considerable emphasis on reducing out-of-wedlock pregnancies, particularly among teenagers. Perhaps the focus should be on unwanted pregnancies and better preparation for parenting among those who do have children. Many school systems are trying to bring a greater awareness of the responsibilities of parenting to both young men and women.

These concerns lead to important policy questions about how children's needs are addressed. Should we have a "child welfare system" focused on the basic needs of children and their families, or should it be a "child protection system" focused on those cases in which serious harm is wrought on a child?[91] If it is to be a child protection system, should that system be in the hands of social welfare authorities who seek to make the family better or in the hands of law enforcement officials who seek retribution and punishment from adults who harm children in their care? Of course, both of these approaches are needed—basic services for families when parents need some help in performing their role, and legal intervention when they are in flagrant violation of society's standards, especially when they do not respond to social services. One group of social workers has suggested a transformation of the current child protective system into local "Children's Authorities" developed on the principle of public safety which would require responsible behavior from adults and afford children the same legal protections as adults.[92]

SOCIAL SERVICES FOR OLDER AMERICANS

As Chapters 3 and 4 indicated, the quality of life of older Americans has improved considerably. But there remains a significant portion of older Americans who spend the last portion of their lives in need. As life spans increase, those in higher income brackets are also likely to need health care services, assistance in independent living, protection, and long-term care. The Social Security program (discussed in Chapter 4) is an important piece of legislation for older Americans; SSI (see Chapter 5) and Medicare and Medicaid (see Chapter 8) are also crucial in maintaining a high quality of life for older people. Another vital component in meeting the needs of older people is social services. Perhaps the most important legislation in this regard is the Older Americans Act (OAA) of 1965.

The goals of the OAA actually sound more like a wish list than a set of objectives that are likely to be achieved by government, but they include

- An adequate income in retirement in accordance with the U.S. standard of living
- The best possible physical and mental health that science can make available without regard to economic status
- Suitable housing that is independently selected, designed, and located, with reference to special needs and available at costs older citizens can afford
- Full restorative services for those who require institutional care
- Opportunity for employment with no discriminatory personnel practices because of age
- Retirement in health, honor, and dignity—after years of contribution to the economy
- Pursuit of meaningful activity within the widest range of civic, cultural, and recreational opportunities
- Efficient community services, including access to low-cost transportation, that provide a choice in supported living arrangements and social assistance in a coordinated manner, and that are readily available when needed
- Immediate benefit from proven research knowledge that can sustain and improve health and happiness
- Freedom, independence, and the free exercise of individual initiative in planning and managing one's own life

Although the country has yet to make a real dent in achieving many of these objectives, the act does provide the framework for a modest array of services to older citizens. In order to qualify for services under the OAA, a person must be at least 60 years old. Income is generally not used to determine eligibility, but getting services to the poor elderly is of special concern.

The OAA created an "aging network" to express the concerns of older Americans (see Figure 10-1).[93] The network operates at the federal, regional, state, and local levels. At the federal level is the Administration on Aging (AoA), which is part of the U.S.

FIGURE 10-1

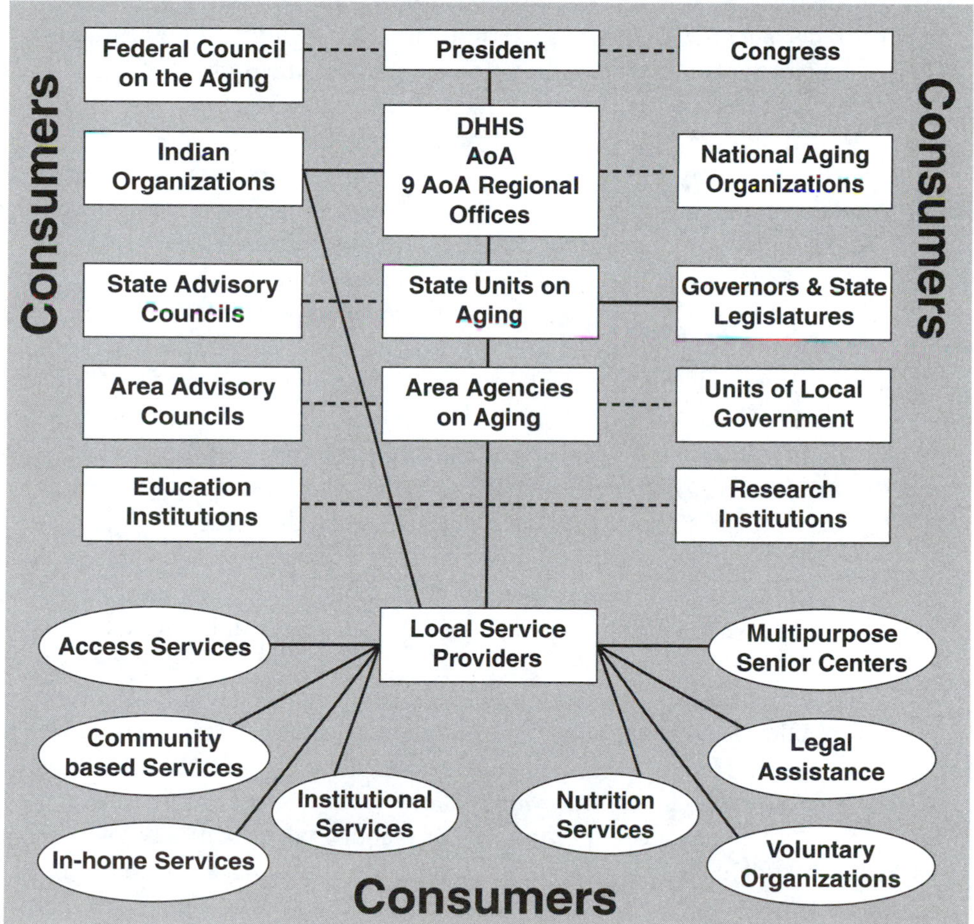

Source: Administration on Aging, Washington, DC, http://www.aoa.dhhs.gov/aoa/pages/aoa.html#OAA.

Department of Health and Human Services. The AoA's primary function is to provide technical assistance to state and local governments in developing and implementing services for older people; it also conducts some program evaluations and research on aging and acts as a national clearinghouse on information about older people. To assist in its efforts, the AoA has nine regional offices across the United States.

At the state level, some of the agencies on aging are part of the state's human services or welfare department, and others are free-standing cabinet-level agencies. These state offices assist in implementing federal policies and act as advocates for elderly citizens. They make the needs and problems of the aged known to the AoA, and also to their own state legislatures, which determine how state programs for older people will be funded and administered.

Actually, most help the elderly receive—about 80 percent of it—is provided by family and friends.[94] But when families and friends cannot meet all these needs, local agencies also try to respond. At the local level there are about 660 Area Agencies on Aging (AAAs). Each AAA is guided by an advisory council primarily composed of older people. The AAAs perform their advocacy function by assessing the needs of older people in their communities and distributing funds to community agencies that deliver services directly to the aged. Among the social services provided are nutrition programs, senior centers, information and referral, transportation, homemaker and chore services, legal counseling, escort services, home repair and renovation, home health aid, shopping assistance, visitation, and telephone assurance (phone calls to the elderly for reassurance and to check on their needs).

The OAA and the aging network are important adjuncts to the major cash assistance and health programs for America's older population. These social service programs provide important links to the community and help to keep the elderly involved in the mainstream of U.S. life and out of institutions. Advocacy groups for older Americans are concerned that services be well publicized to ensure they are used.

In addition to services for older citizens, family caretakers of the elderly may also need services if they are to continue to be a mainstay of support. For example, respite care provides relief to spouses, adult children, and other caretakers, so they can go shopping, have a few hours of free time, or take a vacation. Many families cannot afford to purchase respite care and do without it or rely on other family members and friends when relief is needed. The Family and Medical Leave Act signed by President Clinton in 1993 (also see Chapter 11) allows greater flexibility to many workers who need time away from the job (although it is unpaid leave) to care for a parent. Other public policies that might encourage greater family involvement in elder care are allowing Medicaid and Medicare to cover more home health care costs. Other means are tax expenditures that would allow families to take more income tax deductions for providing care to their parents or grandparents, especially lower-income families who might otherwise be unable to provide this care.

There have been four White House Conferences on Aging, with older Americans from across the United States participating as delegates. The last one was held in 1995. The conferences have reiterated many of the goals of the OAA. In addition to support for Social Security, Medicare, Medicaid, long-term care services, the Older Americans Act, and research on aging, the 1995 conference focused on newer areas of concern.[95]

Participants noted that the number of ethnic minority elderly will double by the year 2030 and called for services that are sensitive to this dynamic as well as to the large number of women that comprise the older population. They also noted the growing number of grandparents who are raising grandchildren and called for better policies to assist them. Participants also recognized the contributions that older people make, and they called for the Corporation for National Service (see Chapter 9) to recruit 1 million older volunteers to assist their communities.

The U.S. House of Representatives no longer funds its former Permanent Select Committee on Aging. The Senate has had a Special Committee on Aging since 1961. Special committees have no legislative authority, but they can bring attention to issues of concern. State legislatures generally have committees whose functions also include consideration of the needs of the elderly. Over the years about half the states have periodically convened "Silver Haired Legislatures" composed of older residents who discuss the needs of their age cohort and report to the governors and state legislatures. In addition to these advisory groups, older people throughout the country have organized in an effort to make their needs known. The most prominent organization of older Americans is the nonpartisan American Association of Retired Persons (AARP). With more than 32 million members, it can be called the country's largest advocacy group. A smaller but also vocal association is the Gray Panthers, which has a particular interest in intergenerational issues.

Although the goals of the Older Americans Act have remained largely the same, there has been increased emphasis on home and community-based services designed to reduce the need for nursing home and other institutional care.[96] When older people can no long care for themselves or when caretakers are unable to encourage them to eat or perform other self-care activities, their situation is termed "self abuse." Another serious situation is maltreatment by others. Most states have statutes that prohibit the physical and psychological abuse of elders and exploitation of their resources (unauthorized use of their income or assets). These types of abuse may occur in the older person's home, the home of a caretaker, or in an institution such as a nursing home. Penalties for citizens who do not report elder abuse vary, and in many cases, there is no real penalty. The identification of elder abuse is complicated by several issues. For example, even those older people capable of reporting the abuse may not do so for fear that loss of their caretaker will result in their being placed in an institution. When the abuser is a loved one, the older person may not want to risk intervention by social service workers or legal action by law enforcement. Elder abuse laws are not as well developed as child abuse laws, but in most areas adult protective service workers or law enforcement officers can be called on to intervene.

One civil rights issue for the elderly that is growing in scope is **guardianship** or **conservatorship.**[97] Guardianship may empower another to make personal and/or financial decisions for another, while conservatorship provides only for financial decisions.[98] Guardians are appointed by courts when it appears that an older person is no longer competent to manage his or her daily affairs. In most states these are probate courts that also deal with child custody and adults in need of treatment for mental illness. Once a guardian is appointed, the older person may be stripped of rights and decision-making power over where to live, how to spend money, whether to receive treatment, and so forth. Guardianship is defined under state law, and these laws have come under increasing scrutiny as more older people are subjected to guardianship. Concerns are that many guardianship decisions are made without sufficient information. Decisions may be based on the viewpoint of the individual who believes guardianship is needed rather than on any convincing evidence. The older person may not even be given an opportunity for legal representation. In many cases, supervision of guardians is also lax. The elderly can be robbed of assets and treated poorly by guardians who may be relatives or someone previously unknown to them.

In some areas, guardianship has become a new business for entrepreneurs because guardians may be paid a fee for their services. Some states have overhauled their guardianship programs to better protect older individuals. In many areas, guardianship is used only as a last resort. In some cases, bill-paying or other financial management services provided by volunteers can prevent the need for guardianship; or durable power of attorney (a voluntary process) is used, which can leave the older person with more rights intact by giving another individual limited powers such as in financial matters. Although useful in helping the elderly maintain their civil rights, these systems can also result in inappropriate use of an individual's financial resources, because many voluntary programs also lack oversight. At a minimum, closer supervision of existing systems is needed, since good alternatives seem to be few.

Two demonstrable effects of the total package of cash, health, and social services for older Americans have been "(1) an increase in the ability of the aged to maintain homes apart from younger relatives, and (2) an increase in proprietary nursing home beds for the sick aged."[99] Other demonstrable effects come from the Nursing Home Reform Act of 1987 (part of that year's Omnibus Budget and Reconciliation Act). For example, there is substantially less use of physical restraints and greater protections of nursing home patients' rights.[100] Still, patient abuses and violations of care procedures are too common. Tensions remain between the nursing home industry and regulatory bodies in trying to remedy problems.

Each year the Senate Special Committee on Aging reviews a range of federal legislation, programs, and issues pertinent to older Americans, including the Older Americans Act and other social service programs. One of its recent reports notes that the $1.4 billion allocated for the OAA has left its programs "overextended and underfunded," thus requiring AAAs to raise funding from many other sources.[101] The report also notes that a major challenge lies in coordinating the various service programs that are available. The report expressed concern that the federal budget deficit had held back expansion of the OAA, but there is optimism that the current healthy economy will invigorate efforts to assist older Americans.

SUMMARY

Social services include many types of programs, including child and adult day care, mental health care, treatment for alcohol and drug abuse, juvenile delinquency prevention services, child welfare programs, and nursing home care. Not all social services are directed toward those in poverty. People from all walks of life may require social services. Social services are provided by public agencies, private not-for-profit and profit-making organizations, religious organizations, and self-help groups. The Title XX Social Services Block Grant is a major vehicle for funding social services.

The Community Mental Health Act of 1963 was the landmark legislation that encouraged the building and staffing of community mental health centers across the country. The bulk of funds for these programs now comes from state governments, but the federal government does contribute. The current federal funding mechanisms are the Substance Abuse Prevention and Treatment Block Grant and the Community Mental Health Services Block Grant.

The United States has no comprehensive social policy for families and children, largely because of the belief that families should be relatively free from governmental intervention. However, state laws govern various aspects of family relations, such as intervention in cases of child abuse and neglect. The 1980 Child Welfare and Adoption Assistance Act, along with amendments to the act in 1997, is currently considered the most important child welfare legislation. This legislation focuses on keeping families together whenever possible and finding other permanent homes when children cannot be returned to their original families.

The most important legislation that recognizes the social service needs of the elderly is the Older Americans Act of 1965. The act emphasizes nutrition programs and services that increase the ability of the elderly to remain in the community. The Administration on Aging is the federal agency which administers this act by determining the needs of older Americans and by encouraging states and communities to provide services that address these needs.

NOTES

1. This overview of services relies on Alfred J. Kahn, *Social Policy and Social Services* (New York: Random House, 1979), pp. 12–13.

2. Steven Rathgeb Smith and Michael Lipsky, *Nonprofits for Hire: The Welfare State in the Age of Contracting* (Cambridge, MA: Harvard University Press, 1993).

3. See Robert Morris, *Social Policy of the American Welfare State: An Introduction to Policy Analysis* (New York: Harper & Row, 1979), p. 120.

4. U.S. Department of Health, Education and Welfare, *First Annual Report to Congress on Title XX of the Social Security Act* (Washington, DC: Department of Health, Education, and Welfare, 1977), p. 1; Martha Derthick, *Uncontrollable Spending for Social Services Grants* (Washington, DC: The Brookings Institution, 1975).

5. Committee on Ways and Means, U.S. House of Representatives, *1998 Green Book: Background Material and Data on Programs Within the Jurisdiction of the Committee on Ways and Means* (Washington, DC: U.S. Government Printing Office, 1998), pp. 713, 714.

6. John L. Palmer and Isabel V. Sawhill, eds., *The Reagan Record* (Cambridge, MA: Ballinger, 1984), p. 376.

7. Committee on Ways and Means, *1998 Green Book*, pp. 718–719.

8. David Mechanic, *Mental Health and Social Policy*, 3rd ed. (Englewood Cliffs, NJ: Prentice Hall, 1989), chapter 2.

9. For a critique of the DSM see Stuart A. Kirk and Herb Kutchins, *The Selling of the DSM: The Rhetoric of Science in Psychiatry* (Hawthorne, NY: Aldine de Gruyter, 1992); Herb Kutchins and Stuart A. Kirk, *Driving Us Crazy: DSM, the Psychiatric Bible and the Creation of Mental Disorders* (New York: Free Press, 1997).

10. C. Aaron McNeece and Diana M. DiNitto, *Chemical Dependency: A Systems Approach*, 2nd ed. (Boston: Allyn and Bacon, 1998).

11. Ronald C. Kessler, Katherine A. McGonagle, Shanyang Zhao, Christopher B. Nelson, Michael Hughes, Suzann Eshleman, Hans-Ulrich Wittchen, and Kenneth S. Kendler, "Lifetime and 12-Month Prevalence of DSM-III-R

Psychiatric Disorders in the United States: Results from the National Comorbidity Survey," *Archives of General Psychiatry,* Vol. 51, No. 8, 1994, pp. 8–19.

12. Ronald C. Kessler, Christopher B. Nelson, Katherine A. McGonagle, Mark J. Edlund, Richard G. Frank, and Philip J. Leaf, "The Epidemiology of Co-Occurring Addictive and Mental Disorders: Implications for Prevention and Service Utilization," *American Journal of Orthopsychiatry,* Vol. 66, No. 1, 1996, pp. 17–31.

13. Ronald C. Kessler et al., "The 12-Month Prevalence and Correlates of Serious Mental Illness (SMI)," in Ronald W. Manderscheid and Mary Anne Sonnenschein, eds., *Mental Health United States, 1996* (Washington, DC: U.S. Government Printing Office, 1996), pp. 59–70.

14. Robert M. Friedman, Judith W. Katz-Leavy, Ronald W. Manderscheid, and Diane L. Sondheimer, "Prevalence of Serious Emotional Disturbance in Children and Adolescents," in Manderscheid and Sonnenschein, eds., *Mental Health United States, 1996,* pp. 71–89.

15. Substance Abuse and Mental Health Services Administration, Drug Abuse Warning Network (DAWN), "Highlights," http://www.samhsa.gov/oas/dawn/dwn96toc.htm.

16. Data from the 1997 National Household Survey on Drug Abuse rely on Substance Abuse and Mental Health Services Administration, Office of Applied Studies, Preliminary Results from the National Household Survey on Drug Abuse, "Highlights," http://www.samhsa.gov/oas/nhsda/nhsdafls.htm.

17. Kessler et al., "Lifetime and 12-Month Prevalence of DSM-III-R Psychiatric Disorders in the United States . . . ," p. 12.

18. Ibid.

19. Substance Abuse and Mental Health Services Administration, Office of Applied Studies, *Uniform Facility Data Set (UFDS): Data for 1996 and 1980–1996,* December 1997, ftp://ftp.samhsa.gov/pub/ufds/ufds96.evy.

20. See Beatrice A. Rouse, ed., *Substance Abuse and Mental Health Statistics Sourcebook* (Washington, DC: U.S. Government Printing Office, 1995), DHHS Publication No. (SMA)95-3064, p. 3.

21. See Mary Jane England, "The Mental Health Parity Act—Lifting the Benefit Plan Limits," *Health Insurance Underwriter,* January 1997, http://nahu.org/hiu/1-97-16.htm; Congressional Budget Office, "CBO's Estimates of the Impact on Employers of the Mental Health Parity Amendments in H.R. 3103," http://www.fmhi.usf.edu/parity/cboestimate.html; Lawrence K. Cagney and Mary Beth Navin, "Compliance with the Mental Health Parity Act of 1996," September 30, 1997, Debevoise & Plimpton, http://www.altavista.digital.com/cgi-bin/query?pg-q&what-web&kl-XX&9 = mental + .

22. Bruce Lubotsky Levin, Ardis Hanson, Richard Coe, and Ann C. Taylor, *Mental Health Parity: National and State Perspectives: A Report* (Tampa, FL: Louis de la Parte Florida Mental Health Institute, March 1997), http://www.fmhi.usf.edu/parity/parityreport/impact.html.

23. Congressional Budget Office, "CBO's Estimates of the Impact on Employers of the Mental Health Parity Amendments in H.R. 3103."

24. Levin et al., *Mental Health Parity: National and State Perspectives: A Report.*

25. Ibid; also see James W. Luckey, "Justifying Alcohol Treatment on the Basis of Cost Savings: The 'Offset' Literature," *Alcohol Health and Research World,* Fall 1987, pp. 8–15.

26. England, "The Mental Health Parity Act—Lifting the Benefit Plan Limits."

27. Bruce Lubotsky Levin, "Managed Mental Health Care: A National Perspective," in Ronald Manderscheid and Mary Anne Sonnenschein, eds., *Mental Health: United States, 1992,* DHHS Pub. No. (SMA) 92-1942 (Rockville, MD: Center for Mental Health Services and National Institute of Mental Health, 1992), pp. 208–218.

28. I am indebted to Peggy Thweatt for reminding me of the benefits of public sector services.

29. Most of this section relies on Mechanic, *Mental Health and Social Policy,* pp. 83, 86–87, 96–97.

30. Gerald N. Grob, *The State and the Mentally Ill: A History of Worcester State Hospital in Massachusetts, 1830–1920* (Chapel Hill: University of North Carolina Press, 1966), cited in ibid., p. 53.

31. Clara Claiborne Park with Leon N. Shapiro, *You Are Not Alone: Understanding and Dealing with Mental Illness—A Guide for Patients, Doctors, and Other Professionals* (Boston: Little, Brown, 1976), pp. 93–94.

32. See Lucy D. Ozarin, "Community Mental Health: Does It Work? Review of the Evaluation Literature," in Walter E. Barton and Charlotte J. Sanborn, eds., *An Assessment of the Community Mental Health Movement* (Lexington, MA: Health, 1977), pp. 122–123.

33. See E. Fuller Torrey, *Nowhere to Go: The Tragic Odyssey of the Homeless Mentally Ill* (New York: Harper & Row, 1988), chapter 9.

34. Lynn Videka-Sherman, "Harriett M. Bartlett Practice Effectiveness Project, Report to NASW Board of Directors" (Silver Spring, MD: National Association of Social Workers, July 10, 1985).

35. See, for example, Thomas M. Wickizer, Daniel Lessler, and Karen M. Travis, "Controlling Inpatient Psychiatric Utilization Through Managed Care," *American Journal of Psychiatry,* Vol. 153, No. 3, 1996, pp. 339–345; David Mechanic, Mark Schlesinger, and Donna D. McAlpine, "Management of Mental Health and Substance Abuse Services: State of the Art and Early Results," *Milbank Quarterly,* Vol. 73, No. 1, 1995, pp. 19–55.

36. *Report of the Presidential Commission on the Human Immunodeficiency Virus* (Washington, DC: U.S. Government Printing Office, 1988).

37. See U.S. House of Representatives, *The Anti-Drug Abuse Act of 1988: A Guide to Programs for State and Local Anti-Drug Assistance,* Report of the Select Committee on Narcotics Abuse and Control, 101st Congress (Washington, DC: U.S. Government Printing Office, 1989).

38. Office of National Drug Control Policy, *The National Drug Control Strategy, 1998* (Washington, DC: ONDCP), http://www.whitehousedrugpolicy.gov/policy/98ndocs/contents.html, see Section III, "America's Illegal Drug Profile."

39. Data are from the General Accounting Office and the Office of Drug Control Policy and were compiled by the Drug Policy Foundation and reported in Julia Malone, "Clinton Shifts War on Drugs to Treatment, More Police," *Austin American-Statesman,* February 10, 1994, p. A4; also see Executive Office of the President, Office of Management and Budget, *Budget of the United States Government, Fiscal Year 1995* (Washington, DC: U.S. Government Printing Office, 1994), p. 206.

40. Office of National Drug Control Policy, *The National Drug Control Strategy, 1998,* see Section V: "Supporting the Ten-Year Strategy: The National Drug Control Budget, FY 1999-FY2003," Table 2.

41. For a discussion of decriminalization, legalization, and other policy alternatives in the fields of alcoholism and drug abuse, see McNeece and DiNitto, *Chemical Dependency: A Systems Approach,* especially chapter 8.

42. This paragraph relies on Mechanic, *Mental Health and Social Policy,* pp. 215–217; quote is from p. 215.

43. Ibid., p. 222.

44. Thomas S. Szasz, *The Myth of Mental Illness: Foundations of Theory of Personal Conduct,* rev. ed. (New York: Harper & Row, 1974), pp. 267–268.

45. Mechanic, *Mental Health and Social Policy,* pp. 228–230.

46. This account of Brown's situation was described in Charlotte Low, "A Rude Awakening from Civil Liberties," *Insight,* March 21, 1988, pp. 8–9.

47. Charles Krauthammer, "When Liberty Really Means Neglect," *Time,* December 2, 1985, pp. 103–104.

48. See, for example, "Is It Safe to Seek Help at Private Psychiatric Hospitals?" *Mental Health Advocate,* Vol. 9, No. 5, newsletter of the Mental Health Association in Texas, 1991, pp. 1, 4–6.

49. Mark Schlesinger, Robert Dowart, Claudia Hoover, and Sherrie Epstein, "The Determinants of Dumping: A National Study of Economically Motivated Transfers Involving Mental Health Care," *Health Services Research,* Vol. 32, No. 5, 1997, pp. 561–590.

50. Marcia Baum, "Remedies for Psychiatric Hospital Abuses Discussed," *NASW Texas Network,* Vol. 17, No. 2, 1992, newsletter of the National Association of Social Workers/Texas, p. 4.

51. Much of this paragraph relies on Pat Harbolt, "The Fight Against Community Programs," *Access: A Human Services Magazine,* Florida Department of Health and Rehabilitative Services, Vol. 4, No. 4, February–March 1981, pp. 14–18; quote from p. 18.

52. Steven P. Segal, "Deinstitutionalization," in Richard L. Edwards ed.-in-chief, *Encyclopedia of Social Work,* 19th ed. (Washington, DC: National Association of Social Workers, 1995), pp. 704–712.

53. Mark Clements, "What We Say About Mental Illness," *Parade,* October 31, 1993, p. 6.

54. E. Fuller Torrey, "Editorial: Jails and Prisons—America's New Mental Hospitals," *American Journal of Public Health,* Vol. 85, No. 12, December 1995, pp. 1611–1613; "Mentally Ill People More Likely to be Taken to Jail Than Hospital," (Associated Press) *Austin American-Statesman,* October 3, 1997, p. B3.

55. Mechanic, *Mental Health and Social Policy.*

56. These data and accompanying references are summarized in Ingrid D. Goldstrom, Ronald W. Manderscheid, and Lawrence A. Rudolph, "Mental Health Services in State Adult Correctional Facilities," in Manderscheid and Sonnenschein, *Mental Health: United States, 1992,* pp. 231–232.

57. This historical account relies on Stephen J. Pfohl, "The Discovery of Child Abuse," *Social Problems,* Vol. 24, No. 3, 1977, pp. 310–323; Diana M. DiNitto and C. Aaron McNeece, *Social Work: Issues and Opportunities in a Challenging Profession* (Englewood Cliffs, NJ: Prentice Hall, 1990), chapter 9; Sallie A. Watkins, "The Mary Ellen Myth: Correcting Child Welfare History," *Social Work,* Vol. 35, No. 6, 1990, pp. 500–503.

58. Watkins, "The Mary Ellen Myth."

59. Robert H. Bremner, ed., *Children and Youth in America: A Documentary,* Vol. 2 (Cambridge, MA: Harvard University Press, 1974), pp. 247–248.

60. The remainder of this section relies on Pfohl, "The Discovery of Child Abuse."

61. C. Henry Kempe et al., "The Battered-Child Syndrome," *Journal of the American Medical Association,* Vol. 181, July 7, 1962, pp. 105–112.

62. See Michael R. Petit and Patrick A. Curtis, *Child Abuse and Neglect: A Look at the States, 1997 CWLA Stat Book* (Washington, DC: CWLA Press, 1997).

63. The 1996 data on child abuse and neglect are from U.S. Department of Health and Human Services, Children's Bureau, *Child Maltreatment 1996: Reports from the States to the National Child Abuse and Neglect Data System* (Washington, DC: U.S. Government Printing Office, 1998).

64. U.S. Department of Health and Human Services, National Center on Child Abuse and Neglect, *Third National Incidence Study of Child Abuse and Neglect (NIS-3): Final Report* (Washington, DC: U.S. Government Printing Office, 1996).

65. Tamar Lewin (*New York Times*), "2 Polls Find Wide Abuse of Children," *Austin American-Statesman*, December 7, 1995, pp. A1, 10.

66. Henry Maas and Richard Engler, *Children in Need of Parents* (New York: Columbia University Press, 1959).

67. See Bruce Bellingham and Joseph Byers, "Foster Care and Child Protection Services," in Allen W. Imershein, Mary K. Pugh Mathis, C. Aaron McNeece and Associates, *Who Cares for the Children: A Case Study of Policies and Practices* (Dix Hills, NY: General Hall, 1995), pp. 101–121.

68. See U.S. House of Representatives, Committee on Ways and Means, *1996 Green Book: Background Material and Data on Programs within the Jurisdiction of the Committee on Ways and Means* (Washington, DC: U.S. Government Printing Office, 1996) pp. 726–727.

69. American Bar Association and National Resource Center on Legal and Court Issues, *Reasonable Efforts Advisory Panel Meeting* (Washington, DC: American Bar Association, April 21, 1995); also see Committee on Ways and Means, *1996 Green Book*, pp. 727–728.

70. "CWLA on Reasonable Efforts," written comments to the Senate Committee on Labor and Human Resources hearing on reasonable efforts submitted by the Child Welfare League of America, January 27, 1998, http://www.casanet.org/library/reasonable_efforts/cwla.htm.

71. Report by Westat, Inc., cited in Committee on Ways and Means, *1998 Green Book*, pp. 762–763.

72. Information on caseload and cost increases relies on Committee on Ways and Means, *1998 Green Book*, pp. 732–733.

73. Most of the information in the remainder of this paragraph and in the next paragraph is found in Petit and Curtis, *Child Abuse and Neglect: A Look at the States, 1997 CWLA Stat Book*, pp. 72, 73, 82 & 83 and is based on the Child Welfare League of America's *State Agency Survey*, 1996.

74. Data from the U.S. Department of Health and Human Services reported in Committee on Ways and Means, *1998 Green Book*, p. 731.

75. See "Summary of the Adoption and Safe Families Act of 1997 (P. L. 105–89)," Child Welfare League of America, http://www.cwla.org/cwla.hr867.html; Committee on Ways and Means, *1998 Green Book*, p. 738.

76. See Committee on Ways and Means, U.S. House of Representatives, *Overview of Entitlement Programs: 1994 Green Book* (Washington, DC: U.S. Government Printing Office, 1994), p. 658.

77. Marsha Mailick Seltzer and Leonard M. Bloksberg, "Permanency Planning and Its Effects on Foster Children: A Review of the Literature," *Social Work*, Vol. 32, No. 1, 1987, pp. 65–68. For an extensive review of evaluations of the various types of child welfare services, see Alfred Kadushin and Judith A. Martin, *Child Welfare Services*, 4th ed. (New York: Macmillan, 1988).

78. See Mark W. Fraser, Peter Pecora, and David A. Haapala, *Families in Crisis: The Impact of Intensive Family Preservation Services* (New York: Aldine de Gruyter, 1991).

79. Jill Kinney, David Haapala, and Charlotte Booth, *Keeping Families Together: The Homebuilders Model* (New York: Aldine de Gruyter, 1991).

80. Gary Cameron and Jim Vanderwood, *Protecting Children and Supporting Families: Promising Programs and Organizational Realities* (New York: Aldine de Gruyter, 1997), especially chapter 6.

81. Bellingham and Byers, "Foster Care and Child Protection Services."

82. "Law Overhauls Foster Care, Procedural Changes Enacted, Funding Needs Remain," *NASW News*, January 1998, p. 6; "Adoption Law Funding Lack Called Threat," *NASW News*, April 1998, p. 9.

83. Testimony of Randy Burton in *Justice for Children* newsletter (Spring, TX), March 1991, p. 10; also see the Spring 1995 issue for reiteration of this view.

84. Brad Bryant, "Panacea Watch: Permanency Planning," *Focus*, Foster Family-based Treatment Association newsletter, Summer 1993, p. 11.

85. *Professional Social Work Practice in Public Child Welfare, An Agenda for Action* (Portland, ME: University of Southern Maine, 1987).

86. Ibid.; also see Michel McQueen, "Family Crisis, Foster Care System is Strained as Reports of Child Abuse Mount," *Wall Street Journal*, June 15, 1987, pp. 1, 18; Clare Ansberry, "Desperate Straits," *Wall Street Journal*, January 5, 1987, pp. 1, 10.

87. David S. Savage (*Los Angeles Times* Service), "Court Gives Social Workers Immunity from Lawsuits," *Austin American-Statesman*, April 26, 1994, p. C20.

88. See Rudolph Alexander, Jr., "The Legal Liability of Social Workers After DeShaney," *Social Work*, Vol. 38, No. 1, January 1993, pp. 64–68.

89. See Arnold Silverman, "Outcomes of Transracial Adoption," in The Center for the Future of Children, ed., *The Future of Children* (Los Altos, CA: David and Lucille Packard Foundation, 1993), pp. 104–118; Ruth G. McRoy, "An Organizational Dilemma: The Case of Transracial Adoptions," *Journal of Applied Behavioral Science*, Vol. 25, No. 2, 1989, pp. 145–160.

90. Jonathan Kozol, "Spare Us the Cheap Grace," *Time*, December 11, 1995, p. 96.

91. Bellingham and Byers, "Foster Care and Child Protection Services."

92. Lela B. Costin, Howard Jacob Karger, and David Stoesz, *The Politics of Child Abuse in America* (New York: Oxford University Press, 1996).

93. See Linda Hubbard Getze, "Need Help? What the Aging Network Can Do for You," *Modern Maturity* March 1981, pp. 33–36; and see "The Administration on Aging and the Older Americans Act," http://www.aoa.dhhs.gov/aoa/pages/aoa.html#OAA.

94. U.S. National Center for Health Statistics, *Vital Statistics of the United States: 1973 Life Tables* (Rockville, MD: U.S. Department of Health, Education and Welfare, 1975) cited in Mario Tonti and Barbara Silverstone, "Services to Families of the Elderly," in Abraham Monk, ed., *Handbook of Gerontological Services* (New York: Van Nostrand Reinhold Co., 1985), pp. 211–239; Lynn Osterkamp, "Family Caregivers: America's Primary Long-Term Care Resource," *Aging,* No. 358, 1988, pp. 3–5.

95. "White House Conference on Aging Final Report Released," March 6, 1996, http://www.aoa.dhhs.gov/aoa/pr/whcoarep.html; also see M. Fernando Torres-Gil, "Aging Policy in the Clinton Administration," *Journal of Aging & Social Policy,* Vol. 7, No. 2, 1995, pp. 113–118; Roberta R. Greene, "Emerging Issues for Social Workers in the Field of Aging: White House Conference Themes," *Journal of Gerontological Social Work,* Vol. 27, No. 3, 1997, pp. 79–87.

96. Robert B. Hudson, "The Older Americans Act and the Defederalization of Community-based Care," in Paul H. K. Kim, ed., *Services to the Aged: Public Policies and Programs* (New York: Garland Publishing, 1994), pp. 45–75.

97. Paragraphs on guardianship rely on Fred Bayles and Scott McCartney, "Guardians of the Elderly, An Ailing System," a six-part Associated Press series appearing in the *Austin American-Statesman,* September 20–25, 1987, Section A; also see George H. Zimny and George T. Grossberg, *Guardianship of the Elderly: Psychiatric and Judicial Aspects* (New York: Springer, 1998).

98. Zimny and Grossberg, *Guardianship of the Elderly: Psychiatric and Judicial Aspects,* p. 9.

99. Morris, *Social Policy of the American Welfare State,* p. 150.

100. See Bruce C. Vladeck and Marvin Feuerberg, "Unloving Care Revisited," *Generations,* Vol. 19, No. 4, 1995–1996, pp. 9–13.

101. Special Committee on Aging, United States Senate, *Developments in Aging: 1996,* Vol. 1 (Washington, DC: U.S. Government Printing Office, 1997).

CHAPTER

Challenging Social Welfare: Racism and Sexism

Eighty years after women won the right to vote and more than thirty-five years after passage of the Civil Rights Act of 1964, the United States still struggles with racism and sexism. Perhaps Rip Van Winkle would be surprised at the progress that blacks, other ethnic groups, and women have made, but frustration over inequality remains. Poverty and other social problems continue to be concentrated among particular groups—primarily women, blacks, Hispanic Americans, and American Indians.* This chapter explores the history of discrimination in the United States and the quest for gender and ethnic equality through social policy.

GENDER INEQUITIES

The Feminization of Poverty

During the 1980s, "the feminization of poverty"[1] became a catch phrase, but this situation was hardly new. Most poor adults and public assistance recipients have always been women. Some of the earliest state and local welfare programs were mothers' aid and mothers' pension laws, which were followed by the federally assisted Aid to Dependent Children program and later the Aid to Families with Dependent Children program (AFDC) (see Chapter 6). These programs were originally intended to help mothers, not fathers. Even the AFDC-Unemployed Parent program, and later the Family Support Act of 1988 which extended AFDC to certain two-parent families in all states, did not change this emphasis. Traditionally, women "went on welfare" because they were expected to remain at home to care for their young children when their hus-

*In this chapter the terms *black* and *African American* are used interchangeably, as are the terms *Hispanic American* and *Hispanic origin*, and *Native American* and *American Indian*.

bands were unable to support them due to death, disability, or unemployment, or unwilling to support them after divorce or desertion. When women did go to work to support themselves and their families, they were usually forced into low-paying jobs; many of them still are. These factors contributed to a pattern in which women are more likely to be poor and more likely to receive public assistance. They were further exacerbated in the 1970s and 1980s with the rapid increase in the number of female-headed households. The discussion of poverty in Chapter 3 clearly shows that female-headed households are most vulnerable to poverty, and that women who are members of certain ethnic groups are extremely vulnerable.

Women are about 59 percent of all Supplemental Security Income (SSI) recipients and 73 percent of aged SSI recipients.[2] Women are overrepresented in SSI for two reasons. First, they are more likely to be poor because their Social Security benefits are less than men's, and they are less likely to have other sources of income such as pensions. In 1997, the median income of males age 65 and older was $17,768, compared to $10,062 for women,[3] and the percentage of women age 65 and older living alone and in poverty was 22, compared with 14 for men.[4] For older white women, the percentage was 20, compared with 12 for their male counterparts. For older Hispanic and black women, the percentages were 54 and 40, respectively, and for older Hispanic and black men, 45 and 31 percent, respectively. The poverty rates for older men and women living alone are high for all groups, but women are generally in the worst straits. The second reason that women are more likely to receive SSI is that they live longer than men. Therefore, they are more likely to encounter the chronic infirmities that accompany advanced age or disability and drain away resources.

Social welfare aid in the United States developed along two separate tracks: the less generous public assistance programs were instituted largely to help women and children while the more generous social insurance programs were targeted toward male workers.[5] Inequities caused by social policy are to blame for many of the economic problems of older women. When the Social Security system was first adopted, the roles of men and women were different than they are today. Women were less likely to work outside the home, and divorce was less common. The Social Security system reflected the social conditions of the 1930s when most women were considered "dependents" of their working husbands. Since women are poorer than men, they rely more heavily on transfer payments such as Social Security, but their benefits are often minimal. In 1996, the average monthly Social Security retirement benefit paid to women was $644 compared to $838 for men.[6] "Nonmarried women over 65 rely on Social Security for 72 percent of their retirement income. Forty percent of that group rely on Social Security for 90 percent or more of their retirement income."[7]

The Social Security system has not kept pace with the changing roles of men and women. Gender inequities persist for a number of reasons:[8]

1. Women's wages are generally lower than men's (even when they do the same work), resulting in lower Social Security benefits paid to women on retirement or disability.
2. Women are still likely to spend less time in the paid workforce than men because they continue to carry the major unpaid responsibilities for home and child care. This also results in lower Social Security benefits paid to women.

3. A divorced woman who was married for at least ten years is entitled to a Social Security payment equal to half of her former husband's retirement benefits. If this is the woman's only income, it is likely inadequate, and she cannot collect at all based on her former husband's earnings if they were married less than ten years.
4. Widows generally do not qualify for benefits until they are 60 years old unless they are disabled or have children under age 18.
5. Homemakers are not covered on their own unless they have held jobs in the paid labor force.
6. Social Security retirement benefits are often based on the earnings of the primary worker, generally the husband. The wages of a second earner, usually the wife, may not raise the couple's combined Social Security benefits.
7. Couples in which one worker (generally the husband) earned most of the wages may receive higher retirement benefits than those in which the husband and wife earned equal wages.
8. Married workers benefit from Social Security more than single workers. An individual who has never worked can benefit from Social Security payments based on the work of a spouse. Single workers do not receive additional benefits, even though they have made Social Security payments at the same rate as married workers.

Over the years, there have been some efforts to reduce gender inequities in the Social Security programs, but most have brought only a limited number of new recipients to the rolls. One measure allows divorced husbands to claim benefits based on the earnings records of their former wives. Another allows divorced spouses to qualify for benefits at age 62 based on a former spouse's earnings, even if the ex-spouse has not claimed benefits. The overhaul of Social Security in 1983 failed to address the program's major gender inequities, and they remain to be resolved.

As we would expect, couples receive the highest Social Security retirement benefits. Widowed or divorced men receive more than widowed or divorced women, but never-married women now average more than their male counterparts.[9] One improvement in the Social Security retirement system is that average benefits for all groups now exceed the poverty level. In the early 1970s, benefits for unmarried men and women were only two-thirds of the poverty level. And the number of women who quality for benefits based on their own work records has increased considerably. Although many women still receive higher payments based on their husbands' earnings rather than on their own, this is expected to change.

Over the years two major options have been suggested for remedying gender inequities in the Social Security system. The **earnings-sharing** option would divide a couple's earnings equally between the husband and wife for each year they are married. This option would allow benefits to be calculated separately for the husband and the wife whether they remained married or not and would eliminate the ideas of the "primary wage earner" and the "dependent spouse." This option would also recognize that a spouse with primary responsibility for care of the home and children is an equal partner in the marriage. A second option is the **double-decker plan.** Under this option, everyone would be eligible for a basic benefit, whether or not they had ever worked for pay. Individuals with paid work experience would receive a payment in addition to the basic benefit.

Now a third option is being discussed that requires women's careful consideration—the privatization of Social Security. As discussed in Chapter 4, privatization can take many forms. It could also be combined with the double-decker and earnings-sharing plans. The Libertarian Cato Institute recently published a study concluding that privatization would leave all women better off in retirement, but the authors admit that they did not weigh in their calculations the fact that Social Security is much safer than private investments.[10] An organization called Financial Women International cautioned about privatization, saying that "all workers should receive comparable benefits, no matter what the state of the market."[11] A female member of the Social Security Advisory Council issued a stronger opinion, calling privatization "a threat to women" because "the promise of security would disappear."[12] She also noted that privatization might strain marriages in more ways than one, especially in one-earner families, if a working spouse was required to contribute to a stay-at-home spouse's private account. In today's system, stay-at-home spouses get a benefit with no additional contributions from the wage earner.

The Wage Gap

In 1955 the Bureau of Labor Statistics calculated that women earned 64 cents for every dollar earned by men; by 1961 the figure had dropped to 59 cents.[13] As it hovered there, "59 cents" became a well-known refrain of the equal rights movement. It was not until the 1980s that the earnings ratio again consistently exceeded the 60 percent mark. In 1997 women's earnings were about 74 percent of men's. Better news is that in the 25 to 35 age bracket, women working full time earned 84 percent of what men earned.

Over time, many reasons have been offered to explain the difference in earning power:

1. Traditionally, most women were not their families' major wage earners, nor did they earn salaries comparable to men's if they did work.
2. Women's wages were considered secondary or as a supplement to their spouses' wages.
3. Women were considered temporary employees who would leave their jobs to marry and have children; they were not seen as serious about careers.
4. Women's work outside the home was considered an extracurricular activity to fill free time.
5. Women had fewer opportunities to obtain education that would lead to better-paying jobs.
6. Women were forced into certain occupations on the low end of the wage scale.

7. Women also had limited job choices because they were forced to accept employment that did not conflict with the routines of their husbands and children.
8. "Women's work"—cleaning and child rearing in their own homes—has not paid a wage.
9. Some argued that women "preferred" lower-level employment because these jobs were more compatible with characteristics they associated with women, such as nurturing qualities and lack of aggressiveness.

Although many of these explanations are readily dismissed, and even laughable today, there are elements of truth in some of them. Some women do terminate their employment on a temporary or long-term basis to raise families. The unfortunate term "mommy track" has been used to describe women who interrupt their careers or try to juggle both career and children. The term implies that women who want or need careers pay the price, because their multiple responsibilities diminish their chances of career advancement. For example, in 1994 Vassar College was found to have discriminated against a married woman with children who was denied tenure in the biology department. In the past 30 years no married woman in the "hard sciences" had been tenured there. Some women do prefer to select jobs that are compatible with family routines and place family over career; however, most women do not work just for the fun of it. The paid employment of many women is essential to their families' support. Eighteen percent of U.S. families are headed by women alone,[14] and many two-earner families would be in serious financial difficulty without the wife's economic contribution. In addition, many women find their work satisfying, challenging, and an integral component of their lives.

Women comprise 46 percent of the civilian labor force.[15] A growing number have earned advanced degrees and many hold higher-level jobs, but women continue to earn less than men, even when they have the same education. Figure 11-1 shows that among full-time, year-round workers in 1997, women with a high school education earned more than $9,000 less than men with equal education; women with bachelor's or master's degrees also earned considerably less than men with equivalent education. Table 11-1 (page 366) also shows that there are differences between women's and men's earnings among the major ethnic groups in the United States, with women consistently earning less. Earnings differences persist even among men and women in the same occupations who worked full–time, year-round, although inequality is greater in some professions than others (see Table 11-2, page 367). In the sales sector, women earned only 60 cents for every dollar earned by men. Even in the "pink collar" administrative support and clerical sector, women earned only 76 percent of what men earned. Among those in the professional specialties (lawyers, engineers, etc.), the earnings ratio was 70 cents to the dollar. Equality was by far the greatest in farming, forestry, and fishing. Although a portion of the pay differentials between men and women may be explained by the number of years of work experience, gender discrimination and racial discrimination continue to explain part of the gap. Men today may complain about "reverse" discrimination, but for many women, achieving gains in pay and breaking the "glass ceiling" in terms of career advancement continue to be painfully slow processes.

FIGURE 11-1

Median Annual Earnings of Full-Time, Year-Round Workers, 25 Years and Older, by Gender and Education, 1997

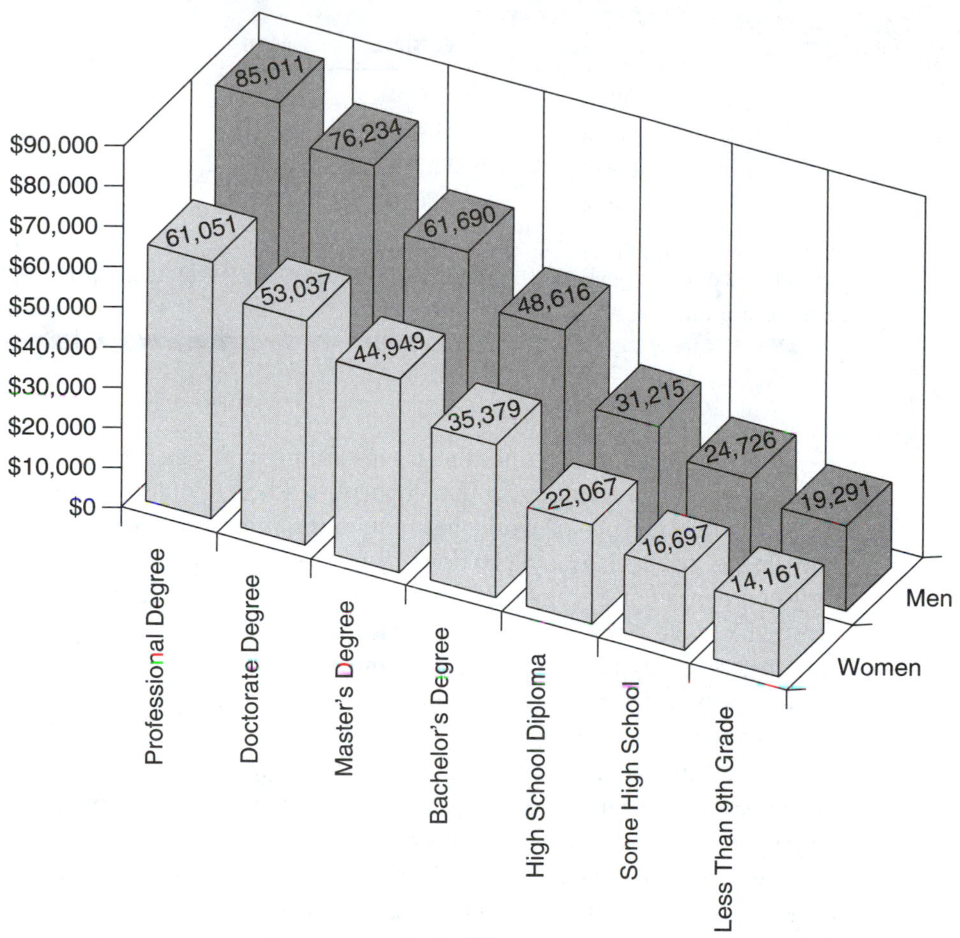

Source: U.S. Bureau of the Census, *Money Income in the United States: 1997,* Current Population Reports, Series P60-200 (Washington, DC: U.S. Government Printing Office, 1998), Table 7, pp. 28–29.

An obvious approach to narrowing the wage gap has been to press for equal pay for equal work. It is difficult, for example, to justify paying a male accountant more than a female accountant if their job responsibilities are the same. According to the Equal Pay Act of 1963, men and women who do the same work are supposed to be paid equally. Those who are not are entitled to use legal channels to settle their grievances. The federal government established the Equal Employment Opportunity Commission (EEOC) to help employees in such cases.

TABLE 11-1

Median Annual Earnings of Full-Time, Year-Round Workers, 25 Years and Older, by Gender and Race or Ethnicity, 1997

	Women	Men
All	$26,029	$35,248
White	26,470	36,118
Black	22,764	26,897
Hispanic[a]	19,676	21,799

Source: U.S. Bureau of the Census, *Money Income in the United States: 1997,* Current Population Reports, Series P60-200 (Washington, DC: U.S. Government Printing Office, 1998), Table 7, pp. 28–29.

[a]May be of any race.

A more recent effort to reduce the gap in earnings between women and men is **comparable worth.**[16] According to this concept, workers should be paid equally when they do *different* types of work that require the same level of responsibility, effort, knowledge, and skill. Many jobs done by men weigh more heavily in terms of monetary compensation because the **dual labor market** creates a situation in which "women's professions"—secretarial, teaching, nursing, social work—tend to be regarded less highly than professions dominated by men. In discussing comparable worth, we are really asking whether the jobs in question are of equal value to society.

While some have called comparable worth a "truly crazy proposal,"[17] others argue that it is a truly rational approach to achieving equality. By 1985, twenty states had passed laws or resolutions making comparable worth a requirement or a goal of state employment. One study found that states most likely to adopt comparable worth policies were those in which state employees had the right to bargain collectively.[18] Two other variables had a significant but lesser impact—whether the state had ratified the Equal Rights Amendment and the percentage of women in the State's House of Representatives. Even when comparable worth policies are adopted, the rub occurs when officials actually attempt to implement them. In theory, most reasonable people can agree on the principle of equal pay for work of equal value, but how do we determine what constitutes different work of equal value? How can we determine if the work of a secretary is comparable to the work of an automobile mechanic? Some contend that even if the value of jobs could be calculated in an agreeable way, the cost of implementing far-reaching comparable worth plans would make it unfeasible. Others feel just as strongly that it is about time that women are paid equitably.

The U.S. Commission on Civil Rights has failed to support comparable worth, saying it would wreak havoc in the marketplace. Thus far the courts have supported salary differentials that appear to arise from labor force competition. For example, in a case against Brown University, a male faculty member accused the university of pay-

TABLE 11-2

Median Annual Earnings of Full-Time, Year-Round Workers, 25 Years and Older in Selected Professions, by Gender, 1997

	Men	Women	Women's Earnings as a Percentage of Men's
Executives, administrators, and managerial	$50,149	$33,037	66%
Professional specialty	50,402	35,417	70
Technical and related support	37,705	27,576	73
Sales	35,655	21,392	60
Administrative support, including clerical	29,442	22,474	76
Precision production, craft, and repairs	31,496	21,649	69
Machine operators, assemblers, and inspectors	26,969	17,683	66
Transportation and material moving	28,227	21,024	74
Handlers, equipment cleaners, helpers, and laborers	21,475	15,774	73
Service workers	22,335	15,964	71
Farming, forestry, and fishing	17,394	17,301	99

Source: U.S. Bureau of the Census, *Money Income in the United States: 1997,* Current Population Reports, Series P60-200 (Washington, DC: U.S. Government Printing Office, 1998), Table 7, pp. 28–29.

ing an equally qualified female faculty member a higher salary. The First Circuit Court ruled in favor of the university, which argued that the female professor was paid more because she had planned to take a position at another school that had offered her a higher salary. Brown wanted to retain her. The university contended that she had greater market value than the male professor, and the court agreed. In another case, nursing faculty at the University of Washington filed suit stating that they were paid less than male faculty in other departments. The Ninth Circuit Court ruled that under Title VII of the Civil Rights Act, suits cannot be brought before the court if salary inequities are due to labor market conditions.

Equal Rights for Women

Women had been organizing to gain equality through political participation long before the suffragette movement, but it was not until 1920 that the Nineteenth Amendment to the U.S. Constitution finally gave women the right to vote. Even with this right, the percentage of women who hold political office has remained small (see Illustration 11-1), but it has grown more rapidly than ever in the last several years. In 1993, Carol Moseley-Braun (D-Illinois) become the first African-American woman to

ILLUSTRATION 11-1

Women in Federal and State Offices

In 1999, women were 4 (28%) of the 14 secretaries in the U.S. Cabinet. Women held 9 (9%) of the 100 seats in the U.S. Senate and 56 (13%) of the 435 seats in the U.S. House of Representatives. Three women (6%) were governors, 18 (36%) lieutenant governors, 10 (20%) state attorney generals, 4 (8%) state comptrollers, 14 (28%) secretaries of state, and 10 (20%) state treasurers. Women held 1,652 (22%) of the 7,424 seats in state legislatures. Washington state had the highest percentage of women in its legislature—41%, and Alabama had the lowest—8%.

Source: Center for the American Woman and Politics (CAWP), National Information Bank on Women in Public Office, Eagleton Institute of Politics, Rutgers University.

serve in the U.S. Senate, and California became the first state to have two women senators simultaneously—Barbara Boxer and Dianne Feinstein (both Democrats). Women still have a long way to go if they want to claim the number of elected positions commensurate with their representation in the population, but President Clinton's political appointments have more dramatically increased the number of women in high-level posts. He appointed Madeleine Albright Secretary of State, making her the highest ranking woman ever to serve in the federal government. He also appointed Janet Reno, the first woman to serve as U.S. Attorney General, and Ruth Bader Ginsburg, the second woman to serve on the U.S. Supreme Court. As the end of his first year in office approached, 37 percent of the more than 500 appointments he made were women, more than the 24 percent of the Bush administration, and far more than other previous presidents.[19]

Since the 1960s, the federal government has attempted to address the inequities women face in employment, education, and the marketplace. The following list contains some of the most notable achievements:

1. The Equal Pay Act of 1963 requires employers to compensate male and female workers equally for performing the same jobs under similar conditions. The law does not cover all employment, but amendments have added to the types of jobs and employers who must comply.
2. Title VII of the Civil Rights Act of 1964 prohibits gender discrimination in employment practices and provides the right to court redress. The Equal Employment Opportunity Commission is charged with interpreting and enforcing Title VII.
3. Executive Order 11246, as amended by Executive Order 11375 in 1967, prohibits employers who practice gender discrimination from receiving federal contracts. Employers are also required to develop "affirmative action" plans to remedy inequities. The

order established the Office of Federal Contract Compliance under the Department of Labor as an enforcement agency.

4. Title IX of the 1972 Education Amendments to the Civil Rights Act prohibits gender discrimination by elementary, secondary, vocational, and professional schools, colleges, and universities that receive federal funds.
5. The Equal Credit Act of 1975 prohibits discrimination by lending institutions based on gender or marital status.
6. The Pregnancy Discrimination Act of 1978, another amendment to the Civil Rights Act, protects women from employment discrimination as a result of childbearing.

The Equal Rights Amendment (ERA) also attempted to guarantee women equality through the U.S. Constitution. It stated,

Section 1. Equality of rights under the law shall not be denied or abridged by the United States or by any state on account of sex.

Section 2. Congress shall have the power to enforce by appropriate legislation the provisions of this Article.

Section 3. This amendment shall take effect two years after the date of ratification.

Proponents of the ERA argued that this guarantee of equality under law should be part of the Constitution—"the supreme law of the land." It is true that a number of existing federal and state laws prohibit gender discrimination, but concerns are that these laws are inadequate to fully address the problem. ERA proponents contend that like many other social policy issues, gender discrimination is best addressed by a national policy rather than by a multitude of federal, state, and local laws, each subject to modification or repeal.

However, opponents of the ERA were successful in halting this proposed constitutional amendment just three states short of the thirty-eight states (three-quarters) needed for ratification. In 1972, the U.S. Congress passed the ERA and set a 1979 deadline for state ratification. By 1978, the amendment had not been ratified. Congress granted an extension of the deadline until June 30, 1982. Despite the endorsement of 450 organizations with 50 million members—unions, churches, civil rights groups, legal associations, educational groups, medical organizations—the ERA failed.[20]

The "stop ERA movement" was based on fears about what *might* happen if the ERA passed. It was argued that the ERA would lead to an extension of military registration and perhaps even a military draft and combat duty for women. The ERA did not specifically address the role of women in the armed services. Other issues—marriage, divorce, child custody, inheritance—were also not specifically mentioned in the ERA. It was thus difficult to predict the long-range consequences of the proposed amendment. Some feared that it would cause laws governing relationships between men and women to change in ways that might disadvantage women. Others claimed that the ERA would not have much impact at all. "Stop ERA" chairperson Phyllis Schafly announced to women: "ERA won't do anything for you. It won't make your husband do half the dirty diapers and dishes. It won't make your ex-husband pay support. I think the defeat of the ERA is a tremendous victory for women's rights."[21]

Do Americans want an ERA? Before the ERA faded from the media, national polls reported that a majority of Americans—both men and women—supported equal rights.[22] Supporters, especially the National Organization for Women, have not given up efforts to see the ERA returned to the national agenda.

In February 1984, the U.S. Supreme Court threw a new monkey wrench into the equal rights and affirmative action arena. In the case of *Grove City v. Bell,* it delivered a ruling affecting the interpretation of Title IX of the Civil Rights Act, which prohibits gender discrimination in federally funded education programs. In a 6–3 vote, the Court declared that Title IX applies only to those individual programs receiving federal aid and not to all programs of an institution. This interpretation was in sharp contrast to the spirit with which Title IX had been applied since its enactment. In 1988 Congress passed the Civil Rights Restoration Act to return Title IX to its original intent. President Reagan thought that this new bill would go too far in regulating churches and private businesses and vetoed the measure, but Congress overrode him.

Family Care

More assistance with child care and other family responsibilities would certainly promote greater equality for women. In 1990 Congress passed several pieces of legislation that increased the federal government's participation in child care. Among them were the Child Care and Development Block Grant (CCDBG) and an expansion of child care services provided through the former AFDC JOBS program (see Chapter 6) so that families could maintain employment rather than risk joining the AFDC rolls. Congress also increased expenditures for the Head Start program and tax credits to help low-income working families pay for child care.

The child care tax credit is one way to help families pay for child care. Some proposals seek to increase the credit. Others claim that this approach penalizes families which choose to use non-paid care while working and those in which one parent does not work and stays at home with the children. They support a larger tax credit for dependents that would help families regardless of their employment and child care choices.[23] This is what happened in 1997 when the Balanced Budget Act included a modest child tax credit (see Chapter 2).

In 1996, the Personal Responsibility and Work Opportunity Reconciliation Act (that instituted large-scale welfare reform) consolidated the CCDBG and AFDC child care programs into a single block grant called the Child Care and Development Fund (CCDF). According to an Urban Institute report, "If every state were to put up enough state dollars to draw down the maximum funds available, CCDF funding in FY 1997 would exceed that provided in FY 1995 in all states. However, to draw down the increased federal funds, states would have to put up on average an additional 70 percent of state dollars over and above their FY 1995 levels."[24] States' reactions to the CCDF are likely to vary. Twenty did not draw down all their AFDC child care allocations in 1994 while others provided considerably more than required. States might also reallocate their child care funding. Since more parents are supposed to go to work under TANF than AFDC, they might divert funds to families receiving public assistance that previously went to other low-income families. The Institute calculates that if states maintain their historical spending levels, the proportion of children needing care who are served under the new legislation will be the same as it was before—about one-third. The affordability of child care, the quality and monitoring of this care, and the low pay afforded child care workers which results in difficulties recruiting and retaining staff are issues of concern to everyone who uses care or provides it.

Obtaining care for disabled adult and elderly family members also presents challenges, primarily to women who generally assume the major caretaker responsibilities. Community day care centers help alleviate some of this burden, and many families purchase home care through the private sector using Medicare, Medicaid, or their own funds. Congress and the Bush administration battled over whether employers should allow workers to take leave when a new baby arrives, a child is sick, or an adult family member needs care. During the Bush years, Congress twice passed family leave bills that would have required some employers to provide twelve weeks of unpaid leave to family members when a new baby arrives or when a spouse, parent, or child had a serious illness. The same leave would have been extended to employees with an illness. Despite strong public support, Bush vetoed both bills saying that while he favored family leave, the bills might force businesses to hire replacement help. Rather than preserve jobs, Bush feared that the bills might result in a net job loss.

President Clinton felt very differently about family leave legislation. On taking office, he moved swiftly to sign the Family and Medical Leave Act of 1993. However, the law exempts businesses with less than fifty workers (thereby excluding half the workforce and the vast majority of businesses), and covered businesses are not required to provide leave to upper-echelon employees. A recent United Nations study found that the U.S. had the least generous maternity benefits of all industrialized countries and that of the 152 countries studied, only six—the U.S., Australia, New Zealand, Lesotho, Swaziland, and Papua New Guinea—have no paid leave requirement.[25]

Sexual Harassment

The Equal Pay Act, the Equal Credit Act, the Family and Medical Leave Act, and similar policies are important to women, but other areas of public policy require attention if women are to enjoy true economic and social equality. A problem that has of late received considerable attention is sexual harassment. The definition found in the Code of Federal Regulations and employed by the Equal Employment Opportunity Commission is

> *Unwelcome sexual advances, requests for sexual favors, and other verbal or physical conduct of a sexual nature constitute sexual harassment when*
>
> 1. *Submission to such conduct is made either explicitly or implicitly a term or condition of an individual's employment or admission to an academic program,*

2. *Submission to or rejection of such conduct is used as the basis for decisions affecting an individual's employment status or academic standing, or*
3. *Such conduct has the purpose or effect of substantially interfering with an individual's performance on the job or in the classroom, or creating an intimidating, hostile, or offensive work or study environment.*[26]

Sexual harassment is prohibited by Title VII of the Civil Rights Act of 1964 and by Title IX of the 1972 Educational Amendments to the Act, but for many years, such behavior was considered harmless and was taken for granted. The damaging effects of such behavior on women as well as men have now come to be recognized in public policy. Under the Civil Rights Act of 1991, those who suffer sexual harassment may collect from $50,000 to $300,000 in damages, depending on the size of the company involved. But making accusations of sexual harassment is not without its risks, as evidenced by law professor Anita Hill when she accused then Supreme Court nominee and now Supreme Court Justice Clarence Thomas of such behavior. Many people were outraged by the poor treatment Hill received during Thomas' Senate confirmation hearings. Some women said they were moved to run for public office because of their disgust with the hearings. Since then, the number of harassment suits has increased, extending even to the President of the United States.

Among the publicized cases of sexual harassment was that of Dr. Frances Conley who resigned her position at Stanford University Medical School after becoming fed up with the sexual harassment she and female medical students had endured over the years (she did return to her job later). The Navy's Tailhook scandal demonstrated personal behavior unbecoming servicemen or any men. In its aftermath, the country learned of situations in other branches of the service in which women who did not go along with such behavior were denied career advancement or left the service altogether. It is probably no coincidence that exposing these scandals has been accompanied by significant promotions of female military personnel and expanded roles for women in duties once off limits to them. Sexual harassment has proved to be a very effective barrier to career advancement for women in all areas of employment.

The U.S. Supreme Court's first major decision in a sexual harassment case came in 1986 in *Meritor Savings Bank v. Vinson,* which stated that Title VII of the Civil Rights Act of 1964 does include sexual harassment. Some lower courts interpreted this decision rather narrowly, applying it only in situations where women were psychologically damaged or no longer able to work in that environment. The second major case came in 1993 when the Court broadened this interpretation. Teresa Harris first brought her sexual harassment case against Forklift Systems in the mid-1980s. Lower courts rejected her case because it did not meet the restrictive definition they had adopted. But Supreme Court Justice Ruth Bader Ginsburg argued that those of one gender should not be subjected to conditions in which they are treated differently from the other gender in the workplace. And Justice Sandra Day O'Connor said that there should be recourse before the behavior becomes psychologically damaging. She added that sufficient proof should be that "the environment would be perceived, and is perceived, as hostile or abusive."

Today, sexual harassment cases are generally divided into two types: the "quid pro quo" type in which sexual favors are demanded or required as a basis for employment decisions, and the "hostile environment type" in which sexual conduct unreasonably interferes with work performance.[27] In Illustration 11-2, which is sure to aggravate many feminists, Camille Paglia defends cases brought on quid pro quo grounds but not on hostile environment grounds. However, in 1998, the Supreme

ILLUSTRATION 11-2

A Call for Lustiness: Just Say No to the Sex Police

Liberal Democrats, who supported Anita Hill against Clarence Thomas in 1991, are waking up to the police state that their rigid rules have created. Now, as allegations fly about presidential sex, we can finally distinguish between genuine sexual coercion and free expression of sexual thought.

As a college teacher, I've long held that no person in power should demand sexual favors in return for a high grade or promotion. Nor should subordinates sexually involved with teachers or managers enjoy an unfair advantage over their peers. Those principles are a genuine contribution to feminist history.

But the secondary "hostile environment" policy, which allows employees to file lawsuits on nebulous grounds of psychological distress, is grotesquely totalitarian. It offends free-speech rights and is predicated on a reactionary female archetype: the prudish Victorian lady who faints at a sexual innuendo. This isn't feminism; it's Puritanism.

The Anita Hill case, far from expanding women's rights, was a disaster for civil liberties. That Hill, an articulate graduate of the Yale Law School, could find no job-preserving way to communicate to her employer her discomfort with mild off-color banter strained credulity. That Thomas could be publicly grilled about trivial lunchtime conversations that occurred 10 years earlier was an outrage worthy of Stalinist Russia.

An antiseptically sex-free workplace is impossible and unnatural. We want a sophisticated art of seduction. Feminist excesses have paralyzed and neutered white, upper-middle-class young men, as should be obvious to any visitor to the campuses of the élite schools. I want a society of lusty men and lusty women whose physical and mental energies are in exuberant free flow. While men must behave honorably (Governors and Presidents should not be dropping their pants in front of female employees or secretly preying on buxom young interns), women must also watch how they dress and behave. For every gross male harasser, there are 10 female sycophants who shamelessly use their sexual attractions to get ahead. We don't want a society of surveillance by old maids and snitches. The proper mission of feminism is to encourage women to take personal responsibility without running to parental authority figures for help.

The fanatic overprotection of women is fast making us an infantile nation. We need to treat sex with greater realism and imagination. Women should be taught not that they are passive wards of the state but that sex is a great human comedy where the joke is always on us.

Source: Camille Paglia, "A Call for Lustiness," *Time,* March 23, 1998, p. 54. Camille Paglia, Professor of Humanities, University of the Arts, Philadelphia.

Court, in *Burlington Industries v. Ellreth* and *Farragher v. City of Boca Raton*, ruled 7 to 2 (Justices Thomas and Scalia dissented in both cases) that employers are liable for sexual harassment in both types of cases even if they did not know of the harassment and even if the threats or abuses were not acted on, as long as the harassment is pervasive or severe.[28] The rulings also indicate that employers may limit their liability by showing that they took care to prevent or correct harassment and that the worker was unreasonable in not trying to correct the situation. In another case, the justices ruled that schools receiving federal funds are liable for the sexual harassment of students only if they knew of it and did not take action, because Title IX of the Civil Rights Act allows schools the opportunity to correct problems. Title VII does not grant this stipulation to employers.

While the definition of sexual harassment remains vague, these rulings have made many more employers take note by educating employees about the types of behaviors that may lead to lawsuits and by being less tolerant of employees who engage in these behaviors.

No Consensus on Abortion Rights

Among the most contentious issues on the country's domestic agenda is abortion. Before the 1960s, abortions were rarely permitted in any states, except in cases where the mother's life was in danger. Then about a quarter of the states made some modifications in their abortion laws, extending them to cases of rape, incest, or when the physical or mental health of the mother was in jeopardy. Obtaining an abortion was still difficult because each case had to be reviewed individually by physicians and by the hospital where the abortion was to be performed.

In 1970, four states (New York, Alaska, Hawaii, and Washington) further liberalized their abortion laws, permitting women to obtain an abortion on the woman's request with her physician's agreement. In 1973 the U.S. Supreme Court made decisions that fundamentally changed abortion policy. In the cases of *Roe v. Wade* and *Doe v. Bolton,* the Court ruled that the Fifth and Fourteenth Amendments to the Constitution, which guarantee all people "life, liberty and property," did not include the life of the unborn fetus. In addition, the First and Fourteenth Amendments guaranteeing personal liberties were said to extend to childbearing decisions. The Court did stipulate some conditions under which abortions could and could not be restricted by the states: (1) during the first three months of pregnancy, the states cannot restrict the mother's decision for an abortion; (2) from the fourth through sixth months of pregnancy, the states cannot restrict abortions, but they can protect the health of the mother by setting standards for how and when abortions can be performed; (3) during the last three months of pregnancy, the states can prohibit all abortions except those to protect the mother's life and health.

Following the Roe and Doe decisions, poor pregnant women were able to obtain federally funded abortions under the Medicaid program. But in 1976, antiabortion groups, with the unflagging support of conservative Representative Henry J. Hyde (R-Illinois), were successful in pushing through "the Hyde Amendment." The amendment prohibited the federal government from paying for abortions except in cases where the mother's life is endangered. It did not prevent states from financing abortions with their own funds. The Hyde amendment also did not restrict women from obtaining privately funded abortions, but necessarily limited their ability to do so if they were unable to cover the costs. The U.S. Supreme Court upheld the Hyde Amendment, declaring that a poor woman does not have the right to a federally financed abortion except when her life is in danger. In 1977, the federal funding ban was lifted in promptly reported cases of rape and incest and in cases where "severe and long-lasting" harm would be caused to the woman, but in 1981 the language was again restricted to permit federally funded abortions only to save the mother's life. In 1989, Congress again approved legislation to add cases of rape and incest, but President Bush vetoed it, and Congress could not muster the two-thirds vote needed in both chambers to override the veto.

In October 1993, Congress passed a law signed by President Clinton reinstating access to Medicaid-financed abortions in cases of rape or incest. Six states already permitted the use of their funds for abortions for poor women with certain restrictions, and thirteen others provided state-funded abortions for poor women on request. The Clinton administration views abortions in cases of rape or incest as "medically necessary," and ordered all states to begin paying for them by March 31, 1994. A protest quickly arose over whether the intent of the law was to allow or to require states to pay for these abortions. Antiabortion activists called the directive an attempt to challenge laws in states with more restrictive abortion policies.[29]

Interpreting abortion rights has kept the U.S. Supreme Court busy. In 1983, it reaffirmed the landmark 1973 decisions concerning the right to abortion and also extended some provisions. Abortions early in the second trimester do not have to be performed in hospitals, because medical advances now make it possible to conduct these procedures safely on an outpatient basis. The Court also struck down regulations adopted in Akron, Ohio, that made it more difficult to obtain an abortion, such as requiring minors to get parental consent and imposing a twenty-four-hour waiting period between the time a woman signed an informed consent form and the time the abortion was actually performed. In 1986, the Court acted again. This time it struck down a Pennsylvania law aimed at discouraging women from obtaining abortions.

But the tenor of the Court began to change. In its 1989 decision in *Webster v. Reproductive Health Services,* the Court upheld a Missouri law that (1) prohibits public hospitals and public employees from performing abortions and from counseling a woman to obtain an abortion unless her life is in danger; (2) requires physicians to determine whether a woman who is at least twenty weeks pregnant is carrying a fetus that is viable (able to survive outside the womb); and (3) declares that life begins at conception. The ruling opened the door for states to pass more restrictive abortion laws. Pennsylvania quickly adopted new regulations, including notification of husbands, twenty-four-hour waiting periods, and prohibition of third-trimester abortions. A wave of additional attempts at more restrictive state laws ensued. In contrast, Maryland bucked the trend and passed a law shoring up abortion rights. Although it met with some stiff opposition, abortion rights advocates hoped it might protect the right to abortion in Maryland should the Supreme Court fail to protect access to abortions.

Opponents of abortion, who usually call themselves "right-to-life" groups, were generally pleased with the 1989 ruling and hoped that it would be a major step in reversing *Roe v. Wade.* These groups oppose the freedom to obtain an abortion and generally base their arguments on religious, moral, and biological grounds, contending that abortion is tantamount to taking a human life. Prolifers demonstrate annually in Washington on the anniversary of the *Roe v. Wade* decision.

Proponents of abortion, who often call themselves the "prochoice" movement, believe that a woman has the right to make decisions about her own body, including abortion. Without recourse to legal abortions, they fear that women may turn to illegal abortions that can result in health risks or even death for the woman. Proponents believe that misery and suffering may be avoided when a woman can make a decision about an unwanted pregnancy. Prochoice groups, including the National Abortion Rights Action League and Planned Parenthood, hold "speakouts" across the country to counteract the antiabortion movement.

Following *Roe v. Wade,* the number of abortions performed annually doubled from an estimated 745,000 in 1973 to about 1.6 million in 1980.[30] In 1995, the abortion rate hit a 20-year low at 20 per 1,000 women.[31] Many reasons have been offered for the drop, including more use of contraceptives and fewer unplanned pregnancies, more decisions to give birth, changing attitudes about abortion, and lack of access to abortions, especially in rural areas.[32]

Prochoice groups grew increasingly concerned about abortion rights during the Republican administrations of the 1980s. The 1973 decision upholding abortion rights was supported 7–2, the 1983 decision 6–3, and the 1986 decision 5–4. In 1989, the restrictions in the Missouri law were also upheld 5–4. President Reagan made three appointments to the court during his terms in office—Sandra Day O'Connor, the first woman ever to serve on the Supreme Court, and Anthony Kennedy and Antonin Scalia. All voted to uphold the Missouri law in 1989. It was the older members of the Court who defended abortion rights. President Bush appointees to the high court, David Souter and Clarence Thomas, were choices that abortion rights advocates feared would further imperil their cause.

In 1992, the U.S. Supreme Court heard yet another case, this time concerning Pennsylvania's new abortion law. In another 5–4 decision, the Court again protected the right to an abortion, but in a 7–2 decision upheld the provisions requiring parental consent for women under age 18, twenty-four-hour waiting periods for almost everyone, and requirements that physicians inform women of their options; it did, however, strike down provisions that required notification of husbands.

While in office, President Reagan tried hard to ban federal funding to family-planning clinics that so much as discussed abortion with patients through what came to be called the "gag rule." Planned Parenthood said it would give up its federal funding rather than obey the rule. The Supreme Court ultimately upheld the gag rule. Congress disagreed, but it was unable to override President Bush's veto of its legislation. The Bush administration did soften the rule by allowing physicians to discuss abortion if there was a medical need for it, but other personnel could only make referrals if women asked for information about abortion. Implementation of Bush's rule was delayed by the courts because the required "notice and comment" period had been bypassed. Many Republicans seem worried that their party's antiabortion stance would hurt them at the polls.

The Democratic presidential administration of Bill Clinton has pursued a far more liberal agenda on abortion. On taking office, Clinton promptly lifted the gag rule. His failed plan for national health care included coverage for abortions. Clinton's appointment of Ruth Bader Ginsburg, a well-known advocate of women's rights, to the Supreme Court renewed hope for stronger support of abortion rights. Prochoice advocates believe that the best way to protect abortion rights is through federal law. The proposed Freedom of Choice Act is intended to do this. It would prevent states from enacting their own restrictions on abortion prior to fetal viability.

Other events in the history of abortion rights stem from the strident efforts of the prolife movement to prevent women from obtaining abortions. Some clinics have been bombed or set on fire. Blockades of abortion clinics have resulted in the arrests of hundreds of members of antiabortion groups. Even if the vast majority of antiabortion activists decry violence, the shooting and bombing deaths of several physicians and staff members have raised serious concerns about how far the more fanatic members of the movement will go.

In an effort to stop harassment at abortion clinics, the National Organization for Women tried several strategies. It was unsuccessful in invoking an 1871 civil rights law that had been used in cases involving the Ku Klux Klan. But NOW filed another lawsuit to invoke federal racketeering and antitrust laws directed at organized crime (called the Racketeer Influenced, Corrupt Organization [RICO] Act of 1970) to prohibit protests at abortion clinics by Operation Rescue and similar organizations. The suit was initially dismissed because the protests involved a political activity, not a commercial activity for profit. Operation Rescue hailed it as a victory for free speech, but when the issue reached the Supreme Court, the justices unanimously agreed that RICO could be invoked if illegal activities are involved. In 1998, under RICO, a Chicago jury found three antiabortion activists guilty of using threats and violence in an attempt to prevent abortions at clinics. Believing that other Supreme Court decisions did not go far enough in protecting entrances to clinics, Congress passed a "buffer zone" law in 1994 that makes it a federal offense to block the entrances to abortion clinics and also to use or threaten force against those seeking or performing abortions. Ardent antiabortion protestors, however, have said it is their duty to continue the opposition to abortion, and suits over what types of protests are permissible continue. In 1994 Operation Rescue and another antiabortion group were ordered to pay $1 million in damages to a Planned Parenthood clinic in Texas, the largest such award to date. Rather than stem the efforts of antiabortionists, some feel that the efforts of antiabortionists have curtailed the number of medical professionals and clinics available to perform abortions.

The latest abortion battle is over a late-term procedure referred to as "partial birth" abortions. Thus far President Clinton has prevented a ban of this procedure, and several states have also seen their efforts to ban the procedure stymied by the courts.

Violence Against Women

Violence against women takes a number of forms. One form is spousal violence which may be directed at husbands or other male partners, but it is most often wives and girlfriends who are the victims. In the late 1970s, some states officially recognized that battered women were not receiving adequate legal protection, and they adopted the position that this amounted to gender discrimination.[33] All states have now enacted some type of legislation to protect abused spouses. Battered spouses have two types of legal recourse: civil and criminal. Civil laws are used to "settle disputes between individuals and to compensate for injuries," while criminal laws are used to "punish acts which are disruptive of social order and to deter other similar acts."[34] Duluth, Minnesota, introduced a strategy for preventing additional incidents of domestic violence that has been adopted by many other jurisdictions:

> *If a police officer has probable cause to believe that a person has, within the preceding four hours, assaulted a spouse, former spouse, or other person with whom he or she resides or has formerly resided, arrest is* mandatory. *The police officer still has the discretion in determining whether or not probable cause exists, but when there is visible sign of injury the officer has no choice but to arrest. A 1984 study conducted by the Minneapolis Police Department and the Police Foundation concluded that arrest was the most significant deterrent to repeat violence when compared to police use of mediation and separation.*[35]

Other forms of violence against women are sexual assault, including rape, and a category that has been more recently defined—stalking. Most women survive victimization with varying degrees of trauma, but this violence can also result in homicide as newspapers accounts seem to indicate all too often. The most important piece of federal legislation which tries to take a comprehensive approach to preventing and intervening in these problems is the Violence Against Women Act (VAWA), part of the Violent Crime Control and Law Enforcement Act of 1994.[36] Prior to this law, the federal response to violence directed at women was weak. The national VAWA Office is located in the U.S. Department of Justice.

VAWA strengthens protective orders through interstate enforcement, prohibits those with restraining orders from possessing a firearm, allows victims to sue for damages, and bolsters restitution orders and "rape shield" laws that prevent a victim's past sexual conduct from being used against her. The act established the National Domestic Violence Hotline (1-800-799-SAFE) and has provided funds to strengthen and streamline the criminal justice system's approach to helping victims, including education for law enforcement officers, prosecutors, and judges and the encouragement of pro-arrest policies and community policing techniques. Guidelines have also been developed to require sex offenders to register with local authorities.

VAWA encourages cooperation between the criminal justice system and agencies such as shelters for battered women, rape crisis programs, and victim-witness programs that have provided the front-line services to victims. The community response is critical because women rely on local law enforcement and courts for protection and to see that justice is served through setting appropriate bail, serving warrants, arresting suspects, and meting out appropriate punishment. Many of the social service agencies that assist women have small budgets and little consistent support. They can help only a fraction of those in need. Services are often crisis-oriented with insufficient long-term help in the form of transportation, housing, and other services such as psychotherapy for women, their children, and the perpetrators.

GAY RIGHTS

Thirty years ago, there was no "gay rights" agenda in this country, only the taboos placed on gay and lesbian relationships. Then, in 1969, a police raid on a gay bar called Stonewall, in Greenwich Village, set off riots that culminated in the birth of the gay rights movement. For many people, gay rights is more than a legal or political issue. The subjects of what "causes" homosexuality, and how many gay men and lesbians there are, are topics of intense debate.

For almost twenty years, the U.S. Supreme Court refused to hear gay rights cases, leaving sodomy laws (which make certain types of sexual acts illegal) and other laws affecting gay men and lesbians to the states. But in 1985, the Court broke its silence and heard the case of *Oklahoma City Board of Education v. National Gay Task Force.* The case involved an Oklahoma law which had permitted school boards to bar from employment teachers who publicly advocated homosexuality. The Gay Rights Task Force criticized the law as a First Amendment violation of free speech while the Board of Education contended that the law was only concerned with those who publicly endorsed certain sexual acts between homosexuals. In its evenly divided 4–4 decision (Justice Powell was ill), the Supreme Court upheld a lower court's ruling that public school teachers cannot be forbidden to advocate homosexuality but that homosexuals can be prohibited from engaging in homosexual acts in public.

Shortly after, in 1986, the U.S. Supreme Court dealt a serious setback to the rights of gay men and lesbians in its decision in *Bowers v. Hardwick* by refusing to strike down Georgia's sodomy law.[37] In 1992, the Kentucky Supreme Court became the first since the *Hardwick* decision to overturn a state antisodomy law; the court ruled that the law violated its state's constitutional right to privacy and equal protection.[38] Defenders of sodomy laws claim that the public has a right to outlaw sexual acts it considers immoral, even if done by consenting adults in private. In Texas, which also has a sodomy law, the state Supreme Court has largely avoided the issue, although it did throw out a lower court's ruling overturning the law. The Texas law remains on the books, but apparently no one is being prosecuted under it. As of early 1998, 24 states and the District of Columbia had repealed their sodomy laws through legislative action, five states' laws had been struck down by the courts, six states had laws making same-sex acts illegal, and fifteen states had sodomy laws that pertained to same-sex and opposite-sex couples.[39]

Sexual behavior is only one aspect of gay and lesbian rights. Various municipalities have taken up the issues of gay and lesbian rights in employment, housing, and other matters, with cities such as San Francisco and St. Louis passing antidiscrimination measures and voters in Houston failing to outlaw such discrimination. In 1992 there was a flurry of state activity over gay rights, much of it spurred by fundamentalist Christians and other conservative groups. A law passed in Colorado would have prohibited the state from enacting gay rights protection and would have caused the repeal of existing local laws supporting gay rights, but the Colorado Supreme Court declared it unconstitutional. The U.S. Supreme Court concurred that the law violated the U.S. Constitution's equal protection clause, "mark[ing] the first time the high court has treated gay rights as a matter of civil rights."[40] When Oregonians failed to approve a tough anti-gay law that would have condemned homosexuality and forbidden protections to gay men and lesbians, some Oregon towns adopted their own anti-gay measures. In 1997, Maine joined ten other states and the District of Columbia with laws supporting gay rights. The measured added "sexual orientation to existing laws banning discrimination in employment, housing, credit and public accommodations."[41] But in 1998 anti-gay forces were successful in overturning the law at the polls. There is no federal law prohibiting discrimination against gay men and lesbians, and sexual orientation is not specifically included in federal hate crimes legislation. Twenty-one states have hate crime statutes that include sexual orientation.[42] Many gay men and lesbians feel that the lack of laws protecting their rights and the laws that expressly deny them protections not only make them targets for discrimination but also for physical attacks or other hate crimes.

Many other public policy issues are also of concern to gay men and lesbians. They want the right to child custody and adoption and the right to name a lover as "next of kin" in case of medical emergencies or other matters. They also wish to prohibit health insurance companies from asking lifestyle questions that may cause them to be denied coverage. In the late 1980s, a handful of cities decided to extend bereavement leave to domestic partners not in traditional marriages, including gay and lesbian partners. Since then, the number of municipal governments and private companies (IBM, American Express, and Walt Disney Co. are among them)[43] extending health care or other benefits to the live-in partners of employees, both gay and straight, has grown. Many companies feel that this helps them to attract the best employees. In 1996 a judge ordered the state of Oregon to provide insurance benefits to the partners of its gay workers, saying that doing otherwise was discriminatory and violated the state's constitution. In 1997, the University of California Board of Regents also extended health care benefits to domestic partners of gay men and lesbians. Most states recognize the rights of gay men and lesbians to child custody and visitation, and about half extend at least some adoption rights to them.[44] Other states take a dimmer view of this. For example, Florida and New Hampshire do not allow them to adopt children.

Marriage between partners of the same gender has now made its way to the public agenda. In 1991 two lesbian couples and a gay male couple sued the state of Hawaii because it refused to issue them a marriage license. Supporters believe that a marriage prohibition violates the equal protection provisions of the U.S. Constitution and constitutes discrimination. Alarmed about the possibility that Hawaii might actually legalize such unions, in 1996, the U.S. Congress passed the Defense of Marriage Act (DOMA). Congress was concerned that the U.S. Constitution's "full faith and credit clause" might require other states to recognize marriages of same-sex couples performed in Hawaii or other states, although there is uncertainty about whether it would. DOMA does not prohibit states from recognizing or legalizing same-sex marriages. It says that states cannot be forced to recognize these unions if they are performed in other states. About 30 states have now enacted laws banning same-sex marriages.[45] Although Hawaii's courts upheld same sex marriages, in 1998, voters in Hawaii and Alaska failed to approve them.

When acquired immune deficiency syndrome (AIDS) was identified, fear resulted in the introduction of state legislation that could have resulted in increased discrimination against gay men. Attempts were made to deny state funds for AIDS prevention to organizations that support the rights of homosexuals, because homosexual acts in many states are illegal. At the federal level, the Helms Amendment, named after ultraconservative Senator Jesse Helms (R-North Carolina), prevents the national Centers for Disease Control from using AIDS education funds in ways that might "encourage homosexuality." Homophobia coupled with fears about AIDS was blamed for increased violence against gays. Eventually the country became more knowledgeable about AIDS and compassion for those with AIDS-related illnesses grew. Though some controversies over AIDS prevention in general continue (such as the distribution of condoms in high schools and of clean needles to drug addicts), the country has moved on to debate a new set of issues with respect to gay men and lesbians.

Among the most vehemently debated has been that of gay men and lesbians serving in the military and in national security positions. In 1949, the U.S. Department of Defense implemented a rule intended to prevent gay men and lesbians from serving in the military, and for several decades, there was no major policy change. In 1988 the U.S. Supreme Court did tell the Central Intelligence Agency that it could not dismiss a gay man without justifying the reason for its action, but the Court avoided the issue of whether gay men and lesbians have employment rights under the "equal protection clause" (Fourteenth Amendment) of the U.S. Constitution, including the right to serve in the military.

Beginning in the early 1990s, some things began to change. In 1991 the case of Sergeant Perry Watkins, a gay soldier, was settled after years in court when he was awarded back pay, an honorable discharge, and full retirement benefits. In 1992 a federal judge ordered the Navy to reinstate Petty Officer Keith Meinhold, who had stated he is gay, but the ruling was based on a technicality and hardly settled the question of gays in the military. As the various branches of the military faced increasing pressure to stop discriminating against gay men and lesbians, President Clinton's desire to drop the ban caused a heated, national debate. Although everyone knows that there are gay men and lesbians in the military, there was considerable opposition both in the military and in Congress to lifting the ban. The president, who is also commander-in-chief of the armed forces, has the authority to lift the ban by executive order, although Congress could overrule him with a two-thirds majority. Those wanting to end the ban declared that sexual orientation has nothing to do with the ability to perform military jobs, while the opposition countered with arguments about close living quarters, security breaches, and low morale. There was some serious Democratic opposition to lifting the ban. So much furor arose over the issue that rather than lift the ban himself, the president decided to go the route he often takes in the face of opposition—the well-known political strategies of negotiation and compromise.

After much political wrangling, in July 1993, the president issued a watered-down policy. Under these new rules, applicants are not to be asked to reveal their sexual orientation, and investigations to determine sexual orientation without cause that sexual conduct codes have been violated are prohibited. As a result, the policy earned the nickname "Don't ask, don't tell, don't pursue." The guidelines also prohibit harassment of gay and lesbian military personnel, but homosexual conduct can be grounds for discharge. According to the Pentagon's guidelines, the definition of homosexual conduct includes acknowledgment of being gay, lesbian, or bisexual. In many circumstances, physical contact, such as holding hands and kissing, can also be construed as homosexual conduct. However, going to gay bars, marching in gay rights demonstrations in civilian attire, or having gay publications would generally not be considered homosexual conduct. Even though the president may have intended for a new spirit to be reflected in the policy, there is concern that the policy is more harmful than helpful for gay men and lesbians because it "has broadened the definition of [homosexual] conduct, and, therefore, is ensnaring many more people."[46]

The courts have not been consistent in their rulings on gays in the military. Some judges believe that the military has a vested interest in keeping gays and lesbians from serving. Others believe that Congress and the president should decide. Another perspective is that sexual orientation is not related to service and using it to keep people out constitutes discrimination.[47] The U.S. Supreme Court has not resolved the issue.

Bill Clinton is the first president to address a gay rights group, and he issued a directive banning discrimination against federal employees who are gay. Most federal agencies already had nondiscrimination policies. The purpose of the executive order was to make the policies uniform. A 1998 challenge to the order failed in the House of Representatives. The Republican party platform opposes gay rights, despite the support the party receives on other issues from a group of gay Republicans who have organized under the name Log Cabin Republicans.

Some school districts are sensitive to the needs of gay, lesbian, and bisexual youth and youth unsure of their sexual identity, and some campuses have organizations of these students. These groups have formed to assist students, particularly in light of the high suicide rate among these youth. The Salt Lake City School Board felt differently about the issue. In 1996 it terminated all student groups on campus rather than allow a gay organization because the federal Equal Access Act of 1984 which arose to support Bible groups also seemed to support the gay student organization.[48] The Utah legislature came to the school board's aid with a law supporting the board's efforts to outlaw gay student groups. In 1997 "a unanimous federal appeals court struck down an Alabama law that sought to keep lesbian, gay, and bisexual student groups off university campuses, saying the law violated the First Amendment rights of students and is wholly unenforceable."[49] The Lambda Legal Defense and Education Fund, the Human Rights Campaign, the American Civil Liberties Union, and other organizations are working to end discrimination based on sexual orientation.

BLACKS, HISPANICS, AND SOCIAL WELFARE

Some people would have us think that race relations have improved tremendously in the United States. Others sway us to believe that the country remains deeply divided along racial lines, pointing to the burning of African American churches, the reaction to the verdict in the O. J. Simpson murder trial, the murder of James Byrd, Jr. in Jasper, Texas, and settlements reached in the case of Texaco's treatment of minority employees and Denny's restaurants' treatment of customers. President Clinton appointed an advisory board to study the issue of race and suggest ways to improve race relations and close the racial gaps in the U.S. In September 1998 the presidential advisory board issued its "One Nation" report, but it received little attention as the country was engrossed in the president's sex scandals and impeachment proceedings. Illustration 11-3 includes some comments on the president's efforts to engage the country in a dialogue on race.

Perhaps the fairest thing that can be said about the living conditions of blacks and Hispanic Americans is that they have improved substantially but not on a par with whites. On the average, blacks are in poorer health than whites, and they do not live as long; they earn less and are more likely to be in poverty, and they are overrepresented in public assistance programs. Poverty and lower earnings also contribute to a less adequate lifestyle for many Americans of Hispanic origin. Table 11-3 (page 386) compares the incomes of these three groups. Twenty–one percent of black and 17 percent of Hispanic-American families earn less than $10,000 annually, compared with 10 percent of white families. White families are more than twice as likely as black or Hispanic-American families to earn over $75,000 annually, and the median income of whites is substantially more than for black or Hispanic-American families.

As described in Chapter 3, poverty rates continue to be more than three times higher for black and Hispanic Americans than for whites. Chapter 3 also showed that while educational attainment is closely related to income for all ethnic groups, even after controlling for education, black and Hispanic Americans are more likely to be poor and less likely to earn as much as whites. Blacks comprise nearly 13 percent of the total U.S. population, but they are 37 percent of families receiving public assistance and 28 percent of SSI recipients.[50] Although the General Accounting Office found that blacks were more likely to be rejected for disability benefits than whites,[51] the proportion of blacks in public assistance programs has served to reinforce stereotypes that they are less motivated to work. These feelings prevail despite recognition of the effects of racial discrimination. According to one report, "surveys show that racial attitudes are the most important reason behind white opposition to welfare programs. Political issues, such as crime and welfare, are viewed as 'coded issues' as they stimulate white Americans'

A Dialogue on Race

President Clinton's promised series of town hall meetings on race opened last week in Akron, Ohio, to mixed reviews. Here is a sampling of opinions from around the country on the meeting and race relations.

No amount of town meetings will seriously undo the racial fears and confusion this nation has lugged around since its inception. We need to use those town meetings as a starting point, not an end in and of themselves. If we fail to do that, many black Americans will continue to be skeptical of Clinton's motives. And many white Americans—particularly those who deny racism's existence—will continue to regard the president as a knee-jerk liberal forcing "old issues" again.

Race is not an old issue, not when it endures as the principal way many people view themselves and others. Race has defined much of the 1990s. Look at the Los Angeles riots, the angry debates on affirmation action, the O. J. Simpson trials. We are not "one nation," no matter how loud we proclaim it. We are, at best, a relatively young nation still forging an identity—and a future.

by Kevin Powell of the Progressive Media Project, which provides commentary from voices of the African American community

Many liberal, mainstream black leaders, and politicians hate to admit it, but there has always been a hidden side of black thought that is less radical and more conservative than it appears at first glance. Six years after the shrill attacks on Clarence Thomas during his Supreme Court confirmation hearings, black opinion has steadily showed a rightward trend on some social issues. In opinion surveys in the *Christian Science Monitor* and *U.S. News & World Report,* 30 percent of blacks called themselves conservatives; 48 percent of blacks blamed themselves, not racism, for not taking full advantage of opportunities; 50 percent favored ending welfare; and a whopping 75 percent backed a constitutional amendment permitting school prayer.

by Earl Ofari Hutchinson, author of "Beyond O. J.: Race, Sex and Class Lessons for America"

While the state of race relations in America is not perfect—consider, for instance, the revival of the Tawana Brawley hoax in New York—it is very different from the epoch that invented affirmative action. Good news about the status of black people in America, and the sea change in attitudes among white Americans, is bad news for dinosaurs who cling to racial quotas.

Even President Clinton may grasp this basic truth. After the cameras were shut off, he engaged (affirmative action opponent) Abigail Thernstrom in a half-hour private discussion praising her book and telling her he had encouraged his staffers to read it. So what does he really think? That affirmative action is as relevant today as in 1964, or that the Democratic Party is so thoroughly committed to racial quotas and preferences that he cannot say publicly what he privately believes?

by Philip Terzian, Providence Journal-Bulletin

continued

ILLUSTRATION 11-3 *(continued)*

The whole atmosphere surrounding discussions of race is one of dogmatism and intimidation that makes dialogue impossible. Too many liberals—black and white alike—find it inconceivable that anyone could honestly disagree with them on racial issues.

A recent op-ed piece in the *New York Times,* for example, explains away those blacks who reject the liberal vision of race by saying that conservative foundations and think tanks have gone after "intellectuals-for-hire" who "were offered money, power, and celebrity in exchange for ideological allegiance." These guns-for-hire "who live very well" were said to include people like Clarence Thomas, Glen Loury and "the economist Thomas Sowell."

In other words, it was the old "sell-out" scenario. How else could anyone possibly disagree with liberals on race?

by Thomas Sowell, author and columnist

In America, the problem is presented by the Clinton administration as largely between blacks and white, but that isn't correct. Most people murdered by whites are white. Most people murdered by blacks are black. When a murder, or any form of brutality, crosses racial lines, it is a very big story. Witness Rodney King or O. J. Simpson. Intra-racial murder and brutality are so common that they don't make the front page. . . .

There are indeed tensions between black and white, Hispanic and non-Hispanic. We can best reduce them not by talking about them, but by reducing the gaps in education and opportunity that are largely ignored while we talk grandly about race and prejudice.

by Otis Pike, Newhouse News Service

Source: Copyright 1997 *Austin American-Statesman.* Reprinted with permission.

anti-black feelings without explicitly raising racial discrimination."[52] In fact, patterns of racial discrimination are so firmly entrenched in U.S. society that the term **institutional racism** has been used to refer to these practices.

Separate But Not Equal

The Fourteenth Amendment to the U.S. Constitution guarantees all citizens equal protection under the law, but this amendment is also an example of how ideas that sound rational can be used to maintain and perpetuate racial discrimination. Until 1954, the Fourteenth Amendment served as legal grounds for *equal* but *separate* protection under the law. Segregation of blacks and whites in public schools, on public buses, and in other public (and private) places was official policy. Although public facilities for blacks were supposed to be equal to facilities for whites (see *Plessy v. Ferguson,* 1896), this was generally not the case. It was not until the middle of the twentieth century that the U.S. Supreme Court overturned the "separate but equal" doctrine set forth in *Plessy v. Ferguson.* The civil rights movement had begun.

TABLE 11-3

Total Money Income of Households by Race or Ethnicity, 1997

Income	Percent of Total White	Percent of Total Black	Percent of Total Hispanic[a]
Under $10,000	10%[b]	21%[b]	17%[b]
$10,000 to $24,999	22	28	30
$25,000 to $49,999	30	29	32
$50,000 to $74,999	19	13	12
$75,000 and over	20	8	9
Median Income	$38,972	$25,050	$26,628

Source: U.S. Bureau of the Census, *Money Income in the United States: 1997,* Current Population Reports, Series P60-200 (Washington, DC: U.S. Government Printing Office, 1998), Table 2, p. 5.

[a]May be of any race

[b]Percentages may not add to 100 due to rounding.

In 1954 a growing dissatisfaction among blacks with the separate but equal doctrine resulted in a U.S. Supreme Court ruling that marked the official recognition of racial inequality in America. Schools in Topeka, Kansas, were segregated but essentially equal in terms of physical conditions and quality of education. However, in the case of *Brown v. Board of Education of Topeka, Kansas,* the Supreme Court ruled that separate was *not* equal. In its decision, the Court took the position that "the policy of separating the races is usually interpreted as denoting the inferiority of the Negro Group." The Court also stated that "segregation with the sanction of law, therefore, has a tendency to retard the education and mental development of Negro children." The *Brown* decision remains a landmark case in the history of equal rights.

However, *de facto* segregation of schools due to neighborhood segregation continues to exist, and has even been exacerbated.[53] When children from inner-city neighborhoods attend their local schools, the schools are almost totally composed of black students. One solution to *de facto* school segregation is busing. In 1971 in the case of *Swann v. Charlotte-Mecklenburg Board of Education,* the U.S. Supreme Court approved court-ordered busing of children to achieve integration in school districts that had a history of discrimination. But, in 1974, in *Milliken v. Bradley,* the Court ruled that mandatory busing across city–suburban boundaries to achieve integration is not required unless segregation has resulted from an official action. As a result, *de facto* segregation occurs in many school districts, especially inner-city districts, more than 45 years after the *Brown* decision.

Busing has been one of the most bitter controversies surrounding public school education in the United States. Parents often reject the idea of sending their child to a school several miles away when a neighborhood school is nearby.[54] Parents—generally white parents—who purposely purchased homes in the school districts they prefer, are often angered when their child must be bused to a school that they feel is inferior. Critics point to the irony of forced busing. They believe busing has contributed to "white flight"—white families moving to avoid busing. Furthermore, they point to the trend toward private-school enrollments, which also thwarts efforts to integrate public schools. In describing its 1996 decision in *Sheff v. O'Neill* concerning the Hartford, Connecticut, public school system, that state's high court said, "racial and ethnic segregation has a pervasive and invidious impact on schools, whether segregation results from intentional conduct or from unorchestrated demographic factors."[55] Other commentators believe that the focus should be less on whether schools are racially balanced and more on whether children are receiving an adequate education. Some see the problem as a class rather than as a race issue because of the way public education is financed. The major source of elementary and secondary school funding is the local property tax, which generally provides schools in middle- and upper-class areas with larger financial bases than schools in poor areas. This has led to a call for equal educational expenditures for all schoolchildren, regardless of their communities' economic status. Despite high high school graduation rates, unequal educational opportunities continue to prevent black and Hispanic Americans from obtaining jobs that would increase their earning capacity and reduce their reliance on welfare programs. Many states have engaged in bitter court battles over the mechanisms used to fund public school education. In Texas, for example, there have been several state constitutional challenges to public school funding. The current plan to equalize funding by calling on wealthier districts to help poorer districts has hardly served to quell the debate. Some wealthier school districts are looking at ways to get around the plan.

The state of public school education in general is alarming. Media accounts suggest that many school systems are in disarray, infested with drugs and violence, and serving children with many social problems that keep them from learning. President Bush called an "education summit" during his first year in office, and he was particularly supportive of federally funded preschool programs like Head Start (see Chapter 9). President Clinton has also voiced strong support for efforts that will help U.S. students reach high educational goals. Congress passed *Goals 2000* designed to set national outcome standards for schoolchildren. There is growing pressure to better prepare young people for employment in a highly competitive, high-technology workforce. But the official role of the federal government in school financing and policy setting remains limited. Educational issues are mostly the responsibility of local and state governments where funding issues remain a concern, and where politics and religion strongly influence curriculums, textbook selection, and policies related to student attendance, suspension, and expulsion. Vouchers which would allow parents greater selection in the schools their children attend have only added to the controversy.

Educators and social researchers also note the lack of progress in integrating institutions of higher education. Colleges and universities that have traditionally enrolled white students and those that have traditionally enrolled black students have failed to become well integrated.[56] Although the role of traditional black colleges remains important, recruitment and retention of black and Hispanic-American students by other institutions of higher learning is high on the list of concerns of academic administrators. There is a particular concern about boosting the college graduation rates of blacks, especially men, and of Hispanics so that members of all ethnic groups will be viable contenders in the workforce.

The Civil Rights Act

Since the 1954 *Brown* decision, the single most important reform with regard to racial equality has been the Civil Rights Act of 1964. The act states,

1. It is unlawful to apply unequal standards in voter registration procedures, or to deny registration for irrelevant errors or omissions on records or applications.
2. It is unlawful to discriminate or segregate persons on the grounds of race, color, religion, or national origin in any public accommodation, including hotels, motels, restaurants, movies, theaters, sports arenas, entertainment houses, and other places that offer to serve the public. This prohibition extends to all establishments whose operations affect interstate commerce or whose discriminatory practices are supported by state action.
3. The attorney general shall undertake civil action on behalf of any person denied equal access to a public accommodation to obtain a federal district court order to secure compliance with the act. If the owner or manager of a public accommodation should continue to discriminate, he would be in contempt of court and subject to peremptory fines and imprisonment without trial by jury.
4. The attorney general shall undertake civil actions on behalf of persons attempting orderly desegregation of public schools.
5. The Commission on Civil Rights, established in the Civil Rights Act of 1957, shall be empowered to investigate deprivations of the right to vote, study, and collect information regarding discrimination in America, and make reports to the President and Congress.
6. Each federal department and agency shall take action to end discrimination in all programs or activities receiving federal financial assistance in any form. This action shall include termination of financial assistance.
7. It shall be unlawful for any employer or labor union with twenty-five or more people after 1965 to discriminate against any individual in any fashion in employment, because of his race, color, religion, sex, or national origin, and an Equal Employment Opportunity Commission shall be established to enforce this provision by investigation, conference, conciliation, persuasion, and if need be, civil action in federal court.

Amendments to the act in 1968 prohibit housing discrimination, yet the balance of racial power has not shifted as dramatically as many African and Hispanic Americans would like. Interestingly, Congress exempted itself from complying with the Civil Rights Act until 1988!

Housing and Racial Discrimination

Housing policy in the United States—public and private, formal and informal—is perhaps the most pervasive remaining tool of racial discrimination. Segregation and discrimination have long been evident in the private housing market and in government housing programs. Section 235 of the 1968 Fair Housing Act became "the largest single subsidized housing program and the most controversial."[57] According to the U.S. Civil Rights Commission, the Federal Housing Administration (FHA) contributed to the sale of inferior homes to blacks and others under section 235 by delegating too much authority to private industry, which had failed to comply with the spirit of the Housing Act and other civil rights legislation.

Redlining has also contributed to inferior living arrangements for blacks and other ethnic groups. This practice occurs when a bank, mortgage company, home insurance company, or other enterprise refuses to finance or insure property in certain areas. Redlined areas are generally those occupied by poor and minority groups. Inability to obtain financing and insurance further depresses the community. It is not only the private sector that has been accused of redlining. During the 1960s, the National Commission on Urban Problems charged the Federal Housing Administration with neglecting loans to poor and black people and with condoning policies that "aided, abetted, and encouraged" neighborhood deterioration.[58] Even today, the U.S. Conference of Mayors claims that redlining is to blame for the low rate of homeownership in urban areas where many members of ethnic minority groups live—49 percent compared to 72 percent in suburban areas.[59]

Studies continue to show that equally qualified blacks are twice as likely as whites to be denied home mortgage loans.[60] African Americans face more segregation barriers in obtaining housing than any other ethnic group; Hispanics, and especially Asians, have fared considerably better in this regard.[61] **Steering** is another practice that contributes to segregation. It occurs when realtors fail to comply with the Fair Housing Act by showing blacks or members of other groups housing only in neighborhoods occupied mostly by those of the same race or ethnicity, and not providing the opportunity to see housing in other areas.

The city of Yonkers, New York, gained national notoriety in 1988 when it refused to implement a housing desegregation order, and Vidor, Texas, earned a similar reputation in 1993 when it failed to integrate a public housing complex. The problem extends well beyond public housing. Neighborhood integration could eliminate the need for busing and other aids, such as magnet schools, to encourage integration in public schools. In order to battle continuing housing discrimination, Congress in 1988 toughened the Department of Housing and Urban Development's enforcement provisions under the Fair Housing Act and added protections against discrimination for people with disabilities and for families with children. In 1997, HUD further stepped up its enforcement program. On a more positive note, in an effort to get their mergers approved, some of the country's large banks "are making multi-million dollar pledges for improved fair lending programs to deprived neighborhoods,"[62] and others have agreed to expand their programs in the wake of accusations against them.[63]

Affirmative Action

Another aspect of equal rights that continues to engender political concern is **affirmative action** policies designed to achieve equality in school admissions and employment for women and members of ethnic minority groups. Affirmative action is based on the notion that women and minorities should be admitted, hired, and promoted in proportion to their representation in the population. But to what extent should affirmative action policies be pursued? Is it enough to use policies that do not discriminate against people because of gender and racial and ethnic background, or should policies go much further in order to reduce imbalances in admissions and employment? Originally, the federal government chose a policy of nondiscrimination. Examples are found in President Truman's decision to desegregate the military in 1946 and in Titles VI and VII of the 1964 Civil Rights Act. Nondiscrimination simply means that preferential treatment will not be given to selected groups.

Those dissatisfied with this method of achieving racial equality thought that a more aggressive approach should be taken. One aspect of this concern spurred a debate as to whether quotas rather than goals should be used to achieve racial equality. **Quotas** are defined as "imposing a fixed, mandatory number or percentage of persons to be hired or promoted, regardless of the number of potential applicants who meet the qualifications," while a **goal** is a

> *numerical objective, fixed realistically in terms of number of vacancies expected, and the number of qualified applicants available. . . . If . . . the employer . . . has demonstrated every good faith effort to include persons from the group which was the object of discrimination . . . but has been unable to do so in sufficient numbers to meet his goal, he is not subject to sanction.*[64]

In addition, an employer is not obligated to hire an unqualified or less qualified person in preference to a prospective employee with better qualifications.

The Philadelphia Plan of 1967 issued by the U.S. Office of Federal Contract Compliance was one of the first examples of an affirmative action plan. It required that those bidding on federal contracts submit plans to employ specific percentages of minority workers. Another quota-type plan was adopted in 1971 by the Federal Aviation Administration. It essentially placed a freeze on hiring any additional employees if every fifth vacant position was not filled by a member of a minority group.

Opponents of quota setting generally believe that giving preferential treatment to members of particular groups violates the equal protection clause (Fourteenth Amendment) of the U.S. Constitution. In 1974 a federal court upheld this belief in its decision that the University of Washington Law School should admit Marco DeFunis, Jr. DeFunis had protested the university's decision to reject his application while admitting blacks with lower grades and test scores. Other cases charging "reverse discrimination" have also been heard by the courts. The U.S. Supreme Court ruled on the issue of admitting less qualified minority applicants over white applicants in the case of Alan Bakke. The Court determined that Bakke had been unfairly denied admission to the University of California Davis Medical School, because his qualifications were stronger than those of some minority candidates admitted to the school. Proponents of the decision hoped the *Bakke* case would help change what they perceived to be a trend of reverse discrimination against whites. Opponents feared that the Bakke decision threatened the future of affirmation action. More recent reverse discrimination charges in California arose when the University of California at Berkeley was accused of discriminating against whites by favoring black, Hispanic, and Filipino applicants, and when complaints were leveled against the University of California system for using more stringent admissions requirements for Asian Americans. Asian Americans generally have higher test scores than other groups, and they have been admitted at rates higher than their representation in the population.

Threats to affirmative action mounted during the Reagan administration. Civil right advocates accused the administration of reversing a pattern of improvement in civil rights that began in the 1960s and had been supported under both Democratic and Republican administrations. Reagan's recommendations for appointments to the U.S. Civil Rights Commission and his attempts to get rid of some members raised the ire of civil rights groups. Controversy also brewed in the U.S. Department of Justice. During the Carter presidency, the department was a strong proponent of civil rights. It had, for example, helped to implement a court decree requiring that the police and fire departments of Indianapolis establish quotas for hiring and promoting women and blacks. But in 1984, the U.S. Supreme Court ruled in the case of *Firefighters Local Union No. 1784 v. Stotts* that the jobs of blacks with less seniority cannot be protected at the expense of jobs of whites with more seniority. The Department of Justice used this decision to get Indianapolis and forty-nine other jurisdictions to abandon the use of quotas. The National Association for the Advancement of Colored People (NAACP) and others called the Department of Justice action illegal.

The Reagan administration also challenged the use of **class action suits** to benefit groups of people. During Reagan's terms, the Equal Employment Opportunity Commission expressed its desire to address cases of discrimination against particular individuals rather than assisting classes of people who have been treated unfairly. William Bradford Reynolds, then head of the Department of Justice, declared that what was needed was a color- and sex-blind society rather than a color- and sex-conscious one. He contended that quotas are a form of discrimination.

The U.S. Supreme Court did deal a victory for affirmative action during the Reagan years with two 1986 decisions (one involved Cleveland firefighters, the other a New York sheet metal workers' union). According to these decisions, "federal judges may set goals and timetables requiring employers guilty of past discrimination to hire or promote specific numbers of minorities, even if the jobs go to people who are not themselves the proven victims of bias."[65] But Supreme Court rulings in 1989 again put affirmative action on shaky ground. In *City of Richmond v. J. A. Croson Co.*, it struck down many state and local "set-aside" programs that gave preference to minority-owned firms in awarding contracts, saying that such programs should be used only to remedy discrimination. The high court said, however, that federal set-aside programs were exempt because of the wide latitude that Congress has in determining what is needed to achieve equality nationally.[66] The decision reportedly caused a severe drop in the contracts awarded to minority-owned businesses. In *Wards Cove Packing Co., Inc. v. Atonio* (a case primarily involving Asian-American and Alaskan native employees of a salmon cannery in Alaska), the Supreme Court placed the onus of proving that an employer intended to discriminate (rather than unintentionally discriminated) on the employee. This reversed the Court's long-standing 1971 decision in *Griggs v. Duke Power,* in which the burden was placed on the employer to show that hiring criteria have a direct relation to the job. Other 1989 decisions also made it easier to challenge affirmative action programs, and more difficult for employees to bring discrimination suits. Many thought that these decisions were ironic given that higher unemployment rates and lesser earnings among women, blacks and Hispanics do not support the contention of reverse discrimination.

During the Reagan years, the NAACP, NOW, and other groups were outraged by the president's position on civil rights and the reductions in the number of discrimination cases pursued by the federal government in education, employment, and housing.[67] They hoped that President Bush's position would indeed be "kinder" and "gentler" to them, but given Bush's lack of action, Congress decided that the real recourse to fair treatment in job bias cases was to pass new civil rights legislation to undo the 1989 Supreme Court rulings. Although expressing strong concern for civil rights, President Bush used one of his trademark vetoes to overturn Congress's 1990 civil rights restoration effort, saying it would lead employers to use quotas to avoid lawsuits. The American Civil Liberties Union accused Bush of using a "smokescreen of 'quotas' to prevent restoration of critically important civil rights laws that give minorities equal access to education, housing, employment and the ballot box."[68] In an attempt to revive the legislation, civil rights and business leaders formed a working group to develop a compromise bill. Their negotiations broke down, however, amid accusations that the Bush administration was pressuring the business leaders to abandon the talks so that "Republican candidates can use the issue of racial quotas in 1992 elections."[69] In 1991 the House of Representatives hammered out a new bill that strengthened antiquota language. The president again rejected the bill, but eventually a compromise emerged that helped to restore the decision in the *Griggs* case and reverse the decision in the *Wards Cove Packing* case. The bill also eliminated a practice called "race norming" in which job-related test scores are adjusted for differences across racial or ethnic groups. The bill further allowed punitive and compensatory damages to be collected for the first time in sexual discrimination (including sexual harassment) cases, as well as in cases of discrimination against people with disabilities and members of religious groups. The bill extended provisions to Senate and White House staff for the first time, with the stipulation that senators who violate the law are personally liable for damages.

Another civil rights stir that arose during the Bush years was questioning whether college scholarships awarded solely on the basis of race violated Title VI of the Civil Rights Act. Since only a tiny fraction of the nation's scholarships are awarded on race alone (most include other criteria such as financial need and merit), there was concern that animosity among ethnic groups was being aroused over a nonissue.[70] In 1993, President Clinton's Secretary of Education Richard Riley announced that such scholarships are a legal remedy to correct past inequities and promised guidelines to help colleges and universities act properly in awarding race-based scholarships.

Among the most controversial affirmative action decisions now being implemented are California's Proposition 209, a referendum put to the states' voters in 1996 which ended affirmative action in hiring and admissions, and the 1996 *Hopwood* decision by the Fifth U.S. Circuit Court of Appeals which put an end to the use of racial preferences in college and university admissions in schools covered by the circuit. The latter case was filed by Cheryl Hopwood, a white woman denied admission to the University of Texas at Austin law school, and three other whites in the same situation. In Texas, many factors can be considered in deciding whether to accept an applicant except race, even though race is as integral a part of one's identity and experience as other characteristics. These events reopened a heated dialogue on affirmative action on campuses. Many people expressed concern that they would create a climate that would dissuade applicants from applying and put schools in California and Texas at a great disadvantage in recruiting qualified minority students.

In 1998 the NAACP reaffirmed its strong support of affirmative action, but a growing group of black conservatives, including some black scholars, feel that affirmative action is no longer helping blacks. For example, businessman Ward Connerly helped spearhead California's Proposition 209. According to Thomas Sowell, a fellow at the Hoover Institution and author of several books on race, "Too many black 'leaders' have a vested interest in the application of old myths. They are like Moses in reverse—leading their people into the welfare state, to a self-imposed isolation from the growing opportunities all around them."[71] Political economist Glenn Loury credits the civil rights movement and affirmative action for doing much to help some (primarily middle-class) blacks, but he is concerned about solutions to the problems of those blacks who remain poor.[72] Loury believes the current problems of black communities must be attacked through "self-help" whether or not government continues to assist. As one newspaper columnist wrote,

> *Self-help is in, while traditional government welfare programs are out. College degrees and consensus-style leadership are a plus, while orthodox civil rights strategies are antiquated.*
>
> *Most important, the political buzzword among emerging black leaders is not discrimination, affirmative action or racism.*
>
> *It is equity—as in economic, educational, and environmental equity.*[73]

Perceptions of the matter may have to do with the definition of affirmative action. One might feel quite differently if it is defined as racial preferences rather than providing opportunity, making sure that minorities are included in the recruitment process, and other equal but nonpreferential treatment. In the wake of *Hopwood,* Texas public universities have begun automatic admissions of undergraduate students who scored in the top 10 percent of their high school classes in order to promote a more diverse and representative student body. Beginning in 2001, California's public university system will begin admitting the top 4 percent.

Voting Rights

One way groups can help themselves is to exercise their right to vote. The abolition of poll taxes and literacy tests were important steps in extending voting rights. Since the mid-1900s many more steps have also been taken to ensure that all groups are provided the same opportunities to vote. Especially important is the 1965 Voting Rights Act, designed to further ensure, protect, and encourage the right to a voice in the electoral process. The act is periodically reviewed by Congress, and constant improvements have been made to promote and protect voting rights. Today the emphasis is on making it even easier to register by doing away with laws requiring people to register in advance of elections and by allowing people to register in public offices, supermarkets, and shopping malls. The National Voter Registration Act signed by President Clinton in 1993 requires states to allow registration by mail.

Many issues of importance are on today's voting rights agenda. Single-member districts, the shape of districts, and cumulative voting (where everyone gets several votes that can all be used for one candidate or spread among candidates) are some methods that have been used to promote representation of all racial and ethnic groups. Of course, cumulative voting is no more effective than having one vote if people fail to exercise their voting rights. More than once the U.S. Supreme Court has found that some voting districts have been drawn to favor blacks or Hispanics, and it has struck down "gerrymandering" by using race as a predominant factor to create voting districts. Attention is now on maintaining the gains that have been made by ethnic minority candidates. Encouraging news was the 1996 reelection of two black incumbents in the state of Georgia to the U.S. House of Representatives after their districts had been redrawn and included mostly whites.

The number of black and Hispanic-American elected officials has increased in recent years, although very few members of any ethnic minority group have ever served in the U.S. Senate. In 1999, among members of the 106th Congress, there were thirty-nine black U.S. representatives (up from twenty-five in 1991). Black mayors have been elected in some of America's larger cities—Los Angeles, Detroit, Cleveland, and New York. The nation's first black governor, Douglas Wilder, was elected by Virginia voters in 1989. In 1999, there were twenty Hispanic-American U.S. representatives. Florida has had an Hispanic governor, and several large cities—Miami, San Antonio, and Denver—have had Hispanic-American mayors. Hispanics are by far the fastest-growing ethnic group in the country, now comprising 11 percent of the population. They will soon become the country's largest ethnic minority group.There are a number of groups promoting the political agenda of Hispanic Americans, such as the National Council of La Raza, the Mexican American Legal Defense and Education Fund (MALDEF), and the League of United Latin American Citizens (LULAC). The number of U.S. residents of Asian ancestry has also grown rapidly, now nearing 4 percent of the U.S. population. There were five Asian American representatives serving in the 106th Congress. By 2050 the United States may look quite different from the way it does today—non-Hispanic whites may be 53 percent of the U.S. population, rather than the 73 percent they are now.[74] Such a major change will certainly be reflected in the country's politics.

NATIVE AMERICANS AND SOCIAL WELFARE

Native Americans are probably the ethnic group most seriously affected by social welfare problems. "Indians [continue to] have the lowest income, worst health and the largest indices of social problems in the U.S."[75] Congress members from states with the largest Native American populations may find it difficult to represent these constituents because Indians' needs often conflict with those of larger, more powerful constituent groups.[76] One Native American, Ben Nighthorse Campbell (R-Colorado), now serves in the U.S. Senate.

There are more than 550 federally recognized tribes,[77] but many Native communities do not have this recognition. Recognition is necessary for Native groups to receive the benefits and services that the government must provide to tribes. Today it seems astonishing that American Indians were not accorded citizenship until 1924, that some remained slaves until 1935, and that New Mexico did not allow them to vote until 1940.[78] Many federal policy decisions have wrought great suffering for the Indian tribes in the United States. Indians have been robbed of land and minerals rights, thus depriving them of a livelihood. They have also faced displacement from their reservations and have encountered problems in adapting to urban life. Many hardships have been attributed to attempts to force Indians to assimilate into the majority culture, even though their family structures, religions, and communication patterns differ substantially from those of whites.

In acknowledging the abuses experienced by Native Americans, the Indian Self-Determination and Education Assistance Act of 1975 emphasized tribal self-government and the establishment of independent health, education, and welfare services, but twenty–five years later it is clear that this legislation has not led to many improvements in the lives of Indian people. One of the worst degradations has been the removal of Indian children from their families to be raised by others, a practice rationalized by welfare professionals who viewed Native American child-rearing practices as overly harsh.[79] The Indian Child Welfare Act of 1978 was designed to remedy problems in the placement of Native American children by restoring greater control over these decisions to Indian tribes. Priority for placement is now given to members of the child's own tribe rather than to non-Indian families.

The Bureau of Indian Affairs (BIA), part of the Department of the Interior, is the primary federal agency responsible for assisting Native Americans in meeting their social welfare needs. Almost all of its employees are Native Americans,[80] but the agency has long been criticized for its paternalistic and authoritarian attitude toward its clientele. Some critics have said, "The BIA takes care of Indians' money, land, children, water, roads, etc. with authority [as] complete as that of a prison."[81] Despite long-standing criticisms, it was not until October 1987 that official action to investigate the bureau began. Senator Daniel Inouye (D-Hawaii), chairperson of the Senate Select Committee on Indian Affairs, called for full investigative hearings after an astonishing series of articles appeared in the *Arizona Republic* claiming "widespread fraud, mismanagement and waste in the almost $3 billion-a-year federal Indian programs."[82] Other accusations were that the government had assisted oil companies in bilking Indians of billions of dollars from oil and gas reserves.[83] The agency responsible for many of the health care needs of Native Americans is the Indian Health Service (IHS), formerly part of the BIA, and now part of the U.S. Department of Health and Human Services. The IHS has also been the target of criticism, including charges of inadequate and incompetent treatment of patients.[84]

In 1980 Edward Carpenter assessed the status of American Indians in a social welfare journal by stating, "that a part of the problem is related to the Indian's cultural diversification and a history of limited tribal cooperation is probably true. However, the impact of the Indian's legal status, the failure of the Congress, and the concomitant administrative morass created by the BIA appear to be the critical variables."[85] Carpenter called for a clarification of the legal status of American Indians, greater accountability on the part of the BIA, and greater use of educational programs by Native Americans, but most important, he called for a hands-off policy by non-Indians and a return to Native Americans of responsibility for planning. Ten years later, a special Senate committee recommended abolishing the BIA and replacing it with a program of direct financial grants to Indian tribes. But such major changes have been met with skepticism by Indians and non-Indians alike,[86] and no such change has taken place. Today the BIA calls itself an agency that "manages for excellence, fostering cooperation and coordination in consultation with Indian tribes while supporting self-determination and tribal sovereignty."[87] The National Congress of American Indians (NCAI) is an advocacy organization which tracks legislative issues of concern to Indian people and is particularly concerned about maintaining Indian sovereignty.[88]

IMMIGRATION AND SOCIAL WELFARE

When white men and women arrived to colonize what is now the United States, they became the first immigrants to set foot on this land. Today, more than one hundred years after the Statue of Liberty—a symbol of freedom for many immigrants—was erected, people from virtually every country and every cultural, ethnic, racial, and religious group inhabit the United States. The majority of Americans are now the descendants of those who came to this country in search of a better life, yet debates about immigration policy are more vehement than ever.

Immigration Policy

U.S. laws regulating immigration have existed since the 1800s. The Chinese Exclusion Act of 1833 and the Oriental Exclusion Law of 1924 severely restricted the entrance of Asian groups, as did the Quota System Law of 1921 and the Immigration Act of 1924. Chinese immigrants were brought to this country in 1864 to do the back-breaking work of building the nation's railroads, but as larger numbers of Asians entered the United States and began to prosper, their successes made Americans uneasy. Immigration policies were more favorable to others, such as northern Europeans, perhaps because of the greater similarity of their physical characteristics to those of many Americans.

The treatment of Japanese-Americans, after Japan attacked Pearl Harbor in 1941 and World War II erupted, is an especially disturbing example of discrimination against Americans of foreign backgrounds. Following the attack, Japanese Americans were interned in ten relocation camps by President Franklin D. Roosevelt for fear that they might threaten U.S. security. Another reason given for their internment was protection from potential harm by Americans who were angered by Japan's attack.[89] Japanese Americans did not believe this action was either necessary or benevolent. They were forced to give up their jobs and their possessions. To prove they were indeed Americans, many volunteered for the armed services. Internment ended in 1943 with the recognition that citizenship and loyalty to one's country, not racial characteristics, make one an American. Not until 1983 did the U.S. government actually acknowledge wrongdoing. The statement came as a result of the work of the Commission on Wartime Relocation and Internment of Civilians. Reparation payments were later approved for the approximately 78,000 remaining survivors of internment.[90]

In 1965 Congress abolished stringent quotas limiting the number of entrants from various countries, but new issues arose. The Vietnam War displaced and impoverished many Vietnamese who later sought refuge in the United States. Of special concern were "Amerasian" children, children born to American servicemen and Vietnamese women. Several thousand of these children lived in poverty in Vietnam because they were not brought to the United States by their fathers or charitable organizations.[91] Considered half-breeds in their place of birth, they were ostracized. Establishing their fathers' identities was difficult; thus many were unable to come to the United States. In other cases, fathers were unable to locate their children, or they faced bureaucratic problems in trying to get their children out of Vietnam. Squalid life conditions in Vietnam left these children and their mothers with little hope for the future, but under the Orderly Departure Program and the Amerasian Homecoming Act of 1987, the United States attempted to bring all these Amerasians (many of whom had reached adulthood) and their families to America.

Another immigration issue to emerge in the 1960s was Cubans seeking political asylum from the communistic Castro regime. As a result of the Cold War, U.S. immigration policy was generous to those seeking asylum for fear of political persecution from communist governments. Freedom flights brought thousands of Cubans to the United States through the early 1970s. Then in 1980 Castro opened the port of Mariel and allowed thousands more Cubans to leave. To accommodate the new influx, President Carter opened several refugee-processing centers in the United States. Many refugees came to join their families in the United States, but the convicted criminals and undesirables that were also sent caused criticism that Castro had used the United States as a dumping ground. Cubans continue to risk their lives to come to the United States. One of the most dramatic escapes occurred when a Cuban pilot flew a small plane from the United States and landed on a highway in Cuba to pick up his wife and sons and bring them to the U.S. Others continue to brave shark-infested waters in small boats, make-shift rafts, and even wind surfers. Cuban refugees have been entitled to privileges not afforded other immigrants, such as temporary public assistance on arrival, and after one year most can become permanent residents. But thirty-five years after the first Cuban exodus, a new wave of immigrants and political pressures caused President Clinton to announce that Cuban refugees would be treated more like refugees from other countries. In 1994 many of those trying to flee were intercepted and detained at the U.S. naval base in Guantanamo Bay, Cuba. The Clinton administration reversed its position in 1996 and granted them asylum but said that those caught at sea in the future would be returned to Cuba.

With the fall of many communistic governments, immigration from a variety of other countries has made headlines. Immigration from the tiny island of Haiti was spurred by both the overwhelming poverty on the island and the repressive Duvalier government. The Duvaliers were eventually overthrown and a democratic election was held, but the elected leader, Jean-Bertrand Aristide, was ousted and exiled to the United States. Efforts to establish an acceptable governing structure resulted in continuing turmoil and violence. Under the Refugee Act of 1980, those seeking asylum are admitted to the United States if they have "a well-founded fear of persecution on account of race, religion, nationality, membership in a particular social group or political opinion"; it does not include those fleeing for "economic" reasons. The Bush administration viewed those coming from Haiti as economic rather than political refugees, despite the country's brutal political situation. Many of those fleeing Haiti were sent to Guantanamo Bay (where many Cuban refugees were then being held). As Haitians fled in larger numbers and the camps filled to capacity, Bush ordered that Haitians intercepted at sea be immediately sent back to Haiti, without offering them legal counsel. There were court challenges to this policy and rulings pro and con amid concern that the plight of these people was not being considered and that they were being turned back to face treacherous waters in rickety boats. Advocates for the Haitians pointed to these daring escapes as evidence that people would risk their lives rather than stay in Haiti. The Clinton administration continued the policy, also encouraging the Haitians not to risk their lives at sea. In 1993 the U.S. Supreme Court upheld the practice of turning the Haitians back, stating that protections offered by the 1952 Immigration and Nationality Act pertain only to those who reach U.S. soil, not those intercepted at sea. Only a small percentage of Haitians requesting political asylum were allowed to enter the United States.

The debate over political or economic refugee status also applies to those coming from Central America. Many blamed the United States for contributing to the political strife in Central America through foreign policies that increased the desire of Central Americans to immigrate to the United States. In 1990, Salvadorans already in the U.S. were temporarily granted stays of deportation, and their work permits were extended. This occurred despite cessation of the country's civil war, after pleas from the Salvadoran president that his country's economy could not incorporate so many returning citizens. Nicaraguans were also allowed to enter the United States after the left-wing Sandinistas took over their country.

The "sanctuary" movement was another aspect of immigration affecting those from certain Central American countries. Americans involved in the movement provided food, clothing, shelter, and jobs to immigrants from El Salvador and Guatemala fleeing right-wing political movements. Sanctuary workers felt their actions were justified even if they were helping people who entered the country illegally. They believed that these individuals should have been treated as political refugees because they faced grave political oppression and persecution in their homeland. But the U.S. Immigration and Naturalization Service (INS) believes that transporting illegal immigrants and related acts are violations of the law. Several sanctuary workers were convicted and jailed for assisting refugees. An improved political climate in Central America may serve to reduce the flow of some immigrants, but poverty remains an important factor in the desire of people from countries such as Mexico and the Central America nations to live in the U.S. From Chinese who are being smuggled into the U.S. in rat-infested boats to those from Russia who wish to escape the harsh life there, the United States with its generous immigration policy looks like an oasis.

How Much Immigration?

In 1997, nearly 800,000 immigrants came to the U.S. through legal channels. Most were approved through family ties, while 91,000 were given employment preferences, and 112,000 were admitted as refugees or asylees due to political persecution in their homeland.[92] The Border Patrol of the INS arrests somewhat more than 1 million individuals trying to enter the country illegally at the extensive Mexican-American border each year,[93] and estimates are that many more enter undetected.[94] As many as 300,000 people who do not have permission to enter are added to the U.S. population each year (about 40 percent initially come legally as students and tourists).[95] Estimates are that about 5 million undocumented individuals currently reside in the U.S.[96]

The National Research Council took a close look at the effects of *legal* immigration on the U.S.[97] It found that immigration provides an overall economic benefit for the country but with some negative effect on the income of high school drop-outs. In the short run and on the average, immigrants use more public services than they pay for in taxes, though the situation varies depending on the immigrant's country of origin. From a macro perspective and in the longrun, there are gains from immigration at the federal level, but losses for states and localities with large immigrant populations. Country of origin also plays a role in determining whether immigrants present an economic cost as does immigrants' age and education. Those who enter during their working years and have higher levels of education make the greatest economic contributions. But what about *illegal* immigration? Is it helpful or harmful? Undocumented workers are useful to farmers or others who hire them as cheap labor at crucial times. But some believe that undocumented workers drive down wages and take jobs away from legally admitted immigrants and Americans. They object to providing services such as health care to undocumented immigrants and to a 1982 U.S. Supreme Court ruling that guarantees their children a public school education. Others counter that these costs are offset by income and Social Security taxes paid on the wages of those who work because undocumented workers do not gain most of the direct benefits from these taxes; for example, they are not entitled to Social Security or public assistance payments.

Two types of approaches have been used to stem illegal immigration—internal and external. Internal approaches occur within the United States, such as punishing employers who hire undocumented workers and enforcing provisions such as deportation of those who entered illegally. External solutions focus on enforcement at the border to prevent those coming illegally from entering in the first place. In a *Wall Street Journal* article, a professor of international economics argued for greater emphasis on external solutions.[98] According to his perspective, internal controls actually increase the number of illegal entrants because INS resources are used to police employers rather than to stop people from entering illegally. Furthermore, he claims that employer sanctions worsen rather than improve the underclass status of documented immigrants by making it more difficult for employers to hire them. Experience in other countries suggests that employer sanctions have not been effective in reducing illegal employment. It may be more effective to keep people out in the first place, because once they enter, the United States often hesitates to deport them.

After years of debate, Congress passed the Immigration Reform and Control Act of 1986, incorporating both internal and external approaches. The law's main features were amnesty for some people who had entered the U.S. illegally, increased enforcement at the border, employer sanctions, and a temporary worker program. Amnesty was the most controversial provision. Under this provision, those who had illegally resided in the United States before 1982, and could prove this, were allowed to remain and obtain citizenship. The irony was that undocumented entrants previously had to hide their residence and were unlikely to have rent receipts or other records to verify their residence. To qualify for amnesty, applicants could not have received welfare (such as AFDC and food stamps) previously and were prohibited from doing so for five years after legalization. The number of people who initially applied for amnesty fell considerably short of official estimates, perhaps due to fear that family and friends who did not qualify for amnesty might be discovered and deported. There was also a substantial fee to apply for amnesty, which might have served as a deterrent, but nearly 3 million people have gained citizenship through this provision.[99] A number of Americans balked at amnesty, contending that it unfairly penalized those who had been waiting to enter the United States through legal channels and that it might encourage even more individuals to enter illegally. Although some of those who are caught without U.S. documents may be able to select "voluntary departure" (which can result in fewer legal consequences, and perhaps gives hope of later returning to the U.S.), individuals may be placed in detention or deported rather than allowed to remain free until a decision on their status is made. Not surprisingly, many who are released never show up for their hearings.

The 1986 law also requires employers to verify that employees are eligible to work in the United States. Violations can result in fines and prison terms if the employer has a pattern of hiring undocumented workers. Some employers have been prosecuted under the law, but many seem to get off lightly. Employers complain that the law unfairly places the burden of proof on them and may cause them to do without needed workers. Human rights advocates remain concerned that despite antidiscrimination laws, those with particular physical characteristics or foreign accents may be unfairly denied jobs. As a concession to some employers, primarily farmers, the law permits hiring foreign workers when domestic workers are not available. It also contains more liberal rules for agricultural workers who want to remain in the country. In 1998, the president of the National Council of La Raza said there is no shortage of agricultural workers in the U.S. and that guest workers desperate for jobs may be vulnerable to abuses by employers.[100] The debate also includes the "high-tech" industries. Employers who claim that the number of work visas should be upped because they cannot find enough qualified Americans face opposition from those who counter that these employees want to bring in foreign workers because they can pay them less than Americans. Even if underqualified, they say that Americans can be provided the additional training necessary to fill these positions.

In retrospect, few people think that the 1986 law did much to deter illegal immigration. Following the 1986 legislation, estimates of immigrants residing illegally in the United States declined, in part because many people were granted amnesty. A decade later, estimates indicated that there were at least as many undocumented individuals residing in the country as there were before the legislation.[101] Recent policies have further increased border patrols and beefed up enforcement efforts. But contrary to what many people might assume, the U.S. foreign-born population is less than 10 percent.[102]

Despite the controversies over immigration, the Immigration Act of 1990 increased the number of people entering the country by making it easier for relatives of new immigrants to join them. The *Congressional Quarterly Almanac* called the law "the most sweeping revision of legal-immigration laws in a quarter century."[103] The law reduced favoritism toward immigrants from certain countries, and increased the abilities of employers to bring in immigrants with skills such as in science and engineering. It also made it more difficult to ban individuals from entering the country because of their political beliefs, sexual orientation, or health status. In 1996, a new Illegal Immigration Act increased border control, and welfare reform legislation added another assault by making most legally admitted immigrants ineligible for TANF (see Chapter 6) and food stamps (see Chapter 7) unless they become citizens. Most newly arrived immigrants are also barred from the SSI program (see Chapter 5). However, the Fourteenth Amendment to the U.S. Constitution adopted in 1868 still entitles anyone born on U.S. soil to citizenship with all the rights and privileges due any American.

Attempts made to count undocumented immigrants in the 1990 census raised a stir because seats in the U.S. House of Representatives and the amount of federal funds received by states and communities for various purposes depend on census figures. The states of California, Florida, Arizona, and Texas filed suit against the federal government, believing that immigrants were undercounted and that state and local budgets have been unfairly burdened with providing services to people who enter illegally. The debate continues into the 2000 census. Democrats want to improve the count of hard-to-reach populations, including immigrants, using statistical sampling for part of the census. This approach has been endorsed by the National Academy of Sciences as a way to improve the tally. Republicans, on the other hand, claim that the method will produce grossly erroneous results and that the Constitution requires a full enumeration, not sampling. In early 1999 the U.S. Supreme Court ruled that an enumeration is necessary for apportioning House seats, the only constitutionally specified purpose of the census. However, the ruling did not preclude using statistical adjustments for other purposes.

Thinking ahead, as the U.S. population grows older, more younger workers of all types will be needed to support the economy and the Social Security retirement and health care system. As these needs become more pressing, the doors to the country may open even wider.

SUMMARY

Racial and gender inequality continue to manifest themselves in many aspects of American life. Women won the right to vote in 1920, but an Equal Rights Amendment to the U.S. Constitution has eluded them. Only recently have the effects of abuses such as domestic violence and sexual harassment been seriously considered in public policy. Other recent movements to secure greater equality for women include passage of the Family and Medical Leave Act of 1993. A particularly contentious social welfare issue that concerns women—and also men—is abortion. The U.S. Supreme Court has upheld the right of women to abortions since its 1973 decision in *Roe v. Wade,* but in recent years it has also upheld a number of state laws restricting access to abortions.

In the last few decades, the rights of gay men and lesbians have made their way to the public policy agenda. Gay men and lesbians have made some progress on the state and local level in gaining equal treatment. The U.S. Supreme Court, however, has refused to overturn state sodomy laws. The much watered-down version of a policy allowing gay men and lesbians to serve in the military, and efforts to ban antidiscrimination laws for gay men and lesbians, attests to the deep-seated controversies that remain over the gay rights agenda in this country.

Black Americans have faced numerous struggles in their fight for civil rights. Not until 1954 did the Supreme Court strike down the "separate but equal" doctrine by stating that separate public facilities can not be equal facilities. The Civil Rights Act of 1964 addressed a number of black Americans' concerns, including equal treatment in employment and access to public facilities. Inequality, however, remains an issue. Even after controlling for education, black Americans earn less than whites.

The vigorous support of civil rights by presidents during the 1960s and 1970s changed during the Reagan and Bush administrations. In the late 1990s, a California state referendum and a court decision in Texas dealt new setbacks to affirmative action policy. Conservative blacks, however, believe that racial preferences are not warranted, and that blacks should focus more on utilizing available educational and economic opportunities.

Hispanic Americans are the fastest-growing ethnic group in the United States. Their political presence at the local and state level is also growing, and they will be an increasingly important political and social force in the years ahead.

Native Americans face the most severe economic and social problems of any ethnic group in this country. The Indian Self-Determination and Education Assistance

Act of 1975 was an attempt to restore to Native Americans planning power over social welfare issues. The many tribal groups do not speak with one voice, and improvements for them are especially slow in coming.

Conditions in Haiti, Mexico, Russia, China, and other countries add to the number of people who want to live in the United States. The large numbers of people entering this country both legally and illegally has resulted in debate over what appropriate immigration policy should be. Legislation in 1986 granted amnesty to many undocumented people residing in the U.S. In 1990 Congress again began permitting an increased number of people to enter the United States. Many immigrants fare quite well, finding jobs and becoming self-sufficient. Those concerned about immigration, however, believe that too many are entering the country to the disadvantage of those already here. As the U.S. population continues to grow older, Americans may develop more generous attitudes toward immigration policy.

NOTES

1. Diana Pearce and Harriette McAdoo, *Women and Children: Alone and in Poverty* (Washington, DC: National Advisory Council on Economic Opportunity, 1981).

2. Committee on Ways and Means, U.S. House of Representatives, *1998 Green Book: Background Material and Data on Programs Within the Jurisdiction of the Committee on Ways and Means* (Washington, DC: U.S. Government Printing Office, 1998), p. 299.

3. U.S. Bureau of the Census, Current Population Reports, *Money Income in the United States: 1997,* Series P60-200 (Washington, DC: U.S. Government Printing Office, 1997), Table 7, pp. 26–27.

4. Poverty figures are from U.S. Bureau of the Census, Current Population Reports, *Poverty in the United States: 1997,* Series P60-201 (Washington, DC: U.S. Government Printing Office, 1998), Table 2, pp. 2–5.

5. See, for example, Barbara J. Nelson, "The Origins of the Two-Channel Welfare State: Workmen's Compensation and Mothers' Aid," in Linda Gordon, ed., *Women, the State, and Welfare* (Madison: University of Wisconsin Press, 1990), pp. 123–150.

6. Committee on Ways and Means, *1998 Green Book,* p. 53.

7. Ekaterina Shirley and Peter Spiegler, *The Benefits of Social Security Privatization for Women,* The Cato Institute, SSP No. 12, July 20, 1998, http://www.cato.org/pubs/ssps/ssp12es.html.

8. See U.S. Department of Health, Education and Welfare, *Social Security and the Changing Roles of Men and Women* (Washington, DC: U.S. Government Printing Office, February 1979), chapters 1 & 2; also see Shirley and Spiegler, *The Benefits of Social Security Privatization for Women.*

9. Information in this paragraph relies on "Women and Social Security," *Social Security Bulletin,* Vol. 48, No. 2, February 1985, pp. 17–26.

10. Shirley and Peter Spiegler, *The Benefits of Social Security Privatization for Women.*

11. Financial Women International, "Position Statement on Social Security Reform," adopted March 1997, 200 North Glebe Road, Suite 814, Arlington, VA 22203-3728, http://www.fwi.org/socsec.htm.

12. Edith U. Fierst, "Privatization of Social Security—A Threat to Women: Part 1," *Womansword,* a newsletter for activists, Vol. 1, Issue 13, February 1997, http://feminist.com/ww9.htm.

13. Data on the earnings ratio are from the U.S. Bureau of the Census and the U.S. Bureau of Labor Statistics and are found in Ida L. Castro, *Equal Pay: A Thirty-Five Year Perspective* (Washington, DC: U.S. Department of Labor, June 10, 1998), Appendix B, pp. 57–58.

14. U.S. Bureau of the Census, *Statistical Abstract of the United States: 1998* (Washington, DC: U.S. Government Printing Office, 1997), Table 69, p. 61.

15. U.S. Bureau of the Census, *Statistical Abstract of the United States: 1998,* Table 648, p. 405; Castro, *Equal Pay,* Appendix A, p. 56.

16. See M. Anne Hill and Mark R. Killingsworth, eds., *Comparable Worth: Analyses and Evidence* (Ithaca, NY: ILR Press, New York State School of Industrial and Labor Relations, Cornell University, 1989); Elaine Sorensen, *Comparable Worth: Is It a Worthy Policy?* (Princeton, NJ: Princeton University Press, 1994).

17. Much of this paragraph relies on Jill Johnson Keeney, "Not a Crazy Proposal," *Louisville Times,* 1984,

reprinted in the *Office Professional,* Vol. 5, No. 2, February 15, 1985, p. 7.

18. Karolyn L. Godbey, "Comparable Worth Policies: Predicting State Level Commitment," *Florida Nursing Review,* Vol. 4, No. 4, April 1990, pp. 19–20.

19. Angie Cannon, "Women Are Holding Historically High Rank in New White House," *Austin American-Statesman,* October 2, 1993, p. A8.

20. National Organization for Women, "ERA Ratification Status Summary," in *ERA Countdown Campaign,* (Washington, DC: NOW, 1981), p. A.

21. Quoted in David Klein, "The ERA Is Wanted Dead or Alive in Florida," *Tallahassee Democrat,* January 21, 1982.

22. These polls are summarized in National Organization for Women, "Strong Public Support for ERA," in *ERA Countdown Campaign* (Washington, DC: NOW, 1981), p. C.

23. Robert Rector (The Heritage Foundation), "Give Parents Who Stay at Home an Even Break," *Austin American-Statesman,* January 30, 1998, p. A15.

24. Much of this paragraph relies on Sharon K. Long and Sandra J. Clark, *The New Child Care Block Grant: State Funding Choices and Their Implications* (Washington, DC: The Urban Institute, 1997), quote from p. 4.

25. International Labour Organization, 1998 Press Releases, "More Than 120 Nations Provide Paid Maternity Leave," February 16, 1998, http://www.ilo.org/public/english/235 press/pr/1998/7.htm; also see Kirstin Downey Grimsley (*The Washington Post*), "Report: U.S. Lags on Benefits for Maternity," *Austin American-Statesman,* February 16, 1998, pp. A1 & 5; "Social Work in the Public Eye," *NASW News,* newsletter of the National Association of Social Workers, April 1998, p. 13.

26. *Code of Federal Regulations,* Vol. 29, Sec. 1604.11.

27. Louis Obdyke, "Small Business Q & A: What Is the Definition of Sexual Harassment?" *Austin American-Statesman,* September 10, 1997, p. D2.

28. See Joan Biskupic, "Court Draws Line on Harassment," *Washington Post,* June 27, 1998, p. A1.

29. Karen Tumulty, "White House May Delay Abortion-Funding Order," *Austin American-Statesman,* December 5, 1993, p. A2.

30. U.S. Bureau of the Census, *Statistical Abstract of the United States: 1992,* (Washington, DC: U.S. Government Printing Office, 1992), pp. 74–75.

31. Lisa M. Koonin, Jack C. Smith, and Merrell Ramick Lilo T. Strauss, "Abortion Surveillance–United States, 1995," Centers for Disease Control, July 3, 1998, http://www.cdc.gov/epo/mmwr/preview/mmwrhtml/00053774.htm.

32. "1995 Abortion Rate Hits Lowest Level in 20 Years," *Austin American-Statesman,* December 5, 1997, p. A8; Barbara Vobejda, "Proportion of Unintended Pregnancies Declines Significantly Since Late 1980s," *The Washington Post,* January 18, 1998, p. A25.

33. U.S. Commission on Civil Rights, *The Federal Response in Domestic Violence* (Washington, DC: U.S. Government Printing Office, January 1982), pp. iv–v; also see Anne Sparks, "Feminists Negotiate the Executive Branch: The Policing of Male Violence," in Cynthia R. Daniels, ed., *Feminists Negotiate the State: The Politics of Domestic Violence* (Lanham, MD: University Press of America, 1997), pp. 35–52.

34. Lisa G. Lerman, "Legal Help for Battered Women," in Joseph J. Costa, ed., *Abuse of Women: Legislation, Reporting, and Prevention* (Lexington, MA: Lexington Books, 1983), p. 29.

35. *Family Violence: The Battered Woman* (Austin: League of Women Voters of Texas Education Fund, 1987), p. 33.

36. See U.S. Department of Justice, Violence Against Women Office, "The Violence Against Women Act," August 4, 1996, http://www.usdoj.gov/vawo/vawafct.htm; Martha R. Burt et al., *1997 Report: Evaluation of the STOP Formula Grants Under the Violence Against Women Act of 1994* (Washington, DC: Urban Institute, March 1997); Rachelle Brooks, "Feminists Negotiate the Legislative Branch: The Violence Against Women Act," in Daniels, *Feminists Negotiate the State*, pp. 65–81.

37. For more information on these and other legal cases, see Arthur S. Leonard, *Sexuality and the Law: An Encyclopedia of Major Legal Cases* (Hamden, CT: Garland, 1993).

38. Ruth Harlow, "Kentucky Ruling a Milestone in Struggle for Gay Rights," *Civil Liberties*, Winter 1992–93, pp. 1, 11.

39. American Civil Liberties Union, "Status of U.S. Sodomy Laws," March 1998, http://www.aclu.org/issues/gay/sodomy.html.

40. The New York Times, "High Court Affirms Gays' Civil Rights," *Austin American-Statesman,* May 21, 1996, pp. A1 & 7.

41. American Civil Liberties Union, "Maine Becomes 10th State with Gay Civil Rights Law, New Hampshire Will Lock Up New England," May 16, 1997, http://www.aclu.org/news/n051697a.html.

42. Human Rights Campaign, "Fighting Anti-Gay Hate Crimes," http://www.hrc.org/issues/hate/index.htm, accessed August 26, 1998.

43. Lori Hawkins, "IBM Adds Benefits for Gay Partners," *Austin American-Statesman,* September 20, 1996, pp. D1 & 2.

44. The remainder of this paragraph relies on American Civil Liberties Union, "ACLU Fact Sheet: Overview of Lesbian and Gay Parenting," May 1997, http://www.aclu.org/issues/gay/parent.html.

45. Randy Thomasson, "Questions and Answers: The California Defense of Marriage Act," *Capitol Resource*

Backgrounder, July 1998, http://www.capitolresource.org/b_doma.htm.

46. Michelle M. Benecke, cited in "Challenges to Old Gay Ban Spark Questions on Military's New Policy," *Miami Herald,* December 19, 1993, p. 7A; this paragraph also relies on "Clinton: Let Military Bar Gay Conduct," *Miami Herald,* July 17, 1993, p. 11A; "Pentagon Outlines Revised Conduct Code for Gays in Military," *Miami Herald,* December 23, 1993, p. 4A; Steven Lee Myers (*New York Times*), "More Gays Forced Out of Service Than Before 'Don't Ask,'" *Austin American-Statesman,* January 23, 1999, p. A21.

47. See American Civil Liberties Union, "Court Upholds 'Don't Ask, Don't Tell," September 8, 1997, http://www.aclu.org/news/w090897a.html; Neil A. Lewis (*The New York Times*), "Court Upholds Military Policy of 'Don't Ask, Don't Tell' for Gays," *Austin American-Statesman,* April 6, 1996, p. 6.

48. Jeff Stryker, "The Gay Team," *Austin American-Statesman,* June 8, 1996, p. A13.

49. "Federal Appeals Court Strikes Down Alabama Law Barring Gay Student Groups from Campus," *American Civil Liberties Freedom Network,* April 30, 1997, http://www.aclu.org/news/n043097e.html.

50. Committee on Ways and Means, *1998 Green Book,* pp. 299 & 440.

51. Stephen Labaton, "GAO: Blacks More Likely to Be Denied Benefits than Whites," *Austin American-Statesman,* May 12, 1992, p. A2.

52. Martin Giles, "'Race Coding' and White Opposition to Welfare," *American Political Science Review,* Vol. 90, No. 3, 1996, pp. 593–604.

53. Gary Orfield, Susan E. Eaton, and the Harvard Project on School Desegregation, *Dismantling Desegregation: The Quiet Reversal of Brown v. Board of Education* (New York: New Press, 1995).

54. Attitudes of black and white parents towards desegregation, busing, and related issues are found in *Time to Move on: African American and White Parents Set an Agenda for Schools,* April 1998, Public Agenda Online, http://www.public agenda.org/moveon/moveon.html.

55. See "With Fairness in Education for All," *Civil Liberties,* November 1997, pp. 1 & 2.

56. "Racial Progress Assessed," *Tallahassee Democrat,* April 9, 1984, p. 3A; Claire V. Handley, coauthor of *Miles to Go: A Report on Black Students and Postsecondary Education in the South* (Atlanta: Southern Education Foundation, 1998) cited in Christi Harlan, "Segregation's Remnants are Seen at Universities," *Austin American-Statesman,* August 26, 1998, p. B7.

57. The remainder of this paragraph relies on Chester W. Hartman, *Housing and Social Policy* (Englewood Cliffs, NJ: Prentice Hall, 1975), pp. 136 & 139.

58. Ibid., p. 139; on the effects of government mortgage policy on blacks' and whites' wealth, see Melvin L. Oliver and Thomas M. Shapiro, *Black Wealth/White Wealth: A New Perspective on Racial Inequality* (New York: Routledge, 1995).

59. U.S. Conference of Mayors, "Mayors Attack Urban Redlining, Mortgagee Discrimination," press release, February 23, 1998, http://www.usmayors.org/USCM/news/press_releases/documents/.

60. Bill Dedman, "Study Finds Racial Lending Gap," *Austin American-Statesman,* January 22, 1989, pp. A1, 16; Constance L. Hays, "Boston Banks to Fight Race Gap in Mortgages," *Champaign-Urbana News Gazette,* January 29, 1990, p. B5; U.S. Conference of Mayors, *America's Homeownership Gap: How Urban Redlining and Mortgagee Discrimination Penalize City Residents,* February 23, 1998, http://www.usmayors.org/USCM/news/press_releases/documents/.

61. Douglas S. Massey and Nancy A. Denton, "Suburbanization and Segregation in U.S. Metropolitan Areas," *American Journal of Sociology,* Vol. 94, No. 3, 1988, pp. 592–626.

62. Rob Wells, "Banks Pledge More to the Underserved," *Austin American-Statesman,* February 13, 1994, p. G10.

63. U.S. Department of Housing and Urban Development, "Cuomo Says HUD to Investigate Mortgage Lending Discrimination as Part of Effort to Close the 'Homeownership Gap,'" press release, March 10, 1998, http://www.hud.gov/pressrel/pr98-107.html.

64. *Federal Policies on Remedies Concerning Equal Employment Opportunity in State and Local Government Personnel Systems,* March 23, 1973, cited in Felix A. Nigro and Lloyd G. Nigro, *The New Public Personnel Administration* (Itasca, IL: Peacock, 1976), p. 21.

65. See Frank Trippet, "A Solid Yes to Affirmative Action," *Time,* July 14, 1986, p. 22.

66. Michael de Courcy Hinds, "Minority Firms Reeling from Ruling on Set-aside Programs," *Austin American-Statesman,* December 25, 1991, pp. A27, 31.

67. For a summary of reductions in litigation, see D. Lee Bawden and John L. Palmer, "Social Policy, Challenging the Welfare State," in John L. Palmer and Isabel V. Sawhill, eds., *The Reagan Record* (Cambridge, MA: Ballinger, 1984), pp. 204–206.

68. From an undated letter to ACLU members from Ira Glasser, executive director of the American Civil Liberties Union, 132 West 43rd St., New York, NY 10036-6599.

69. William M. Welch, "Democrats Angling for Resumption of Civil Rights Talks," *Austin American-Statesman,* April 23, 1991, p. A5.

70. Bob Dart, "Education Department Unveils New Minority Scholarship Policy," *Austin American-Statesman,* December 15, 1992, p. A2; also see Karen Dewitt, "Education Chief Backs Minority Scholarships," *New York Times,* March 19, 1993, p. A15.

71. Thomas Sowell, "Yes, Blacks Can Make It On Their Own," *Time,* September 8, 1997, p. 62.

72. Glenn C. Loury, "The Moral Quandary of the Black Community," *Public Interest,* No. 79, Spring 1985, pp. 9–22.

73. A. Phillips Brooks, "New Black Leaders Shifting from Traditional Civil Rights," *Austin American-Statesman,* November 10, 1993, pp. A10, 12.

74. U.S. Bureau of the Census, *Statistical Abstract of the United States:1998,* Table No. 19, p. 19.

75. Thomas H. Walz and Gary Askerooth, *The Upside Down Welfare State* (Minneapolis: Elwood, 1973), p. 25.

76. Michael P. Shea, "Indians Skeptical of Report Urging Program Overhaul," *Congressional Quarterly,* Vol. 48, No. 2, 1990, pp. 98–100.

77. U.S. Bureau of Indian Affairs, "Answers to Frequently Asked Questions," April 2, 1998, http://www.doi.gov/bia/aitoday/q_and_a.html.

78. Gerald Thomas Wilkinson, "On Assisting Indian People," *Social Casework,* Vol. 61, No. 8, 1980, pp. 451–454.

79. Joseph J. Westermeyer, "Indian Powerlessness in Minnesota," *Society,* Vol. 10, No. 3, March–April 1973, pp. 45–47, 50–52; also see Walz and Askerooth, *The Upside Down Welfare State,* p. 31.

80. Shea, "Indians Skeptical of Report Urging Program Overhaul."

81. Walz and Askerooth, *The Upside Down Welfare State,* p. 25.

82. Chuck Cook, "BIA Ordered to Prepare for Inquiry," *Arizona Republic,* October 16, 1987, pp. A1, 5.

83. Chuck Cook, Mike Masterson, and M. N. Trahant, "Indians Are Sold Out by the U.S.," *Arizona Republic,* October 4, 1987, pp. A1, 18, 20.

84. Chuck Cook, Mike Masterson, and M. N. Trahant, "Child's Suffering Is Cry for Reform," *Arizona Republic,* October 7, 1987, p. A18.

85. Edward M. Carpenter, "Social Services, Policies, and Issues," *Social Casework,* Vol. 61, No. 8, 1980, pp. 455–461.

86. Shea, "Indians Skeptical of Report Urging Program Overhaul."

87. Bureau of Indian Affairs, "Vision Statement," http://www.doi.gov/bia/mission.html, April 2, 1997.

88. National Congress of American Indians, "Current NCAI Advocacy Activities," http://www.ncai.org/issues/issues.html, accessed September 20, 1998.

89. Donald Brieland, Lela B. Costin, and Charles R. Atherton, *Contemporary Social Work: An Introduction to Social Work and Social Welfare,* 2nd ed. (New York: McGraw-Hill, 1980), p. 404.

90. Neil Skene, ed., *Congressional Quarterly Almanac, 1992,* Vol. XLVIII (Washington, DC: Congressional Quarterly, 1993), pp. 335–336.

91. Walter W. Miller, "Vietnamese Society Rife with U.S. 'Footprints,' " *Austin American-Statesman,* April 2, 1985, p. A16.

92. Immigration and Naturalization Service, *Legal Immigration, Fiscal Year 1997,* Annual Report (Washington, DC: U.S. Department of Justice, January 1999), http://www.ins/usdoj.gov/public-affairs/news-releases.legal.pdf.

93. Martha Angle, "Immigration's Bridges Have Ups and Downs," *Congressional Quarterly,* Vol. 51, No. 12, March 20, 1993, p. 710; James E. Garcia and Suzanne Gamboa, "Blockade Successful But Controversial," *Austin American-Statesman,* November 26, 1993, pp. A1, 9.

94. Information from the U.S. Immigration and Naturalization Service, cited in Garcia and Gamboa, "Blockade Successful But Controversial," p. A9.

95. Robert Warren, *State Population Estimates: Legal Permanent Residents and Aliens Eligible for Naturalization* (Washington, DC: Office of Policy and Planning, Immigration and Naturalization Service, 1996) cited in James P. Smith and Barry Edmonston, eds., *The New Americans: Economic, Demographic, and Fiscal Effects of Immigration* (Washington, DC: National Academy Press, 1997), p. 51.

96. Immigration and Naturalization Service, cited in Bureau of the Census, *Statistical Abstract of the United States: 1997* (Washington, DC: U.S. Government Printing Office, 1997), Table 10, p. 12.

97. Smith and Edmonston, *The New Americans: Economic, Demographic, and Fiscal Effects of Immigration.*

98. This argument is based on Jagdish N. Bhagwati, "Control Immigration at the Border," *Wall Street Journal,* February 1, 1985, p. 22.

99. See Smith and Edmonston, *The New Americans: Economic, Demographic, and Fiscal Effects of Immigration,* p. 29.

100. NCLR (National Council of La Raza) "Opposes Guestworker Legislation," Statement of Raul Yzaguirre, president of NCLR, June 24, 1998, http://www.nclr.org/press/063098a.html.

101. Warren, *State Population Estimates: Legal Permanent Residents and Aliens Eligible for Naturalization.*

102. U.S. Bureau of the Census, *Statistical Abstract of the United States: 1998,* Table 57, p. 55.

103. Neil Skene, ed., "Sizable Boost in Immigration Ok'd," *Congressional Quarterly Almanac, 1990,* Vol. XLVI (Washington, DC: Congressional Quarterly, 1991), pp. 474–485.

CHAPTER

Implementing and Evaluating Social Welfare Policy: What Happens After a Law Is Passed

Americans were once confident that if Congress adopted a policy and appropriated money for it, and the executive branch organized a program, hired people, spent money, and carried out the activities designed to implement the policy, then the effects of the policy felt by society would be those intended by the Congress. But today, as the following discussion of implementation and evaluation demonstrates, there is growing concern about the government's ability to solve social problems.

THE POLITICS OF IMPLEMENTATION

Many problems in social welfare policy arise after a law is passed—in the implementation process. Policy implementation includes all the activities designed to carry out the intention of the law: (1) creating, organizing, and staffing agencies to carry out the new policy, or assigning new responsibilities to existing agencies and personnel; (2) issuing directives, rules, regulations, and guidelines to translate policies into specific courses of action; and (3) directing and coordinating both personnel and expenditures toward the achievement of policy objectives.

There is always a gap—sometimes small, sometimes very large—between a policy decision and its implementation. Some scholars of implementation take an almost cynical view of the process:

> *Our normal expectation should be that new programs will fail to get off the ground and that, at best, they will take considerable time to get started. The cards in this world are*

stacked against things happening, as so much effort is required to make them move. The remarkable thing is that new programs work at all.[1]

What are the obstacles to implementation? Why isn't implementation a *rational* activity? Why can't policies be directly implemented in decisions about organization, staffing, spending, regulation, direction, and coordination? The obstacles to successful implementation are many, but they can be categorized in terms of (1) communications, (2) resources, (3) attitudes, and (4) bureaucratic structure.[2]

Communications

The first requirement for effective policy implementation is that the people who are running the program must know what they are supposed to do. Directives must not only be received but must also be clear. Vague, inconsistent, and contradictory directives confuse administrators. Directives give meanings to policies, but these meanings may not be consistent with the original intention of the law. Moreover, poor directives enable people who disagree with the policy to read their own biases into programs. The U.S. Department of Health and Human Services, a major federal government agency, is divided into many offices that are responsible for administering hundreds of programs (see Figure 12-1). These programs affect virtually every individual, every community, and every state in the country. The DHHS constantly struggles with maintaining accurate communications. Similar problems are faced by every other federal, state, and local bureaucracy.

Generally, the more decentralized the administration of a program, and the greater the number of layers of administration through which directives must flow, the less likely it is that policies will be transmitted accurately and consistently. As discussed in Chapter 4, the Social Security retirement program is highly centralized. The Food Stamp Program (see Chapter 7) has uniform eligibility rules but they must be communicated to thousands of state and local eligibility workers. TANF, another public assistance program (see Chapter 6), is much more decentralized with the federal government establishing broad guidelines, and each state setting many of the rules of the program. Other block grant programs give even more discretion to the states. Whatever the advantages of decentralization may be, prompt, consistent, and uniform policy implementation is *not* usually found in a decentralized structure.

Frequently, Congress (and state legislatures) is deliberately vague about public policy. Congress and the president may pass vague and ambiguous laws largely for symbolic reasons—to reassure people that "something" is being done to help with a problem. In these cases, Congress and the president may not really know exactly what to do about the problem. They therefore delegate wide discretion to administrators who act under the "authority" of broad laws to determine what, if anything, actually will be done. Often Congress and the president want to claim credit for the high-sounding principles enacted into law but do not want to accept responsibility for any unpopular actions that administrators must take to implement these principles. It is much easier for political leaders to blame the "bureaucrats" and pretend that government regulations are a product of an "ungovernable" Washington bureaucracy.

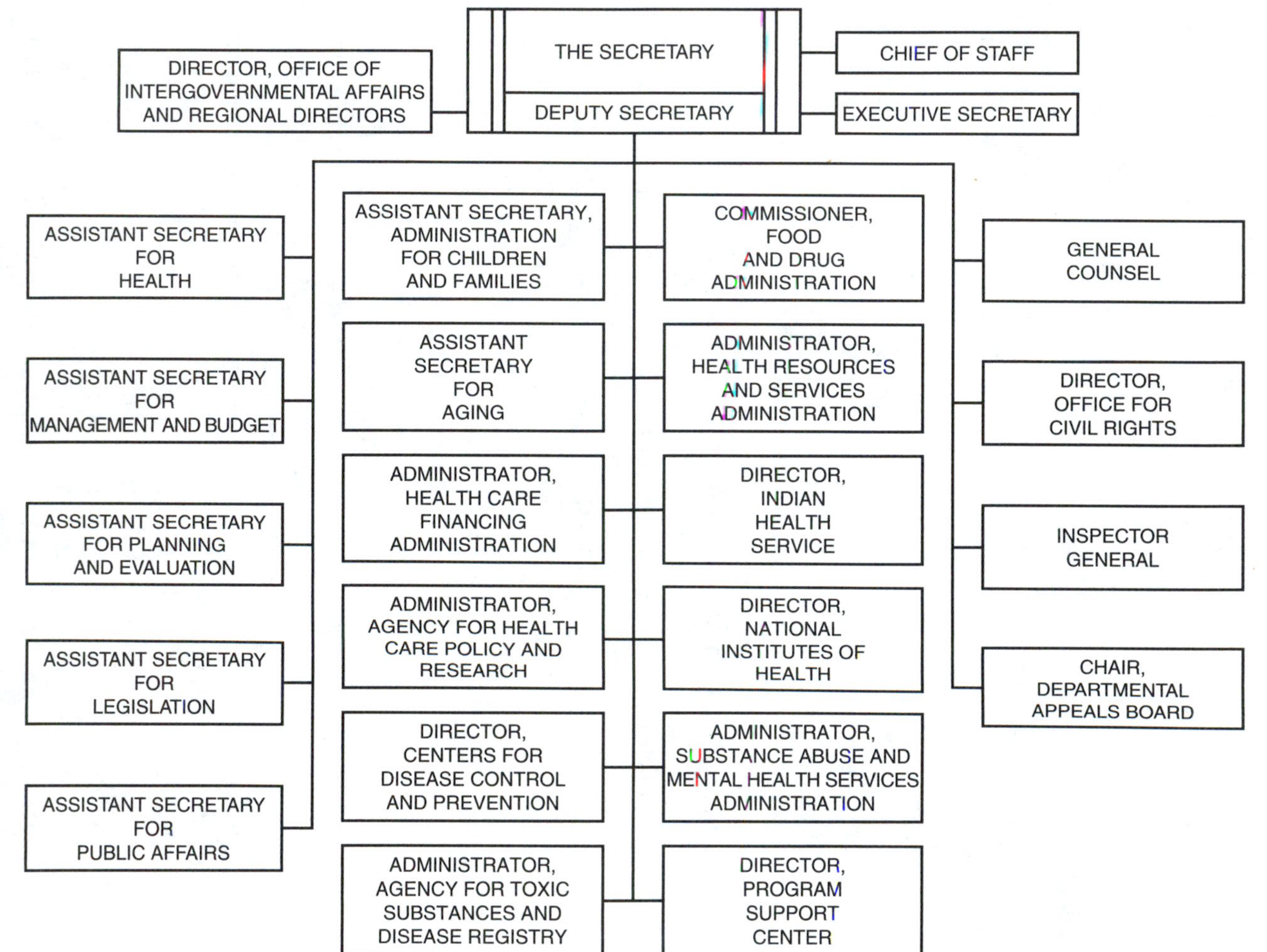

FIGURE 12-1

Structure of the U.S. Department of Health and Human Services

Source: Office of the Federal Register, National Archives and Records Administration, *The United States Government Manual 1998/1999* (Washington, DC: U.S. Government Printing Office, 1998), p. 272.

One of the best examples of this problem occurred during the War on Poverty (also see Chapter 9). In the Economic Opportunity Act of 1964, Congress and President Johnson wrote into the law a provision calling for "maximum feasible participation of the poor" in community action agencies and other programs supported by the Office of Economic Opportunity (OEO). But no one knew exactly what that phrase meant. How were the poor to help plan and run the programs? Did this phrase authorize poverty workers to organize the poor politically? Did this phrase mean that social activists paid by the government should help organize the poor to pressure welfare and housing agencies for better services? The policy was not clear, and its implementation was confusing and frustrating. Eventually, of course, the OEO was abolished, in part because of its problems in administering an unclear mandate from Congress.

Resources

Even if policy directives are clear, accurate, and consistent, when administrators lack the resources to carry out these policies implementation fails. A crucial resource is funds—the money needed to implement new policies. Sometimes new policies require only limited funds to implement, but many new policies and programs seem doomed to fail because insufficient resources are allocated for startup and maintenance functions. An obvious example is the relatively limited amount of funds given to each community to fight the War on Poverty. Another is the lack of child care placements available to ensure that a substantial number of TANF parents are able to obtain and maintain employment (see Chapter 6).

Implementation or **process evaluation studies** can be useful in determining whether modifications in rules, regulations, procedures, or resources are needed as new policies and programs are put into place. For example, an implementation study might help identify areas having difficulty in developing sufficient child care placements to accommodate parents receiving TANF and the obstacles encountered. Some major implementation studies have been conducted of the Job Training Partnership Act[3] and the JOBS programs,[4] but it is generally difficult to acquire the funds needed to conduct these studies. Everyone from policymakers to the public is more interested in outcome evaluation—the final results of the program.

Resources also include staff with the proper skills to carry out their assignments and with the authority and facilities necessary to translate a paper proposal into a functioning public service. It is common for government agencies to claim that problems with implementation arise from undersized staffs. And many of these claims are true. Even adequate funds to hire personnel to carry out a policy are not enough. The personnel must have the skills necessary for the job. Consider concerns about the need to treat sex offenders. There may not be enough highly skilled therapists available to provide this treatment, even if treatment programs were adequately funded. Staffing is especially difficult in new programs, especially those few that are highly innovative and experimental, as was the case during the War on Poverty. There are frequently no ready-made reserves of people who are trained for the program and who know what to do. Yet there is always pressure to show results as quickly as possible, to ensure the continuation of the program the next year.

Sometimes agencies lack the authority, even on paper, to implement policy. Agencies may not be authorized to issue checks to citizens, or to purchase goods or services, or to provide funds to other government agencies, or to withdraw funds in the case of noncompliance, or to go to court to force compliance. Even if agencies do have the necessary authority (for example, to withhold federal funds from a local government agency or a nonprofit corporation), they may be reluctant to exercise this authority because of the adverse political repercussions that might ensue. Agencies that do not have the necessary authority to carry out policy (or agencies that fear that exercising that authority may be politically risky) must rely on persuasion and cooperation. Rather than order local agencies, private corporations, or individual citizens to do something, higher-level officials may consult with them, ask for their cooperation, or appeal to their sense of public service. Successful implementation generally requires goodwill on the part of everyone involved. Agencies or administrators who must continually resort to sanctions will probably be unsuccessful in the long run.

Physical facilities may also be crucial in implementation. Programs generally need offices, telephones, equipment, and supplies. Yet government agencies (especially new ones) often find it difficult to acquire the necessary facilities to carry out their programs. Once again, most government administrators must rely on persuasion and cooperation to get other government agencies to provide them with offices, equipment, travel approvals, and so on.

The opponents of a particular policy may prefer to see resources reduced. One tactic of opponents, even after they lose the fight over the actual policy in Congress, is to try to reduce the size of the budget and staff that is to implement the policy. The political battle does not end with the passing of a law. It continues each year in fights over resources to implement the law. This has certainly been the case with the Legal Services Corporation (LSC), an agency that provides legal aid to low-income people (see Chapter 9). The Reagan administration wanted to abolish the LSC and appointed members to the LSC's board that shared these sentiments. "When Congress refused to . . . cut the corporation's budget further, . . . the board actually hired lobbyists to press the lawmakers for less . . . money."[5] The LSC remains in existence, but it has been in a tenuous position for years.

Attitudes

If administrators and program personnel sympathize with a particular policy, it is likely to be carried out as the original policymakers intended. But when the attitudes of agency administrators and staff personnel differ from those of the policymakers, the implementation process can be anything but smooth. Because administrators always have some discretion (and occasionally a great deal) in implementation, their attitudes toward policies have much to do with how a program is implemented. When people are told to do things with which they do not agree, inevitable slippage will occur between a policy and its implementation.

Generally, social service personnel enter the field because they want to "help people"—especially those who are aged, poor, disabled, or otherwise vulnerable. There is seldom any attitudinal problem in social agencies in implementing policies to expand social services. But highly committed social service personnel may find it very difficult to implement policies to cut back or eliminate social services.

Conservative policymakers are aware of the social service orientation of the "welfare bureaucracy." They do not believe that welfare administrators really try to enforce work provisions of welfare laws, for example, or care about reducing administrative errors.[6] These conservatives say that eligibility requirements have been given liberal interpretation by sympathetic administrators, and they believe that the welfare bureaucracy is directly responsible for much of the growth in caseloads over the years. They see welfare administrators as a major obstacle to policies designed to tighten eligibility, reduce overlapping benefits, and encourage work. Conservatives therefore try to impose fiscal sanctions on state agencies that fail to keep error rates below a certain level. Even if these sanctions fail to prove effective, opponents of public assistance want to make their point.

In government agencies, it is generally impossible to remove staff simply because they disagree with a policy. Direct pressures are generally unavailable. Pay increases are primarily across the board, and promotions are infrequent and often based on seniority. "Selling" a policy—winning support through persuasion—remains a more effective strategy to overcoming opposition than threatening sanctions. If those who implement policy cannot be convinced that the policy is good for their clients or themselves, perhaps they can be convinced that it is less offensive than other alternatives that might be imposed by policymakers.

Bureaucracy

Despite widespread distaste for the word "bureaucracy,"[7] nearly all public functions are handled by this type of organization. Previously established organizations and procedures in bureaucracies often hinder implementation of new policies and programs. Bureaucratic "inertia" slows changes in policy. Administrators become accustomed to certain ways of doing things (called *standard operating procedures*), and administrative structures generally remain in place long after their original functions have changed or even disappeared.

Standard operating procedures (SOPs) are routines that enable officials to perform numerous tasks every day; SOPs save time. If every worker had to invent a new way of doing things for every case, there would not be enough time to help very many people. SOPs bring consistency in handling cases; rules can be applied more uniformly.

However, SOPs can also obstruct policy implementation. "Once requirements and practices are instituted, they tend to remain in force long after the conditions that spawned them have disappeared."[8] Routines are not regularly re-examined; they tend to persist even when policies or times change. If SOPs are not revised to reflect policy changes, these changes are not implemented. Moreover, many people prefer the stability and familiarity of existing routines, and they are reluctant to revise their patterns. Organizations have spent time, effort, and money in developing these routines. These "sunk costs" commit organizations to limit change as much as possible.

SOPs can make it difficult to handle nonconforming cases in an individual fashion. Frustrations arise for social service employees when they attempt to help people in need who do not meet specific eligibility criteria. Even though particular cases may not conform to prewritten SOPs, many administrators and staff try to force them into one or another of the established classifications. Over time, these frustrations with bureaucracy may lead to staff "burnout." This occurs frequently among child welfare workers. Their job turnover is high because often they can intervene in only the most serious cases, and even in these cases they may be unable to do what in their professional judgment is necessary.

Bureaucractic organization also affects workers' abilities to implement policy, especially when responsibility for a policy is dispersed among many governmental units. The number of governments has proliferated. There are now more than 87,000 governments in the U.S.: a national government, fifty state governments, about 3,000 county governments, over 19,000 city governments, and nearly 17,000 township governments, as well as nearly 14,000 school districts, and about 35,000 special districts.[9] Even within the national government, many departments have responsibility for social welfare programs. For example, the U.S. Department of Health and Human Services has responsibility for TANF and Medicaid; the U.S. Department of Agriculture administers the Food Stamp and WIC programs; and the U.S. Department of Labor administers the JTPA and Job Corps programs. A similar dispersement of responsibility for social welfare programs may occur at the state level. The descriptions of TANF in Chapter 6 and the Food Stamp Program in Chapter 7 illustrate the difficulties clients face in dealing with what are supposed to be rational bureaucracies. All of us have been frustrated by bureaucracies from public agencies such as the IRS to private agencies such as insurance companies. These situations must be even more frustrating for those who are ill, disabled, or have little formal education.

The more governments and agencies involved with a particular policy, and the more independent their decisions, the greater the problems of implementation. Every government and every agency becomes concerned with its own "turf"—areas each considers its exclusive responsibility. The national government and the states frequently struggle over how states will implement federal regulations. State governments often fight with the national government to hold onto their traditional areas of authority, particularly when the federal government imposes regulations on them (such as requirements to expand Medicaid eligibility) but fails to provide sufficient funding for the new mandate, or when the states perceive that federal rules and regulations are unfair (see, for example, the discussion on fraud, abuse, and error in Chapter 7).

Proponents of particular programs may insist to Congress that their programs be administered by separate agencies that are largely independent of traditional executive departments or other agencies. These proponents believe their projects are special. They fear that consolidating program responsibilities will downgrade the emphasis that a separate department will give to their particular program. For example, advocates of special programs for alcoholics do not want to merge the National Institute on Alcohol Abuse and Alcoholism with the National Institute on Drug Abuse, despite the number of people who abuse both alcohol and other drugs. They fear that a merger will reduce attention to alcohol problems because the public views illegal drugs as the greater menace to society (see Chapter 10).

Actually, some separation of programs is probably desirable. The argument for federalism—the division of governmental responsibilities between the national government and the fifty state governments—is that it allows each state to deal more directly with the particular conditions confronting its residents. Government "closer to home" is sometimes thought to be more flexible, manageable, and personal than a distant bureaucracy in Washington.

However, when programs and services are fragmented, policy coordination is difficult. This is true whether we are talking about the distribution of responsibilities among different agencies at the national, state, or local government level, or the division of responsibilities between the national government and the fifty states. Uniformity is lost. Consider, for example, that every state in the nation has its own, separate TANF program. These are state-administered programs that operate with federal financial assistance. As we saw in Chapter 6, program rules and maximum payments to families vary widely among the states.

The federal government does recognize the maze involved in applying for public assistance benefits, and it has considered ways to reduce the red tape. In 1990 the Secretary of the USDA was directed to develop an Advisory Committee on Welfare Simplification and Coordination.[10] The committee was charged with recommending policies that will help program administrators more efficiently serve those who qualify for more than one program. The committee studied differences in eligibility requirements across programs such as food stamps, AFDC, Medicaid, and public housing to see how they might impede receiving benefits from multiple programs. In 1993, the committee recommended replacing the country's [public assistance] programs with "one, family-focused, client-oriented comprehensive program" that "should be overseen by only one committee in the House and Senate," rather than "the 24 congressional subcommittees [that] oversee the various welfare programs."[11] It also suggested a single application form and the same means tests for programs, yet there is little serious effort to move in these directions.

Making bureaucracy more rational is a challenge to every social welfare administrator. In an effort to follow the rules and respond to so many in need, administrators may forget that they are helping consumers or clients. Administrators rarely ask for clients' input. In 1993, President Clinton instituted the National Performance Review (NPR) headed by Vice President Al Gore in an attempt to "reinvent government" by increasing efficiency and reducing the "trust deficit" between citizens and the federal government.

EVALUATING SOCIAL POLICY

In recent years, interest in **policy evaluation**—learning about the consequences of public policy—has grown. Government agencies regularly report how much money they spend, how many people receive various services, and how much these services cost. Congressional committees regularly receive testimony from influential individuals and groups about how popular or unpopular various programs and services are. But even if programs and policies are well organized, adequately funded, efficiently operated, appropriately used, and politically popular, the questions still arise "So what?" "Do they make a difference?" "Do these programs have any beneficial effects on society?" "What about people not receiving the benefits or services?" "What is the relationship between the costs of the program and the benefits to society?" and "Could we be doing something else of more benefit to society with the money and human resources devoted to these programs?"

Can the federal government answer these questions? Can it say, for example, that TANF and Medicaid, family preservation programs, or community mental health services are accomplishing their objectives? that their benefits to society exceed their costs? that there are no better or less costly means of achieving the same ends? In 1970, one surprisingly candid report by the liberally-oriented think tank, the Urban Institute, argued convincingly that the federal government did *not* know whether most of its social service programs were worthwhile:

> *The most impressive finding about the evaluation of social programs in the federal government is that substantial work in this field has been almost nonexistent.*
>
> *Few significant studies have been undertaken. Most of those carried out have been poorly conceived. Many small studies around the country have been carried out with such lack of uniformity of design and objective that the results rarely are comparable or responsive to the questions facing policy makers. . . .*
>
> *The impact of activities that cost the public millions, sometimes billions, of dollars has not been measured. One cannot point with confidence to the difference, if any, that most social programs cause in the lives of Americans.*[12]

In the 1980s there was still considerable pessimism about social service program evaluation. Take, for example, comments by two social scientists on the state of job creation and training programs:

> *Despite nearly twenty years of continuous federal involvement, . . . we still have to do a good deal of guesswork about what will work and for whom. We have had substantial and on-going difficulties in identifying what works, for whom, and why. This has been, in large part, because of an unwillingness on the part of Congress and policy makers to allow for adequate experimentation in the delivery of employment and training services.*[13]

In the 1990s some people were more optimistic about the future of program evaluation. According to a *New York Times* story lauding evaluations of job training programs,

> *Recent experiments designed and monitored by the Manpower Demonstration Research Corporation, a nonprofit organization spun off from the Ford Foundation in 1974, have had enormous impact on the direction of welfare reform. And with admirers in high*

places, the experimenters are likely to influence everything from the design of public schools that work to so-called managed competition in health care, in which prepaid health plans such as HMOs would compete for the insurance business of consumers.[14]

But with people's lives hanging in the balance and with the price tags that accompany programs today, we need far more definitive information in many areas of social policy on what works, for whom, and why.

Policy Evaluation as a Rational Activity

From a rational perspective, policy evaluation involves more than just learning about the consequences of public policy. Consider the following definitions by scholars in the field:

> *Policy evaluation is the objective, systematic, empirical examination of the effects ongoing policies and programs have on their target in terms of the goals they are meant to achieve.*[15]
>
> *Evaluation research is viewed by its partisans as a way to increase the rationality of policy making. With objective information on the outcomes of programs, wise decisions can be made on budget allocations and program planning. Programs that yield good results will be expanded; those that make poor showings will be abandoned or drastically modified.*[16]
>
> Formal evaluation *is an approach which uses scientific methods to produce reliable and valid information about policy outcomes but evaluates such outcomes on the basis of policy-program objectives that have been formally announced by policy makers and program administrators. The major assumption of formal evaluation is that formally announced goals and objectives are appropriate measures of the worth or value of policies and programs.*[17]

These definitions of policy evaluation assume that the goals and objectives of programs and policies are clear, that we know how to measure progress toward these goals, that we know how to measure costs, and that we can impartially weigh benefits against costs in evaluating a public program. In short, these definitions view policy evaluation as a rational activity. If we were to undertake a truly rational evaluation, we would want to address all the questions about program conceptualization and design, monitoring, and utility described in Illustration 12-1, "Rational Evaluation: What Questions to Ask" and we would consider the model of evaluation shown in Figure 12-2. Evaluative research might be directed at any of the linkages in the policy process suggested in this diagram. For example, one might want to inquire about whether the agency's objectives are consistent with the legislated goals, whether the program's administrative structure is effective in meeting program objectives, or whether the program's activities have any impact on society.

Ideally, the evaluation of a program would include all its effects on real-world conditions. Evaluators would want to (1) identify and rank all the goals of a program;

ILLUSTRATION 12-1

Rational Evaluation: What Questions to Ask

Several ideal, rational models of program evaluation have been proposed. Social scientists Peter Rossi and Howard Freeman suggest that rational evaluation include three important types of questions:

1. *Program Conceptualization and Design Questions*

   Is a social problem appropriately conceptualized?

   What is the extent of the problem and the distribution of the target population?

   Is the program designed to meet its intended objectives?

   Is there a coherent rationale underlying it?

   Have chances of successful delivery been maximized?

   What are the projected or existing costs?

   What is the relationship between costs and benefits?

2. *Program Monitoring Questions*

   Is the program reaching the specified target population?

   Are the intervention efforts being conducted as specified in the program design?

3. *Program Utility Questions*

   Is the program effective in achieving its intended goals?

   Can the results of the program be explained by some alternative process that does not include the program?

   What are the costs to deliver services and benefits to program participants?

   Is the program an efficient use of resources, compared with alternative uses of resources?

Source: Peter H. Rossi and Howard E. Freeman, *Evaluation: A Systematic Approach,* 4th ed. (Newbury Park, CA: Sage Publications, 1989), pp. 45, 46, 52, copyright © 1989 by Sage Publications, Inc. Reprinted by permission of Sage Publications, Inc. Also see Peter H. Rossi and Howard E. Freeman, *Evaluation: A Systematic Approach,* 6th ed. (Newbury Park, CA: Sage Publications, 1998).

FIGURE 12-2

A Rational Model of Program Evaluation

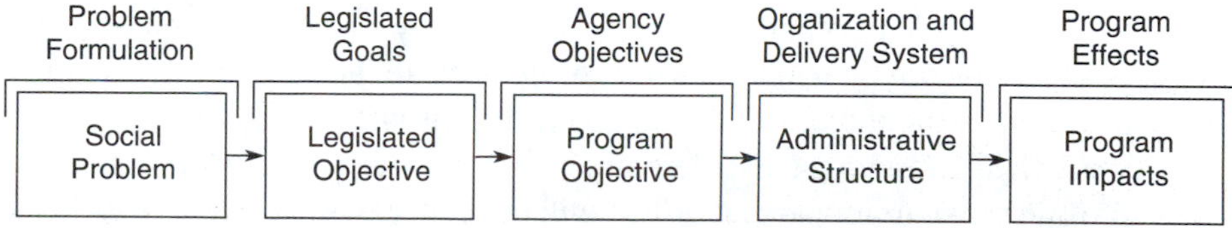

Source: Adapted from Dennis N. T. Perkins, "Evaluating Social Interventions: A Conceptual Schema," *Evaluation Quarterly,* Vol. 1, No. 4, 1977, p. 642, copyright ©1977 by Sage Publications, Inc. Reprinted by permission of Sage Publications, Inc.

(2) devise measures to describe progress toward these goals; (3) identify the "target" situation or group for which the program was designed; (4) identify nontarget groups who might be affected indirectly by the program ("spillover" effects), and nontarget groups who are similar to the target groups but did not participate in the program or receive its direct benefits ("control group"); (5) measure program effects on target and nontarget groups over as long a period of time as possible; (6) identify and measure the costs of the program in terms of all the resources allocated to it; and (7) identify and measure the indirect costs of the program, including the loss of opportunities to pursue other activities.

Identifying target groups in social welfare programs means defining the segment of the population for whom the program is intended—the poor, the sick, the ill housed, and so on. Then, the desired effect of the program on the target population must be determined. Is it to change their physical or economic conditions—their health, their nutrition, their income? Or is it to change their behavior—put them to work or improve their parenting skills? Or perhaps it is to change their knowledge, attitudes, awareness, or interests—to pressure slum landlords into improving housing conditions, to increase voter turnout among poor persons and ethnic minorities, to discourage unrest, riots, and violence among inner-city residents. If multiple effects are intended, what are the priorities (rankings) among different effects? What are the possible unintended effects (side effects) on target groups—for example, does public housing achieve better physical environments for the urban poor at the cost of increasing their segregation and isolation from the mainstream of the community?

In making these identifications and measurements, the evaluators must not confuse policy **outputs** (what governments do) with policy **impacts** (what consequences these government actions have). Benefits should not be measured in terms of government activity alone. For example, the number of dollars spent per member of a target group (per pupil educational expenditures, per capita welfare or health expenditures) is not really a measure of the impact of government activity. We cannot be content with counting how many times a bird flaps its wings; we must learn how far the bird has flown. In assessing the impact of public policy, we cannot simply count the number of dollars spent or clients served; rather, we must identify the changes in individuals, groups, and society brought about by public policies.

Identifying the effects of a program on nontarget groups is equally important. For example, what effects will the change from AFDC to TANF have on social workers, social welfare bureaucracies, working families who are not receiving public assistance, taxpayers, and others? Nontarget effects may turn out to be costs (such as the displacement of poor residents as a result of urban renewal), but they can also be benefits (such as the increased income to physicians who see Medicare patients).

Evaluators must also determine whether the program's goals are supposed to be long range or immediate. When will the benefits and costs be felt? Is the program designed for a short-term, emergency situation, or is it a long-term, developmental effort? Many impact studies show that new or innovative programs have short-term positive effects—for example, Head Start and other educational programs. The newness of the program, or the realization by the target group that is being given special treatment and being watched closely, may create measurable changes (the **Hawthorne** or **halo**

effect). But these positive effects may disappear as the novelty and enthusiasm of the new program wear off. Longitudinal studies that assess the far-reaching impacts of social welfare programs are rarely conducted due to constraints of time and money. This leaves policymakers and the public with little information to assess the positive and negative consequences of many social welfare programs.

Perhaps the most difficult problem confronting evaluators is weighing costs against benefits. Benefits may be measured in terms of bettering human conditions—greater educational attainment, longer life spans, better nutrition, steady employment, and so on. Costs are usually measured in dollars, but many of the values of education, health, or self-esteem cannot be measured in dollars alone. Cost savings are not the only goals that society wants to achieve. It is difficult to pursue rational evaluation when benefits and costs are measured in different ways.

The Many Faces of Program Evaluation

Most governments make some attempt to assess the utility of their programs. These efforts usually take one or more of the following forms.

Public Hearings

Public hearings are the most common type of program review. Frequently legislative committees ask agency heads to give formal or informal testimony regarding the accomplishments of their programs. This usually occurs near budget time. At the state and local level citizen input may also be requested. In addition, written "program reports" or "annual reports" may be provided to legislators and interested citizens by agencies as a "public information" activity. However, testimonials and reports of program administrators and those served by the program are not very objective means of program evaluation. Unless there has been substantial wrongdoing, public hearings frequently magnify the benefits and minimize the costs of programs.

Site Visits

Occasionally teams of legislators, high-ranking federal or state officials, or expert consultants (or some combination of all of these people) will descend on agencies to conduct investigations "in the field." These teams can interview workers and clients and directly observe the operation of the agency. They can accumulate impressions about how programs are being run, whether they have competent staffs, whether the programs seem to be having beneficial effects, and perhaps even whether or not the clients (target groups) are pleased with the services. But site visits can also provide a biased view of the program. Program staff are usually on their best behavior, and clients that meet with the site visit team are usually hand-picked.

Program Measures

The evaluation data developed by the agencies themselves usually describe program or output measures—for example, the number of people enrolled in work and training programs, the number of hospital beds available, or the number of people treated by mental health programs. Less frequently, these measures also indicate the impact these numbers have on society—for example, reductions in poverty figures, decreases in criminal activity by drug addicts, the success of work trainees in later finding and holding useful employment in the nation's workforce, or improvements in parenting skills that lessen the need for intervention by child protective service programs.

Comparison with Professional Standards

In some areas of social welfare activity, professional associations have developed their own "standards" of benefits and services. These standards may be expressed in terms of the maximum number of cases that a mental health, child welfare, or public assistance case worker can handle effectively, or the minimum number of hospital beds required by a population of 100,000 people, or in other ways. Actual governmental outputs can be compared with these "ideal" outputs. Although this kind of study may be helpful, it still focuses on the outputs and not on the impacts that government activities have on the conditions of target and nontarget groups. Though the standards are usually developed by professionals, these individuals may lack concrete data on which to determine the ideal levels of benefits and services. Although having too many cases can obviously result in insufficient attention to each client, and too many hospital beds waste resources, there is very little hard evidence that these supposedly ideal levels of government outputs have any significant impact on society.

Formal Research Designs

Another rational approach is to conduct formal evaluation studies employing the techniques of scientific research. In the opinion of many social scientists,[18] the most highly regarded, though least frequently used, approach is the **classic experimental design.** This design employs two groups—an **experimental group** and a **control group**—that are theoretically equivalent in every way except that the policy has been applied only to the experimental group. In order to ensure that control and experimental groups are comparable, research subjects are assigned randomly to the two groups and the program must be applied only to the experimental group. After the application of the policy for a given length of time, its impact is measured by comparing the status of the experimental group with the status of the control group. The postprogram status of both groups must be carefully measured. Also, every effort must be made to make certain that any observed postprogram differences between the two groups can be attributed to the program and not to some other intervening cause that affected one of the groups as the program was administered. This classic research design (see Figure 12-3) is preferred because it provides the best opportunity for estimating changes that can be directly attributed to policies and programs.

Although revered by many, the classic experimental design has been increasingly criticized by a number of scholars, not because it can be methodologically difficult to carry out, but because it is reductionistic. Methodologically, it is difficult to avoid contamination (the introduction of extraneous factors) in social science research. Many studies of new medications use double-blind procedures in which neither the

FIGURE 12-3

Classic Experimental Research Design

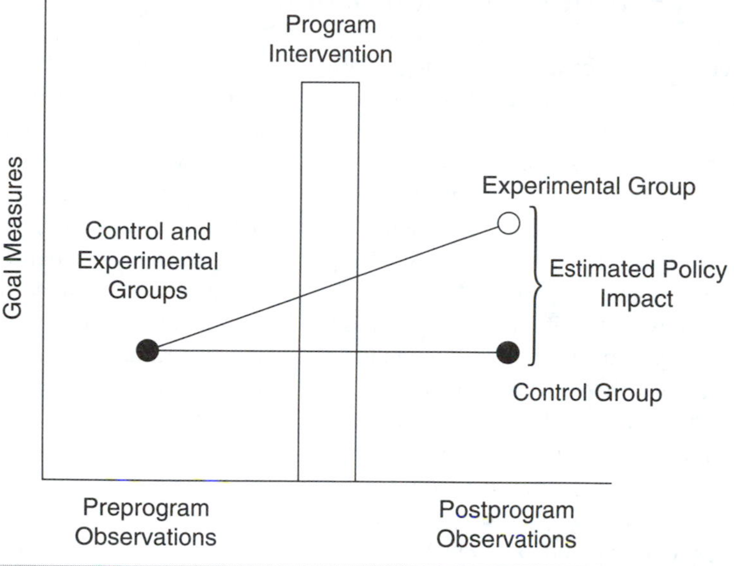

person administering the medication nor the research subject taking the "medication" know whether it is the real thing or a placebo. Such studies are nearly impossible when it comes to social interventions in which both those administering the social intervention (for example, a job training program or drug rehabilitation services) and those receiving the intervention know who is in the experimental group and who is in the control group. More importantly, most controlled experiments can be called reductionistic because they focus on narrowly defined interventions and narrowly defined outcomes. As described by Lisbeth Schorr in Illustration 12-2, controlled studies may not be well suited to studying complex interventions offered to individuals who face myriad problems and changing life circumstances. If there is hope for bridging the gap between rational evaluation and politics, perhaps the model of "theoretical evaluation" she suggests will help.

Even when one wants to conduct controlled experiments in public policy, it is frequently impossible to do so because sometimes the human beings involved cannot be placed arbitrarily in experimental or control groups just for the sake of program evaluation. Indeed, if experimental and control groups are really identical, the application of public policy to one group of citizens and not the other may violate the "equal protection of the laws" clause of the Fourteenth Amendment to the U.S. Constitution. In addition to legal issues, differential treatment of people with the same social problems raises ethical concerns. Social workers and other professionals may find it unacceptable to deny what may be a promising treatment to clients, regardless of

ILLUSTRATION 12-2

Is Theory-Based Evaluation Better?

It will not be easy to break with the dogma of experimental designs using random assignment as the only source of reliable knowledge. Swarthmore economics professor Robinson G. Hollister, a leading figure in evaluation circles since the mid-1960s, says that experimental designs are "like the nectar of the gods: once you've had a taste of the pure stuff it is hard to settle for the flawed alternatives." And the nectar of the gods of experimental design have intoxicated not only evaluators but also policy makers and funders.

The "flawed alternatives" may provide less certainty about what, exactly, caused the observed effects but do offer a broader range of information that may turn out to be more useful in making judgments about what really matters. The new evaluators embrace both the old and the new, in the belief that there is knowledge worth having and acting on even if it is not absolutely certain knowledge. They do not reject—on grounds of messiness or complexity—information that can shed light on real-world efforts that promise to improve outcomes.

The new approaches to the evaluation of complex interventions share at least four attributes: They are built on a strong theoretical and conceptual base, emphasize shared interests rather than adversarial relationships between evaluators and program people, employ multiple methods and perspectives, and offer both rigor and relevance. . . .

To illustrate how a theory-based approach could illuminate both the design and evaluation of an early childhood program, here is an example of a rough theory of change: Children whose experiences during infancy and early childhood equip them to enter school "ready to learn" are more likely to succeed at school than children who enter school not "ready to learn." More children will be ready for school learning if the community can reduce early deficits in health care, nutrition, child care, and preschool experiences; if families feel safe and protected in the neighborhood; and if the community is able to support families in ways that contribute to children's developing trust, curiosity, self-control, and the ability to interact with others.

Once theories have been articulated, evaluators work with program people to identify, on the basis of experience and research, what needs to be in place to accomplish the agreed-upon outcomes. In the case of the "ready to learn" theory, the steps leading to school readiness might include the availability to all low-income families of accessible, responsive, high-quality health care for infants, children, and pregnant women; child care that combines developmentally appropriate care, education, and family support; child protective services; family support programs; adequate nutrition; adequate income; and supportive community norms. Interim outcome measures, which would be apparent before long-term outcomes, might include higher rates of pregnant women receiving prompt and continuing prenatal care; higher rates of infants and preschool children receiving preventive health care, including immunizations; higher rates of three- and four-year-olds in Head Start and other high-quality child care/education settings; higher rates of infants and toddlers receiving care in high-quality settings; fewer confirmed and repeat instances of child abuse

continued

ILLUSTRATION 12-2 *(continued)*

and neglect; and lower rates of inappropriate out-of-home placements. . . .

The theories-of-change approach to evaluation, then, has evaluators, practitioners, and researchers working together to construct a conceptual map that links the most important parts of an intervention together. As these conceptual maps accumulate, are refined through experience, and systematically analyzed, they will provide an ever richer and more reliable understanding of all the links along the causal chain leading to improved outcomes for children, families, and communities.

Source: From *COMMON PURPOSE* by Lisbeth B. Schorr. Copyright © 1997 Lisbeth Bamberger Schorr. Used by permission of Doubleday, a division of Random House, Inc.

the need for better program evaluation. Frequently, it is only possible to conduct studies that compare individuals and groups that have participated in programs with those that have not, or to compare cities, states, and nations that have programs with those that do not. Comparisons are made of the extent to which the groups that participated in the program achieved the desired goals in relation to those groups that did not participate. Such studies are called **quasiexperimental** because subjects are not randomly assigned to experimental and control groups—researchers cannot really be sure that the two groups were alike before the experiment began. They must try to eliminate the possibility that any difference between the two groups in goal achievement was caused by some factor other than experience with the program. For example, the job records of JTPA participants may be compared with those who did not participate. Following the quasiexperiment, if the JTPA group did not have higher employment rates and greater earnings than other groups, it may be because JTPA participants were less skilled to begin with. If they were more successful, it may be because the JTPA officials "creamed off" the local unemployed and gave services only to those who already possessed skills and job experience. Thus, quasiexperimental research designs (see Figure 12-4), like most social science research, still leave room for discussion and disagreement about the utility of social welfare programs.

Another type of research design involves a comparison of conditions before and after a policy or program has been adopted. Usually only the target group is examined. This design may be the only choice in jurisdictions where no control or comparison group can be identified. The simplest before–after or **pretest–posttest** study involves taking one measure before the program is implemented and one after the program is administered, but this is a very weak design. When several observations are made before and several observations are made after, this is generally referred to as a **time series** design (see Figure 12-4). These studies are also intended to show program impacts, but it is still very difficult to know whether any changes that might have occurred were due to the program itself or were a result of other

FIGURE 12-4

Quasiexperimental Research Design

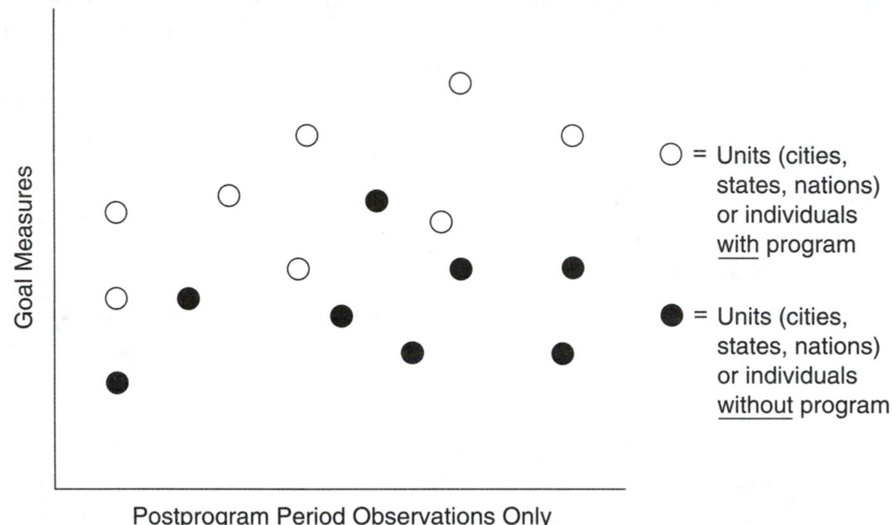

changes occurring in society at the same time. For example, a program evaluator may be faced with the problem of determining whether a high school drug education program reduced the frequency of students' drug use or whether a decrease in the supply of drugs that occurred simultaneously in the community was responsible for this effect.

Policy Evaluation as a Political Activity

Policy and program evaluation may resemble rational, scientific inquiry, but it can never really be separated from politics. Let us consider just a few of the political problems that make rational policy evaluation difficult, if not impossible.

Unclear, Ambiguous Program Goals

Evaluators are often told to evaluate a program and yet are not informed of its goals or purposes. Reading the language of the original legislation that established the program may not be very helpful; legislative language is frequently fuzzy—"improve the conditions of life of the poor," or "enhance the quality of life," are examples. Even interviews with the original legislative sponsors (Congressmembers, state legislators, county commissioners, or city council members) may produce ambiguous, or even contradictory, goals. There is also a "confusion between policy ends and policy means. . . . While federal and state governments are committed to 'doing something'

FIGURE 12-5

Time Series Research Design

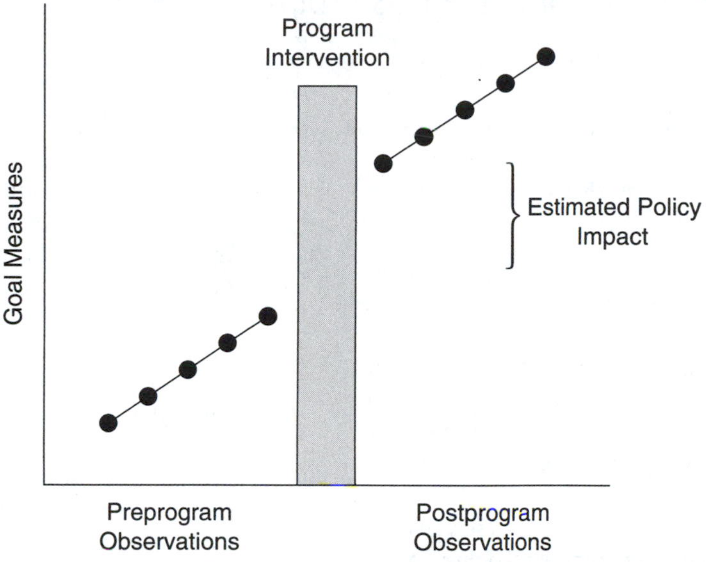

about certain vulnerable populations, the end product of their efforts has not been specified."[19] Often the evaluators, at the risk of offending someone, must define the goals or purposes themselves. In this way, evaluation itself becomes a political activity.

Symbolic Goals

Many programs and policies have primarily symbolic value. They are not designed so much to change social conditions as they are to make groups feel that their government "cares." Of course, an agency does not welcome a study that reveals its efforts have no tangible effects. Indeed, such a finding, if widely publicized, is likely to reduce the symbolic impact of the program by telling target groups or other supporters of its uselessness.

Unhappy Findings

Agencies and administrators usually have a heavy investment—organizational, financial, psychological—in current programs and policies. They are predisposed against findings that these programs do not work, involve excessive costs, or have unexpected negative consequences. If a negative report is issued, the agency may adopt a variety of strategies to offset the findings, as suggested in Illustration 12-3, "What to Do If Your Agency's Program Receives a Negative Evaluation."

ILLUSTRATION 12-3

What to Do If Your Agency's Program Receives a Negative Evaluation

What if you are faced with clear evidence that your favorite program is useless, or even counterproductive? Here is a tongue-in-cheek list of last-ditch efforts to save it.

1. Claim that the effects of the program are long range and cannot be adequately measured for many years.
2. Argue that the effects of the program are general and intangible, and that these effects cannot be identified with the crude methodology, including statistical measures, used in the evaluation.
3. If the classic experimental research design was used, claim that withholding services or benefits from the control group was unfair; and claim that there were no differences between the control and experimental groups because both groups had knowledge of the experiment.
4. If a quasiexperimental design was used, claim that initial differences between the experimental and comparison groups make the results useless.
5. If a time series research design was used, claim that there were no differences between the "before" and "after" observations because of other coinciding variables that hid the program's effects. That is to say, claim that the participants' condition would be even worse without the program.
6. Argue that the lack of differences between the people receiving the program services and those not receiving them only means that the program is not sufficiently intensive and indicates the need to spend more resources on the program.
7. Argue that the failure to identify positive program effects is due to the inadequacy of the evaluation research design and of bias on the part of the evaluators.

Program Interference

Most serious evaluation studies involve some burdens on ongoing program activities. Accomplishing an agency's day-to-day business is generally a higher priority in the minds of program administrators and line workers than making special arrangements for evaluation. Evaluation also requires funds, facilities, time, and personnel, all of which administrators may not want to sacrifice from their programs.

Usefulness of Evaluations

Program administrators are clearly dissatisfied with evaluative studies that conclude, "The program is not achieving the desired results." Not only is such a finding a threat to the agency, but standing alone, it fails to tell administrators why the program is failing. Evaluations are better received by agencies when they include some action recommendations that might conceivably rescue the program. But even when studies show programs to be failures, the usual reaction is to patch things up and try again. Few programs are ever abolished.

Evaluation by Whom?

A central political issue is who will do the evaluation. From the agency's perspective, the evaluation should be done by the agency itself. This type of "in-house" evaluation is most likely to produce favorable results. The next best thing, from the agency's perspective, is to allow the agency to contract with a private firm for an "outside" evaluation. A private firm that wants to win future contracts from the agency, or from any other agency, is very hesitant about producing totally negative evaluations. The worst evaluation arrangement, from the agency's perspective, is to have an outside evaluation conducted by an independent office (for example, the Congressional Budget Office, the General Accounting Office, or a state comptroller's office or auditor general's office). Agency staff fear that outsiders do not understand clearly the nature of their work or the problems faced by the clients they serve and that this will hurt the program.

Threats to Everyone

Political obstacles to evaluation operate at all levels of the social service delivery system. Evaluation is threatening to elected officials because it might imply that they have developed poor policies, passed inadequate laws, provided inadequate funding in relation to need, or funded ineffective programs. Evaluation is threatening to social service administrators because it might suggest that they have done a poor job of implementing and managing the policies and programs developed by legislators. Evaluation is threatening to social service workers because it might indicate that they are not adequately skilled in delivering and providing social services to clients. Finally, evaluation can be threatening to clients because the process may invade their privacy, place additional pressure on them in times of personal crisis, and make them feel even more conspicuous about receiving social services.

Politics at Work: Evaluating the Guaranteed Annual Income Experiments

Perhaps the most well-known example of an attempt by the federal government to experiment with public policy is the New Jersey Graduated Work Incentive Experiment funded by the Office of Economic Opportunity. The experiment was designed to resolve some serious questions about the effect of welfare payments on the incentives for poor people to work.[20] In order to learn more about the effects of the welfare system on human behavior and, more important, to learn about the possible effects of guaranteed family income proposals, the OEO funded a three-year social experiment involving 1,350 families in New Jersey and Pennsylvania. The research was conducted by the Institute for Research on Poverty at the University of Wisconsin.

Debates over welfare reform had generated certain questions that social science could presumably answer with careful, controlled experimentation. Would a guaranteed family income reduce the incentive to work? If payments were made to poor families with employable male heads, would the men drop out of the labor force? Would the level of the income guarantee or the steepness of the reductions in payments due to increases in earnings make any difference in work behavior? Because the United States did not provide a guaranteed minimum income to families, because welfare payments to families were not tapered off gradually in relation to earnings, and because many states at that time did not make welfare payments to two-parent families in which the primary breadwinner was unemployed, these questions could only be directly answered through policy experimentation.

But experimentation raised some serious initial problems for the OEO.[21] Costs were one concern. Any experiment involving substantial payments to a fair sampling of families would be expensive. For example, if payments averaged $1,000 per year per family, and if each family had to be observed for three years, and if 1,000 families were to be involved, a minimum of $3 million (a modest sum by today's standards, but substantial then) would be spent even before any consideration of the costs of administration, data collection, analysis, and reporting. Ideally a national sample should have been used, but it would have been more expensive to monitor than a local sample, and differences in employment conditions across the country would have made it difficult to sort out the effects of income payments from variations in local job availability. By concentrating the sample in one region, it was hoped that local conditions would be held constant. Also ideally, all types of low-income families should have been included, but that procedure would have necessitated a larger sample and greater expense. So only poor families with an able-bodied male between the ages of 18 and 58 were selected.

To ascertain the effects of different levels of guaranteed income, four guarantee levels were established. Some families were chosen to receive 50 percent of the federal government's official poverty-level income, others 75 percent, others 100 percent, and still others 125 percent. To ascertain the effects of graduated payments in relation to earnings, some families had their payments reduced by 30 percent of their outside earnings, others by 50 percent, and still others by 70 percent. Finally, a control sample was observed—low-income families who received no payments at all.

The experiment was initiated in August 1968 and continued until September 1972. But political events moved swiftly and soon engulfed the study. In 1969, President Nixon proposed the Family Assistance Plan (FAP), which would have guaranteed all families a minimum income of 50 percent of the poverty level with a payment reduction of 50 percent for outside earnings (also see Chapter 6). The Nixon administration had not waited to learn the results of the OEO experiment before introducing the FAP. Nixon wanted welfare reform to be his priority domestic legislation, and the FAP bill was symbolically numbered HR 1 (House of Representatives Bill 1).

After the FAP was introduced, the Nixon administration pressured the OEO to produce favorable evidence—specifically, evidence that a guaranteed income at the levels proposed in the FAP would not reduce incentives to work among the poor. The

OEO obliged by hastily publishing a short report, "Preliminary Results of the New Jersey Graduated Work Incentive Experiment," that purported to show that there were no differences in the outside earnings of families receiving guaranteed incomes (the experimental group) and those not (the control group).[22]

The director of the research, economist Harold Watts of the University of Wisconsin, warned that "the evidence from this preliminary and crude analysis of the results is less than ideal," but he concluded that "no evidence has been found in the urban experiment to support the belief that negative-tax type income maintenance programs will produce large disincentives and consequent reductions in earnings."[23] Moreover, the early results indicated that families in all experimental groups, with different guaranteed minimums and different graduated payment schedules, behaved similarly to each other and to the control group receiving no payments. Predictably, later results confirmed the preliminary results, which were used to assist the FAP in Congress.[24]

However, when the Rand Corporation (which was not responsible for the design of the original study) later reanalyzed data from the Graduated Work Incentive Experiment, markedly different results were produced.[25] Rand reported that the Wisconsin researchers working for OEO had originally chosen New Jersey because it had no state welfare programs for "intact" families—families with a mother and an able-bodied, working-age father. The guaranteed incomes were offered to these intact families to compare their work behavior with similar intact families who received no such payments. But six months after the experiment began, New Jersey changed its state law and offered all poor families rather substantial welfare benefits. This meant that for most of the period of the experiment, the control group was offered benefits equivalent to those given the experimental group—an obvious violation of the experimental research design. The OEO-funded University of Wisconsin researchers failed to consider this factor. Thus, they found no significant differences between the work behaviors of experimental and control groups, and they implied that a national guaranteed income would not be a disincentive to work. The Rand Corporation researchers, in contrast, considered the New Jersey state welfare program in their estimates of work behavior. Rand concluded that recipients of a guaranteed annual income would work six and one-half fewer hours per week than they would work in the absence of such a program. In short, the Rand study suggested that a guaranteed annual income would produce a substantial disincentive to work.

The Rand study was published in 1978 after Congress's enthusiasm for welfare reform via a guaranteed annual income program had already cooled. Rand's results confirmed the intuition of many members of Congress that a guaranteed annual income would reduce willingness to work. The Rand study also suggested that a national program might be very costly and involve some payments to nearly half the nation's families (!), noting that its estimates of high costs and work disincentives may "seriously understate the expected cost of an economy-wide . . . program."

A similar but larger and longer experiment with cash payments and work-related earnings deductions was later conducted in Denver and Seattle.[26] It was called the Seattle-Denver Income Maintenance Experiment or SIME/DIME for short. SIME/DIME added job counseling and training for some participants. The SIME/DIME study also found substantially lower earnings and hours worked for both husbands and wives across the various payment and earnings deduction groups. The job services also failed to increase earnings or hours of work, and the time and effort spent in them "generally hurt the labor market positions of participants."

In spite of this evidence about what does *not* work, perhaps the more important conclusion to be drawn from the guaranteed annual income studies is that they did not identify for policymakers the types of social welfare programs and circumstances that *will* promote incentives to work and reduce poverty. A more recent example of controversy over program evaluation concerns the Drug Abuse Resistance Education (D.A.R.E.) program. D.A.R.E. is near and dear to the hearts of many, but evaluations show that it is ineffective in preventing or reducing drug use.[27] Nevertheless the program remains a favorite in many communities.

SUMMARY

Implementing public policy can be a difficult task for administrators of social welfare programs. Implementation involves a number of activities, including organizing and staffing agencies, translating policies into specific courses of action, and spending funds to operate programs. One major obstacle to successful implementation can come in determining the intent of social policies, which is not always clearly defined in legislation. Other problems may include obtaining sufficient resources, overcoming negative attitudes toward a program, and seeing that bureaucratic structures do not prevent the program from operating smoothly.

Americans know how difficult it is to remedy social problems. As a result, policymakers are increasingly concerned with obtaining evidence about whether social welfare policies and programs are effective, even though most policy and program decisions boil down to politics in the end. A rational approach to evaluation includes identifying and ranking program goals and objectives, developing ways to measure these goals, identifying target groups as well as nontarget groups that might be affected, measuring tangible and intangible program effects, and measuring direct and indirect program costs. Several types of research designs are used to conduct evaluative studies of social welfare policies and programs: experimental designs, quasi-experimental designs, and time series designs. Experimental designs are often preferred because they provide the greatest confidence in determining policy and program results. But they are not always feasible and may fail to capture the information needed in addressing complex social problems.

Policy evaluation is no less political than other aspects of the policy process. Evaluation is political for several reasons. Program goals and objectives are not always clear, but evaluators must evaluate something, even if everyone does not agree. Some program goals are more symbolic than tangible, and the symbolic goals are often more difficult to evaluate. No administrator wants to receive a negative program evaluation. Administrators generally criticize unfavorable evaluations and take steps to counteract negative findings. Evaluations often disrupt the agency's day-to-day work and take time and resources from other activities. Also, an evaluation may not provide useful information about how to improve the program. In-house evaluations tend to be positive, and outside evaluations are more likely to be critical or ambivalent about the program. The well-known evaluations of the New Jersey Graduated Work Incentive Experiment are but one example of the politics of policy evaluation.

NOTES

1. Jeffrey Pressman and Aaron Wildavsky, *Implementation* (Berkeley: University of California Press, 1973), p. 109.

2. This discussion relies on George C. Edwards, *Implementing Public Policy* (Washington, DC: Congressional Quarterly, 1980).

3. Fred Doolittle and Linda Traeger, *Implementing the National JTPA Study* (New York: Manpower Demonstration Research Corporation, 1990).

4. Jan L. Hagen and Irene Lurie, *Implementing JOBS: Initial State Choices* (Albany: Nelson A. Rockefeller College of Public Affairs and Policy, University at Albany, State University of New York, March 1992).

5. Richard Lacayo, "The Sad Fate of Legal Aid," *Time,* June 20, 1988, p. 59.

6. See Daniel P. Moynihan, *The Politics of a Guaranteed Income* (New York: Vintage Books, 1973), p. 220.

7. Larry B. Hill, ed., *The State of Public Bureaucracy* (Armonk, NY: Sharpe, 1992).

8. Herbert Kaufman, *Red Tape* (Washington, DC: Brookings Institution, 1977), p. 13.

9. U.S. Bureau of the Census, *Statistical Abstract of the United States: 1998* (Washington, DC: U.S. Government Printing Office, 1998), Table 497, p. 305.

10. *Federal Register,* Vol. 58, No. 38, March 1, 1993, p. 11830.

11. Richard Whitmire, "Study: Single State Agency Should Direct Welfare," Gannatt News Service, Tuesday, June 29, 1993.

12. Joseph S. Wholey, John W. Scanlon, Hugh G. Duffy, James S. Fukumoto, and Leona M. Vogt, *Federal Evaluation Policy* (Washington, DC: Urban Institute, 1970), p. 15.

13. Laurie J. Bassi and Orley Ashenfelter, "The Effect of Direct Job Creation and Training Programs on Low-Skilled Workers," in Sheldon H. Danzinger and Daniel H. Weinberg, eds., *Fighting Poverty: What Works and What Doesn't* (Cambridge, MA: Harvard University Press, 1986), p. 150.

14. Peter Passell, "Like a New Drug, Social Programs Are Put to the Test," *New York Times,* March 9, 1993, pp. C1, 10.

15. David Nachmias, *Policy Evalution* (New York: St. Martin's, 1979), p. 4.

16. Carol H. Weiss, *Evaluation Research: Methods of Assessing Program Effectiveness* (Englewood Cliffs, NJ: Prentice Hall, 1972), p. 2.

17. William N. Dunn, *Public Policy Analysis: An Introduction* (Englewood Cliffs, NJ: Prentice Hall, 1981), p. 345.

18. For further discussion of classic experimental research see Fred N. Kerlinger, *Foundations of Behavioral Research,* 3rd ed. (New York: Holt, Rinehart, & Winston, 1986), especially chapter 19; Allen Rubin and Earl Babbie, *Research Methods for Social Work* (Pacific Grove, CA: Brooks/Cole, 1993), especially chapter 9. For a discussion of the need for this type of research in the area of public policy, see Bassie and Ashenfelter, "The Effects of Direct Job Creation and Training Programs on Low-Skilled Workers."

19. Robert Morris, *Social Policy of the American Welfare State: An Introduction to Policy Analysis* (New York: Harper & Row, 1979), p. 133.

20. See Harold M. Watts, "Graduated Work Incentives: An Experiment in Negative Taxation," *American Economic Review,* Vol. 59, May 1969, pp. 463–472.

21. For a discussion of the Graduated Work Incentive Experiment also see Alice M. Rivlin, *Systematic Thinking for Social Action* (Washington, DC: Brookings Institution, 1971).

22. Office of Economic Opportunity, *Preliminary Results of the New Jersey Graduated Work Incentive Experiment* (Washington, DC: Office of Economic Opportunity, February 18, 1970).

23. Harold M. Watts, *Adjusted and Extended Preliminary Results from the Urban Graduated Work Incentive Experiment* (Madison: Institute for Research on Poverty, University of Wisconsin, rev. June 10, 1970), p. 40.

24. David Kershaw and Jerelyn Fair, eds., *Final Report of the New Jersey Graduated Work Incentive Experiment,* Vol. 4 (Princeton, NJ: University of Wisconsin, Institute for Research on Poverty and Mathematica, 1974).

25. John F. Cogan, *Negative Income Taxation and Labor Supply: New Evidence from the New Jersey-Pennsylvania Experiment* (Santa Monica, CA: Rand, 1978).

26. Stanford Research Institute, *Final Report of the Seattle-Denver Income Maintenance Experiment* (Washington, DC: U.S. Government Printing Office, 1983), quote from p. 250.

27. Christopher L. Ringwalt, Jody M. Green, Susan T. Ennett, Ronaldo Iachan, Richard Clayton, and Carl G. Leukfeld, *Past and Future Directions of the D.A.R.E. Program: Draft Final Report* (Research Triangle Park, NC: Research Triangle Institute, June 1994).

Name Index

Note: Page numbers in italics indicate an illustration, table, or chart.

Subject Index

Note: Page numbers in italics indicate an illustration, table, or chart.

PRACTICE TEST

CHAPTER 1: Politics, Rationalism and Social Welfare

Multiple Choice

1. Income maintenance refers to social welfare programs that include the following elements with the exception of:
   a. public welfare
   b. social services
   c. social security
   d. social insurance.

2. A social welfare policy is defined as anything a __________ chooses to do, or not to do, that affects the quality of life of its people.
   a. agency
   b. society
   c. political party
   d. government

3. In a rational approach, it is necessary to do all of the following except:
   a. all possible alternatives must be identified and considered.
   b. policy makers must calculate the ratio of benefits to costs for each alternative.
   c. all policies must be fair.
   d. all values must be known and weighted.

4. Which group is most likely to favor letting business run social welfare programs?
   a. Libertarians
   b. Radical
   c. Liberals
   d. Conservatives

5. Which group would favor turning social welfare over to the non-profit sector?
   a. Liberals
   b. Conservatives
   c. Libertarians
   d. Radical

6. Which group would favor large federal programs like social security?
   a. Radical
   b. Liberals
   c. Conservatives
   d. Libertarians

7. Political action committees:
   a. are groups that try to discuss current affairs in a fair and objective way.
   b. are influential in American politics.
   c. do not provide money for candidate elections.
   d. are not influential in American politics.

8. Which group is most likely to favor letting business run social welfare programs?
   a. Liberals
   b. Conservatives
   c. Radical
   d. Libertarians

True/False

1. In the political approach, policy is rational if politicians like it.

   TRUE
   FALSE

2. According to Wolpert, it possible for private philanthropy to substitute for public social welfare.

   TRUE
   FALSE

3. The National Association of Social Workers has a Political Action Committee.

   TRUE
   FALSE

4. Not considering a question or issue is the same as making a decision.

   TRUE
   FALSE

5. Getting publicity for a social problem is one way that the media participates in agenda setting.

   TRUE
   FALSE

6. Target groups are the segment of the population for which the policy is intended.

   TRUE
   FALSE

7. A more stringent form of rationality (as compared to comprehensive rationality) is bounded rationality.

   TRUE
   FALSE

8. Incremental policy-making builds on existing policies and programs.

   TRUE
   FALSE

9. According to the book, crisis makes policy-makers look at new ideas.

   TRUE
   FALSE

10. Well-funded interest groups can have a big impact on the policy-making process.

    TRUE
    FALSE

Chapter 2: Government and Social Welfare

Multiple Choice

1. Early social welfare in the United States was heavily influenced by the social welfare system in what nation?
   - **a.** Sweden
   - **b.** Spain
   - **c.** Germany
   - **d.** England

2. The Poor Laws replaced
   - **a.** more comprehensive legislation.
   - **b.** Mutual Aid.
   - **c.** less comprehensive legislation.
   - **d.** more punitive legislation.
   - **e.** less punitive legislation.

3. Indoor Relief originally referred to
   - **a.** settlement acts.
   - **b.** workhouses.
   - **c.** relief inside your home.
   - **d.** money to purchase housing.
   - **e.** relief inside someone else's home.

4. The Statute of Laborers was designed to address what problem?
   - **a.** the plague
   - **b.** Henry VIII
   - **c.** Reganomics
   - **d.** labor shortages

5. The first federal social insurance program in the United States was
   - **a.** Temporary Aid to Needy Families.
   - **b.** the Economic Opportunity Act
   - **c.** the Poor Law.
   - **d.** the Social Security Act.

6. Poverty during the great depression was due largely to personal fault, according to
   - **a.** liberals.
   - **b.** conservatives.
   - **c.** libertarians.
   - **d.** radicals.

7. Roosevelt's program to help America survive the depression was called
   - **a.** the New Society.
   - **b.** the Fair Deal.
   - **c.** the New Deal.
   - **d.** the Great Society.

8. Which piece of legislation began the War on Poverty?
   - **a.** The Economic Opportunity Act
   - **b.** The Family Support Act
   - **c.** The Social Security Act
   - **d.** The New Deal

9. In the early 1980s there were major reductions in social welfare spending. Which President led this attack?
   - **a.** Bush
   - **b.** Reagan
   - **c.** Nixon
   - **d.** Carter

10. Which is not a part of the current social welfare policy scene in the United States?
    - **a.** Federalism
    - **b.** Cost reductions
    - **c.** Privatization
    - **d.** Centralizing responsibility in the federal government

True/False

1. In early America, Warning Out referred to encouraging new arrivals to move on if they appeared to lack financial support.

   TRUE
   FALSE

2. Harrington's Other American demonstrated that poverty still existed in America.

   TRUE
   FALSE

3. Residency requirements are a historical theme in welfare.

   TRUE
   FALSE

4. The workhouses are an example of indoor relief.

   TRUE
   FALSE

5. Rural to Urban migration led to a number of social problems that eventually overwhelmed state and local government and led to federal involvement.

   TRUE
   FALSE

6. The welfare rights movement is a product of the last four decades.

   TRUE
   FALSE

7. Residency requirements returned with welfare reform in 1996.

   TRUE
   FALSE

8. Tax expenditures include loopholes, deductions, and credits, which provide benefits to wealthier people.

   TRUE
   FALSE

9. Reagan's cuts in social welfare were partly justified by supply side economics.

   TRUE
   FALSE

10. Block grants were an important part of Reagan's social welfare strategy.

    TRUE
    FALSE

Chapter 3: Defining Poverty

Multiple Choice

1. Which president declared War on Poverty?
   a. Nixon
   b. Reagan
   c. Johnson
   d. Roosevelt

2. Structural approaches to poverty are favored by
   a. conservatives.
   b. libertarians.
   c. liberals and radicals.

3. Which of the following is a structural approach to poverty?
   a. Dual Labor Market Theory
   b. Orthodox Economic Theory
   c. Human Capital Theory

4. The GINI coefficient is a measure of
   a. poverty.
   b. inequality.
   c. malnutrition.
   d. culture.

5. Which choice represents the two approaches to counting in-kind benefits?
   a. Market Value and Recipient Approaches
   b. Market Value and Purchase Approaches
   c. Market Value and Purchase Approaches
   d. Recipient and Cost Recovery Approaches

6. Among the causes of homelessness are
   a. lack of affordable housing.
   b. poverty.
   c. mental illness and substance abuse.
   d. All of the above

True/False

1. Defining poverty is a political activity.
   TRUE
   FALSE

2. Poverty levels are adjusted every five years using the CPI.
   TRUE
   FALSE

3. The poverty line was originally defined as the cost of the low cost food budget multiplied by three.
   TRUE
   FALSE

4. The number of people in poverty declined in the 1960s and began to rise again in the late 1970s.
   TRUE
   FALSE

5. Human capital theory holds that poverty occurs because the poor lack education, skills, knowledge, etc.
   TRUE
   FALSE

6. More whites are poor than blacks.
   TRUE
   FALSE

7. Poverty is almost exclusively an urban problem.
   TRUE
   FALSE

8. All measures of poverty involve deprivation.
   TRUE
   FALSE

9. Among the highest poverty rates are those for female householders without husbands.

TRUE
FALSE

10. Most welfare clients are long term recipients.

TRUE
FALSE

Chapter 4: Preventing Poverty: The Social Insurance Programs

Multiple Choice

1. The oldest social insurance program in the United States is
   a. Workers Compensation.
   b. Aid to Families with Dependent children.
   c. Unemployment Compensation.
   d. Old Age, Survivors, Disability, and Health Insurance.

2. In relation to the rest of the world, the United States was _________ to enact social insurance legislation.
   a. first
   b. earlier than most
   c. later than most
   d. unwilling

3. The Social Security Program in the United States was created during
   a. the Civil War.
   b. the Industrial Revolution.
   c. the Great Depression.
   d. the War on Poverty.

4. Unemployment compensation covers:
   a. everyone who is unemployed or underemployed.
   b. only certain unemployed people.
   c. everyone who is unemployed and some who are underemployed.
   d. a very small portion of the unemployed.

5. What percentage of unemployed people do not receive unemployment insurance benefits?
   a. 10%
   b. 40%
   c. 65%
   d. 90%

6. Which of the following make the task of social security financing more difficult?
   a. The aging population
   b. Greater longevity
   c. COLAs
   d. All are true

7. Unemployment compensation is administered by which agency?
   a. Department of Health and Human Services
   b. Department of Commerce
   c. Department of Labor
   d. Department of Income Security

8. Being officially unemployed means that you are ________ and ________.
   a. not working and receiving unemployment insurance
   b. not working and actively looking for work
   c. not working full time and seeking work
   d. not working and not looking for work

True/False

1. All workers are covered by social security.

   TRUE
   FALSE

2. All persons who are without work are counted as unemployed in the official statistics.

   TRUE
   FALSE

3. The federal government has a fund to help states that have exhausted their unemployment compensation funds.

   TRUE
   FALSE

4. COLA refers to the increases in social security payments that occur when the Consumer Price Index increases.

   TRUE
   FALSE

5. Payments made to social security are really a tax.

   TRUE
   FALSE

6. If you are working but underpaid you may be eligible for unemployment compensation.

   TRUE
   FALSE

7. Privatization could involve private investment of social security funds.

   TRUE
   FALSE

8. Unemployment compensation programs generally require a search for work.

   TRUE
   FALSE

Chapter 5: Helping the Deserving Poor: Aged, Blind and Disabled

Multiple Choice

1. The SSI program was proceeded by all of the following except
   a. ATPD.
   b. AB.
   c. OAA.
   d. FAP.

2. Which is not a situation that makes one eligible for SSI?
   a. Unemployed
   b. Disabled
   c. Blind
   d. Aged

3. Which is NOT true of general assistance?
   a. Limited funds
   b. Run by state and local government
   c. Federally assisted
   d. Designed for adults

True/False

1. In order to qualify for SSI, it is first necessary to apply for everything else for which you might be eligible.

   TRUE
   FALSE

2. Vocational Rehabilitation works with any disabled person.

   TRUE
   FALSE

3. Selecting the most desirable clients in vocational rehabilitation is called milking.

   TRUE
   FALSE

4. The Americans with Disabilities Act was a major step forward for disabled Americans.

   TRUE
   FALSE

5. In 1972 Congress federalized the adult categorical assistance program and created SSI.

   TRUE
   FALSE

6. Critics argued that SSI checks are funding drug and alcohol habits.

   TRUE
   FALSE

7. Contemporary programming for the disabled have included, as goals, deinstitutionalization, normalization, and independent living.

   TRUE
   FALSE

8. General Assistance is welfare provided by states and local communities.

   TRUE
   FALSE

9. The federal government monitors General Assistance.

   TRUE
   FALSE

10. Most states pay General Assistance in cash.

    TRUE
    FALSE

Chapter 6: Ending Welfare As We Know It: Temporary Assistance for Needy Families

Multiple Choice

1. The Program that was in place to help children and families prior to the passage of the Personal Responsibility and Work Opportunity Act of 1996 was
   - a. Aid to Families.
   - b. Mothers Assistance.
   - c. Welfare.
   - d. Aid to Families with Dependent Children.

2. The term "family cap" refers to
   - a. limits on the number of new children for which a family on welfare can receive benefits.
   - b. limitations on the number of children that a family on welfare is allowed to have.
   - c. matching hats for all welfare recipients.
   - d. limits on the number of new children a family on welfare is allowed to have.

3. Most AFDC families have
   - a. two children or less.
   - b. over six children.
   - c. three or four children.
   - d. five or six children.

4. Learnfare Programs
   - a. provided funding for welfare recipients who wanted to return to school.
   - b. reduced payments if a student missed school.
   - c. provided welfare payments for mothers in high school.
   - d. made receipt of TANF contingent on passing a test.

5. Welfare reform, as enacted in 1996,
   - a. was exactly what President Clinton desired.
   - b. included a number of provisions that the President was concerned about.
   - c. was not signed by President Clinton.
   - d. was more liberal than the legislation desired by the White House.

True/False

1. The Man in the House Rule and Midnight Raids were part of the AFDC program.

   TRUE
   FALSE

2. Child Support Enforcement is a part of both AFDC and TANF.

   TRUE
   FALSE

3. The work requirement in TANF was not part of AFDC.

   TRUE
   FALSE

4. All states provided the same benefits for AFDC.

   TRUE
   FALSE

5. Like AFDC, TANF is considered an entitlement.

   TRUE
   FALSE

6. Single parents are more likely to be poor.

   TRUE
   FALSE

7. The FEDERAL time limit for TANF is two years.

   TRUE
   FALSE

8. The National Directory of New Hires is an aid in Child Support Enforcement.

   TRUE
   FALSE

9. Child Support Enforcement recovers the majority of support payments owed for welfare recipients.

   TRUE
   FALSE

10. TANF recipients in states with higher benefits receive lower food stamp payments than those with higher TANF benefits.

    TRUE
    FALSE

Chapter 7: Fighting Hunger: Nutrition Policy and Programs in the United States

Multiple Choice

1. The Food Stamp program partially replaced
   a. the School Lunch Program.
   b. the WIC Program.
   c. the Commodity Food Program.

2. The Food Stamp program is administered by
   a. the Labor Department.
   b. the Department of Health And Human Services.
   c. the Food Service Department.
   d. the US Agriculture Department.

3. Which of the following is targeted at preventing malnutrition for young children and their mothers?
   a. WIC
   b. Food Stamps
   c. Meals on Wheels
   d. Commodity Foods

4. Which of the following is targeted at preventing malnutrition for those who are homebound?
   a. Commodity Foods
   b. Meals on Wheels
   c. WIC
   d. Food Stamps

5. In 1996, the food stamp program was changed in all the ways stated below except:
   a. many people no longer qualify
   b. stiffer work requirements for recipients
   c. eligibility rules were made more stringent
   d. converted to a Block Grant

True/False

1. More than half of the families receiving food stamps have children.
   TRUE
   FALSE

2. Income is not considered when applying for food stamps.
   TRUE
   FALSE

3. Only the elderly can receive meals-on-wheels.
   TRUE
   FALSE

4. WIC is designed to meet the needs of young children and their mothers.
   TRUE
   FALSE

5. Commodity food distribution began in the 1930s.
   TRUE
   FALSE

6. Many people in the United States suffer from malnutrition.
   TRUE
   FALSE

7. The Food Stamp program was created in 1964.
   TRUE
   FALSE

8. There were reductions in Food Stamps as a consequence of welfare reform in 1996.
   TRUE
   FALSE

9. The National School Lunch Act was signed in 1971 by President Nixon.

   TRUE
   FALSE

10. Electronic Benefit transfer operates on the same ideas as a debit card.

   TRUE
   FALSE

Chapter 8: Improving Health Care: Treating the Nation's Ills

Multiple Choice

1. Medicaid is primarily for
   a. the poor.
   b. the chronically ill.
   c. children.
   d. the elderly or disabled with Social Security.

2. Medicare and Medicaid were created during the _____________ administration.
   a. Roosevelt
   b. Nixon
   c. Johnson
   d. Kennedy

3. Prescription drugs are generally not covered by:
   a. private insurance.
   b. Medicaid.
   c. HMOs.
   d. Medicare.

True/False

1. The Struggle for national health care began in the Johnson administration.

   TRUE
   FALSE

2. Medicaid is partially funded by the states.

   TRUE
   FALSE

3. Medicare is partially funded by the states.

   TRUE
   FALSE

4. There is a positive relationship between low incomes and chronic health problems.

   TRUE
   FALSE

5. All social security recipients receive Medicaid.

   TRUE
   FALSE

6. Medicare pays for prescription drugs.

   TRUE
   FALSE

7. Good medical care does not always mean good health.

   TRUE
   FALSE

8. EPSDT is part of the Medicare program.

   TRUE
   FALSE

9. Medicare has two parts that provide different coverage.

   TRUE
   FALSE

10. Medicare pays for prescription drugs.

    TRUE
    FALSE

Chapter 9: Changing Paradigms in the Poverty Wars: Victories, Defeats, and Stalemates

Multiple Choice

1. The legislation that was the centerpiece of the War on Poverty was:
   a. the Social Security Act.
   b. the Family Assistance Plan.
   c. the Economic Opportunity Act.
   d. the Poverty Prevention Act.

2. Which of the following is not a program designed to prepare people for work?
   a. MDTA
   b. Job Corps
   c. Head Start
   d. JTPA
   e. CETA

3. Which program was NOT part of the War on Poverty?
   a. MDTA
   b. Head Start
   c. Legal Services
   d. AFDC
   e. Job Corps

4. The part of the War on Poverty that focused on community organization, citizen participation, and empowerment to the greatest extent was:
   a. Legal Services
   b. Job Corps
   c. Head Start
   d. Community Action Agency

5. Which War on Poverty program focused on Jobs for teenagers and young adults?
   a. Job Corps
   b. Head Start
   c. MDTA
   d. Work Study

6. Which of the following programs is most identified with a make-work job strategy?
   a. Head Start
   b. CETA
   c. Job Corp
   d. JTPA

7. Which was NOT a major problem of the CETA program?
   a. Shortage of clients
   b. Creaming
   c. Substitution

8. Which is not a volunteer service program?
   a. Job Corp
   b. The Peace Corps
   c. Americorp
   d. VISTA

True/False

1. There are exceptions to the minimum wage.

   TRUE
   FALSE

2. Head Start tries to provide compensatory education for low income children.

   TRUE
   FALSE

3. The unemployment rates for minority youth are much lower than for non-minority adults.

   TRUE
   FALSE

4. The War on Poverty fell victim to politics.

   TRUE
   FALSE

5. The original evaluations of Head Start were not positive.

   TRUE
   FALSE

6. The War on Poverty raised the expectations of the poor but did not deliver on many of its promises. This lead to frustration.

   TRUE
   FALSE

7. Empowerment zones offer special incentives for businesses to locate there.

   TRUE
   FALSE

Chapter 10: Providing Social Services: Help for Children, the Elderly and People with Mental Illness

Multiple Choice

1. Which is NOT true about Community Mental Health Centers?
   - a. Were a product of the Community Mental Health Centers Act of 1963
   - b. Aimed at prevention of hospitalization
   - c. Are no longer required to provide the essential services provided in earlier legislation
   - d. Are not funded by block grants

2. A study by the National Association of Social Workers found that
   - a. short term treatment worked better than long term treatment.
   - b. long term treatment worked better than short term treatment.
   - c. time in treatment was irrelevant.
   - d. effectiveness depended on worker experience.

3. Prior to the Reagan Administration, funding for Mental Health, Alcoholism, and Drug Abuse were
   - a. funded at a lower level.
   - b. funded separately.
   - c. funded only by the states.
   - d. paid for only from client fees.

4. The Charities Organization Society was
   - a. a form of local government.
   - b. an early provider of social services.
   - c. a military organization.
   - d. a self-help group.

5. Child welfare legislation focuses on all of the following problems except
   - a. foster care drift
   - b. family reunification.
   - c. permanent homes for children.
   - d. the need for more adoptive children.

6. Substitute care refers to
   - a. adoption.
   - b. foster care.
   - c. group homes.
   - d. all are correct.

7. The legislation that governs many social services for the elderly is called
   - a. the Senior Citizens Act.
   - b. the Adult Social Services Act.
   - c. the Older Americans Act.
   - d. None are correct

8. At the local level, advocacy and services for the elderly are coordinated and sometimes provided by
   - a. local health departments.
   - b. area agencies on aging.
   - c. White House Conferences on Aging.
   - d. Administration on Aging.

True/False

1. At one time mental health commitments were handled informally.

   TRUE
   FALSE

2. Szasz rejects all involuntary mental health commitments.

   TRUE
   FALSE

3. Child abuse was not considered a problem until relatively recently.

   TRUE
   FALSE

4. The United States has a well-articulated family policy.

   TRUE
   FALSE

5. Mary Ellen was a famous child welfare case from the late 1800s.

   TRUE
   FALSE

6. Child Maltreatment is separate from Abuse and Neglect.

   TRUE
   FALSE

7. According to the text, child and adult protection can only be provided by public agencies.

   TRUE
   FALSE

8. Non-profit agencies are also called proprietary agencies.

   TRUE
   FALSE

9. Alcoholics Anonymous is an example of a self-help group.

   TRUE
   FALSE

10. A substantial portion of the population has mental health or substance abuse problems.

    TRUE
    FALSE

11. Consumers of mental health services enjoy more rights today than in the past.

    TRUE
    FALSE

12. Elder abuse is a growing problem.

    TRUE
    FALSE

Chapter 11: Challenging Social Welfare: Racism and Sexism

Multiple Choice

1. Which of the following best describes the relationship between sexism, racism and social policy?
   - **a.** Sexism, but not racism, is reflected in social policy.
   - **b.** Sexism and racism are not reflected in social policy.
   - **c.** Racism, but not sexism, is reflected in social policy.
   - **d.** Sexism and racism are reflected in social policy.

2. Redlining means that
   - **a.** banks, insurance, and mortgage companies refuse to deal with certain types of people.
   - **b.** banks, insurance, and mortgage companies refuse to do business in certain areas.
   - **c.** certain areas prohibit Banks, insurance, and mortgage companies from doing business in their community.

3. Studies have shown that African Americans are
   - **a.** twice as likely as whites to be denied home mortgage loans.
   - **b.** four times as likely as whites to qualify for home mortgage loans.
   - **c.** half as likely as whites to be denied for home mortgage loans.
   - **d.** twice as likely as whites to qualify for home mortgage loans.

4. Brown vs. Board of Education of Topeka struck down the idea of
   - **a.** separate but equal.
   - **b.** school busing.
   - **c.** literacy tests.
   - **d.** racial quotas.

5. The Civil Right Act of 1964
   - **a.** mandated school busing.
   - **b.** protected only African Americans.
   - **c.** was overturned in 1980.
   - **d.** protected the right to vote.

True/False

1. In today's economy, women are often paid less then men for equal work.

   TRUE
   FALSE

2. There is a relationship between the likelihood of being poor and membership in an at-risk group.

   TRUE
   FALSE

3. Sexual harassment is a form of discrimination.

   TRUE
   FALSE

4. Discrimination in housing is a major problem.

   TRUE
   FALSE

5. Nearly 60 percent of the SSI recipients are women.

   TRUE
   FALSE

6. Women's wages are lower than men's and they stay in the paid workforce a shorter time.

   TRUE
   FALSE

7. In 1997, women made 74 cents for every dollar made by men.

   TRUE
   FALSE

8. Women make less than men at every educational level.

   TRUE
   FALSE

9. Comparative work means the same pay for the same exact work.

   TRUE
   FALSE

10. Rights for gap people are a relatively recent development.

    TRUE
    FALSE

11. Affirmative action has been hotly debated in recent political dialog.

    TRUE
    FALSE

Chapter 12: What Happens After a Law Is Passed

Multiple Choice

1. Program implementation, according to the text, is a
   a. completely rational process.
   b. completely political process.
   c. mix of political and rational considerations.

2. The program evaluation model, advocated by Schorr uses a __________ approach.
   a. political
   b. rational
   c. program theory or theory of change approach
   d. Black Box Model

3. In a ___________ design there is an experimental group and a control group to which subjects are randomly assigned. Only the experimental group gets the intervention.
   a. qualitative
   b. quasi experimental
   c. classical experimental
   d. pre-experimental

4. Most social scientists would say that __________ are the most powerful designs for evaluating causality.
   a. classical Experimental
   b. pre-Experimental
   c. qualitative
   d. quasi experimental

True/False

1. Program evaluation, according to the text, is a completely rational process.
   TRUE
   FALSE

2. Program participants often see the evaluation process as a political problem.
   TRUE
   FALSE

3. The move toward evaluation is relatively recent.
   TRUE
   FALSE

4. Management and staff usually welcome program evaluation.
   TRUE
   FALSE

5. Social programs typically have clear, easy to evaluate outcome statements.
   TRUE
   FALSE

6. Poor evaluation results always lead to a loss of funding.
   TRUE
   FALSE

7. Formal Research Designs are easy to apply in program settings.
   TRUE
   FALSE

8. Programs are usually implemented so as to faithfully represent the Congressional intent.
   TRUE
   FALSE

9. The Pre-test-Post-test design is very powerful.
   TRUE
   FALSE